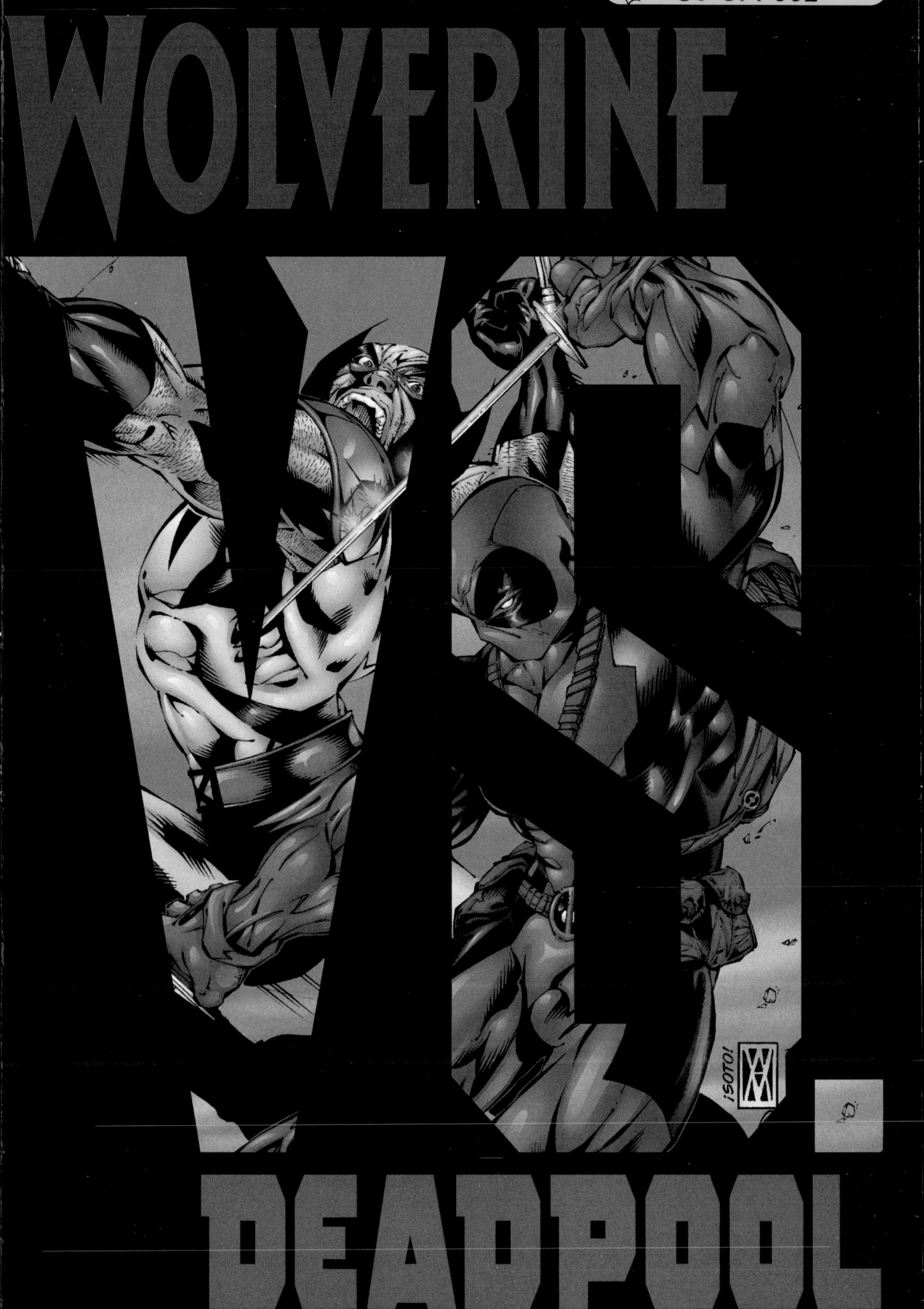
WOLVERINE
VS.
DEADPOOL
¡SOTO!

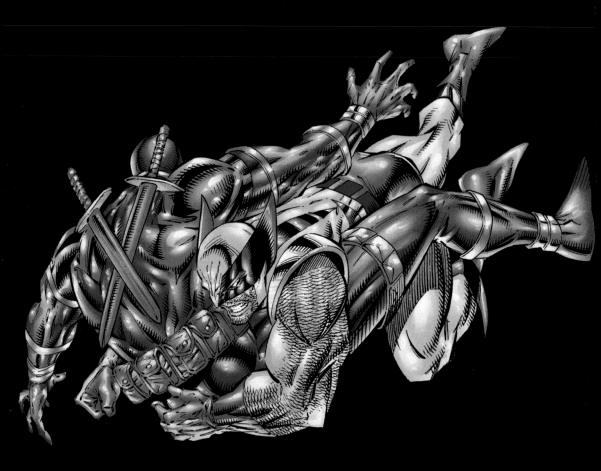

Wolverine created by **Len Wein** & **John Romita Sr.**   Deadpool created by **Rob Liefeld** & **Fabian Nicieza**

front cover artists **Simone Bianchi** & **Simone Peruzzi**   back cover artists **Rob Liefeld** & **Kevin Senft**

collection editor **Mark D. Beazley**

assistant editor **Caitlin O'Connell**

associate managing editor **Kateri Woody**

associate manager, digital assets **Joe Hochstein**

senior editor, special projects **Jennifer Grünwald**

vp production & special projects **Jeff Youngquist**

research & layout **Jeph York**

book designer **Adam Del Re**

svp print, sales & marketing **David Gabriel**

editor in chief **Axel Alonso**

chief creative officer **Joe Quesada**

publisher **Dan Buckley**

executive producer **Alan Fine**

WOLVERINE VS. DEADPOOL. Contains material originally published in magazine form as WOLVERINE #88, #154-155, and ANNUAL '95 and '99; DEADPOOL #27; CABLE & DEADPOOL #43-44; WOLVERINE ORIGINS #21-25; and WOLVERINE/DEADPOOL: THE DECOY #1. First printing 2017. ISBN# 978-1-302-90466-1. Published by MARVEL WORLDWIDE, INC. a subsidiary of MARVEL ENTERTAINMENT, LLC. OFFICE OF PUBLICATION: 135 West 50th Street, New York, NY 10020. Copyright © 2017 MARVEL No similarity between any of the names, characters, persons, and/or institutions in this magazine with those of any living or dead person or institution is intended, and any such similarity which may exist is purely coincidental. **Printed in the U.S.A.** ALAN FINE, President, Marvel Entertainment; DAN BUCKLEY, President, TV, Publishing & Brand Management; JOE QUESADA, Chief Creative Officer; TOM BREVOORT, SVP of Publishing; DAVID BOGART, SVP of Business Affairs & Operations, Publishing & Partnership; C.B. CEBULSKI, VP of Brand Management & Development, Asia; DAVID GABRIEL, SVP of Sales & Marketing, Publishing; JEFF YOUNGQUIST, VP of Production & Special Projects; DAN CARR, Executive Director of Publishing Technology; ALEX MORALES, Director of Publishing Operations; SUSAN CRESPI, Production Manager; STAN LEE, Chairman Emeritus. For information regarding advertising in Marvel Comics or on Marvel.com, please contact Vit DeBellis, Integrated Sales Manager, at vdebellis@marvel.com. For Marvel subscription inquiries, please call 888-511-5480. **Manufactured between 12/30/2016 and 2/6/2017 by QUAD/GRAPHICS WASECA, WASECA, MN, USA.**

10 9 8 7 6 5 4 3 2 1

WOLVERINE VS. DEADPOOL

WRITERS

Larry Hama, Chris Golden, Joe Kelly, Marc Andreyko, Rob Liefeld,
Eric Stephenson, Fabian Nicieza, Daniel Way & Stuart Moore

PENCILERS

Ben Herrera, Walter McDaniel, Rob Liefeld, Ron Lim,
Steve Dillon & Shawn Crystal with Adam Kubert & Fabio Laguna

INKERS

Vince Russell, Whitney McFarland, Norm Rapmund,
Jeremy Freeman, Steve Dillon & Shawn Crystal with Mark Farmer,
Tim Townsend, Walden Wong, Scott Koblish & John Dell

COLORISTS

Marie Javins, Ian Laughlin, Kevin Somers,
Gina Going, Digital Broome, Gotham,
Avalon's Matt Milla & John Rauch with Sotocolor

LETTERERS

Pat Brosseau, Dave Sharpe, VC's Cory Petit,
Jeff Eckleberry, Michael Heisler &
Revenge Graphics, and Richard Starkings &
Comicraft's Troy Peteri & co.

ASSISTANT EDITORS

Ben Raab, Paul Tutrone,
Pete Franco & Aubrey Sitterson

EDITORS

Bob Harras, Mark Powers,
Matt Idelson, Nicole Boose,
John Barber & Sebastian Girner

GROUP EDITOR

Axel Alonso (*Wolverine: Origins*)

VP DIGITAL CONTENT & PROGRAMMING

ASSOCIATE PRODUCER

DIGITAL PRODUCTION MANAGER

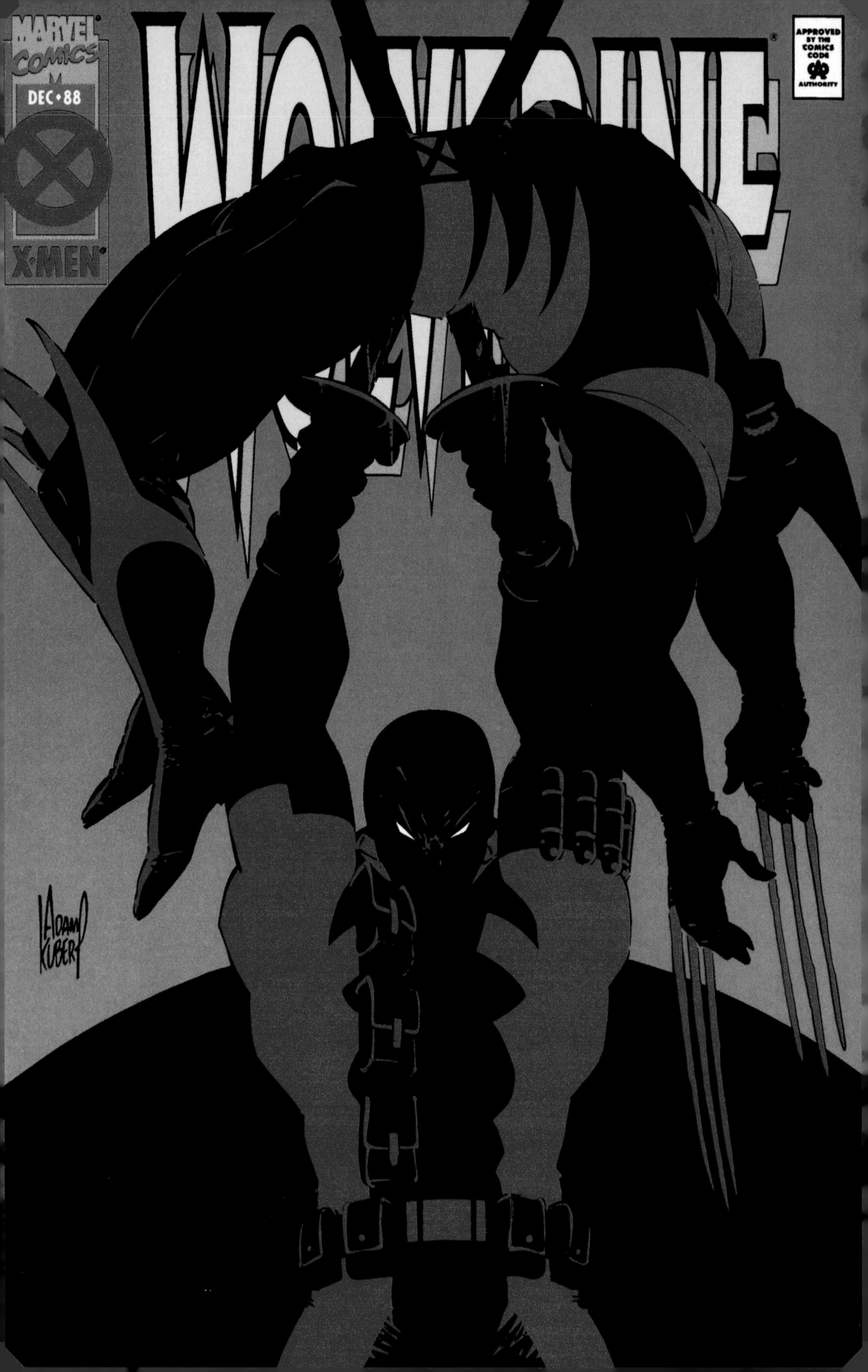
MARVEL COMICS
DEC • 88
X-MEN
APPROVED BY THE COMICS CODE AUTHORITY
ADAM KUBERT

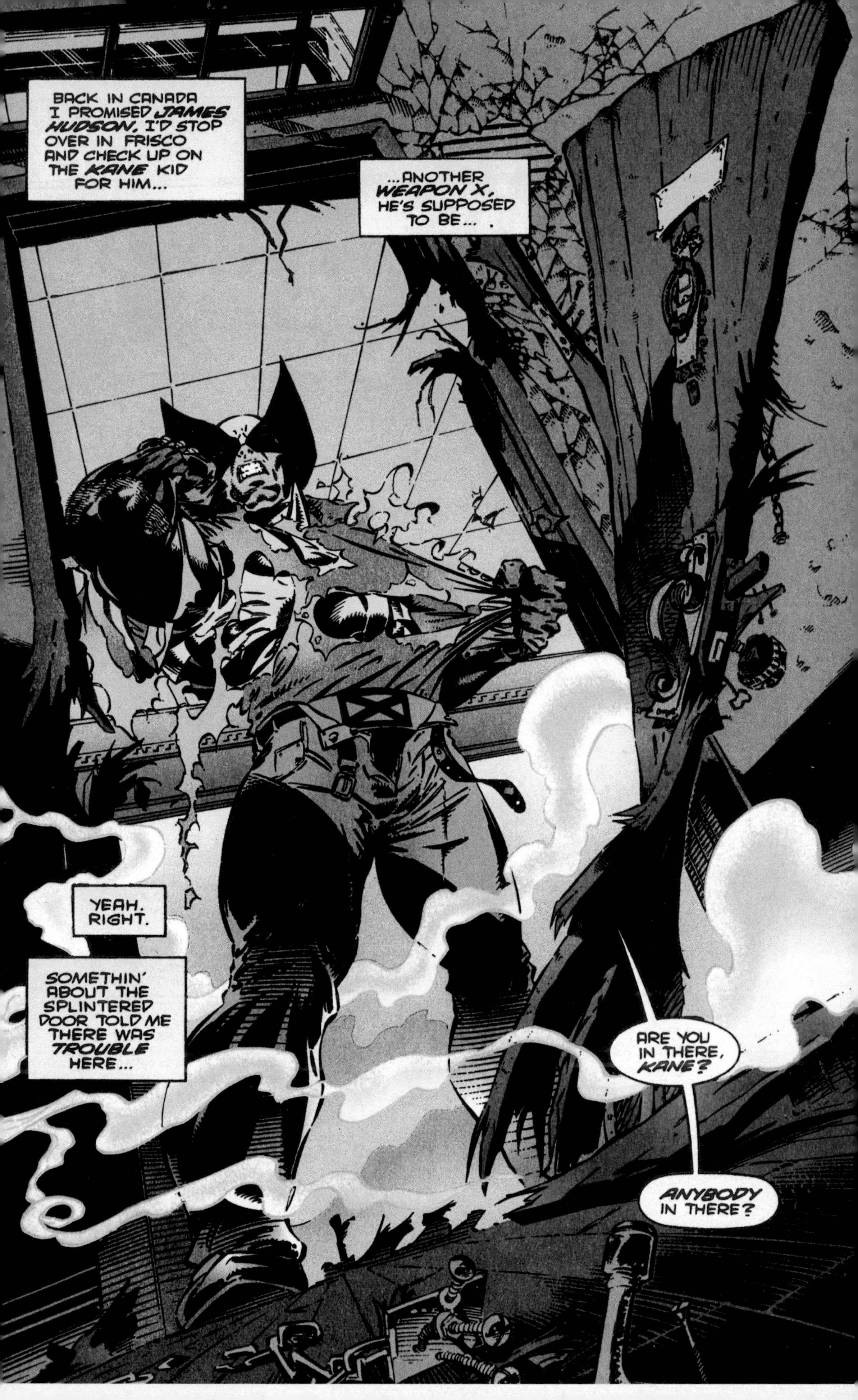
BACK IN CANADA I PROMISED JAMES HUDSON, I'D STOP OVER IN FRISCO AND CHECK UP ON THE KANE KID FOR HIM...
...ANOTHER WEAPON X, HE'S SUPPOSED TO BE... .
YEAH. RIGHT.
SOMETHIN' ABOUT THE SPLINTERED DOOR TOLD ME THERE WAS TROUBLE HERE...
ARE YOU IN THERE, KANE?
ANYBODY IN THERE?

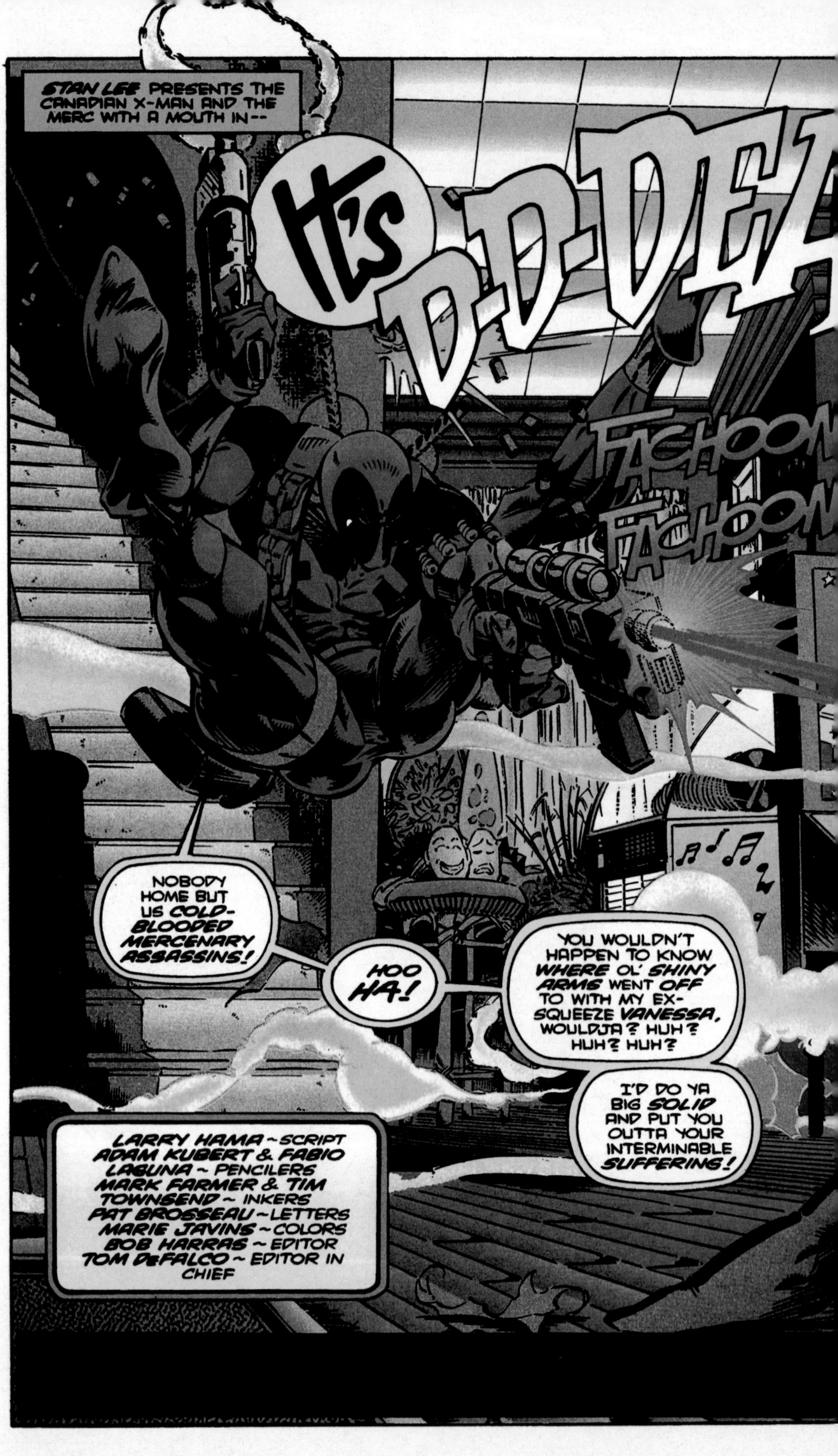

STAN LEE PRESENTS THE CANADIAN X-MAN AND THE MERC WITH A MOUTH IN--
IT'S D-D-DEA
FACHOOM
FACHOOM
NOBODY HOME BUT US COLD-BLOODED MERCENARY ASSASSINS!
HOO HA!
YOU WOULDN'T HAPPEN TO KNOW WHERE OL' SHINY ARMS WENT OFF TO WITH MY EX-SQUEEZE VANESSA, WOULDJA? HUH? HUH? HUH?
I'D DO YA BIG SOLID AND PUT YOU OUTTA YOUR INTERMINABLE SUFFERING!
LARRY HAMA ~ SCRIPT ADAM KUBERT & FABIO LAGUNA ~ PENCILERS MARK FARMER & TIM TOWNSEND ~ INKERS PAT BROSSEAU ~ LETTERS MARIE JAVINS ~ COLORS BOB HARRAS ~ EDITOR TOM DeFALCO ~ EDITOR IN CHIEF

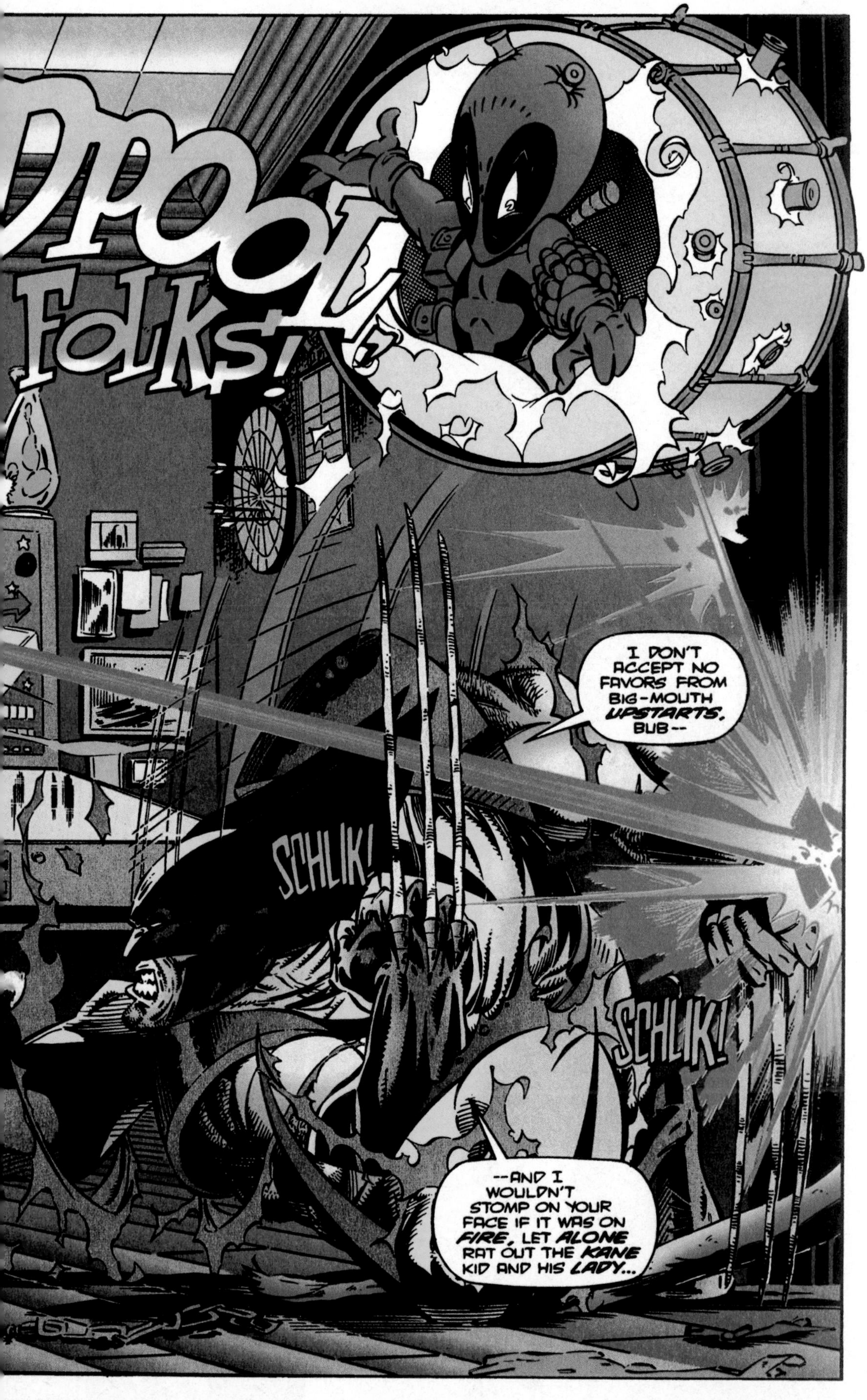

...POOL, Folks!
I DON'T ACCEPT NO FAVORS FROM BIG-MOUTH UPSTARTS, BUB--
SCHLIK!
SCHLIK!
--AND I WOULDN'T STOMP ON YOUR FACE IF IT WAS ON FIRE, LET ALONE RAT OUT THE KANE KID AND HIS LADY...

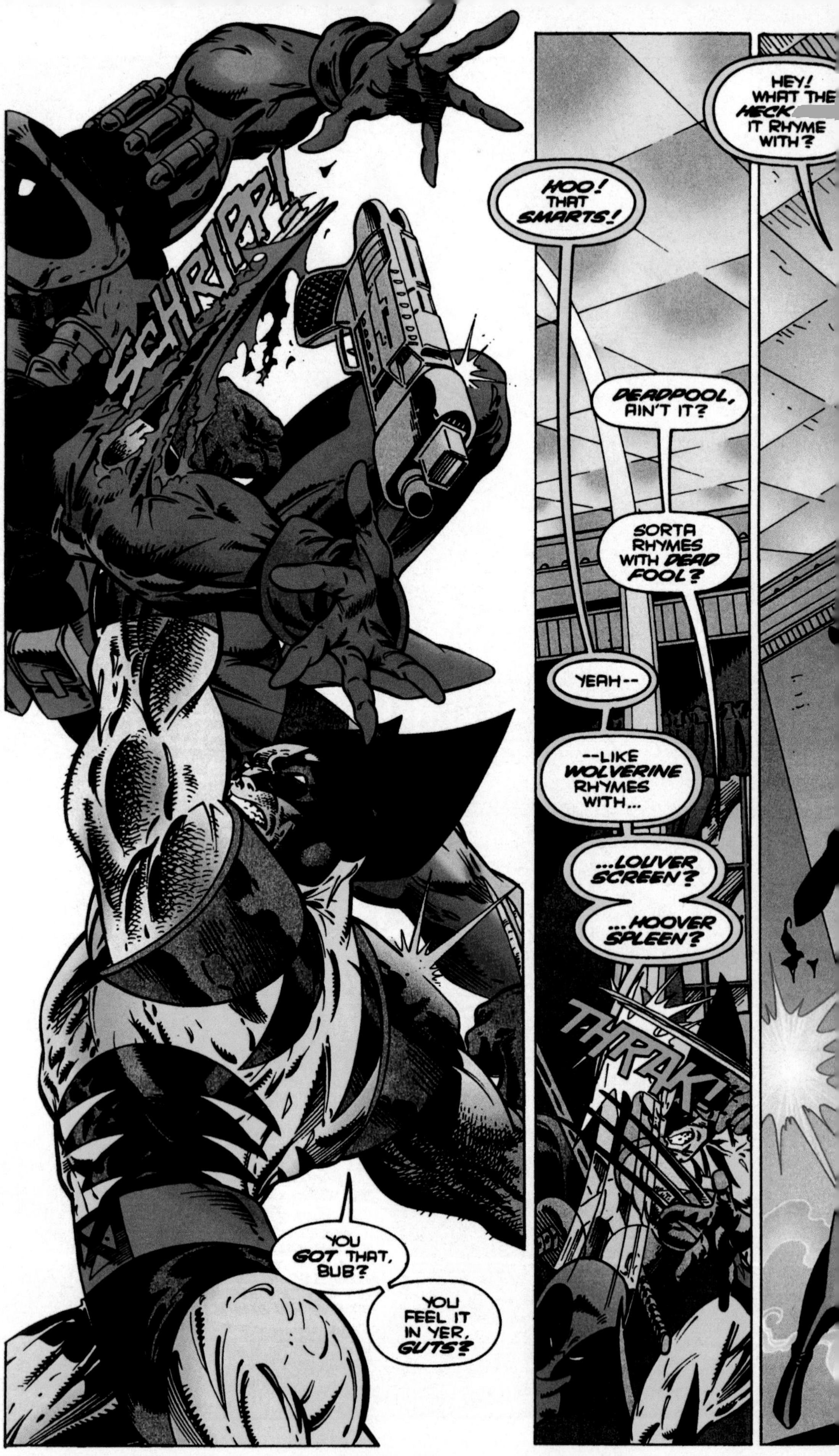
SCHRIPP!
YOU GOT THAT, BUB?
YOU FEEL IT IN YER, GUTS?
HOO! THAT SMARTS!
DEADPOOL, AIN'T IT?
SORTA RHYMES WITH DEAD FOOL?
YEAH--
--LIKE WOLVERINE RHYMES WITH...
...LOUVER SCREEN?
...HOOVER SPLEEN?
THRAK!
HEY! WHAT THE HECK IT RHYME WITH?

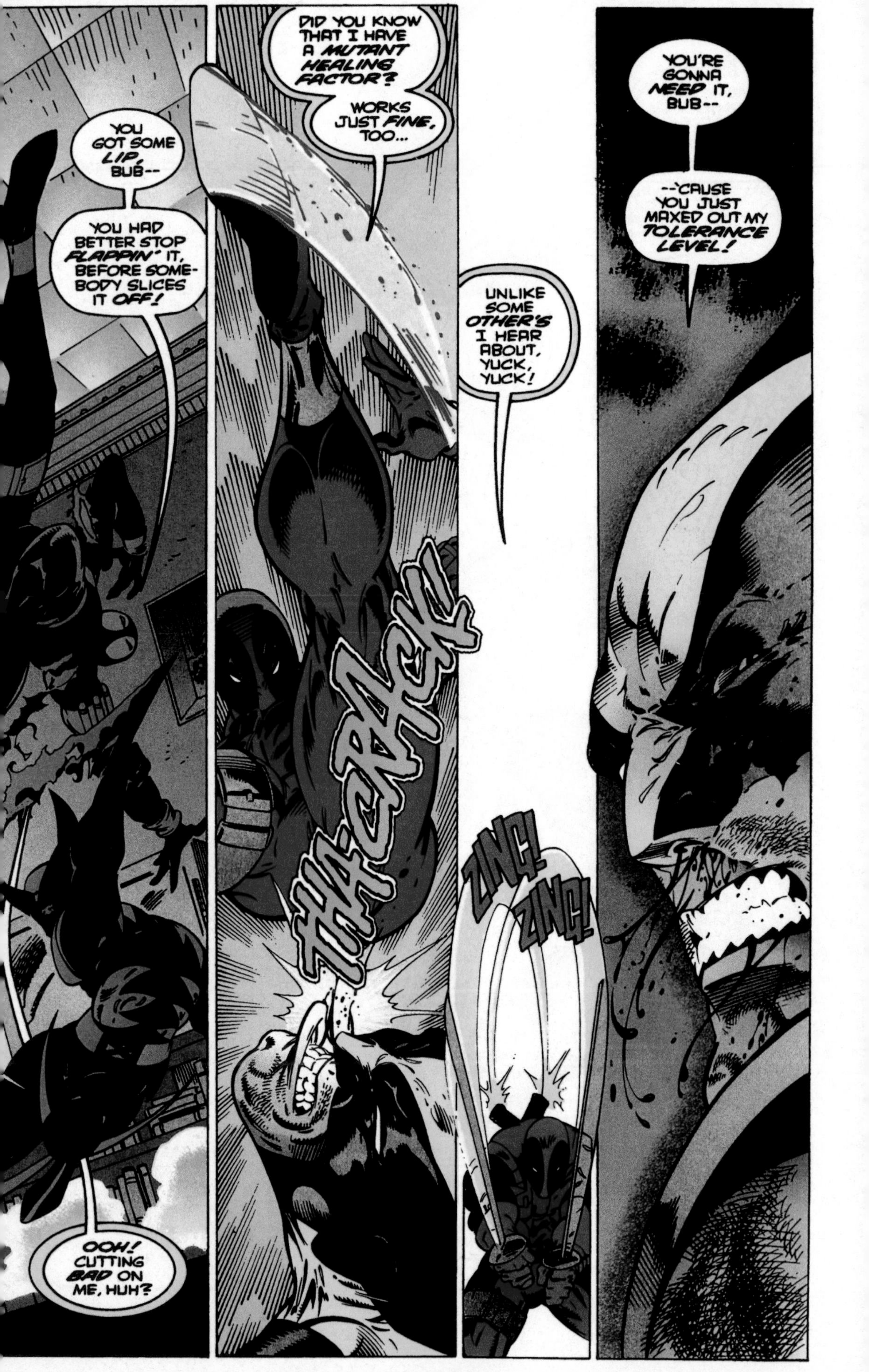
YOU GOT SOME LIP, BUB--
YOU HAD BETTER STOP FLAPPIN' IT, BEFORE SOME-BODY SLICES IT OFF!
OOH! CUTTING BAD ON ME, HUH?
DID YOU KNOW THAT I HAVE A MUTANT HEALING FACTOR?
WORKS JUST FINE, TOO...
THA-CHAK!
UNLIKE SOME OTHER'S I HEAR ABOUT, YUCK, YUCK!
ZING! ZING!
YOU'RE GONNA NEED IT, BUB--
--'CAUSE YOU JUST MAXED OUT MY TOLERANCE LEVEL!

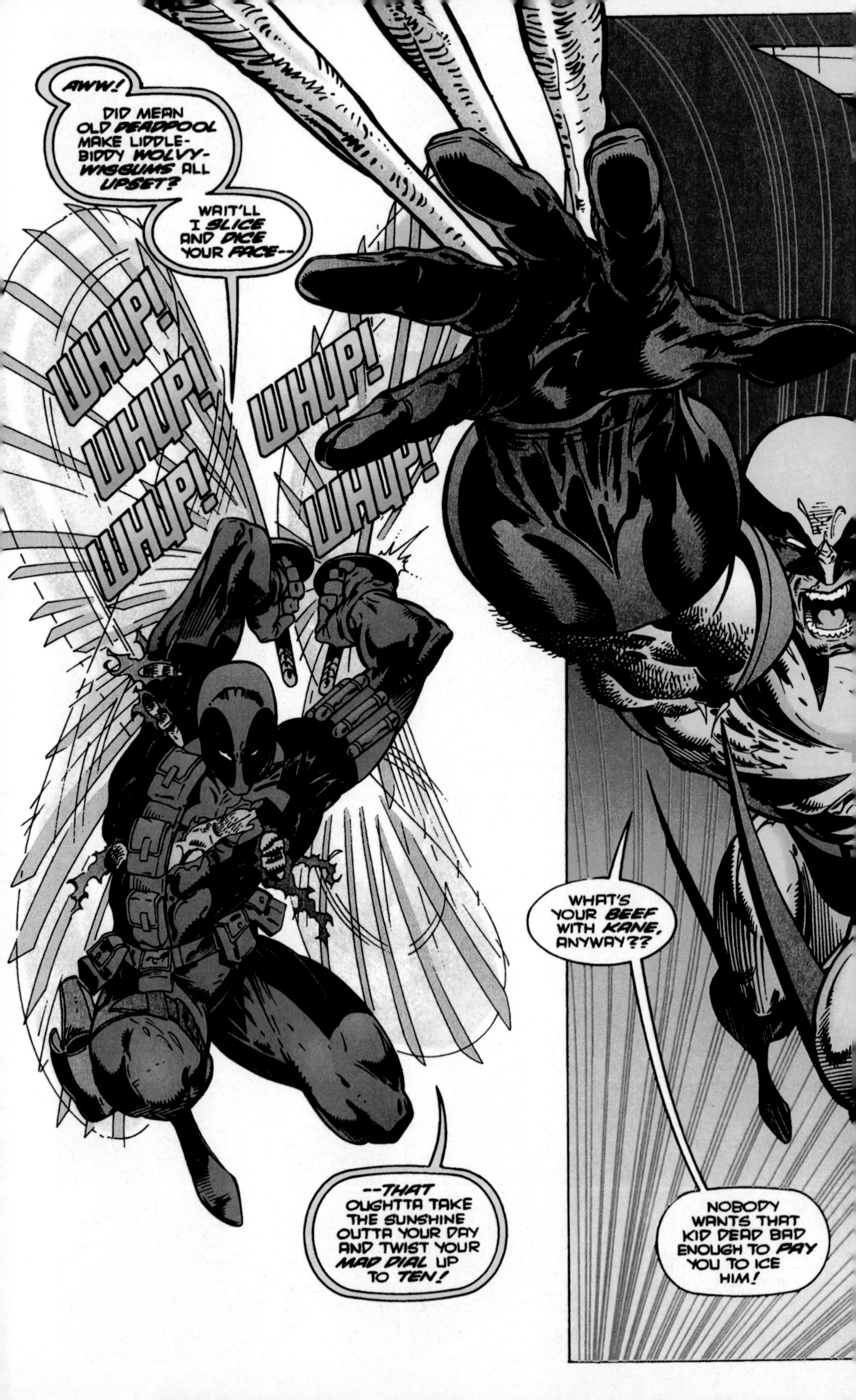
AWW! DID MEAN OLD DEADPOOL MAKE LIDDLE-BIDDY WOLVY-WIGGUMS ALL UPSET?
WAIT'LL I SLICE AND DICE YOUR FACE--
WHUP! WHUP! WHUP! WHUP! WHUP!
--THAT OUGHTTA TAKE THE SUNSHINE OUTTA YOUR DAY AND TWIST YOUR MAD DIAL UP TO TEN!
WHAT'S YOUR BEEF WITH KANE, ANYWAY??
NOBODY WANTS THAT KID DEAD BAD ENOUGH TO PAY YOU TO ICE HIM!

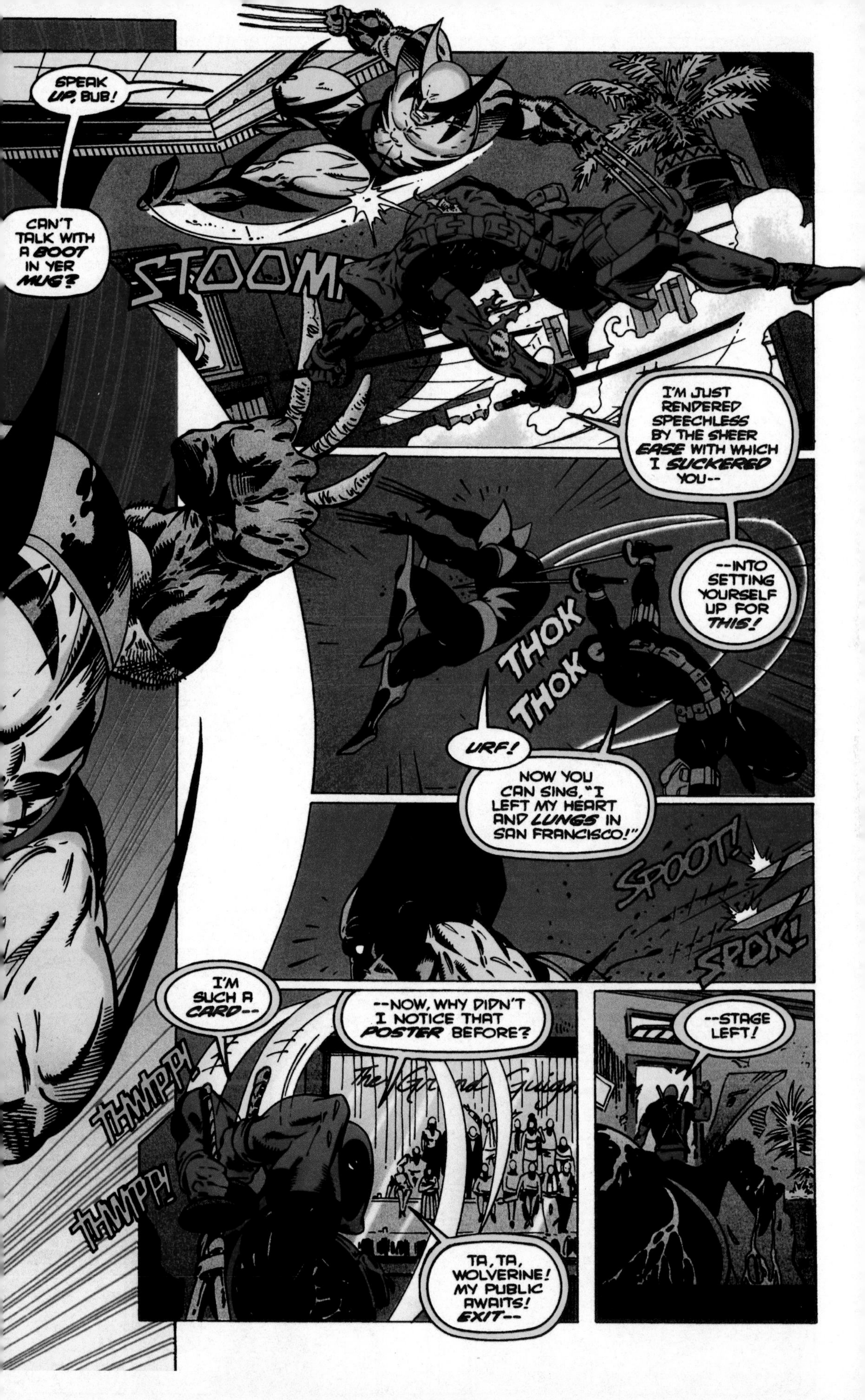
SPEAK UP, BUB!
CAN'T TALK WITH A BOOT IN YER MUG?
STOOM
I'M JUST RENDERED SPEECHLESS BY THE SHEER EASE WITH WHICH I SUCKERED YOU--
--INTO SETTING YOURSELF UP FOR THIS!
THOK
THOK
URF!
NOW YOU CAN SING, "I LEFT MY HEART AND LUNGS IN SAN FRANCISCO!"
SPOOT!
SPOK!
I'M SUCH A CARD--
--NOW, WHY DIDN'T I NOTICE THAT POSTER BEFORE?
THWPP!
THWPP!
TA, TA, WOLVERINE! MY PUBLIC AWAITS! EXIT--
--STAGE LEFT!

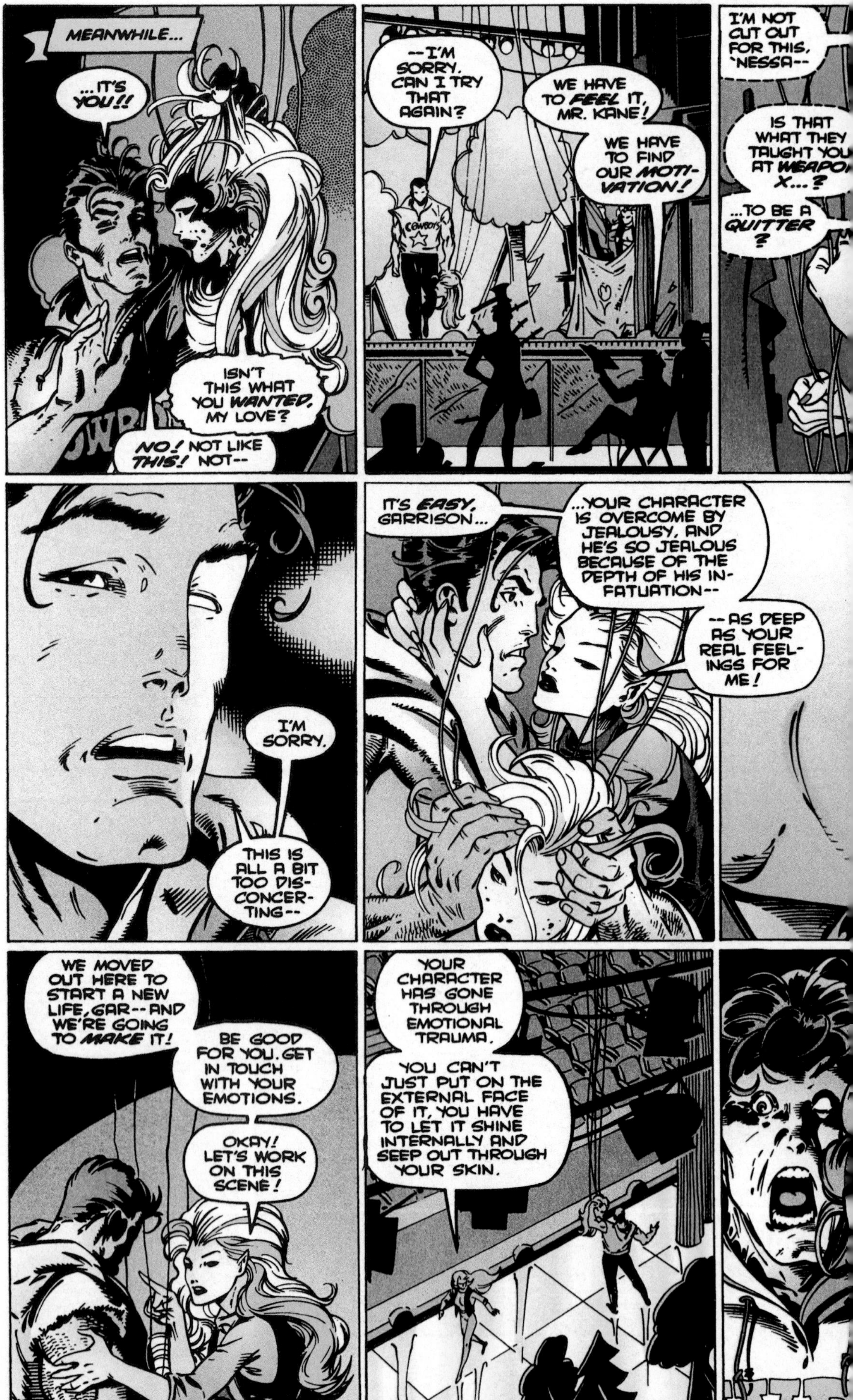

1
MEANWHILE...
...IT'S YOU!!
ISN'T THIS WHAT YOU WANTED, MY LOVE?
NO! NOT LIKE THIS! NOT--
--I'M SORRY. CAN I TRY THAT AGAIN?
WE HAVE TO FEEL IT, MR. KANE!
WE HAVE TO FIND OUR MOTI-VATION!
I'M NOT CUT OUT FOR THIS, 'NESSA--
IS THAT WHAT THEY TAUGHT YOU AT WEAPO X...?
...TO BE A QUITTER?
I'M SORRY.
THIS IS ALL A BIT TOO DIS-CONCER-TING--
IT'S EASY, GARRISON...
...YOUR CHARACTER IS OVERCOME BY JEALOUSY, AND HE'S SO JEALOUS BECAUSE OF THE DEPTH OF HIS IN-FATUATION--
--AS DEEP AS YOUR REAL FEEL-INGS FOR ME!
WE MOVED OUT HERE TO START A NEW LIFE, GAR--AND WE'RE GOING TO MAKE IT!
BE GOOD FOR YOU. GET IN TOUCH WITH YOUR EMOTIONS.
OKAY! LET'S WORK ON THIS SCENE!
YOUR CHARACTER HAS GONE THROUGH EMOTIONAL TRAUMA.
YOU CAN'T JUST PUT ON THE EXTERNAL FACE OF IT, YOU HAVE TO LET IT SHINE INTERNALLY AND SEEP OUT THROUGH YOUR SKIN.

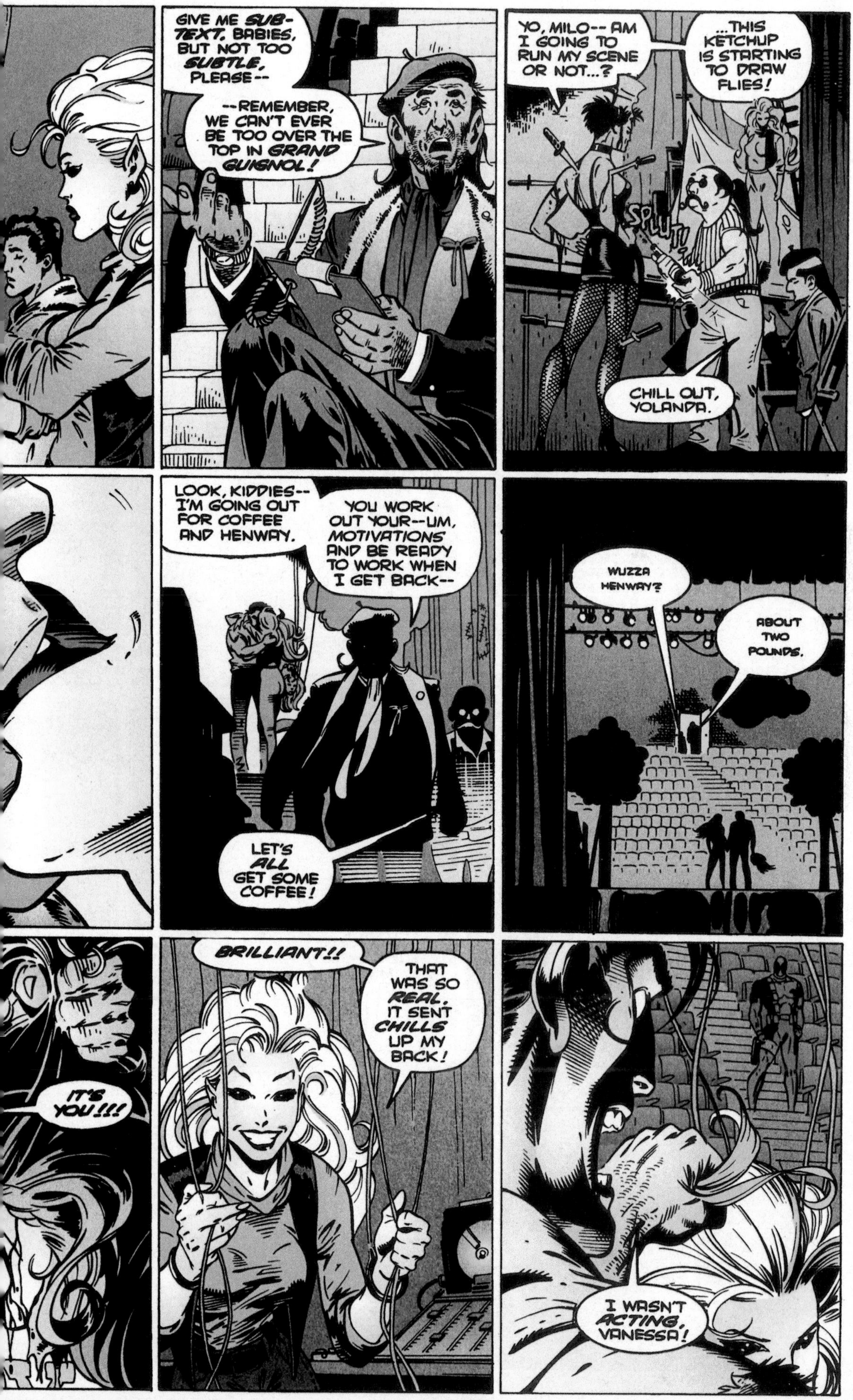
GIVE ME SUB-TEXT, BABIES, BUT NOT TOO SUBTLE, PLEASE--
--REMEMBER, WE CAN'T EVER BE TOO OVER THE TOP IN GRAND GUIGNOL!
YO, MILO-- AM I GOING TO RUN MY SCENE OR NOT...?
...THIS KETCHUP IS STARTING TO DRAW FLIES!
SPLUT!
CHILL OUT, YOLANDA.
LOOK, KIDDIES-- I'M GOING OUT FOR COFFEE AND HENWAY.
YOU WORK OUT YOUR--UM, MOTIVATIONS AND BE READY TO WORK WHEN I GET BACK--
LET'S ALL GET SOME COFFEE!
WUZZA HENWAY?
ABOUT TWO POUNDS.
IT'S YOU!!!
BRILLIANT!!
THAT WAS SO REAL. IT SENT CHILLS UP MY BACK!
I WASN'T ACTING, VANESSA!

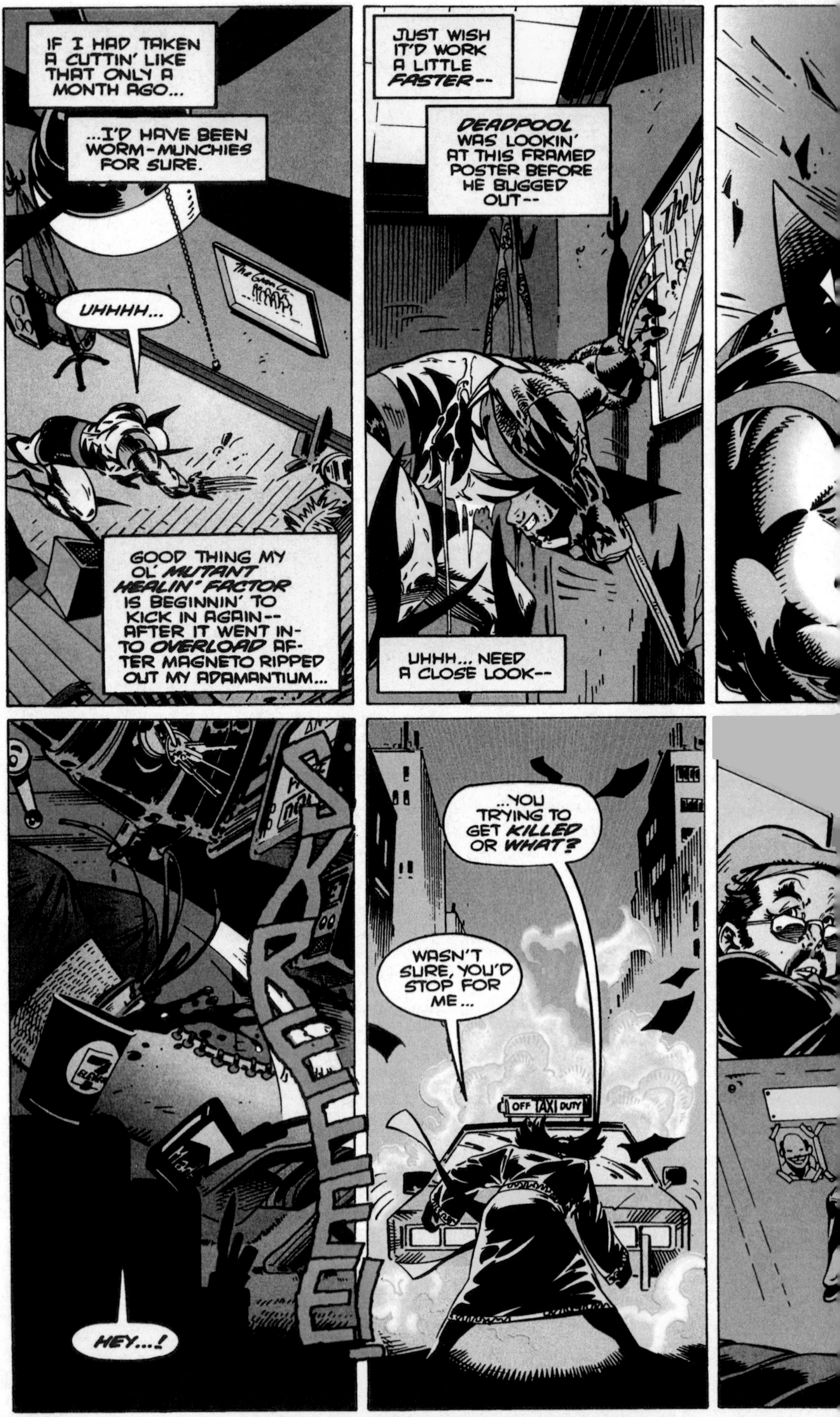

IF I HAD TAKEN A CUTTIN' LIKE THAT ONLY A MONTH AGO...
...I'D HAVE BEEN WORM-MUNCHIES FOR SURE.
UHHHH...
GOOD THING MY OL' MUTANT HEALIN' FACTOR IS BEGINNIN' TO KICK IN AGAIN-- AFTER IT WENT INTO OVERLOAD AFTER MAGNETO RIPPED OUT MY ADAMANTIUM...
JUST WISH IT'D WORK A LITTLE FASTER--
DEADPOOL WAS LOOKIN' AT THIS FRAMED POSTER BEFORE HE BUGGED OUT--
UHHH... NEED A CLOSE LOOK--
SKREEEEE
HEY...!
...YOU TRYING TO GET KILLED OR WHAT?
WASN'T SURE, YOU'D STOP FOR ME...
OFF TAXI DUTY

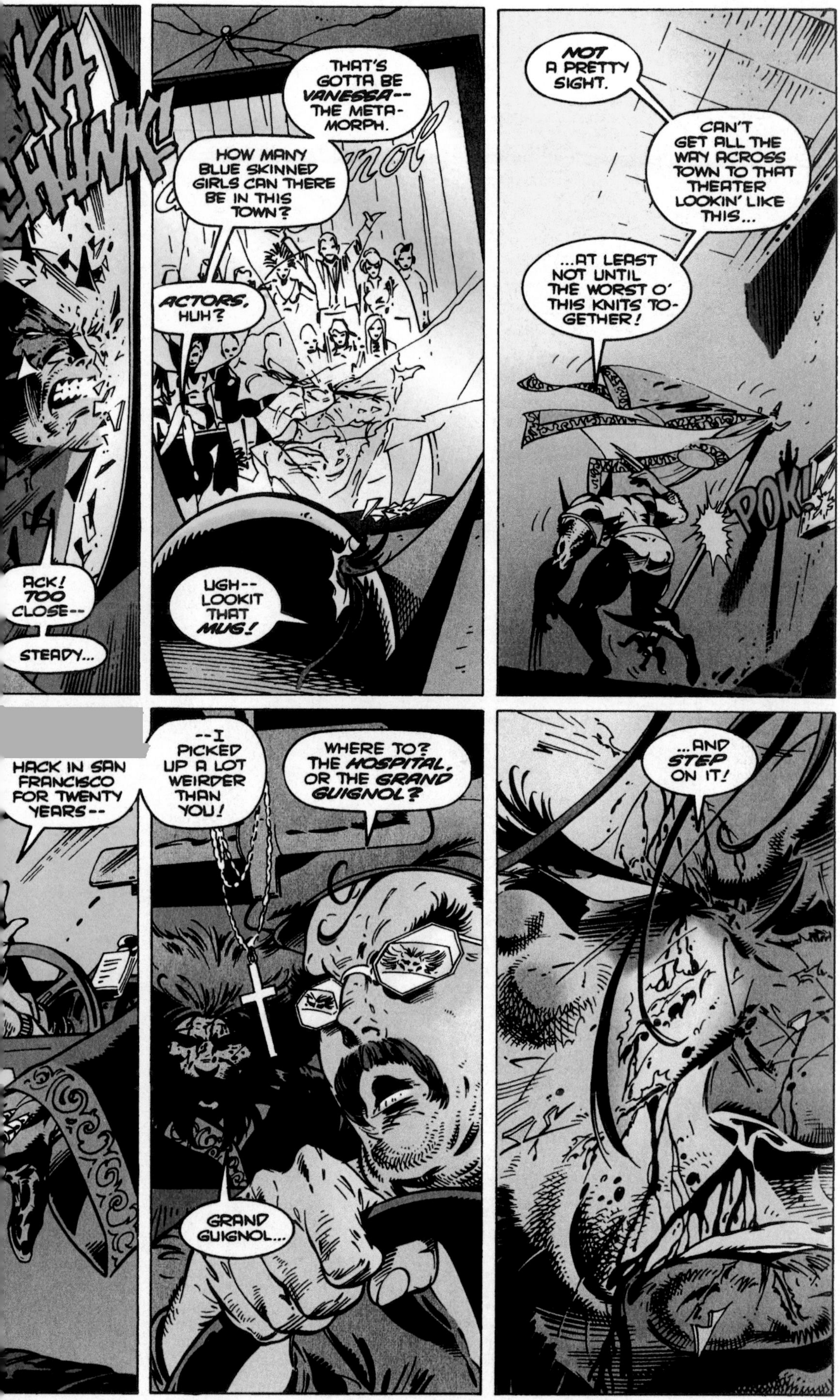
KA-CHUNK!
ACK! TOO CLOSE--
STEADY...
THAT'S GOTTA BE VANESSA-- THE METAMORPH.
HOW MANY BLUE SKINNED GIRLS CAN THERE BE IN THIS TOWN?
ACTORS, HUH?
UGH-- LOOKIT THAT MUG!
NOT A PRETTY SIGHT.
CAN'T GET ALL THE WAY ACROSS TOWN TO THAT THEATER LOOKIN' LIKE THIS...
...AT LEAST NOT UNTIL THE WORST O' THIS KNITS TOGETHER!
POK!
HACK IN SAN FRANCISCO FOR TWENTY YEARS--
--I PICKED UP A LOT WEIRDER THAN YOU!
WHERE TO? THE HOSPITAL, OR THE GRAND GUIGNOL?
GRAND GUIGNOL...
...AND STEP ON IT!

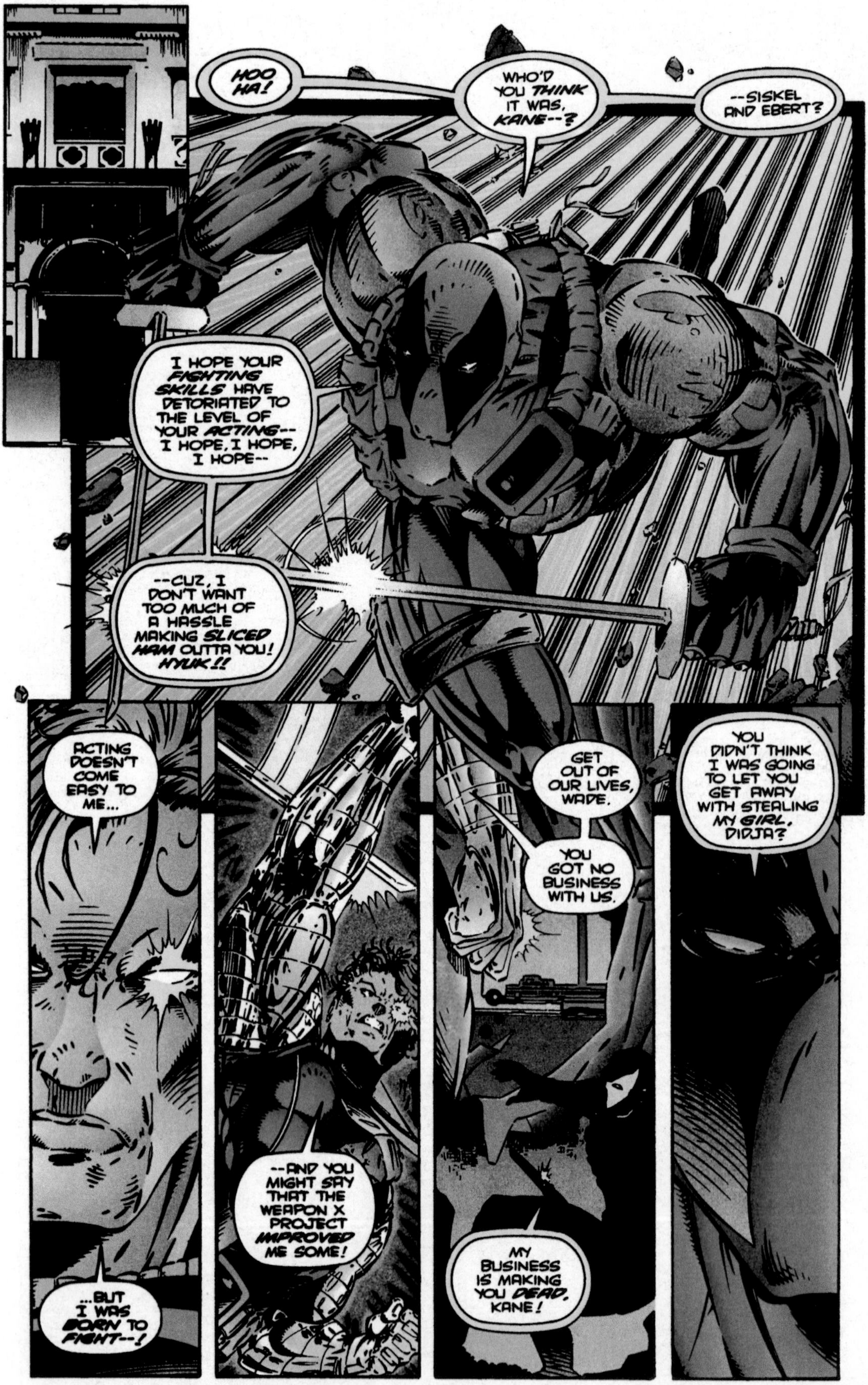
HOO HA!
WHO'D YOU THINK IT WAS, KANE--?
--SISKEL AND EBERT?
I HOPE YOUR FIGHTING SKILLS HAVE DETORIATED TO THE LEVEL OF YOUR ACTING-- I HOPE, I HOPE, I HOPE--
--CUZ, I DON'T WANT TOO MUCH OF A HASSLE MAKING SLICED HAM OUTTA YOU! HYUK!!
ACTING DOESN'T COME EASY TO ME...
...BUT I WAS BORN TO FIGHT--!
--AND YOU MIGHT SAY THAT THE WEAPON X PROJECT IMPROVED ME SOME!
GET OUT OF OUR LIVES, WADE.
YOU GOT NO BUSINESS WITH US.
MY BUSINESS IS MAKING YOU DEAD, KANE!
YOU DIDN'T THINK I WAS GOING TO LET YOU GET AWAY WITH STEALING MY GIRL, DIDJA?

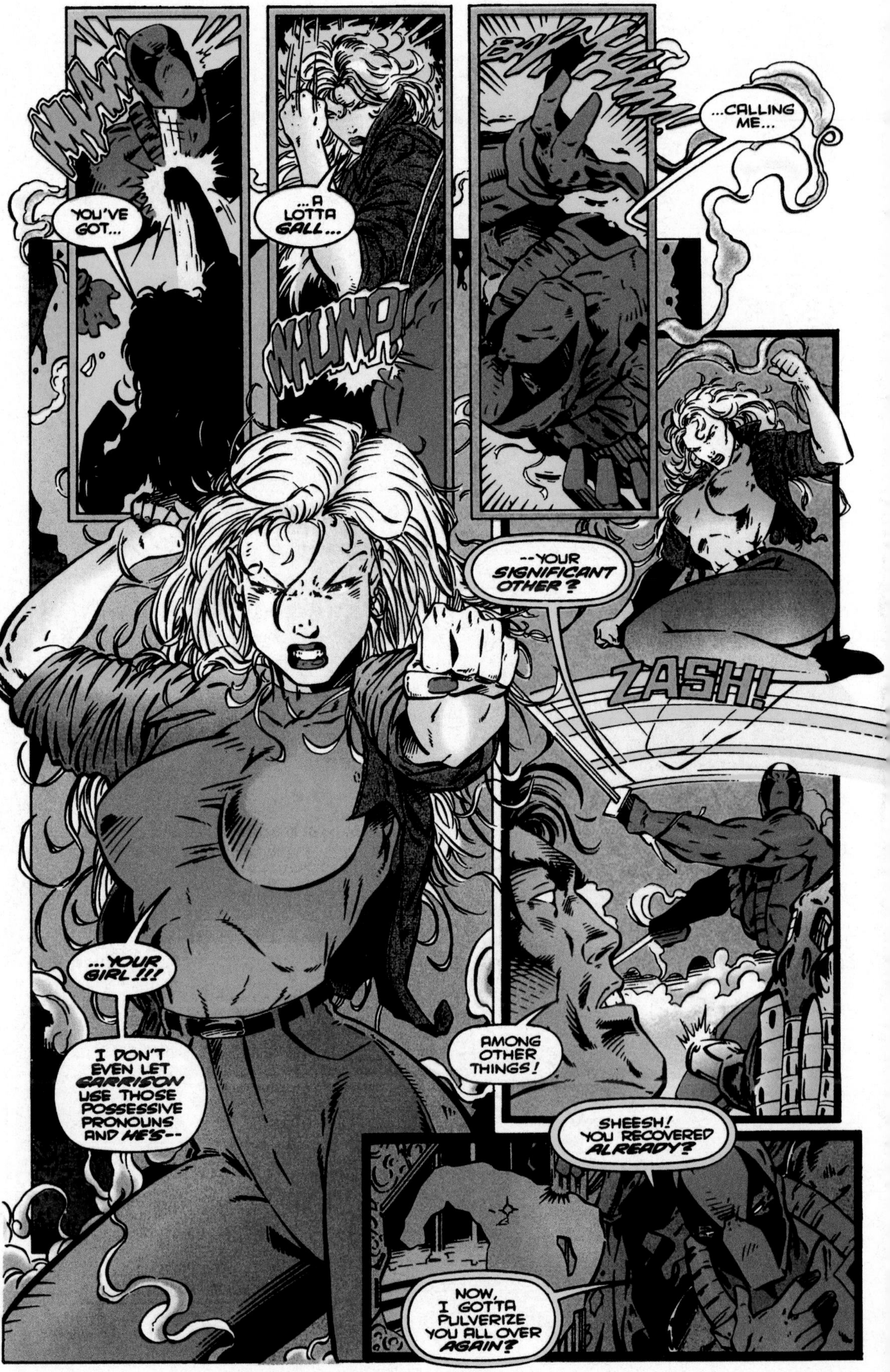
WHAM!
YOU'VE GOT...
...A LOTTA GALL...
WHUMP!
...CALLING ME...
--YOUR SIGNIFICANT OTHER?
ZASH!
...YOUR GIRL!!!
I DON'T EVEN LET GARRISON USE THOSE POSSESSIVE PRONOUNS AND HE'S--
AMONG OTHER THINGS!
SHEESH! YOU RECOVERED ALREADY?
NOW, I GOTTA PULVERIZE YOU ALL OVER AGAIN?

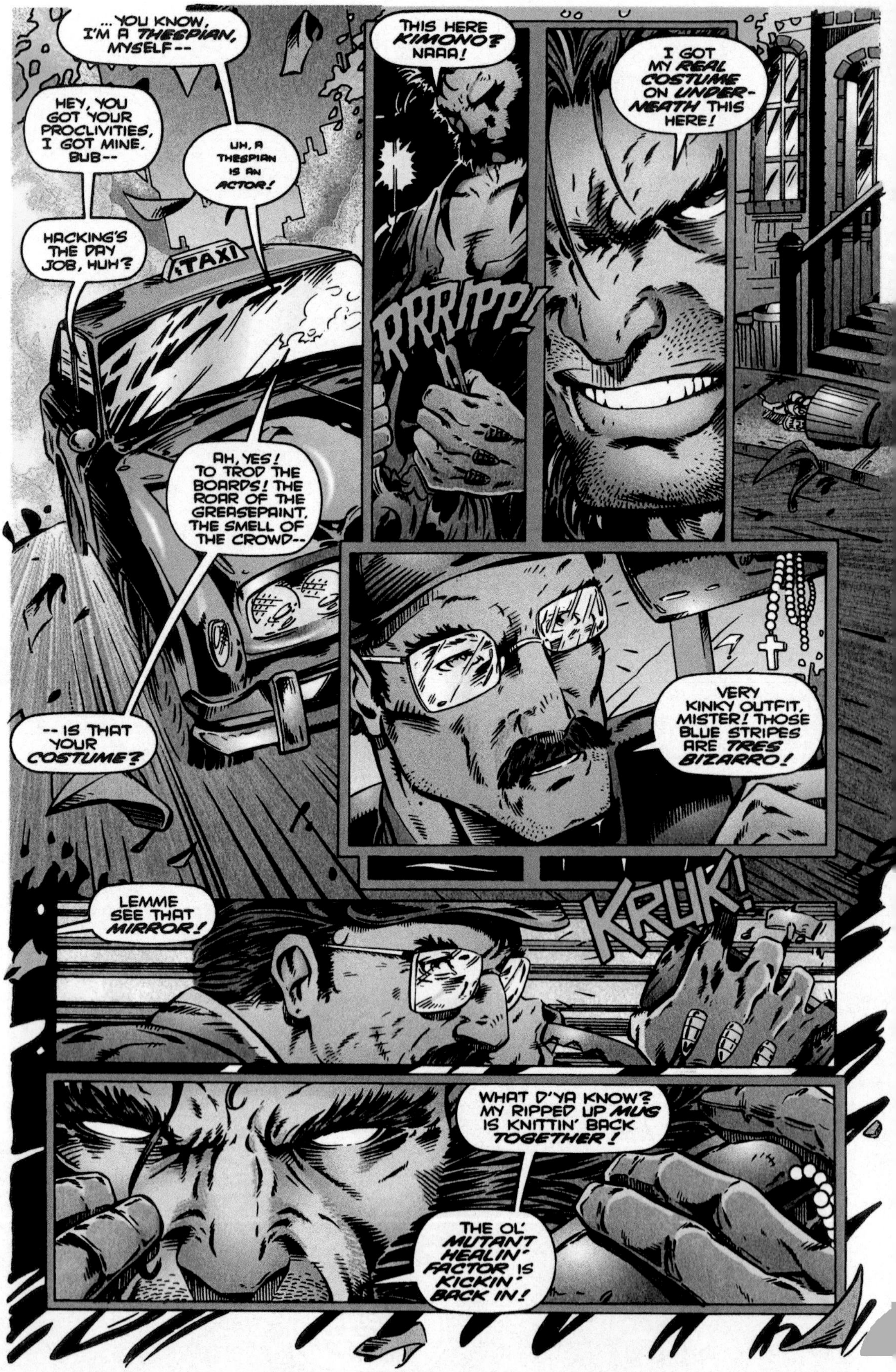
...YOU KNOW, I'M A THESPIAN, MYSELF--
HEY, YOU GOT YOUR PROCLIVITIES, I GOT MINE, BUB--
UH, A THESPIAN IS AN ACTOR!
HACKING'S THE DAY JOB, HUH?
TAXI
AH, YES! TO TROD THE BOARDS! THE ROAR OF THE GREASEPAINT, THE SMELL OF THE CROWD--
--IS THAT YOUR COSTUME?
THIS HERE KIMONO? NAAA!
RRRIPP!
I GOT MY REAL COSTUME ON UNDERNEATH THIS HERE!
VERY KINKY OUTFIT, MISTER! THOSE BLUE STRIPES ARE TRES BIZARRO!
LEMME SEE THAT MIRROR!
KRUK!
WHAT D'YA KNOW? MY RIPPED UP MUG IS KNITTIN' BACK TOGETHER!
THE OL' MUTANT HEALIN' FACTOR IS KICKIN' BACK IN!

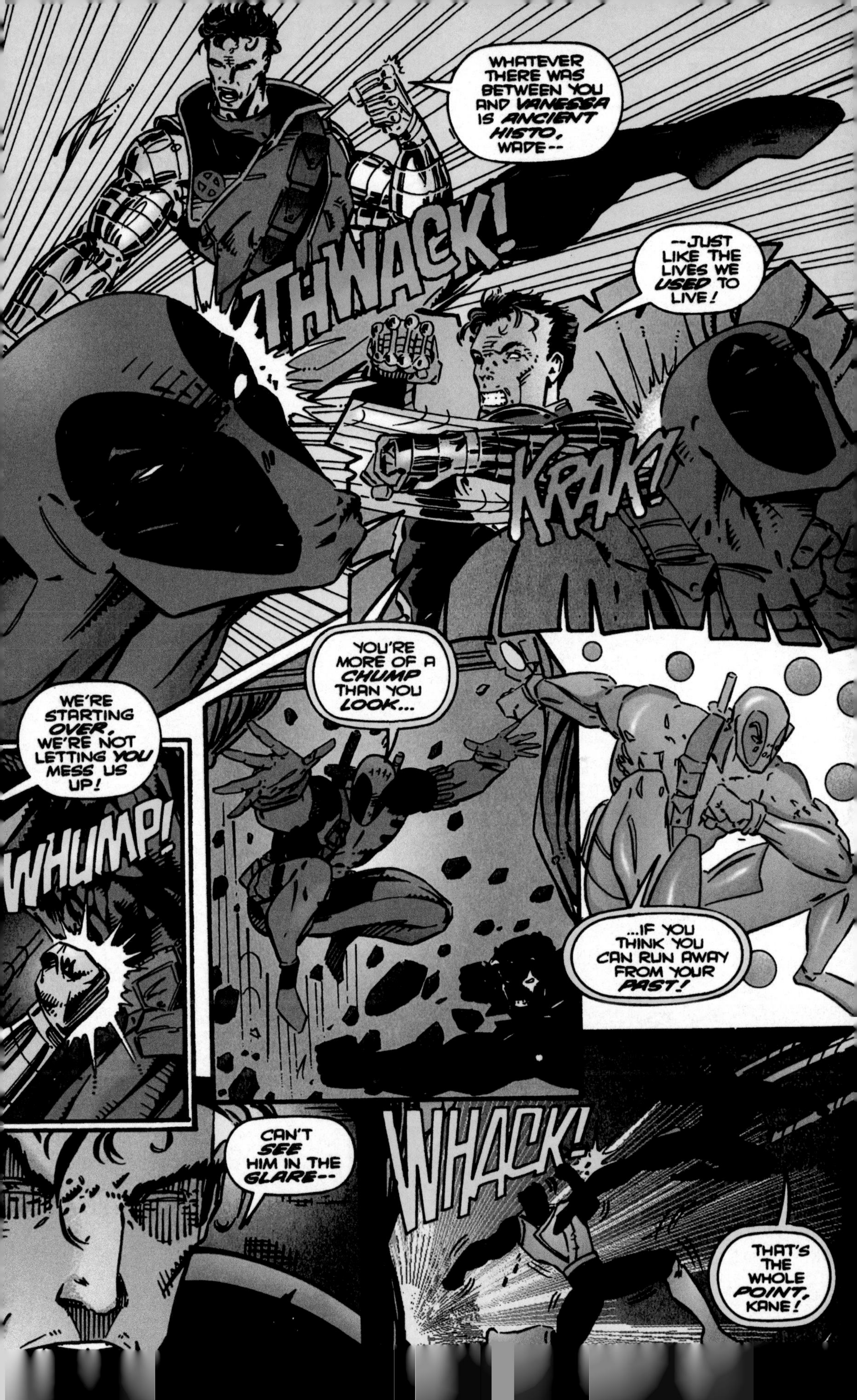
WHATEVER THERE WAS BETWEEN YOU AND VANESSA IS ANCIENT HISTO, WADE--
THWACK!
--JUST LIKE THE LIVES WE USED TO LIVE!
KRAK!
WE'RE STARTING OVER, WE'RE NOT LETTING YOU MESS US UP!
WHUMP!
YOU'RE MORE OF A CHUMP THAN YOU LOOK...
...IF YOU THINK YOU CAN RUN AWAY FROM YOUR PAST!
CAN'T SEE HIM IN THE GLARE--
WHACK!
THAT'S THE WHOLE POINT, KANE!

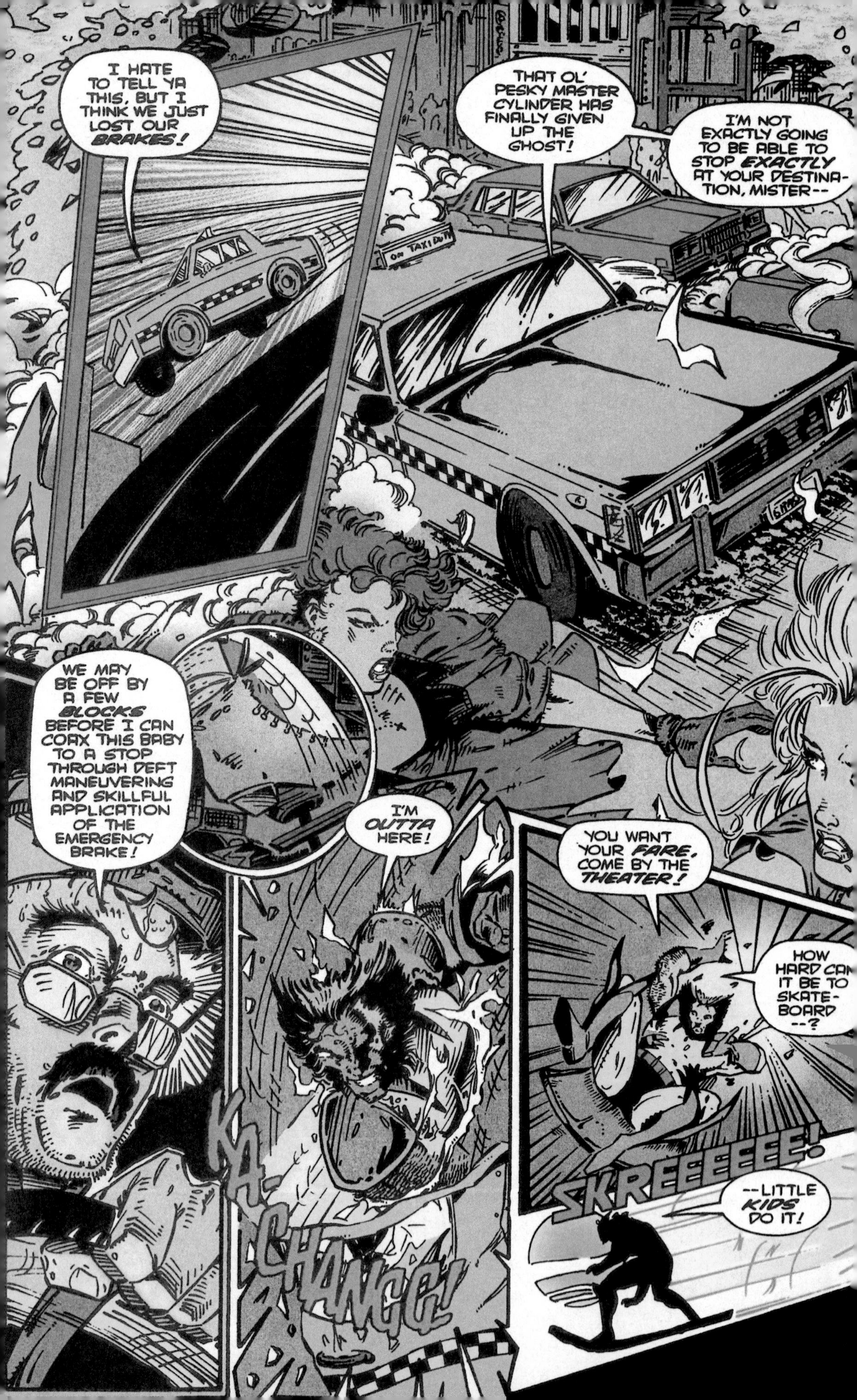
I HATE TO TELL YA THIS, BUT I THINK WE JUST LOST OUR BRAKES!
THAT OL' PESKY MASTER CYLINDER HAS FINALLY GIVEN UP THE GHOST!
I'M NOT EXACTLY GOING TO BE ABLE TO STOP EXACTLY AT YOUR DESTINATION, MISTER--
WE MAY BE OFF BY A FEW BLOCKS BEFORE I CAN COAX THIS BABY TO A STOP THROUGH DEFT MANEUVERING AND SKILLFUL APPLICATION OF THE EMERGENCY BRAKE!
I'M OUTTA HERE!
KA-CHANGG!
YOU WANT YOUR FARE, COME BY THE THEATER!
HOW HARD CAN IT BE TO SKATE-BOARD --?
SKREEEEEEE!
--LITTLE KIDS DO IT!

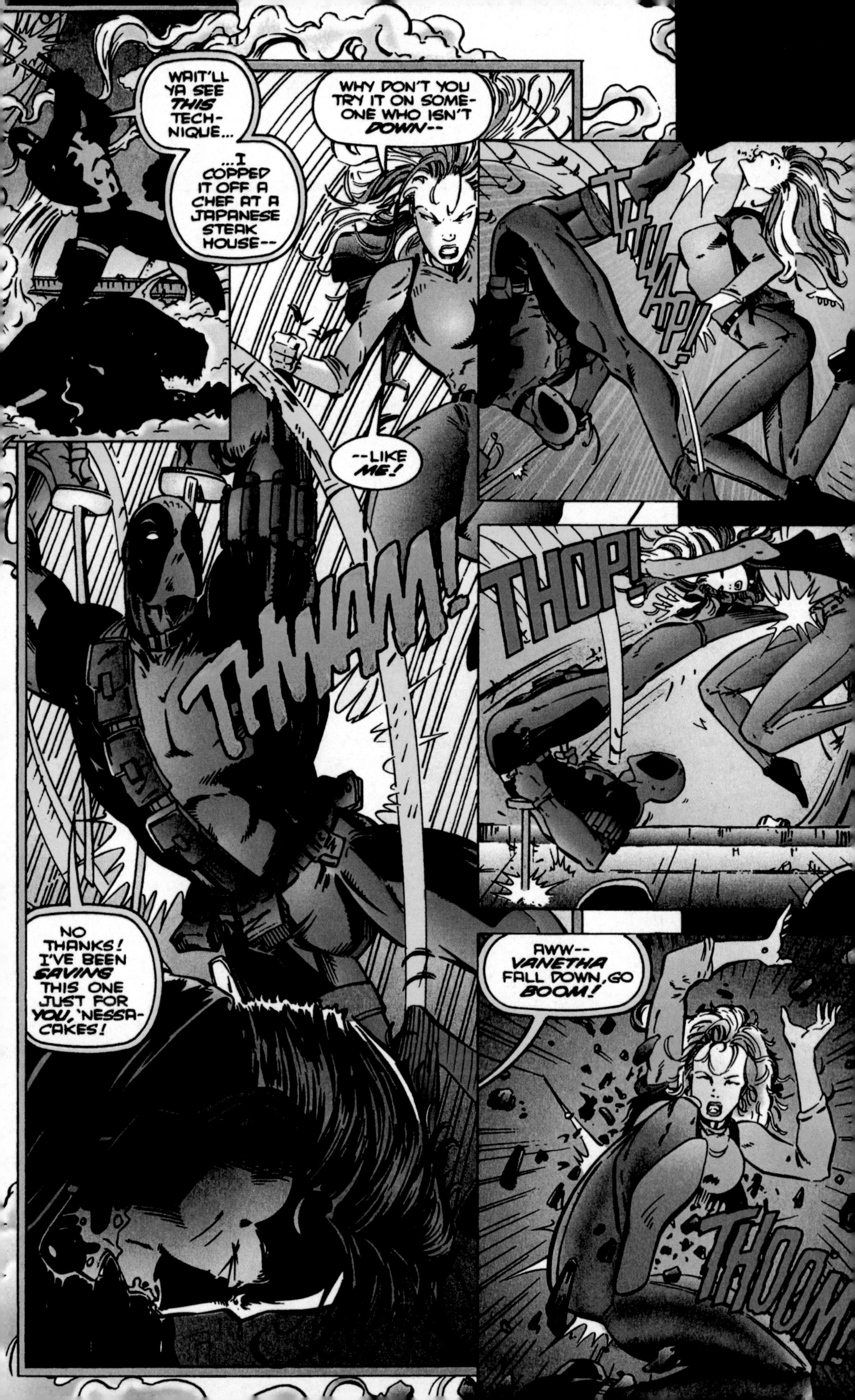

WAIT'LL YA SEE THIS TECHNIQUE...
...I COPPED IT OFF A CHEF AT A JAPANESE STEAK HOUSE--
WHY DON'T YOU TRY IT ON SOMEONE WHO ISN'T DOWN--
THWAP!
--LIKE ME!
THWAM!
THOP!
NO THANKS! I'VE BEEN SAVING THIS ONE JUST FOR YOU, 'NESSA-CAKES!
AWW-- VANETHA FALL DOWN, GO BOOM!
THOOM!

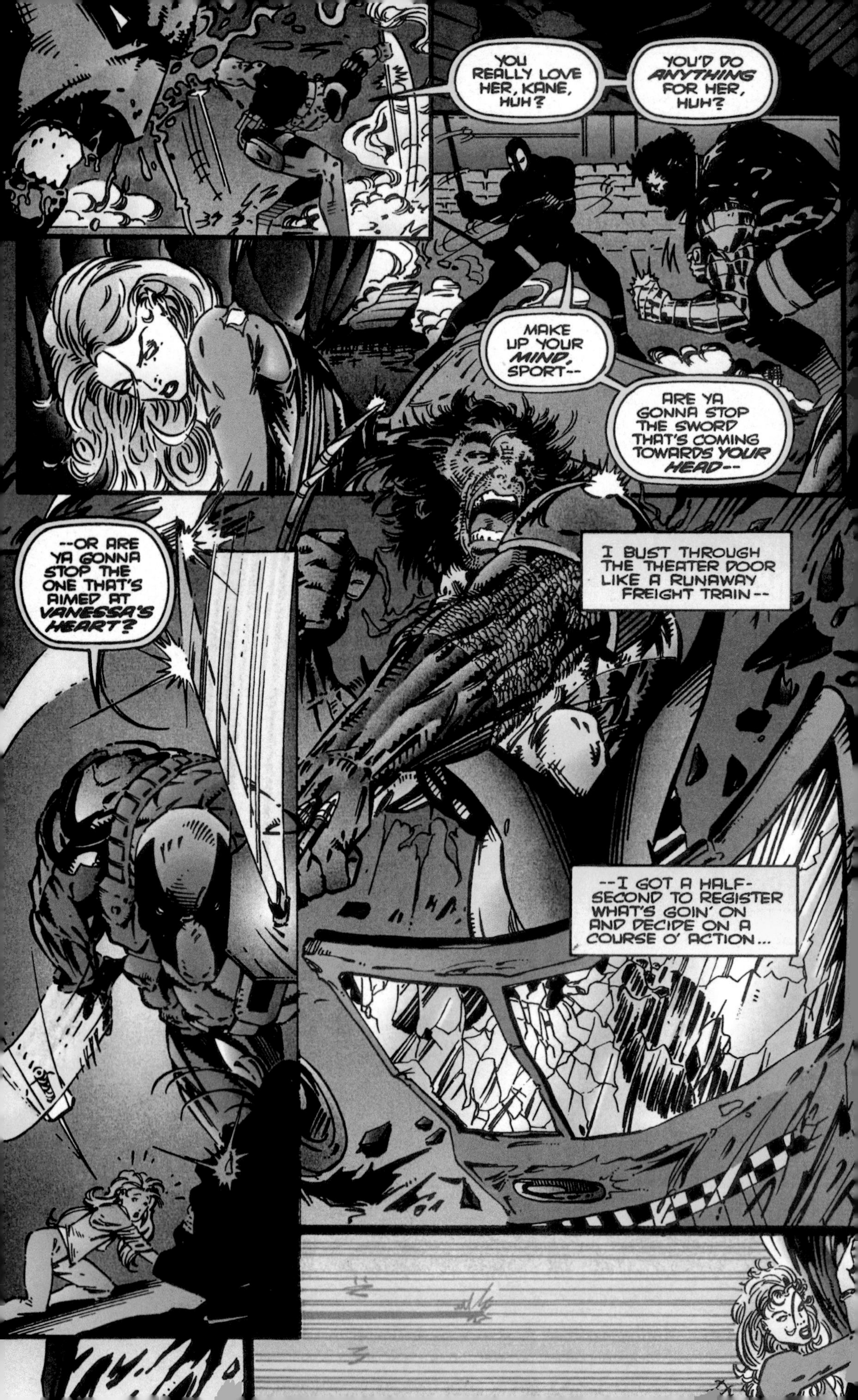
YOU REALLY LOVE HER, KANE, HUH?
YOU'D DO ANYTHING FOR HER, HUH?
MAKE UP YOUR MIND, SPORT--
ARE YA GONNA STOP THE SWORD THAT'S COMING TOWARDS YOUR HEAD--
--OR ARE YA GONNA STOP THE ONE THAT'S AIMED AT VANESSA'S HEART?
I BUST THROUGH THE THEATER DOOR LIKE A RUNAWAY FREIGHT TRAIN--
--I GOT A HALF-SECOND TO REGISTER WHAT'S GOIN' ON AND DECIDE ON A COURSE O' ACTION...

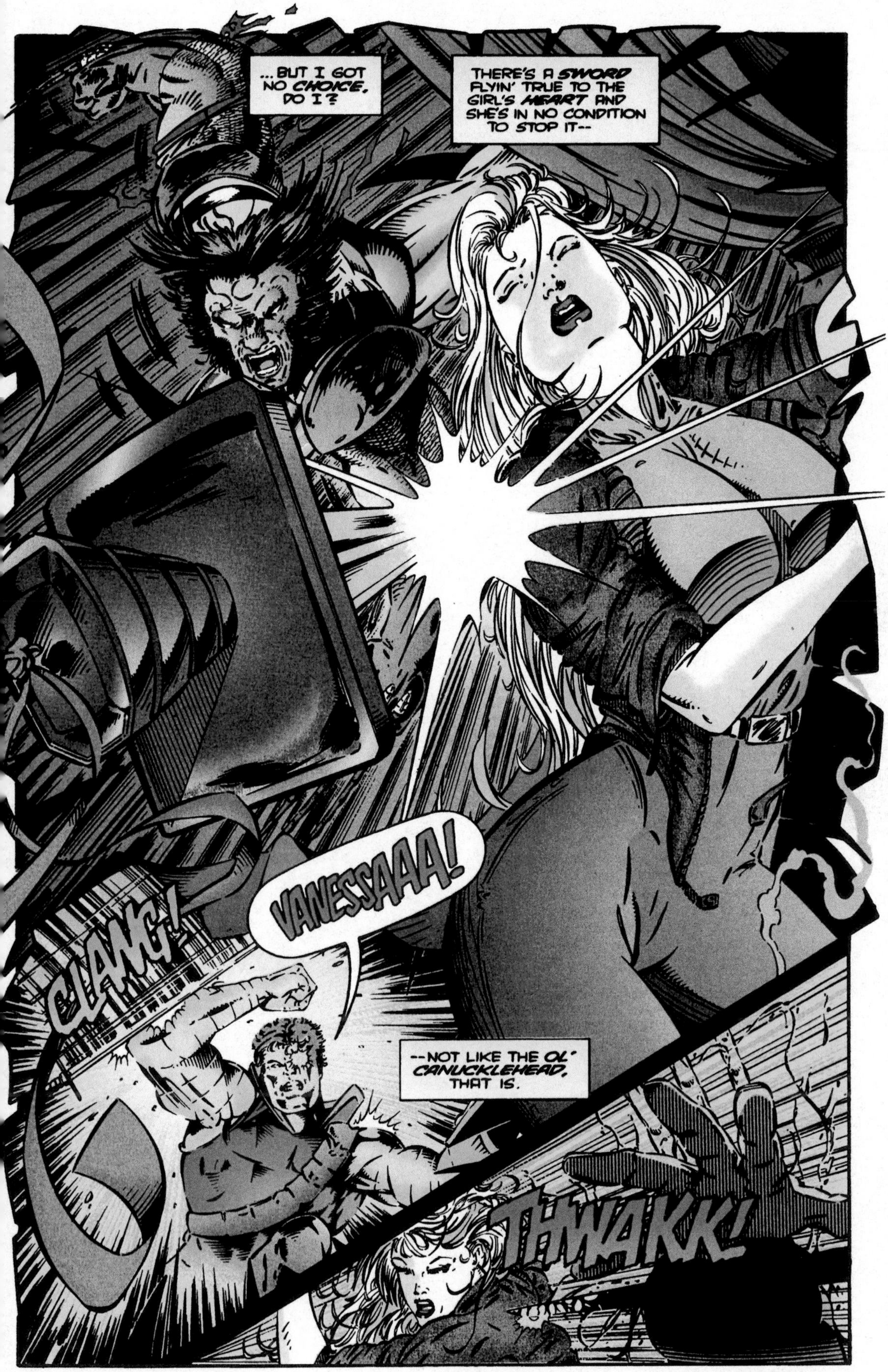
...BUT I GOT NO CHOICE, DO I?
THERE'S A SWORD FLYIN' TRUE TO THE GIRL'S HEART AND SHE'S IN NO CONDITION TO STOP IT--
VANESSAAA!
CLANG!
--NOT LIKE THE OL' CANUCKLEHEAD, THAT IS.
THWAKK!

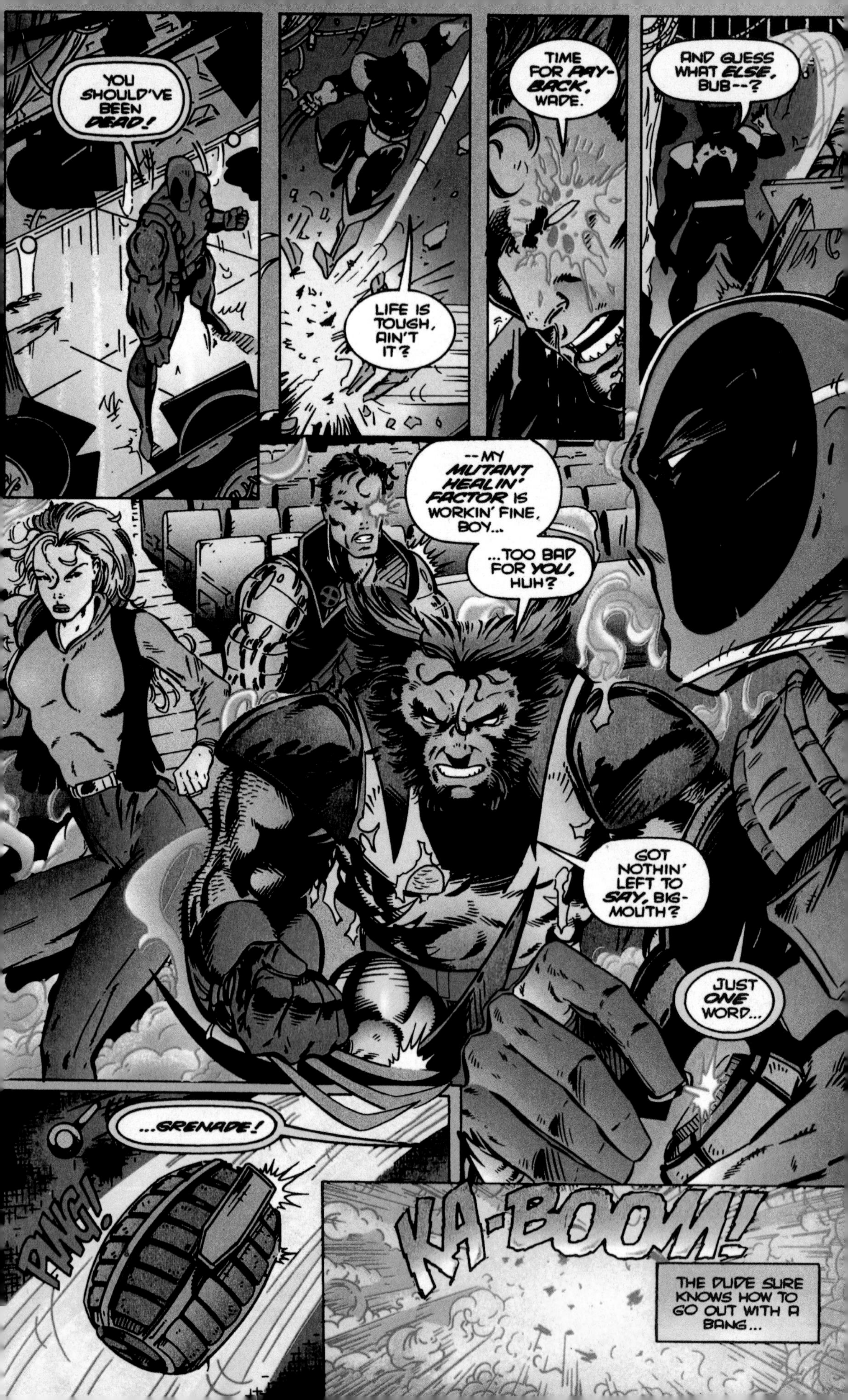

YOU SHOULD'VE BEEN DEAD!
LIFE IS TOUGH, AIN'T IT?
TIME FOR PAY-BACK, WADE.
AND GUESS WHAT ELSE, BUB--?
--MY MUTANT HEALIN' FACTOR IS WORKIN' FINE, BOY...
...TOO BAD FOR YOU, HUH?
GOT NOTHIN' LEFT TO SAY, BIG-MOUTH?
JUST ONE WORD...
...GRENADE!
PING!
KA-BOOM!
THE DUDE SURE KNOWS HOW TO GO OUT WITH A BANG...

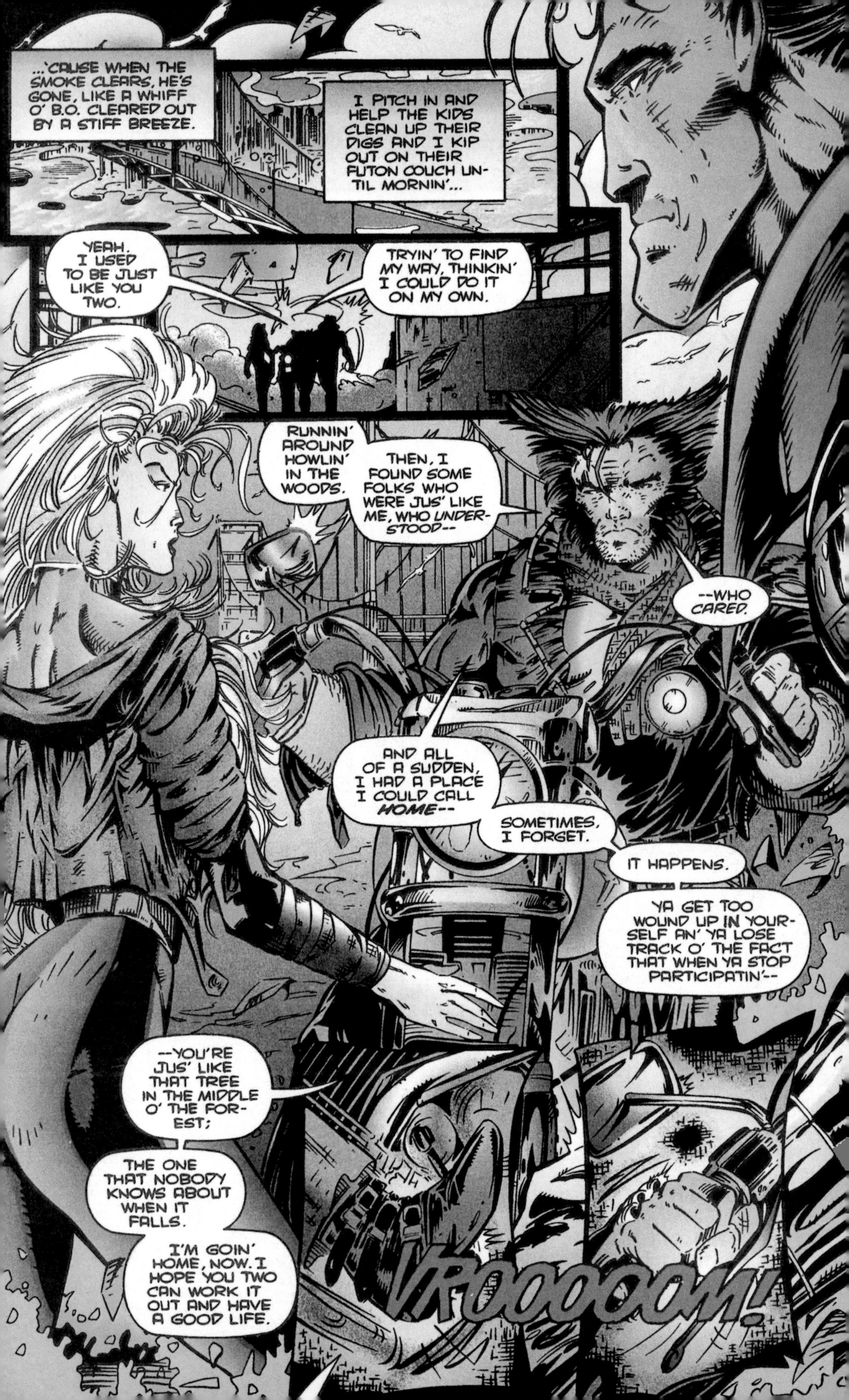
...'CAUSE WHEN THE SMOKE CLEARS, HE'S GONE, LIKE A WHIFF O' B.O. CLEARED OUT BY A STIFF BREEZE.
I PITCH IN AND HELP THE KIDS CLEAN UP THEIR DIGS AND I KIP OUT ON THEIR FUTON COUCH UNTIL MORNIN'...
YEAH. I USED TO BE JUST LIKE YOU TWO.
TRYIN' TO FIND MY WAY, THINKIN' I COULD DO IT ON MY OWN.
RUNNIN' AROUND HOWLIN' IN THE WOODS.
THEN, I FOUND SOME FOLKS WHO WERE JUS' LIKE ME, WHO UNDERSTOOD--
--WHO CARED.
AND ALL OF A SUDDEN, I HAD A PLACE I COULD CALL HOME--
SOMETIMES, I FORGET.
IT HAPPENS.
YA GET TOO WOUND UP IN YOURSELF AN' YA LOSE TRACK O' THE FACT THAT WHEN YA STOP PARTICIPATIN'--
--YOU'RE JUS' LIKE THAT TREE IN THE MIDDLE O' THE FOREST;
THE ONE THAT NOBODY KNOWS ABOUT WHEN IT FALLS.
I'M GOIN' HOME, NOW. I HOPE YOU TWO CAN WORK IT OUT AND HAVE A GOOD LIFE.
VROOOOOOM!

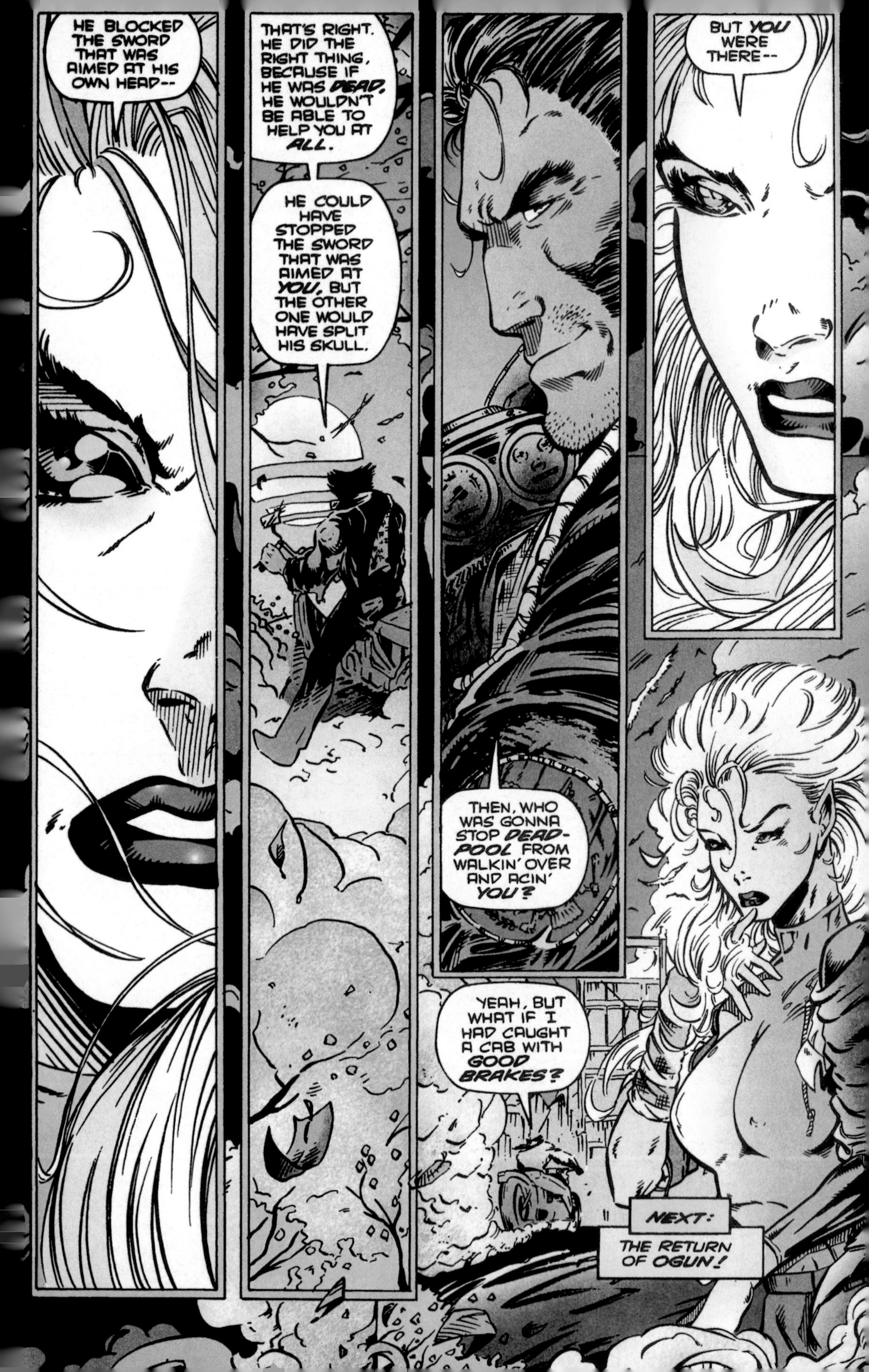
HE BLOCKED THE SWORD THAT WAS AIMED AT HIS OWN HEAD--
THAT'S RIGHT. HE DID THE RIGHT THING, BECAUSE IF HE WAS DEAD, HE WOULDN'T BE ABLE TO HELP YOU AT ALL.
HE COULD HAVE STOPPED THE SWORD THAT WAS AIMED AT YOU, BUT THE OTHER ONE WOULD HAVE SPLIT HIS SKULL.
THEN, WHO WAS GONNA STOP DEADPOOL FROM WALKIN' OVER AND ACIN' YOU?
BUT YOU WERE THERE--
YEAH, BUT WHAT IF I HAD CAUGHT A CAB WITH GOOD BRAKES?
NEXT:
THE RETURN OF OGUN!

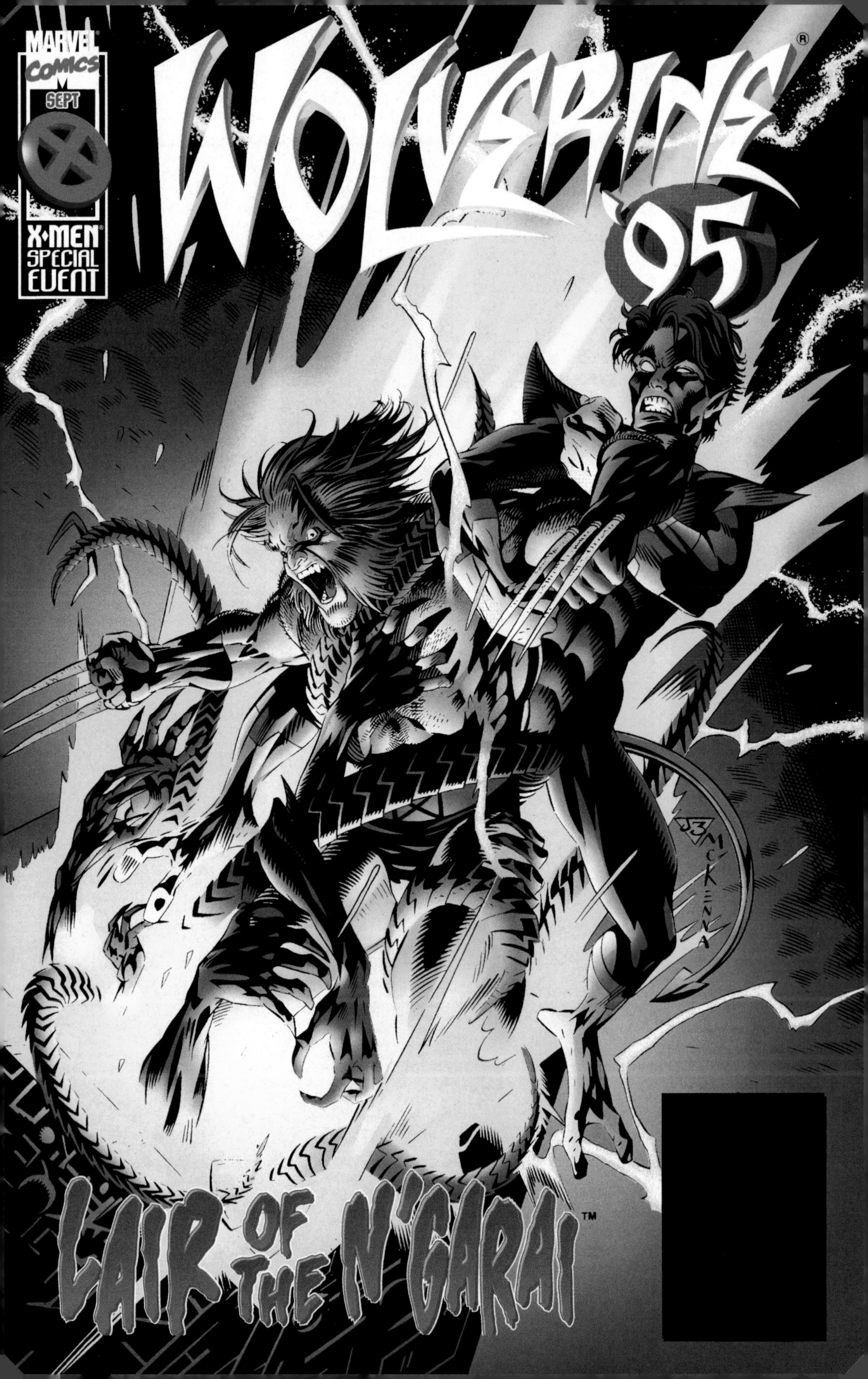
MARVEL COMICS
SEPT
X-MEN SPECIAL EVENT
WOLVERINE ®
'95
LAIR OF THE N'GARAI ™

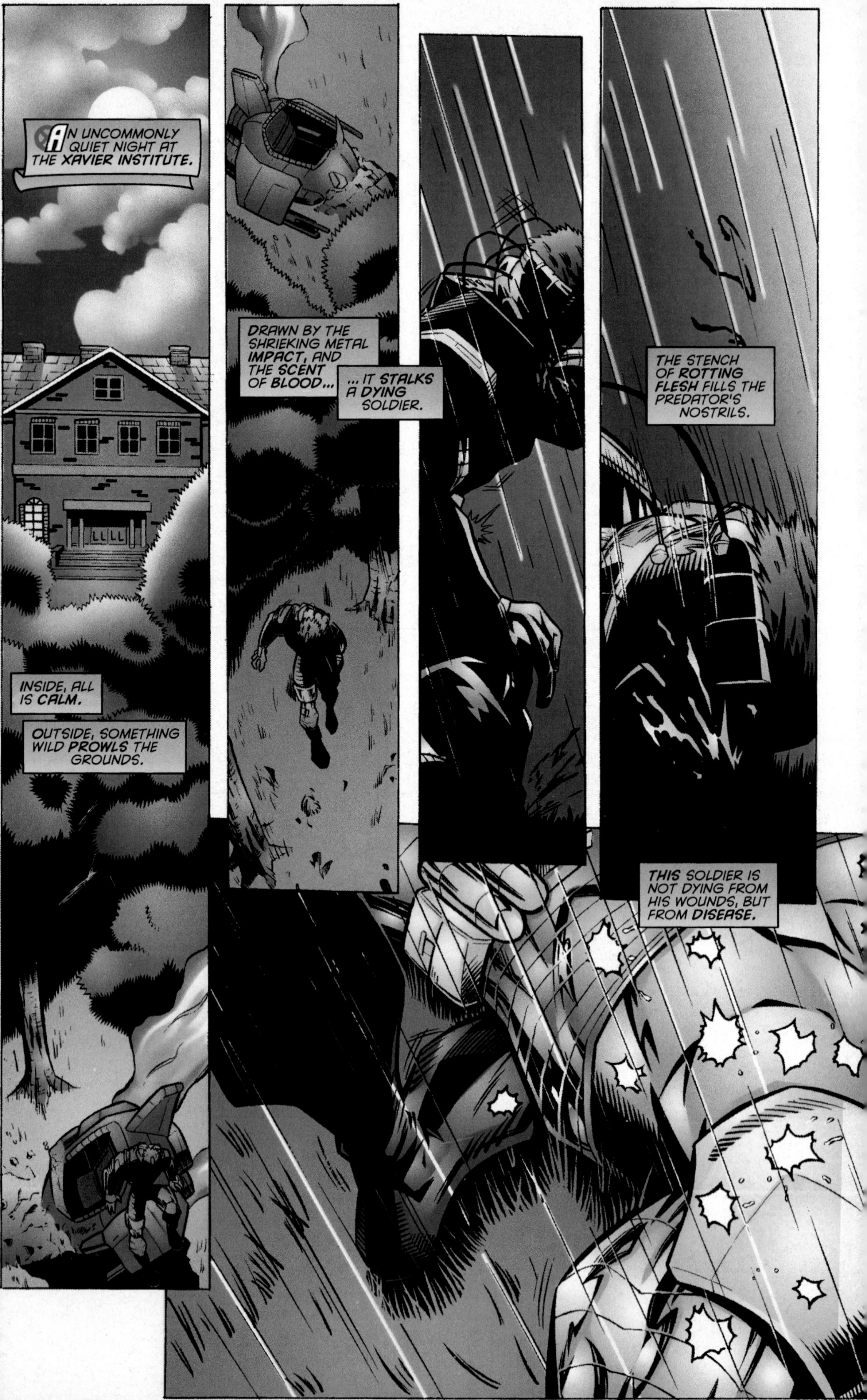
AN UNCOMMONLY QUIET NIGHT AT THE XAVIER INSTITUTE.
INSIDE, ALL IS CALM.
OUTSIDE, SOMETHING WILD PROWLS THE GROUNDS.
DRAWN BY THE SHRIEKING METAL IMPACT, AND THE SCENT OF BLOOD...
...IT STALKS A DYING SOLDIER.
THE STENCH OF ROTTING FLESH FILLS THE PREDATOR'S NOSTRILS.
THIS SOLDIER IS NOT DYING FROM HIS WOUNDS, BUT FROM DISEASE.

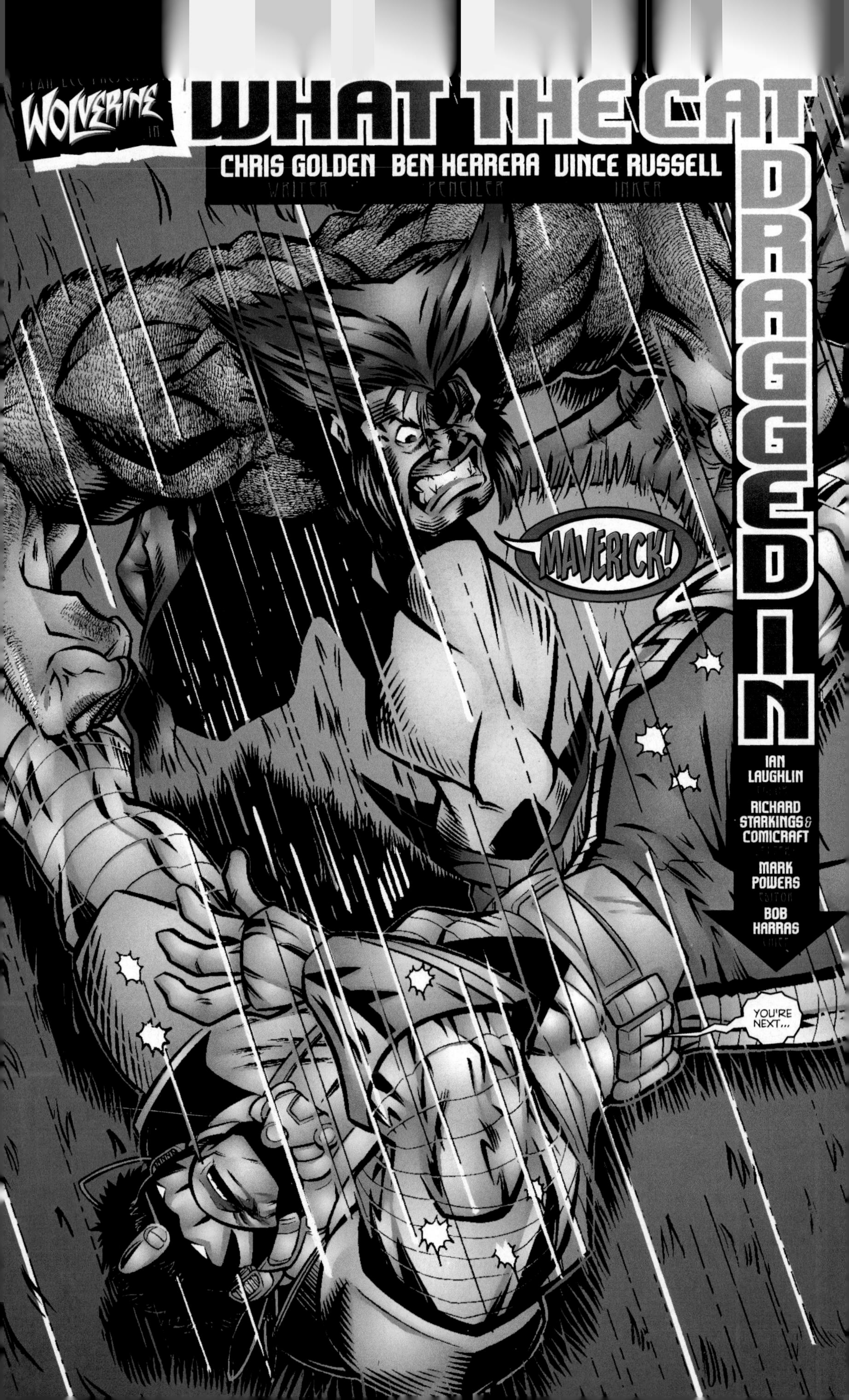

WOLVERINE IN
WHAT THE CAT DRAGGED IN
CHRIS GOLDEN WRITER
BEN HERRERA PENCILER
VINCE RUSSELL INKER
IAN LAUGHLIN
RICHARD STARKINGS & COMICRAFT
MARK POWERS EDITOR
BOB HARRAS
MAVERICK!
YOU'RE NEXT...

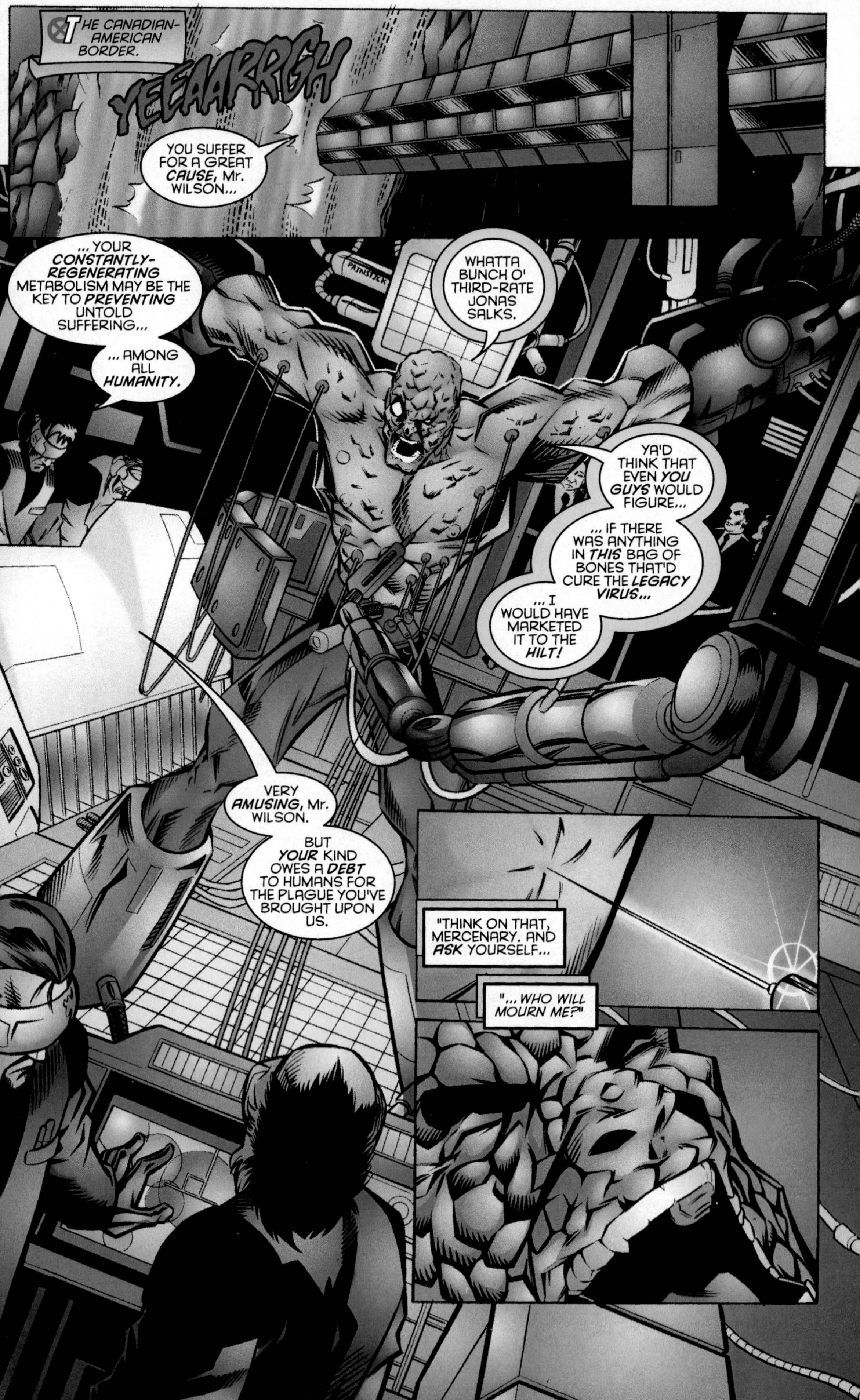
THE CANADIAN-AMERICAN BORDER.
YEEAARRGH
YOU SUFFER FOR A GREAT CAUSE, Mr. WILSON...
...YOUR CONSTANTLY-REGENERATING METABOLISM MAY BE THE KEY TO PREVENTING UNTOLD SUFFERING...
...AMONG ALL HUMANITY.
WHATTA BUNCH O' THIRD-RATE JONAS SALKS.
YA'D THINK THAT EVEN YOU GUYS WOULD FIGURE...
...IF THERE WAS ANYTHING IN THIS BAG OF BONES THAT'D CURE THE LEGACY VIRUS...
...I WOULD HAVE MARKETED IT TO THE HILT!
VERY AMUSING, Mr. WILSON.
BUT YOUR KIND OWES A DEBT TO HUMANS FOR THE PLAGUE YOU'VE BROUGHT UPON US.
"THINK ON THAT, MERCENARY. AND ASK YOURSELF...
"...WHO WILL MOURN ME?"

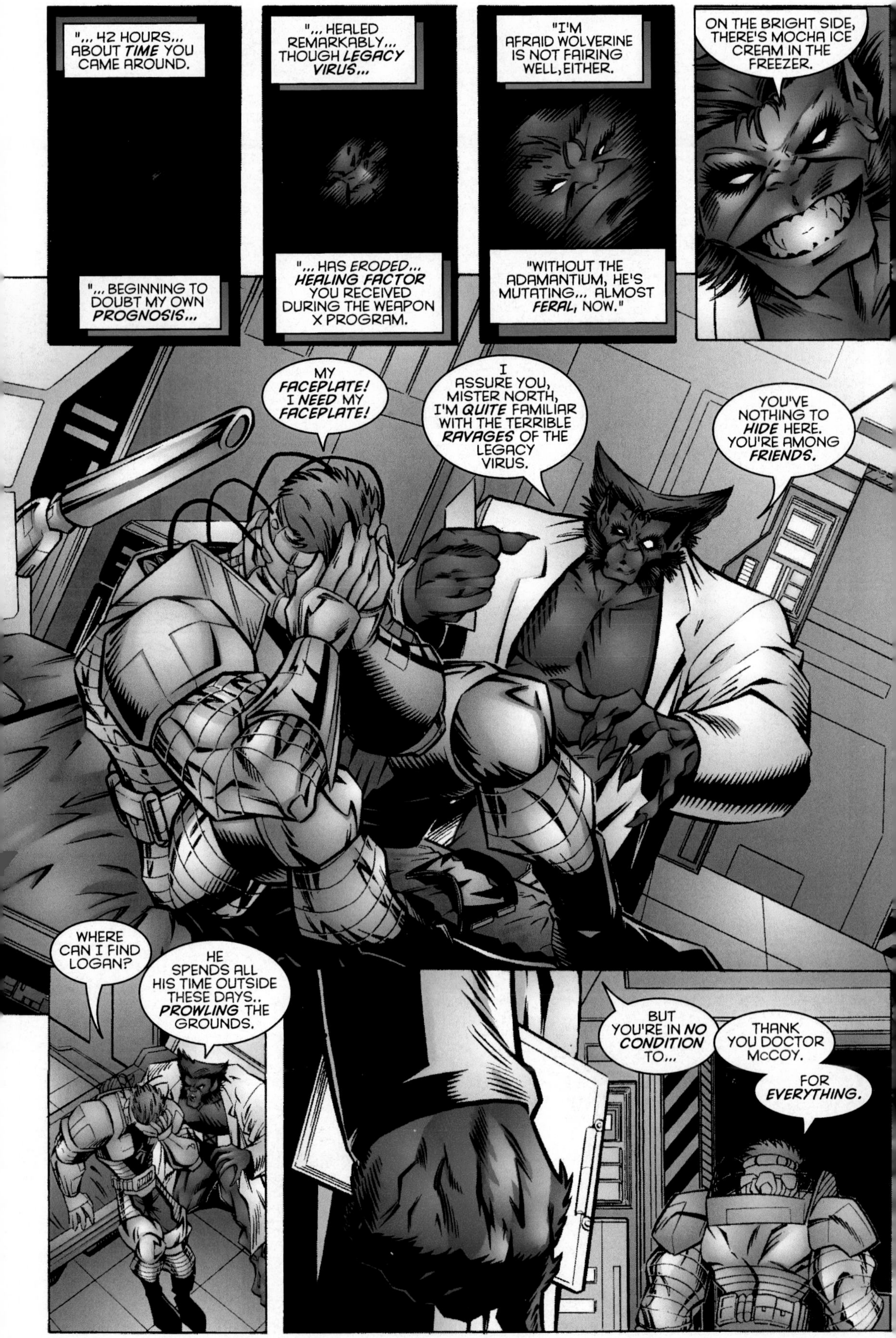
"... 42 HOURS... ABOUT *TIME* YOU CAME AROUND.
"... BEGINNING TO DOUBT MY OWN *PROGNOSIS*...
"... HEALED REMARKABLY... THOUGH *LEGACY VIRUS*...
"... HAS *ERODED*... *HEALING FACTOR* YOU RECEIVED DURING THE WEAPON X PROGRAM.
"I'M AFRAID WOLVERINE IS NOT FAIRING WELL, EITHER.
"WITHOUT THE ADAMANTIUM, HE'S MUTATING... ALMOST *FERAL*, NOW."
ON THE BRIGHT SIDE, THERE'S MOCHA ICE CREAM IN THE FREEZER.
MY *FACEPLATE!* I *NEED* MY *FACEPLATE!*
I ASSURE YOU, MISTER NORTH, I'M *QUITE* FAMILIAR WITH THE TERRIBLE *RAVAGES* OF THE LEGACY VIRUS.
YOU'VE NOTHING TO *HIDE* HERE. YOU'RE AMONG *FRIENDS*.
WHERE CAN I FIND LOGAN?
HE SPENDS ALL HIS TIME OUTSIDE THESE DAYS.. *PROWLING* THE GROUNDS.
BUT YOU'RE IN *NO CONDITION* TO...
THANK YOU DOCTOR McCOY.
FOR *EVERYTHING*.

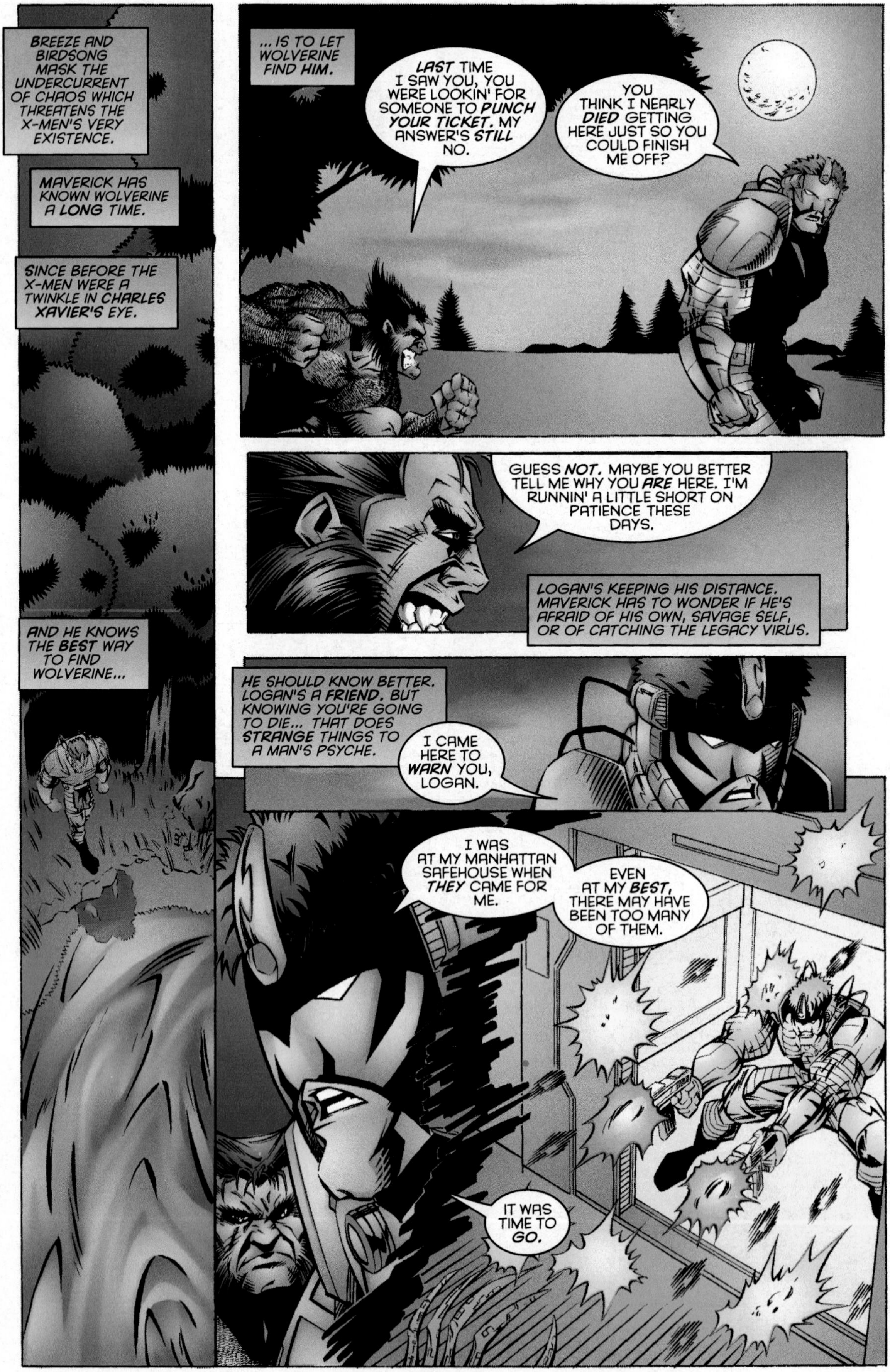

BREEZE AND BIRDSONG MASK THE UNDERCURRENT OF CHAOS WHICH THREATENS THE X-MEN'S VERY EXISTENCE.
MAVERICK HAS KNOWN WOLVERINE A LONG TIME.
SINCE BEFORE THE X-MEN WERE A TWINKLE IN CHARLES XAVIER'S EYE.
AND HE KNOWS THE BEST WAY TO FIND WOLVERINE...
...IS TO LET WOLVERINE FIND HIM.
LAST TIME I SAW YOU, YOU WERE LOOKIN' FOR SOMEONE TO PUNCH YOUR TICKET. MY ANSWER'S STILL NO.
YOU THINK I NEARLY DIED GETTING HERE JUST SO YOU COULD FINISH ME OFF?
GUESS NOT. MAYBE YOU BETTER TELL ME WHY YOU ARE HERE. I'M RUNNIN' A LITTLE SHORT ON PATIENCE THESE DAYS.
LOGAN'S KEEPING HIS DISTANCE. MAVERICK HAS TO WONDER IF HE'S AFRAID OF HIS OWN, SAVAGE SELF, OR OF CATCHING THE LEGACY VIRUS.
HE SHOULD KNOW BETTER. LOGAN'S A FRIEND. BUT KNOWING YOU'RE GOING TO DIE... THAT DOES STRANGE THINGS TO A MAN'S PSYCHE.
I CAME HERE TO WARN YOU, LOGAN.
I WAS AT MY MANHATTAN SAFEHOUSE WHEN THEY CAME FOR ME.
EVEN AT MY BEST, THERE MAY HAVE BEEN TOO MANY OF THEM.
IT WAS TIME TO GO.

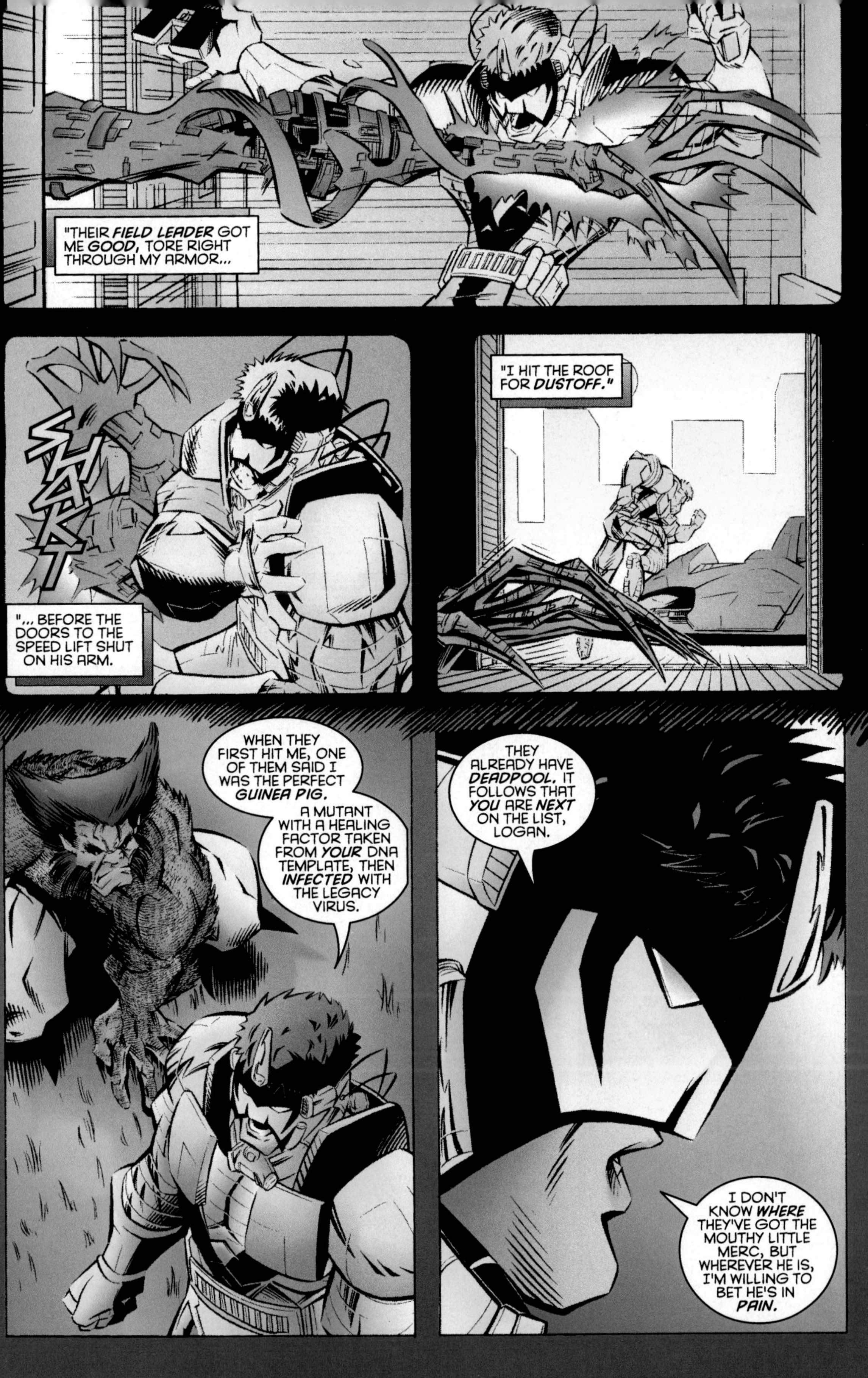
"THEIR FIELD LEADER GOT ME GOOD, TORE RIGHT THROUGH MY ARMOR...
SHAKT
"... BEFORE THE DOORS TO THE SPEED LIFT SHUT ON HIS ARM.
"I HIT THE ROOF FOR DUSTOFF."
WHEN THEY FIRST HIT ME, ONE OF THEM SAID I WAS THE PERFECT GUINEA PIG.
A MUTANT WITH A HEALING FACTOR TAKEN FROM YOUR DNA TEMPLATE, THEN INFECTED WITH THE LEGACY VIRUS.
THEY ALREADY HAVE DEADPOOL. IT FOLLOWS THAT YOU ARE NEXT ON THE LIST, LOGAN.
I DON'T KNOW WHERE THEY'VE GOT THE MOUTHY LITTLE MERC, BUT WHEREVER HE IS, I'M WILLING TO BET HE'S IN PAIN.

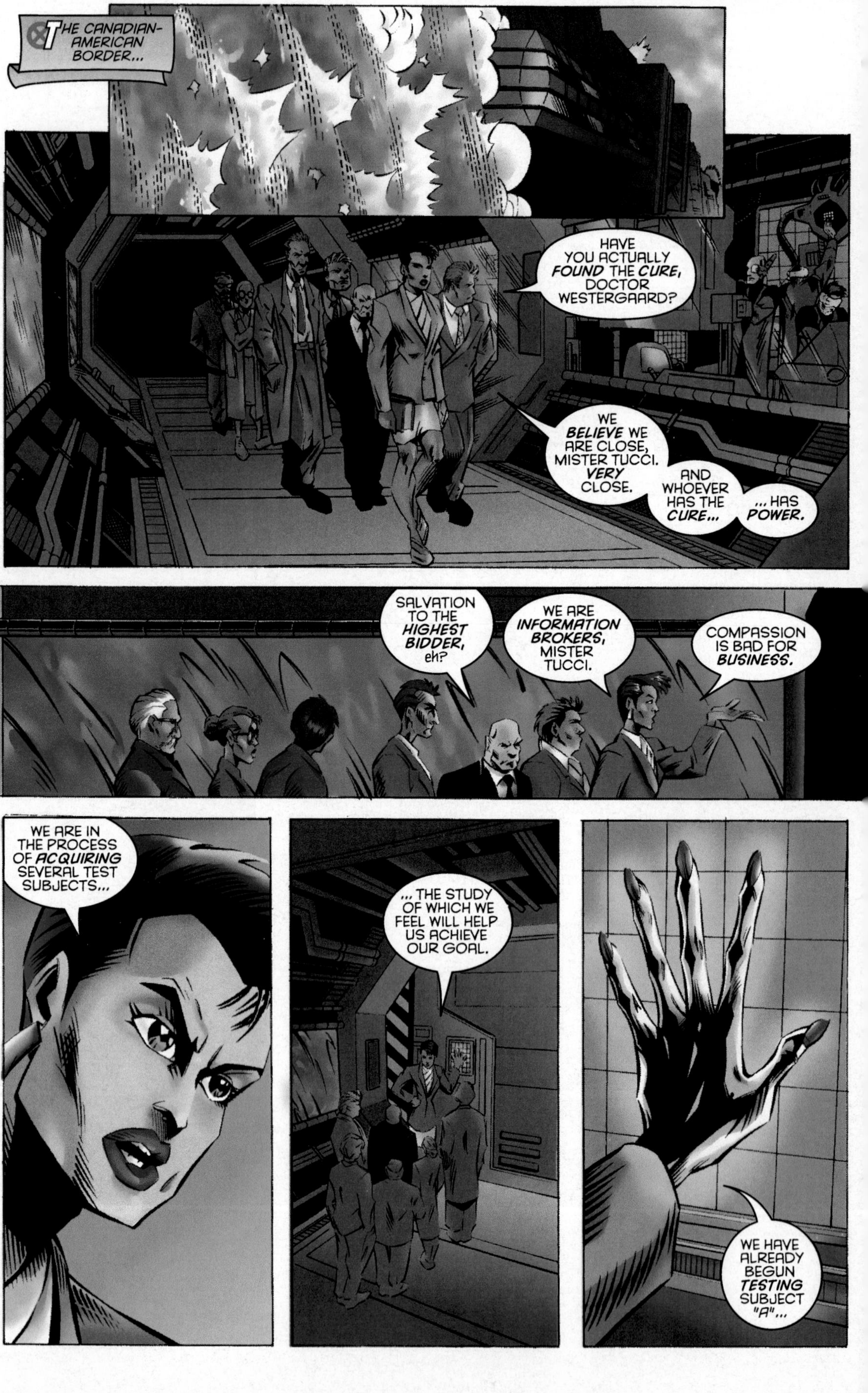
THE CANADIAN-AMERICAN BORDER...
HAVE YOU ACTUALLY FOUND THE CURE, DOCTOR WESTERGAARD?
WE BELIEVE WE ARE CLOSE, MISTER TUCCI. VERY CLOSE.
AND WHOEVER HAS THE CURE...
...HAS POWER.
SALVATION TO THE HIGHEST BIDDER, eh?
WE ARE INFORMATION BROKERS, MISTER TUCCI.
COMPASSION IS BAD FOR BUSINESS.
WE ARE IN THE PROCESS OF ACQUIRING SEVERAL TEST SUBJECTS...
...THE STUDY OF WHICH WE FEEL WILL HELP US ACHIEVE OUR GOAL.
WE HAVE ALREADY BEGUN TESTING SUBJECT "A"...

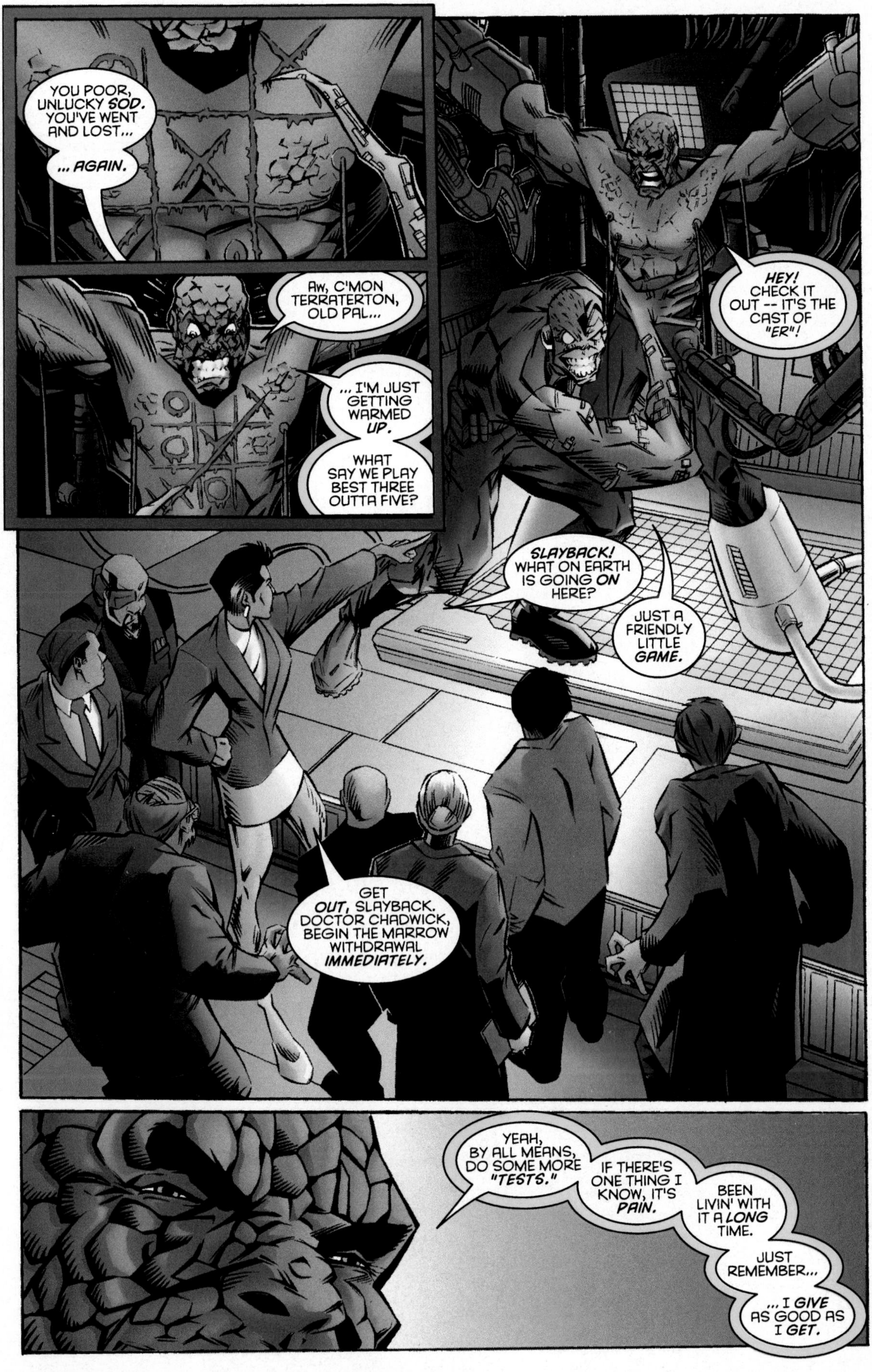
YOU POOR, UNLUCKY SOD. YOU'VE WENT AND LOST...
... AGAIN.
AW, C'MON TERRATERTON, OLD PAL...
... I'M JUST GETTING WARMED UP.
WHAT SAY WE PLAY BEST THREE OUTTA FIVE?
HEY! CHECK IT OUT -- IT'S THE CAST OF "ER"!
SLAYBACK! WHAT ON EARTH IS GOING ON HERE?
JUST A FRIENDLY LITTLE GAME.
GET OUT, SLAYBACK. DOCTOR CHADWICK, BEGIN THE MARROW WITHDRAWAL IMMEDIATELY.
YEAH, BY ALL MEANS, DO SOME MORE "TESTS."
IF THERE'S ONE THING I KNOW, IT'S PAIN.
BEEN LIVIN' WITH IT A LONG TIME.
JUST REMEMBER...
... I GIVE AS GOOD AS I GET.

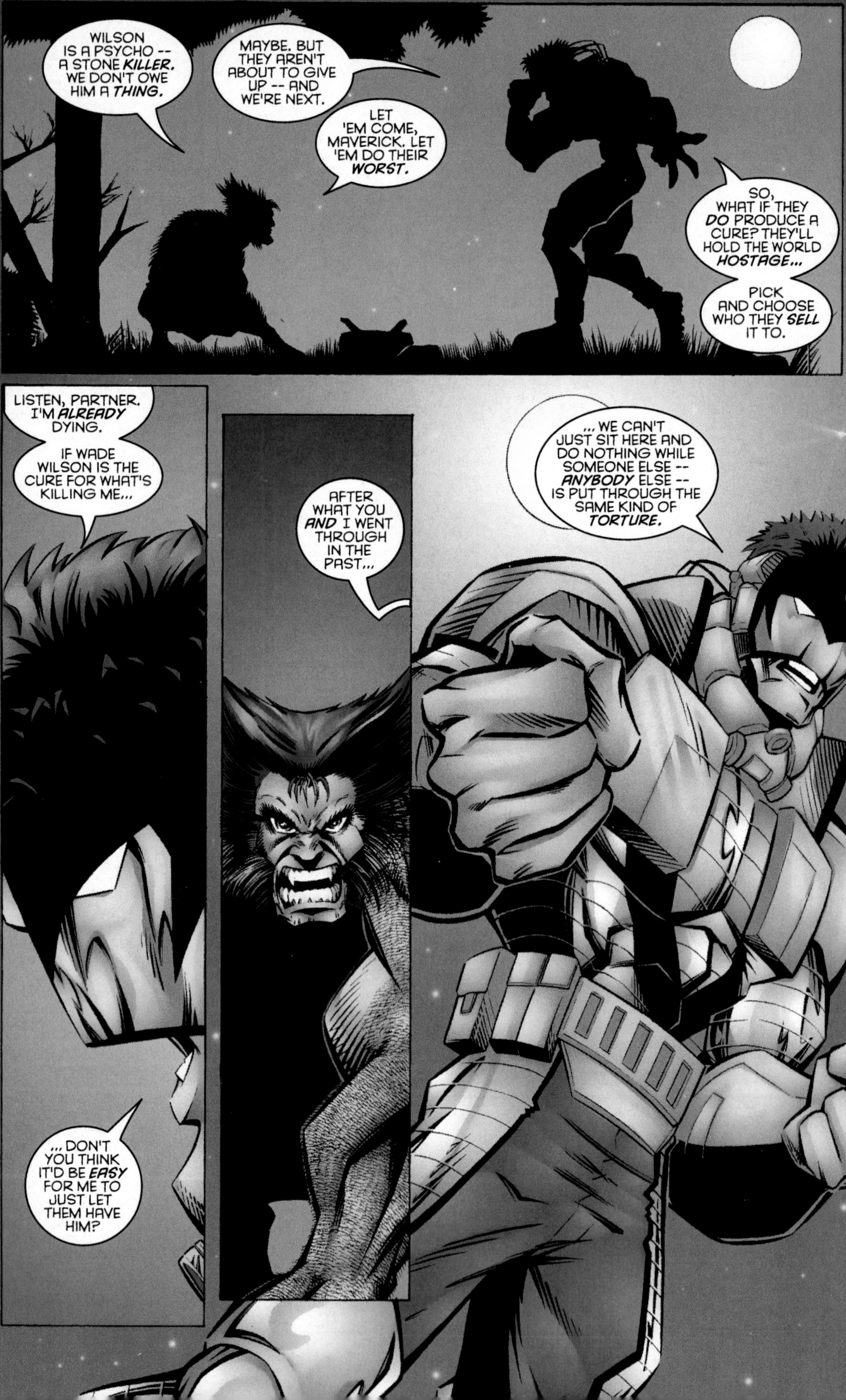
WILSON IS A PSYCHO -- A STONE KILLER. WE DON'T OWE HIM A THING.
MAYBE. BUT THEY AREN'T ABOUT TO GIVE UP -- AND WE'RE NEXT.
LET 'EM COME, MAVERICK. LET 'EM DO THEIR WORST.
SO, WHAT IF THEY DO PRODUCE A CURE? THEY'LL HOLD THE WORLD HOSTAGE...
PICK AND CHOOSE WHO THEY SELL IT TO.
LISTEN, PARTNER. I'M ALREADY DYING.
IF WADE WILSON IS THE CURE FOR WHAT'S KILLING ME...
...DON'T YOU THINK IT'D BE EASY FOR ME TO JUST LET THEM HAVE HIM?
AFTER WHAT YOU AND I WENT THROUGH IN THE PAST...
...WE CAN'T JUST SIT HERE AND DO NOTHING WHILE SOMEONE ELSE -- ANYBODY ELSE -- IS PUT THROUGH THE SAME KIND OF TORTURE.

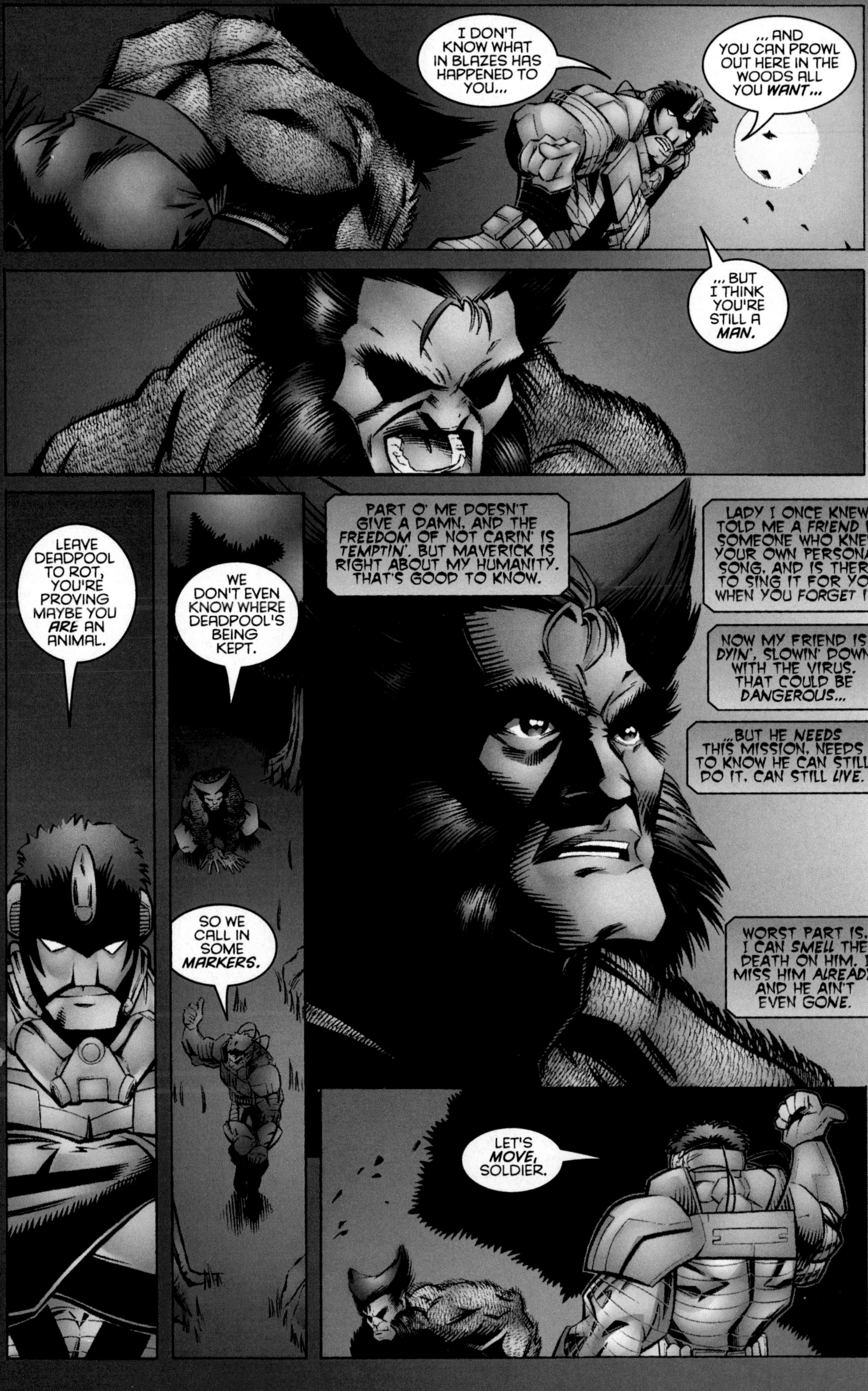
I DON'T KNOW WHAT IN BLAZES HAS HAPPENED TO YOU...
...AND YOU CAN PROWL OUT HERE IN THE WOODS ALL YOU *WANT*...
...BUT I THINK YOU'RE STILL A *MAN.*
LEAVE DEADPOOL TO ROT, YOU'RE PROVING MAYBE YOU *ARE* AN ANIMAL.
WE DON'T EVEN KNOW WHERE DEADPOOL'S BEING KEPT.
SO WE CALL IN SOME *MARKERS.*
PART O' ME DOESN'T GIVE A DAMN, AND THE *FREEDOM OF NOT CARIN'* IS *TEMPTIN'*. BUT MAVERICK IS RIGHT ABOUT MY HUMANITY. THAT'S GOOD TO KNOW.
LADY I ONCE KNEW TOLD ME A *FRIEND* IS SOMEONE WHO KNEW YOUR OWN PERSONAL SONG, AND IS THERE TO SING IT FOR YOU WHEN YOU FORGET IT.
NOW MY FRIEND IS *DYIN'*, SLOWIN' DOWN WITH THE VIRUS. THAT COULD BE *DANGEROUS...*
...BUT HE *NEEDS* THIS MISSION, NEEDS TO KNOW HE CAN STILL DO IT. CAN STILL *LIVE.*
WORST PART IS, I CAN *SMELL* THE DEATH ON HIM. I MISS HIM *ALREADY*, AND HE AIN'T EVEN *GONE.*
LET'S *MOVE*, SOLDIER.

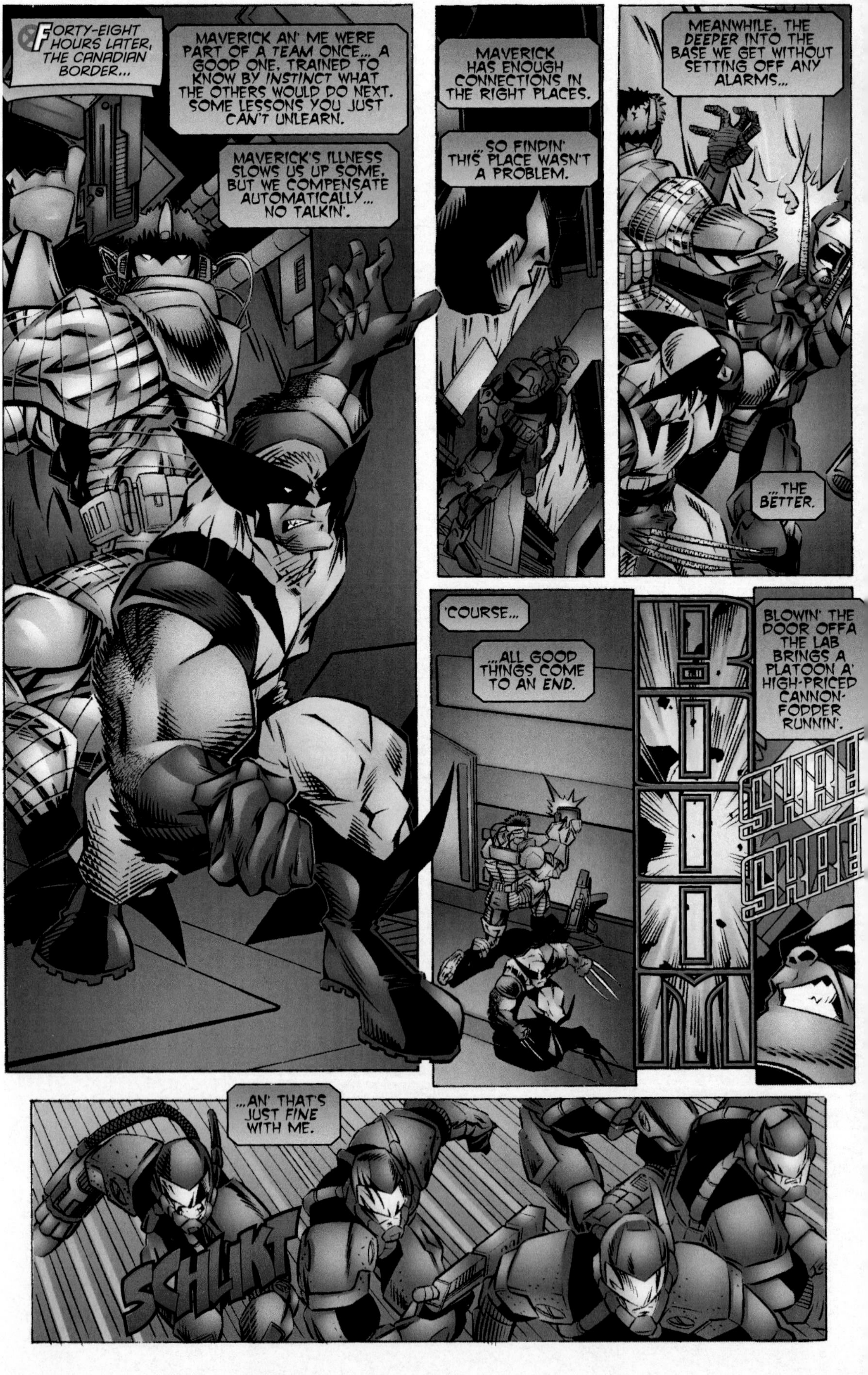
FORTY-EIGHT HOURS LATER, THE CANADIAN BORDER...
MAVERICK AN' ME WERE PART OF A TEAM ONCE... A GOOD ONE, TRAINED TO KNOW BY INSTINCT WHAT THE OTHERS WOULD DO NEXT. SOME LESSONS YOU JUST CAN'T UNLEARN.
MAVERICK'S ILLNESS SLOWS US UP SOME, BUT WE COMPENSATE AUTOMATICALLY... NO TALKIN'.
MAVERICK HAS ENOUGH CONNECTIONS IN THE RIGHT PLACES.
...SO FINDIN' THIS PLACE WASN'T A PROBLEM.
MEANWHILE, THE DEEPER INTO THE BASE WE GET WITHOUT SETTING OFF ANY ALARMS...
...THE BETTER.
'COURSE...
...ALL GOOD THINGS COME TO AN END.
BLOWIN' THE DOOR OFFA THE LAB BRINGS A PLATOON A' HIGH-PRICED CANNON-FODDER RUNNIN'.
...AN' THAT'S JUST FINE WITH ME.
SCHLIKT

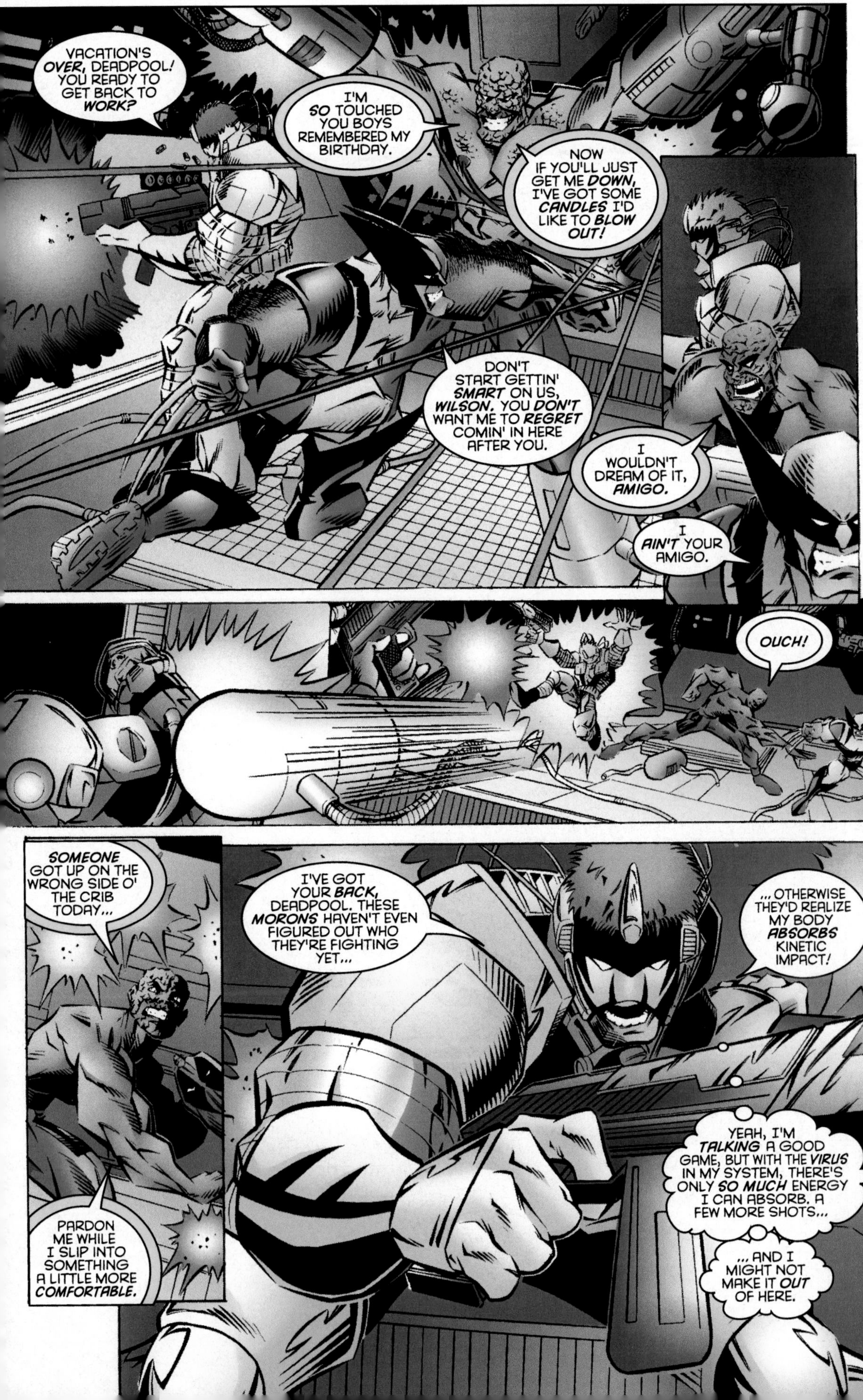
VACATION'S OVER, DEADPOOL! YOU READY TO GET BACK TO WORK?
I'M SO TOUCHED YOU BOYS REMEMBERED MY BIRTHDAY.
NOW IF YOU'LL JUST GET ME DOWN, I'VE GOT SOME CANDLES I'D LIKE TO BLOW OUT!
DON'T START GETTIN' SMART ON US, WILSON. YOU DON'T WANT ME TO REGRET COMIN' IN HERE AFTER YOU.
I WOULDN'T DREAM OF IT, AMIGO.
I AIN'T YOUR AMIGO.
OUCH!
SOMEONE GOT UP ON THE WRONG SIDE O' THE CRIB TODAY...
PARDON ME WHILE I SLIP INTO SOMETHING A LITTLE MORE COMFORTABLE.
I'VE GOT YOUR BACK, DEADPOOL. THESE MORONS HAVEN'T EVEN FIGURED OUT WHO THEY'RE FIGHTING YET...
...OTHERWISE THEY'D REALIZE MY BODY ABSORBS KINETIC IMPACT!
YEAH, I'M TALKING A GOOD GAME, BUT WITH THE VIRUS IN MY SYSTEM, THERE'S ONLY SO MUCH ENERGY I CAN ABSORB. A FEW MORE SHOTS...
...AND I MIGHT NOT MAKE IT OUT OF HERE.

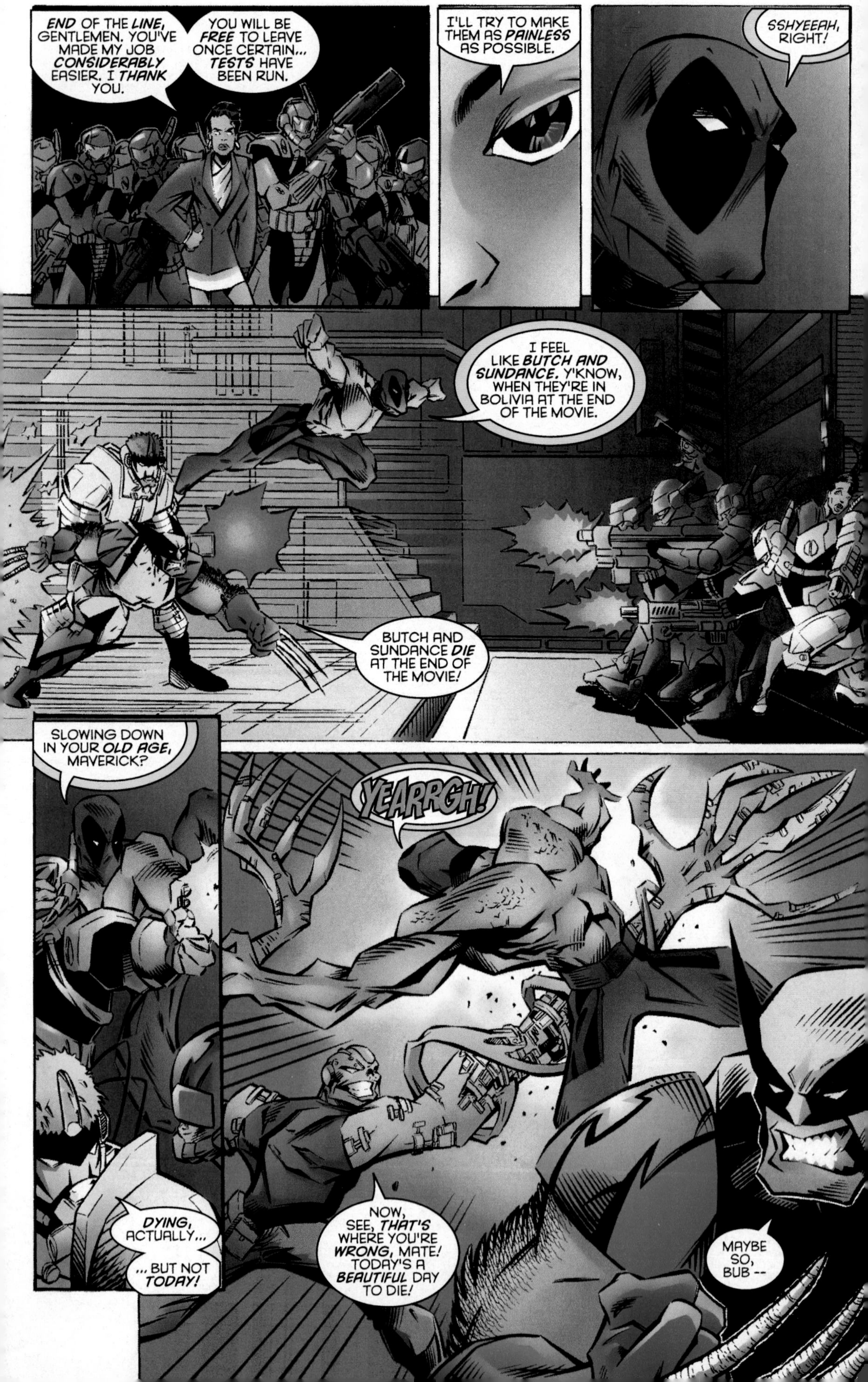

END OF THE LINE, GENTLEMEN. YOU'VE MADE MY JOB CONSIDERABLY EASIER. I THANK YOU.
YOU WILL BE FREE TO LEAVE ONCE CERTAIN... TESTS HAVE BEEN RUN.
I'LL TRY TO MAKE THEM AS PAINLESS AS POSSIBLE.
SSHYEEAH, RIGHT!
I FEEL LIKE BUTCH AND SUNDANCE. Y'KNOW, WHEN THEY'RE IN BOLIVIA AT THE END OF THE MOVIE.
BUTCH AND SUNDANCE DIE AT THE END OF THE MOVIE!
SLOWING DOWN IN YOUR OLD AGE, MAVERICK?
YEARRGH!
DYING, ACTUALLY...
...BUT NOT TODAY!
NOW, SEE, THAT'S WHERE YOU'RE WRONG, MATE! TODAY'S A BEAUTIFUL DAY TO DIE!
MAYBE SO, BUB --

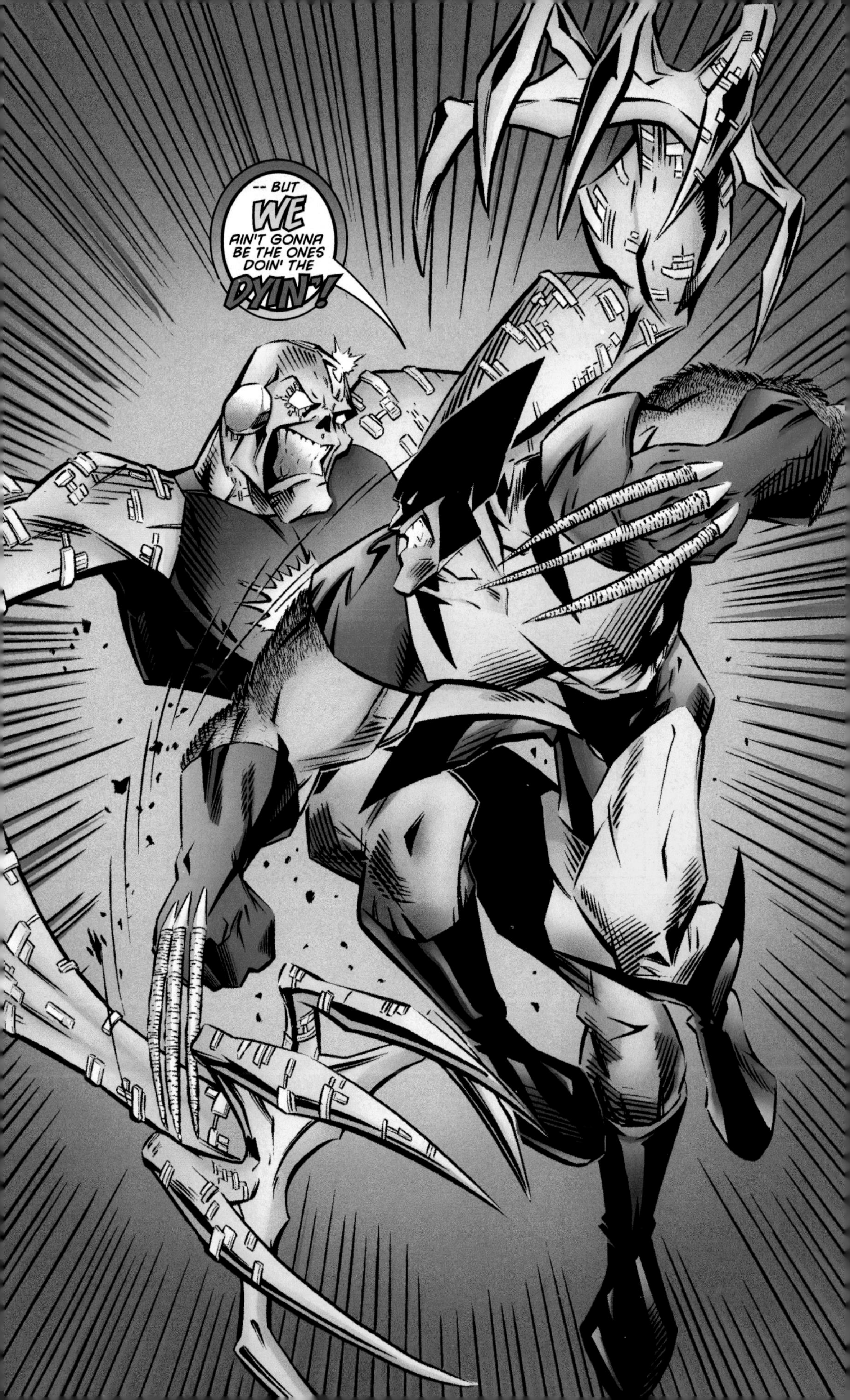
-- BUT WE AIN'T GONNA BE THE ONES DOIN' THE DYIN'!

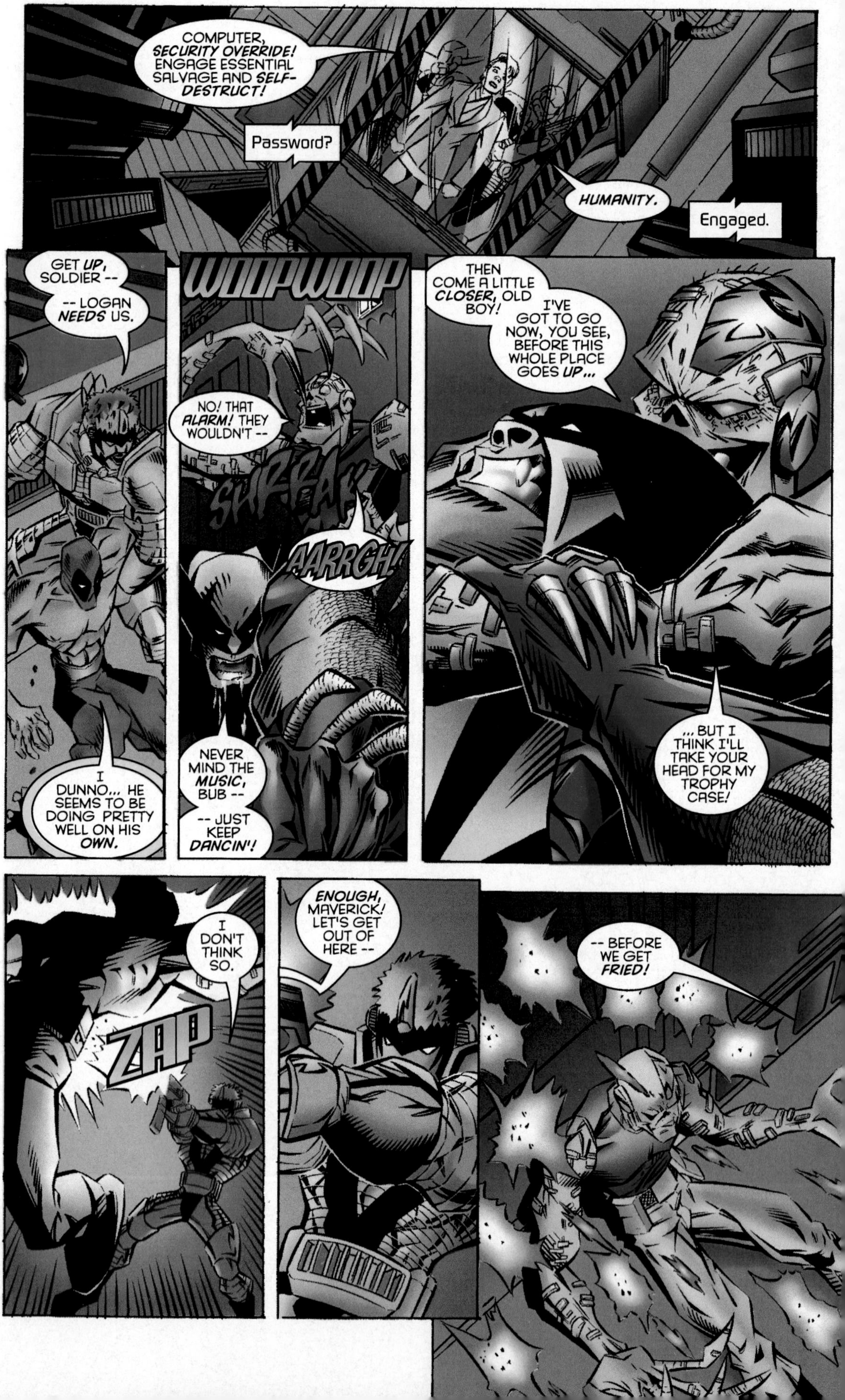
COMPUTER, SECURITY OVERRIDE! ENGAGE ESSENTIAL SALVAGE AND SELF-DESTRUCT!
Password?
HUMANITY.
Engaged.
GET UP, SOLDIER --
-- LOGAN NEEDS US.
I DUNNO... HE SEEMS TO BE DOING PRETTY WELL ON HIS OWN.
WOOPWOOP
NO! THAT ALARM! THEY WOULDN'T --
AARRGH!
NEVER MIND THE MUSIC, BUB --
-- JUST KEEP DANCIN'!
THEN COME A LITTLE CLOSER, OLD BOY!
I'VE GOT TO GO NOW, YOU SEE, BEFORE THIS WHOLE PLACE GOES UP...
... BUT I THINK I'LL TAKE YOUR HEAD FOR MY TROPHY CASE!
I DON'T THINK SO.
ZAP
ENOUGH, MAVERICK! LET'S GET OUT OF HERE --
-- BEFORE WE GET FRIED!

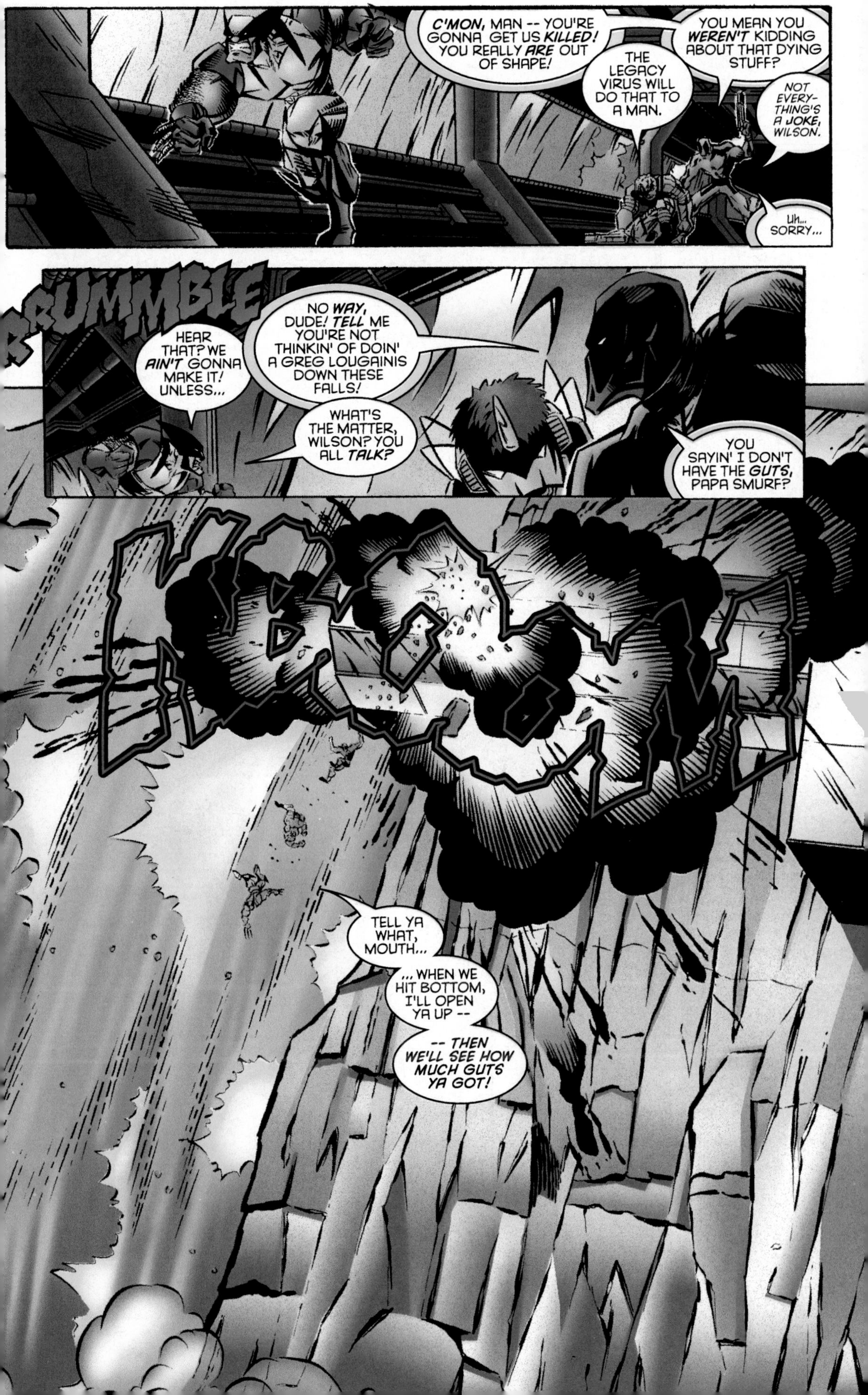
C'MON, MAN -- YOU'RE GONNA GET US KILLED! YOU REALLY ARE OUT OF SHAPE!
THE LEGACY VIRUS WILL DO THAT TO A MAN.
YOU MEAN YOU WEREN'T KIDDING ABOUT THAT DYING STUFF?
NOT EVERYTHING'S A JOKE, WILSON.
UH... SORRY...
RUMMBLE
HEAR THAT? WE AIN'T GONNA MAKE IT! UNLESS...
NO WAY, DUDE! TELL ME YOU'RE NOT THINKIN' OF DOIN' A GREG LOUGAINIS DOWN THESE FALLS!
WHAT'S THE MATTER, WILSON? YOU ALL TALK?
YOU SAYIN' I DON'T HAVE THE GUTS, PAPA SMURF?
TELL YA WHAT, MOUTH...
...WHEN WE HIT BOTTOM, I'LL OPEN YA UP --
-- THEN WE'LL SEE HOW MUCH GUTS YA GOT!

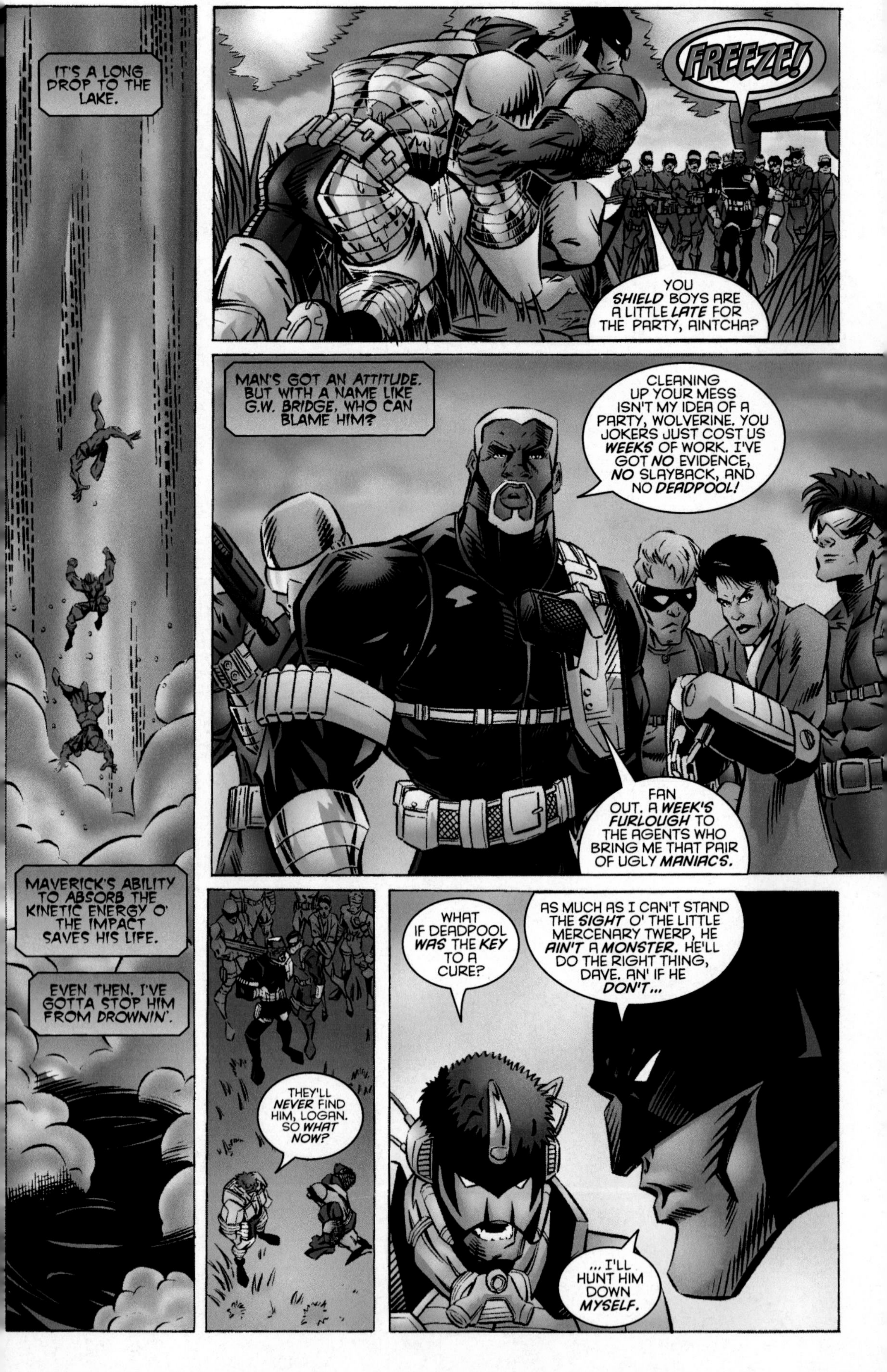
IT'S A LONG DROP TO THE LAKE.
FREEZE!
YOU SHIELD BOYS ARE A LITTLE LATE FOR THE PARTY, AINTCHA?
MAN'S GOT AN ATTITUDE. BUT WITH A NAME LIKE G.W. BRIDGE, WHO CAN BLAME HIM?
CLEANING UP YOUR MESS ISN'T MY IDEA OF A PARTY, WOLVERINE. YOU JOKERS JUST COST US WEEKS OF WORK. I'VE GOT NO EVIDENCE, NO SLAYBACK, AND NO DEADPOOL!
FAN OUT. A WEEK'S FURLOUGH TO THE AGENTS WHO BRING ME THAT PAIR OF UGLY MANIACS.
MAVERICK'S ABILITY TO ABSORB THE KINETIC ENERGY O' THE IMPACT SAVES HIS LIFE.
EVEN THEN, I'VE GOTTA STOP HIM FROM DROWNIN'.
THEY'LL NEVER FIND HIM, LOGAN. SO WHAT NOW?
WHAT IF DEADPOOL WAS THE KEY TO A CURE?
AS MUCH AS I CAN'T STAND THE SIGHT O' THE LITTLE MERCENARY TWERP, HE AIN'T A MONSTER. HE'LL DO THE RIGHT THING, DAVE. AN' IF HE DON'T...
...I'LL HUNT HIM DOWN MYSELF.

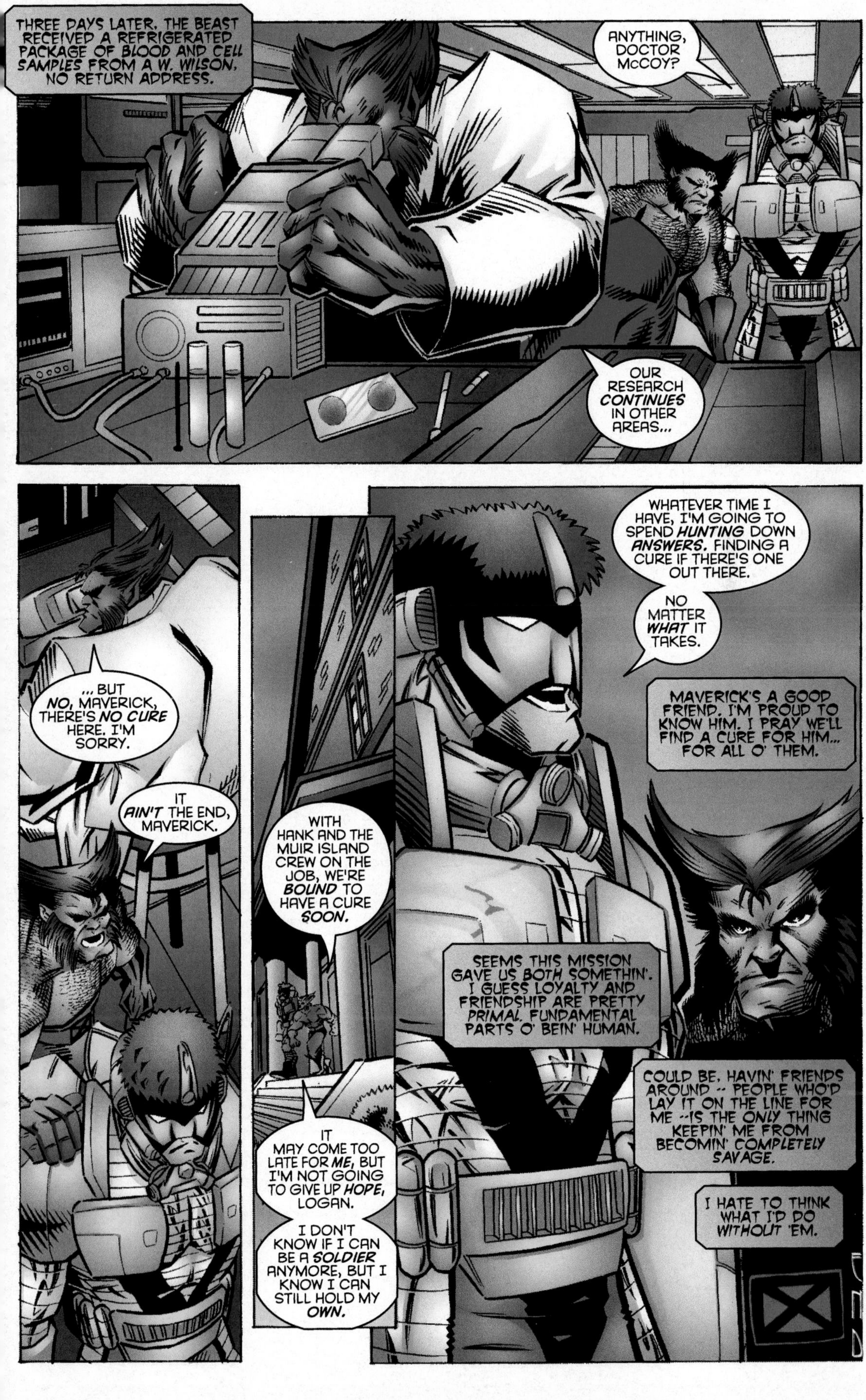
THREE DAYS LATER, THE BEAST RECEIVED A REFRIGERATED PACKAGE OF BLOOD AND CELL SAMPLES FROM A W. WILSON, NO RETURN ADDRESS.
ANYTHING, DOCTOR McCOY?
OUR RESEARCH CONTINUES IN OTHER AREAS...
...BUT NO, MAVERICK, THERE'S NO CURE HERE. I'M SORRY.
IT AIN'T THE END, MAVERICK.
WITH HANK AND THE MUIR ISLAND CREW ON THE JOB, WE'RE BOUND TO HAVE A CURE SOON.
IT MAY COME TOO LATE FOR ME, BUT I'M NOT GOING TO GIVE UP HOPE, LOGAN.
I DON'T KNOW IF I CAN BE A SOLDIER ANYMORE, BUT I KNOW I CAN STILL HOLD MY OWN.
WHATEVER TIME I HAVE, I'M GOING TO SPEND HUNTING DOWN ANSWERS. FINDING A CURE IF THERE'S ONE OUT THERE.
NO MATTER WHAT IT TAKES.
MAVERICK'S A GOOD FRIEND. I'M PROUD TO KNOW HIM. I PRAY WE'LL FIND A CURE FOR HIM... FOR ALL O' THEM.
SEEMS THIS MISSION GAVE US BOTH SOMETHIN'. I GUESS LOYALTY AND FRIENDSHIP ARE PRETTY PRIMAL. FUNDAMENTAL PARTS O' BEIN' HUMAN.
COULD BE. HAVIN' FRIENDS AROUND -- PEOPLE WHO'D LAY IT ON THE LINE FOR ME --IS THE ONLY THING KEEPIN' ME FROM BECOMIN' COMPLETELY SAVAGE.
I HATE TO THINK WHAT I'D DO WITHOUT 'EM.

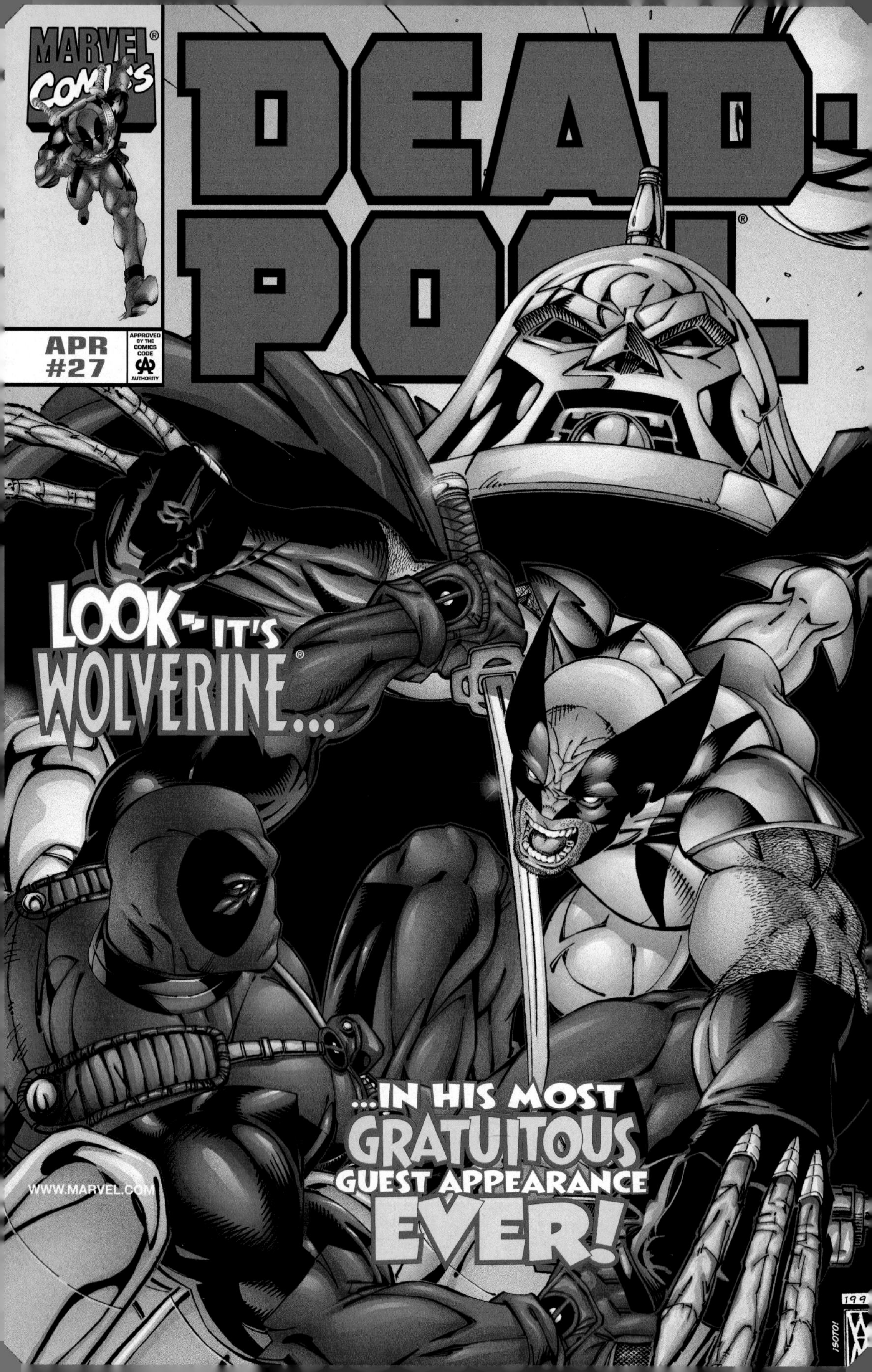
MARVEL COMICS
DEADPOOL
APR #27
APPROVED BY THE COMICS CODE AUTHORITY
LOOK-- IT'S WOLVERINE...
...IN HIS MOST GRATUITOUS GUEST APPEARANCE EVER!
WWW.MARVEL.COM

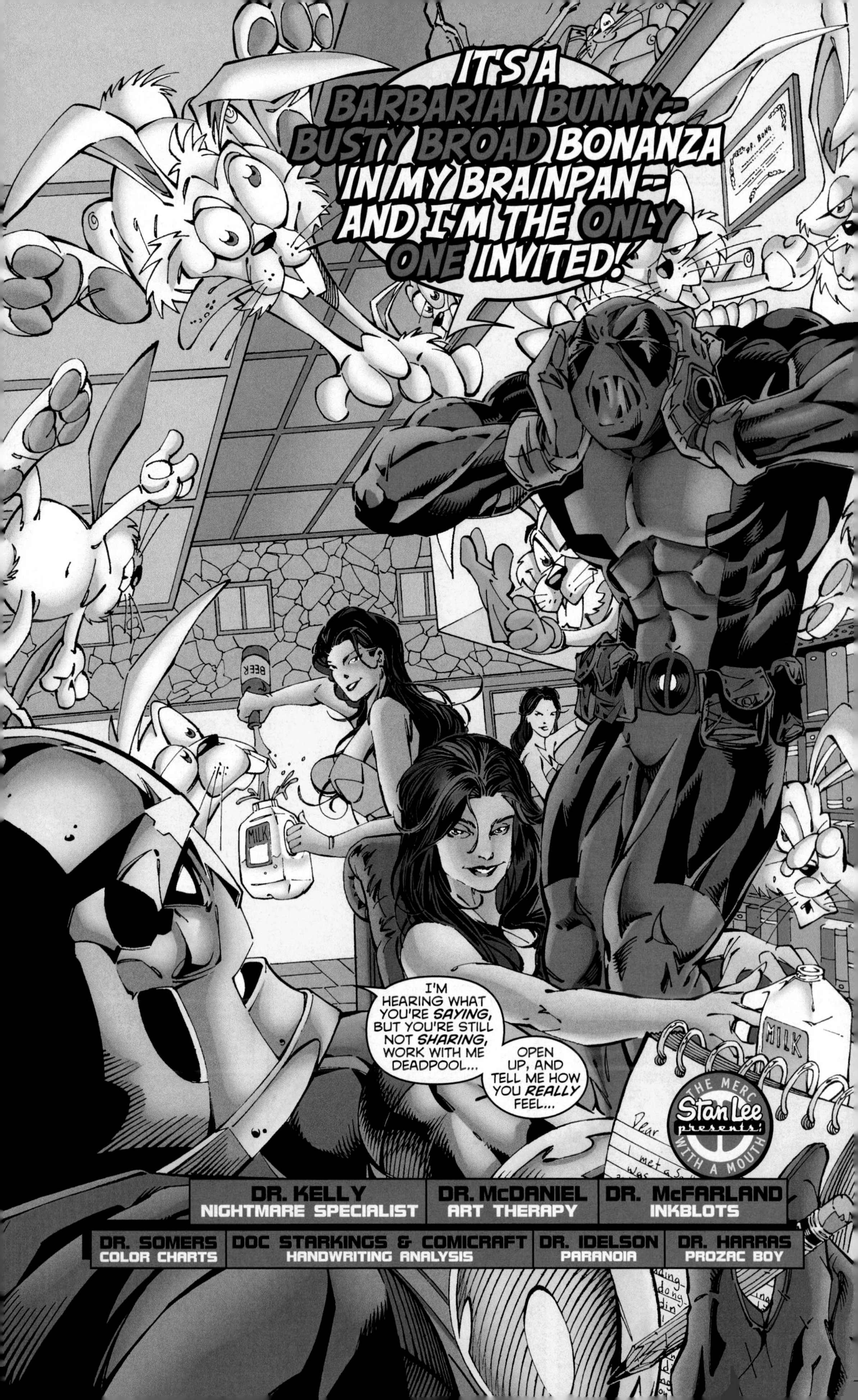
IT'S A BARBARIAN BUNNY-- BUSTY BROAD BONANZA IN MY BRAINPAN-- AND I'M THE ONLY ONE INVITED!
BEER
MILK
I'M HEARING WHAT YOU'RE *SAYING*, BUT YOU'RE STILL NOT *SHARING*, WORK WITH ME DEADPOOL...
OPEN UP, AND TELL ME HOW YOU *REALLY* FEEL...
MILK
THE MERC WITH A MOUTH
Stan Lee presents:
DR. KELLY NIGHTMARE SPECIALIST
DR. McDANIEL ART THERAPY
DR. McFARLAND INKBLOTS
DR. SOMERS COLOR CHARTS
DOC STARKINGS & COMICRAFT HANDWRITING ANALYSIS
DR. IDELSON PARANOIA
DR. HARRAS PROZAC BOY

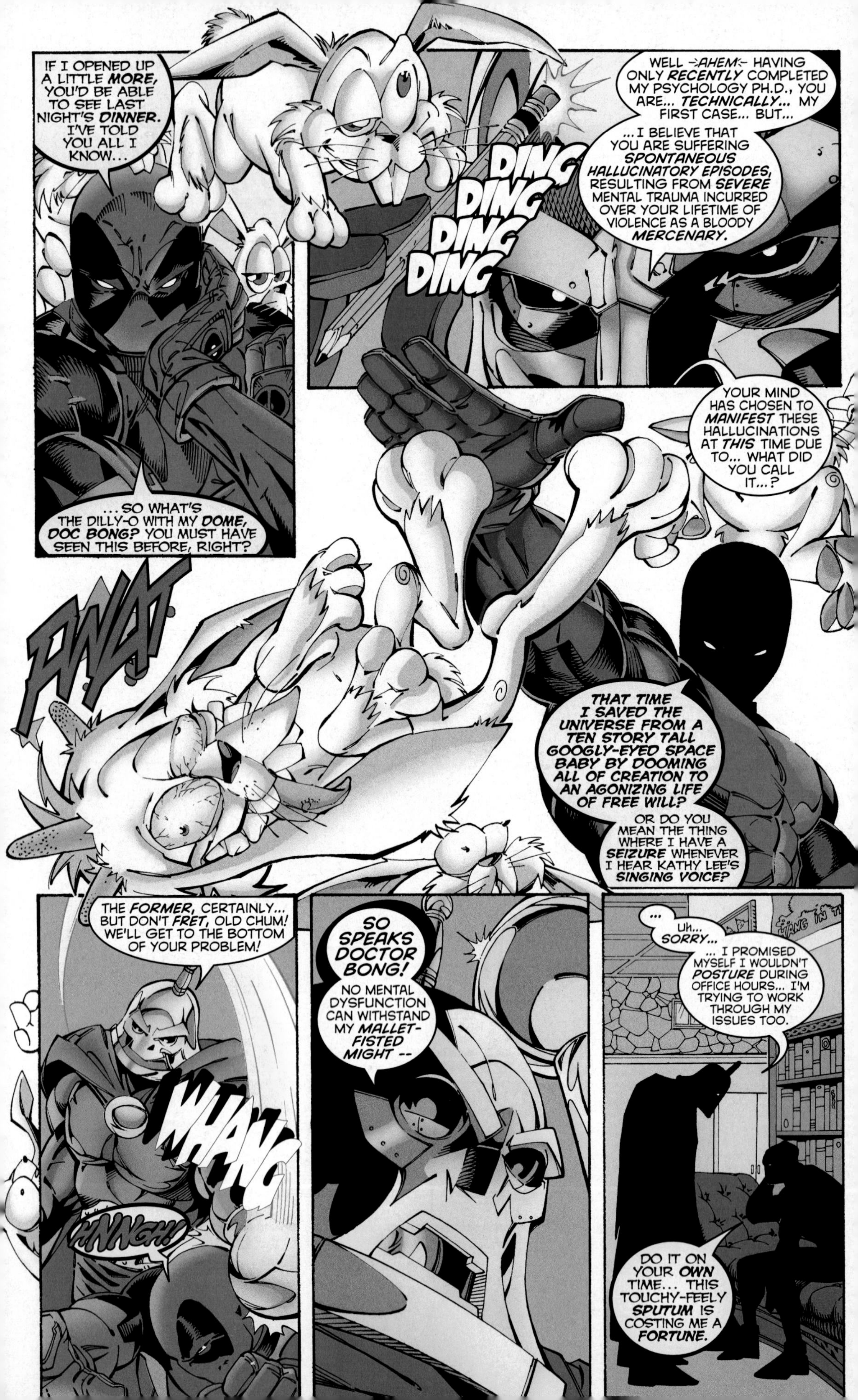
IF I OPENED UP A LITTLE MORE, YOU'D BE ABLE TO SEE LAST NIGHT'S DINNER. I'VE TOLD YOU ALL I KNOW...
WELL -AHEM- HAVING ONLY RECENTLY COMPLETED MY PSYCHOLOGY PH.D., YOU ARE... TECHNICALLY... MY FIRST CASE... BUT...
...I BELIEVE THAT YOU ARE SUFFERING SPONTANEOUS HALLUCINATORY EPISODES, RESULTING FROM SEVERE MENTAL TRAUMA INCURRED OVER YOUR LIFETIME OF VIOLENCE AS A BLOODY MERCENARY.
DING DING DING DING
YOUR MIND HAS CHOSEN TO MANIFEST THESE HALLUCINATIONS AT THIS TIME DUE TO... WHAT DID YOU CALL IT...?
...SO WHAT'S THE DILLY-O WITH MY DOME, DOC BONG? YOU MUST HAVE SEEN THIS BEFORE, RIGHT?
PWAT
THAT TIME I SAVED THE UNIVERSE FROM A TEN STORY TALL GOOGLY-EYED SPACE BABY BY DOOMING ALL OF CREATION TO AN AGONIZING LIFE OF FREE WILL?
OR DO YOU MEAN THE THING WHERE I HAVE A SEIZURE WHENEVER I HEAR KATHY LEE'S SINGING VOICE?
THE FORMER, CERTAINLY... BUT DON'T FRET, OLD CHUM! WE'LL GET TO THE BOTTOM OF YOUR PROBLEM!
WHANG
HNNGH!
SO SPEAKS DOCTOR BONG!
NO MENTAL DYSFUNCTION CAN WITHSTAND MY MALLET-FISTED MIGHT --
... UH... SORRY...
... I PROMISED MYSELF I WOULDN'T POSTURE DURING OFFICE HOURS... I'M TRYING TO WORK THROUGH MY ISSUES TOO.
DO IT ON YOUR OWN TIME... THIS TOUCHY-FEELY SPUTUM IS COSTING ME A FORTUNE.

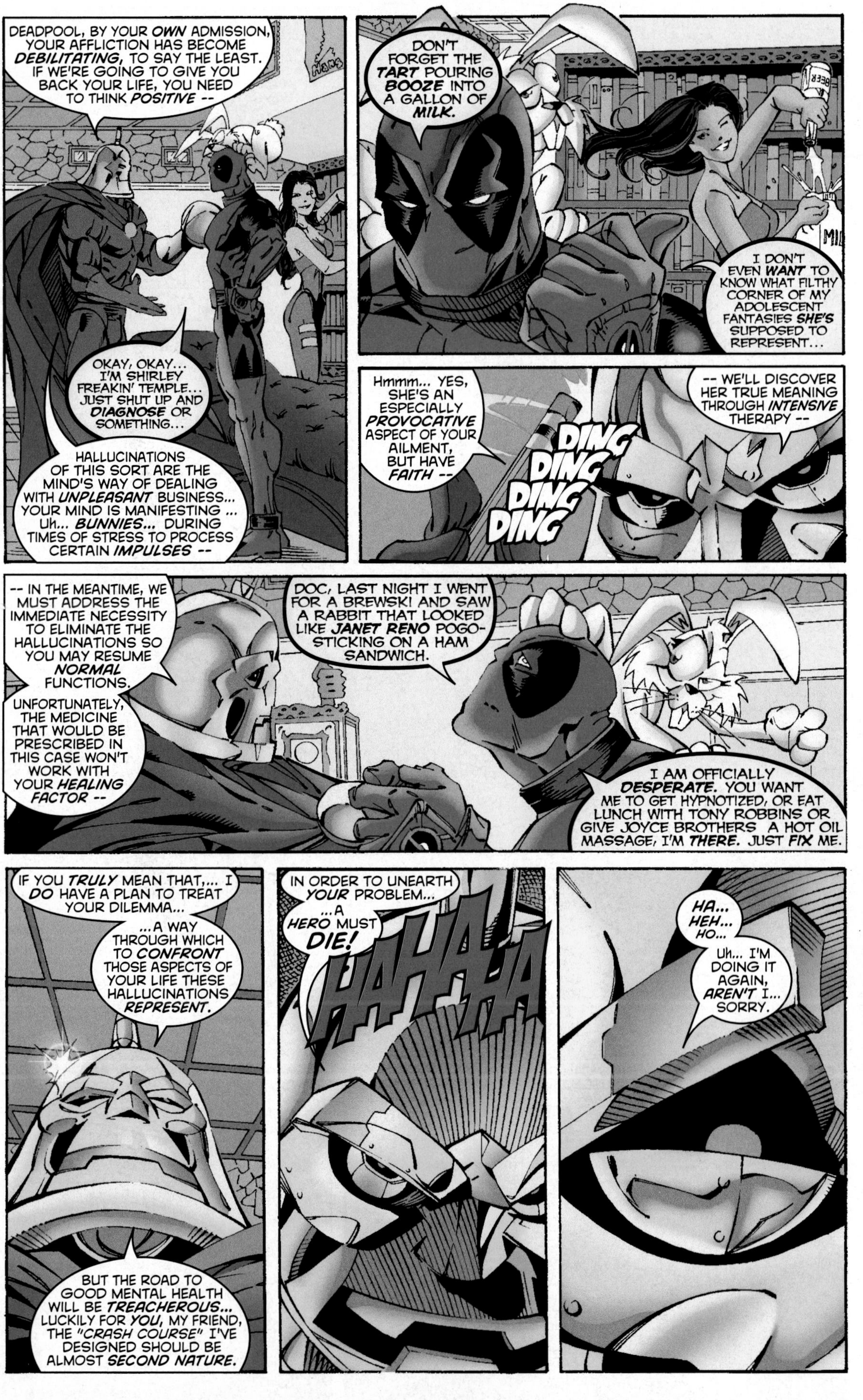
DEADPOOL, BY YOUR OWN ADMISSION, YOUR AFFLICTION HAS BECOME DEBILITATING, TO SAY THE LEAST. IF WE'RE GOING TO GIVE YOU BACK YOUR LIFE, YOU NEED TO THINK POSITIVE --
OKAY, OKAY... I'M SHIRLEY FREAKIN' TEMPLE... JUST SHUT UP AND DIAGNOSE OR SOMETHING...
HALLUCINATIONS OF THIS SORT ARE THE MIND'S WAY OF DEALING WITH UNPLEASANT BUSINESS... YOUR MIND IS MANIFESTING ... Uh... BUNNIES... DURING TIMES OF STRESS TO PROCESS CERTAIN IMPULSES --
DON'T FORGET THE TART POURING BOOZE INTO A GALLON OF MILK.
BEER
I DON'T EVEN WANT TO KNOW WHAT FILTHY CORNER OF MY ADOLESCENT FANTASIES SHE'S SUPPOSED TO REPRESENT...
Hmmm... YES, SHE'S AN ESPECIALLY PROVOCATIVE ASPECT OF YOUR AILMENT, BUT HAVE FAITH --
-- WE'LL DISCOVER HER TRUE MEANING THROUGH INTENSIVE THERAPY --
DING DING DING DING
-- IN THE MEANTIME, WE MUST ADDRESS THE IMMEDIATE NECESSITY TO ELIMINATE THE HALLUCINATIONS SO YOU MAY RESUME NORMAL FUNCTIONS.
UNFORTUNATELY, THE MEDICINE THAT WOULD BE PRESCRIBED IN THIS CASE WON'T WORK WITH YOUR HEALING FACTOR --
DOC, LAST NIGHT I WENT FOR A BREWSKI AND SAW A RABBIT THAT LOOKED LIKE JANET RENO POGO-STICKING ON A HAM SANDWICH.
I AM OFFICIALLY DESPERATE. YOU WANT ME TO GET HYPNOTIZED, OR EAT LUNCH WITH TONY ROBBINS OR GIVE JOYCE BROTHERS A HOT OIL MASSAGE, I'M THERE. JUST FIX ME.
IF YOU TRULY MEAN THAT,... I DO HAVE A PLAN TO TREAT YOUR DILEMMA...
...A WAY THROUGH WHICH TO CONFRONT THOSE ASPECTS OF YOUR LIFE THESE HALLUCINATIONS REPRESENT.
BUT THE ROAD TO GOOD MENTAL HEALTH WILL BE TREACHEROUS... LUCKILY FOR YOU, MY FRIEND, THE "CRASH COURSE" I'VE DESIGNED SHOULD BE ALMOST SECOND NATURE.
IN ORDER TO UNEARTH YOUR PROBLEM... ...A HERO MUST DIE!
HAHAHA
HA... HEH... HO...
Uh... I'M DOING IT AGAIN, AREN'T I... SORRY.

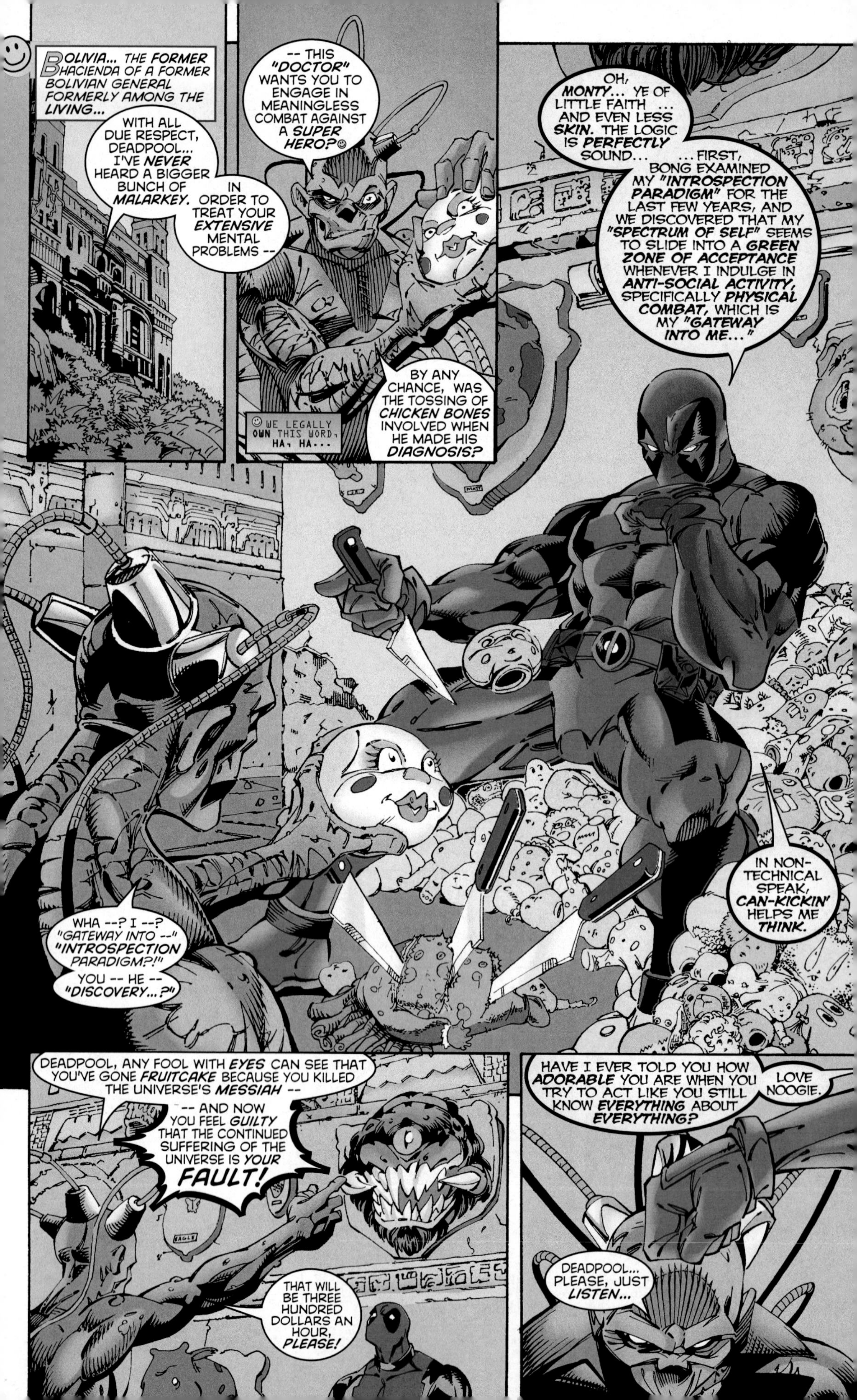
BOLIVIA... THE FORMER HACIENDA OF A FORMER BOLIVIAN GENERAL FORMERLY AMONG THE LIVING...
WITH ALL DUE RESPECT, DEADPOOL... I'VE NEVER HEARD A BIGGER BUNCH OF MALARKEY.
IN ORDER TO TREAT YOUR EXTENSIVE MENTAL PROBLEMS --
-- THIS "DOCTOR" WANTS YOU TO ENGAGE IN MEANINGLESS COMBAT AGAINST A SUPER HERO?
WE LEGALLY OWN THIS WORD, HA, HA...
BY ANY CHANCE, WAS THE TOSSING OF CHICKEN BONES INVOLVED WHEN HE MADE HIS DIAGNOSIS?
OH, MONTY... YE OF LITTLE FAITH ... AND EVEN LESS SKIN. THE LOGIC IS PERFECTLY SOUND...
... FIRST, BONG EXAMINED MY "INTROSPECTION PARADIGM" FOR THE LAST FEW YEARS, AND WE DISCOVERED THAT MY "SPECTRUM OF SELF" SEEMS TO SLIDE INTO A GREEN ZONE OF ACCEPTANCE WHENEVER I INDULGE IN ANTI-SOCIAL ACTIVITY, SPECIFICALLY PHYSICAL COMBAT, WHICH IS MY "GATEWAY INTO ME..."
IN NON-TECHNICAL SPEAK, CAN-KICKIN' HELPS ME THINK.
WHA --? I --? "GATEWAY INTO --" "INTROSPECTION PARADIGM?!" YOU -- HE -- "DISCOVERY...?"
DEADPOOL, ANY FOOL WITH EYES CAN SEE THAT YOU'VE GONE FRUITCAKE BECAUSE YOU KILLED THE UNIVERSE'S MESSIAH --
-- AND NOW YOU FEEL GUILTY THAT THE CONTINUED SUFFERING OF THE UNIVERSE IS YOUR FAULT!
THAT WILL BE THREE HUNDRED DOLLARS AN HOUR, PLEASE!
HAVE I EVER TOLD YOU HOW ADORABLE YOU ARE WHEN YOU TRY TO ACT LIKE YOU STILL KNOW EVERYTHING ABOUT EVERYTHING?
LOVE NOOGIE.
DEADPOOL... PLEASE, JUST LISTEN...

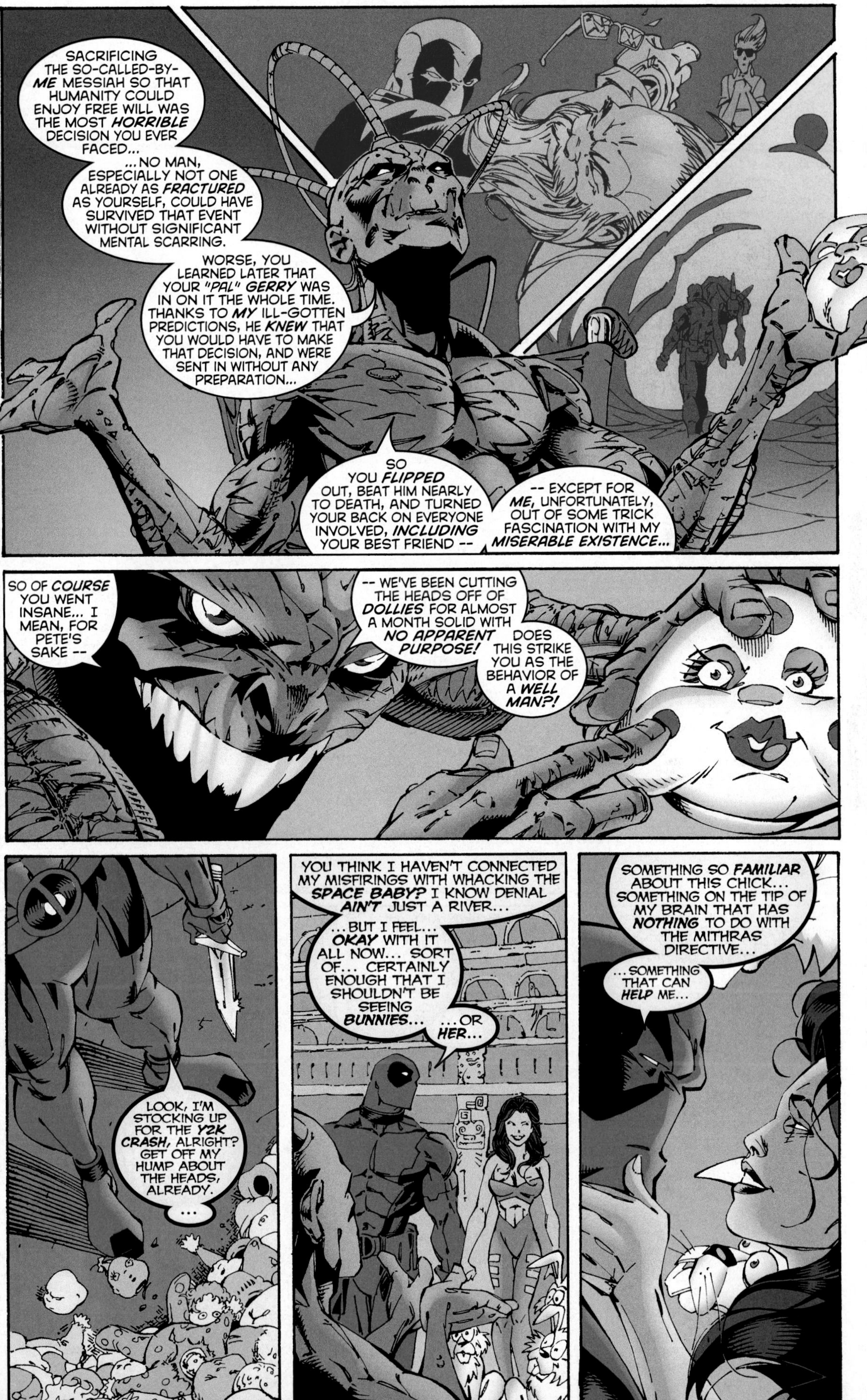
SACRIFICING THE SO-CALLED-BY-ME MESSIAH SO THAT HUMANITY COULD ENJOY FREE WILL WAS THE MOST HORRIBLE DECISION YOU EVER FACED...
...NO MAN, ESPECIALLY NOT ONE ALREADY AS FRACTURED AS YOURSELF, COULD HAVE SURVIVED THAT EVENT WITHOUT SIGNIFICANT MENTAL SCARRING.
WORSE, YOU LEARNED LATER THAT YOUR "PAL" GERRY WAS IN ON IT THE WHOLE TIME. THANKS TO MY ILL-GOTTEN PREDICTIONS, HE KNEW THAT YOU WOULD HAVE TO MAKE THAT DECISION, AND WERE SENT IN WITHOUT ANY PREPARATION...
SO YOU FLIPPED OUT, BEAT HIM NEARLY TO DEATH, AND TURNED YOUR BACK ON EVERYONE INVOLVED, INCLUDING YOUR BEST FRIEND --
-- EXCEPT FOR ME, UNFORTUNATELY, OUT OF SOME TRICK FASCINATION WITH MY MISERABLE EXISTENCE...
SO OF COURSE YOU WENT INSANE... I MEAN, FOR PETE'S SAKE --
-- WE'VE BEEN CUTTING THE HEADS OFF OF DOLLIES FOR ALMOST A MONTH SOLID WITH NO APPARENT PURPOSE!
DOES THIS STRIKE YOU AS THE BEHAVIOR OF A WELL MAN?!
LOOK, I'M STOCKING UP FOR THE Y2K CRASH, ALRIGHT? GET OFF MY HUMP ABOUT THE HEADS, ALREADY.
...
YOU THINK I HAVEN'T CONNECTED MY MISFIRINGS WITH WHACKING THE SPACE BABY? I KNOW DENIAL AIN'T JUST A RIVER...
...BUT I FEEL... OKAY WITH IT ALL NOW... SORT OF... CERTAINLY ENOUGH THAT I SHOULDN'T BE SEEING BUNNIES...
...OR HER...
SOMETHING SO FAMILIAR ABOUT THIS CHICK... SOMETHING ON THE TIP OF MY BRAIN THAT HAS NOTHING TO DO WITH THE MITHRAS DIRECTIVE...
...SOMETHING THAT CAN HELP ME...

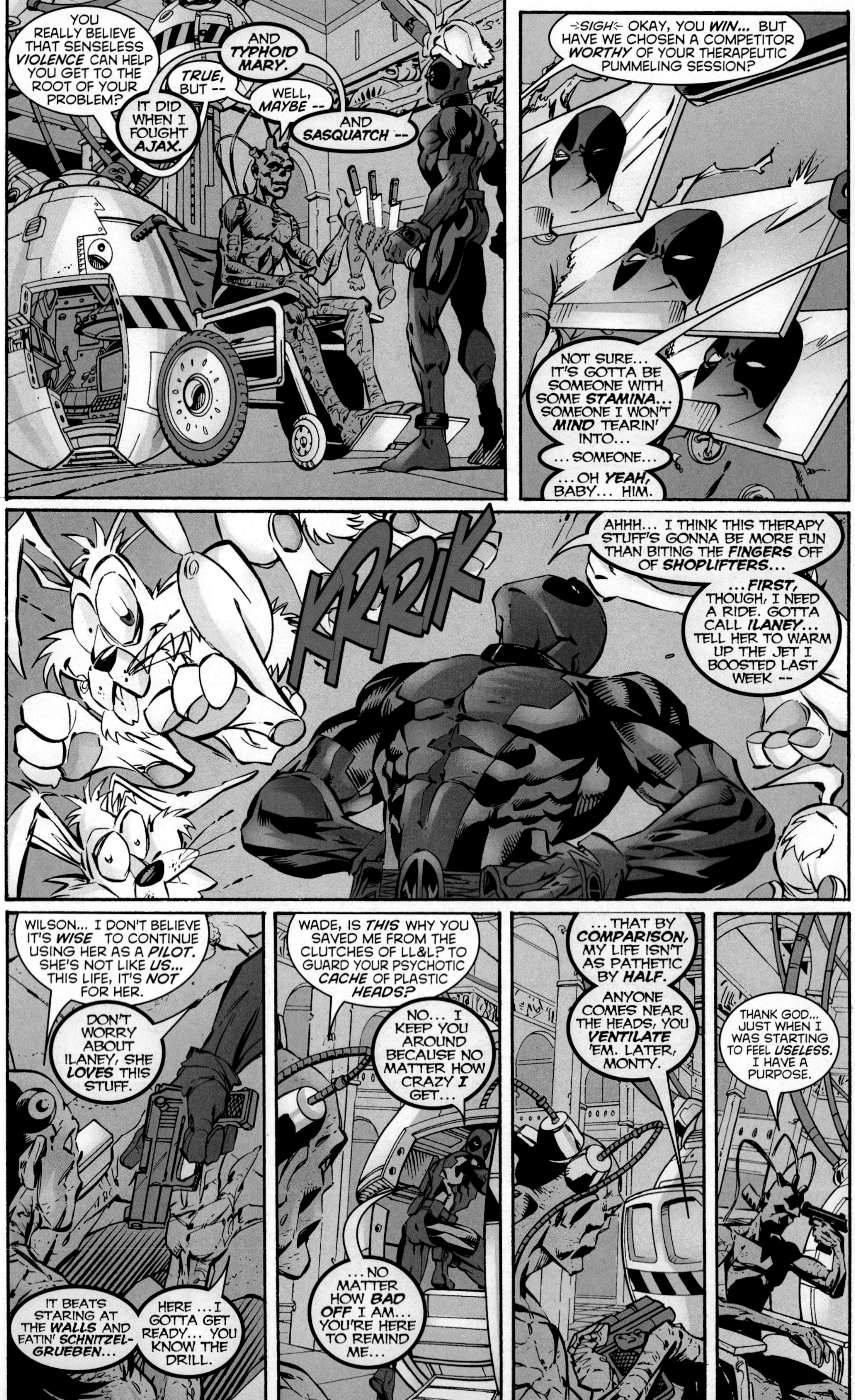

YOU REALLY BELIEVE THAT SENSELESS VIOLENCE CAN HELP YOU GET TO THE ROOT OF YOUR PROBLEM?
IT DID WHEN I FOUGHT AJAX.
TRUE, BUT --
AND TYPHOID MARY.
WELL, MAYBE --
AND SASQUATCH --
>SIGH< OKAY, YOU WIN... BUT HAVE WE CHOSEN A COMPETITOR WORTHY OF YOUR THERAPEUTIC PUMMELING SESSION?
NOT SURE... IT'S GOTTA BE SOMEONE WITH SOME STAMINA... SOMEONE I WON'T MIND TEARIN' INTO...
...SOMEONE...
...OH YEAH, BABY... HIM.
KRRIK
AHHH... I THINK THIS THERAPY STUFF'S GONNA BE MORE FUN THAN BITING THE FINGERS OFF OF SHOPLIFTERS...
...FIRST, THOUGH, I NEED A RIDE. GOTTA CALL ILANEY... TELL HER TO WARM UP THE JET I BOOSTED LAST WEEK --
WILSON... I DON'T BELIEVE IT'S WISE TO CONTINUE USING HER AS A PILOT. SHE'S NOT LIKE US... THIS LIFE, IT'S NOT FOR HER.
DON'T WORRY ABOUT ILANEY, SHE LOVES THIS STUFF.
IT BEATS STARING AT THE WALLS AND EATIN' SCHNITZEL-GRUEBEN...
HERE ...I GOTTA GET READY... YOU KNOW THE DRILL.
WADE, IS THIS WHY YOU SAVED ME FROM THE CLUTCHES OF LL&L? TO GUARD YOUR PSYCHOTIC CACHE OF PLASTIC HEADS?
NO... I KEEP YOU AROUND BECAUSE NO MATTER HOW CRAZY I GET...
...NO MATTER HOW BAD OFF I AM... YOU'RE HERE TO REMIND ME...
...THAT BY COMPARISON, MY LIFE ISN'T AS PATHETIC BY HALF.
ANYONE COMES NEAR THE HEADS, YOU VENTILATE 'EM. LATER, MONTY.
THANK GOD... JUST WHEN I WAS STARTING TO FEEL USELESS. I HAVE A PURPOSE.

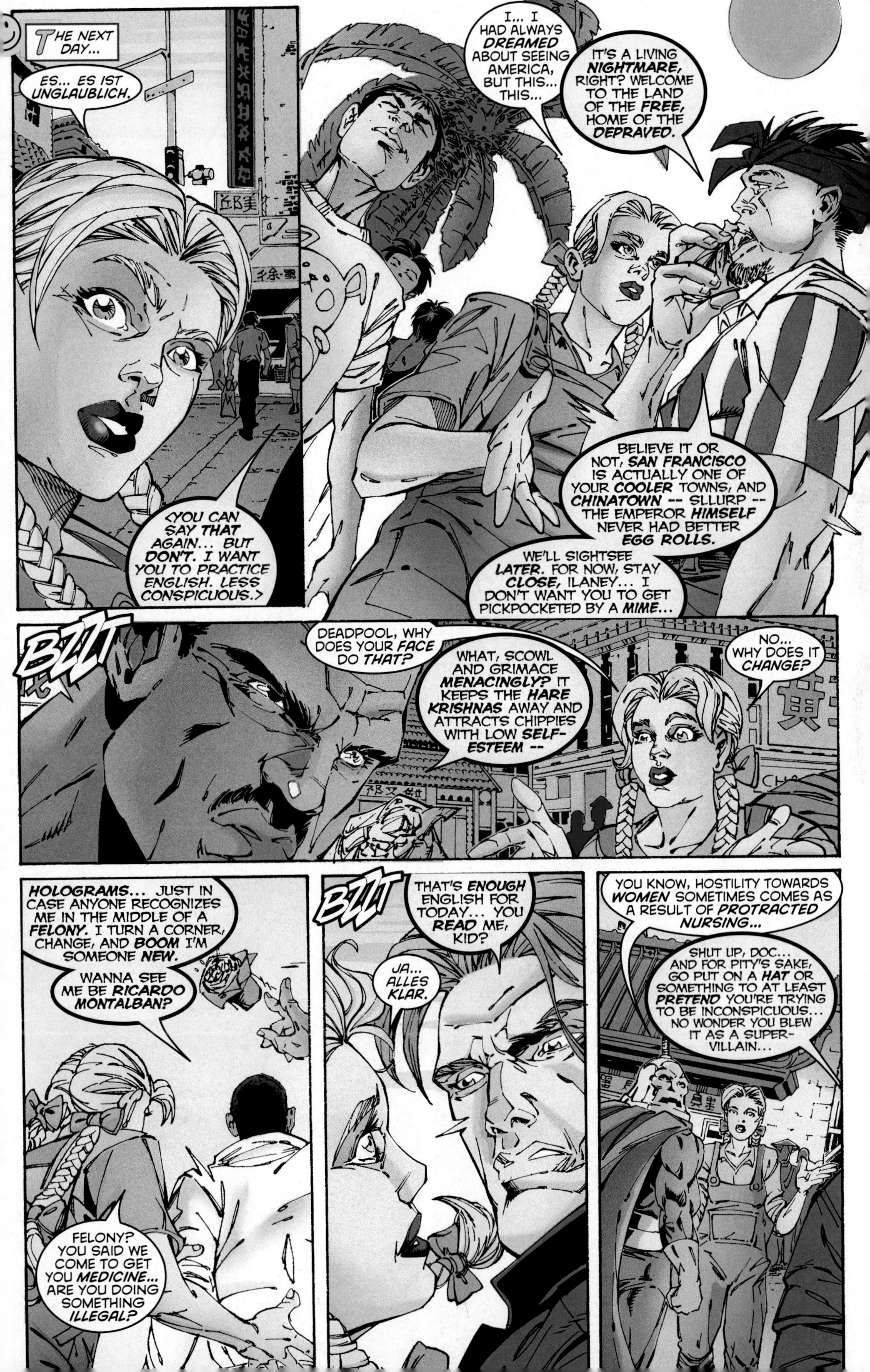
THE NEXT DAY...
ES... ES IST UNGLAUBLICH.
<YOU CAN SAY THAT AGAIN... BUT DON'T. I WANT YOU TO PRACTICE ENGLISH. LESS CONSPICUOUS.>
I... I HAD ALWAYS DREAMED ABOUT SEEING AMERICA, BUT THIS... THIS...
IT'S A LIVING NIGHTMARE, RIGHT? WELCOME TO THE LAND OF THE FREE, HOME OF THE DEPRAVED.
BELIEVE IT OR NOT, SAN FRANCISCO IS ACTUALLY ONE OF YOUR COOLER TOWNS, AND CHINATOWN -- SLLURP -- THE EMPEROR HIMSELF NEVER HAD BETTER EGG ROLLS.
WE'LL SIGHTSEE LATER. FOR NOW, STAY CLOSE, ILANEY... I DON'T WANT YOU TO GET PICKPOCKETED BY A MIME...
BZZZT
DEADPOOL, WHY DOES YOUR FACE DO THAT?
WHAT, SCOWL AND GRIMACE MENACINGLY? IT KEEPS THE HARE KRISHNAS AWAY AND ATTRACTS CHIPPIES WITH LOW SELF-ESTEEM --
NO... WHY DOES IT CHANGE?
HOLOGRAMS... JUST IN CASE ANYONE RECOGNIZES ME IN THE MIDDLE OF A FELONY. I TURN A CORNER, CHANGE, AND BOOM I'M SOMEONE NEW.
WANNA SEE ME BE RICARDO MONTALBAN?
FELONY? YOU SAID WE COME TO GET YOU MEDICINE... ARE YOU DOING SOMETHING ILLEGAL?
BZZZT
THAT'S ENOUGH ENGLISH FOR TODAY... YOU READ ME, KID?
JA... ALLES KLAR.
YOU KNOW, HOSTILITY TOWARDS WOMEN SOMETIMES COMES AS A RESULT OF PROTRACTED NURSING...
SHUT UP, DOC... AND FOR PITY'S SAKE, GO PUT ON A HAT OR SOMETHING TO AT LEAST PRETEND YOU'RE TRYING TO BE INCONSPICUOUS... NO WONDER YOU BLEW IT AS A SUPER-VILLAIN...

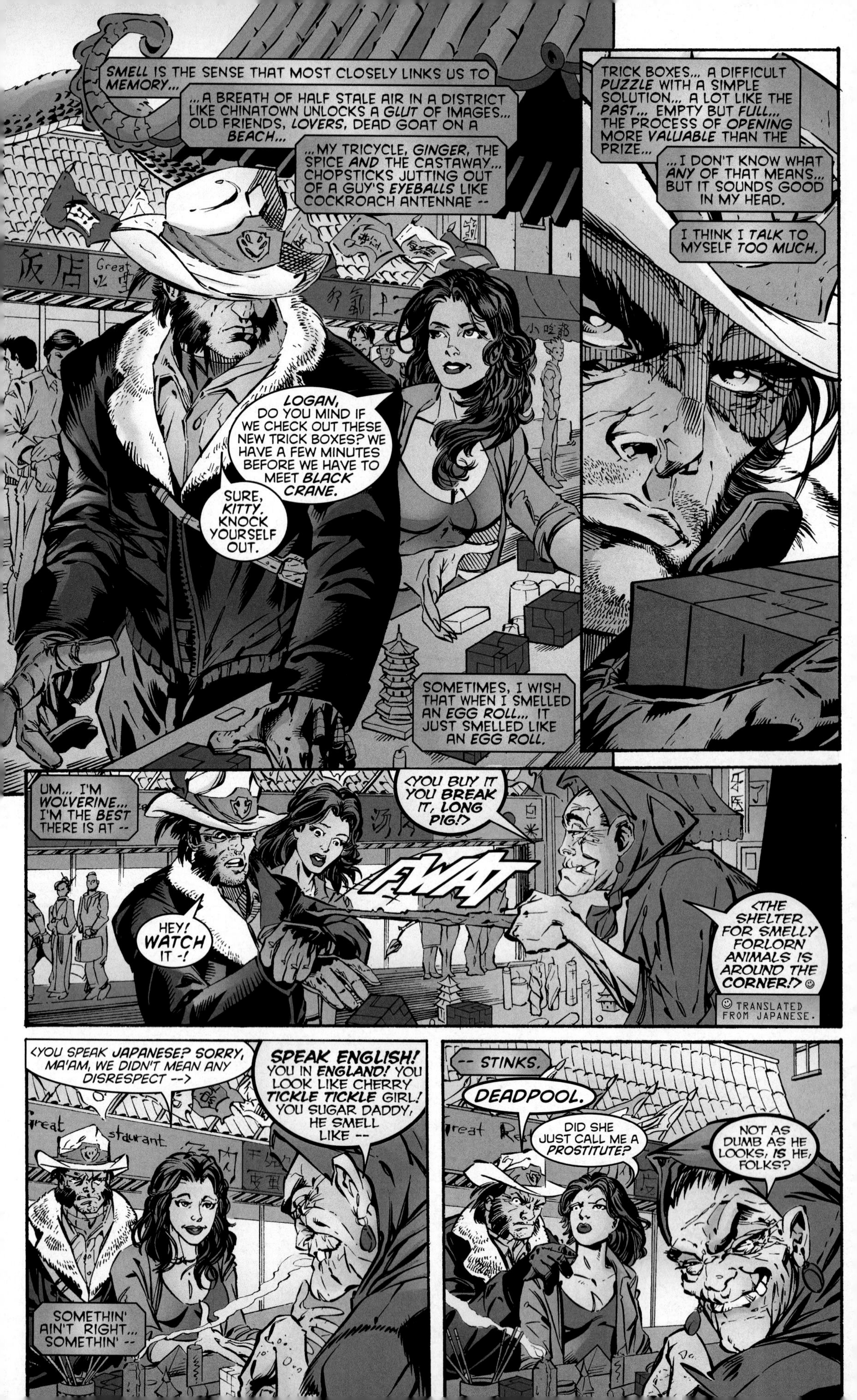
SMELL IS THE SENSE THAT MOST CLOSELY LINKS US TO MEMORY...
...A BREATH OF HALF STALE AIR IN A DISTRICT LIKE CHINATOWN UNLOCKS A GLUT OF IMAGES... OLD FRIENDS, LOVERS, DEAD GOAT ON A BEACH...
...MY TRICYCLE, GINGER, THE SPICE AND THE CASTAWAY... CHOPSTICKS JUTTING OUT OF A GUY'S EYEBALLS LIKE COCKROACH ANTENNAE --
LOGAN, DO YOU MIND IF WE CHECK OUT THESE NEW TRICK BOXES? WE HAVE A FEW MINUTES BEFORE WE HAVE TO MEET BLACK CRANE.
SURE, KITTY. KNOCK YOURSELF OUT.
SOMETIMES, I WISH THAT WHEN I SMELLED AN EGG ROLL... IT JUST SMELLED LIKE AN EGG ROLL.
TRICK BOXES... A DIFFICULT PUZZLE WITH A SIMPLE SOLUTION... A LOT LIKE THE PAST... EMPTY BUT FULL... THE PROCESS OF OPENING MORE VALUABLE THAN THE PRIZE...
...I DON'T KNOW WHAT ANY OF THAT MEANS... BUT IT SOUNDS GOOD IN MY HEAD.
I THINK I TALK TO MYSELF TOO MUCH.
UM... I'M WOLVERINE... I'M THE BEST THERE IS AT --
<YOU BUY IT YOU BREAK IT, LONG PIG!>
FWAT
HEY! WATCH IT -!
<THE SHELTER FOR SMELLY FORLORN ANIMALS IS AROUND THE CORNER!> ☺
☺ TRANSLATED FROM JAPANESE.
<YOU SPEAK JAPANESE? SORRY, MA'AM, WE DIDN'T MEAN ANY DISRESPECT -->
SPEAK ENGLISH! YOU IN ENGLAND! YOU LOOK LIKE CHERRY TICKLE TICKLE GIRL! YOU SUGAR DADDY, HE SMELL LIKE --
SOMETHIN' AIN'T RIGHT... SOMETHIN' --
-- STINKS.
DEADPOOL.
DID SHE JUST CALL ME A PROSTITUTE?
NOT AS DUMB AS HE LOOKS, IS HE, FOLKS?

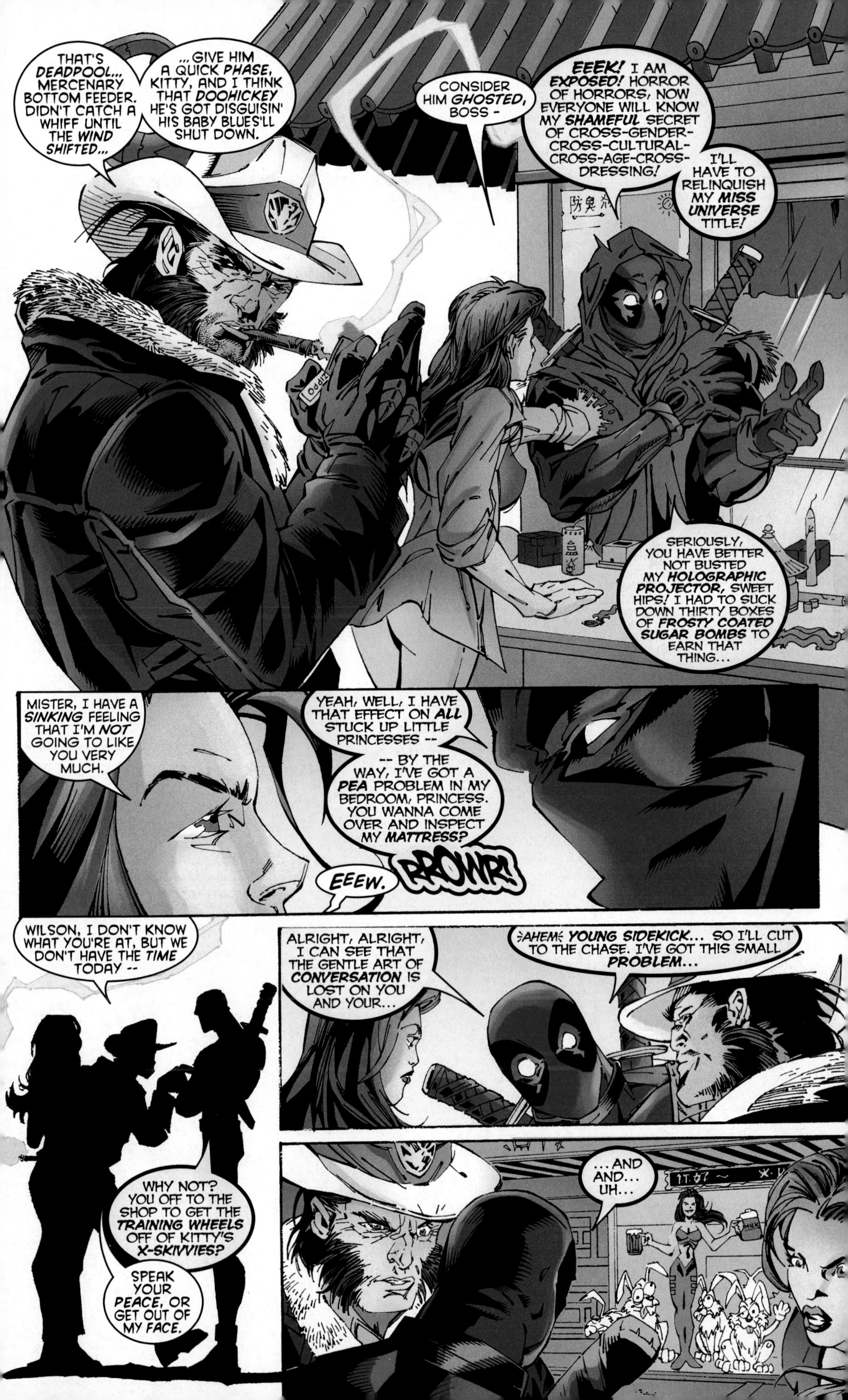
THAT'S DEADPOOL... MERCENARY BOTTOM FEEDER. DIDN'T CATCH A WHIFF UNTIL THE WIND SHIFTED...
...GIVE HIM A QUICK PHASE, KITTY, AND I THINK THAT DOOHICKEY HE'S GOT DISGUISIN' HIS BABY BLUES'LL SHUT DOWN.
CONSIDER HIM GHOSTED, BOSS -
EEEK! I AM EXPOSED! HORROR OF HORRORS, NOW EVERYONE WILL KNOW MY SHAMEFUL SECRET OF CROSS-GENDER-CROSS-CULTURAL-CROSS-AGE-CROSS-DRESSING!
I'LL HAVE TO RELINQUISH MY MISS UNIVERSE TITLE!
SERIOUSLY, YOU HAVE BETTER NOT BUSTED MY HOLOGRAPHIC PROJECTOR, SWEET HIPS! I HAD TO SUCK DOWN THIRTY BOXES OF FROSTY COATED SUGAR BOMBS TO EARN THAT THING...
MISTER, I HAVE A SINKING FEELING THAT I'M NOT GOING TO LIKE YOU VERY MUCH.
YEAH, WELL, I HAVE THAT EFFECT ON ALL STUCK UP LITTLE PRINCESSES --
-- BY THE WAY, I'VE GOT A PEA PROBLEM IN MY BEDROOM, PRINCESS. YOU WANNA COME OVER AND INSPECT MY MATTRESS?
EEEW.
RROWR!
WILSON, I DON'T KNOW WHAT YOU'RE AT, BUT WE DON'T HAVE THE TIME TODAY --
ALRIGHT, ALRIGHT, I CAN SEE THAT THE GENTLE ART OF CONVERSATION IS LOST ON YOU AND YOUR...
AHEM YOUNG SIDEKICK... SO I'LL CUT TO THE CHASE. I'VE GOT THIS SMALL PROBLEM...
WHY NOT? YOU OFF TO THE SHOP TO GET THE TRAINING WHEELS OFF OF KITTY'S X-SKIVVIES?
SPEAK YOUR PEACE, OR GET OUT OF MY FACE.
...AND AND... UH...

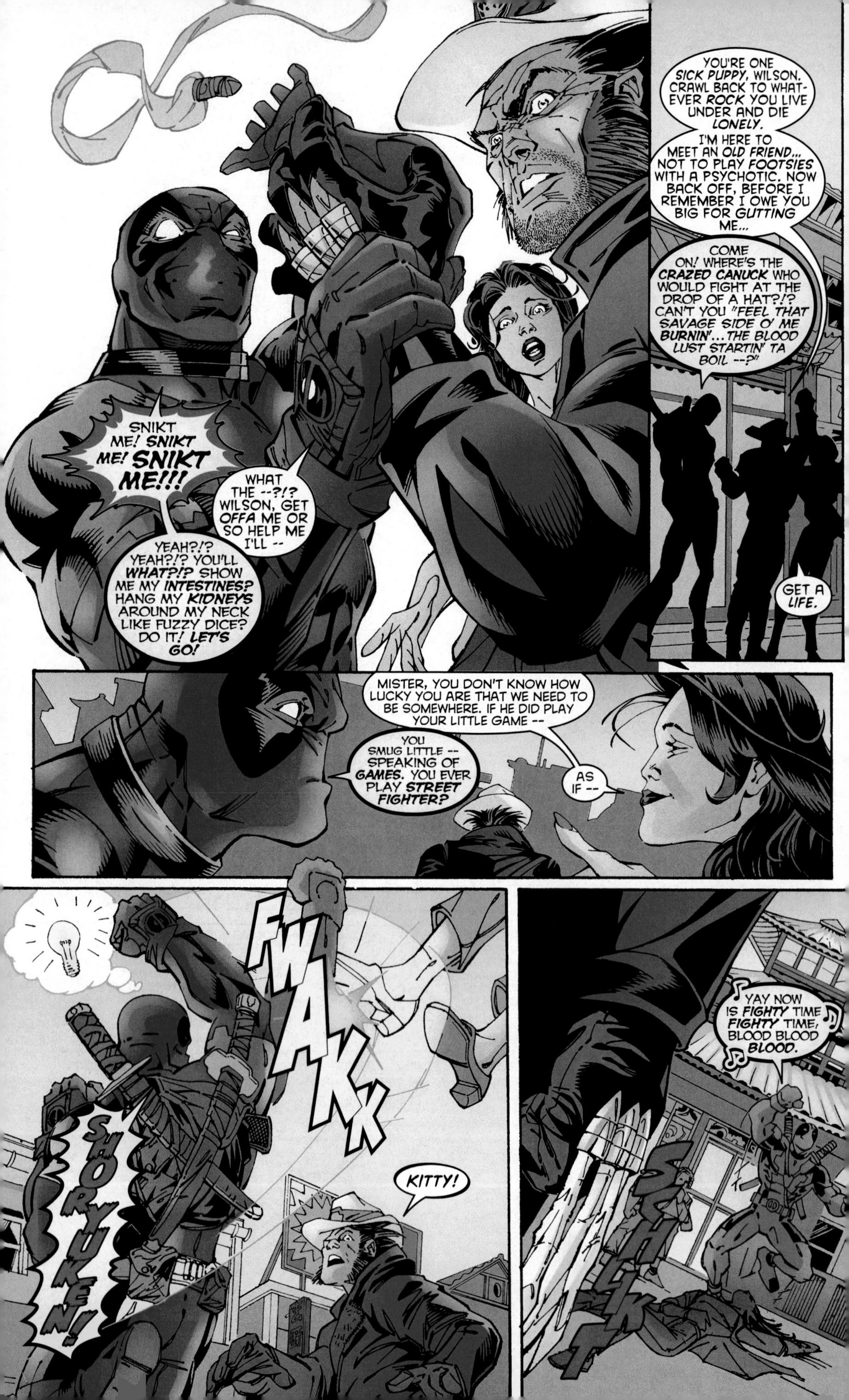
YOU'RE ONE SICK PUPPY, WILSON. CRAWL BACK TO WHAT-EVER ROCK YOU LIVE UNDER AND DIE LONELY.
I'M HERE TO MEET AN OLD FRIEND... NOT TO PLAY FOOTSIES WITH A PSYCHOTIC. NOW BACK OFF, BEFORE I REMEMBER I OWE YOU BIG FOR GUTTING ME...
COME ON! WHERE'S THE CRAZED CANUCK WHO WOULD FIGHT AT THE DROP OF A HAT?!? CAN'T YOU "FEEL THAT SAVAGE SIDE O' ME BURNIN'... THE BLOOD LUST STARTIN' TA BOIL --?"
GET A LIFE.
SNIKT ME! SNIKT ME! SNIKT ME!!!
WHAT THE --?!? WILSON, GET OFFA ME OR SO HELP ME I'LL --
YEAH?!? YEAH?!? YOU'LL WHAT?!? SHOW ME MY INTESTINES? HANG MY KIDNEYS AROUND MY NECK LIKE FUZZY DICE? DO IT! LET'S GO!
MISTER, YOU DON'T KNOW HOW LUCKY YOU ARE THAT WE NEED TO BE SOMEWHERE. IF HE DID PLAY YOUR LITTLE GAME --
YOU SMUG LITTLE -- -- SPEAKING OF GAMES. YOU EVER PLAY STREET FIGHTER?
AS IF --
FWAKK
SHORYUKEN!
KITTY!
YAY NOW IS FIGHTY TIME FIGHTY TIME, BLOOD BLOOD BLOOD.
SHLAKK

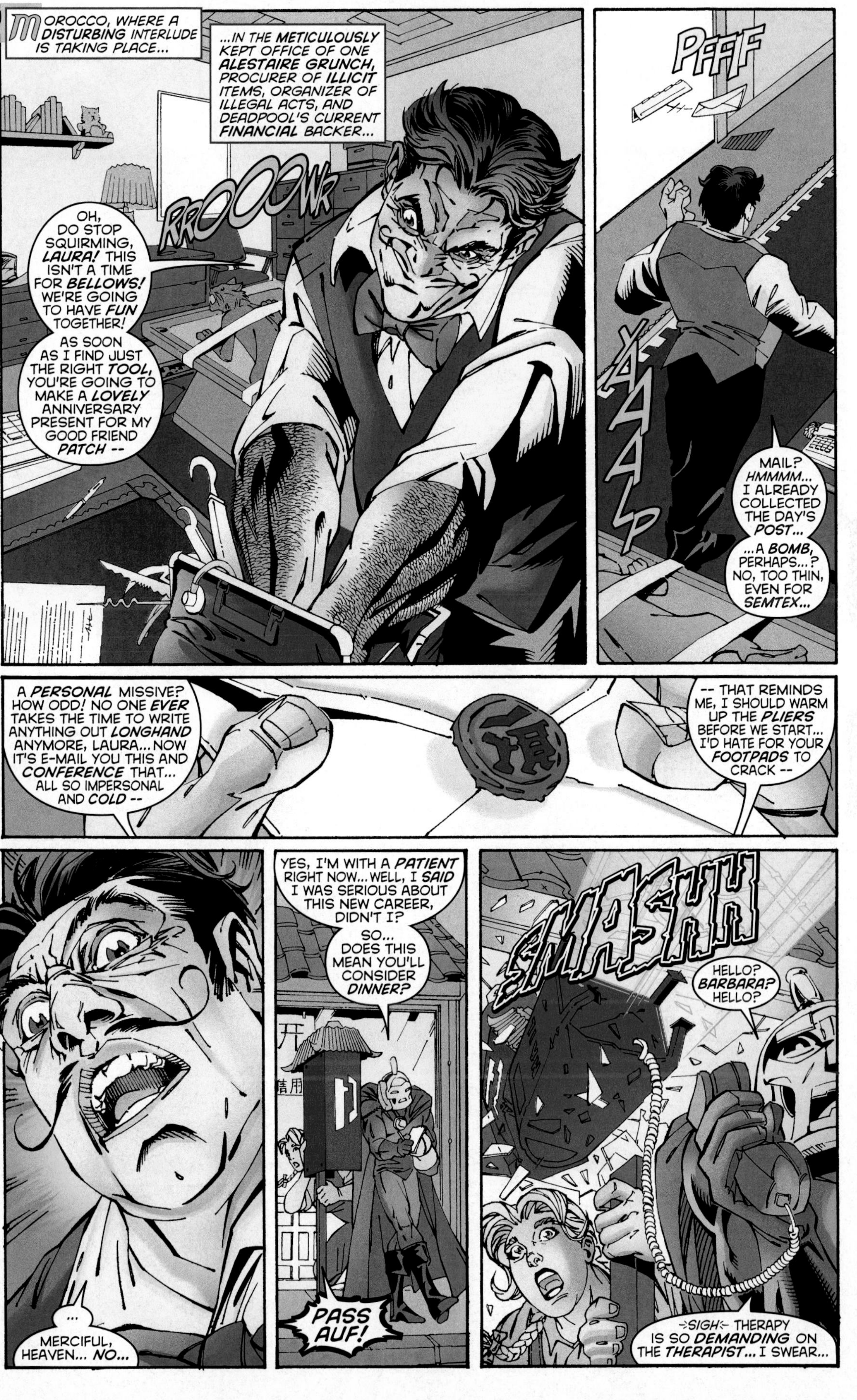
MOROCCO, WHERE A DISTURBING INTERLUDE IS TAKING PLACE...
...IN THE METICULOUSLY KEPT OFFICE OF ONE ALESTAIRE GRUNCH, PROCURER OF ILLICIT ITEMS, ORGANIZER OF ILLEGAL ACTS, AND DEADPOOL'S CURRENT FINANCIAL BACKER...
RROOOONR
OH, DO STOP SQUIRMING, LAURA! THIS ISN'T A TIME FOR BELLOWS! WE'RE GOING TO HAVE FUN TOGETHER!
AS SOON AS I FIND JUST THE RIGHT TOOL, YOU'RE GOING TO MAKE A LOVELY ANNIVERSARY PRESENT FOR MY GOOD FRIEND PATCH --
PFFF
YAAAALP
MAIL? HMMMM... I ALREADY COLLECTED THE DAY'S POST...
...A BOMB, PERHAPS...? NO, TOO THIN, EVEN FOR SEMTEX...
A PERSONAL MISSIVE? HOW ODD! NO ONE EVER TAKES THE TIME TO WRITE ANYTHING OUT LONGHAND ANYMORE, LAURA... NOW IT'S E-MAIL YOU THIS AND CONFERENCE THAT... ALL SO IMPERSONAL AND COLD --
-- THAT REMINDS ME, I SHOULD WARM UP THE PLIERS BEFORE WE START... I'D HATE FOR YOUR FOOTPADS TO CRACK --
... MERCIFUL HEAVEN... NO...
YES, I'M WITH A PATIENT RIGHT NOW... WELL, I SAID I WAS SERIOUS ABOUT THIS NEW CAREER, DIDN'T I?
SO... DOES THIS MEAN YOU'LL CONSIDER DINNER?
PASS AUF!
SMASHH
HELLO? BARBARA? HELLO?
SIGH THERAPY IS SO DEMANDING ON THE THERAPIST... I SWEAR...

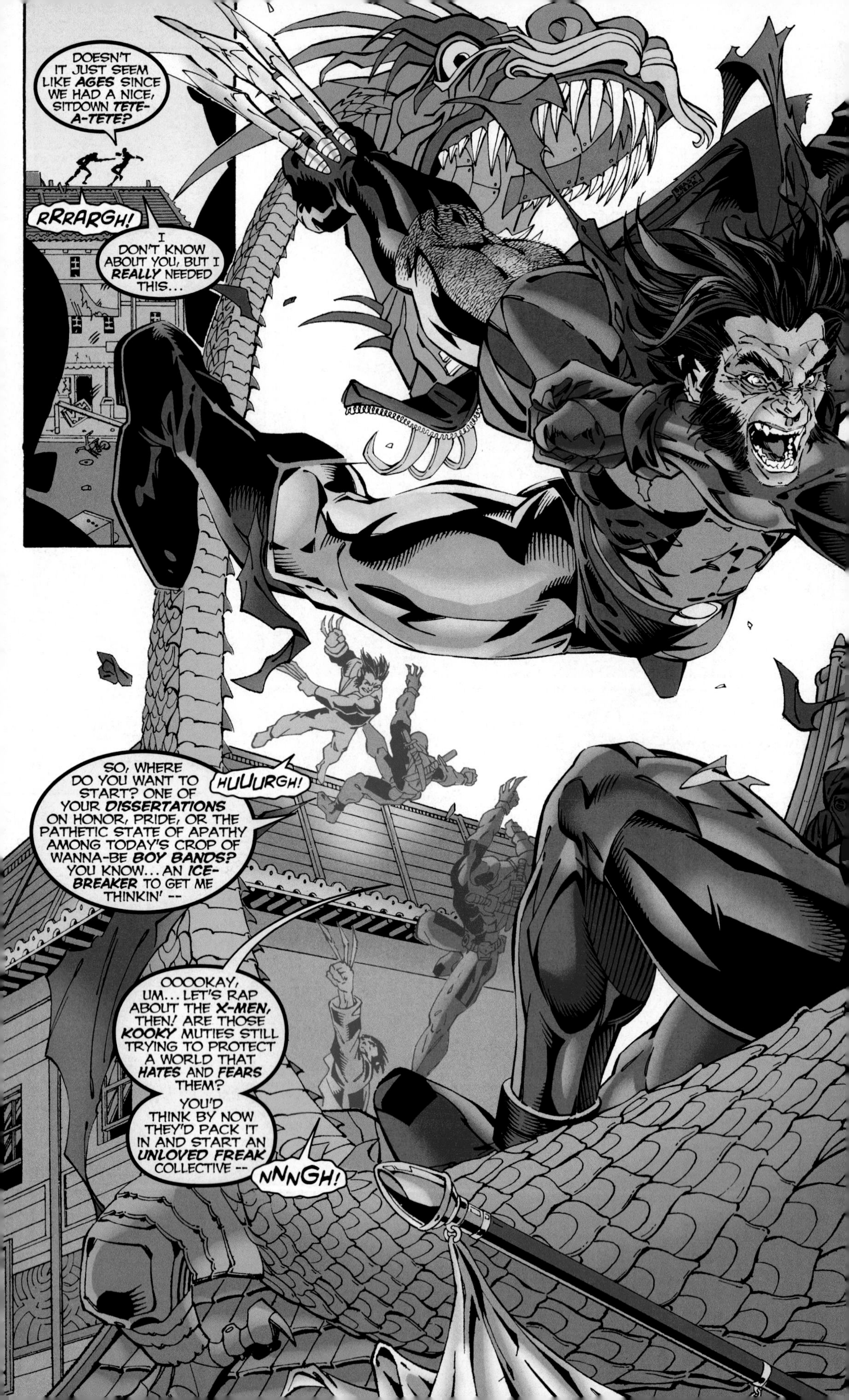
DOESN'T IT JUST SEEM LIKE AGES SINCE WE HAD A NICE, SITDOWN TETE-A-TETE?
RRRARGH!
I DON'T KNOW ABOUT YOU, BUT I REALLY NEEDED THIS...
SO, WHERE DO YOU WANT TO START? ONE OF YOUR DISSERTATIONS ON HONOR, PRIDE, OR THE PATHETIC STATE OF APATHY AMONG TODAY'S CROP OF WANNA-BE BOY BANDS? YOU KNOW... AN ICE-BREAKER TO GET ME THINKIN' --
HUUURGH!
OOOOKAY, UM... LET'S RAP ABOUT THE X-MEN, THEN! ARE THOSE KOOKY MUTIES STILL TRYING TO PROTECT A WORLD THAT HATES AND FEARS THEM?
YOU'D THINK BY NOW THEY'D PACK IT IN AND START AN UNLOVED FREAK COLLECTIVE --
NNNGH!

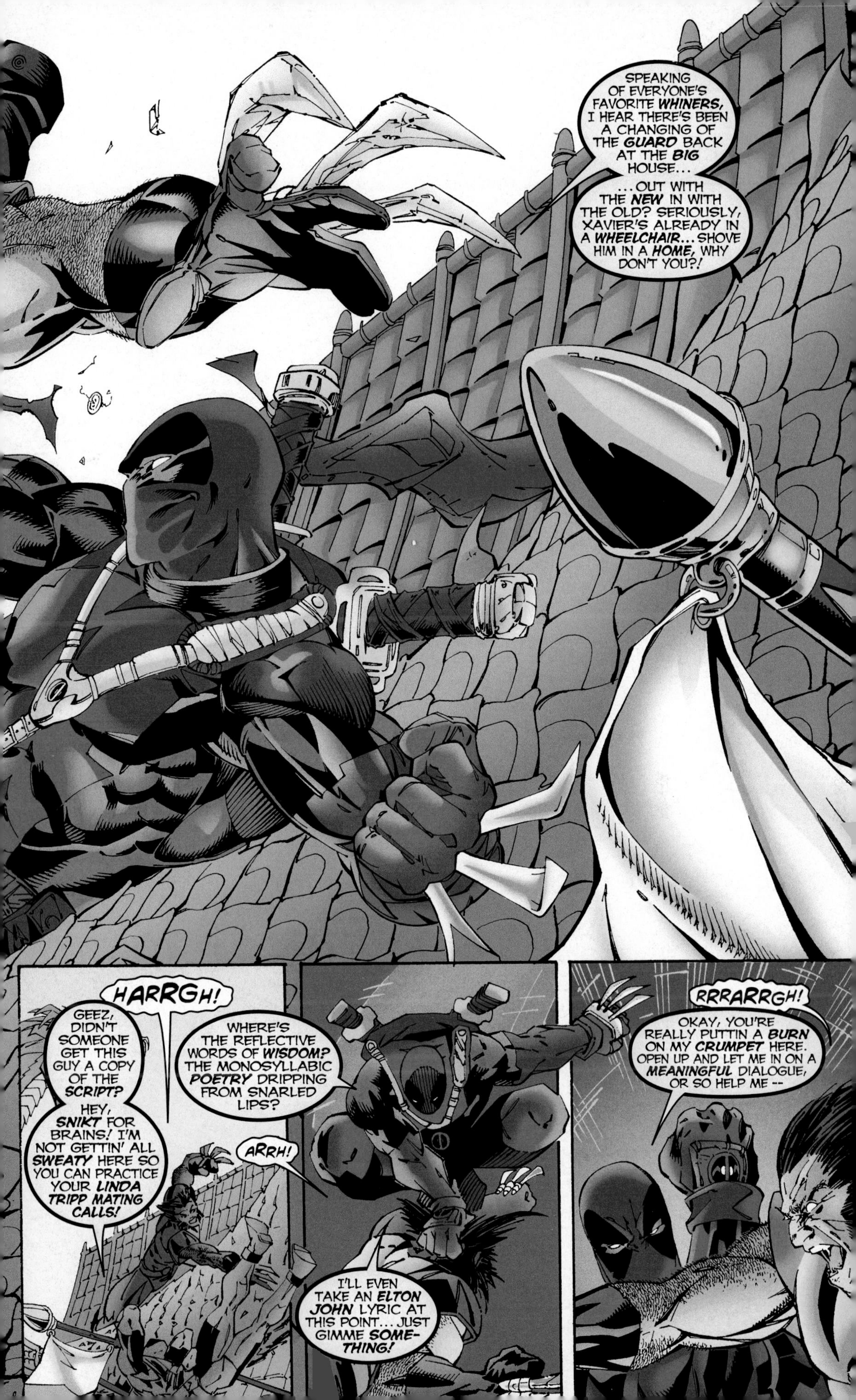
SPEAKING OF EVERYONE'S FAVORITE **WHINERS,** I HEAR THERE'S BEEN A CHANGING OF THE **GUARD** BACK AT THE **BIG** HOUSE...
...OUT WITH THE **NEW** IN WITH THE OLD? SERIOUSLY, XAVIER'S ALREADY IN A **WHEELCHAIR**... SHOVE HIM IN A **HOME,** WHY DON'T YOU?!
HARRGH!
GEEZ, DIDN'T SOMEONE GET THIS GUY A COPY OF THE **SCRIPT?**
HEY, **SNIKT** FOR BRAINS! I'M NOT GETTIN' ALL **SWEATY** HERE SO YOU CAN PRACTICE YOUR **LINDA TRIPP MATING CALLS!**
WHERE'S THE REFLECTIVE WORDS OF **WISDOM?** THE MONOSYLLABIC **POETRY** DRIPPING FROM SNARLED LIPS?
ARRH!
I'LL EVEN TAKE AN **ELTON JOHN** LYRIC AT THIS POINT... JUST GIMME **SOME-THING!**
RRRARRGH!
OKAY, YOU'RE REALLY PUTTIN A **BURN** ON MY **CRUMPET** HERE. OPEN UP AND LET ME IN ON A **MEANINGFUL** DIALOGUE, OR SO HELP ME --

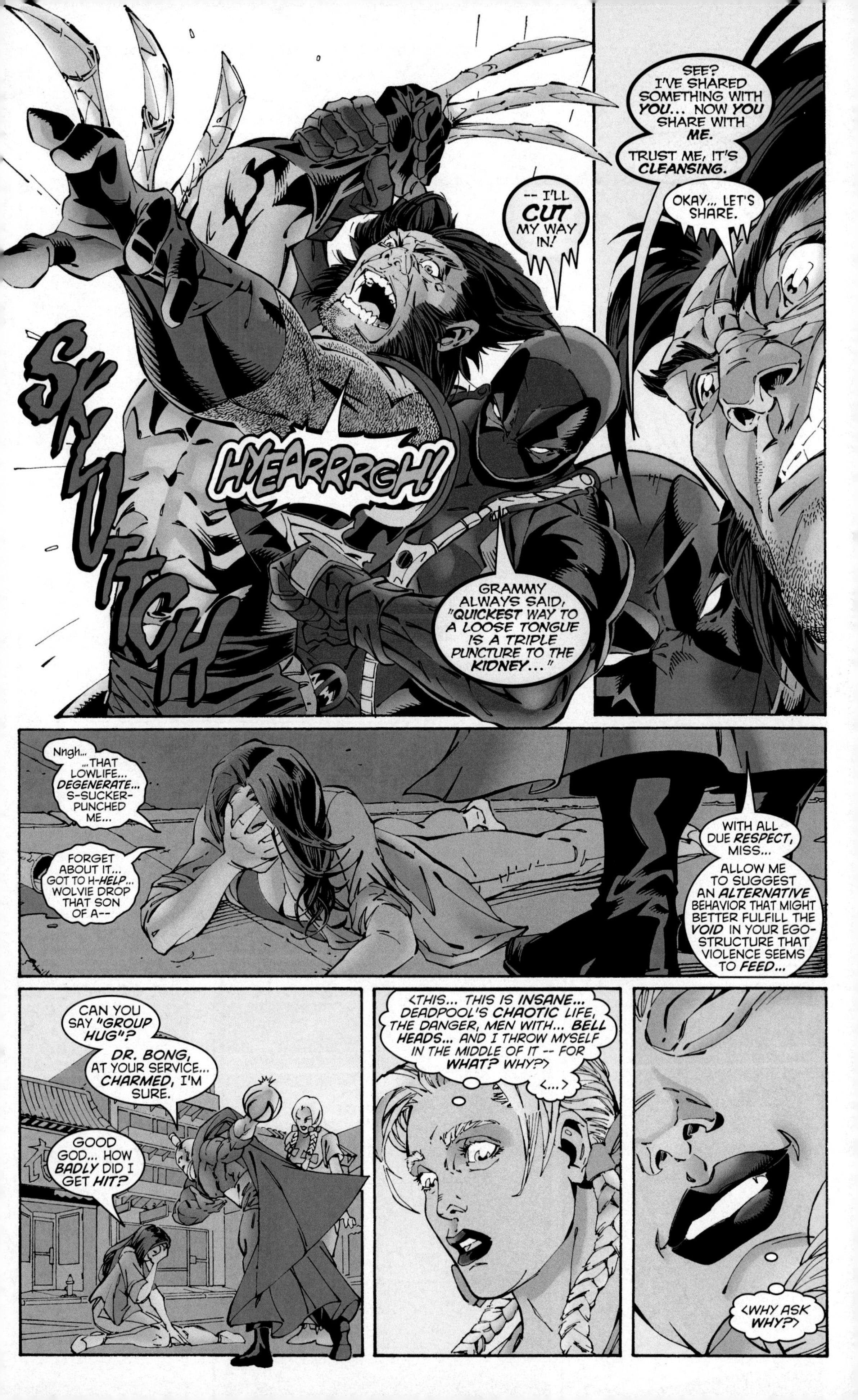
SEE? I'VE SHARED SOMETHING WITH YOU... NOW YOU SHARE WITH ME.
TRUST ME, IT'S CLEANSING.
OKAY... LET'S SHARE.
-- I'LL CUT MY WAY IN!
SKLUTCH
HYEARRRGH!
GRAMMY ALWAYS SAID, "QUICKEST WAY TO A LOOSE TONGUE IS A TRIPLE PUNCTURE TO THE KIDNEY..."
Nngh... ...THAT LOWLIFE... DEGENERATE... S-SUCKER-PUNCHED ME...
FORGET ABOUT IT... GOT TO H-HELP... WOLVIE DROP THAT SON OF A--
WITH ALL DUE RESPECT, MISS...
ALLOW ME TO SUGGEST AN ALTERNATIVE BEHAVIOR THAT MIGHT BETTER FULFILL THE VOID IN YOUR EGO-STRUCTURE THAT VIOLENCE SEEMS TO FEED...
CAN YOU SAY "GROUP HUG"?
DR. BONG, AT YOUR SERVICE... CHARMED, I'M SURE.
GOOD GOD... HOW BADLY DID I GET HIT?
<THIS... THIS IS INSANE... DEADPOOL'S CHAOTIC LIFE, THE DANGER, MEN WITH... BELL HEADS... AND I THROW MYSELF IN THE MIDDLE OF IT -- FOR WHAT? WHY?>
<...>
<WHY ASK WHY?>

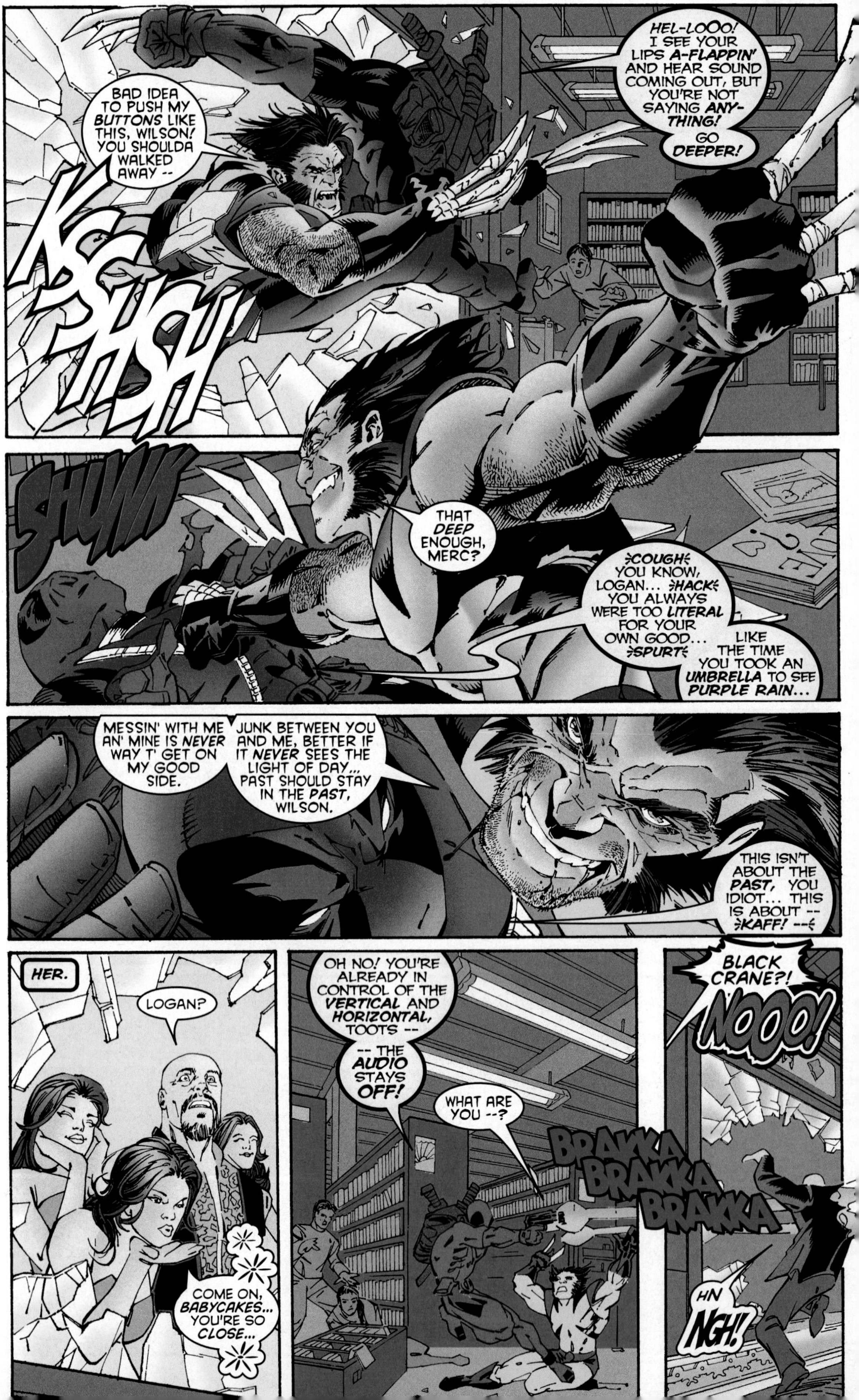
BAD IDEA TO PUSH MY BUTTONS LIKE THIS, WILSON! YOU SHOULDA WALKED AWAY --
KSSHHH
HEL-LOOO! I SEE YOUR LIPS A-FLAPPIN' AND HEAR SOUND COMING OUT, BUT YOU'RE NOT SAYING ANY-THING!
GO DEEPER!
SHUNK
THAT DEEP ENOUGH, MERC?
COUGH YOU KNOW, LOGAN... HACK YOU ALWAYS WERE TOO LITERAL FOR YOUR OWN GOOD... SPURT
LIKE THE TIME YOU TOOK AN UMBRELLA TO SEE PURPLE RAIN...
MESSIN' WITH ME AN' MINE IS NEVER WAY T' GET ON MY GOOD SIDE.
JUNK BETWEEN YOU AND ME, BETTER IF IT NEVER SEES THE LIGHT OF DAY... PAST SHOULD STAY IN THE PAST, WILSON.
THIS ISN'T ABOUT THE PAST, YOU IDIOT... THIS IS ABOUT -- KAFF! --
HER.
LOGAN?
COME ON, BABYCAKES... YOU'RE SO CLOSE...
OH NO! YOU'RE ALREADY IN CONTROL OF THE VERTICAL AND HORIZONTAL, TOOTS --
-- THE AUDIO STAYS OFF!
WHAT ARE YOU --?
BRAKKA BRAKKA BRAKKA
BLACK CRANE?!
NOOO!
HN NGH!

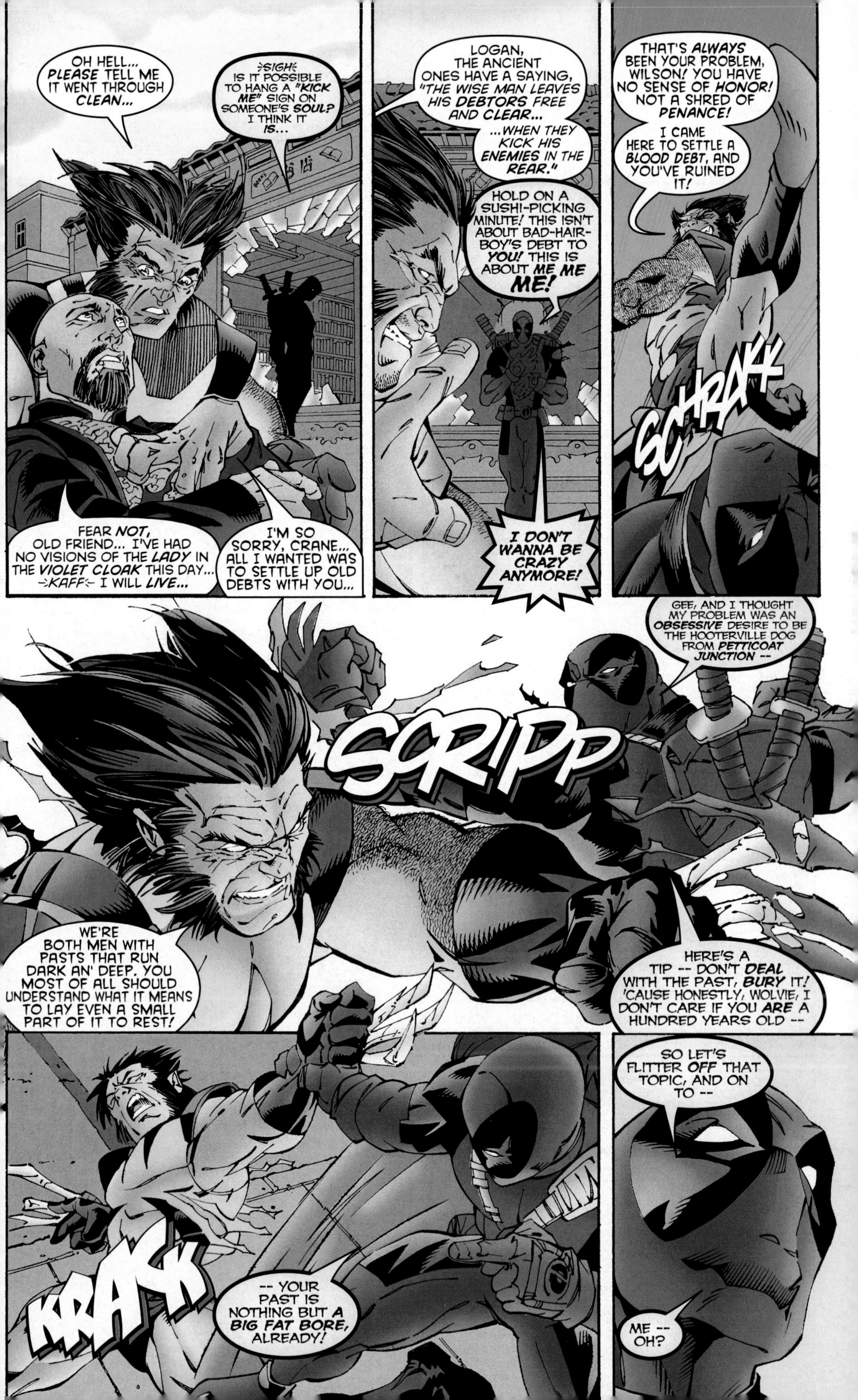
OH HELL... PLEASE TELL ME IT WENT THROUGH CLEAN...
⇛SIGH⇚ IS IT POSSIBLE TO HANG A "KICK ME" SIGN ON SOMEONE'S SOUL? I THINK IT IS...
FEAR NOT, OLD FRIEND... I'VE HAD NO VISIONS OF THE LADY IN THE VIOLET CLOAK THIS DAY... ⇛KAFF⇚ I WILL LIVE...
I'M SO SORRY, CRANE... ALL I WANTED WAS TO SETTLE UP OLD DEBTS WITH YOU...
LOGAN, THE ANCIENT ONES HAVE A SAYING, "THE WISE MAN LEAVES HIS DEBTORS FREE AND CLEAR...
...WHEN THEY KICK HIS ENEMIES IN THE REAR."
HOLD ON A SUSHI-PICKING MINUTE! THIS ISN'T ABOUT BAD-HAIR-BOY'S DEBT TO YOU! THIS IS ABOUT ME ME ME!
I DON'T WANNA BE CRAZY ANYMORE!
THAT'S ALWAYS BEEN YOUR PROBLEM, WILSON! YOU HAVE NO SENSE OF HONOR! NOT A SHRED OF PENANCE!
I CAME HERE TO SETTLE A BLOOD DEBT, AND YOU'VE RUINED IT!
SCHRAK
GEE, AND I THOUGHT MY PROBLEM WAS AN OBSESSIVE DESIRE TO BE THE HOOTERVILLE DOG FROM PETTICOAT JUNCTION --
SCRIPP
WE'RE BOTH MEN WITH PASTS THAT RUN DARK AN' DEEP. YOU MOST OF ALL SHOULD UNDERSTAND WHAT IT MEANS TO LAY EVEN A SMALL PART OF IT TO REST!
HERE'S A TIP -- DON'T DEAL WITH THE PAST, BURY IT! 'CAUSE HONESTLY, WOLVIE, I DON'T CARE IF YOU ARE A HUNDRED YEARS OLD --
KRAK
-- YOUR PAST IS NOTHING BUT A BIG FAT BORE, ALREADY!
SO LET'S FLITTER OFF THAT TOPIC, AND ON TO --
ME -- OH?

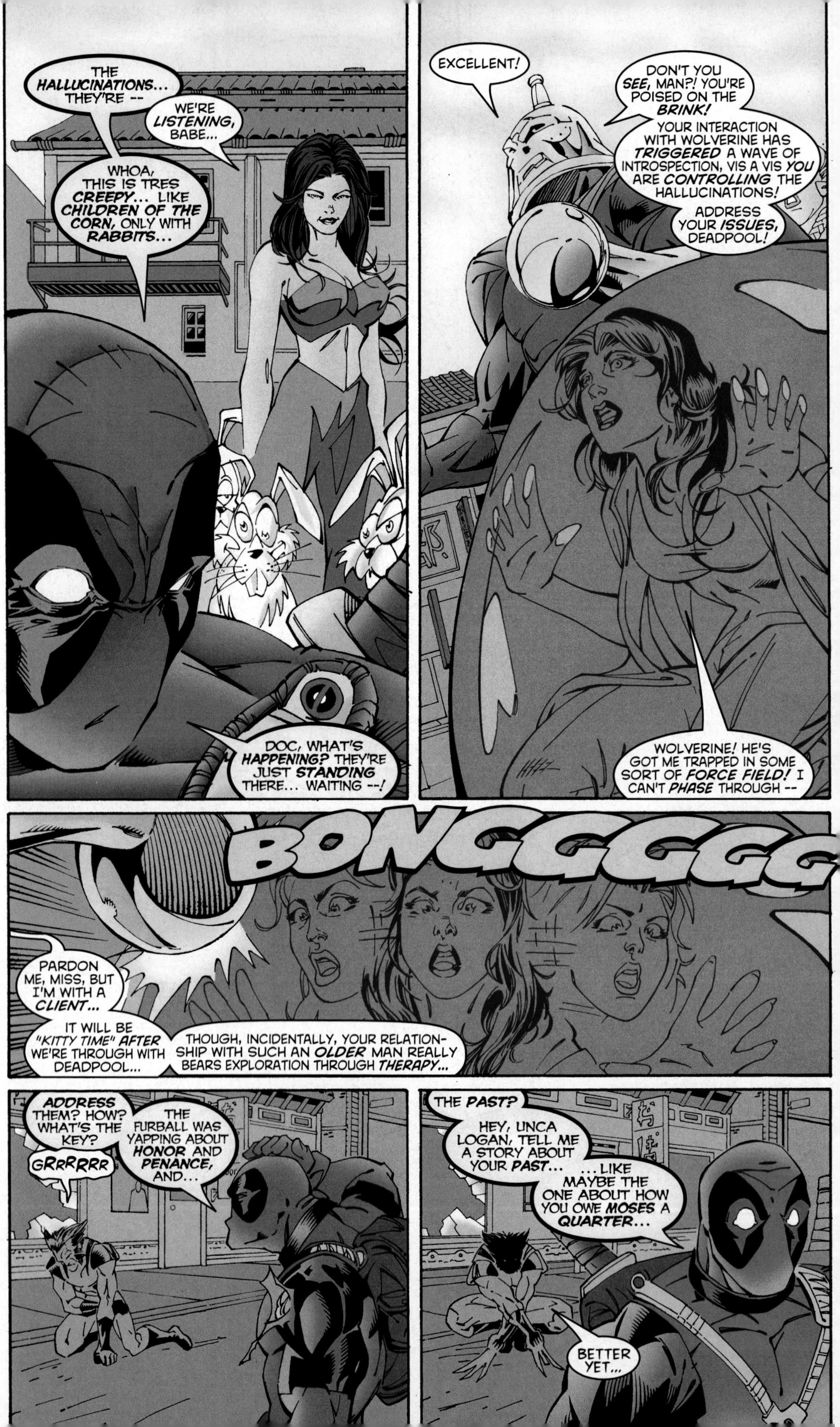
THE HALLUCINATIONS... THEY'RE --
WE'RE LISTENING, BABE...
WHOA, THIS IS TRES CREEPY... LIKE CHILDREN OF THE CORN, ONLY WITH RABBITS...
DOC, WHAT'S HAPPENING? THEY'RE JUST STANDING THERE... WAITING --!
EXCELLENT!
DON'T YOU SEE, MAN?! YOU'RE POISED ON THE BRINK!
YOUR INTERACTION WITH WOLVERINE HAS TRIGGERED A WAVE OF INTROSPECTION, VIS A VIS YOU ARE CONTROLLING THE HALLUCINATIONS!
ADDRESS YOUR ISSUES, DEADPOOL!
WOLVERINE! HE'S GOT ME TRAPPED IN SOME SORT OF FORCE FIELD! I CAN'T PHASE THROUGH --
BONGGGGG
PARDON ME, MISS, BUT I'M WITH A CLIENT...
IT WILL BE "KITTY TIME" AFTER WE'RE THROUGH WITH DEADPOOL...
THOUGH, INCIDENTALLY, YOUR RELATIONSHIP WITH SUCH AN OLDER MAN REALLY BEARS EXPLORATION THROUGH THERAPY...
ADDRESS THEM? HOW? WHAT'S THE KEY?
GRRRRRR
THE FURBALL WAS YAPPING ABOUT HONOR AND PENANCE, AND...
THE PAST?
HEY, UNCA LOGAN, TELL ME A STORY ABOUT YOUR PAST...
...LIKE MAYBE THE ONE ABOUT HOW YOU OWE MOSES A QUARTER...
BETTER YET...

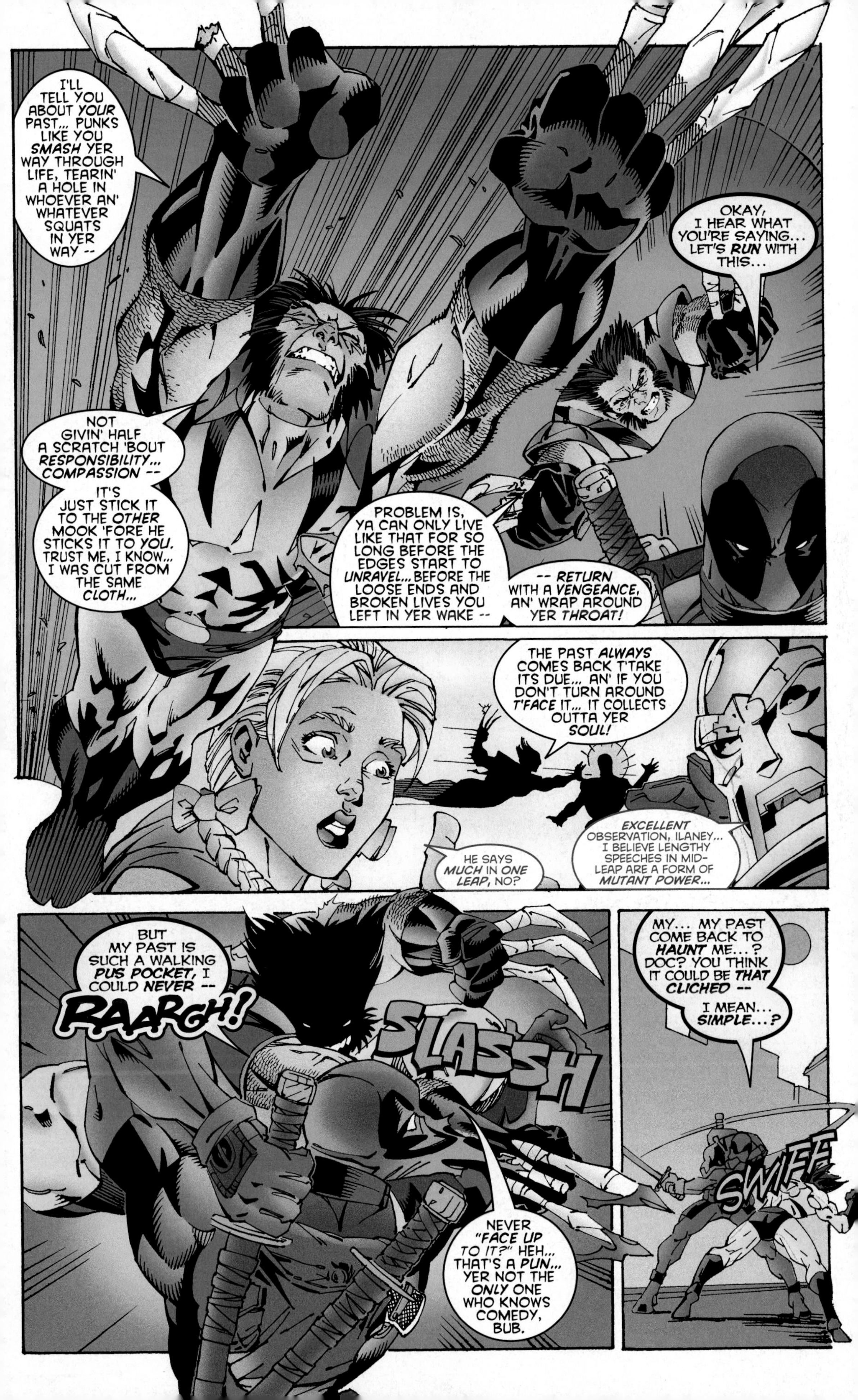

I'LL TELL YOU ABOUT YOUR PAST... PUNKS LIKE YOU SMASH YER WAY THROUGH LIFE, TEARIN' A HOLE IN WHOEVER AN' WHATEVER SQUATS IN YER WAY --
OKAY, I HEAR WHAT YOU'RE SAYING... LET'S RUN WITH THIS...
NOT GIVIN' HALF A SCRATCH 'BOUT RESPONSIBILITY... COMPASSION --
IT'S JUST STICK IT TO THE OTHER MOOK 'FORE HE STICKS IT TO YOU. TRUST ME, I KNOW... I WAS CUT FROM THE SAME CLOTH...
PROBLEM IS, YA CAN ONLY LIVE LIKE THAT FOR SO LONG BEFORE THE EDGES START TO UNRAVEL... BEFORE THE LOOSE ENDS AND BROKEN LIVES YOU LEFT IN YER WAKE --
-- RETURN WITH A VENGEANCE, AN' WRAP AROUND YER THROAT!
THE PAST ALWAYS COMES BACK T'TAKE ITS DUE... AN' IF YOU DON'T TURN AROUND T'FACE IT... IT COLLECTS OUTTA YER SOUL!
HE SAYS MUCH IN ONE LEAP, NO?
EXCELLENT OBSERVATION, ILANEY... I BELIEVE LENGTHY SPEECHES IN MID-LEAP ARE A FORM OF MUTANT POWER...
BUT MY PAST IS SUCH A WALKING PUS POCKET, I COULD NEVER --
RAARGH!
SLASSH
NEVER "FACE UP TO IT?" HEH... THAT'S A PUN... YER NOT THE ONLY ONE WHO KNOWS COMEDY, BUB.
MY... MY PAST COME BACK TO HAUNT ME...? DOC? YOU THINK IT COULD BE THAT CLICHED --
I MEAN... SIMPLE...?
SWIFF

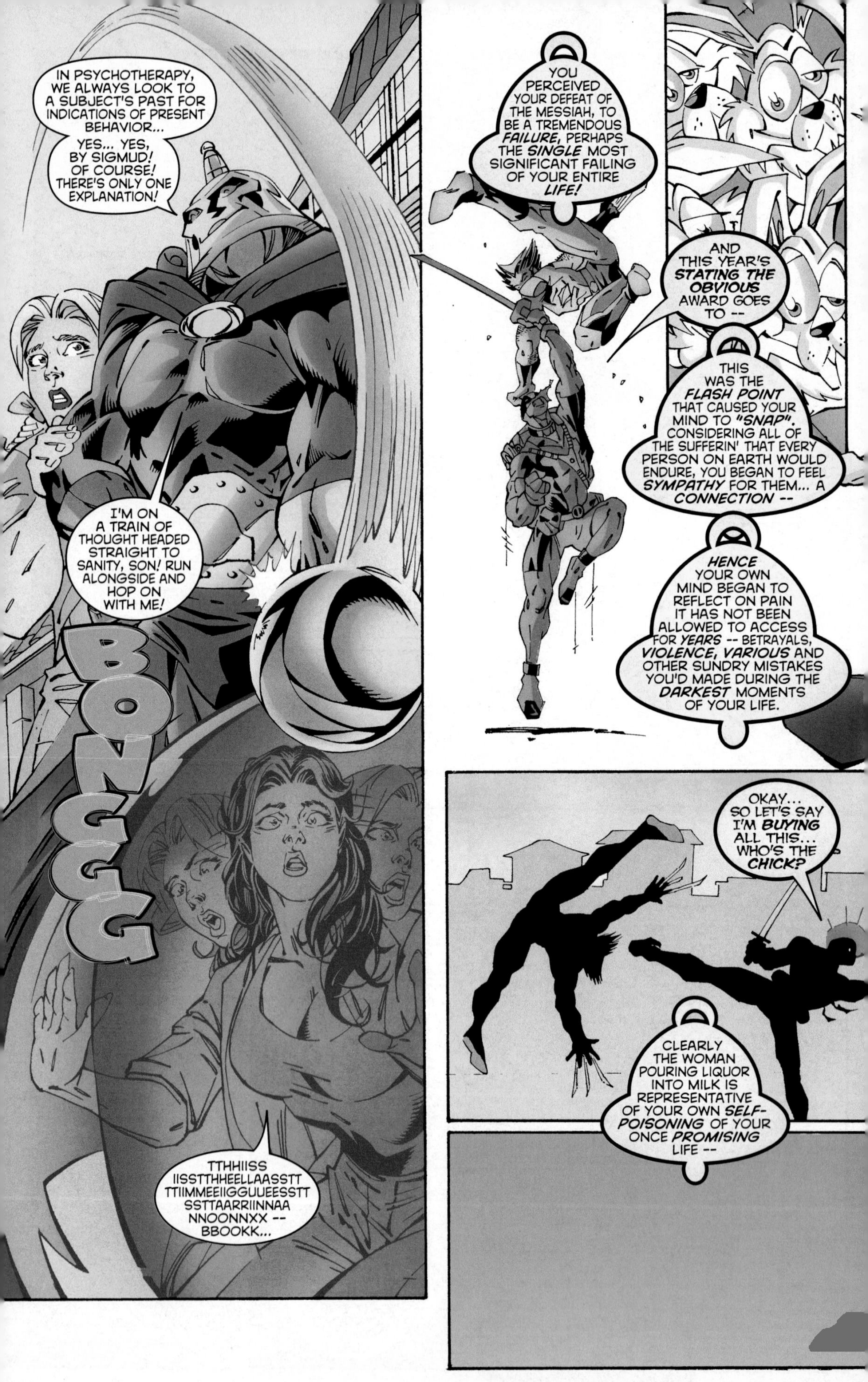
IN PSYCHOTHERAPY, WE ALWAYS LOOK TO A SUBJECT'S PAST FOR INDICATIONS OF PRESENT BEHAVIOR...
YES... YES, BY SIGMUD! OF COURSE! THERE'S ONLY ONE EXPLANATION!
YOU PERCEIVED YOUR DEFEAT OF THE MESSIAH, TO BE A TREMENDOUS FAILURE, PERHAPS THE SINGLE MOST SIGNIFICANT FAILING OF YOUR ENTIRE LIFE!
AND THIS YEAR'S STATING THE OBVIOUS AWARD GOES TO --
THIS WAS THE FLASH POINT THAT CAUSED YOUR MIND TO "SNAP". CONSIDERING ALL OF THE SUFFERIN' THAT EVERY PERSON ON EARTH WOULD ENDURE, YOU BEGAN TO FEEL SYMPATHY FOR THEM... A CONNECTION --
I'M ON A TRAIN OF THOUGHT HEADED STRAIGHT TO SANITY, SON! RUN ALONGSIDE AND HOP ON WITH ME!
HENCE YOUR OWN MIND BEGAN TO REFLECT ON PAIN IT HAS NOT BEEN ALLOWED TO ACCESS FOR YEARS -- BETRAYALS, VIOLENCE, VARIOUS AND OTHER SUNDRY MISTAKES YOU'D MADE DURING THE DARKEST MOMENTS OF YOUR LIFE.
BONGGG
OKAY... SO LET'S SAY I'M BUYING ALL THIS... WHO'S THE CHICK?
CLEARLY THE WOMAN POURING LIQUOR INTO MILK IS REPRESENTATIVE OF YOUR OWN SELF-POISONING OF YOUR ONCE PROMISING LIFE --
TTHHIISS IISSTTHHEELLAASSTT TTIIMMEEIIGGUUEESSTT SSTTAARRIINNAA NNOONNXX -- BBOOKK...

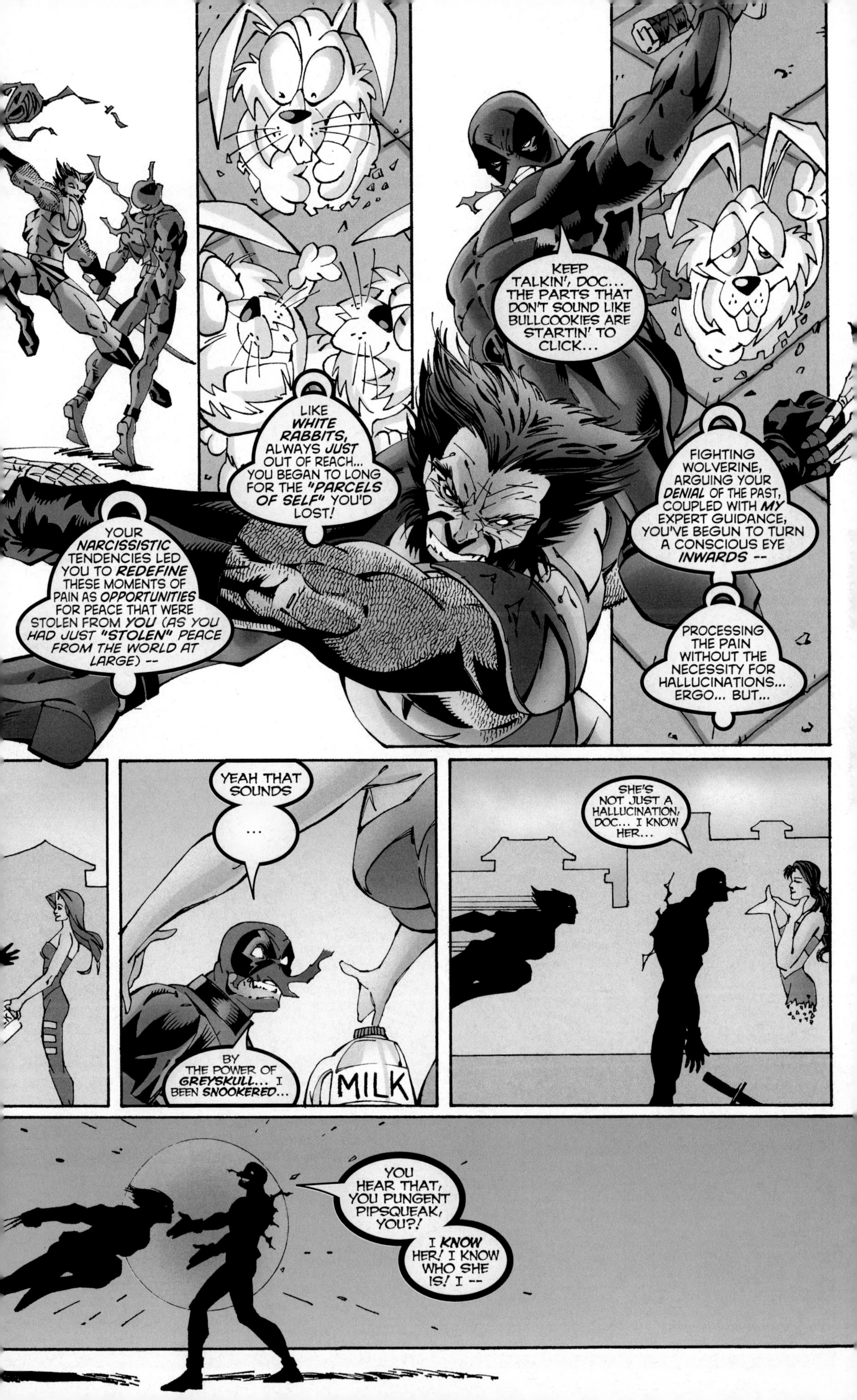
KEEP TALKIN', DOC... THE PARTS THAT DON'T SOUND LIKE BULLCOOKIES ARE STARTIN' TO CLICK...
YOUR NARCISSISTIC TENDENCIES LED YOU TO REDEFINE THESE MOMENTS OF PAIN AS OPPORTUNITIES FOR PEACE THAT WERE STOLEN FROM YOU (AS YOU HAD JUST "STOLEN" PEACE FROM THE WORLD AT LARGE) --
LIKE WHITE RABBITS, ALWAYS JUST OUT OF REACH... YOU BEGAN TO LONG FOR THE "PARCELS OF SELF" YOU'D LOST!
FIGHTING WOLVERINE, ARGUING YOUR DENIAL OF THE PAST, COUPLED WITH MY EXPERT GUIDANCE, YOU'VE BEGUN TO TURN A CONSCIOUS EYE INWARDS --
PROCESSING THE PAIN WITHOUT THE NECESSITY FOR HALLUCINATIONS... ERGO... BUT...
YEAH THAT SOUNDS
...
BY THE POWER OF GREYSKULL... I BEEN SNOOKERED...
MILK
SHE'S NOT JUST A HALLUCINATION, DOC... I KNOW HER...
YOU HEAR THAT, YOU PUNGENT PIPSQUEAK, YOU?!
I KNOW HER! I KNOW WHO SHE IS! I --

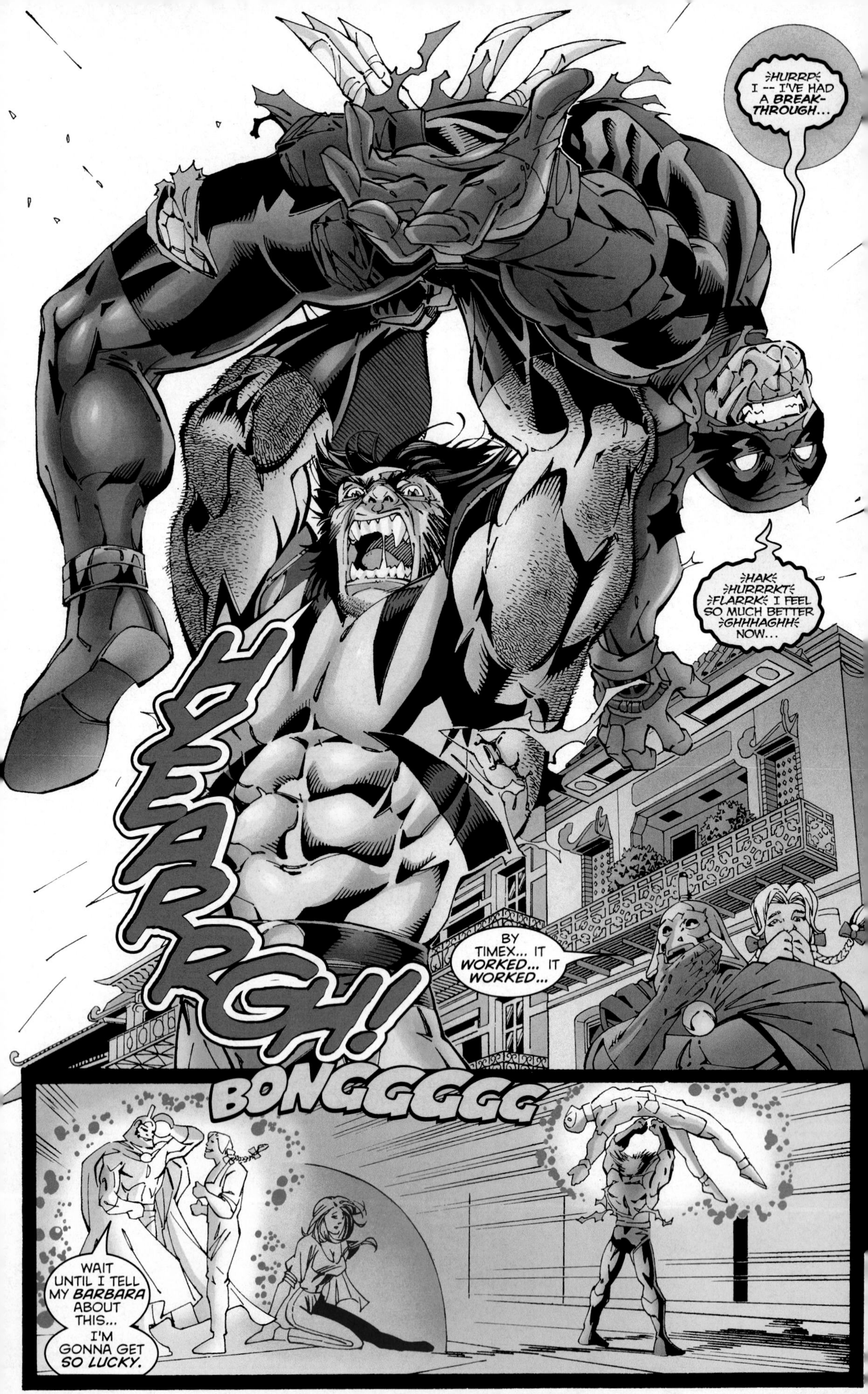
HURRP I -- I'VE HAD A BREAK-THROUGH...
HAK *HURRRKT* *FLARRK* I FEEL SO MUCH BETTER *GHHHAGHH* NOW...
HBLARRGH!
BY TIMEX... IT WORKED... IT WORKED...
BONGGGGG
WAIT UNTIL I TELL MY BARBARA ABOUT THIS... I'M GONNA GET SO LUCKY.

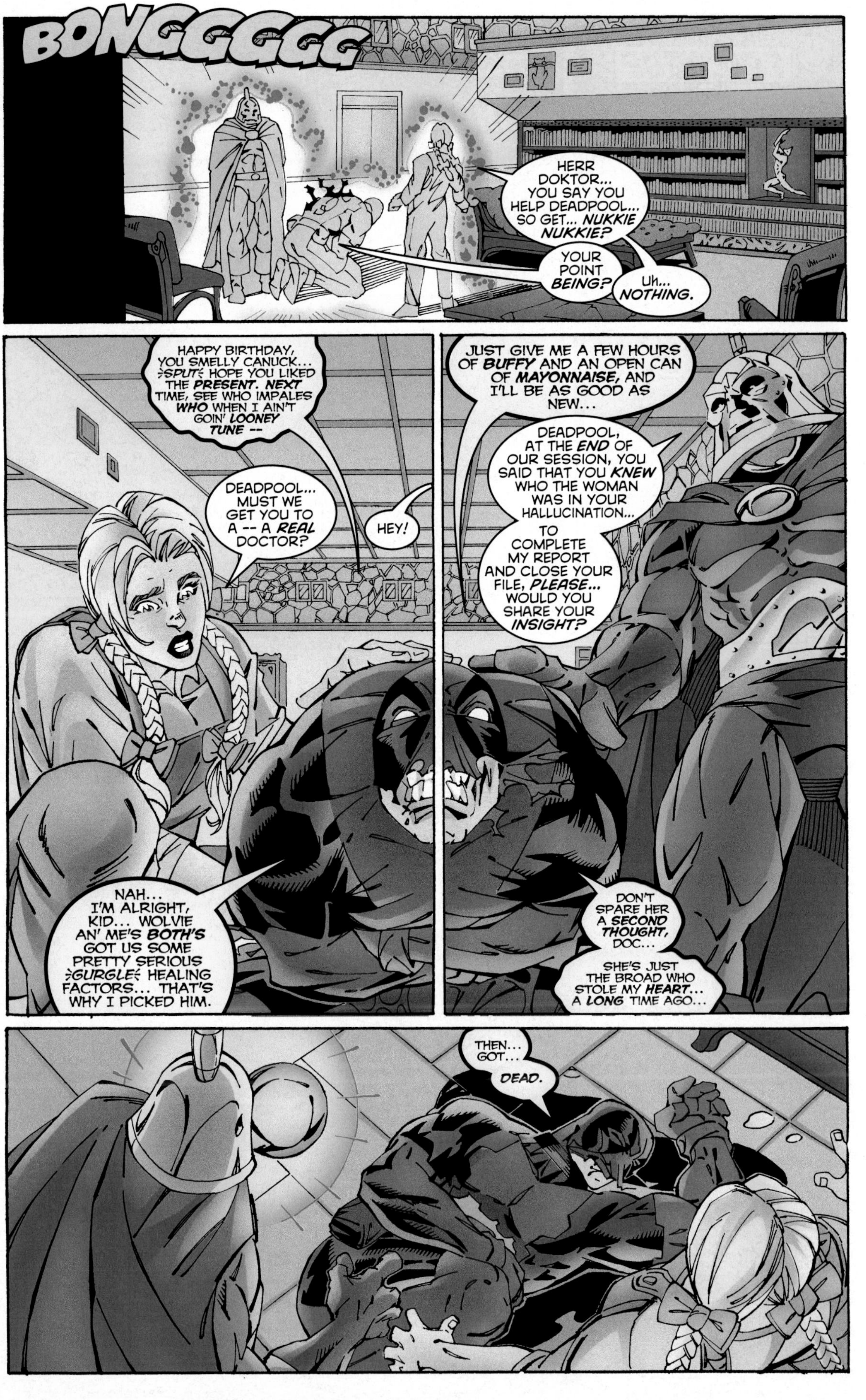
BONGGGGGG
HERR DOKTOR... YOU SAY YOU HELP DEADPOOL... SO GET... NUKKIE NUKKIE?
YOUR POINT BEING?
Uh... NOTHING.
HAPPY BIRTHDAY, YOU SMELLY CANUCK... SPUT HOPE YOU LIKED THE PRESENT. NEXT TIME, SEE WHO IMPALES WHO WHEN I AIN'T GOIN' LOONEY TUNE --
DEADPOOL... MUST WE GET YOU TO A -- A REAL DOCTOR?
HEY!
JUST GIVE ME A FEW HOURS OF BUFFY AND AN OPEN CAN OF MAYONNAISE, AND I'LL BE AS GOOD AS NEW...
DEADPOOL, AT THE END OF OUR SESSION, YOU SAID THAT YOU KNEW WHO THE WOMAN WAS IN YOUR HALLUCINATION...
TO COMPLETE MY REPORT AND CLOSE YOUR FILE, PLEASE... WOULD YOU SHARE YOUR INSIGHT?
NAH... I'M ALRIGHT, KID... WOLVIE AN' ME'S BOTH'S GOT US SOME PRETTY SERIOUS GURGLE HEALING FACTORS... THAT'S WHY I PICKED HIM.
DON'T SPARE HER A SECOND THOUGHT, DOC...
SHE'S JUST THE BROAD WHO STOLE MY HEART... A LONG TIME AGO...
THEN... GOT... DEAD.

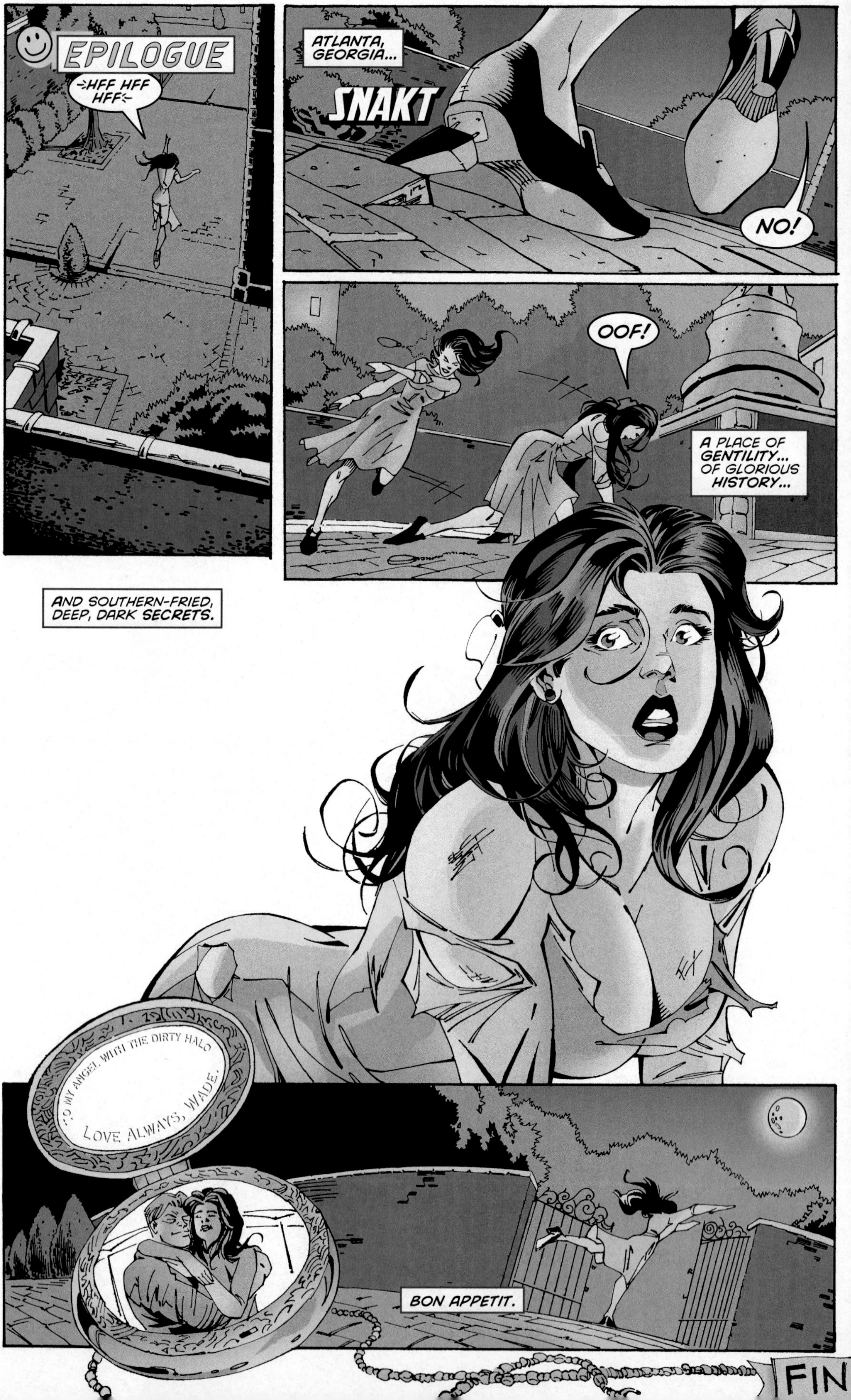
EPILOGUE
HFF HFF HFF
ATLANTA, GEORGIA...
SNAKT
NO!
OOF!
A PLACE OF GENTILITY... OF GLORIOUS HISTORY...
AND SOUTHERN-FRIED, DEEP, DARK SECRETS.
TO MY ANGEL WITH THE DIRTY HALO
LOVE ALWAYS, WADE.
BON APPETIT.
FIN

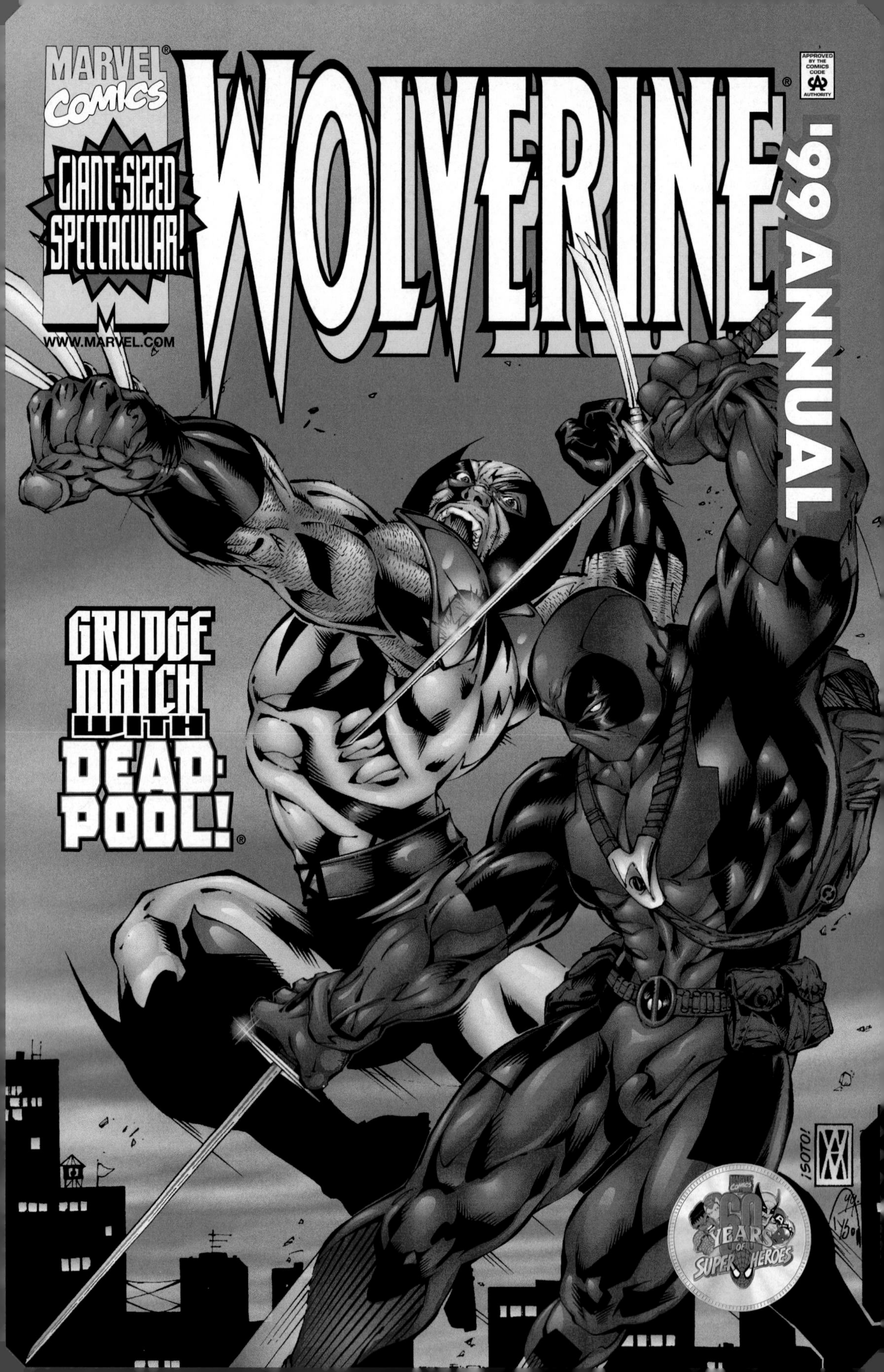
MARVEL COMICS
GIANT-SIZED SPECTACULAR!
WWW.MARVEL.COM
WOLVERINE
'99 ANNUAL
APPROVED BY THE COMICS CODE AUTHORITY
GRUDGE MATCH WITH DEADPOOL!
60 YEARS OF SUPER HEROES

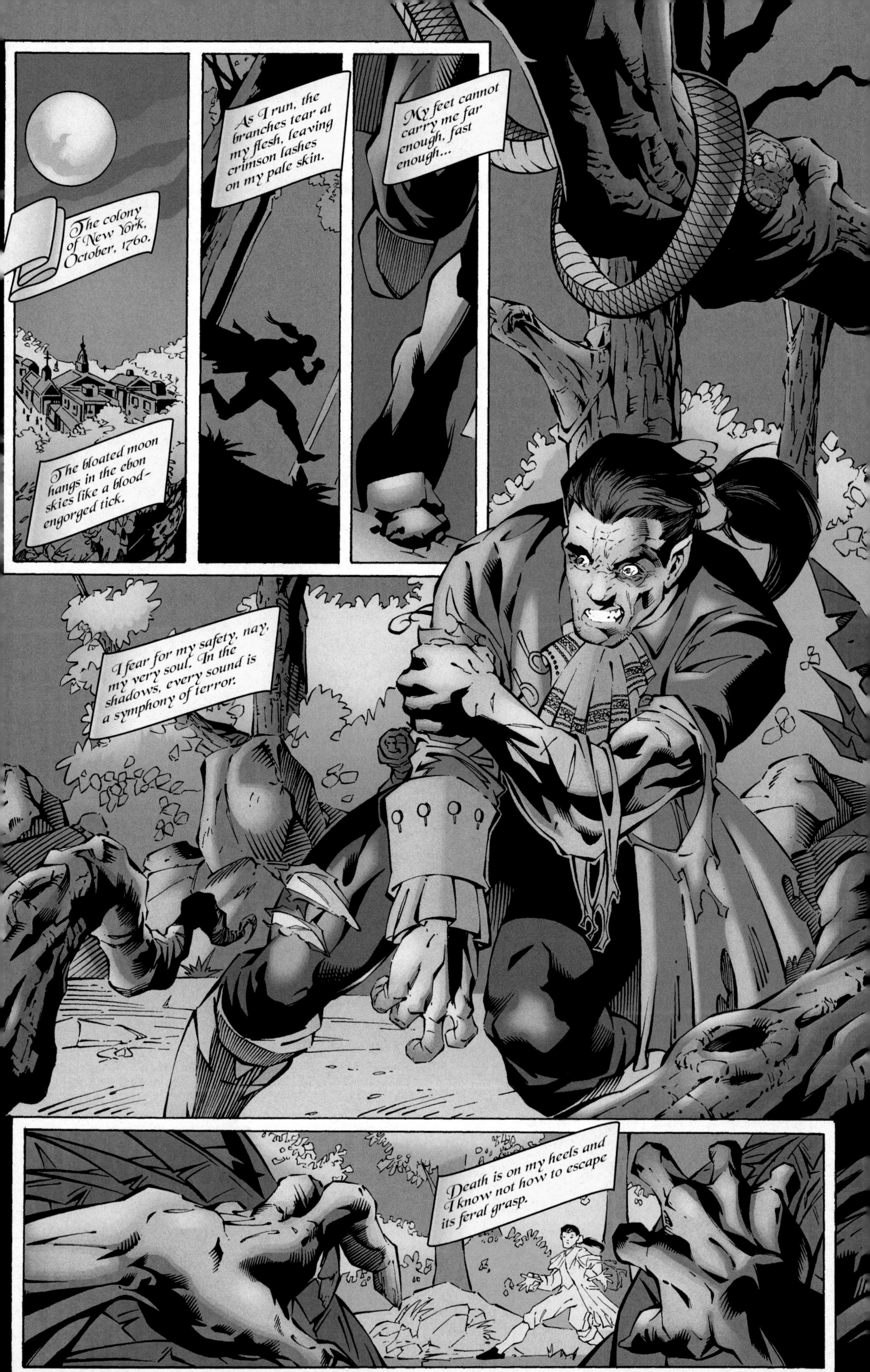
The colony of New York, October, 1760.
The bloated moon hangs in the ebon skies like a blood-engorged tick.
As I run, the branches tear at my flesh, leaving crimson lashes on my pale skin.
My feet cannot carry me far enough, fast enough...
I fear for my safety, nay, my very soul. In the shadows, every sound is a symphony of terror.
Death is on my heels and I know not how to escape its feral grasp.

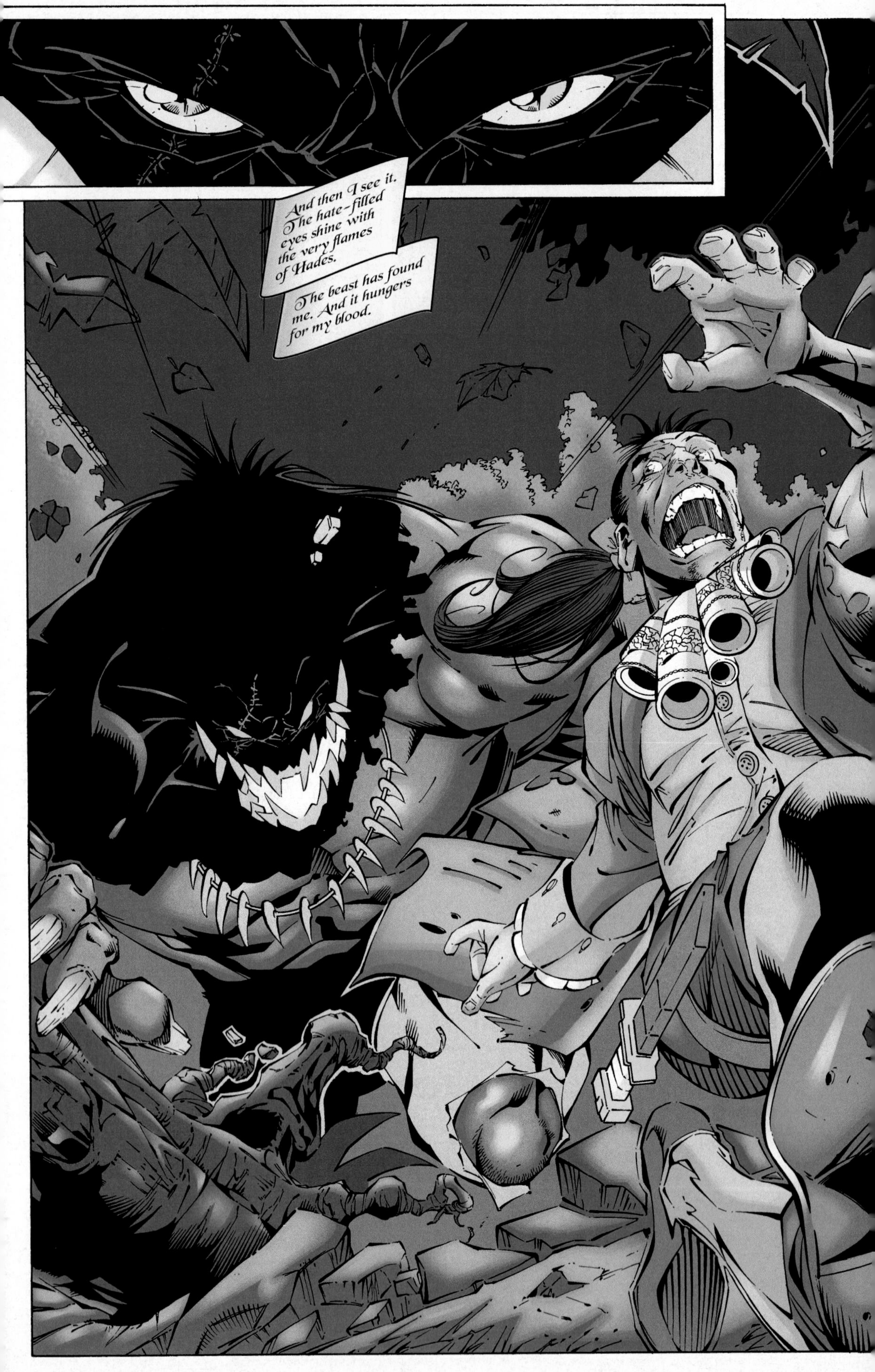
And then I see it. The hate-filled eyes shine with the very flames of Hades.
The beast has found me. And it hungers for my blood.

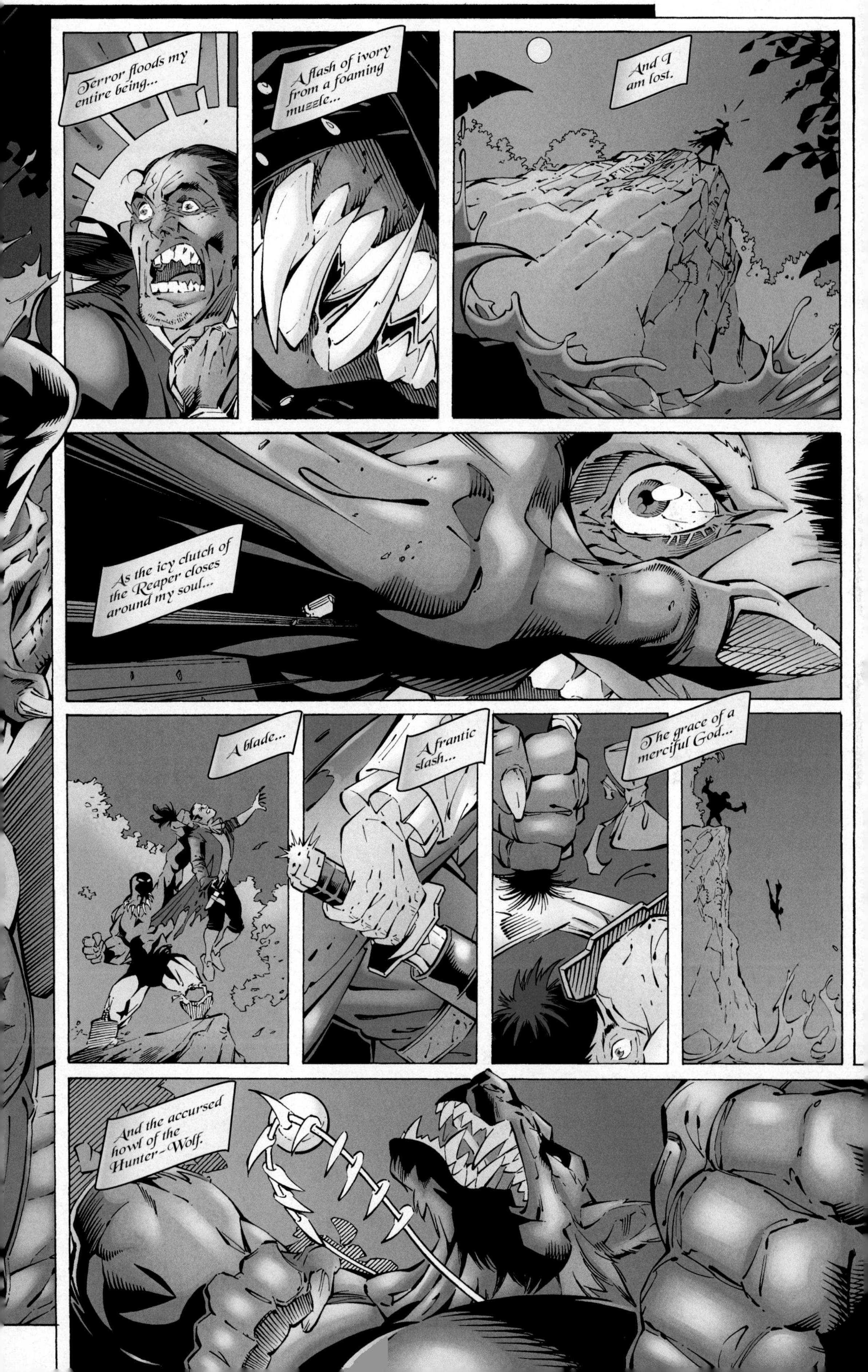
Terror floods my entire being...
A flash of ivory from a foaming muzzle...
And I am lost.
As the icy clutch of the Reaper closes around my soul...
A blade...
A frantic slash...
The grace of a merciful God...
And the accursed howl of the Hunter-Wolf.

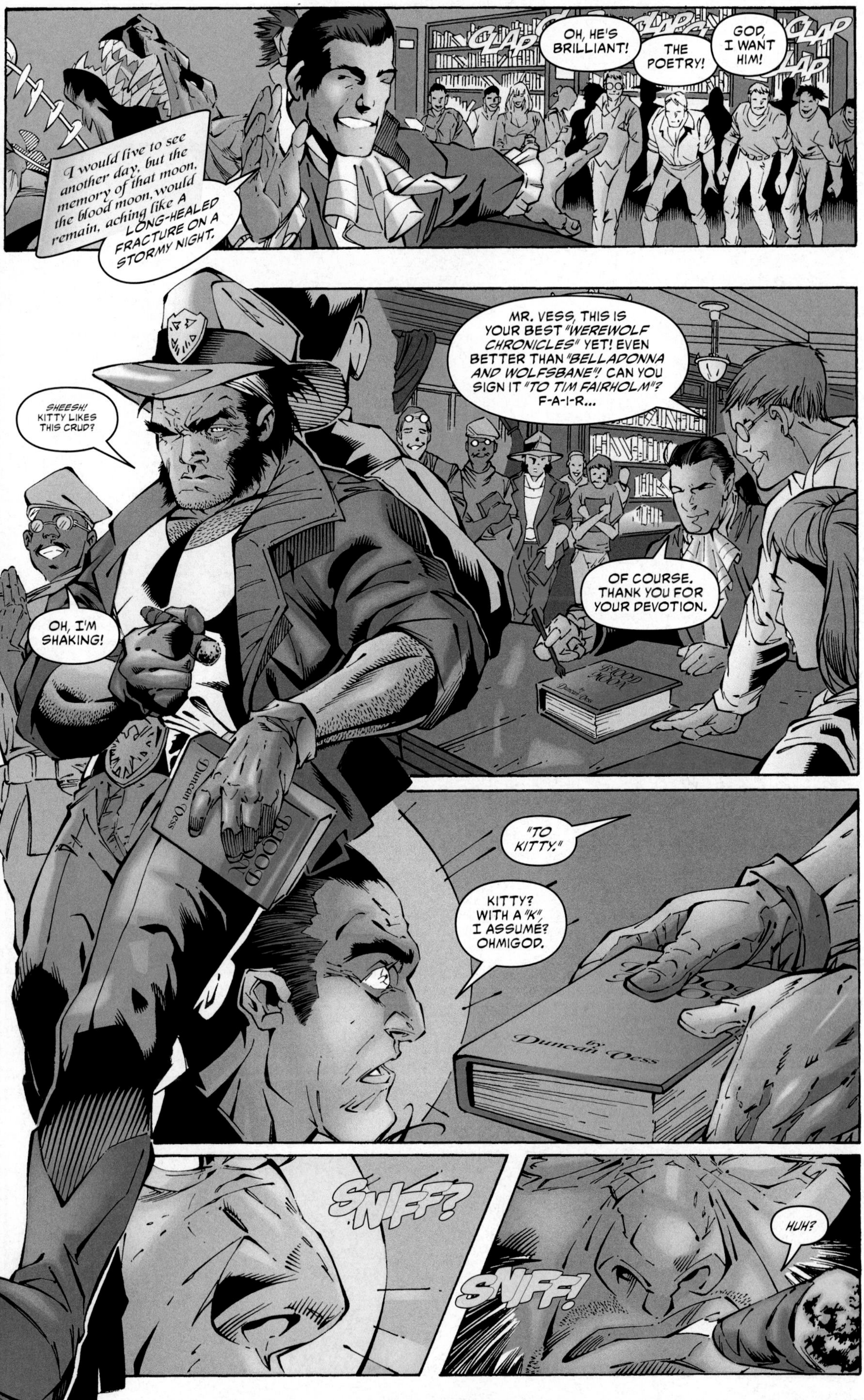
CLAP CLAP CLAP CLAP CLAP
OH, HE'S BRILLIANT!
THE POETRY!
GOD, I WANT HIM!
I would live to see another day, but the memory of that moon, the blood moon, would remain, aching like a LONG-HEALED FRACTURE ON A STORMY NIGHT.
MR. VESS, THIS IS YOUR BEST "WEREWOLF CHRONICLES" YET! EVEN BETTER THAN "BELLADONNA AND WOLFSBANE"! CAN YOU SIGN IT "TO TIM FAIRHOLM"? F-A-I-R...
SHEESH! KITTY LIKES THIS CRUD?
OF COURSE. THANK YOU FOR YOUR DEVOTION.
OH, I'M SHAKING!
"TO KITTY."
KITTY? WITH A "K," I ASSUME? OHMIGOD.
by Duncan Vess
SNIFF?
SNIFF!
HUH?

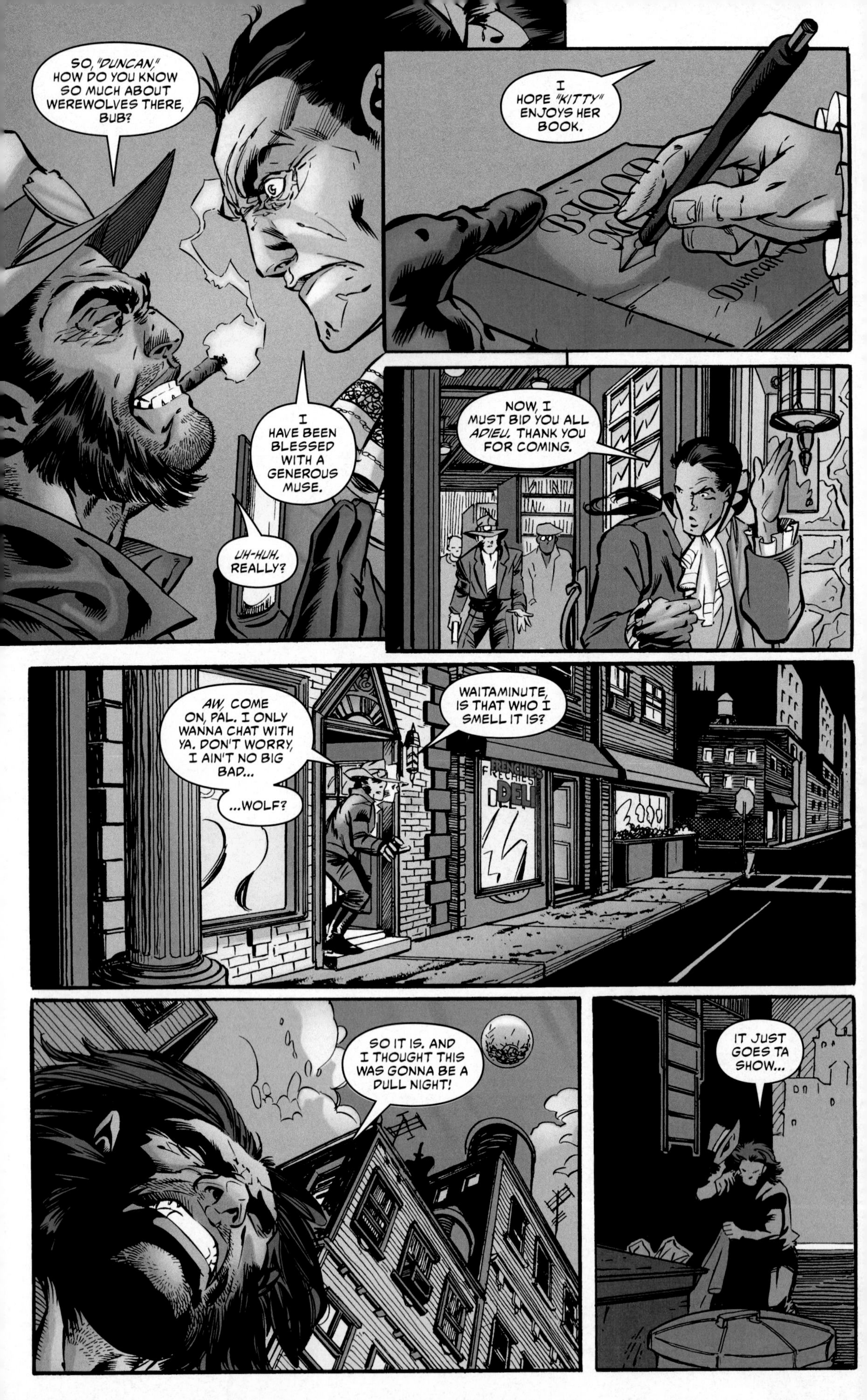
SO, "DUNCAN," HOW DO YOU KNOW SO MUCH ABOUT WEREWOLVES THERE, BUB?
I HAVE BEEN BLESSED WITH A GENEROUS MUSE.
UH-HUH. REALLY?
I HOPE "KITTY" ENJOYS HER BOOK.
Duncan
NOW, I MUST BID YOU ALL ADIEU. THANK YOU FOR COMING.
AW, COME ON, PAL. I ONLY WANNA CHAT WITH YA. DON'T WORRY, I AIN'T NO BIG BAD...
...WOLF?
WAITAMINUTE, IS THAT WHO I SMELL IT IS?
FRENCHIE'S DELI
SO IT IS. AND I THOUGHT THIS WAS GONNA BE A DULL NIGHT!
IT JUST GOES TA SHOW...

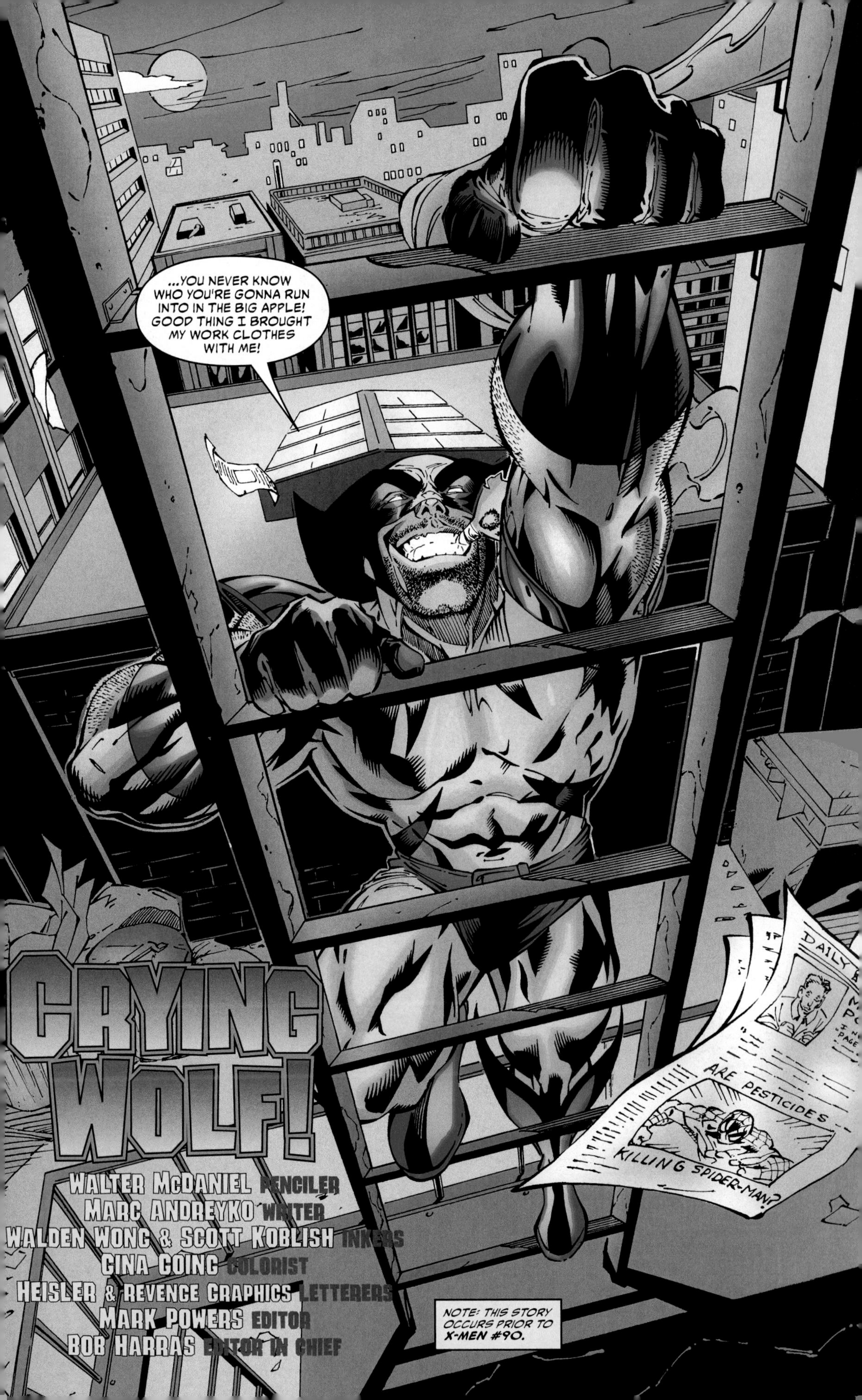
...YOU NEVER KNOW WHO YOU'RE GONNA RUN INTO IN THE BIG APPLE! GOOD THING I BROUGHT MY WORK CLOTHES WITH ME!
ARE PESTICIDES KILLING SPIDER-MAN?
CRYING WOLF!
WALTER McDANIEL PENCILER
MARC ANDREYKO WRITER
WALDEN WONG & SCOTT KOBLISH INKERS
GINA GOING COLORIST
HEISLER & REVENGE GRAPHICS LETTERERS
MARK POWERS EDITOR
BOB HARRAS EDITOR IN CHIEF
NOTE: THIS STORY OCCURS PRIOR TO X-MEN #90.

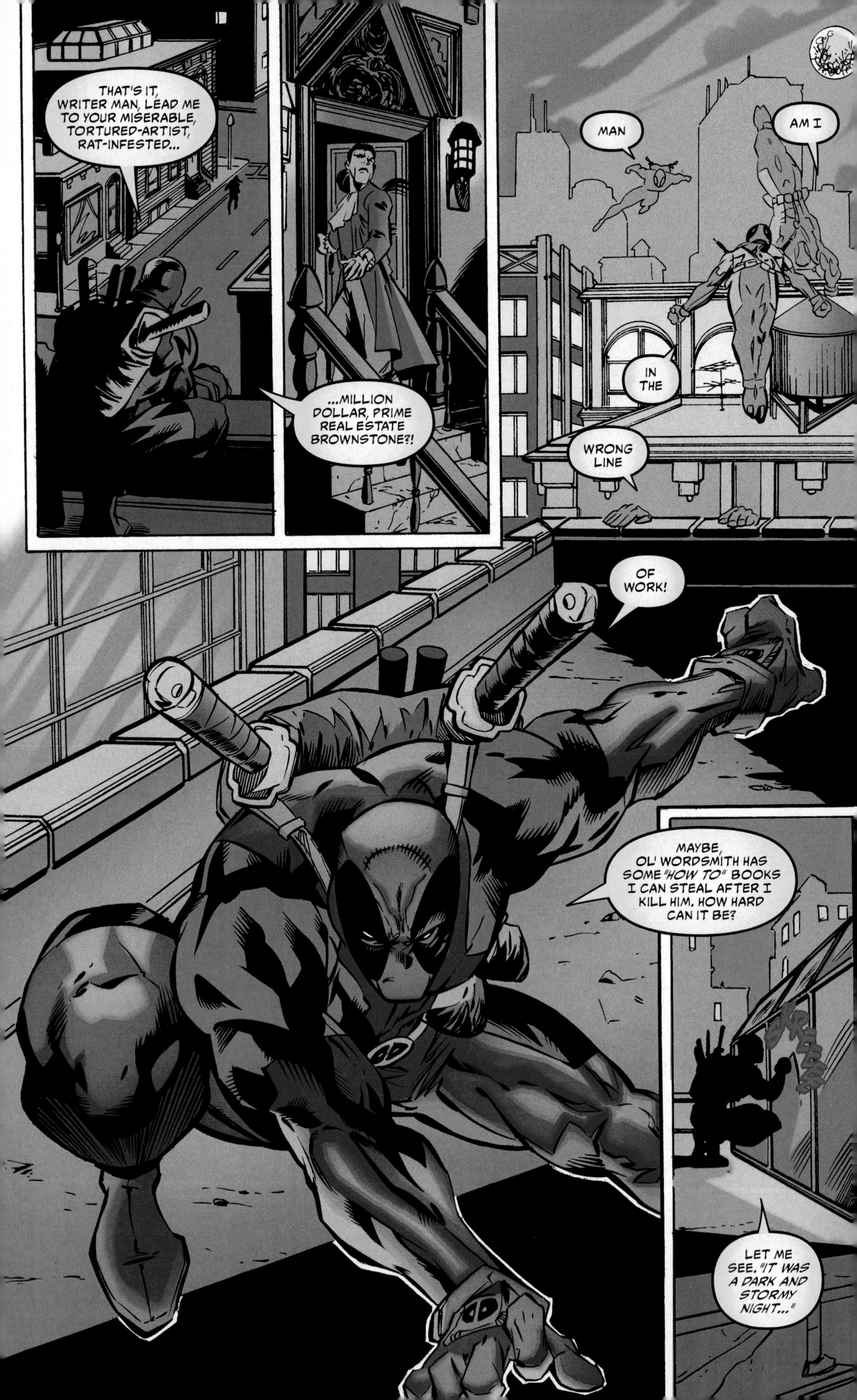
THAT'S IT, WRITER MAN, LEAD ME TO YOUR MISERABLE, TORTURED-ARTIST, RAT-INFESTED...
...MILLION DOLLAR, PRIME REAL ESTATE BROWNSTONE?!
MAN
AM I
IN THE
WRONG LINE
OF WORK!
MAYBE, OL' WORDSMITH HAS SOME "HOW TO" BOOKS I CAN STEAL AFTER I KILL HIM. HOW HARD CAN IT BE?
LET ME SEE. "IT WAS A DARK AND STORMY NIGHT..."

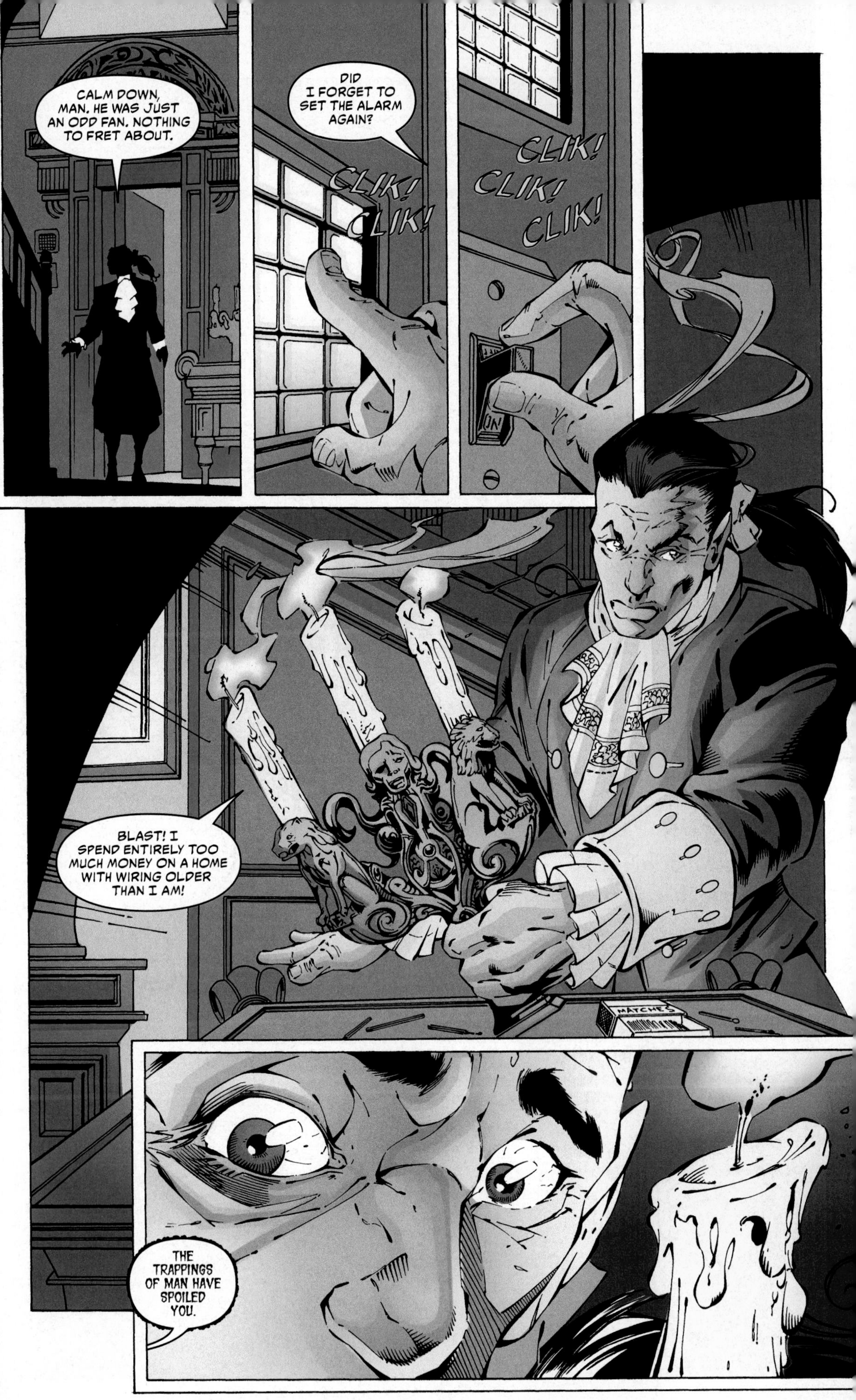
CALM DOWN, MAN. HE WAS JUST AN ODD FAN. NOTHING TO FRET ABOUT.
DID I FORGET TO SET THE ALARM AGAIN?
CLIK! CLIK!
CLIK! CLIK! CLIK!
ON
BLAST! I SPEND ENTIRELY TOO MUCH MONEY ON A HOME WITH WIRING OLDER THAN I AM!
MATCHES
THE TRAPPINGS OF MAN HAVE SPOILED YOU.

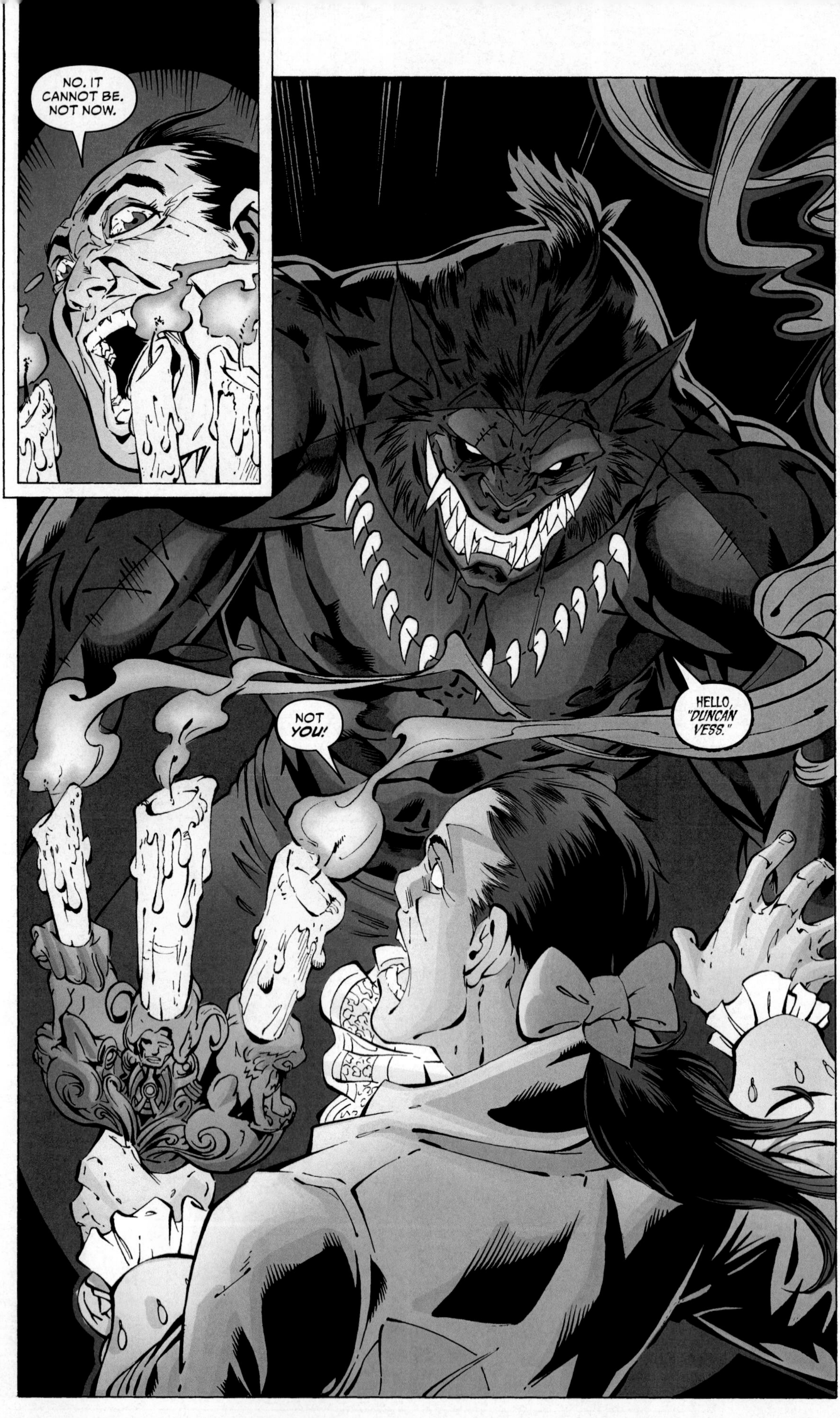
NO. IT CANNOT BE. NOT NOW.
HELLO, "DUNCAN VESS."
NOT YOU!

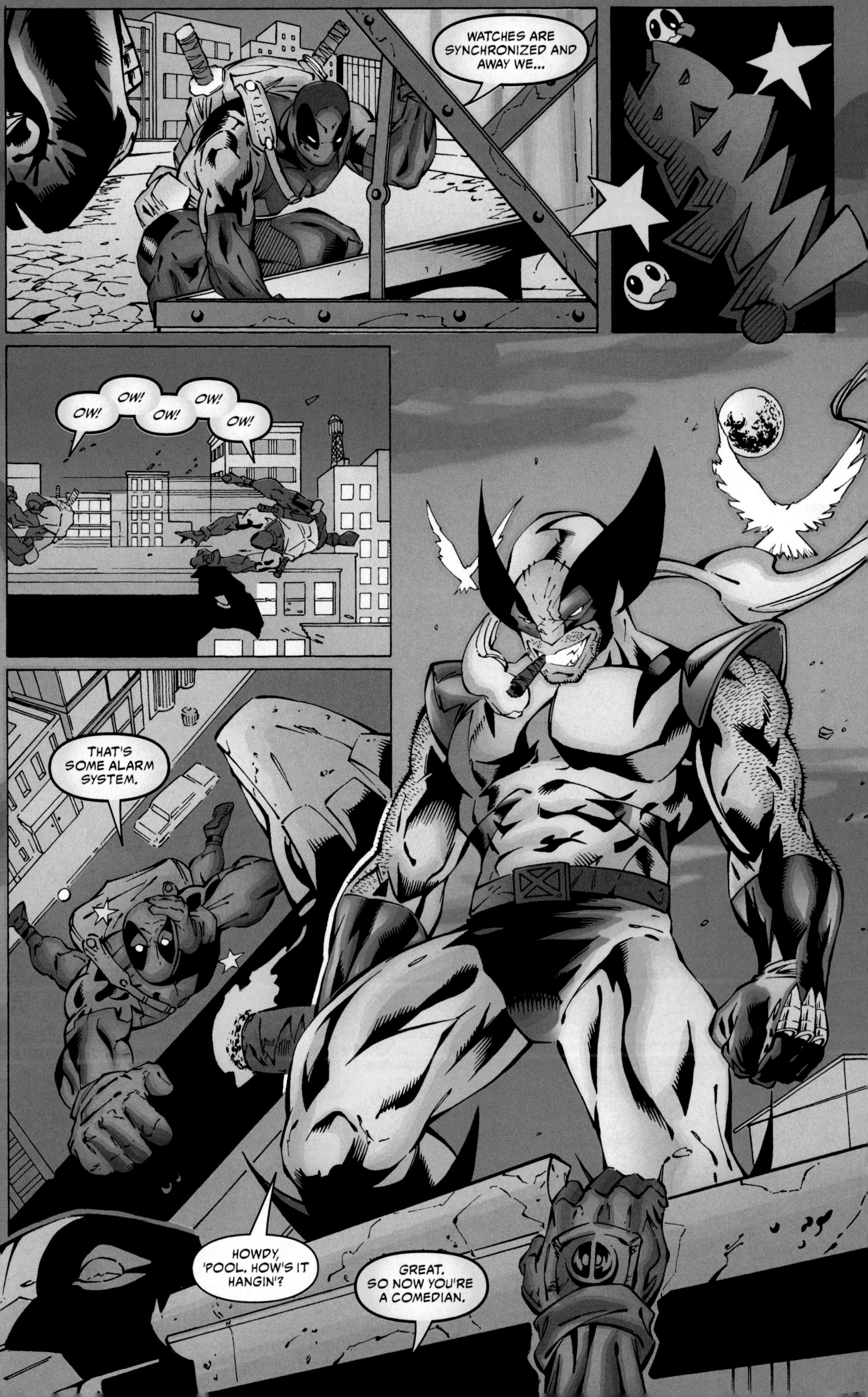
WATCHES ARE SYNCHRONIZED AND AWAY WE...
BAM!
OW!
OW!
OW!
OW!
OW!
THAT'S SOME ALARM SYSTEM.
HOWDY, 'POOL. HOW'S IT HANGIN'?
GREAT. SO NOW YOU'RE A COMEDIAN.

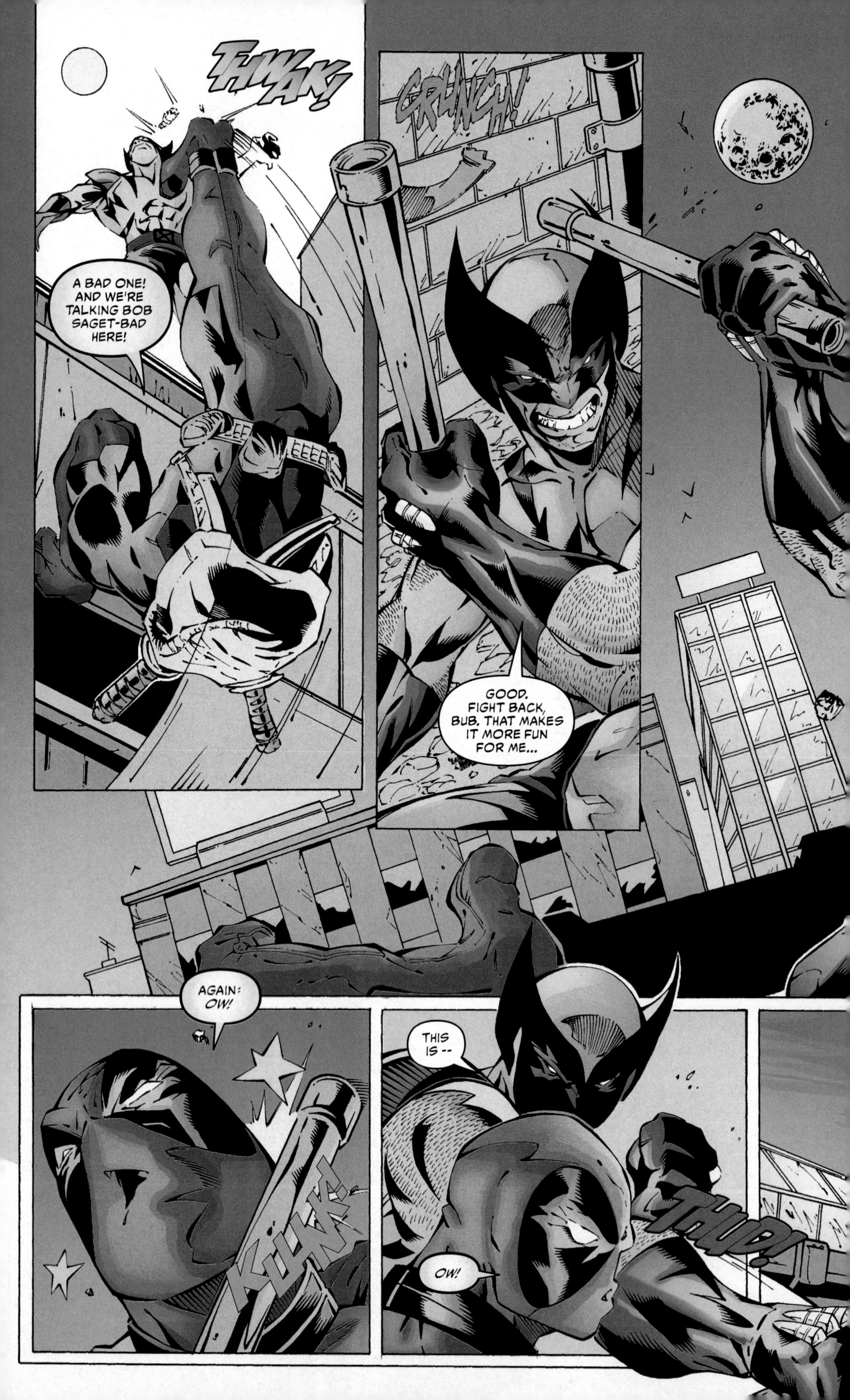
THWAK!
A BAD ONE! AND WE'RE TALKING BOB SAGET-BAD HERE!
CRUNCH!
GOOD. FIGHT BACK, BUB. THAT MAKES IT MORE FUN FOR ME...
AGAIN: OW!
KLUNK!
THIS IS --
THUD!
OW!

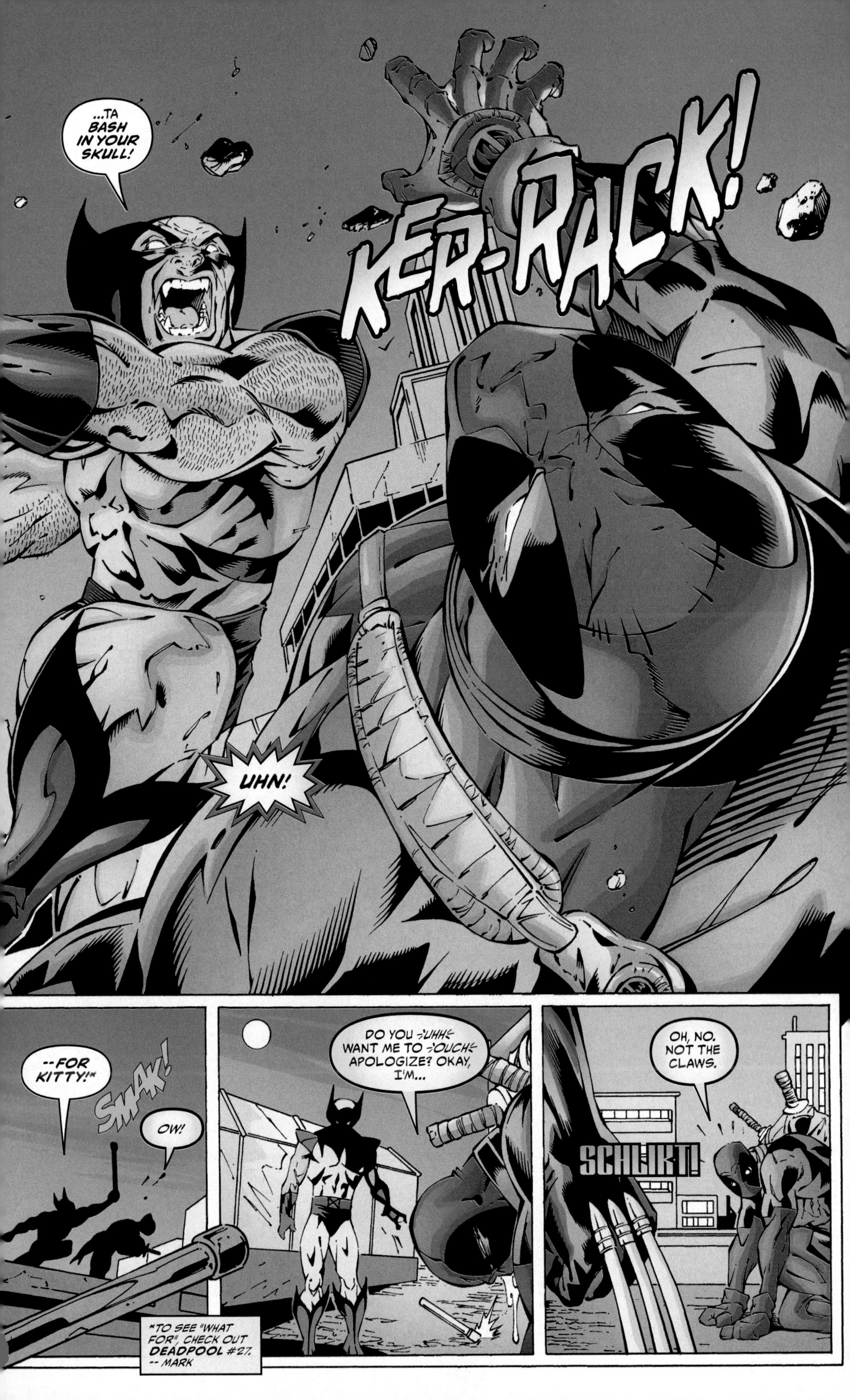
...TA BASH IN YOUR SKULL!
KER-RACK!
UHN!
--FOR KITTY!*
SMAK!
OW!
*TO SEE "WHAT FOR", CHECK OUT DEADPOOL #27. -- MARK
DO YOU -UHH- WANT ME TO -OUCH- APOLOGIZE? OKAY, I'M...
OH, NO. NOT THE CLAWS.
SCHLIKT!

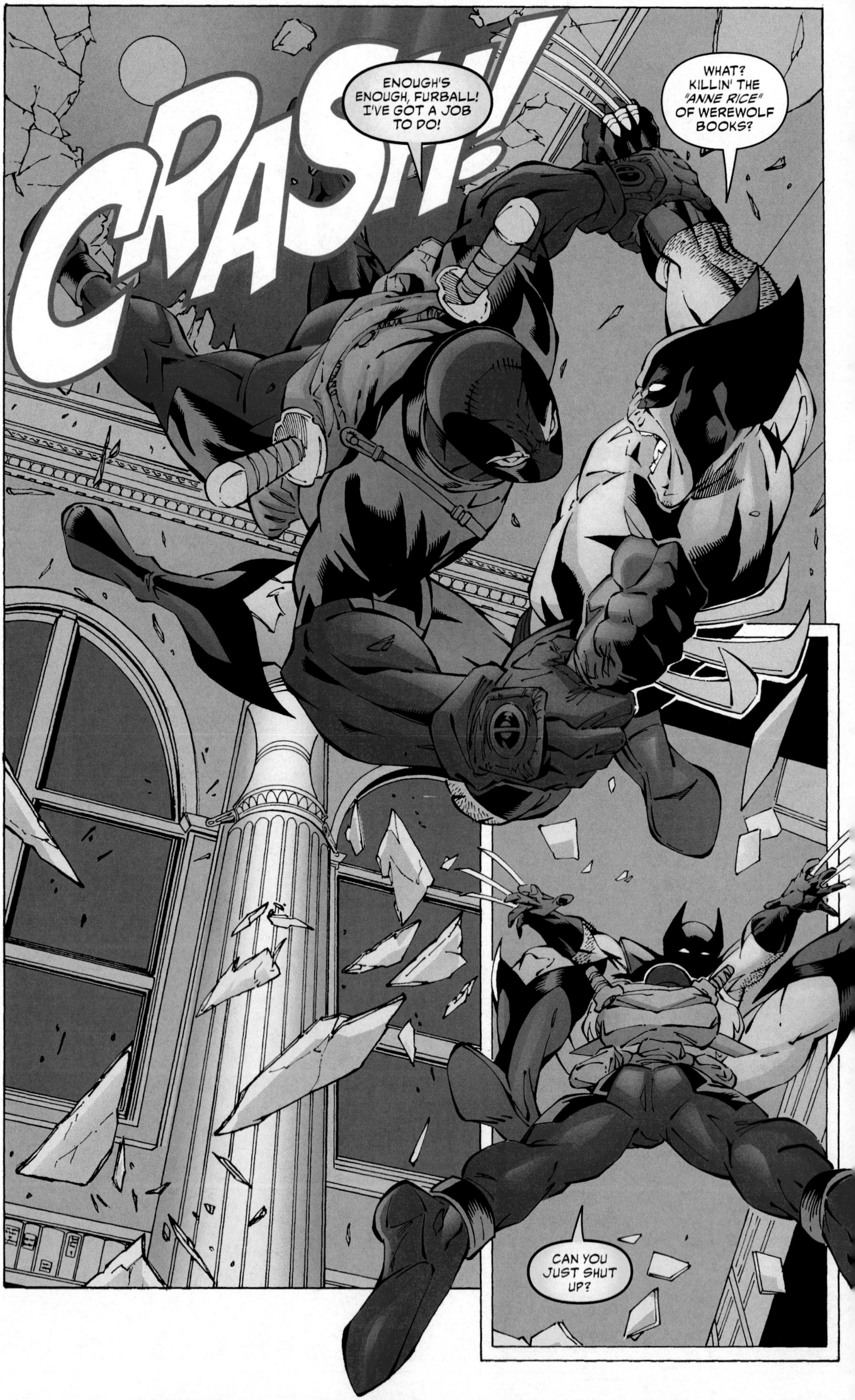
CRASH!
ENOUGH'S ENOUGH, FURBALL! I'VE GOT A JOB TO DO!
WHAT? KILLIN' THE "ANNE RICE" OF WEREWOLF BOOKS?
CAN YOU JUST SHUT UP?

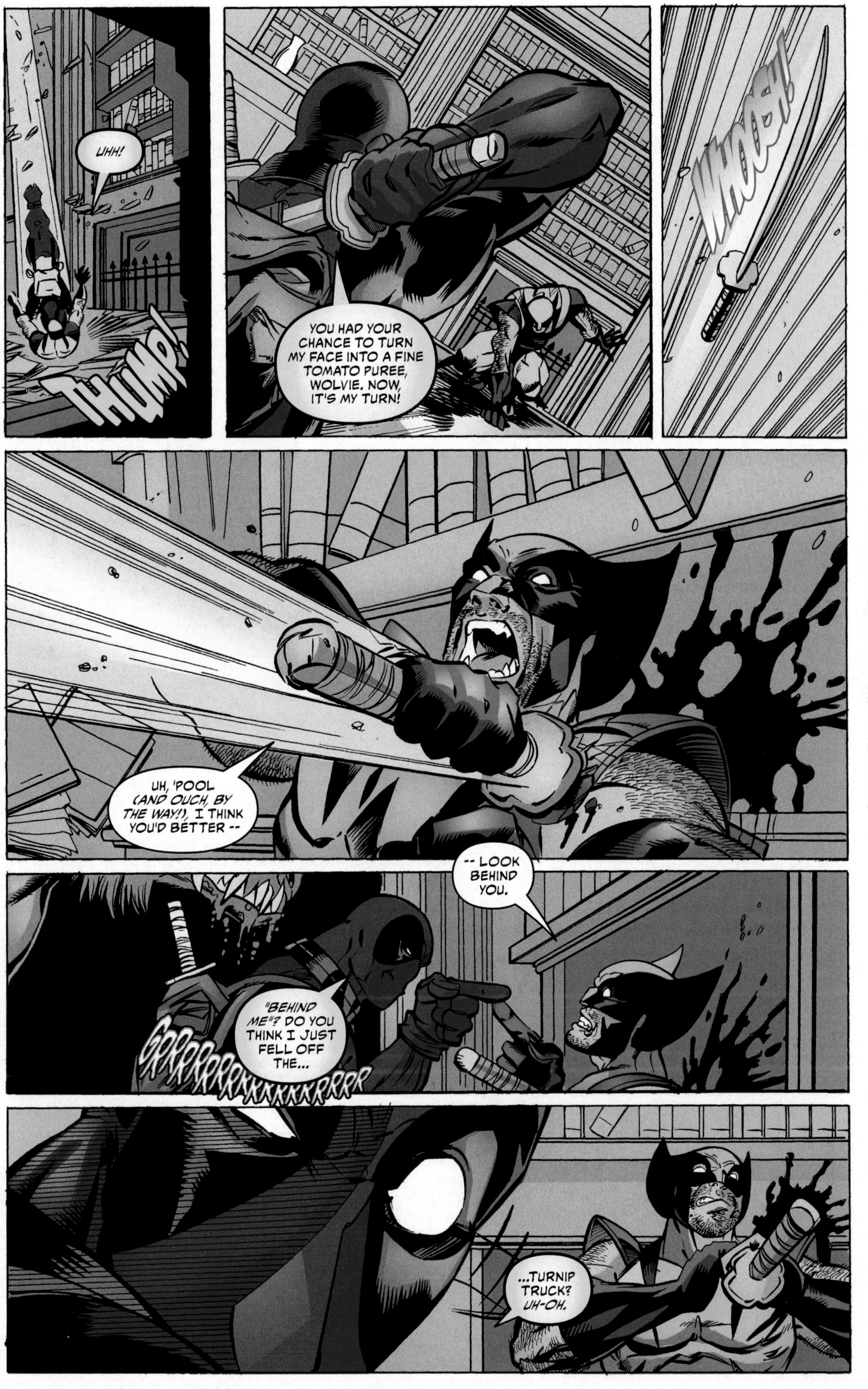
UHH!
THUMP!
YOU HAD YOUR CHANCE TO TURN MY FACE INTO A FINE TOMATO PUREE, WOLVIE. NOW, IT'S MY TURN!
WHOOSH!
UH, 'POOL (AND OUCH, BY THE WAY!), I THINK YOU'D BETTER --
-- LOOK BEHIND YOU.
"BEHIND ME"? DO YOU THINK I JUST FELL OFF THE...
GRRRRRRRRRRRRRRRRRRR
...TURNIP TRUCK? UH-OH.

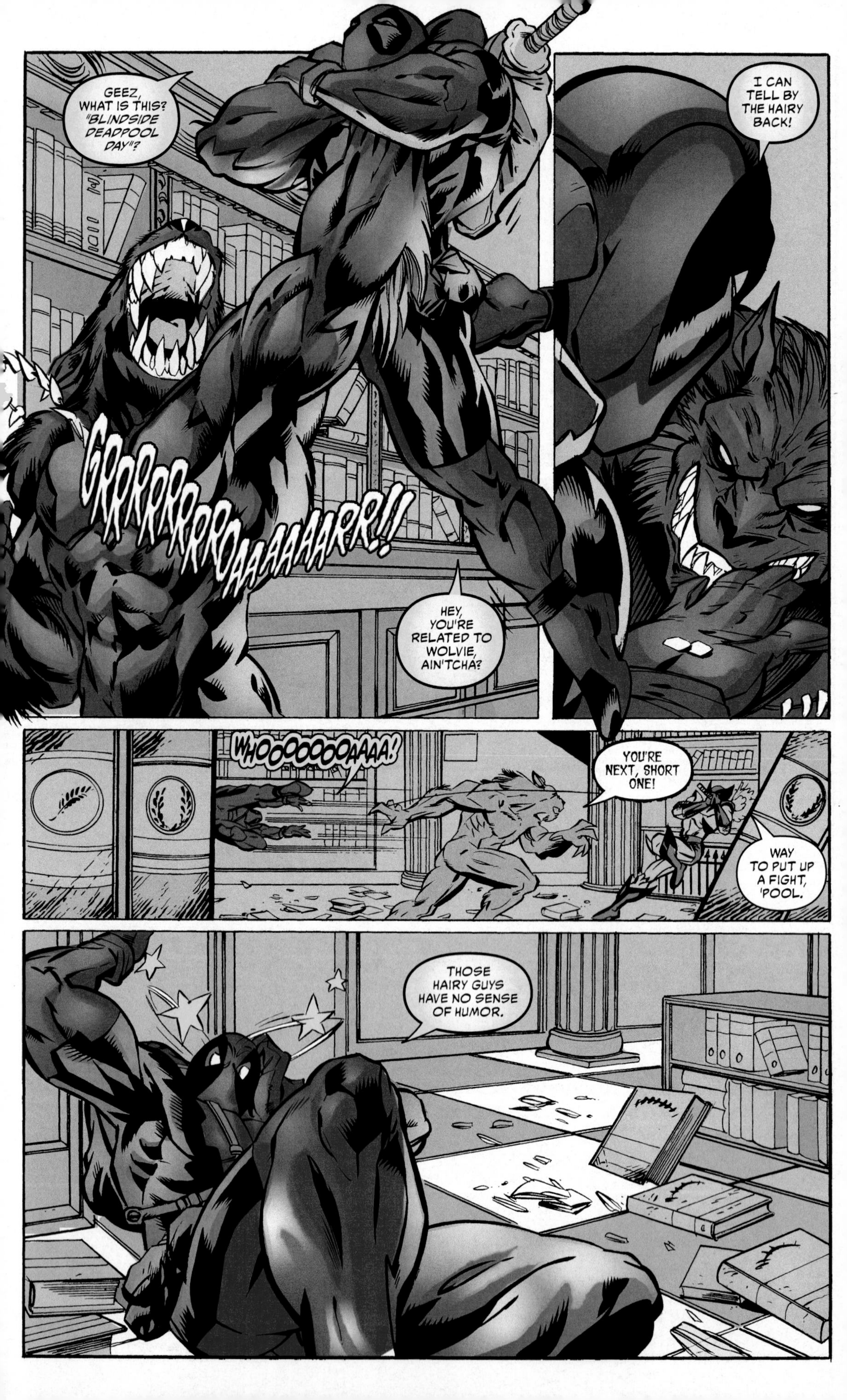
GEEZ, WHAT IS THIS? "BLINDSIDE DEADPOOL DAY"?
GRRRRRRRROAAAAAARR!!
HEY, YOU'RE RELATED TO WOLVIE, AIN'TCHA?
I CAN TELL BY THE HAIRY BACK!
WHOOOOOOOAAAA!
YOU'RE NEXT, SHORT ONE!
WAY TO PUT UP A FIGHT, 'POOL.
THOSE HAIRY GUYS HAVE NO SENSE OF HUMOR.

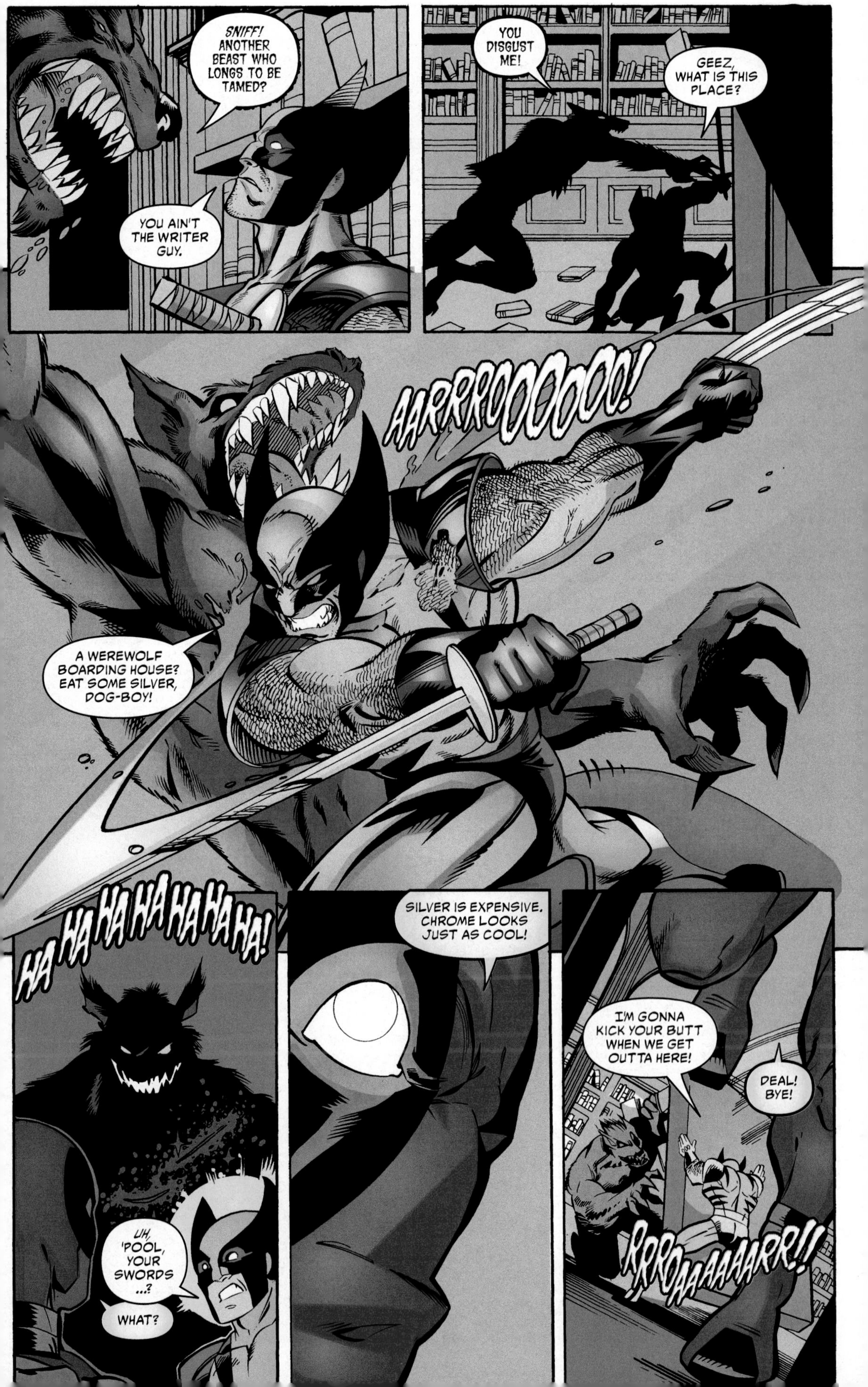
SNIFF! ANOTHER BEAST WHO LONGS TO BE TAMED?
YOU AIN'T THE WRITER GUY.
YOU DISGUST ME!
GEEZ, WHAT IS THIS PLACE?
AARRROOOOOO!
A WEREWOLF BOARDING HOUSE? EAT SOME SILVER, DOG-BOY!
HA HA HA HA HA HA HA HA!
UH, 'POOL, YOUR SWORDS ...?
WHAT?
SILVER IS EXPENSIVE. CHROME LOOKS JUST AS COOL!
I'M GONNA KICK YOUR BUTT WHEN WE GET OUTTA HERE!
DEAL! BYE!
RRROAAAAAARR!!

CARE TO TELL ME WHAT EXACTLY IS GOIN' ON HERE?

DON'T LOOK AT ME! I WAS HIRED TO KILL A PRETENTIOUS WRITER, NO WEREWOLVES WERE PART OF THE DEAL!

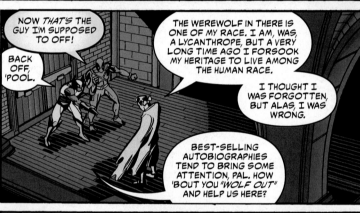

NOW *THAT'S* THE GUY I'M SUPPOSED TO OFF!

BACK OFF, 'POOL.

THE WEREWOLF IN THERE IS ONE OF MY RACE. I AM, WAS, A LYCANTHROPE, BUT A VERY LONG TIME AGO I FORSOOK MY HERITAGE TO LIVE AMONG THE HUMAN RACE.

I THOUGHT I WAS FORGOTTEN, BUT ALAS, I WAS WRONG.

BEST-SELLING AUTOBIOGRAPHIES TEND TO BRING SOME ATTENTION, PAL. HOW 'BOUT YOU *"WOLF OUT"* AND HELP US HERE?

PERHAPS I CAN CLEAR THINGS UP.

I...I CAN'T.

SMASH!

DING-DING! ROUND TWO!

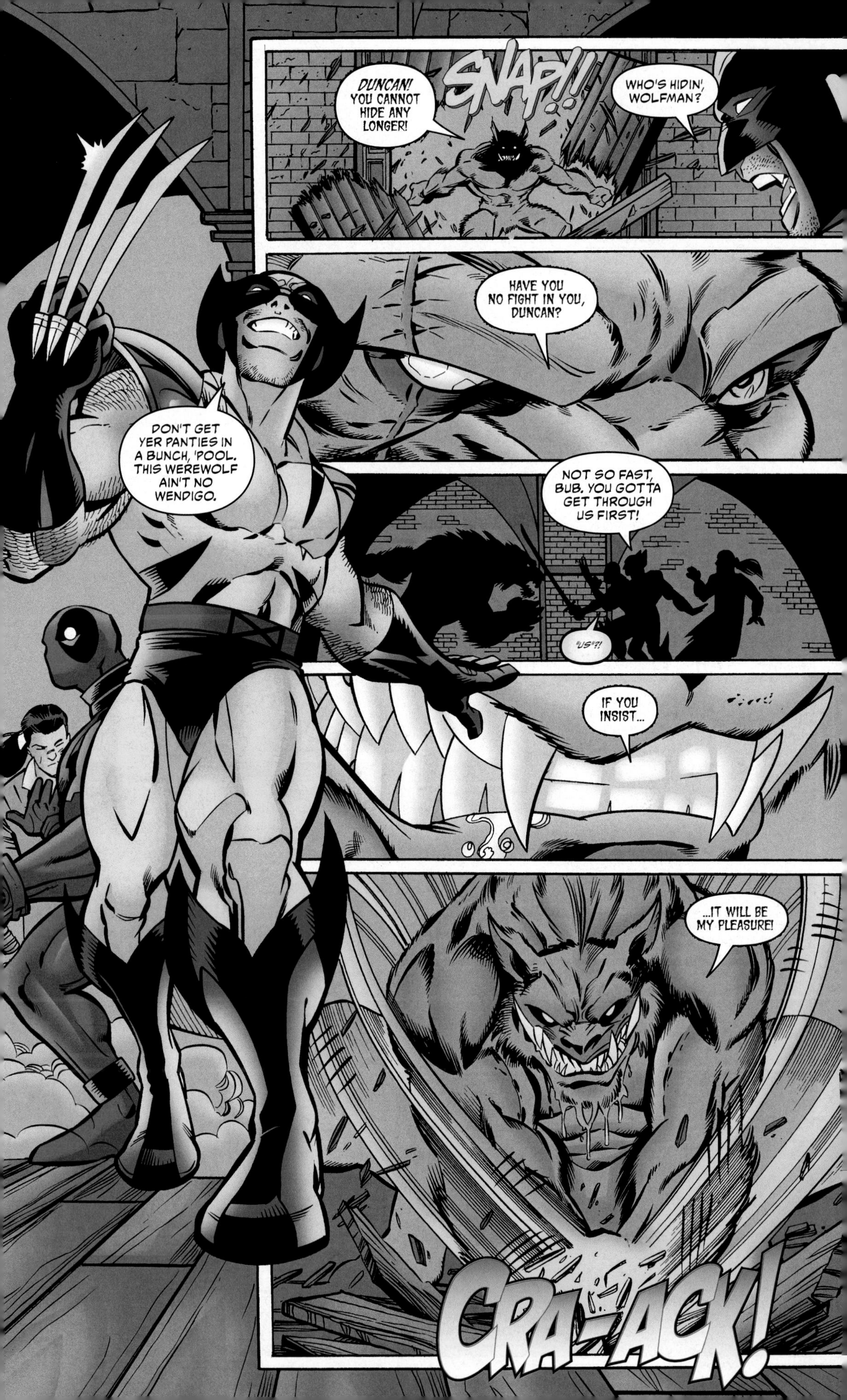
DUNCAN! YOU CANNOT HIDE ANY LONGER!
SNAP!!
WHO'S HIDIN', WOLFMAN?
HAVE YOU NO FIGHT IN YOU, DUNCAN?
DON'T GET YER PANTIES IN A BUNCH, 'POOL. THIS WEREWOLF AIN'T NO WENDIGO.
NOT SO FAST, BUB. YOU GOTTA GET THROUGH US FIRST!
"US"?!
IF YOU INSIST...
...IT WILL BE MY PLEASURE!
CRA-ACK!

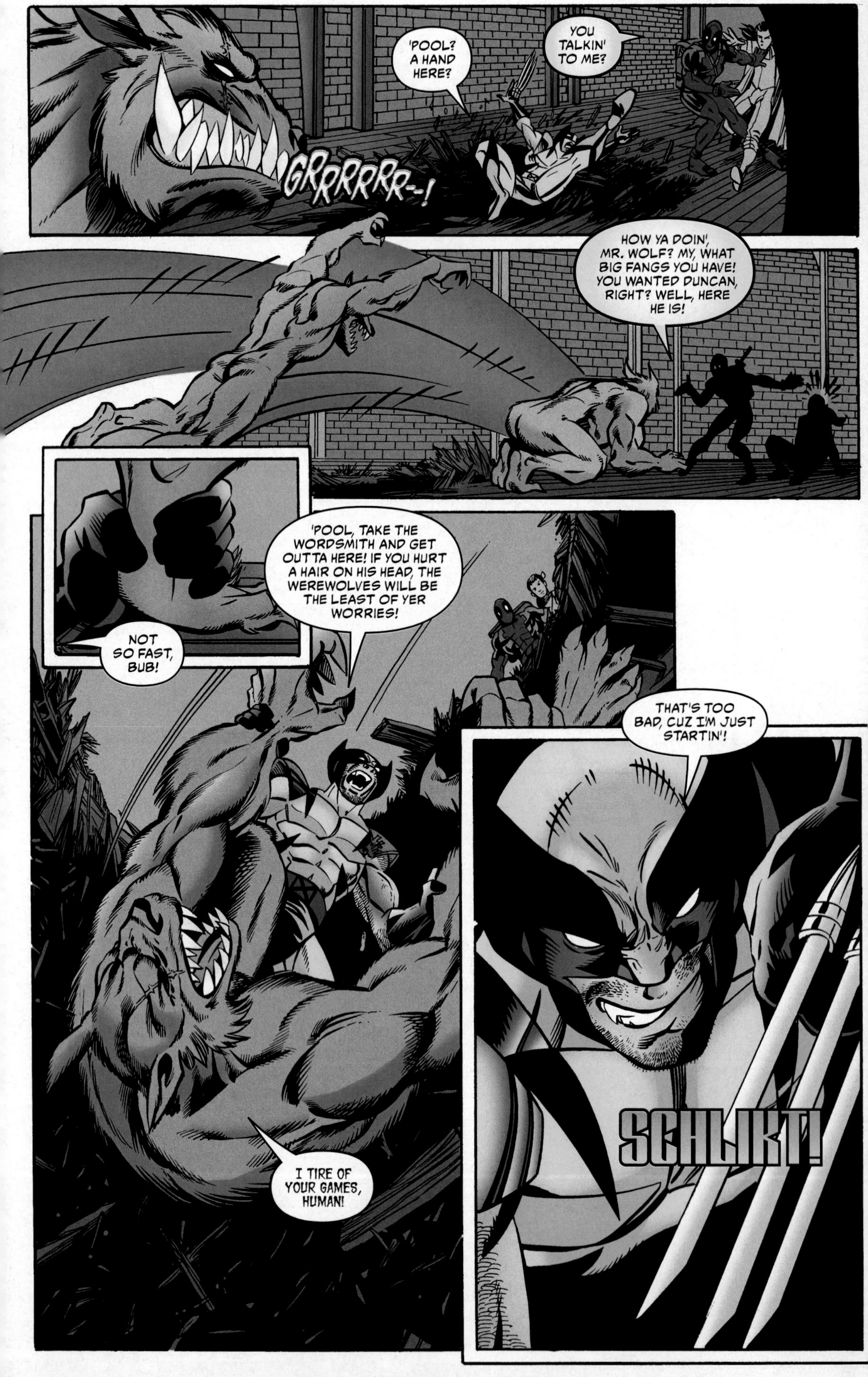

'POOL? A HAND HERE?
YOU TALKIN' TO ME?
GRRRRRR--!
HOW YA DOIN', MR. WOLF? MY, WHAT BIG FANGS YOU HAVE! YOU WANTED DUNCAN, RIGHT? WELL, HERE HE IS!
NOT SO FAST, BUB!
'POOL, TAKE THE WORDSMITH AND GET OUTTA HERE! IF YOU HURT A HAIR ON HIS HEAD, THE WEREWOLVES WILL BE THE LEAST OF YER WORRIES!
I TIRE OF YOUR GAMES, HUMAN!
THAT'S TOO BAD, CUZ I'M JUST STARTIN'!
SCHLIKT!

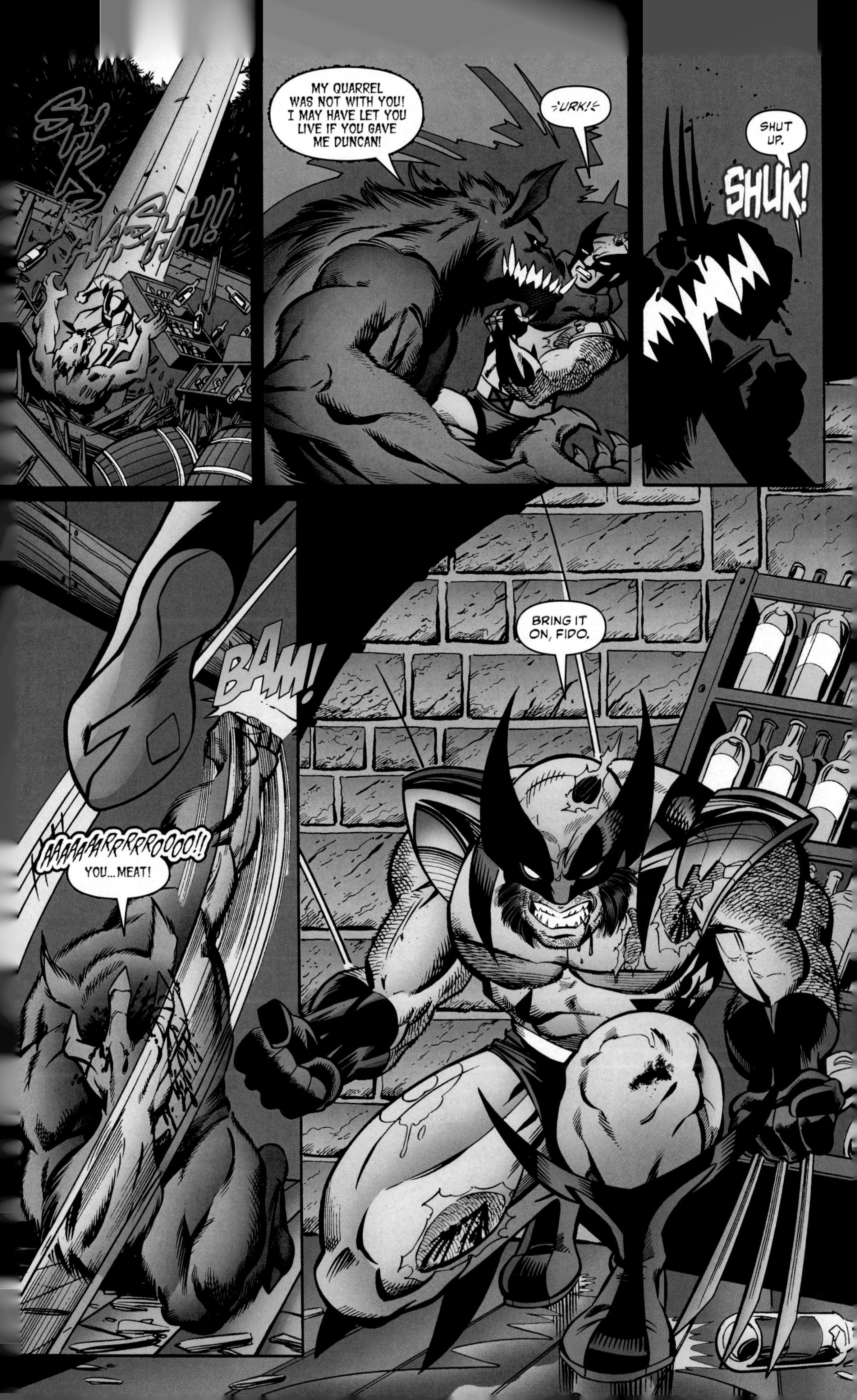
SHK
KRAASHH!
MY QUARREL WAS NOT WITH YOU! I MAY HAVE LET YOU LIVE IF YOU GAVE ME DUNCAN!
URK!
SHUT UP.
SHUK!
BAM!
AAAAAARRRRROOOO!!
YOU...MEAT!
BRING IT ON, FIDO.

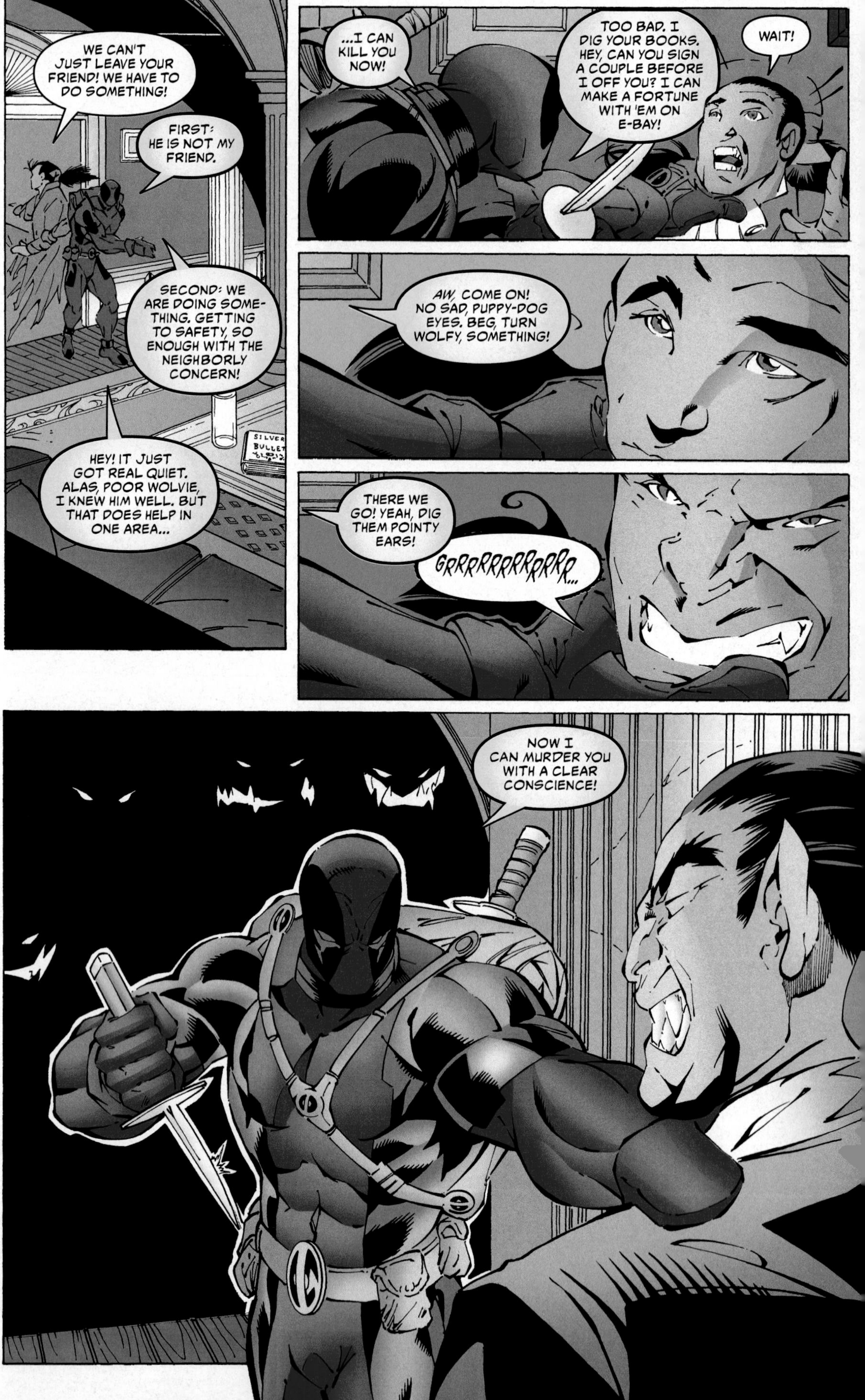
WE CAN'T JUST LEAVE YOUR FRIEND! WE HAVE TO DO SOMETHING!
FIRST: HE IS NOT MY FRIEND.
SECOND: WE ARE DOING SOMETHING. GETTING TO SAFETY, SO ENOUGH WITH THE NEIGHBORLY CONCERN!
HEY! IT JUST GOT REAL QUIET. ALAS, POOR WOLVIE, I KNEW HIM WELL. BUT THAT DOES HELP IN ONE AREA...
SILVER BULLET
...I CAN KILL YOU NOW!
TOO BAD. I DIG YOUR BOOKS. HEY, CAN YOU SIGN A COUPLE BEFORE I OFF YOU? I CAN MAKE A FORTUNE WITH 'EM ON E-BAY!
WAIT!
AW, COME ON! NO SAD, PUPPY-DOG EYES. BEG, TURN WOLFY, SOMETHING!
THERE WE GO! YEAH, DIG THEM POINTY EARS!
GRRRRRRRRRRR...
NOW I CAN MURDER YOU WITH A CLEAR CONSCIENCE!

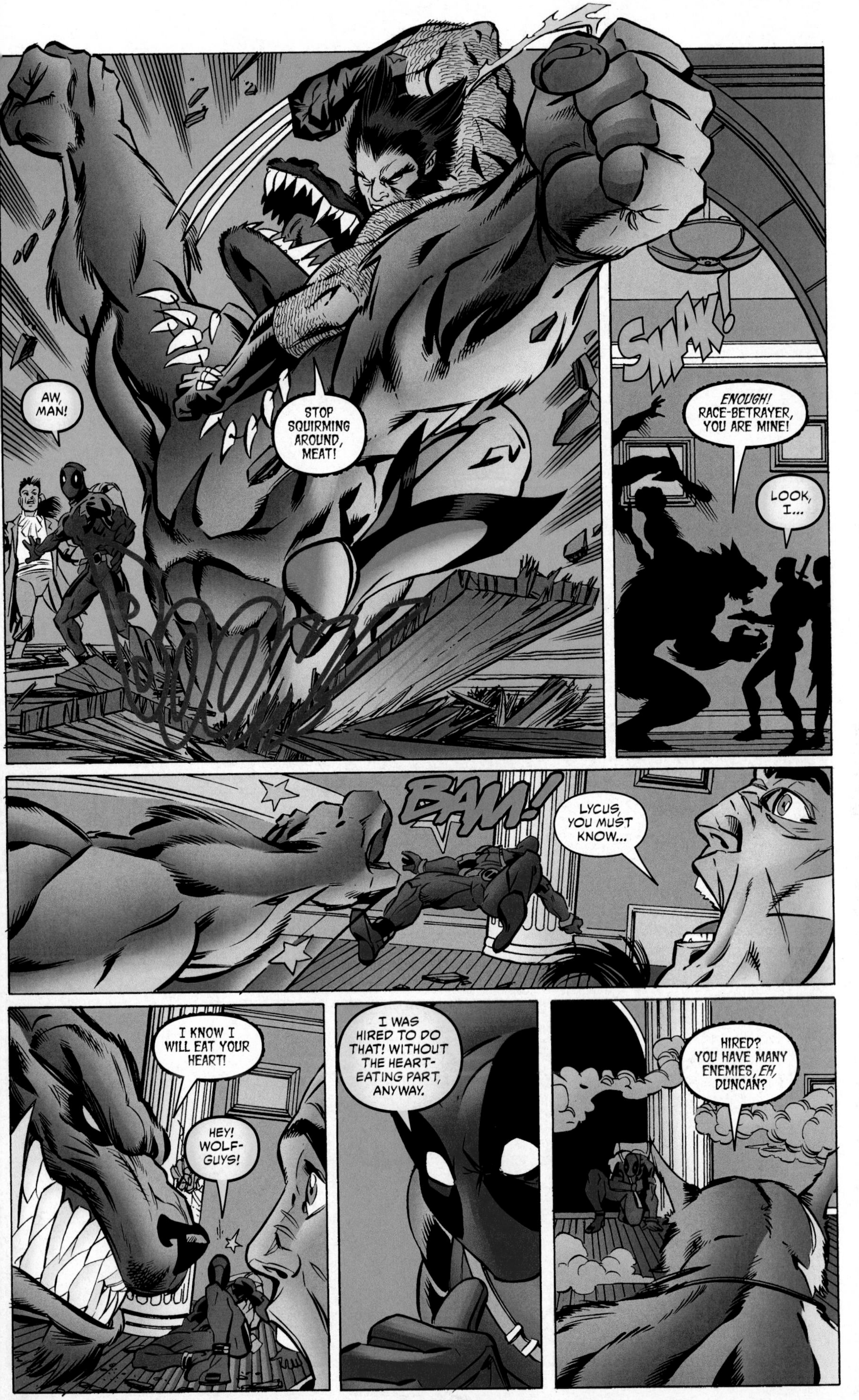

AW, MAN!
STOP SQUIRMING AROUND, MEAT!
SMAK!
ENOUGH! RACE-BETRAYER, YOU ARE MINE!
LOOK, I...
BAM!
LYCUS, YOU MUST KNOW...
I KNOW I WILL EAT YOUR HEART!
HEY! WOLF-GUYS!
I WAS HIRED TO DO THAT! WITHOUT THE HEART-EATING PART, ANYWAY.
HIRED? YOU HAVE MANY ENEMIES, EH, DUNCAN?

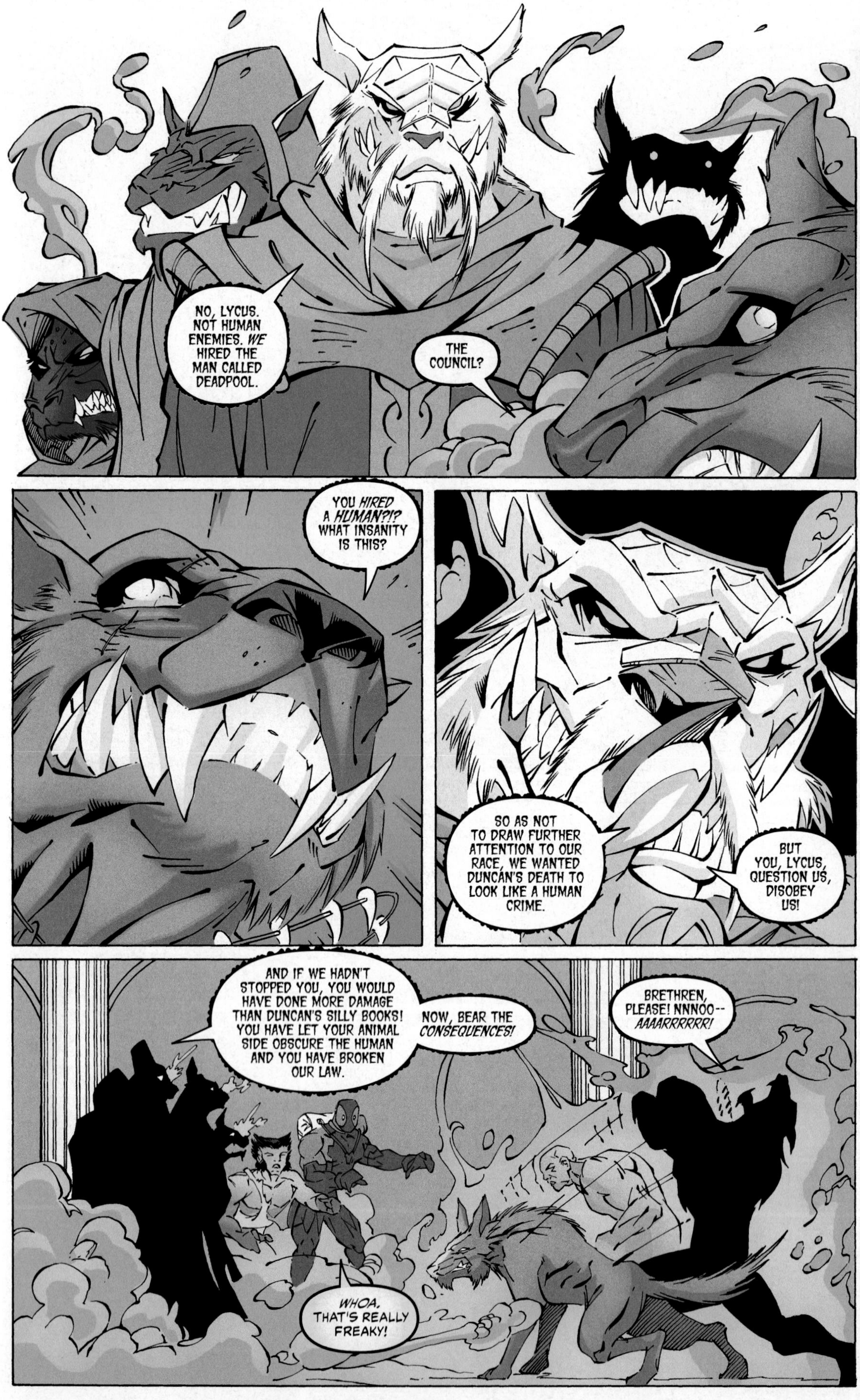
NO, LYCUS. NOT HUMAN ENEMIES. *WE* HIRED THE MAN CALLED DEADPOOL.
THE COUNCIL?
YOU *HIRED* A *HUMAN?!?* WHAT INSANITY IS THIS?
SO AS NOT TO DRAW FURTHER ATTENTION TO OUR RACE, WE WANTED DUNCAN'S DEATH TO LOOK LIKE A HUMAN CRIME.
BUT YOU, LYCUS, QUESTION US, DISOBEY US!
AND IF WE HADN'T STOPPED YOU, YOU WOULD HAVE DONE MORE DAMAGE THAN DUNCAN'S SILLY BOOKS! YOU HAVE LET YOUR ANIMAL SIDE OBSCURE THE HUMAN AND YOU HAVE BROKEN OUR LAW.
NOW, BEAR THE *CONSEQUENCES!*
BRETHREN, PLEASE! NNNOO-- *AAAARRRRRR!*
WHOA. THAT'S REALLY FREAKY!

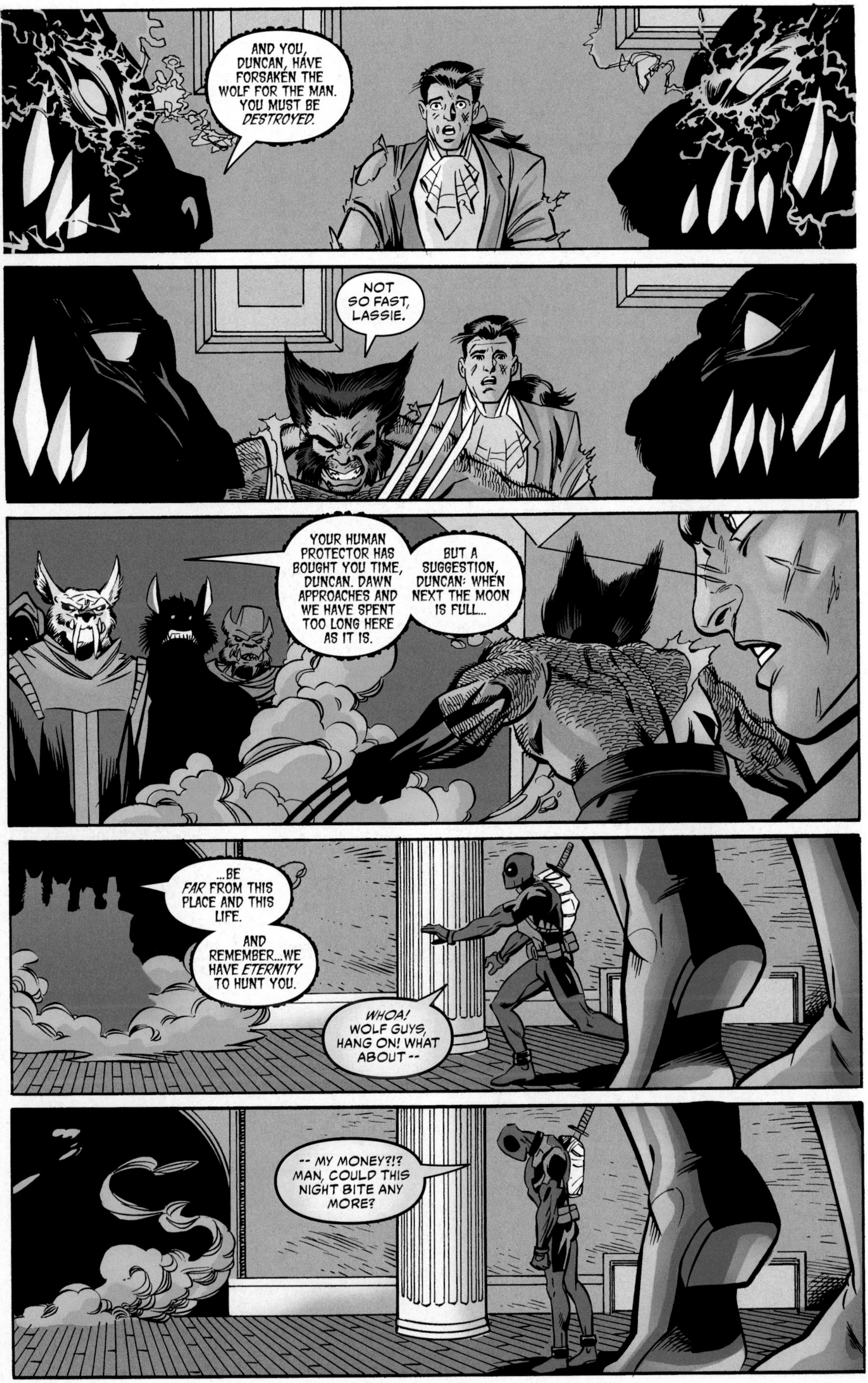
AND YOU, DUNCAN, HAVE FORSAKEN THE WOLF FOR THE MAN. YOU MUST BE *DESTROYED.*
NOT SO FAST, LASSIE.
YOUR HUMAN PROTECTOR HAS BOUGHT YOU TIME, DUNCAN. DAWN APPROACHES AND WE HAVE SPENT TOO LONG HERE AS IT IS.
BUT A SUGGESTION, DUNCAN: WHEN NEXT THE MOON IS FULL...
...BE *FAR* FROM THIS PLACE AND THIS LIFE.
AND REMEMBER...WE HAVE *ETERNITY* TO HUNT YOU.
WHOA! WOLF GUYS, HANG ON! WHAT ABOUT --
-- MY MONEY?!? MAN, COULD THIS NIGHT BITE ANY MORE?

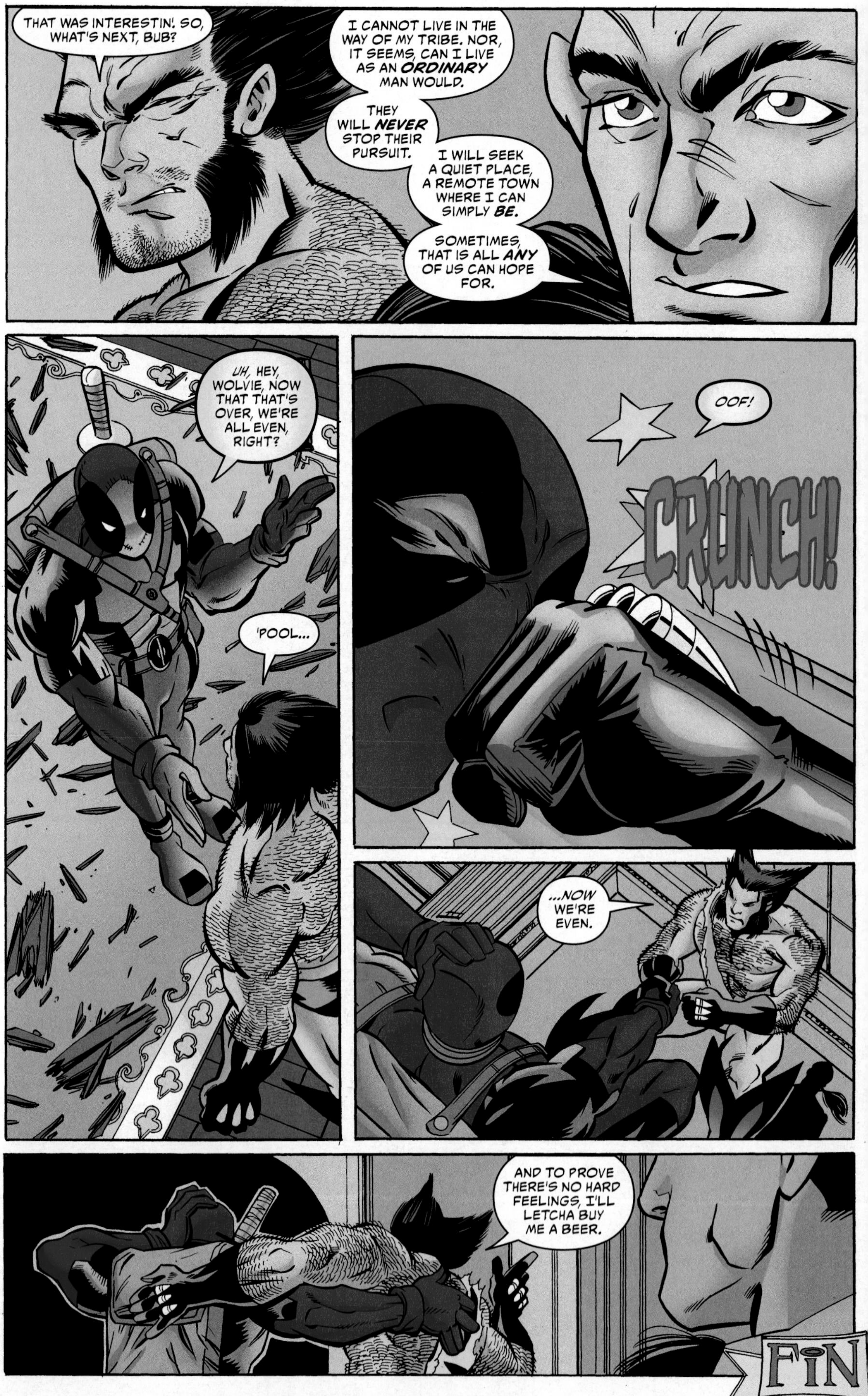
THAT WAS INTERESTIN'. SO, WHAT'S NEXT, BUB?
I CANNOT LIVE IN THE WAY OF MY TRIBE. NOR, IT SEEMS, CAN I LIVE AS AN ORDINARY MAN WOULD.
THEY WILL NEVER STOP THEIR PURSUIT.
I WILL SEEK A QUIET PLACE, A REMOTE TOWN WHERE I CAN SIMPLY BE.
SOMETIMES, THAT IS ALL ANY OF US CAN HOPE FOR.
UH, HEY, WOLVIE, NOW THAT THAT'S OVER, WE'RE ALL EVEN, RIGHT?
'POOL...
OOF!
CRUNCH!
...NOW WE'RE EVEN.
AND TO PROVE THERE'S NO HARD FEELINGS, I'LL LETCHA BUY ME A BEER.
FIN

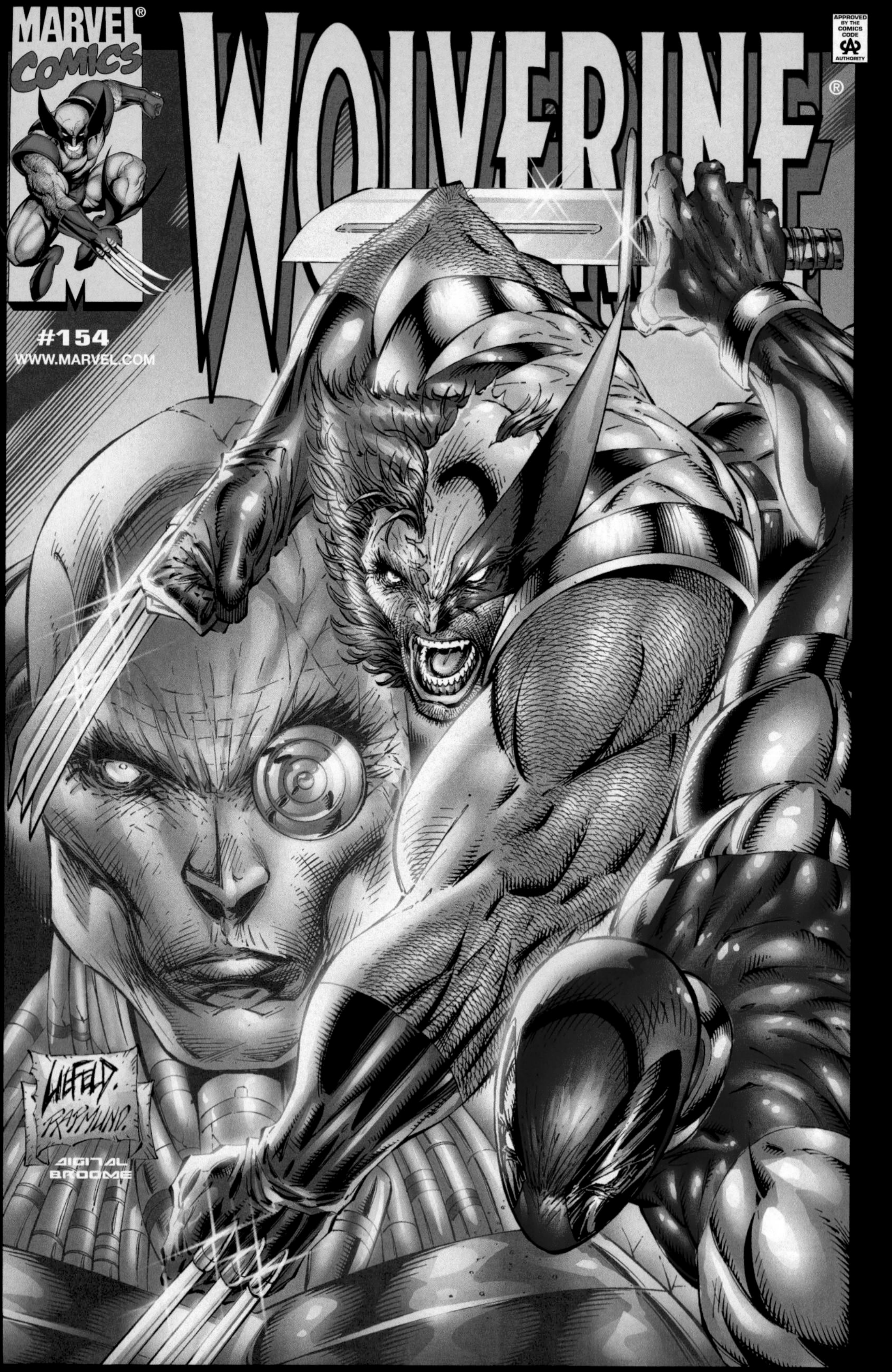
MARVEL COMICS
WOLVERINE
APPROVED BY THE COMICS CODE AUTHORITY
#154
WWW.MARVEL.COM
LIEFELD
RAPMUND
DIGITAL BROOME

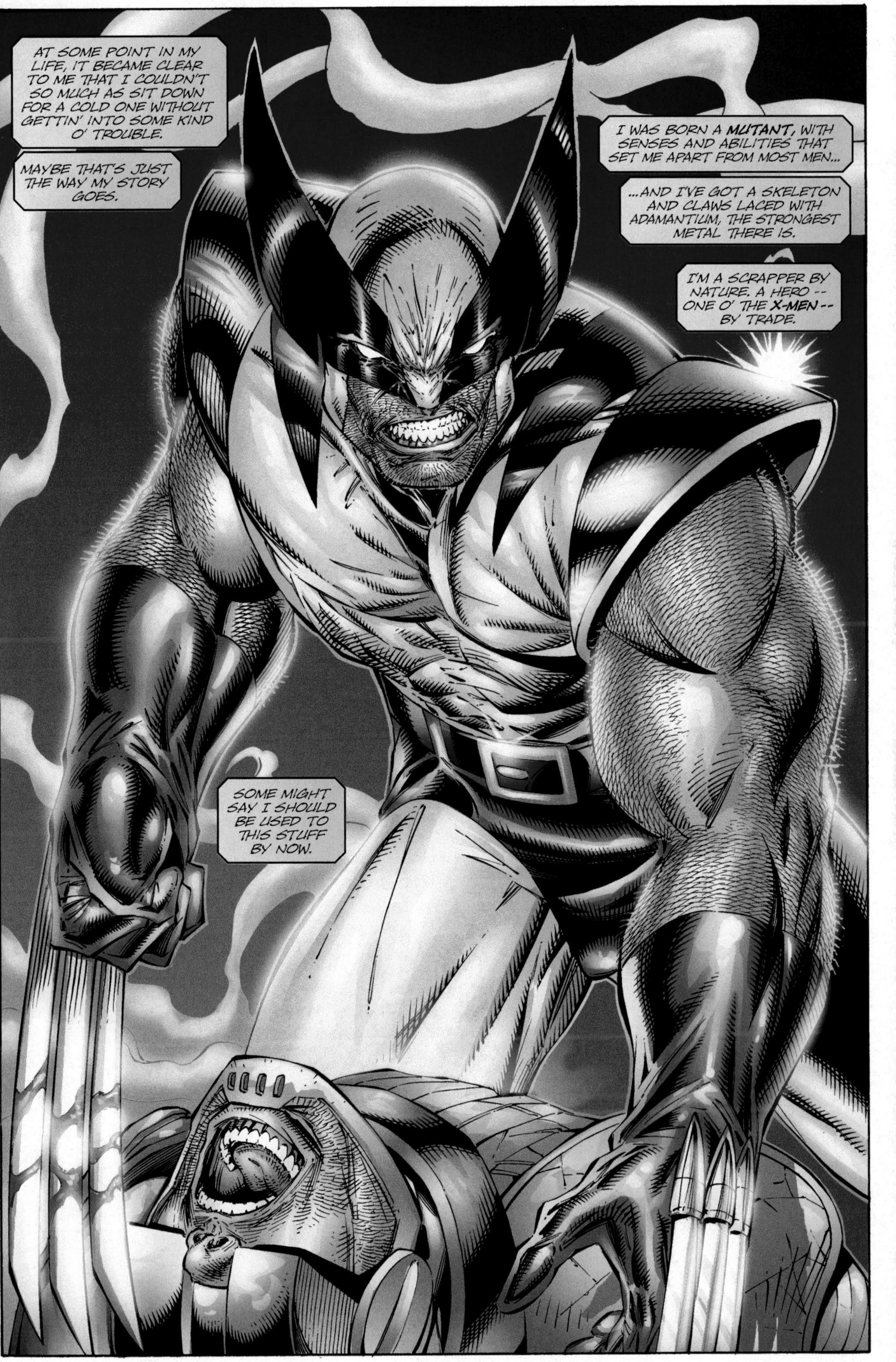
AT SOME POINT IN MY LIFE, IT BECAME CLEAR TO ME THAT I COULDN'T SO MUCH AS SIT DOWN FOR A COLD ONE WITHOUT GETTIN' INTO SOME KIND O' TROUBLE.
MAYBE THAT'S JUST THE WAY MY STORY GOES.
I WAS BORN A MUTANT, WITH SENSES AND ABILITIES THAT SET ME APART FROM MOST MEN...
...AND I'VE GOT A SKELETON AND CLAWS LACED WITH ADAMANTIUM, THE STRONGEST METAL THERE IS.
I'M A SCRAPPER BY NATURE. A HERO -- ONE O' THE X-MEN -- BY TRADE.
SOME MIGHT SAY I SHOULD BE USED TO THIS STUFF BY NOW.

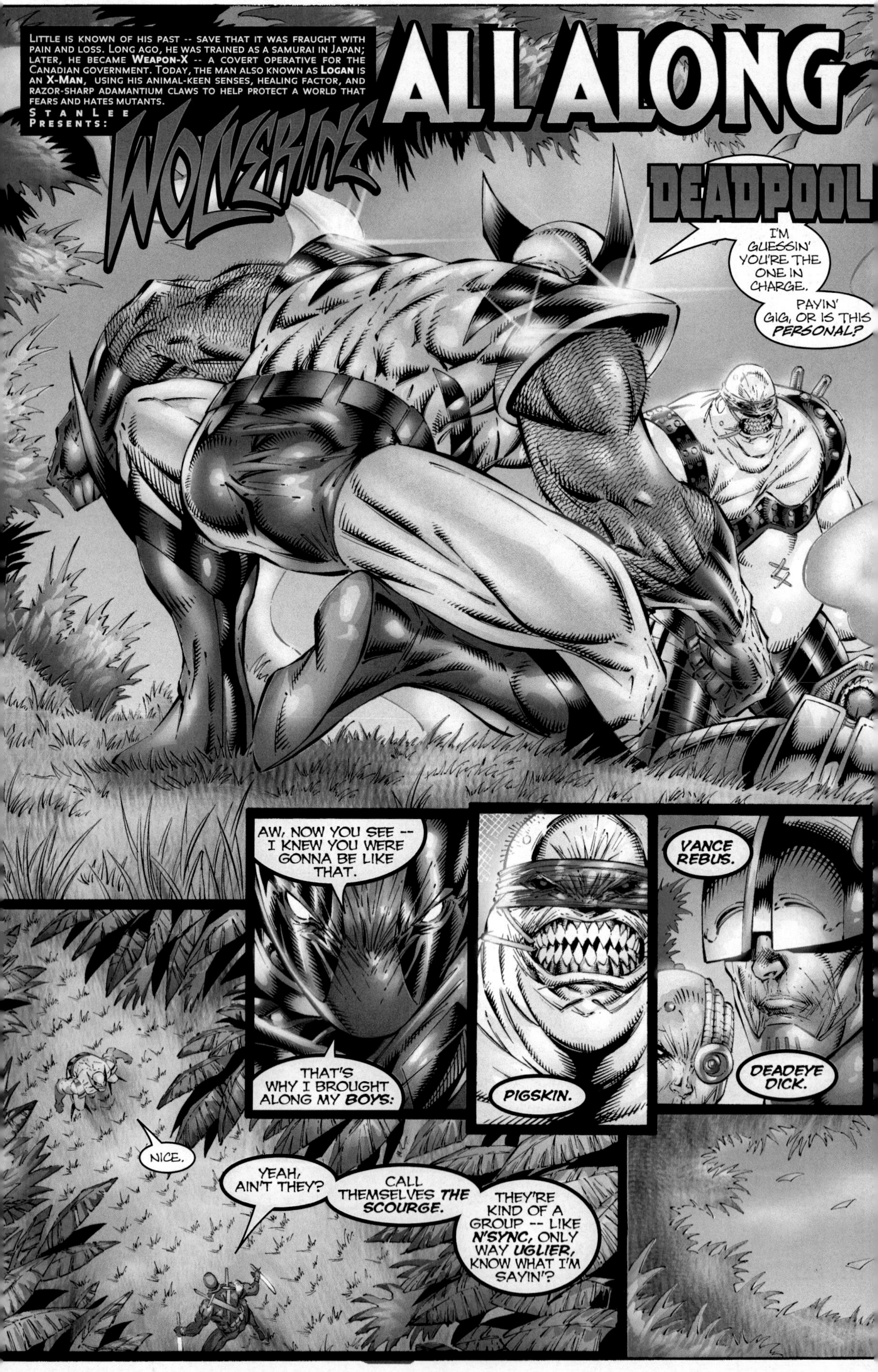
Little is known of his past -- save that it was fraught with pain and loss. Long ago, he was trained as a samurai in Japan; later, he became Weapon-X -- a covert operative for the Canadian government. Today, the man also known as Logan is an X-Man, using his animal-keen senses, healing factor, and razor-sharp adamantium claws to help protect a world that fears and hates mutants.
Stan Lee Presents:
Wolverine
All Along
Deadpool
I'M GUESSIN' YOU'RE THE ONE IN CHARGE.
PAYIN' GIG, OR IS THIS PERSONAL?
AW, NOW YOU SEE -- I KNEW YOU WERE GONNA BE LIKE THAT.
THAT'S WHY I BROUGHT ALONG MY BOYS:
PIGSKIN.
VANCE REBUS.
DEADEYE DICK.
NICE.
YEAH, AIN'T THEY?
CALL THEMSELVES THE SCOURGE.
THEY'RE KIND OF A GROUP -- LIKE N'SYNC, ONLY WAY UGLIER, KNOW WHAT I'M SAYIN'?

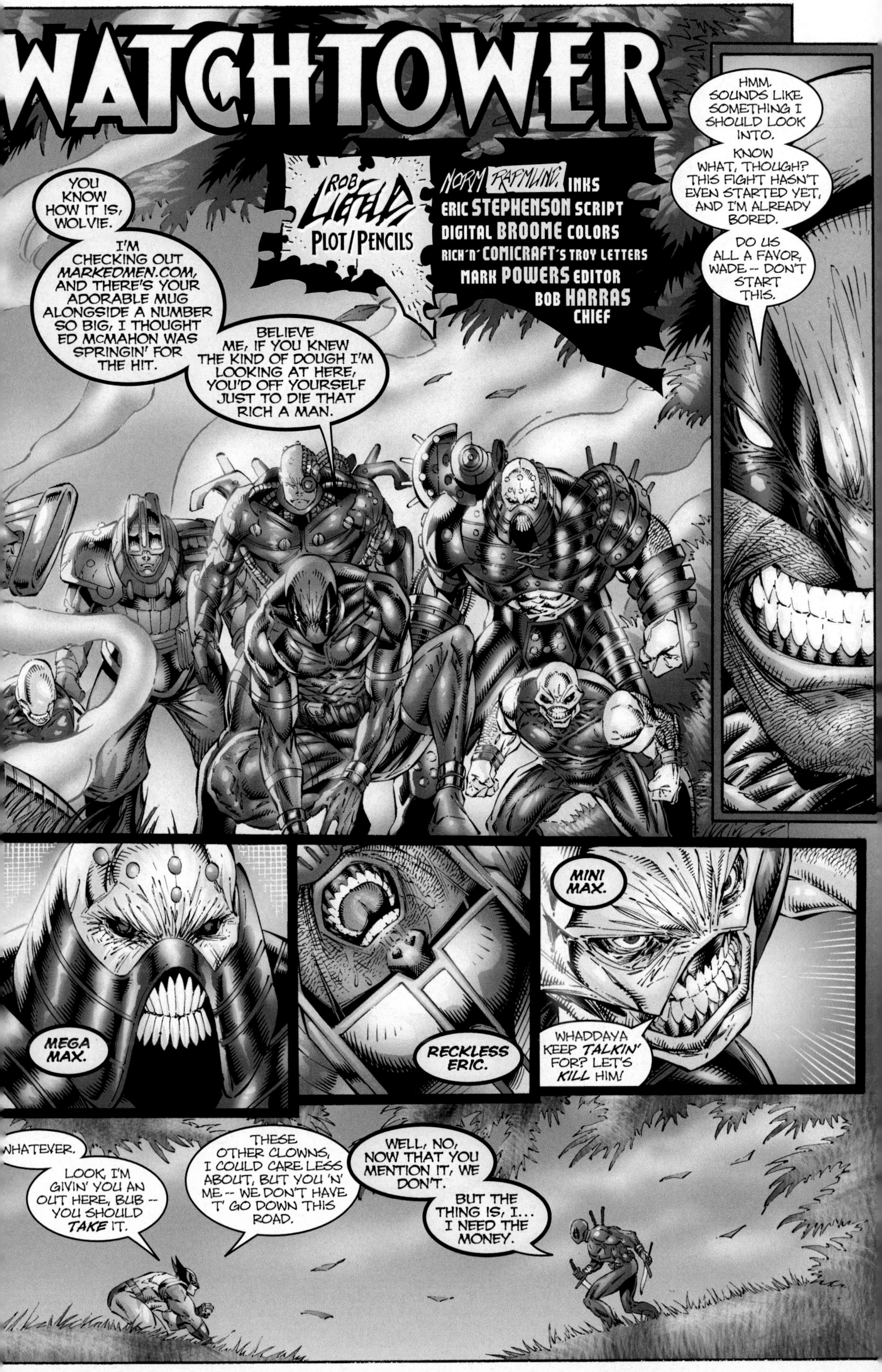
WATCHTOWER
ROB LIEFELD PLOT/PENCILS
NORM RAPMUND INKS
ERIC STEPHENSON SCRIPT
DIGITAL BROOME COLORS
RICH 'N' COMICRAFT'S TROY LETTERS
MARK POWERS EDITOR
BOB HARRAS CHIEF
YOU KNOW HOW IT IS, WOLVIE.
I'M CHECKING OUT MARKEDMEN.COM, AND THERE'S YOUR ADORABLE MUG ALONGSIDE A NUMBER SO BIG, I THOUGHT ED McMAHON WAS SPRINGIN' FOR THE HIT.
BELIEVE ME, IF YOU KNEW THE KIND OF DOUGH I'M LOOKING AT HERE, YOU'D OFF YOURSELF JUST TO DIE THAT RICH A MAN.
HMM. SOUNDS LIKE SOMETHING I SHOULD LOOK INTO.
KNOW WHAT, THOUGH? THIS FIGHT HASN'T EVEN STARTED YET, AND I'M ALREADY BORED.
DO US ALL A FAVOR, WADE -- DON'T START THIS.
MEGA MAX.
RECKLESS ERIC.
MINI MAX.
WHADDAYA KEEP TALKIN' FOR? LET'S KILL HIM!
WHATEVER.
LOOK, I'M GIVIN' YOU AN OUT HERE, BUB -- YOU SHOULD TAKE IT.
THESE OTHER CLOWNS, I COULD CARE LESS ABOUT, BUT YOU 'N' ME -- WE DON'T HAVE T' GO DOWN THIS ROAD.
WELL, NO, NOW THAT YOU MENTION IT, WE DON'T.
BUT THE THING IS, I... I NEED THE MONEY.

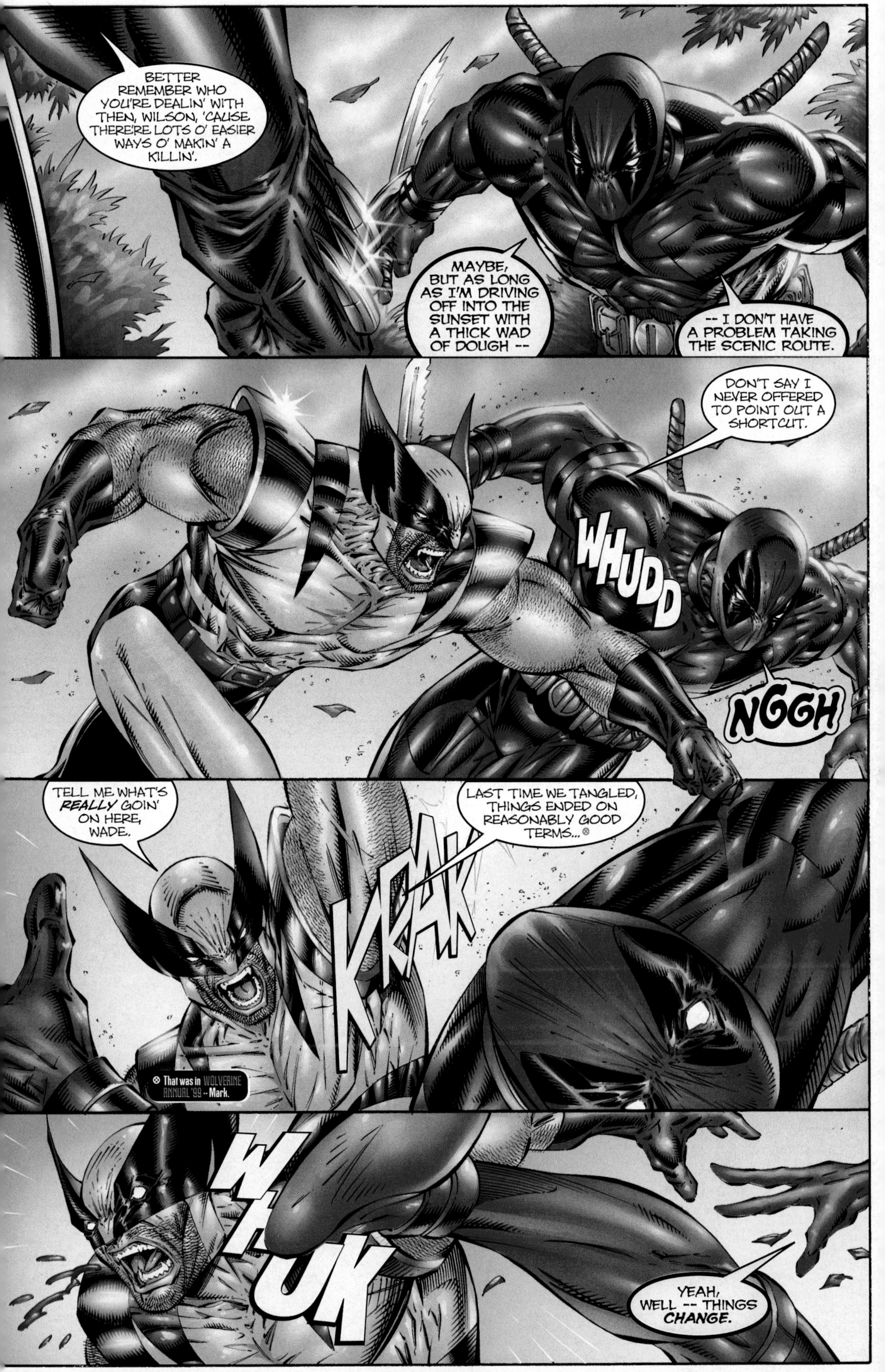
BETTER REMEMBER WHO YOU'RE DEALIN' WITH THEN, WILSON, 'CAUSE THERE'RE LOTS O' EASIER WAYS O' MAKIN' A KILLIN'.
MAYBE, BUT AS LONG AS I'M DRIVING OFF INTO THE SUNSET WITH A THICK WAD OF DOUGH --
-- I DON'T HAVE A PROBLEM TAKING THE SCENIC ROUTE.
DON'T SAY I NEVER OFFERED TO POINT OUT A SHORTCUT.
WHUDD
NGGH
TELL ME WHAT'S *REALLY* GOIN' ON HERE, WADE.
LAST TIME WE TANGLED, THINGS ENDED ON REASONABLY GOOD TERMS...⊗
KRAK
⊗ That was in WOLVERINE ANNUAL '99 -- Mark.
WHUK
YEAH, WELL -- THINGS *CHANGE.*

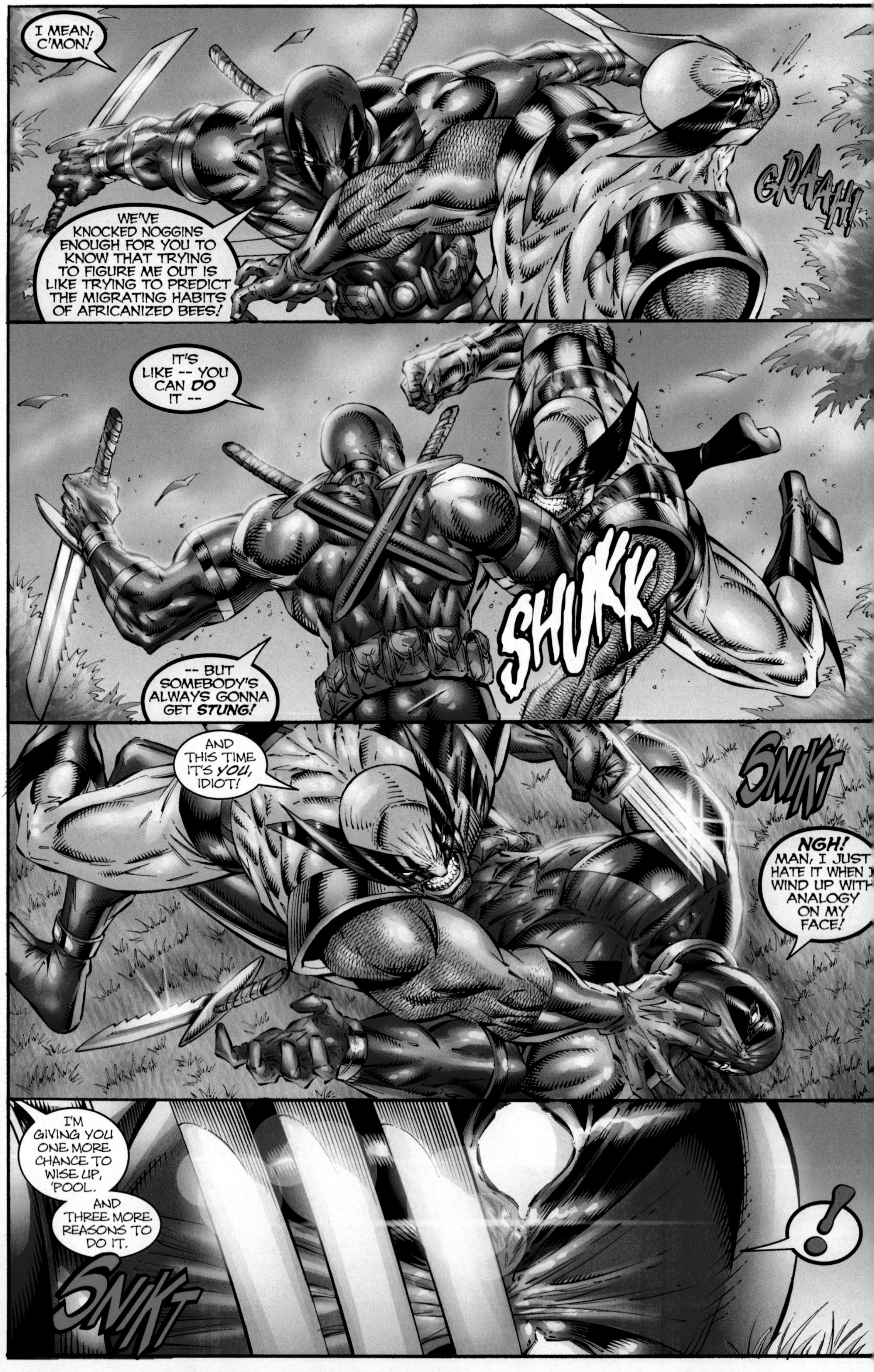
I MEAN, C'MON!
WE'VE KNOCKED NOGGINS ENOUGH FOR YOU TO KNOW THAT TRYING TO FIGURE ME OUT IS LIKE TRYING TO PREDICT THE MIGRATING HABITS OF AFRICANIZED BEES!
GRAAHH
IT'S LIKE -- YOU CAN DO IT --
SHUKK
-- BUT SOMEBODY'S ALWAYS GONNA GET STUNG!
AND THIS TIME IT'S YOU, IDIOT!
SNIKT
NGH! MAN, I JUST HATE IT WHEN I WIND UP WITH ANALOGY ON MY FACE!
I'M GIVING YOU ONE MORE CHANCE TO WISE UP, 'POOL.
AND THREE MORE REASONS TO DO IT.
SNIKT
!

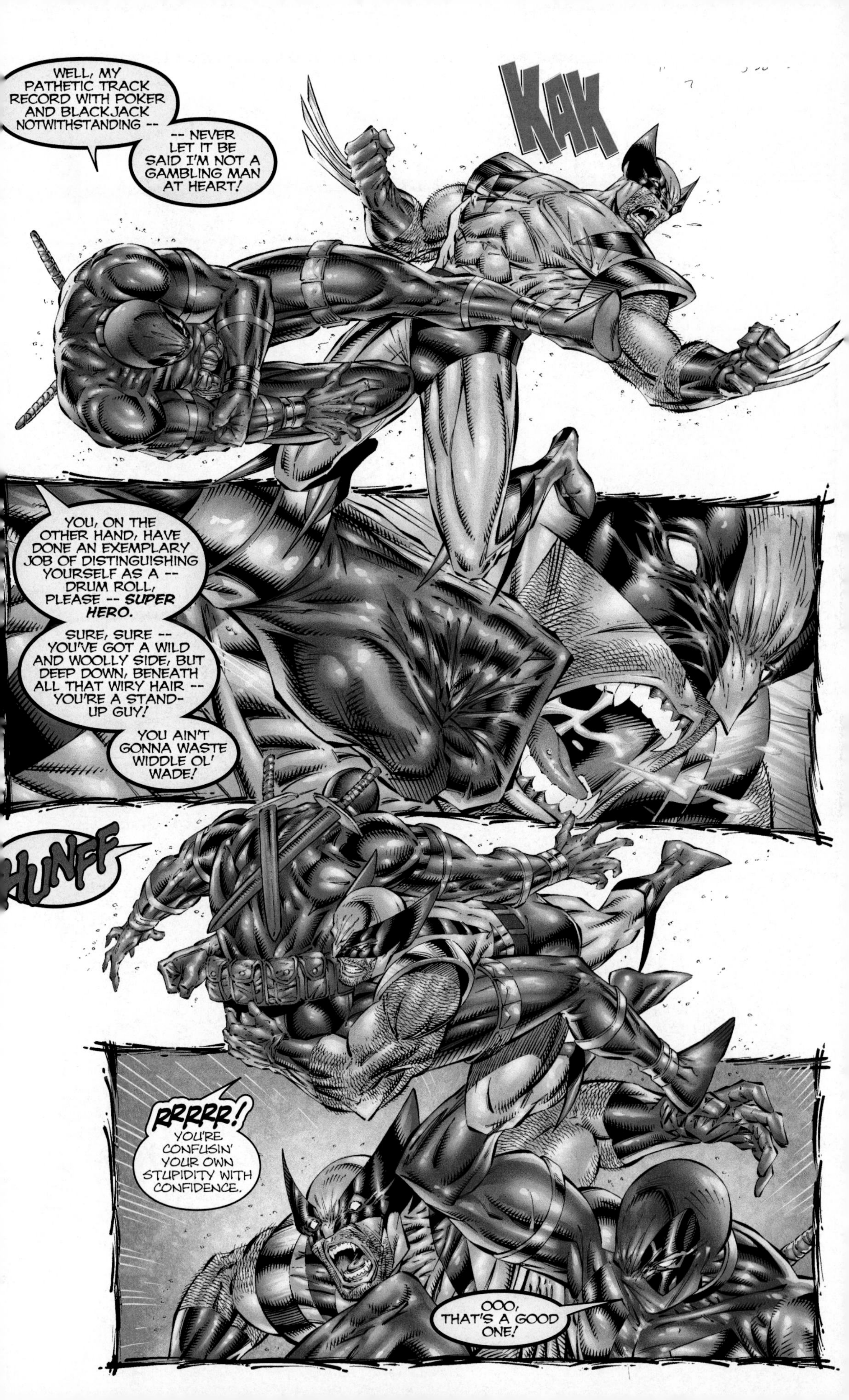

WELL, MY PATHETIC TRACK RECORD WITH POKER AND BLACKJACK NOTWITHSTANDING --
-- NEVER LET IT BE SAID I'M NOT A GAMBLING MAN AT HEART!
KAK
YOU, ON THE OTHER HAND, HAVE DONE AN EXEMPLARY JOB OF DISTINGUISHING YOURSELF AS A -- DRUM ROLL, PLEASE -- **SUPER HERO.**
SURE, SURE -- YOU'VE GOT A WILD AND WOOLLY SIDE, BUT DEEP DOWN, BENEATH ALL THAT WIRY HAIR -- YOU'RE A STAND-UP GUY!
YOU AIN'T GONNA WASTE WIDDLE OL' WADE!
HUNFF
RRRRR! YOU'RE CONFUSIN' YOUR OWN STUPIDITY WITH CONFIDENCE.
OOO, THAT'S A GOOD ONE!

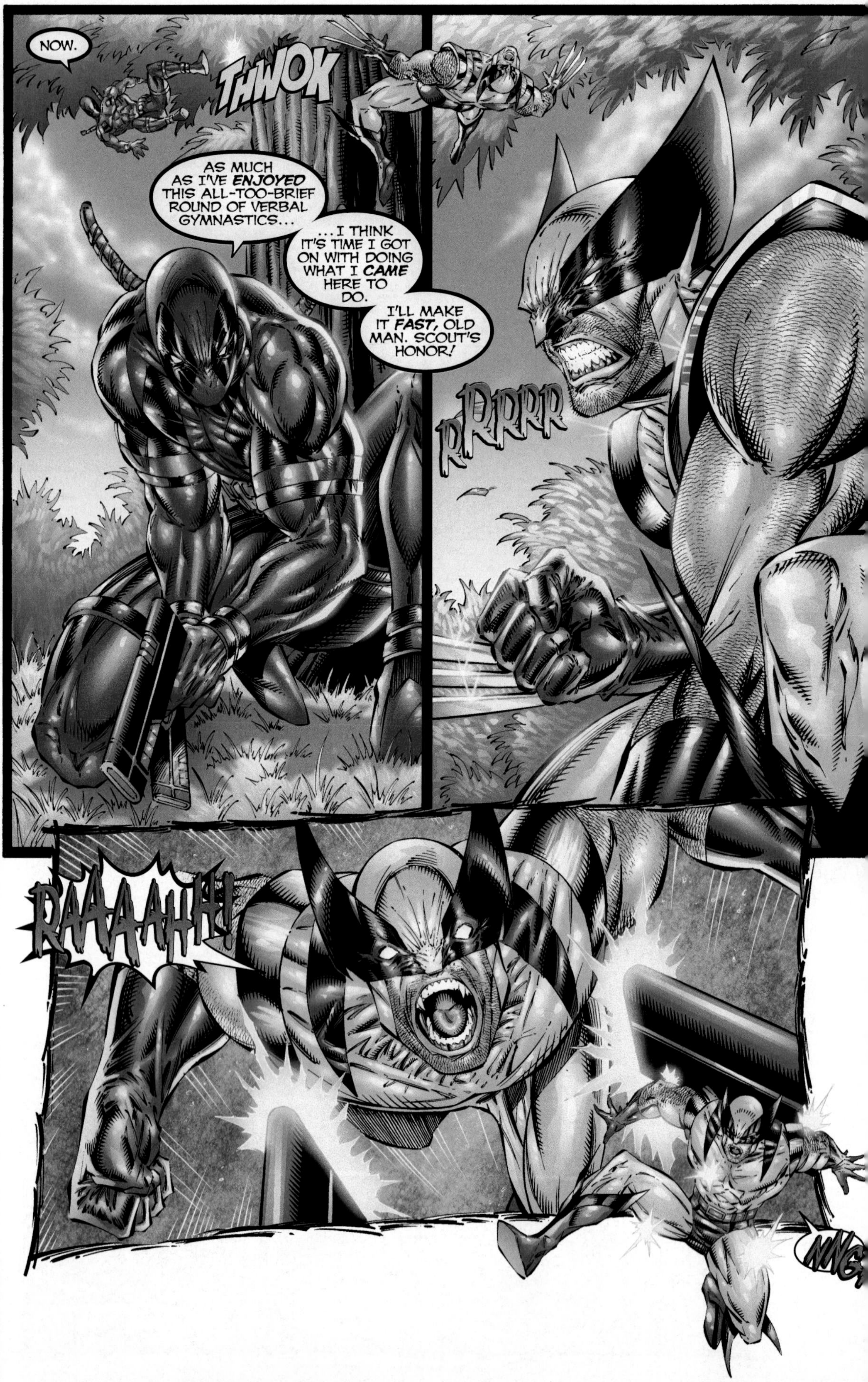
NOW.
THWOK
AS MUCH AS I'VE ENJOYED THIS ALL-TOO-BRIEF ROUND OF VERBAL GYMNASTICS...
...I THINK IT'S TIME I GOT ON WITH DOING WHAT I CAME HERE TO DO.
I'LL MAKE IT FAST, OLD MAN. SCOUT'S HONOR!
RRRRR
RAAAAHH!
NNG!

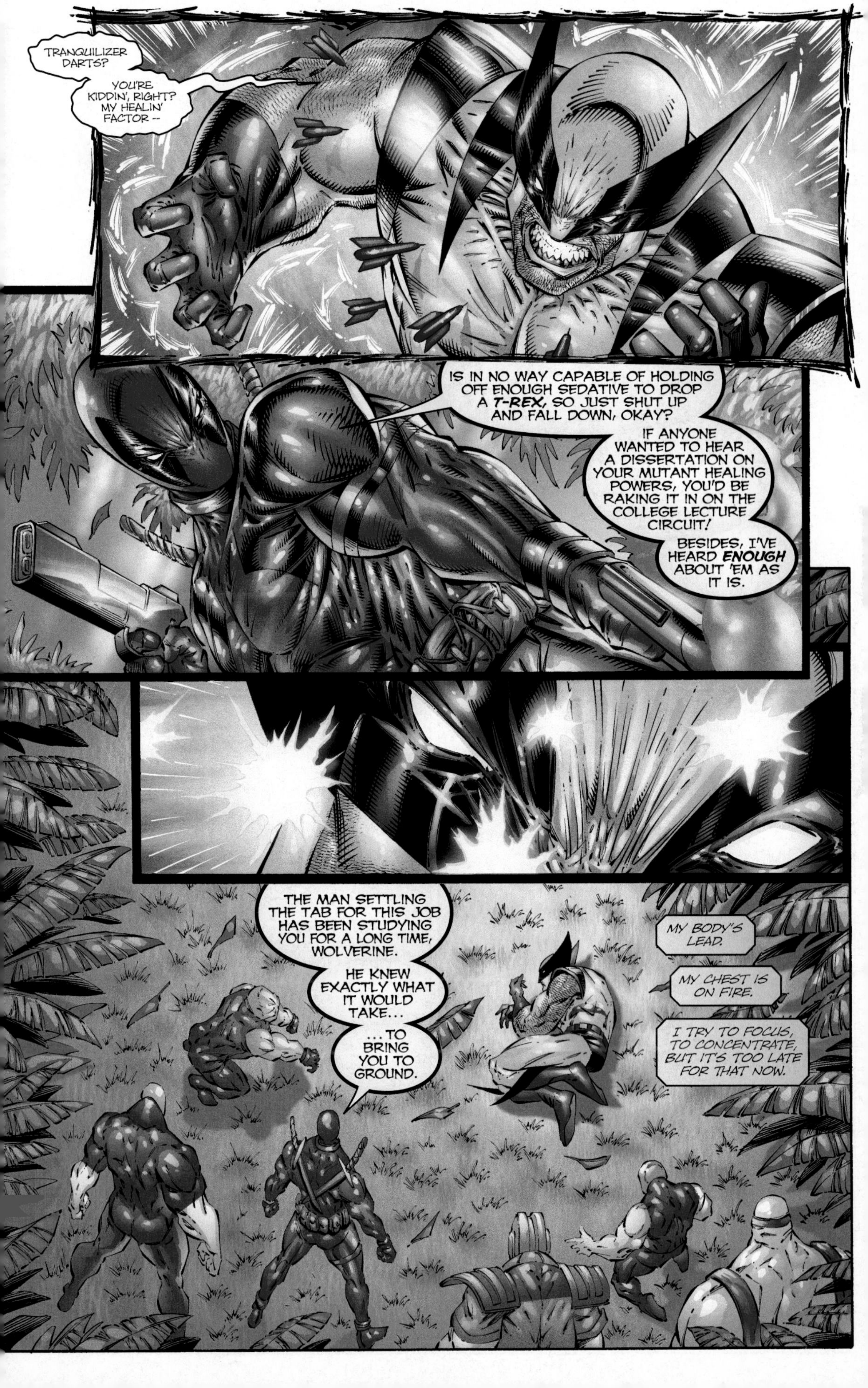
TRANQUILIZER DARTS?
YOU'RE KIDDIN', RIGHT? MY HEALIN' FACTOR --
IS IN NO WAY CAPABLE OF HOLDING OFF ENOUGH SEDATIVE TO DROP A T-REX, SO JUST SHUT UP AND FALL DOWN, OKAY?
IF ANYONE WANTED TO HEAR A DISSERTATION ON YOUR MUTANT HEALING POWERS, YOU'D BE RAKING IT IN ON THE COLLEGE LECTURE CIRCUIT!
BESIDES, I'VE HEARD ENOUGH ABOUT 'EM AS IT IS.
THE MAN SETTLING THE TAB FOR THIS JOB HAS BEEN STUDYING YOU FOR A LONG TIME, WOLVERINE.
HE KNEW EXACTLY WHAT IT WOULD TAKE...
...TO BRING YOU TO GROUND.
MY BODY'S LEAD.
MY CHEST IS ON FIRE.
I TRY TO FOCUS, TO CONCENTRATE, BUT IT'S TOO LATE FOR THAT NOW.

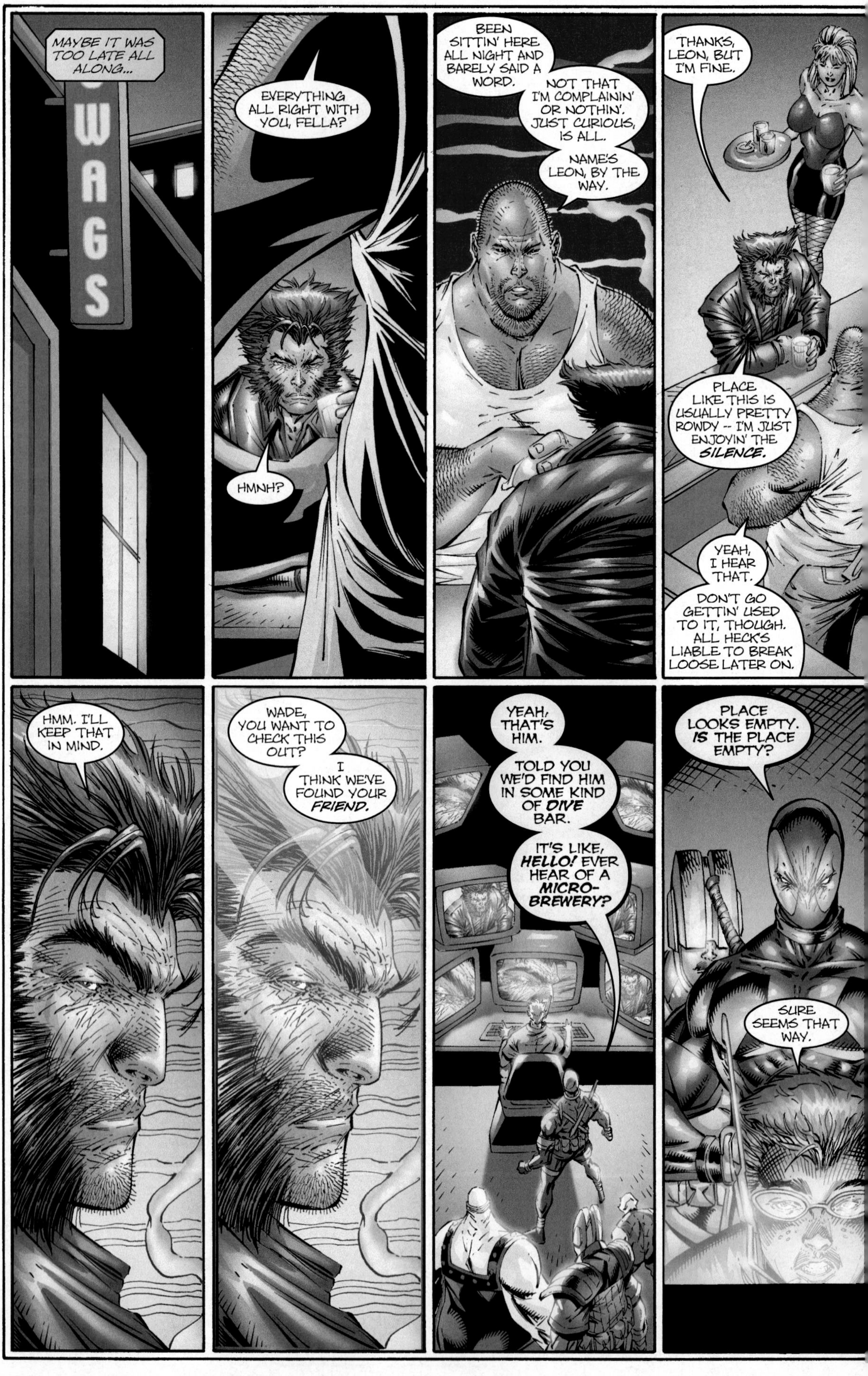

MAYBE IT WAS TOO LATE ALL ALONG...
EVERYTHING ALL RIGHT WITH YOU, FELLA?
HMNH?
BEEN SITTIN' HERE ALL NIGHT AND BARELY SAID A WORD.
NOT THAT I'M COMPLAININ' OR NOTHIN'. JUST CURIOUS, IS ALL.
NAME'S LEON, BY THE WAY.
THANKS, LEON, BUT I'M FINE.
PLACE LIKE THIS IS USUALLY PRETTY ROWDY -- I'M JUST ENJOYIN' THE SILENCE.
YEAH, I HEAR THAT.
DON'T GO GETTIN' USED TO IT, THOUGH. ALL HECK'S LIABLE TO BREAK LOOSE LATER ON.
HMM. I'LL KEEP THAT IN MIND.
WADE, YOU WANT TO CHECK THIS OUT?
I THINK WE'VE FOUND YOUR FRIEND.
YEAH, THAT'S HIM.
TOLD YOU WE'D FIND HIM IN SOME KIND OF DIVE BAR.
IT'S LIKE, HELLO! EVER HEAR OF A MICRO-BREWERY?
PLACE LOOKS EMPTY. IS THE PLACE EMPTY?
SURE SEEMS THAT WAY.

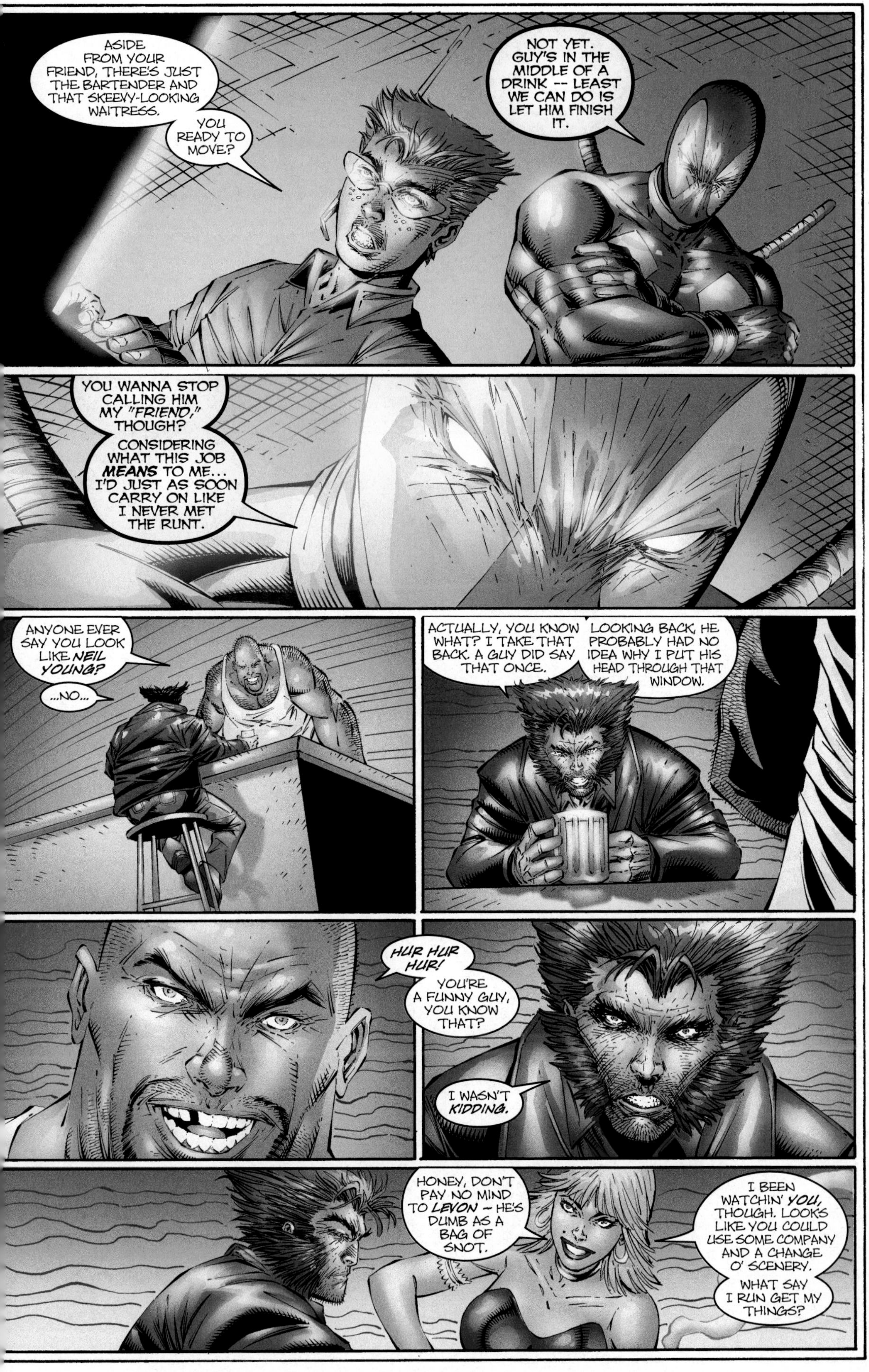
ASIDE FROM YOUR FRIEND, THERE'S JUST THE BARTENDER AND THAT SKEEVY-LOOKING WAITRESS.
YOU READY TO MOVE?
NOT YET. GUY'S IN THE MIDDLE OF A DRINK -- LEAST WE CAN DO IS LET HIM FINISH IT.
YOU WANNA STOP CALLING HIM MY "FRIEND," THOUGH?
CONSIDERING WHAT THIS JOB MEANS TO ME... I'D JUST AS SOON CARRY ON LIKE I NEVER MET THE RUNT.
ANYONE EVER SAY YOU LOOK LIKE NEIL YOUNG?
...NO...
ACTUALLY, YOU KNOW WHAT? I TAKE THAT BACK. A GUY DID SAY THAT ONCE.
LOOKING BACK, HE PROBABLY HAD NO IDEA WHY I PUT HIS HEAD THROUGH THAT WINDOW.
HUR HUR HUR!
YOU'RE A FUNNY GUY, YOU KNOW THAT?
I WASN'T KIDDING.
HONEY, DON'T PAY NO MIND TO LEVON -- HE'S DUMB AS A BAG OF SNOT.
I BEEN WATCHIN' YOU, THOUGH. LOOKS LIKE YOU COULD USE SOME COMPANY AND A CHANGE O' SCENERY.
WHAT SAY I RUN GET MY THINGS?

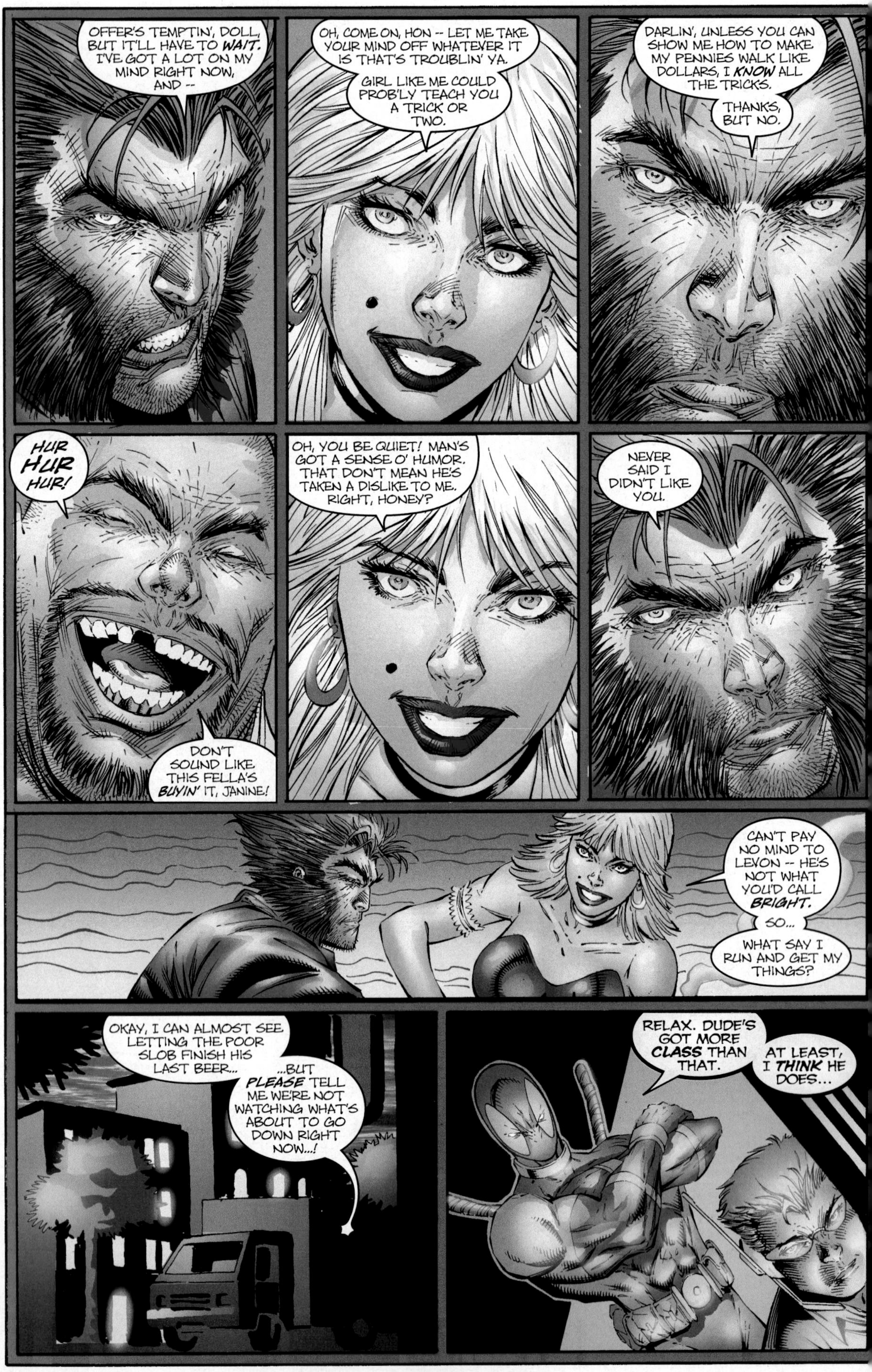

OFFER'S TEMPTIN', DOLL, BUT IT'LL HAVE TO WAIT. I'VE GOT A LOT ON MY MIND RIGHT NOW, AND --
OH, COME ON, HON -- LET ME TAKE YOUR MIND OFF WHATEVER IT IS THAT'S TROUBLIN' YA.
GIRL LIKE ME COULD PROB'LY TEACH YOU A TRICK OR TWO.
DARLIN', UNLESS YOU CAN SHOW ME HOW TO MAKE MY PENNIES WALK LIKE DOLLARS, I KNOW ALL THE TRICKS.
THANKS, BUT NO.
HUR HUR HUR!
DON'T SOUND LIKE THIS FELLA'S BUYIN' IT, JANINE!
OH, YOU BE QUIET! MAN'S GOT A SENSE O' HUMOR. THAT DON'T MEAN HE'S TAKEN A DISLIKE TO ME. RIGHT, HONEY?
NEVER SAID I DIDN'T LIKE YOU.
CAN'T PAY NO MIND TO LEVON -- HE'S NOT WHAT YOU'D CALL BRIGHT.
SO...
WHAT SAY I RUN AND GET MY THINGS?
OKAY, I CAN ALMOST SEE LETTING THE POOR SLOB FINISH HIS LAST BEER...
...BUT PLEASE TELL ME WE'RE NOT WATCHING WHAT'S ABOUT TO GO DOWN RIGHT NOW...!
RELAX. DUDE'S GOT MORE CLASS THAN THAT.
AT LEAST, I THINK HE DOES...

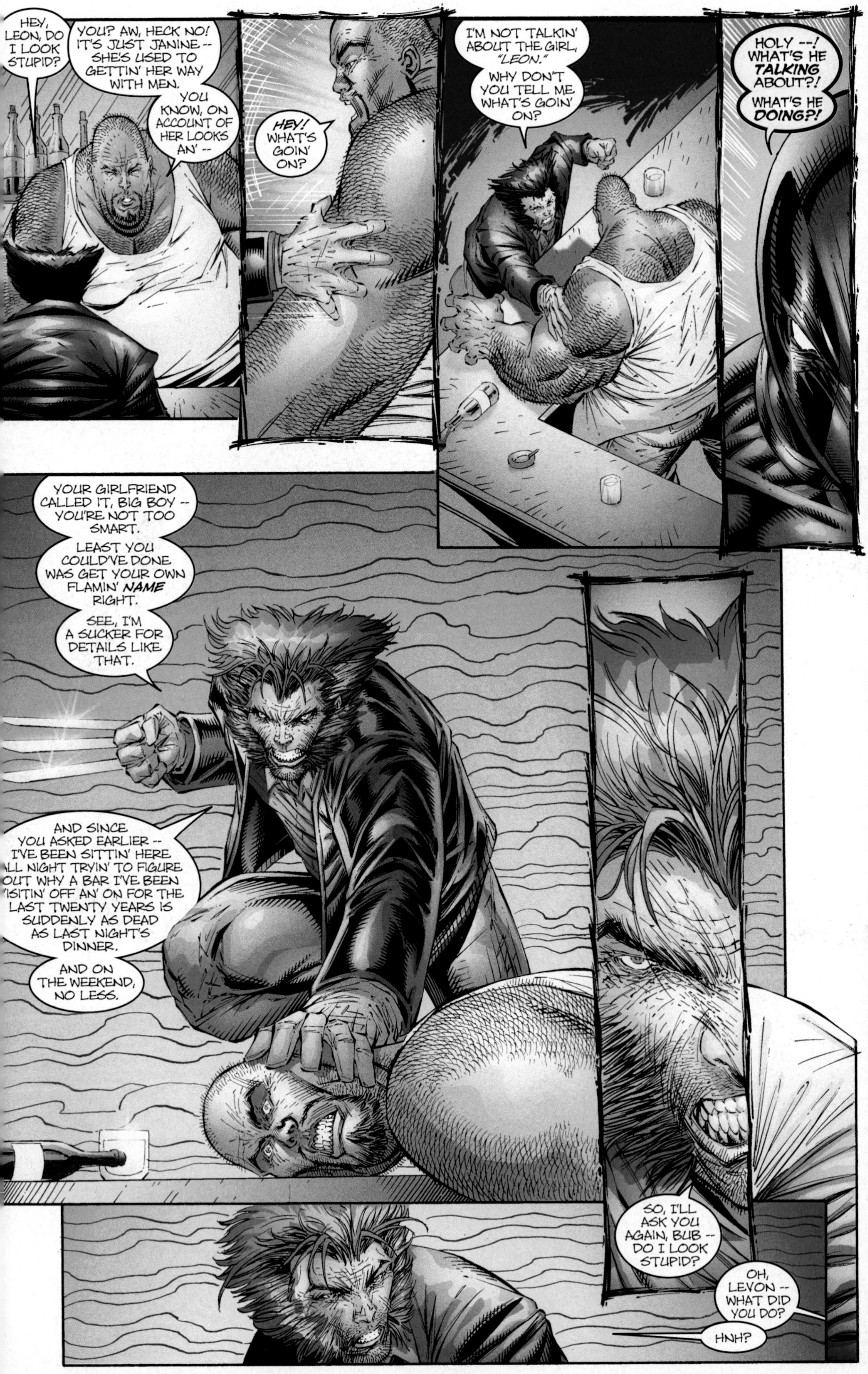
HEY, LEON, DO I LOOK STUPID?
YOU? AW, HECK NO! IT'S JUST JANINE -- SHE'S USED TO GETTIN' HER WAY WITH MEN.
YOU KNOW, ON ACCOUNT OF HER LOOKS AN' --
HEY! WHAT'S GOIN' ON?
I'M NOT TALKIN' ABOUT THE GIRL, "LEON."
WHY DON'T YOU TELL ME WHAT'S GOIN' ON?
HOLY --! WHAT'S HE TALKING ABOUT?!
WHAT'S HE DOING?!
YOUR GIRLFRIEND CALLED IT, BIG BOY -- YOU'RE NOT TOO SMART.
LEAST YOU COULD'VE DONE WAS GET YOUR OWN FLAMIN' NAME RIGHT.
SEE, I'M A SUCKER FOR DETAILS LIKE THAT.
AND SINCE YOU ASKED EARLIER -- I'VE BEEN SITTIN' HERE ALL NIGHT TRYIN' TO FIGURE OUT WHY A BAR I'VE BEEN VISITIN' OFF AN' ON FOR THE LAST TWENTY YEARS IS SUDDENLY AS DEAD AS LAST NIGHT'S DINNER.
AND ON THE WEEKEND, NO LESS.
SO, I'LL ASK YOU AGAIN, BUB -- DO I LOOK STUPID?
OH, LEVON -- WHAT DID YOU DO?
HNH?

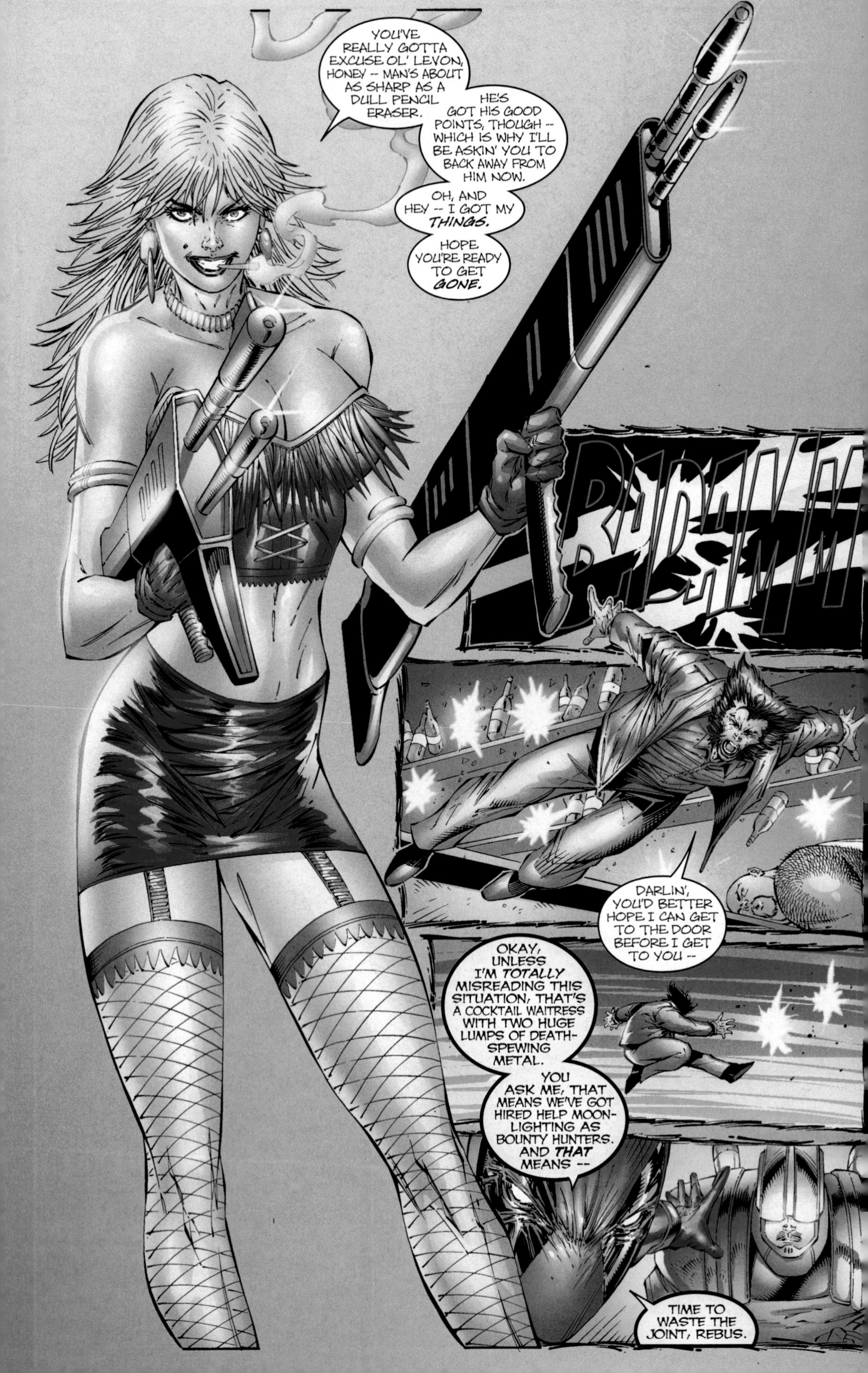

YOU'VE REALLY GOTTA EXCUSE OL' LEVON, HONEY -- MAN'S ABOUT AS SHARP AS A DULL PENCIL ERASER.
HE'S GOT HIS GOOD POINTS, THOUGH -- WHICH IS WHY I'LL BE ASKIN' YOU TO BACK AWAY FROM HIM NOW.
OH, AND HEY -- I GOT MY *THINGS.*
HOPE YOU'RE READY TO GET *GONE.*
DARLIN', YOU'D BETTER HOPE I CAN GET TO THE DOOR BEFORE I GET TO YOU --
OKAY, UNLESS I'M *TOTALLY* MISREADING THIS SITUATION, THAT'S A COCKTAIL WAITRESS WITH TWO HUGE LUMPS OF DEATH-SPEWING METAL.
YOU ASK ME, THAT MEANS WE'VE GOT HIRED HELP MOON-LIGHTING AS BOUNTY HUNTERS. AND *THAT* MEANS --
TIME TO WASTE THE JOINT, REBUS.

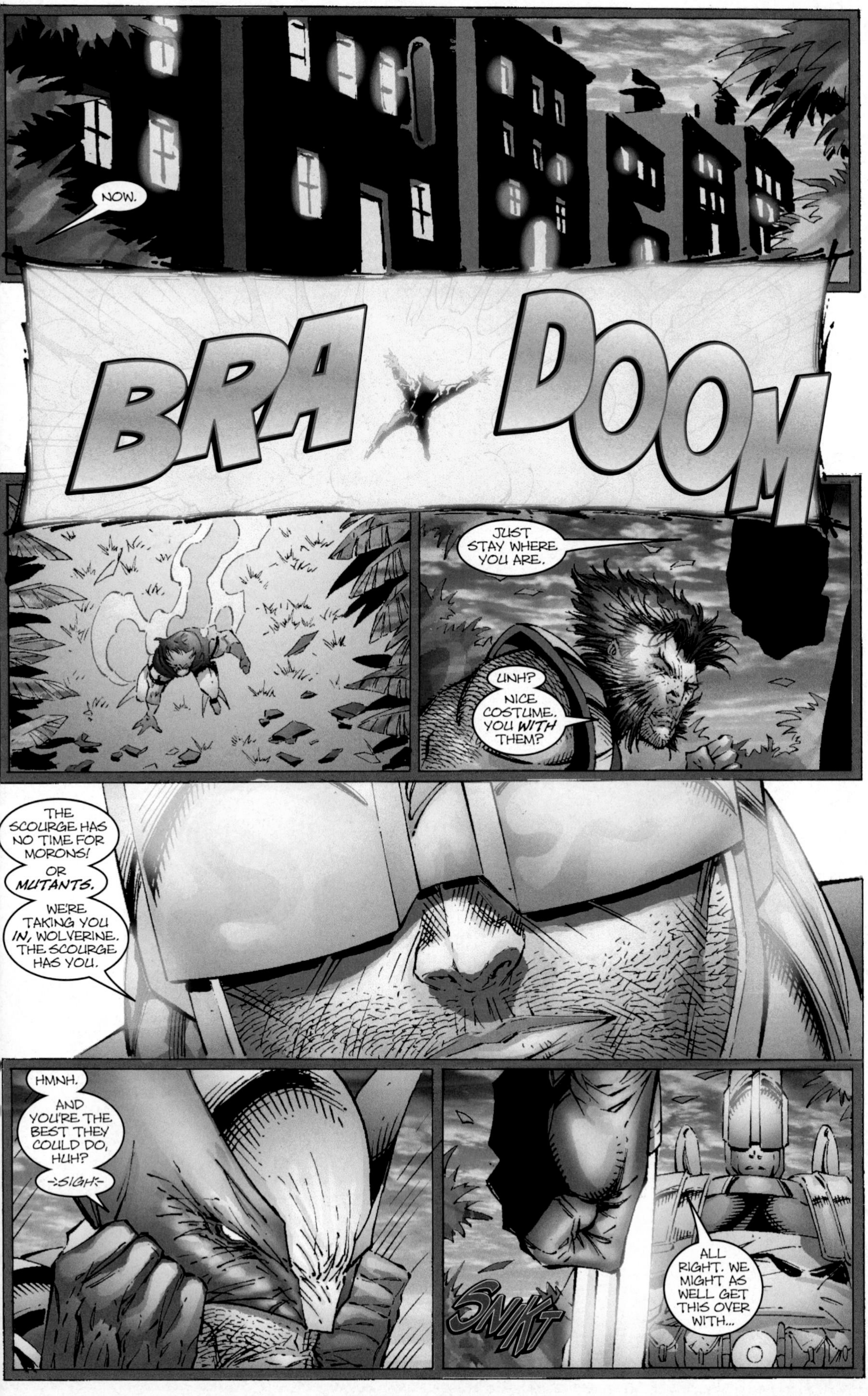
NOW.
BRA-DOOM
JUST STAY WHERE YOU ARE.
UNH? NICE COSTUME. YOU WITH THEM?
THE SCOURGE HAS NO TIME FOR MORONS!
OR MUTANTS.
WE'RE TAKING YOU IN, WOLVERINE. THE SCOURGE HAS YOU.
HMNH.
AND YOU'RE THE BEST THEY COULD DO, HUH?
-SIGH-
SNIKT
ALL RIGHT. WE MIGHT AS WELL GET THIS OVER WITH...

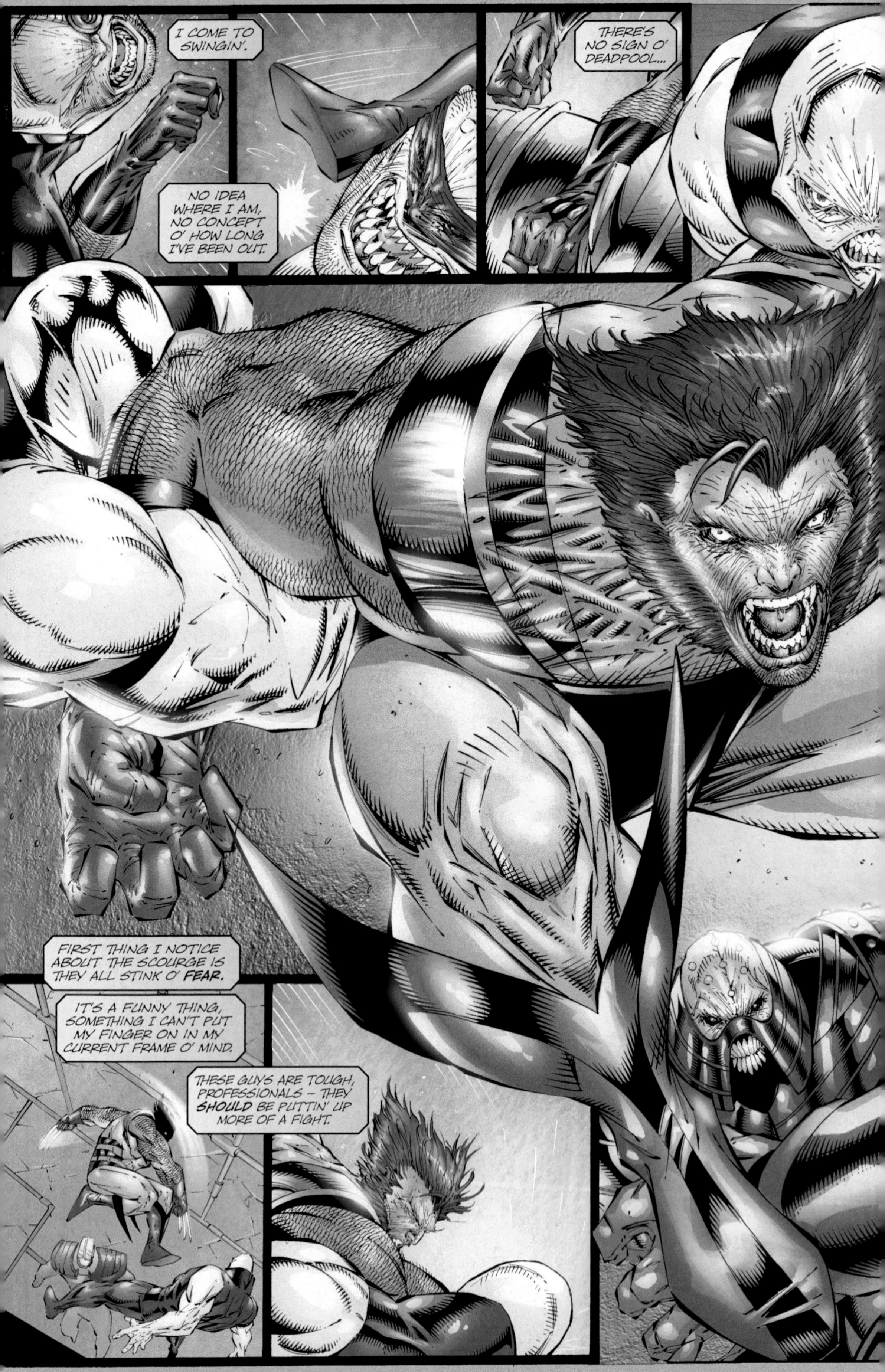
I COME TO SWINGIN'.
NO IDEA WHERE I AM, NO CONCEPT O' HOW LONG I'VE BEEN OUT.
THERE'S NO SIGN O' DEADPOOL...
FIRST THING I NOTICE ABOUT THE SCOURGE IS THEY ALL STINK O' FEAR.
IT'S A FUNNY THING, SOMETHING I CAN'T PUT MY FINGER ON IN MY CURRENT FRAME O' MIND.
THESE GUYS ARE TOUGH, PROFESSIONALS -- THEY SHOULD BE PUTTIN' UP MORE OF A FIGHT.

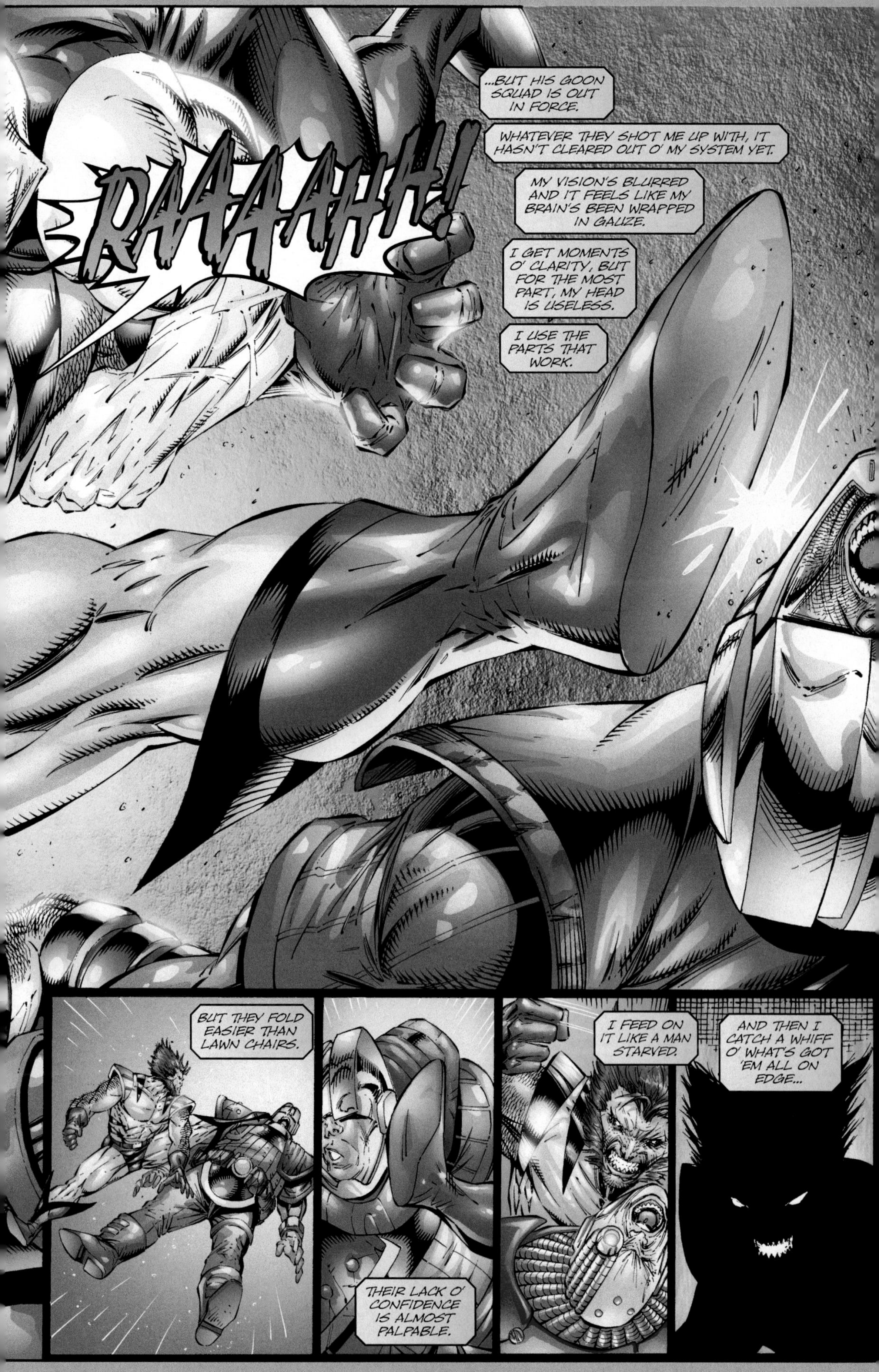
...BUT HIS GOON SQUAD IS OUT IN FORCE.
WHATEVER THEY SHOT ME UP WITH, IT HASN'T CLEARED OUT O' MY SYSTEM YET.
MY VISION'S BLURRED AND IT FEELS LIKE MY BRAIN'S BEEN WRAPPED IN GAUZE.
I GET MOMENTS O' CLARITY, BUT FOR THE MOST PART, MY HEAD IS USELESS.
I USE THE PARTS THAT WORK.
RAAAAHH!
BUT THEY FOLD EASIER THAN LAWN CHAIRS.
THEIR LACK O' CONFIDENCE IS ALMOST PALPABLE.
I FEED ON IT LIKE A MAN STARVED.
AND THEN I CATCH A WHIFF O' WHAT'S GOT 'EM ALL ON EDGE...

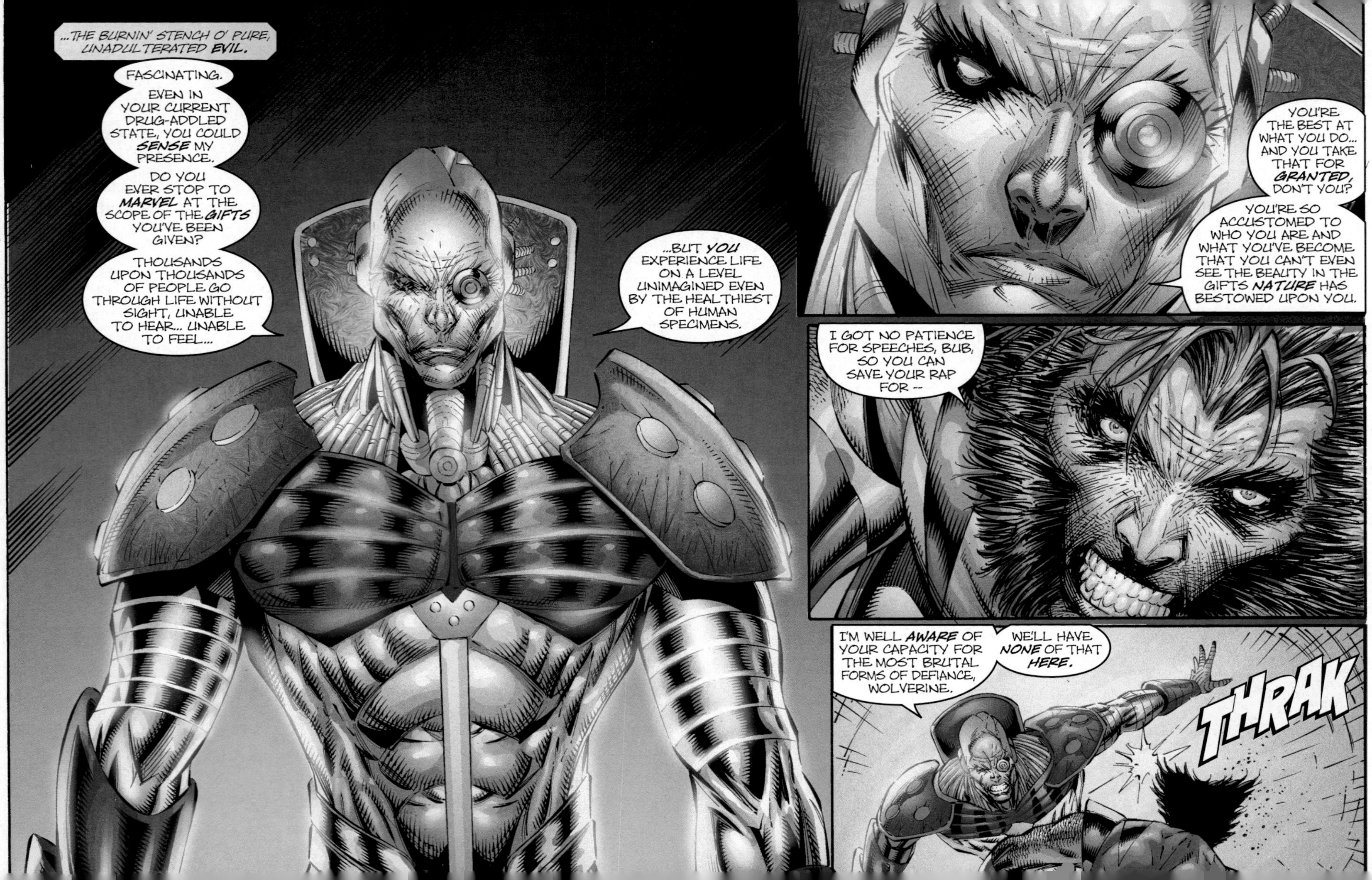
...THE BURNIN' STENCH O' PURE, UNADULTERATED EVIL.
FASCINATING.
EVEN IN YOUR CURRENT DRUG-ADDLED STATE, YOU COULD SENSE MY PRESENCE.
DO YOU EVER STOP TO MARVEL AT THE SCOPE OF THE GIFTS YOU'VE BEEN GIVEN?
THOUSANDS UPON THOUSANDS OF PEOPLE GO THROUGH LIFE WITHOUT SIGHT, UNABLE TO HEAR... UNABLE TO FEEL...
...BUT YOU EXPERIENCE LIFE ON A LEVEL UNIMAGINED EVEN BY THE HEALTHIEST OF HUMAN SPECIMENS.
YOU'RE THE BEST AT WHAT YOU DO... AND YOU TAKE THAT FOR GRANTED, DON'T YOU?
YOU'RE SO ACCUSTOMED TO WHO YOU ARE AND WHAT YOU'VE BECOME THAT YOU CAN'T EVEN SEE THE BEAUTY IN THE GIFTS NATURE HAS BESTOWED UPON YOU.
I GOT NO PATIENCE FOR SPEECHES, BUB, SO YOU CAN SAVE YOUR RAP FOR --
I'M WELL AWARE OF YOUR CAPACITY FOR THE MOST BRUTAL FORMS OF DEFIANCE, WOLVERINE.
WE'LL HAVE NONE OF THAT HERE.
THRAK

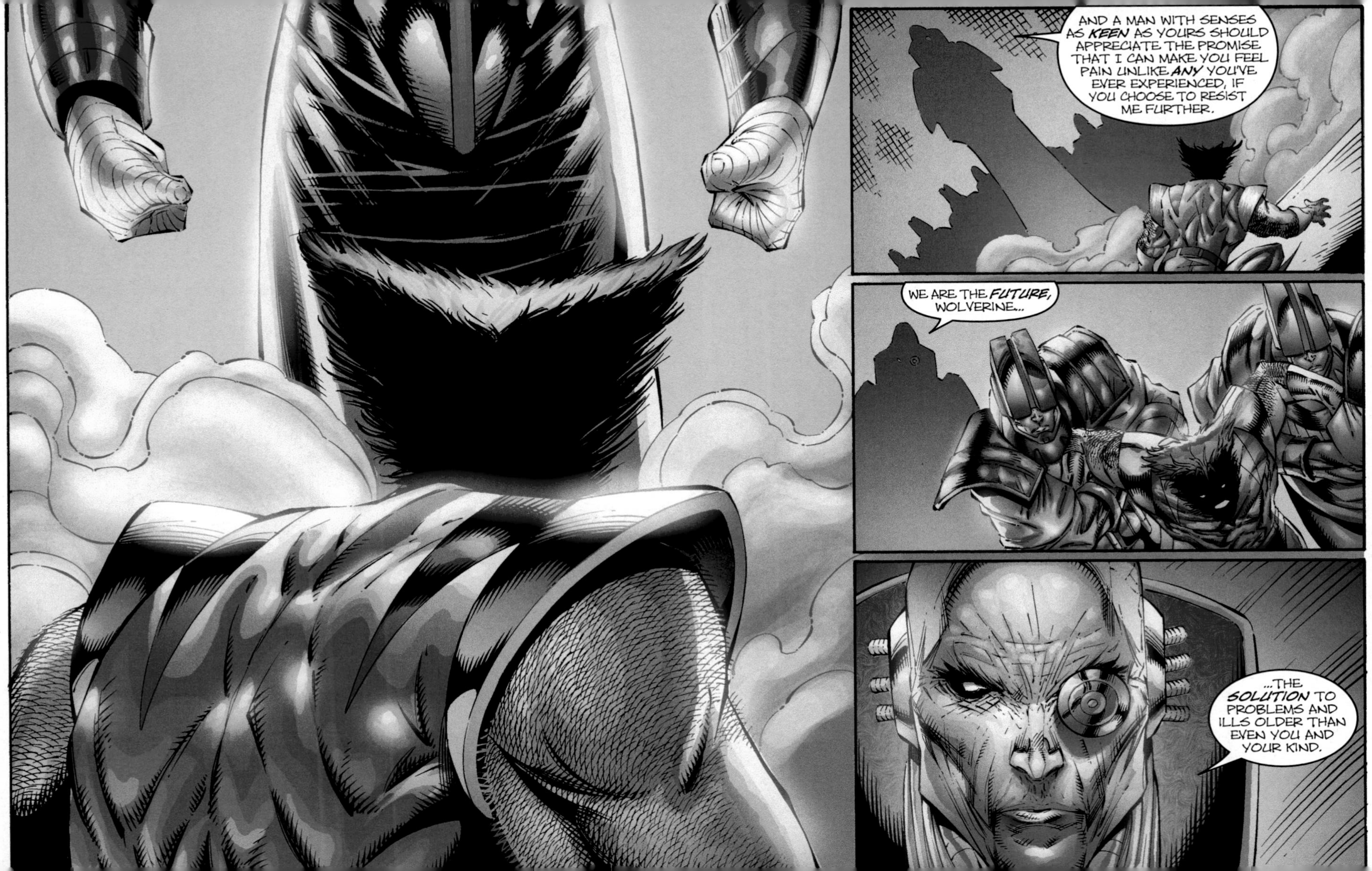
AND A MAN WITH SENSES AS **KEEN** AS YOURS SHOULD APPRECIATE THE PROMISE THAT I CAN MAKE YOU FEEL PAIN UNLIKE **ANY** YOU'VE EVER EXPERIENCED, IF YOU CHOOSE TO RESIST ME FURTHER.
WE ARE THE ***FUTURE,*** WOLVERINE...
...THE ***SOLUTION*** TO PROBLEMS AND ILLS OLDER THAN EVEN YOU AND YOUR KIND.

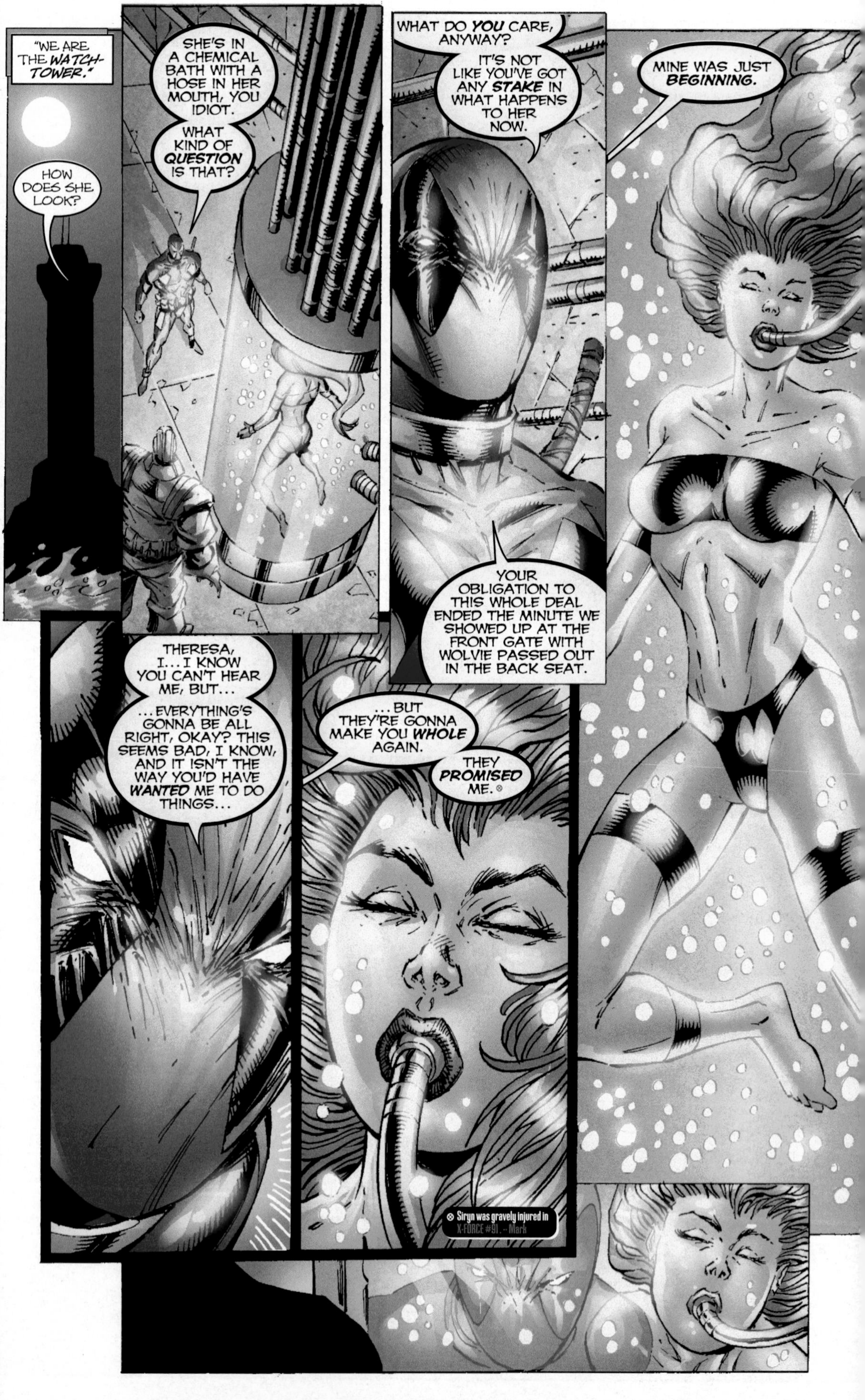
"WE ARE THE WATCH-TOWER."
HOW DOES SHE LOOK?
SHE'S IN A CHEMICAL BATH WITH A HOSE IN HER MOUTH, YOU IDIOT.
WHAT KIND OF QUESTION IS THAT?
WHAT DO YOU CARE, ANYWAY?
IT'S NOT LIKE YOU'VE GOT ANY STAKE IN WHAT HAPPENS TO HER NOW.
YOUR OBLIGATION TO THIS WHOLE DEAL ENDED THE MINUTE WE SHOWED UP AT THE FRONT GATE WITH WOLVIE PASSED OUT IN THE BACK SEAT.
MINE WAS JUST BEGINNING.
THERESA, I... I KNOW YOU CAN'T HEAR ME, BUT...
...EVERYTHING'S GONNA BE ALL RIGHT, OKAY? THIS SEEMS BAD, I KNOW, AND IT ISN'T THE WAY YOU'D HAVE WANTED ME TO DO THINGS...
...BUT THEY'RE GONNA MAKE YOU WHOLE AGAIN.
THEY PROMISED ME.
Siryn was gravely injured in X-FORCE #91. --Mark

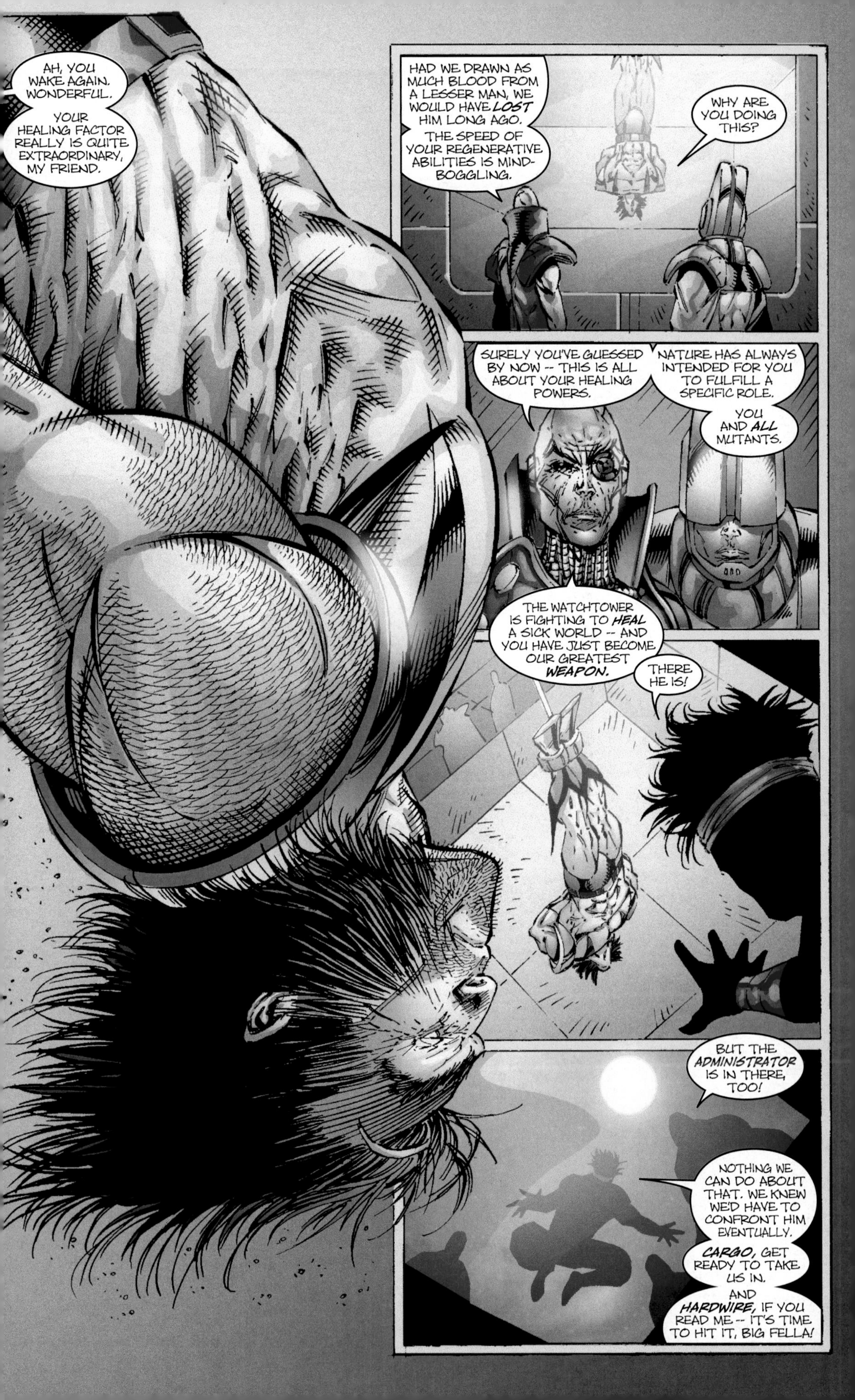
AH, YOU WAKE AGAIN. WONDERFUL.
YOUR HEALING FACTOR REALLY IS QUITE EXTRAORDINARY, MY FRIEND.
HAD WE DRAWN AS MUCH BLOOD FROM A LESSER MAN, WE WOULD HAVE LOST HIM LONG AGO.
THE SPEED OF YOUR REGENERATIVE ABILITIES IS MIND-BOGGLING.
WHY ARE YOU DOING THIS?
SURELY YOU'VE GUESSED BY NOW -- THIS IS ALL ABOUT YOUR HEALING POWERS.
NATURE HAS ALWAYS INTENDED FOR YOU TO FULFILL A SPECIFIC ROLE.
YOU AND ALL MUTANTS.
THE WATCHTOWER IS FIGHTING TO HEAL A SICK WORLD -- AND YOU HAVE JUST BECOME OUR GREATEST WEAPON.
THERE HE IS!
BUT THE ADMINISTRATOR IS IN THERE, TOO!
NOTHING WE CAN DO ABOUT THAT. WE KNEW WE'D HAVE TO CONFRONT HIM EVENTUALLY.
CARGO, GET READY TO TAKE US IN.
AND HARDWIRE, IF YOU READ ME -- IT'S TIME TO HIT IT, BIG FELLA!

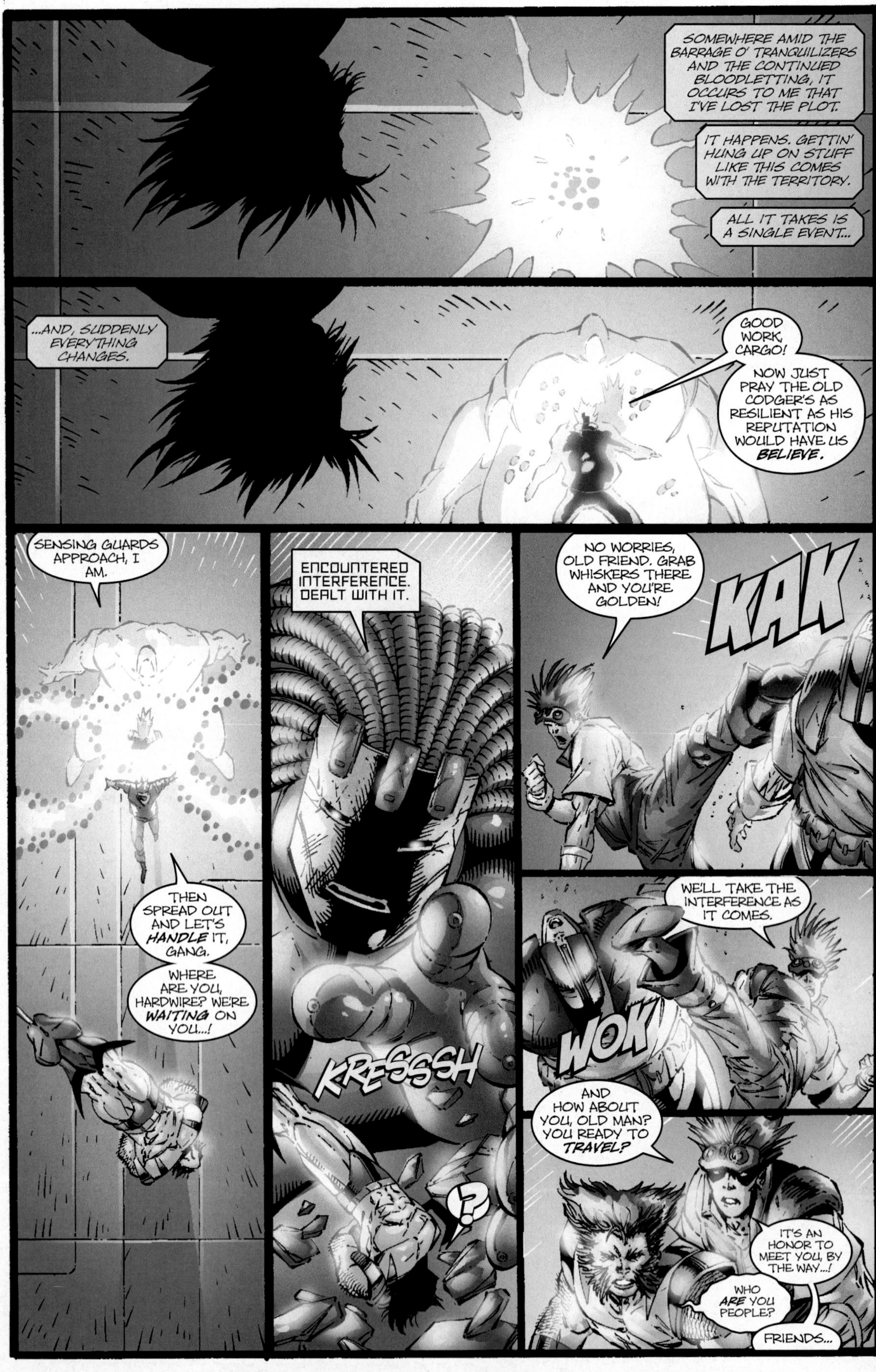

SOMEWHERE AMID THE BARRAGE O' TRANQUILIZERS AND THE CONTINUED BLOODLETTING, IT OCCURS TO ME THAT I'VE LOST THE PLOT.
IT HAPPENS. GETTIN' HUNG UP ON STUFF LIKE THIS COMES WITH THE TERRITORY.
ALL IT TAKES IS A SINGLE EVENT...
...AND, SUDDENLY EVERYTHING CHANGES.
GOOD WORK, CARGO!
NOW JUST PRAY THE OLD CODGER'S AS RESILIENT AS HIS REPUTATION WOULD HAVE US BELIEVE.
SENSING GUARDS APPROACH, I AM.
THEN SPREAD OUT AND LET'S HANDLE IT, GANG.
WHERE ARE YOU, HARDWIRE? WE'RE WAITING ON YOU...!
ENCOUNTERED INTERFERENCE. DEALT WITH IT.
KRESSSH
?
NO WORRIES, OLD FRIEND. GRAB WHISKERS THERE AND YOU'RE GOLDEN!
KAK
WE'LL TAKE THE INTERFERENCE AS IT COMES.
WOK
AND HOW ABOUT YOU, OLD MAN? YOU READY TO TRAVEL?
IT'S AN HONOR TO MEET YOU, BY THE WAY...!
WHO ARE YOU PEOPLE?
FRIENDS...

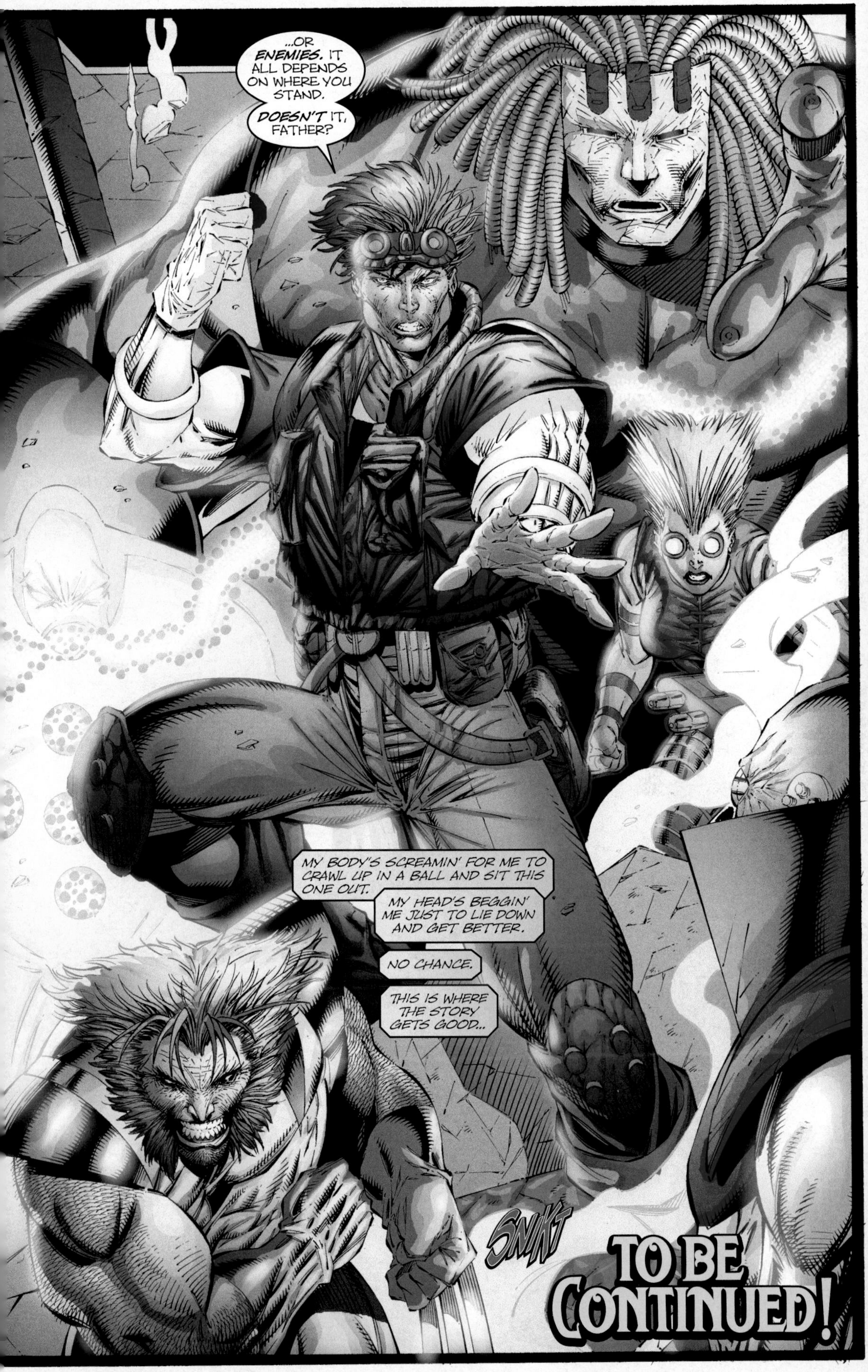
...OR ENEMIES. IT ALL DEPENDS ON WHERE YOU STAND.
DOESN'T IT, FATHER?
MY BODY'S SCREAMIN' FOR ME TO CRAWL UP IN A BALL AND SIT THIS ONE OUT.
MY HEAD'S BEGGIN' ME JUST TO LIE DOWN AND GET BETTER.
NO CHANCE.
THIS IS WHERE THE STORY GETS GOOD...
SNIKT
TO BE CONTINUED!

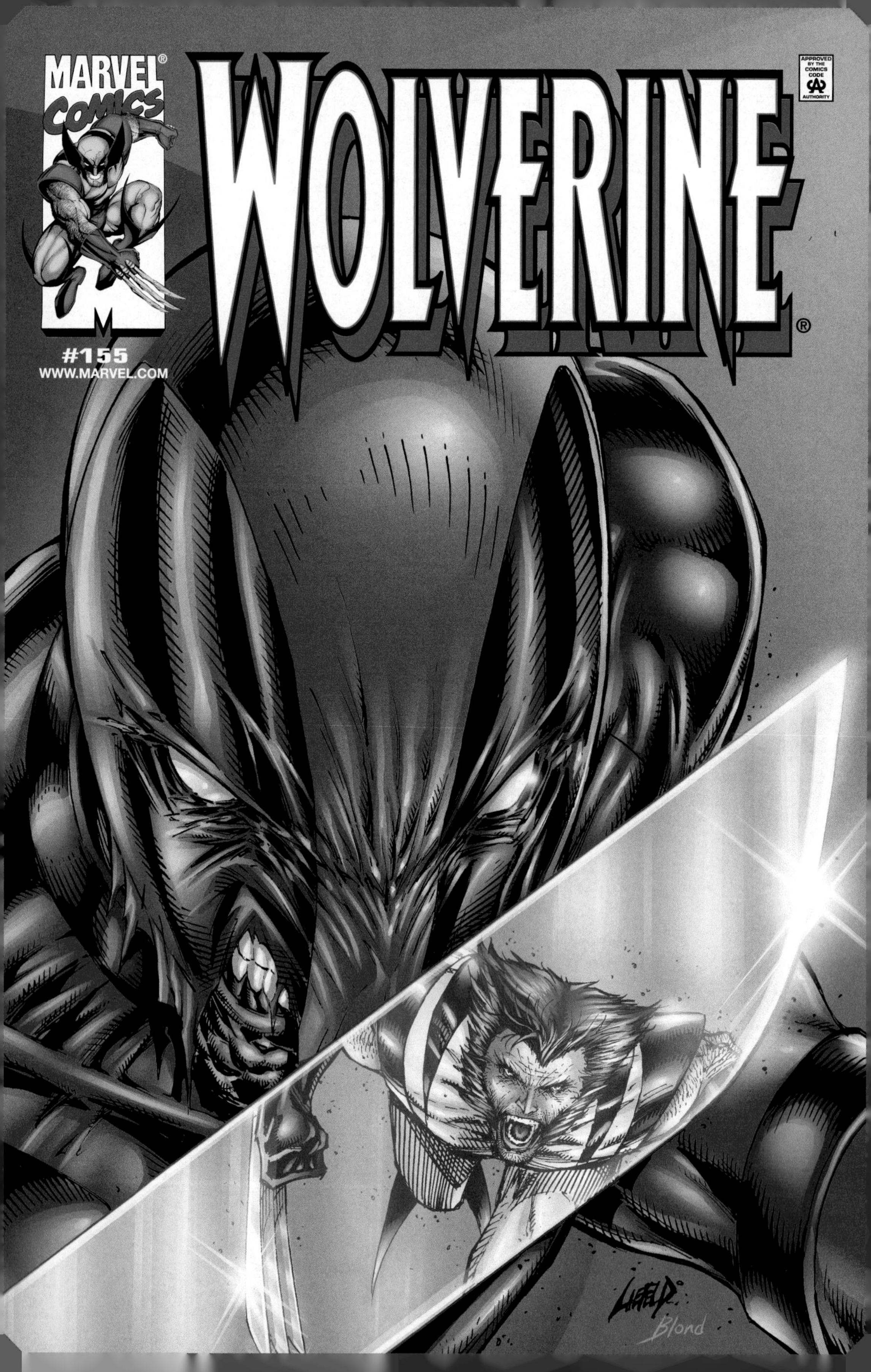
MARVEL
COMICS
WOLVERINE
#155
WWW.MARVEL.COM
APPROVED BY THE COMICS CODE AUTHORITY
LIEFELD
Blond

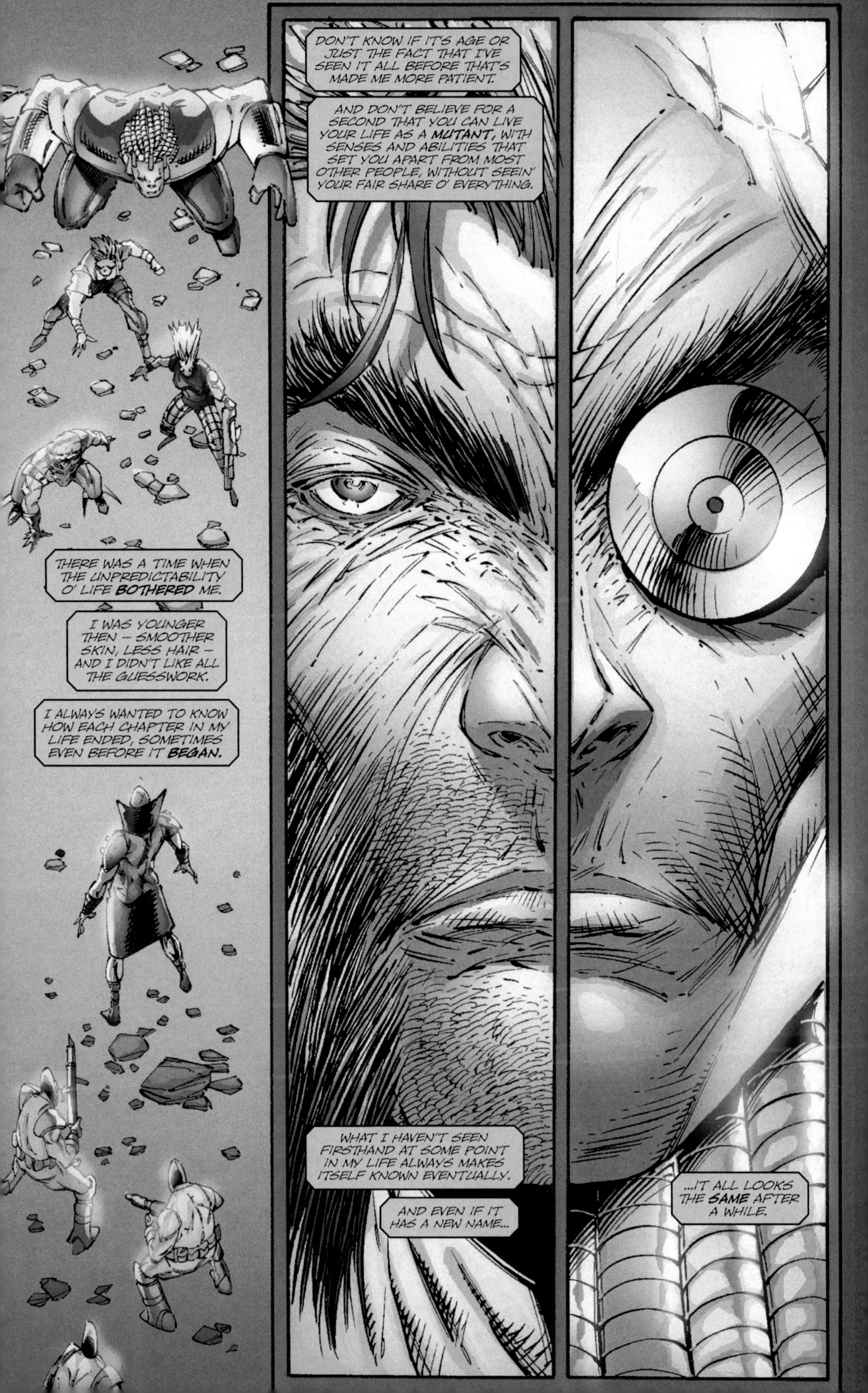

THERE WAS A TIME WHEN THE UNPREDICTABILITY O' LIFE BOTHERED ME.
I WAS YOUNGER THEN -- SMOOTHER SKIN, LESS HAIR -- AND I DIDN'T LIKE ALL THE GUESSWORK.
I ALWAYS WANTED TO KNOW HOW EACH CHAPTER IN MY LIFE ENDED, SOMETIMES EVEN BEFORE IT BEGAN.
DON'T KNOW IF IT'S AGE OR JUST THE FACT THAT I'VE SEEN IT ALL BEFORE THAT'S MADE ME MORE PATIENT.
AND DON'T BELIEVE FOR A SECOND THAT YOU CAN LIVE YOUR LIFE AS A MUTANT, WITH SENSES AND ABILITIES THAT SET YOU APART FROM MOST OTHER PEOPLE, WITHOUT SEEIN' YOUR FAIR SHARE O' EVERYTHING.
WHAT I HAVEN'T SEEN FIRSTHAND AT SOME POINT IN MY LIFE ALWAYS MAKES ITSELF KNOWN EVENTUALLY.
AND EVEN IF IT HAS A NEW NAME...
...IT ALL LOOKS THE SAME AFTER A WHILE.

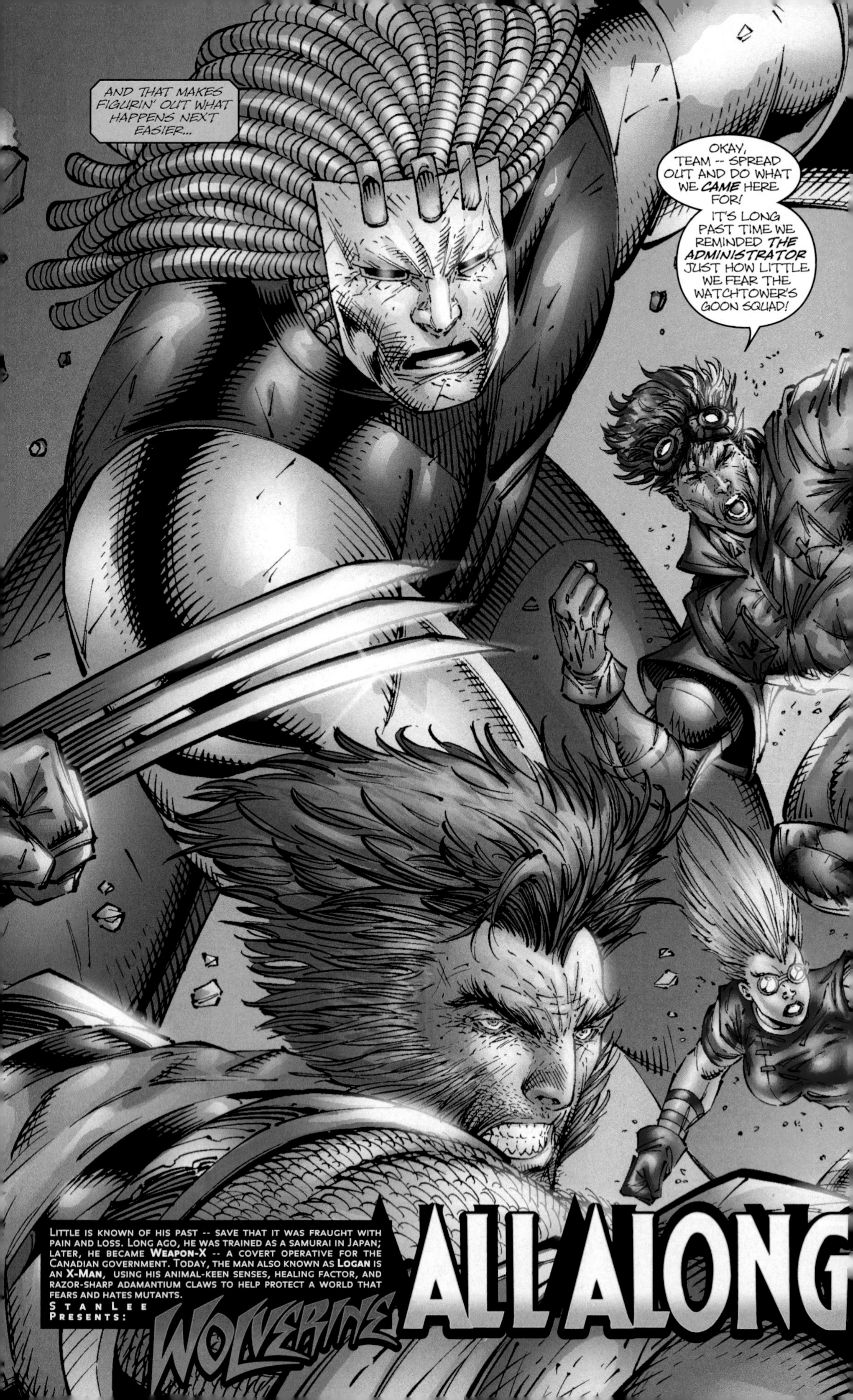
AND THAT MAKES FIGURIN' OUT WHAT HAPPENS NEXT EASIER...
OKAY, TEAM -- SPREAD OUT AND DO WHAT WE CAME HERE FOR!
IT'S LONG PAST TIME WE REMINDED THE ADMINISTRATOR JUST HOW LITTLE WE FEAR THE WATCHTOWER'S GOON SQUAD!
LITTLE IS KNOWN OF HIS PAST -- SAVE THAT IT WAS FRAUGHT WITH PAIN AND LOSS. LONG AGO, HE WAS TRAINED AS A SAMURAI IN JAPAN; LATER, HE BECAME WEAPON-X -- A COVERT OPERATIVE FOR THE CANADIAN GOVERNMENT. TODAY, THE MAN ALSO KNOWN AS LOGAN IS AN X-MAN, USING HIS ANIMAL-KEEN SENSES, HEALING FACTOR, AND RAZOR-SHARP ADAMANTIUM CLAWS TO HELP PROTECT A WORLD THAT FEARS AND HATES MUTANTS.
STAN LEE PRESENTS:
WOLVERINE
ALL ALONG

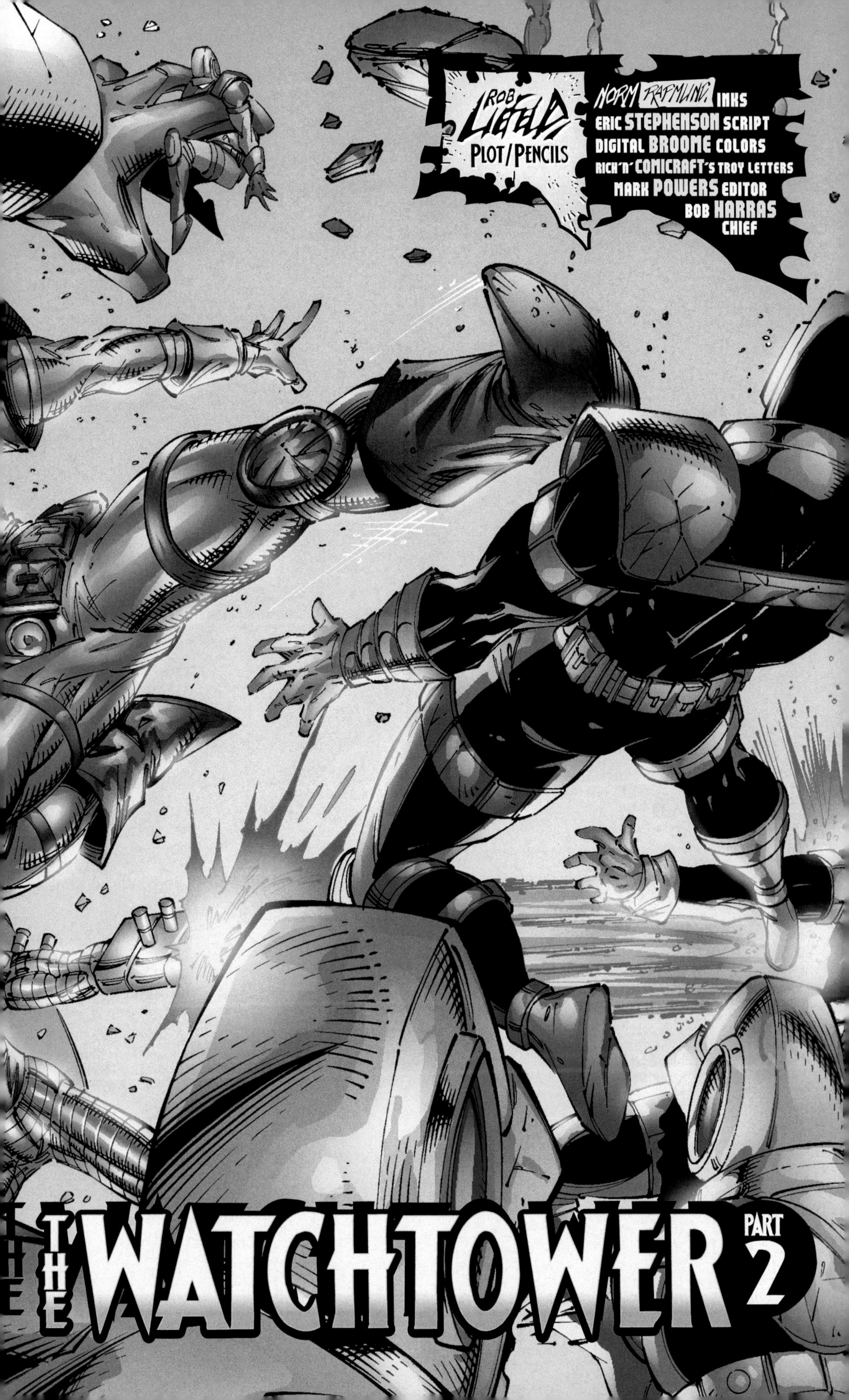
ROB LIEFELD PLOT/PENCILS
NORM RAPMUND INKS
ERIC STEPHENSON SCRIPT
DIGITAL BROOME COLORS
RICH'N' COMICRAFT'S TROY LETTERS
MARK POWERS EDITOR
BOB HARRAS CHIEF
THE WATCHTOWER PART 2

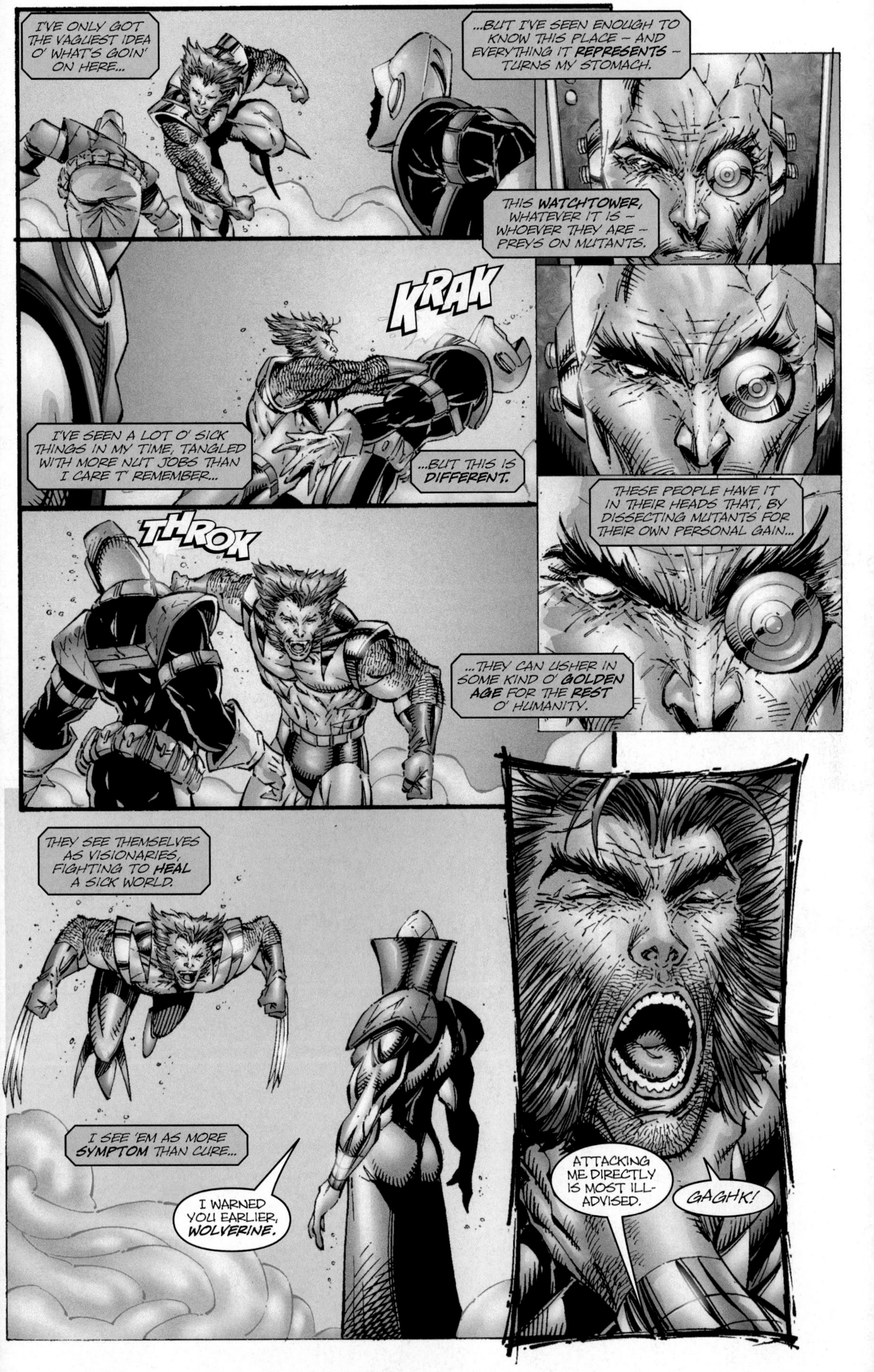
I'VE ONLY GOT THE VAGUEST IDEA O' WHAT'S GOIN' ON HERE...
...BUT I'VE SEEN ENOUGH TO KNOW THIS PLACE -- AND EVERYTHING IT REPRESENTS -- TURNS MY STOMACH.
THIS WATCHTOWER, WHATEVER IT IS -- WHOEVER THEY ARE -- PREYS ON MUTANTS.
KRAK
I'VE SEEN A LOT O' SICK THINGS IN MY TIME, TANGLED WITH MORE NUT JOBS THAN I CARE T' REMEMBER...
...BUT THIS IS DIFFERENT.
THROK
THESE PEOPLE HAVE IT IN THEIR HEADS THAT, BY DISSECTING MUTANTS FOR THEIR OWN PERSONAL GAIN...
...THEY CAN USHER IN SOME KIND O' GOLDEN AGE FOR THE REST O' HUMANITY.
THEY SEE THEMSELVES AS VISIONARIES, FIGHTING TO HEAL A SICK WORLD.
I SEE 'EM AS MORE SYMPTOM THAN CURE...
I WARNED YOU EARLIER, WOLVERINE.
ATTACKING ME DIRECTLY IS MOST ILL-ADVISED.
GAGHK!

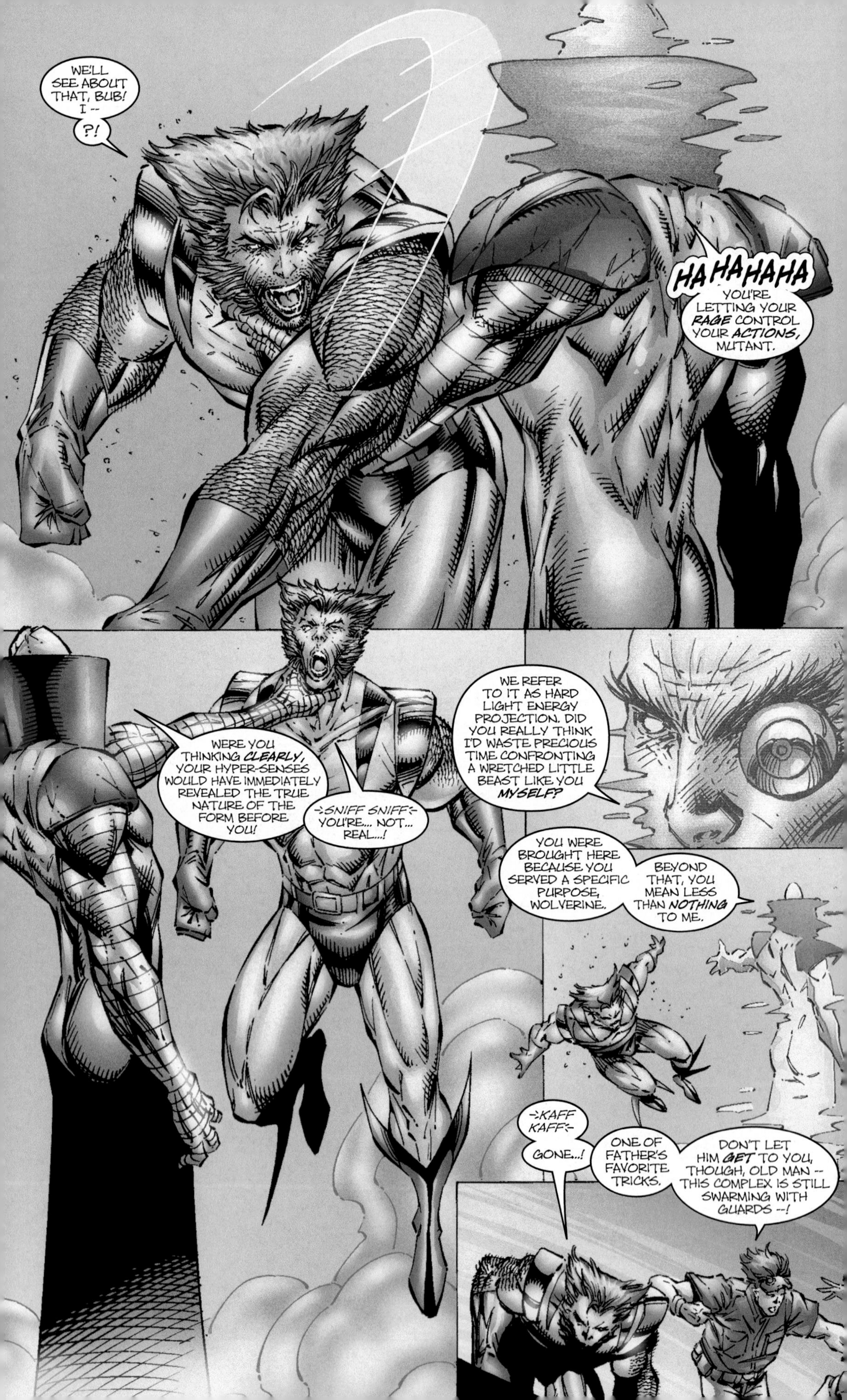
WE'LL SEE ABOUT THAT, BUB! I --
?!
HAHAHAHA
YOU'RE LETTING YOUR RAGE CONTROL YOUR ACTIONS, MUTANT.
WERE YOU THINKING CLEARLY, YOUR HYPER-SENSES WOULD HAVE IMMEDIATELY REVEALED THE TRUE NATURE OF THE FORM BEFORE YOU!
-SNIFF SNIFF- YOU'RE... NOT... REAL...!
WE REFER TO IT AS HARD LIGHT ENERGY PROJECTION. DID YOU REALLY THINK I'D WASTE PRECIOUS TIME CONFRONTING A WRETCHED LITTLE BEAST LIKE YOU MYSELF?
YOU WERE BROUGHT HERE BECAUSE YOU SERVED A SPECIFIC PURPOSE, WOLVERINE.
BEYOND THAT, YOU MEAN LESS THAN NOTHING TO ME.
-KAFF KAFF-
GONE...!
ONE OF FATHER'S FAVORITE TRICKS.
DON'T LET HIM GET TO YOU, THOUGH, OLD MAN -- THIS COMPLEX IS STILL SWARMING WITH GUARDS --!

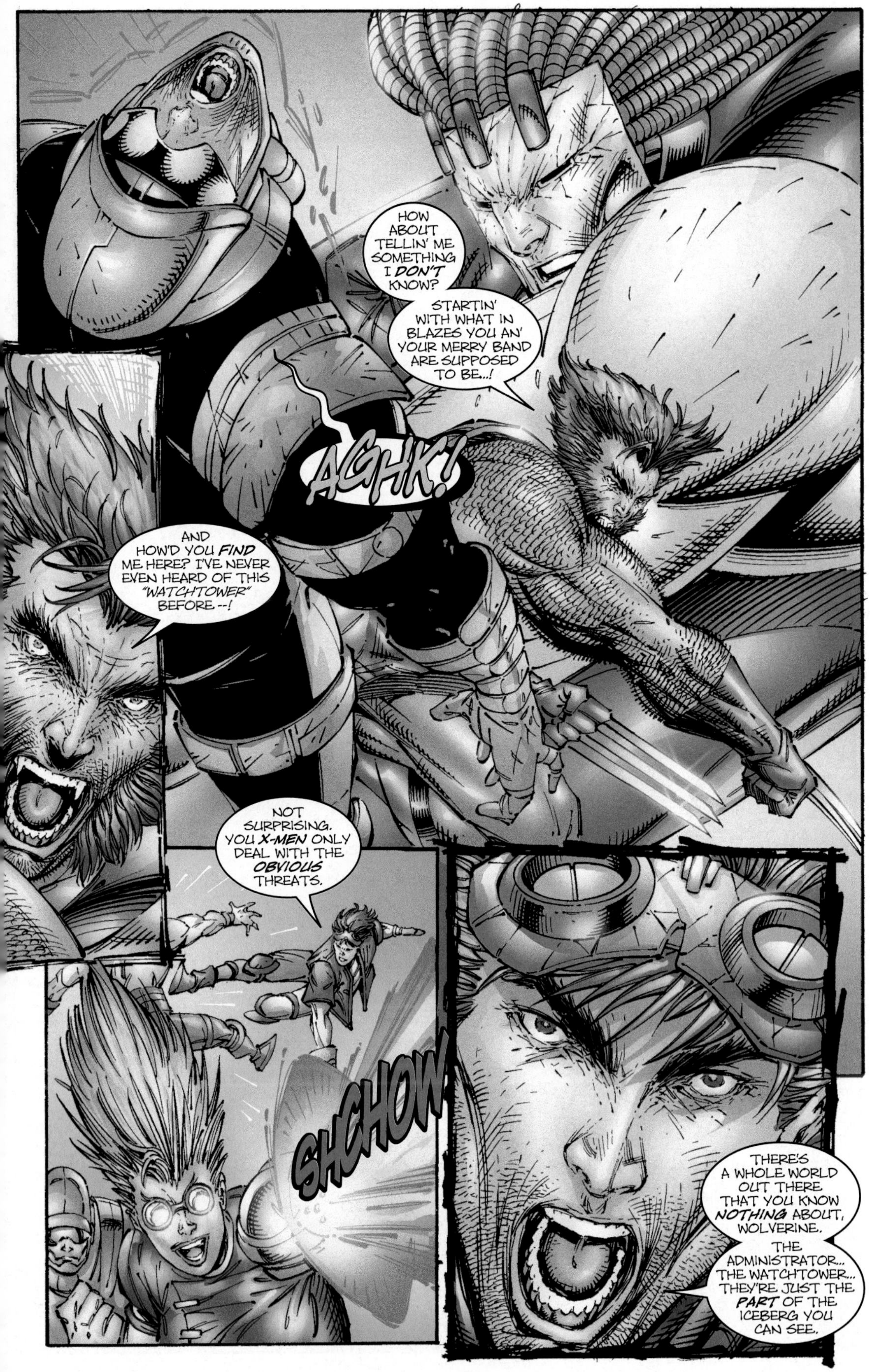
HOW ABOUT TELLIN' ME SOMETHING I DON'T KNOW?
STARTIN' WITH WHAT IN BLAZES YOU AN' YOUR MERRY BAND ARE SUPPOSED TO BE...!
AGHK!
AND HOW'D YOU FIND ME HERE? I'VE NEVER EVEN HEARD OF THIS "WATCHTOWER" BEFORE --!
NOT SURPRISING. YOU X-MEN ONLY DEAL WITH THE OBVIOUS THREATS.
SHCHOW
THERE'S A WHOLE WORLD OUT THERE THAT YOU KNOW NOTHING ABOUT, WOLVERINE.
THE ADMINISTRATOR... THE WATCHTOWER... THEY'RE JUST THE PART OF THE ICEBERG YOU CAN SEE.

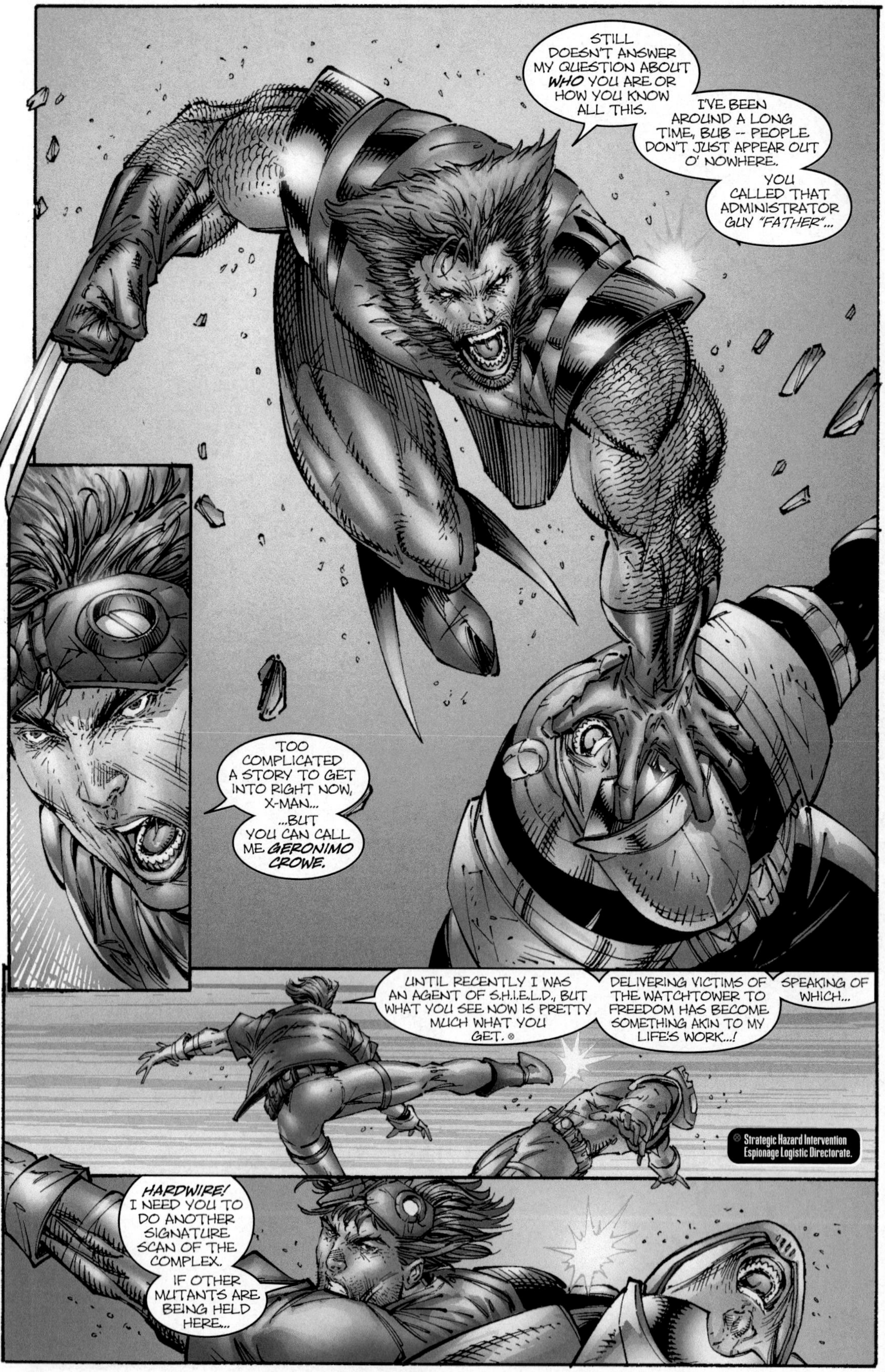
STILL DOESN'T ANSWER MY QUESTION ABOUT WHO YOU ARE OR HOW YOU KNOW ALL THIS.
I'VE BEEN AROUND A LONG TIME, BUB -- PEOPLE DON'T JUST APPEAR OUT O' NOWHERE.
YOU CALLED THAT ADMINISTRATOR GUY "FATHER"...
TOO COMPLICATED A STORY TO GET INTO RIGHT NOW, X-MAN...
...BUT YOU CAN CALL ME GERONIMO CROWE.
UNTIL RECENTLY I WAS AN AGENT OF S.H.I.E.L.D., BUT WHAT YOU SEE NOW IS PRETTY MUCH WHAT YOU GET.
DELIVERING VICTIMS OF THE WATCHTOWER TO FREEDOM HAS BECOME SOMETHING AKIN TO MY LIFE'S WORK...!
SPEAKING OF WHICH...
Strategic Hazard Intervention Espionage Logistic Directorate.
HARDWIRE! I NEED YOU TO DO ANOTHER SIGNATURE SCAN OF THE COMPLEX.
IF OTHER MUTANTS ARE BEING HELD HERE...

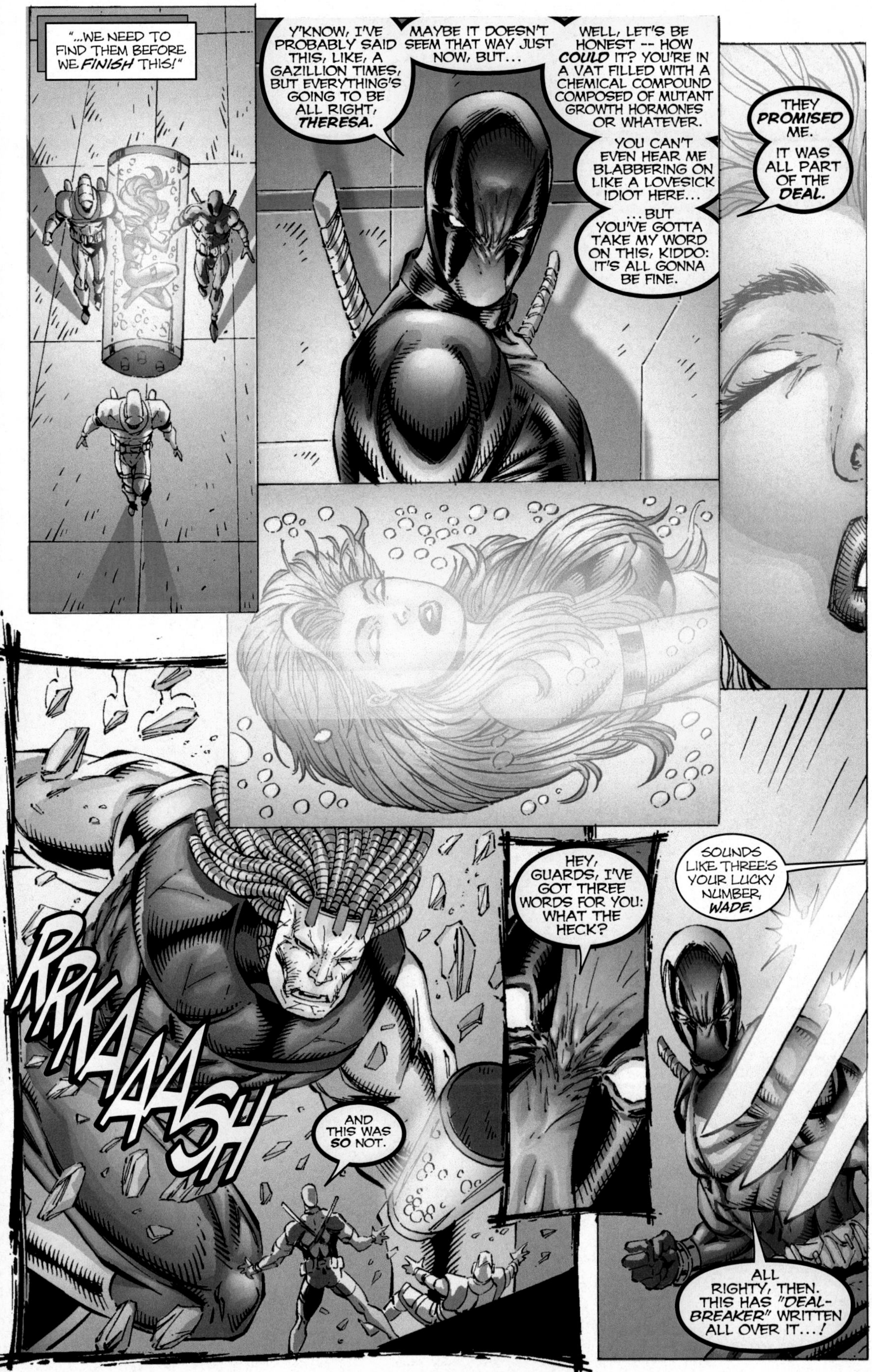
"...WE NEED TO FIND THEM BEFORE WE FINISH THIS!"
Y'KNOW, I'VE PROBABLY SAID THIS, LIKE, A GAZILLION TIMES, BUT EVERYTHING'S GOING TO BE ALL RIGHT, THERESA.
MAYBE IT DOESN'T SEEM THAT WAY JUST NOW, BUT...
WELL, LET'S BE HONEST -- HOW COULD IT? YOU'RE IN A VAT FILLED WITH A CHEMICAL COMPOUND COMPOSED OF MUTANT GROWTH HORMONES OR WHATEVER.
YOU CAN'T EVEN HEAR ME BLABBERING ON LIKE A LOVESICK IDIOT HERE...
...BUT YOU'VE GOTTA TAKE MY WORD ON THIS, KIDDO: IT'S ALL GONNA BE FINE.
THEY PROMISED ME.
IT WAS ALL PART OF THE DEAL.
RRKAAASH
AND THIS WAS SO NOT.
HEY, GUARDS, I'VE GOT THREE WORDS FOR YOU: WHAT THE HECK?
SOUNDS LIKE THREE'S YOUR LUCKY NUMBER, WADE.
ALL RIGHTY, THEN. THIS HAS "DEAL-BREAKER" WRITTEN ALL OVER IT...!

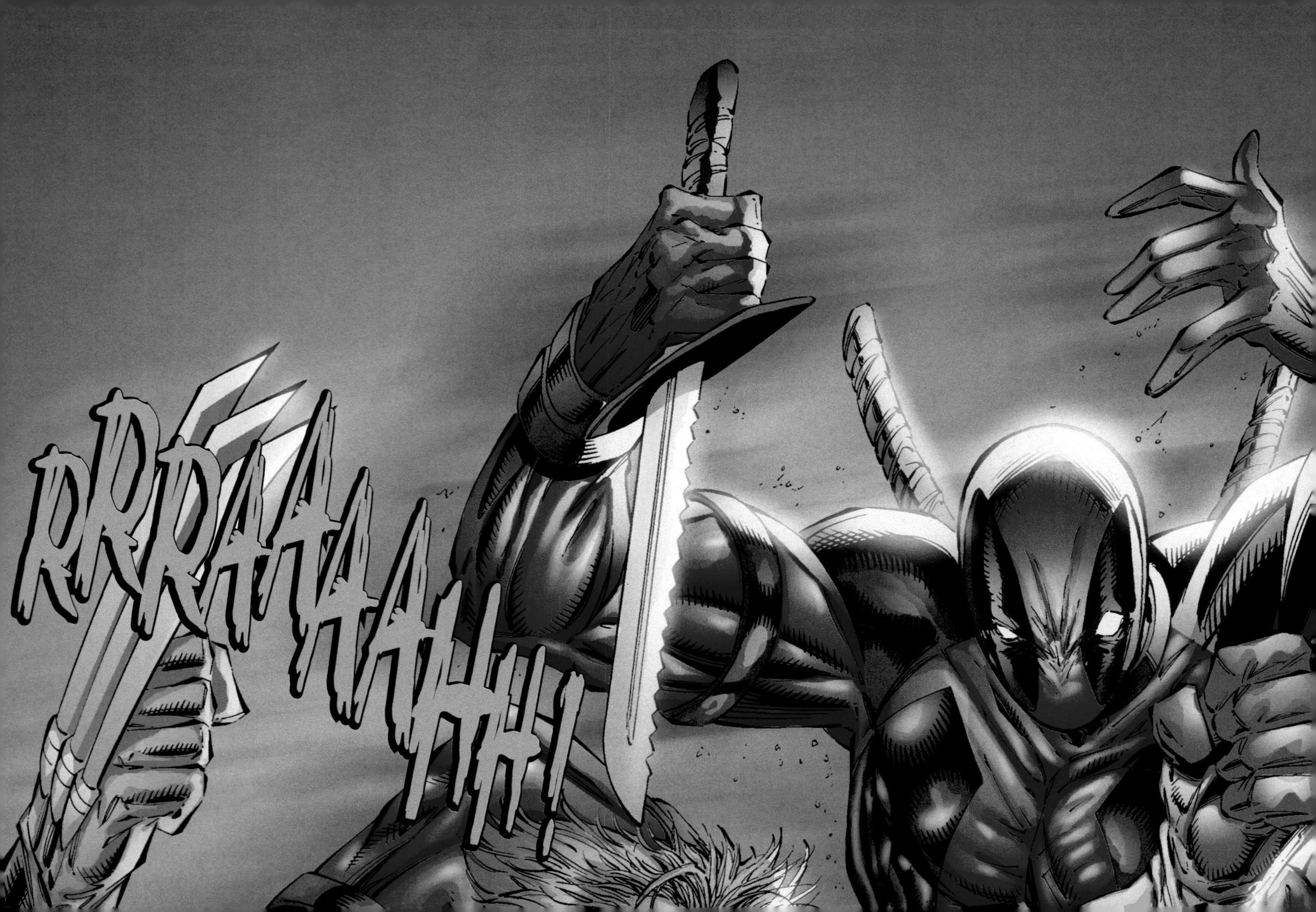
RRRAAAAAHH!

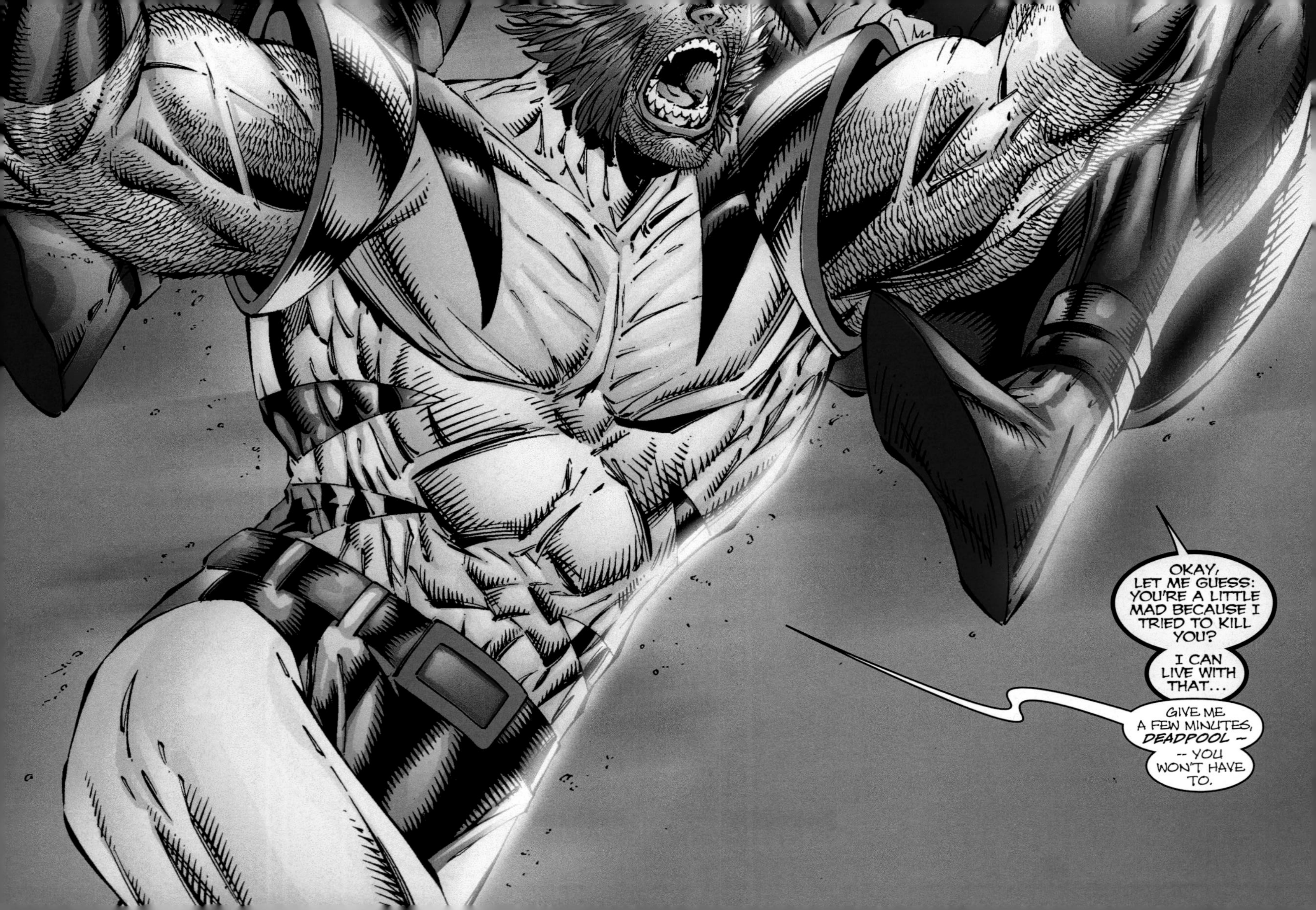
OKAY, LET ME GUESS: YOU'RE A LITTLE MAD BECAUSE I TRIED TO KILL YOU?
I CAN LIVE WITH THAT...
GIVE ME A FEW MINUTES, *DEADPOOL* --
-- YOU WON'T HAVE TO.

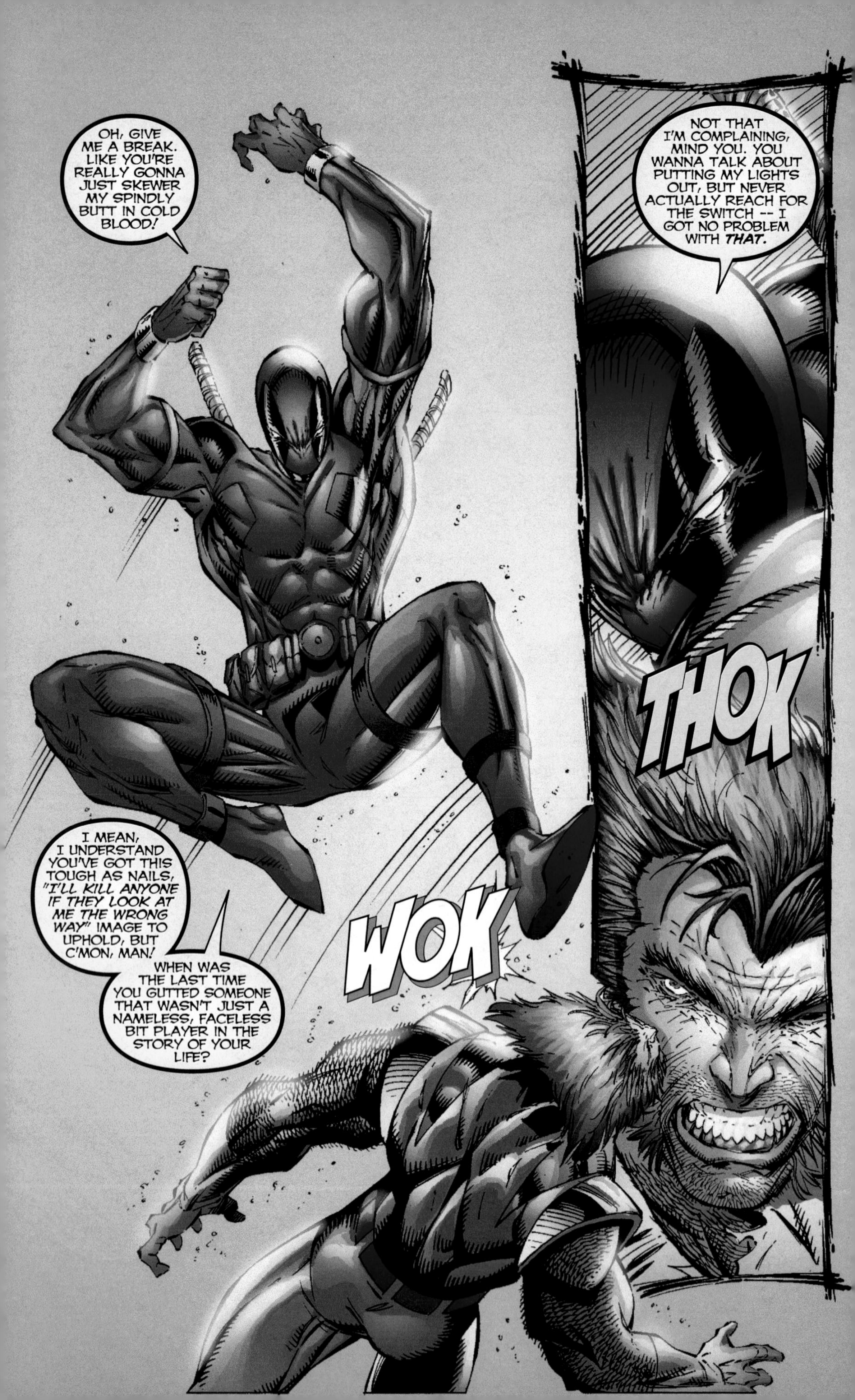
OH, GIVE ME A BREAK. LIKE YOU'RE REALLY GONNA JUST SKEWER MY SPINDLY BUTT IN COLD BLOOD!
NOT THAT I'M COMPLAINING, MIND YOU. YOU WANNA TALK ABOUT PUTTING MY LIGHTS OUT, BUT NEVER ACTUALLY REACH FOR THE SWITCH -- I GOT NO PROBLEM WITH *THAT.*
THOK
I MEAN, I UNDERSTAND YOU'VE GOT THIS TOUGH AS NAILS, *"I'LL KILL ANYONE IF THEY LOOK AT ME THE WRONG WAY"* IMAGE TO UPHOLD, BUT C'MON, MAN!
WHEN WAS THE LAST TIME YOU GUTTED SOMEONE THAT WASN'T JUST A NAMELESS, FACELESS BIT PLAYER IN THE STORY OF YOUR LIFE?
WOK

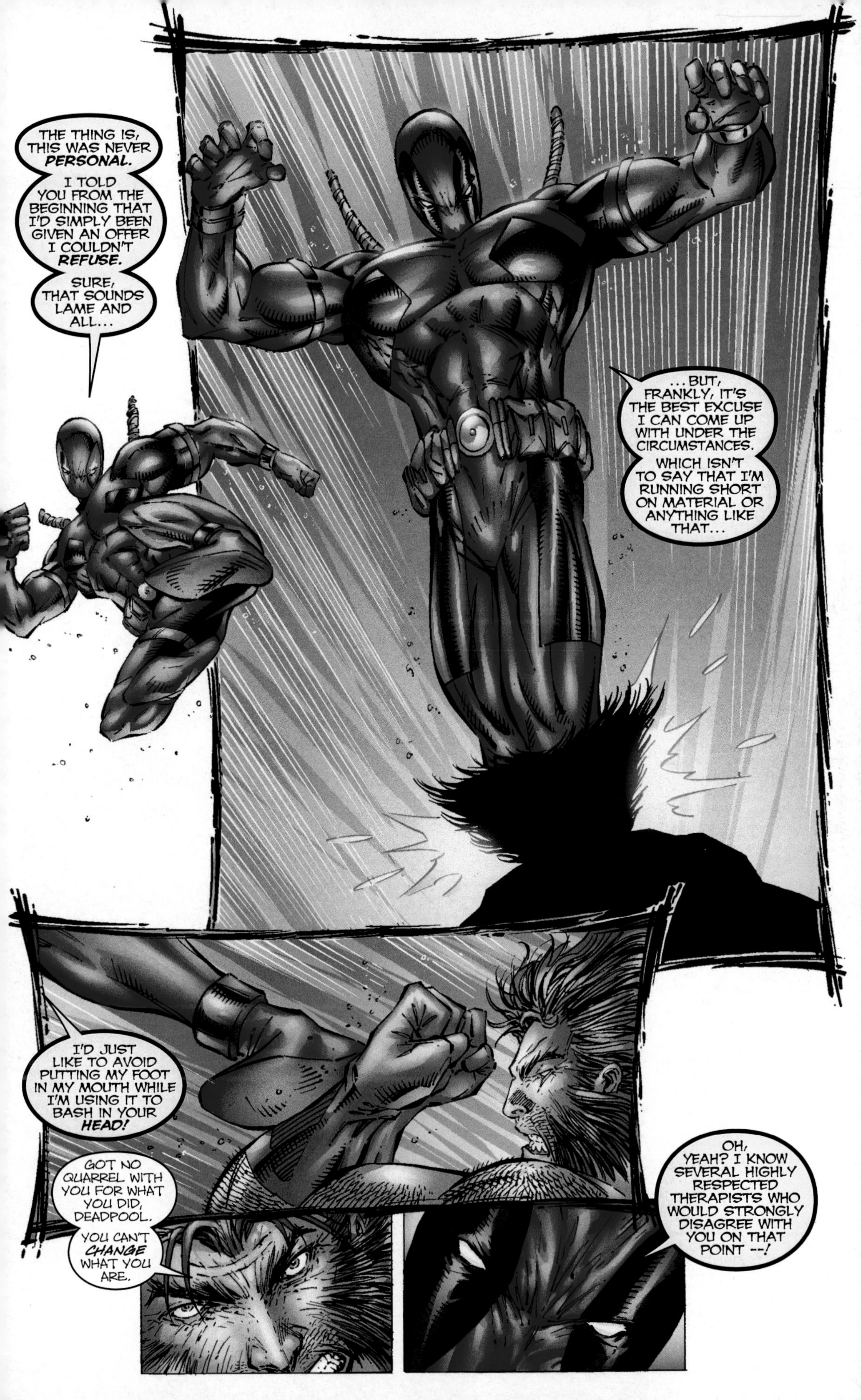
THE THING IS, THIS WAS NEVER ***PERSONAL.***
I TOLD YOU FROM THE BEGINNING THAT I'D SIMPLY BEEN GIVEN AN OFFER I COULDN'T ***REFUSE.***
SURE, THAT SOUNDS LAME AND ALL...
...BUT, FRANKLY, IT'S THE BEST EXCUSE I CAN COME UP WITH UNDER THE CIRCUMSTANCES.
WHICH ISN'T TO SAY THAT I'M RUNNING SHORT ON MATERIAL OR ANYTHING LIKE THAT...
I'D JUST LIKE TO AVOID PUTTING MY FOOT IN MY MOUTH WHILE I'M USING IT TO BASH IN YOUR ***HEAD!***
GOT NO QUARREL WITH YOU FOR WHAT YOU DID, DEADPOOL.
YOU CAN'T ***CHANGE*** WHAT YOU ARE.
OH, YEAH? I KNOW SEVERAL HIGHLY RESPECTED THERAPISTS WHO WOULD STRONGLY DISAGREE WITH YOU ON THAT POINT --!

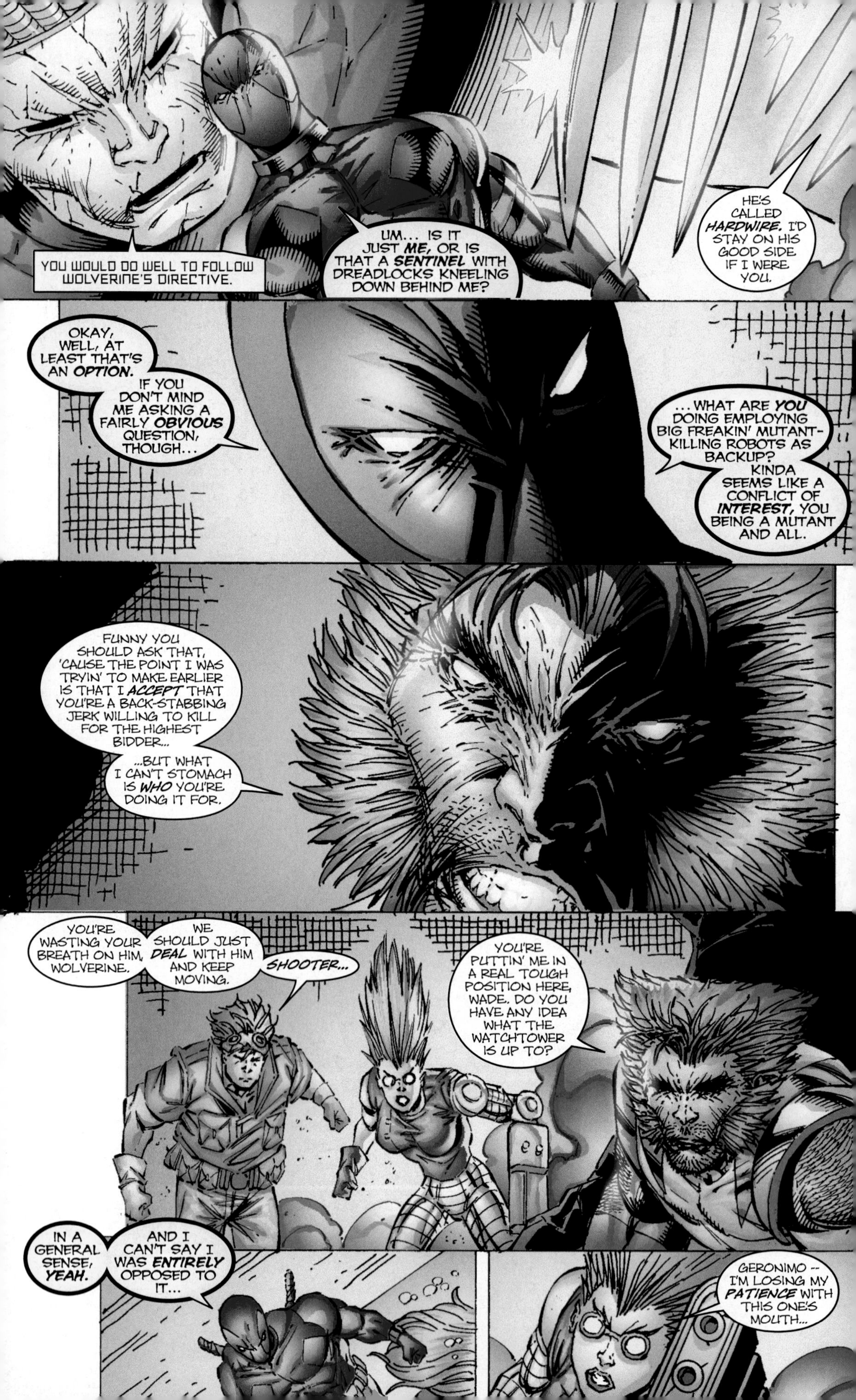
YOU WOULD DO WELL TO FOLLOW WOLVERINE'S DIRECTIVE.
UM... IS IT JUST ME, OR IS THAT A SENTINEL WITH DREADLOCKS KNEELING DOWN BEHIND ME?
HE'S CALLED HARDWIRE. I'D STAY ON HIS GOOD SIDE IF I WERE YOU.
OKAY, WELL, AT LEAST THAT'S AN OPTION.
IF YOU DON'T MIND ME ASKING A FAIRLY OBVIOUS QUESTION, THOUGH...
...WHAT ARE YOU DOING EMPLOYING BIG FREAKIN' MUTANT-KILLING ROBOTS AS BACKUP?
KINDA SEEMS LIKE A CONFLICT OF INTEREST, YOU BEING A MUTANT AND ALL.
FUNNY YOU SHOULD ASK THAT, 'CAUSE THE POINT I WAS TRYIN' TO MAKE EARLIER IS THAT I ACCEPT THAT YOU'RE A BACK-STABBING JERK WILLING TO KILL FOR THE HIGHEST BIDDER...
...BUT WHAT I CAN'T STOMACH IS WHO YOU'RE DOING IT FOR.
YOU'RE WASTING YOUR BREATH ON HIM, WOLVERINE.
WE SHOULD JUST DEAL WITH HIM AND KEEP MOVING.
SHOOTER...
YOU'RE PUTTIN' ME IN A REAL TOUGH POSITION HERE, WADE. DO YOU HAVE ANY IDEA WHAT THE WATCHTOWER IS UP TO?
IN A GENERAL SENSE, YEAH.
AND I CAN'T SAY I WAS ENTIRELY OPPOSED TO IT...
GERONIMO -- I'M LOSING MY PATIENCE WITH THIS ONE'S MOUTH...

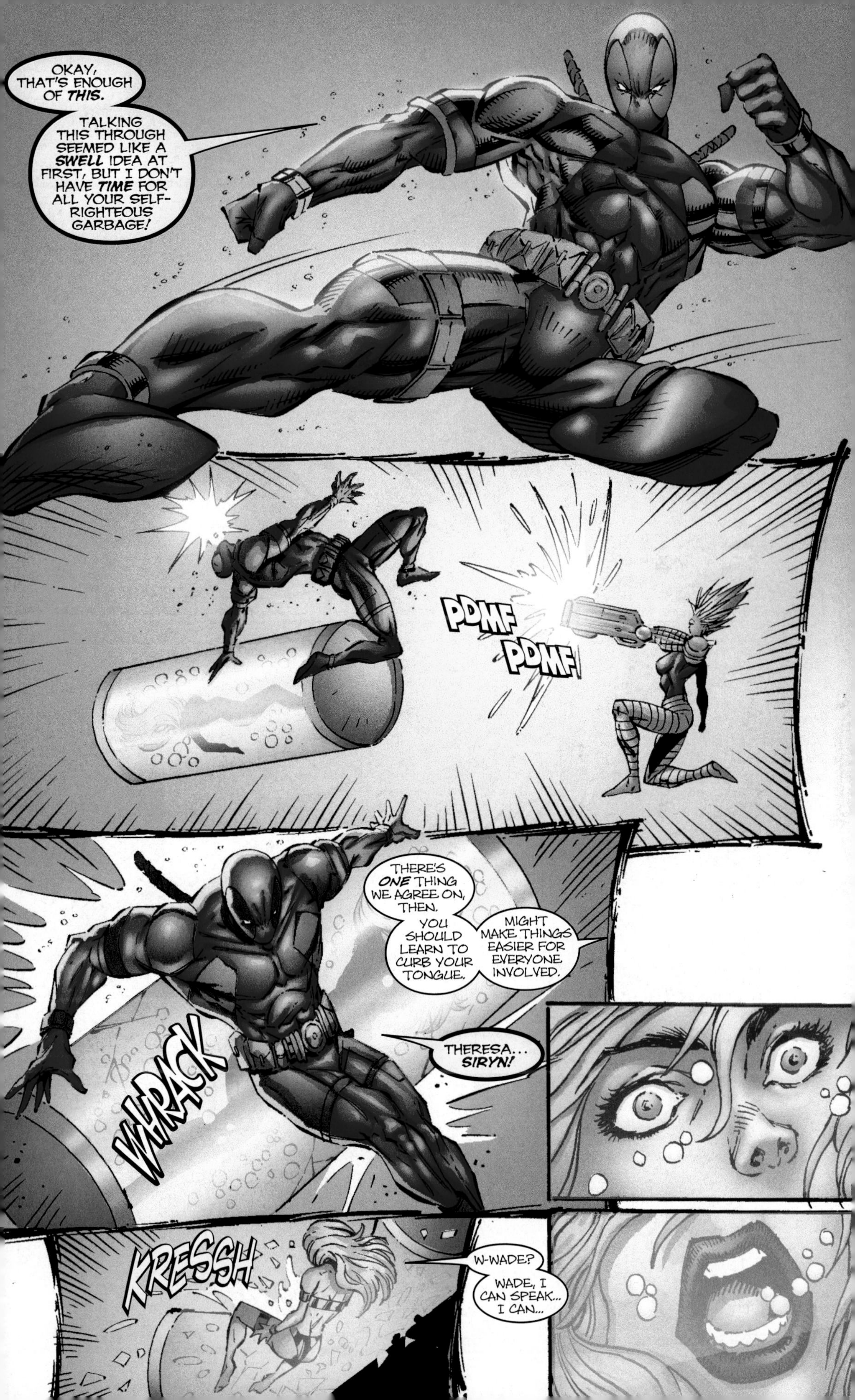
OKAY, THAT'S ENOUGH OF THIS.
TALKING THIS THROUGH SEEMED LIKE A SWELL IDEA AT FIRST, BUT I DON'T HAVE TIME FOR ALL YOUR SELF-RIGHTEOUS GARBAGE!
PDMF
PDMF
THERE'S ONE THING WE AGREE ON, THEN.
YOU SHOULD LEARN TO CURB YOUR TONGUE.
MIGHT MAKE THINGS EASIER FOR EVERYONE INVOLVED.
WHRACK
THERESA... SIRYN!
KRESSH
W-WADE?
WADE, I CAN SPEAK... I CAN...

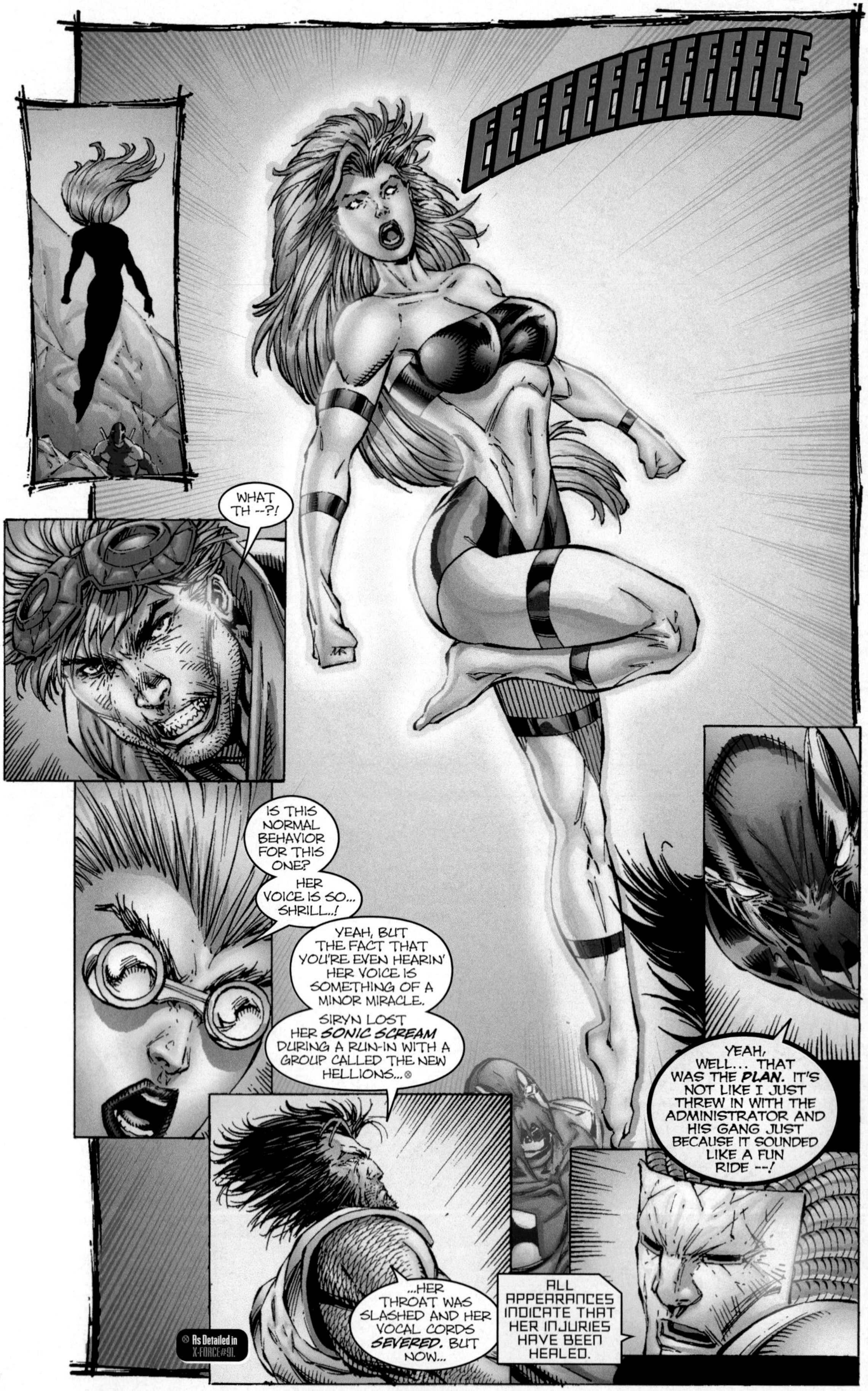
EEEEEEEEEEEEE
WHAT TH --?!
IS THIS NORMAL BEHAVIOR FOR THIS ONE?
HER VOICE IS SO... SHRILL...!
YEAH, BUT THE FACT THAT YOU'RE EVEN HEARIN' HER VOICE IS SOMETHING OF A MINOR MIRACLE.
SIRYN LOST HER SONIC SCREAM DURING A RUN-IN WITH A GROUP CALLED THE NEW HELLIONS...⊗
...HER THROAT WAS SLASHED AND HER VOCAL CORDS SEVERED. BUT NOW...
ALL APPEARANCES INDICATE THAT HER INJURIES HAVE BEEN HEALED.
YEAH, WELL... THAT WAS THE PLAN. IT'S NOT LIKE I JUST THREW IN WITH THE ADMINISTRATOR AND HIS GANG JUST BECAUSE IT SOUNDED LIKE A FUN RIDE --!
⊗ As Detailed in X-FORCE #91.

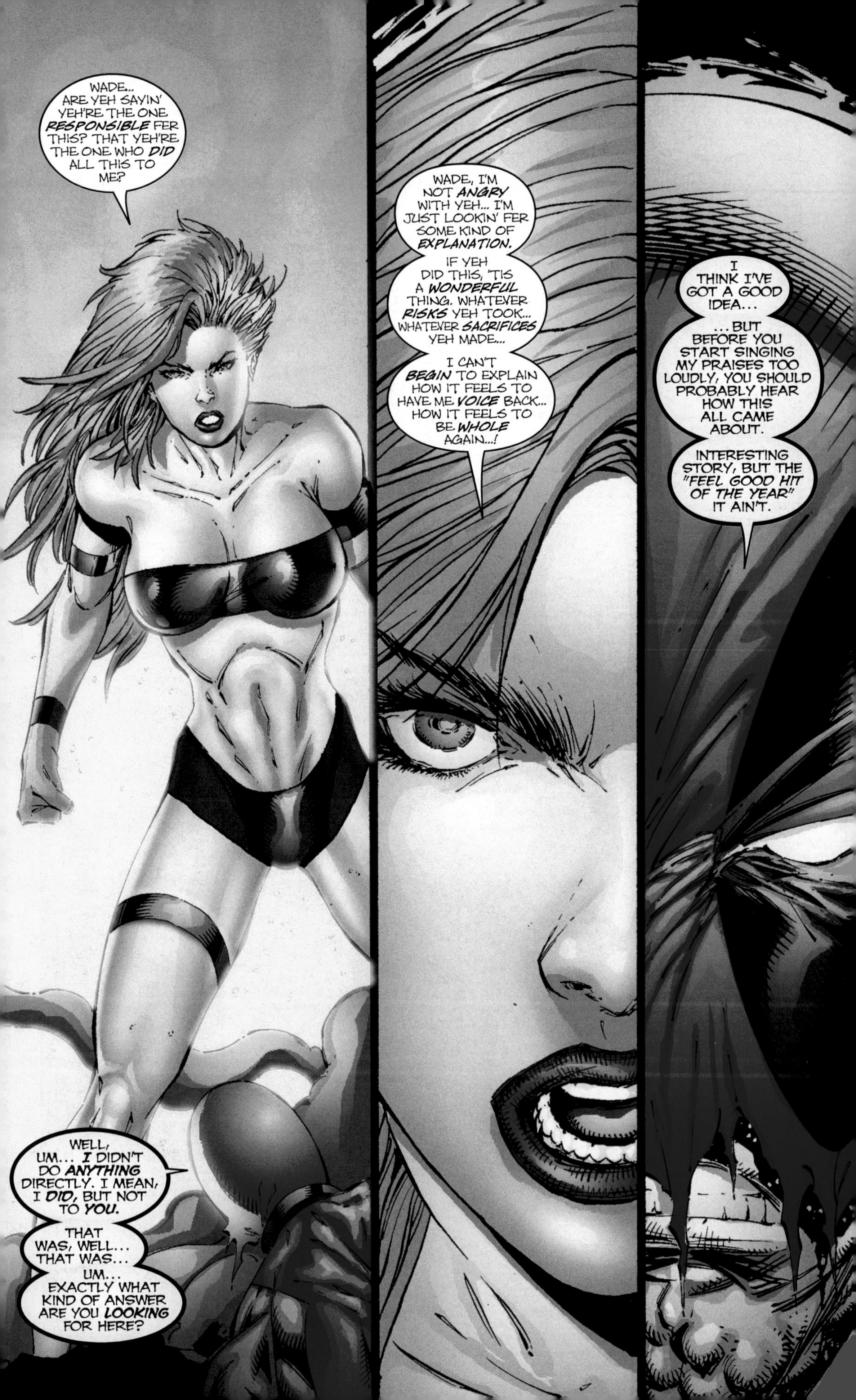
WADE... ARE YEH SAYIN' YEH'RE THE ONE RESPONSIBLE FER THIS? THAT YEH'RE THE ONE WHO DID ALL THIS TO ME?
WELL, UM... I DIDN'T DO ANYTHING DIRECTLY. I MEAN, I DID, BUT NOT TO YOU.
THAT WAS, WELL... THAT WAS... UM...
EXACTLY WHAT KIND OF ANSWER ARE YOU LOOKING FOR HERE?
WADE, I'M NOT ANGRY WITH YEH... I'M JUST LOOKIN' FER SOME KIND OF EXPLANATION.
IF YEH DID THIS, 'TIS A WONDERFUL THING. WHATEVER RISKS YEH TOOK... WHATEVER SACRIFICES YEH MADE...
I CAN'T BEGIN TO EXPLAIN HOW IT FEELS TO HAVE ME VOICE BACK... HOW IT FEELS TO BE WHOLE AGAIN...!
I THINK I'VE GOT A GOOD IDEA...
... BUT BEFORE YOU START SINGING MY PRAISES TOO LOUDLY, YOU SHOULD PROBABLY HEAR HOW THIS ALL CAME ABOUT.
INTERESTING STORY, BUT THE "FEEL GOOD HIT OF THE YEAR" IT AIN'T.

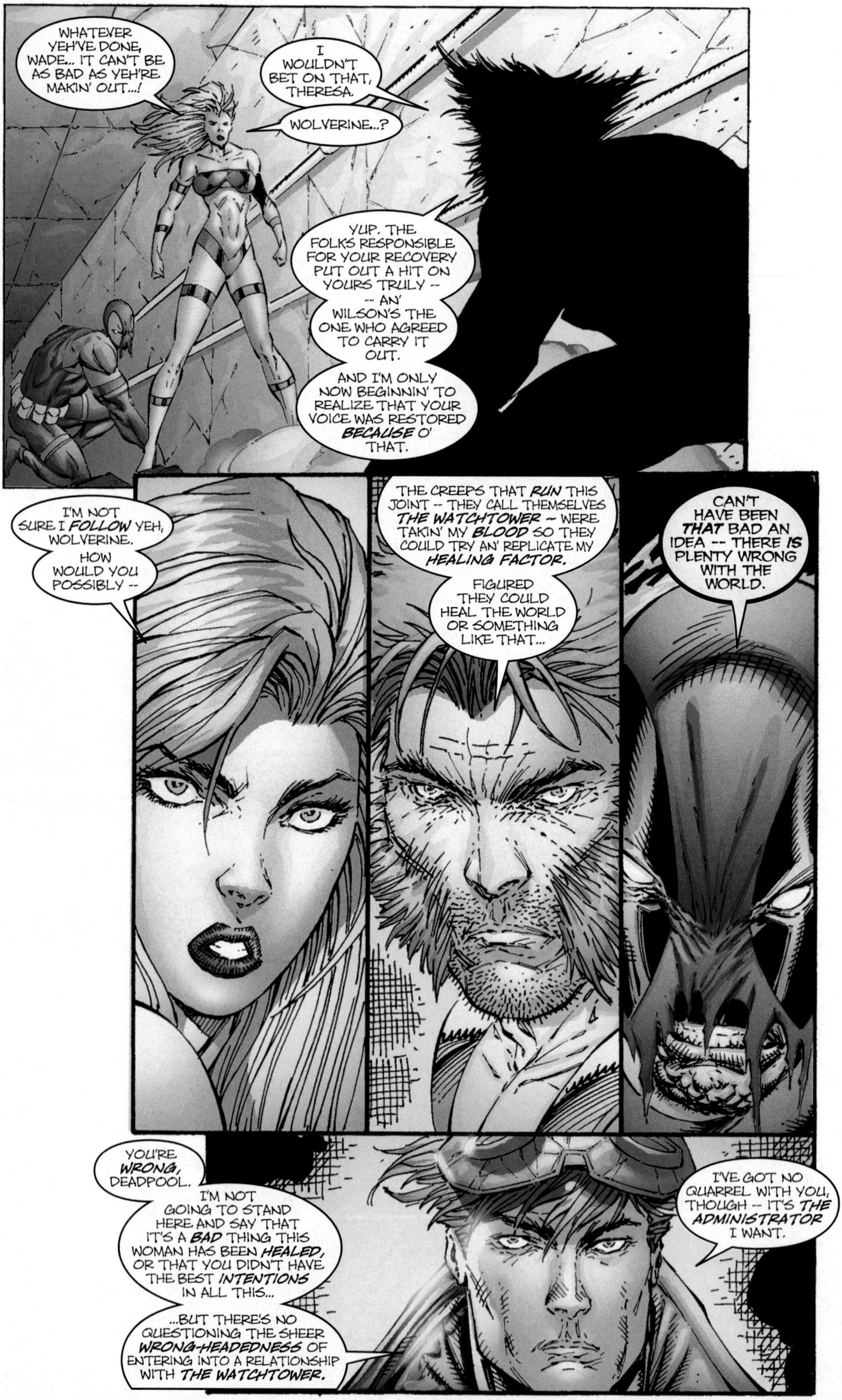
WHATEVER YEH'VE DONE, WADE... IT CAN'T BE AS BAD AS YEH'RE MAKIN' OUT...!
I WOULDN'T BET ON THAT, THERESA.
WOLVERINE...?
YUP. THE FOLKS RESPONSIBLE FOR YOUR RECOVERY PUT OUT A HIT ON YOURS TRULY --
-- AN' WILSON'S THE ONE WHO AGREED TO CARRY IT OUT.
AND I'M ONLY NOW BEGINNIN' TO REALIZE THAT YOUR VOICE WAS RESTORED BECAUSE O' THAT.
I'M NOT SURE I FOLLOW YEH, WOLVERINE.
HOW WOULD YOU POSSIBLY --
THE CREEPS THAT RUN THIS JOINT -- THEY CALL THEMSELVES THE WATCHTOWER -- WERE TAKIN' MY BLOOD SO THEY COULD TRY AN' REPLICATE MY HEALING FACTOR.
FIGURED THEY COULD HEAL THE WORLD OR SOMETHING LIKE THAT...
CAN'T HAVE BEEN THAT BAD AN IDEA -- THERE IS PLENTY WRONG WITH THE WORLD.
YOU'RE WRONG, DEADPOOL.
I'M NOT GOING TO STAND HERE AND SAY THAT IT'S A BAD THING THIS WOMAN HAS BEEN HEALED, OR THAT YOU DIDN'T HAVE THE BEST INTENTIONS IN ALL THIS...
...BUT THERE'S NO QUESTIONING THE SHEER WRONG-HEADEDNESS OF ENTERING INTO A RELATIONSHIP WITH THE WATCHTOWER.
I'VE GOT NO QUARREL WITH YOU, THOUGH -- IT'S THE ADMINISTRATOR I WANT.

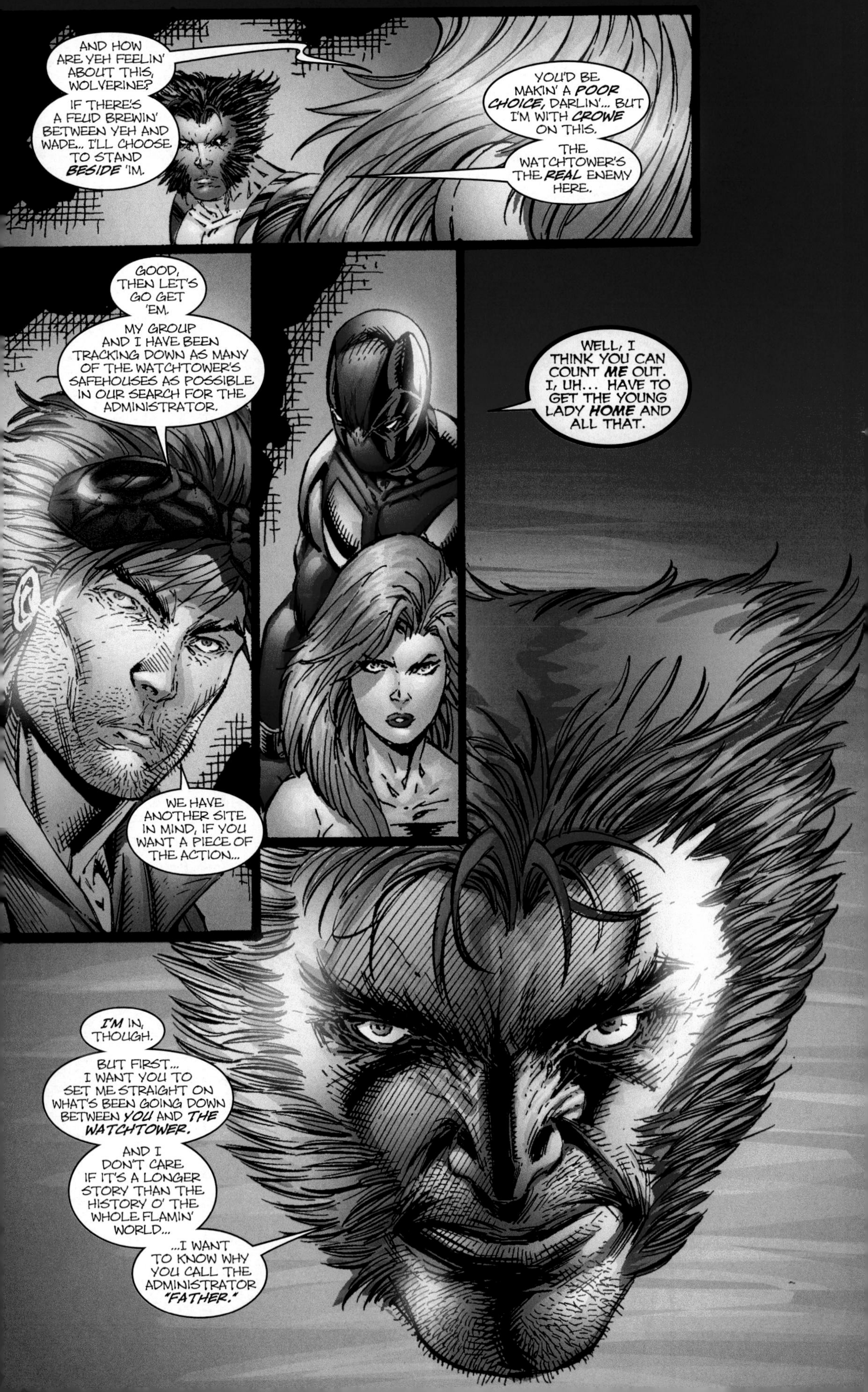
AND HOW ARE YEH FEELIN' ABOUT THIS, WOLVERINE?
IF THERE'S A FEUD BREWIN' BETWEEN YEH AND WADE... I'LL CHOOSE TO STAND BESIDE 'IM.
YOU'D BE MAKIN' A POOR CHOICE, DARLIN'... BUT I'M WITH CROWE ON THIS.
THE WATCHTOWER'S THE REAL ENEMY HERE.
GOOD, THEN LET'S GO GET 'EM.
MY GROUP AND I HAVE BEEN TRACKING DOWN AS MANY OF THE WATCHTOWER'S SAFEHOUSES AS POSSIBLE IN OUR SEARCH FOR THE ADMINISTRATOR.
WE HAVE ANOTHER SITE IN MIND, IF YOU WANT A PIECE OF THE ACTION...
WELL, I THINK YOU CAN COUNT ME OUT. I, UH... HAVE TO GET THE YOUNG LADY HOME AND ALL THAT.
I'M IN, THOUGH.
BUT FIRST... I WANT YOU TO SET ME STRAIGHT ON WHAT'S BEEN GOING DOWN BETWEEN YOU AND THE WATCHTOWER.
AND I DON'T CARE IF IT'S A LONGER STORY THAN THE HISTORY O' THE WHOLE FLAMIN' WORLD...
...I WANT TO KNOW WHY YOU CALL THE ADMINISTRATOR "FATHER."

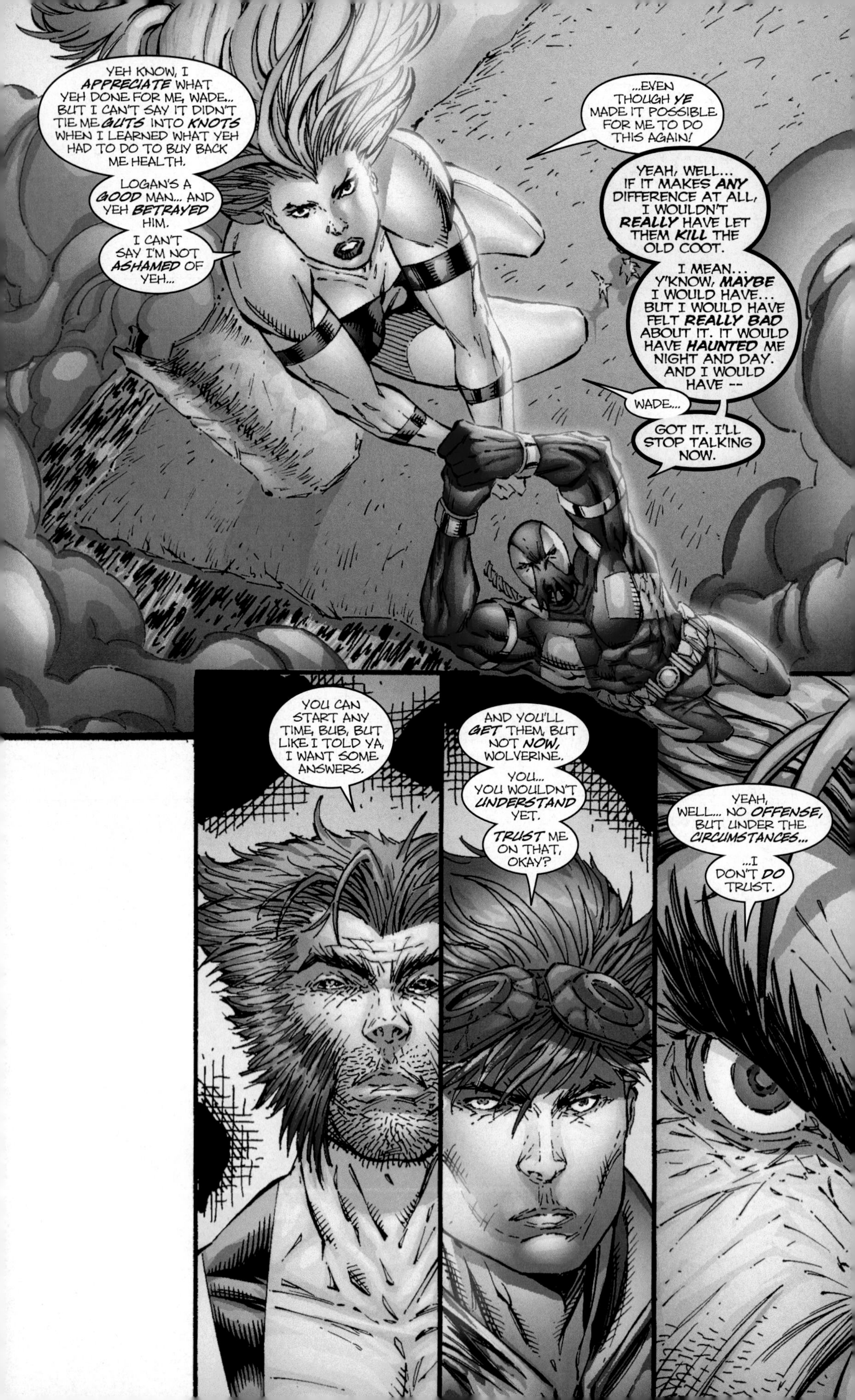
YEH KNOW, I APPRECIATE WHAT YEH DONE FOR ME, WADE... BUT I CAN'T SAY IT DIDN'T TIE ME GUTS INTO KNOTS WHEN I LEARNED WHAT YEH HAD TO DO TO BUY BACK ME HEALTH.
LOGAN'S A GOOD MAN... AND YEH BETRAYED HIM.
I CAN'T SAY I'M NOT ASHAMED OF YEH...
...EVEN THOUGH YE MADE IT POSSIBLE FOR ME TO DO THIS AGAIN!
YEAH, WELL... IF IT MAKES ANY DIFFERENCE AT ALL, I WOULDN'T REALLY HAVE LET THEM KILL THE OLD COOT.
I MEAN... Y'KNOW, MAYBE I WOULD HAVE... BUT I WOULD HAVE FELT REALLY BAD ABOUT IT. IT WOULD HAVE HAUNTED ME NIGHT AND DAY. AND I WOULD HAVE --
WADE...
GOT IT. I'LL STOP TALKING NOW.
YOU CAN START ANY TIME, BUB, BUT LIKE I TOLD YA, I WANT SOME ANSWERS.
AND YOU'LL GET THEM, BUT NOT NOW, WOLVERINE.
YOU... YOU WOULDN'T UNDERSTAND YET.
TRUST ME ON THAT, OKAY?
YEAH, WELL... NO OFFENSE, BUT UNDER THE CIRCUMSTANCES...
...I DON'T DO TRUST.

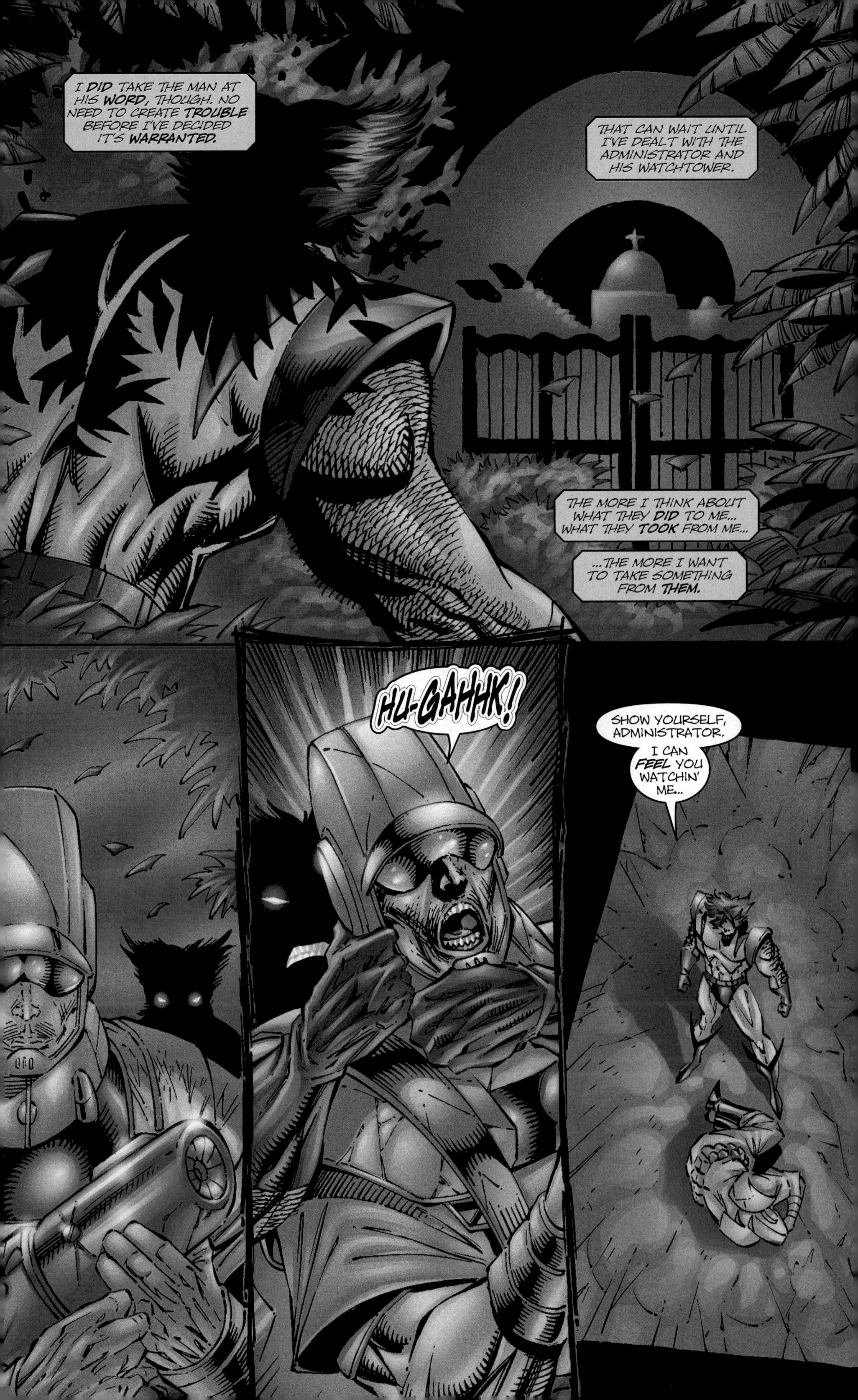
I DID TAKE THE MAN AT HIS WORD, THOUGH. NO NEED TO CREATE TROUBLE BEFORE I'VE DECIDED IT'S WARRANTED.
THAT CAN WAIT UNTIL I'VE DEALT WITH THE ADMINISTRATOR AND HIS WATCHTOWER.
THE MORE I THINK ABOUT WHAT THEY DID TO ME... WHAT THEY TOOK FROM ME...
...THE MORE I WANT TO TAKE SOMETHING FROM THEM.
HU-GAHHK!
SHOW YOURSELF, ADMINISTRATOR.
I CAN FEEL YOU WATCHIN' ME...

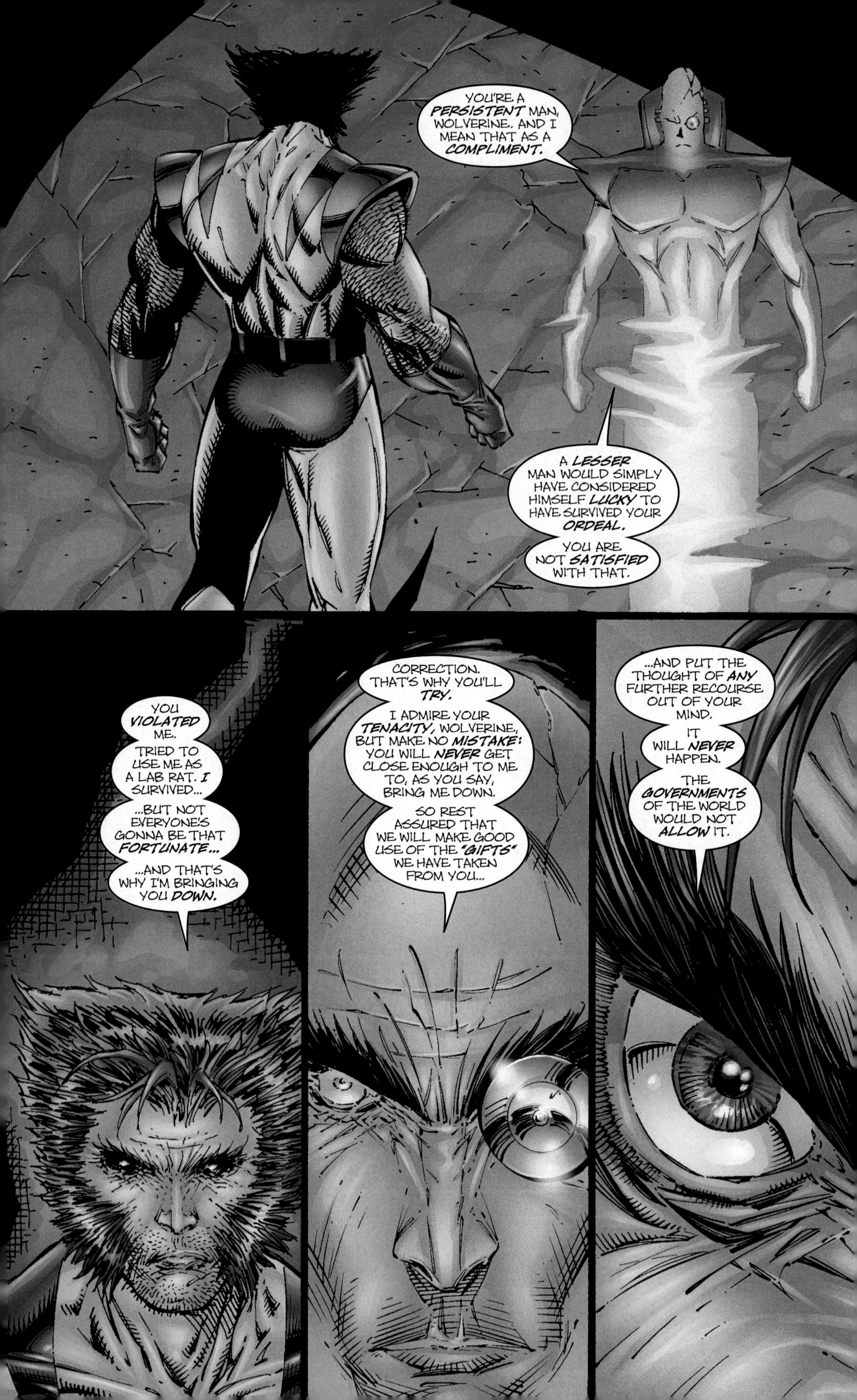
YOU'RE A PERSISTENT MAN, WOLVERINE. AND I MEAN THAT AS A COMPLIMENT.
A LESSER MAN WOULD SIMPLY HAVE CONSIDERED HIMSELF LUCKY TO HAVE SURVIVED YOUR ORDEAL.
YOU ARE NOT SATISFIED WITH THAT.
YOU VIOLATED ME.
TRIED TO USE ME AS A LAB RAT. I SURVIVED...
...BUT NOT EVERYONE'S GONNA BE THAT FORTUNATE...
...AND THAT'S WHY I'M BRINGING YOU DOWN.
CORRECTION. THAT'S WHY YOU'LL TRY.
I ADMIRE YOUR TENACITY, WOLVERINE, BUT MAKE NO MISTAKE: YOU WILL NEVER GET CLOSE ENOUGH TO ME TO, AS YOU SAY, BRING ME DOWN.
SO REST ASSURED THAT WE WILL MAKE GOOD USE OF THE "GIFTS" WE HAVE TAKEN FROM YOU...
...AND PUT THE THOUGHT OF ANY FURTHER RECOURSE OUT OF YOUR MIND.
IT WILL NEVER HAPPEN.
THE GOVERNMENTS OF THE WORLD WOULD NOT ALLOW IT.

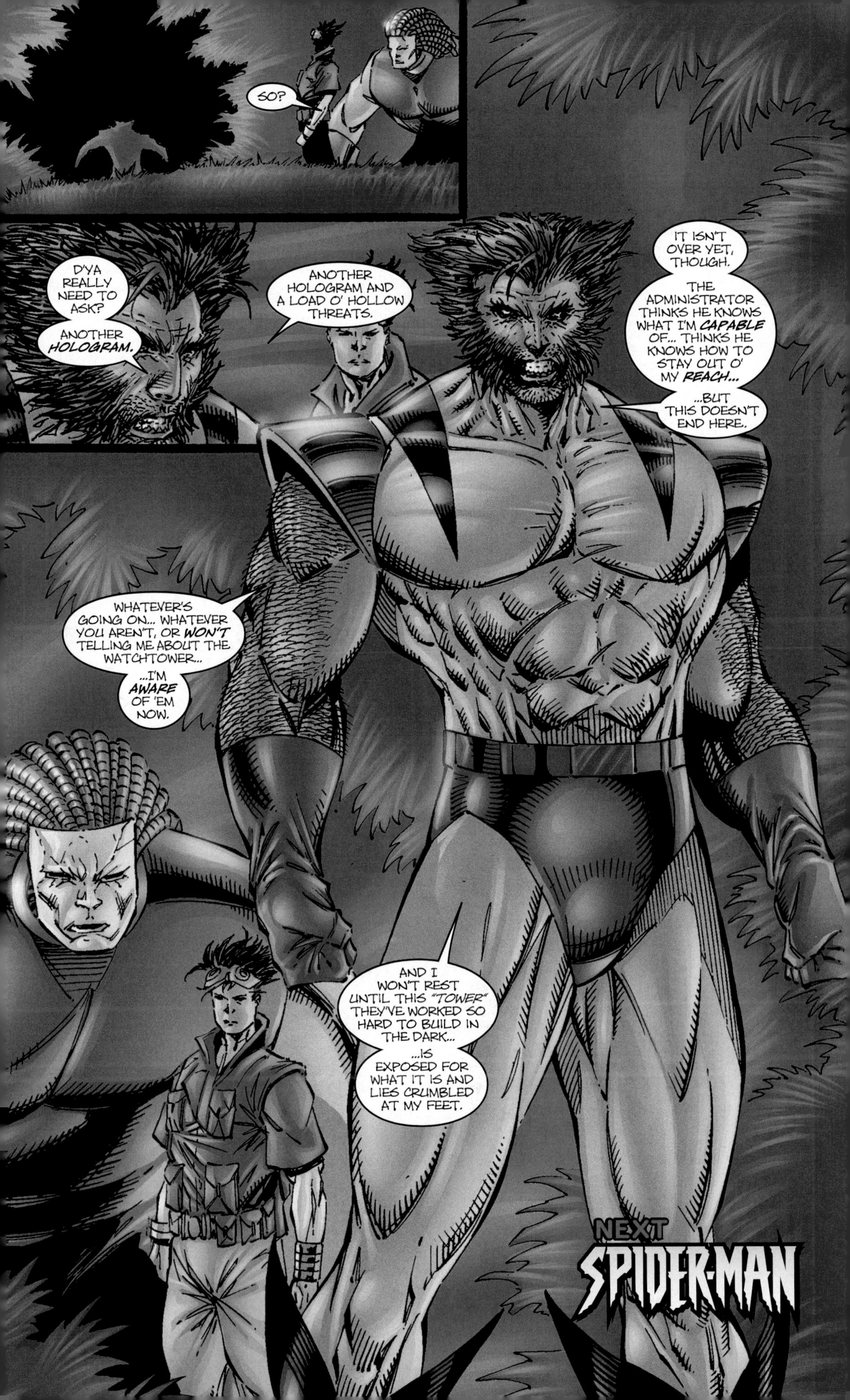
SO?
D'YA REALLY NEED TO ASK?
ANOTHER *HOLOGRAM.*
ANOTHER HOLOGRAM AND A LOAD O' HOLLOW THREATS.
IT ISN'T OVER YET, THOUGH.
THE ADMINISTRATOR THINKS HE KNOWS WHAT I'M *CAPABLE* OF... THINKS HE KNOWS HOW TO STAY OUT O' MY *REACH*...
...BUT THIS DOESN'T END HERE.
WHATEVER'S GOING ON... WHATEVER YOU AREN'T, OR *WON'T* TELLING ME ABOUT THE WATCHTOWER...
...I'M *AWARE* OF 'EM NOW.
AND I WON'T REST UNTIL THIS *"TOWER"* THEY'VE WORKED SO HARD TO BUILD IN THE DARK...
...IS EXPOSED FOR WHAT IT IS AND LIES CRUMBLED AT MY FEET.
NEXT
SPIDER-MAN

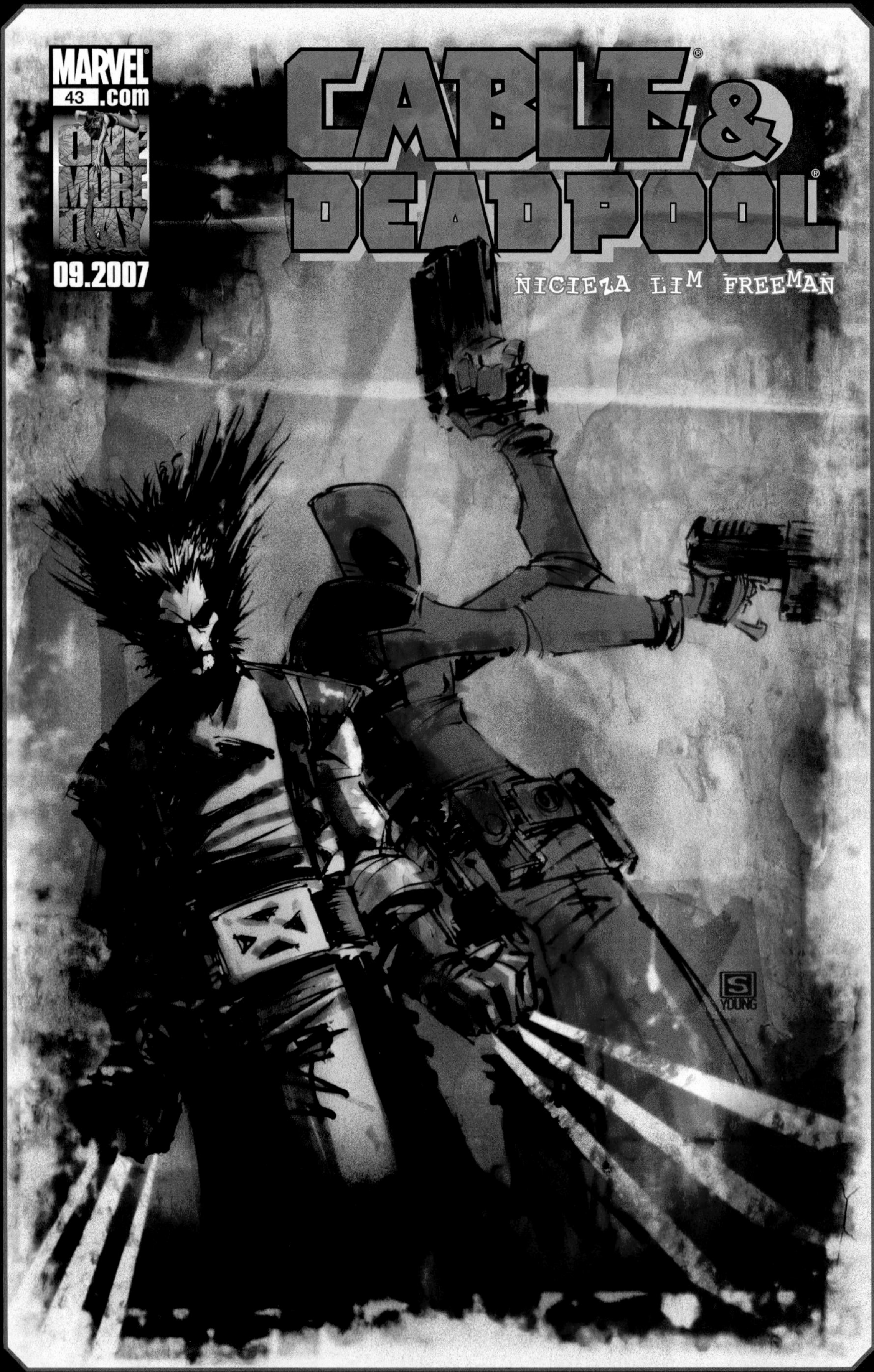
MARVEL
43 .com
ONE MORE DAY
09.2007
CABLE & DEADPOOL
NICIEZA LIM FREEMAN
S YOUNG

WITH FRIENDS LIKE THESE--?

FABIAN NICIEZA-WRITER RON LIM-PENCILER
JEREMY FREEMAN-INKER GOTHAM-COLORISTS
DAVE SHARPE-LETTERER SKOTTIE YOUNG-COVER
NICOLE BOOSE-EDITOR JOE QUESADA-EDITOR IN CHIEF DAN BUCKLEY-PUBLISHER

IRENE MERRYWEATHER

I WAS NATHAN'S CHIEF OF STAFF...AND HIS FRIEND. IT'S BEEN SIX WEEKS SINCE... SINCE HE *DIED*.

I'M BACK IN *NEW YORK* NOW. SEVEN-FIGURE BOOK DEALS ARE FALLING IN MY LAP.

WHAT SHOULD A FORMER REPORTER DO WHEN THE GREATEST OPPORTUNITY OF HER LIFE IS WRITING AN *OBITUARY* FOR THE MAN SHE LOVED?

DOMINO

I SPENT FIRST THREE WEEKS DEBRIEFING *S.H.I.E.L.D.* ABOUT HOW CABLE'S SOUTH PACIFIC HAVEN, *PROVIDENCE*, WAS MAULED BY THE ALIEN *HECATOMB*...

...AND HOW HE WAS KILLED BY THE *MARAUDERS*.

I SPENT THE NEXT THREE WEEKS DRINKING. ENOUGH. TIME TO MOVE FORWARD. BUT WHAT DIRECTION DO YOU TAKE WHEN YOU HAVE NOWHERE TO GO...?

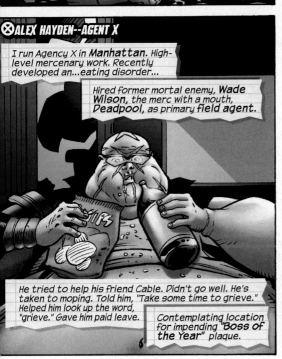

ALEX HAYDEN--AGENT X

I run Agency X in *Manhattan*. High-level mercenary work. Recently developed an...eating disorder...

Hired former mortal enemy, *Wade Wilson*, the merc with a mouth, *Deadpool*, as primary field *agent*.

He tried to help his friend Cable. Didn't go well. He's taken to moping. Told him, "Take some time to grieve." Helped him look up the word, "grieve." Gave him paid leave.

Contemplating location for impending "Boss of the Year" plaque.

BOB, AGENT OF HYDRA

WHERE DO I LOOK? THIS WAY-- NO--WHERE? THERE?

THAT'S WHERE THEY ARE? DO THEY KNOW MY REAL NAME? I MEAN, *BOB*, SURE, SAYS IT OVER MY HEAD, BUT LAST NAME AND STUFF?

I-- I HAVE A FAMILY...I ONLY JOINED *HYDRA* 'CAUSE MY WIFE WAS NAGGIN' THAT I COULDN'T FIND A JOB WITH HEALTH INSURANCE, SO...

WHAT? I'M OUT OF SPACE ALREADY...?

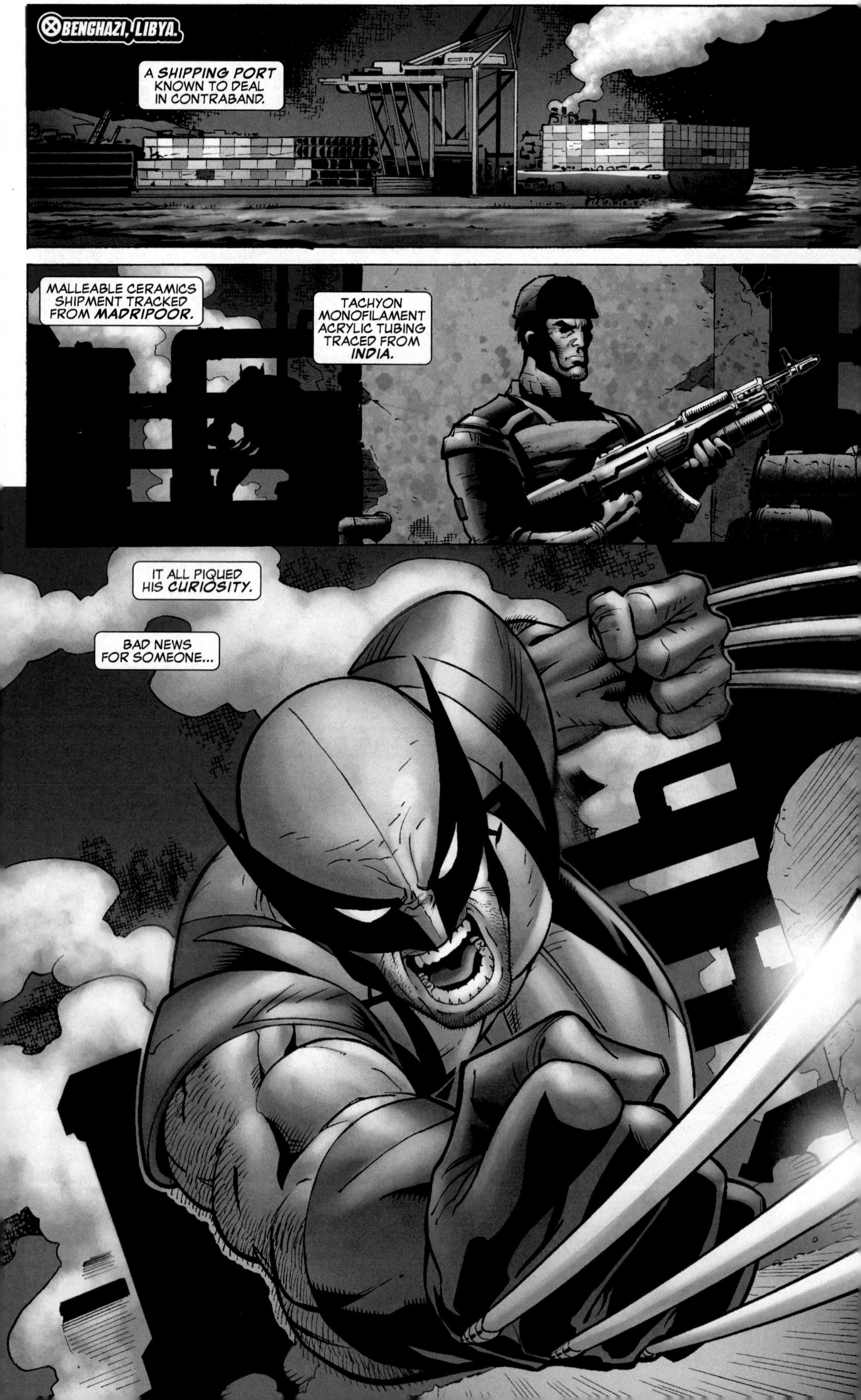
BENGHAZI, LIBYA.
A SHIPPING PORT KNOWN TO DEAL IN CONTRABAND.
MALLEABLE CERAMICS SHIPMENT TRACKED FROM MADRIPOOR.
TACHYON MONOFILAMENT ACRYLIC TUBING TRACED FROM INDIA.
IT ALL PIQUED HIS CURIOSITY.
BAD NEWS FOR SOMEONE...

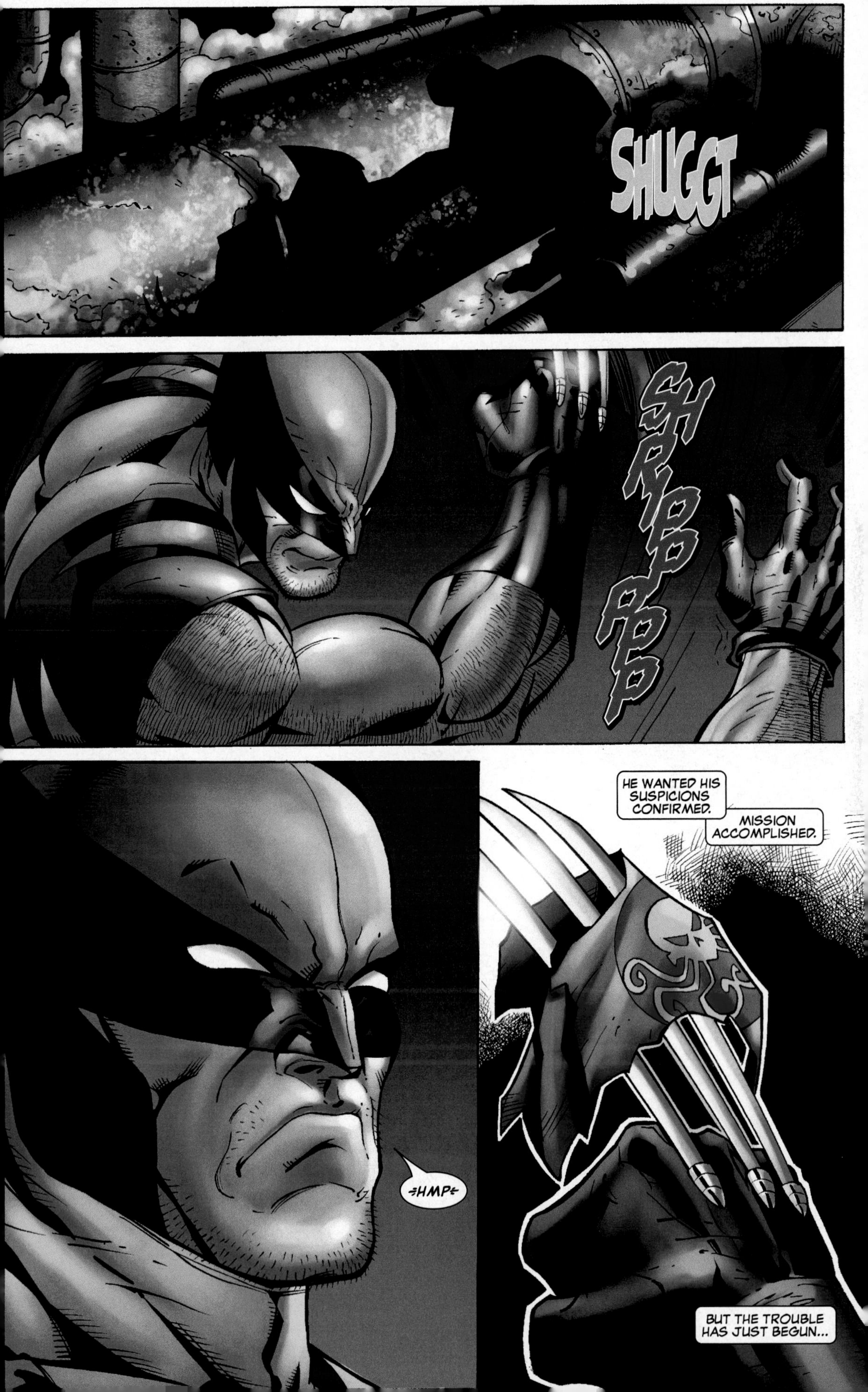
SHUGGT
SHRRPPPP
HE WANTED HIS SUSPICIONS CONFIRMED.
MISSION ACCOMPLISHED.
HMP
BUT THE TROUBLE HAS JUST BEGUN...

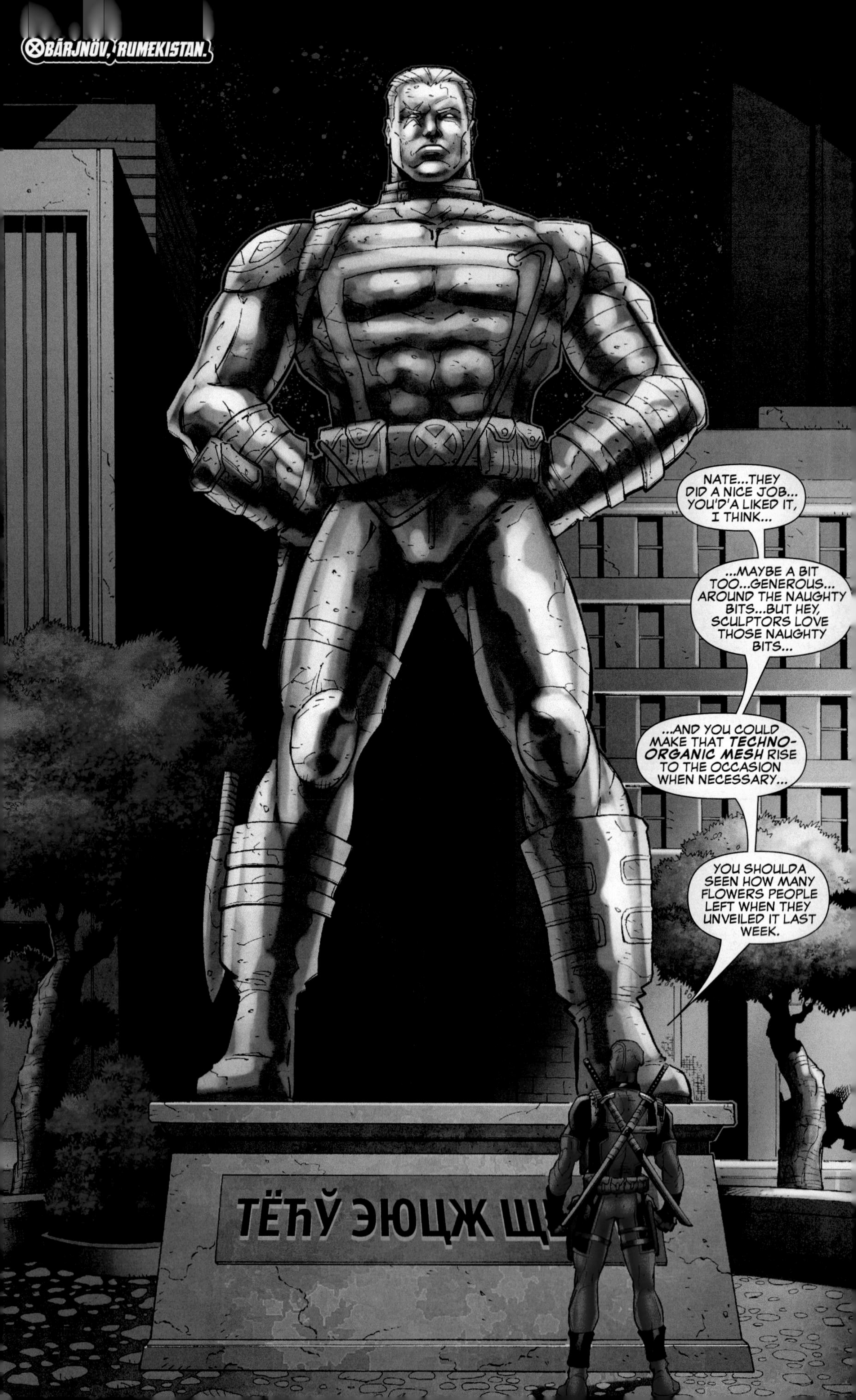
BÁRJNÖV, RUMEKISTAN.
NATE...THEY DID A NICE JOB... YOU'D'A LIKED IT, I THINK...
...MAYBE A BIT TOO...GENEROUS... AROUND THE NAUGHTY BITS...BUT HEY, SCULPTORS LOVE THOSE NAUGHTY BITS...
...AND YOU COULD MAKE THAT TECHNO-ORGANIC MESH RISE TO THE OCCASION WHEN NECESSARY...
YOU SHOULDA SEEN HOW MANY FLOWERS PEOPLE LEFT WHEN THEY UNVEILED IT LAST WEEK.

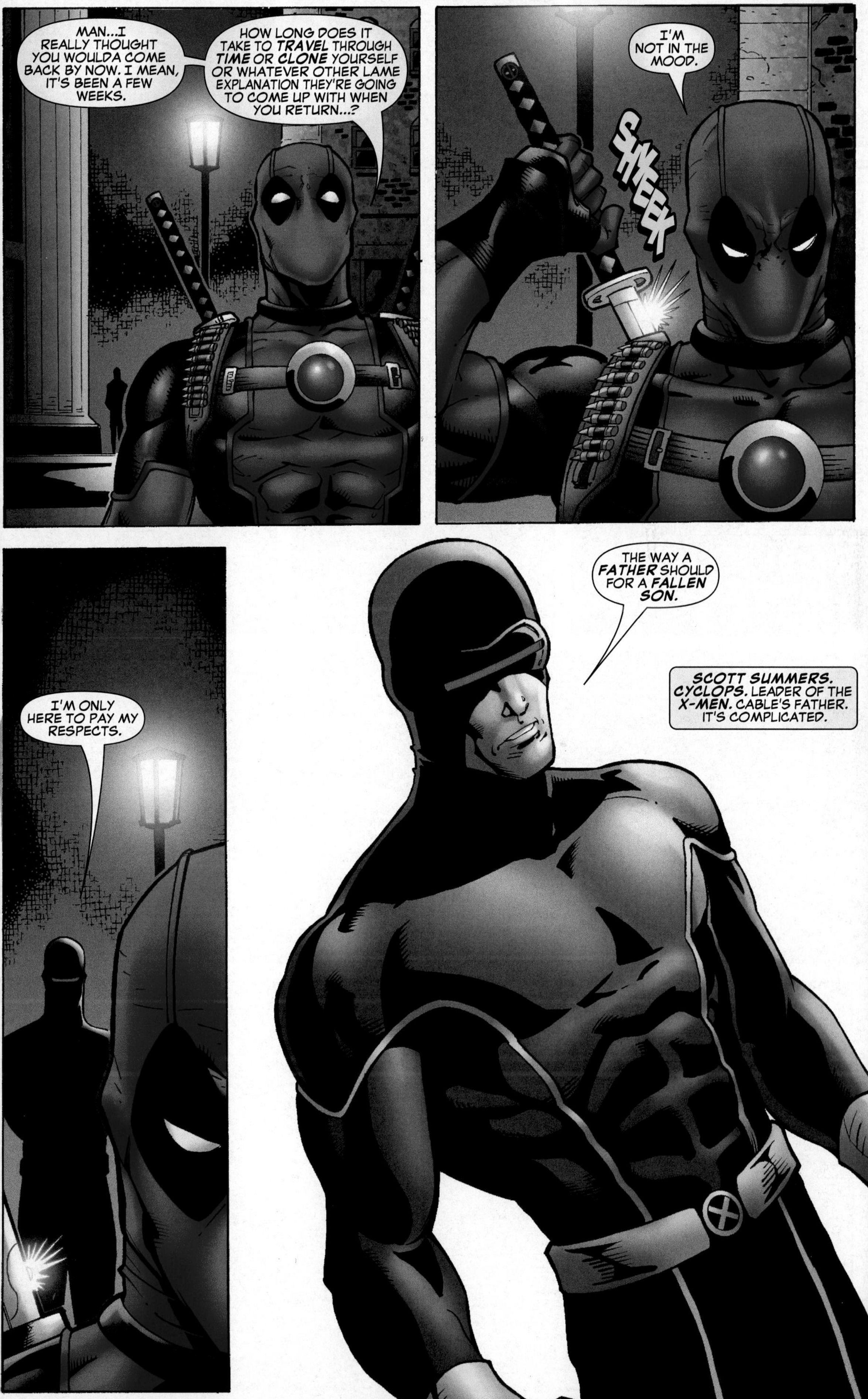
MAN...I REALLY THOUGHT YOU WOULDA COME BACK BY NOW. I MEAN, IT'S BEEN A FEW WEEKS.
HOW LONG DOES IT TAKE TO TRAVEL THROUGH TIME OR CLONE YOURSELF OR WHATEVER OTHER LAME EXPLANATION THEY'RE GOING TO COME UP WITH WHEN YOU RETURN...?
I'M NOT IN THE MOOD.
SHEEEK
I'M ONLY HERE TO PAY MY RESPECTS.
THE WAY A FATHER SHOULD FOR A FALLEN SON.
SCOTT SUMMERS. CYCLOPS. LEADER OF THE X-MEN. CABLE'S FATHER. IT'S COMPLICATED.

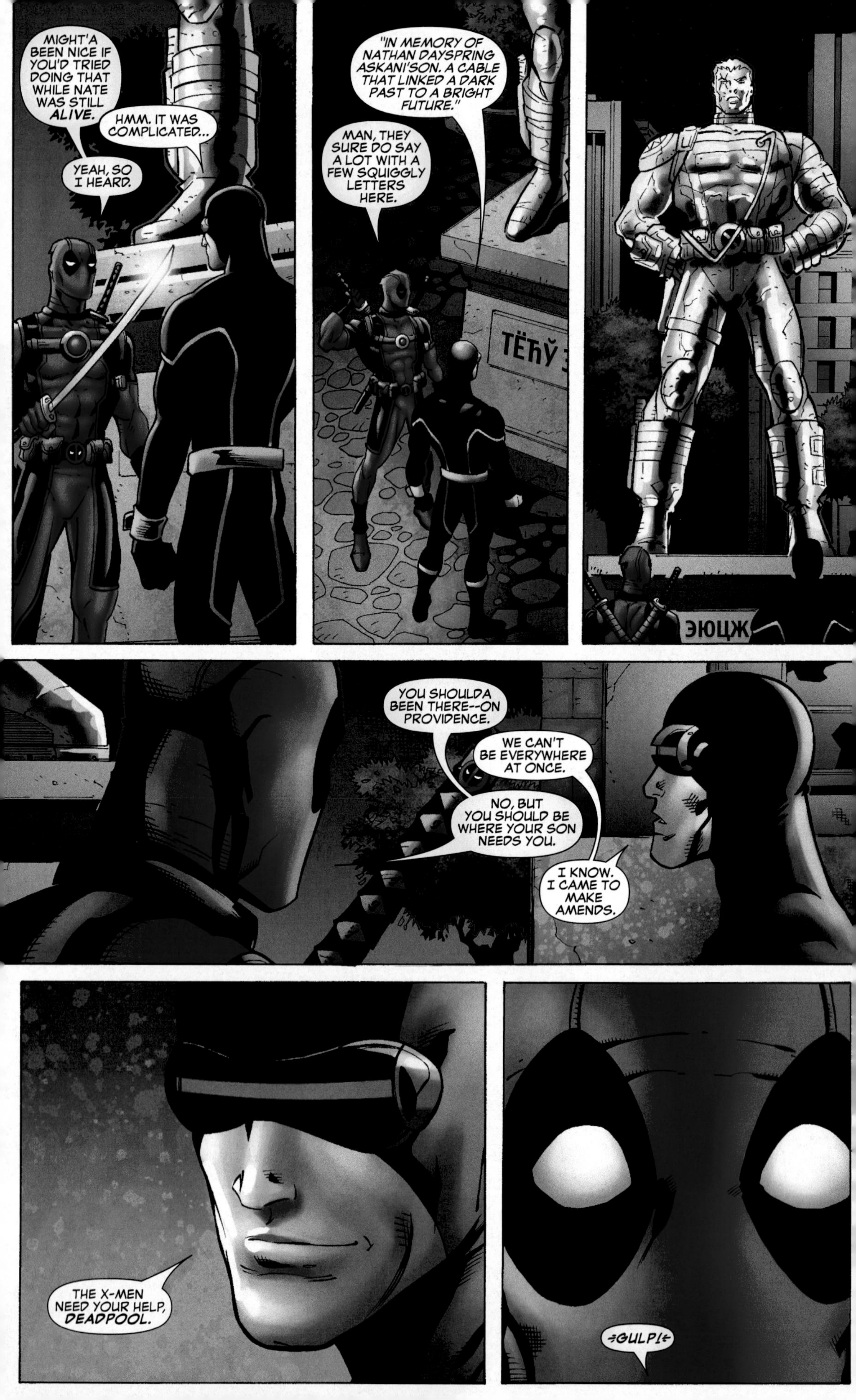
MIGHT'A BEEN NICE IF YOU'D TRIED DOING THAT WHILE NATE WAS STILL ALIVE.
HMM. IT WAS COMPLICATED...
YEAH, SO I HEARD.
"IN MEMORY OF NATHAN DAYSPRING ASKANI'SON. A CABLE THAT LINKED A DARK PAST TO A BRIGHT FUTURE."
MAN, THEY SURE DO SAY A LOT WITH A FEW SQUIGGLY LETTERS HERE.
YOU SHOULDA BEEN THERE--ON PROVIDENCE.
WE CAN'T BE EVERYWHERE AT ONCE.
NO, BUT YOU SHOULD BE WHERE YOUR SON NEEDS YOU.
I KNOW. I CAME TO MAKE AMENDS.
THE X-MEN NEED YOUR HELP, DEADPOOL.
=GULP!=

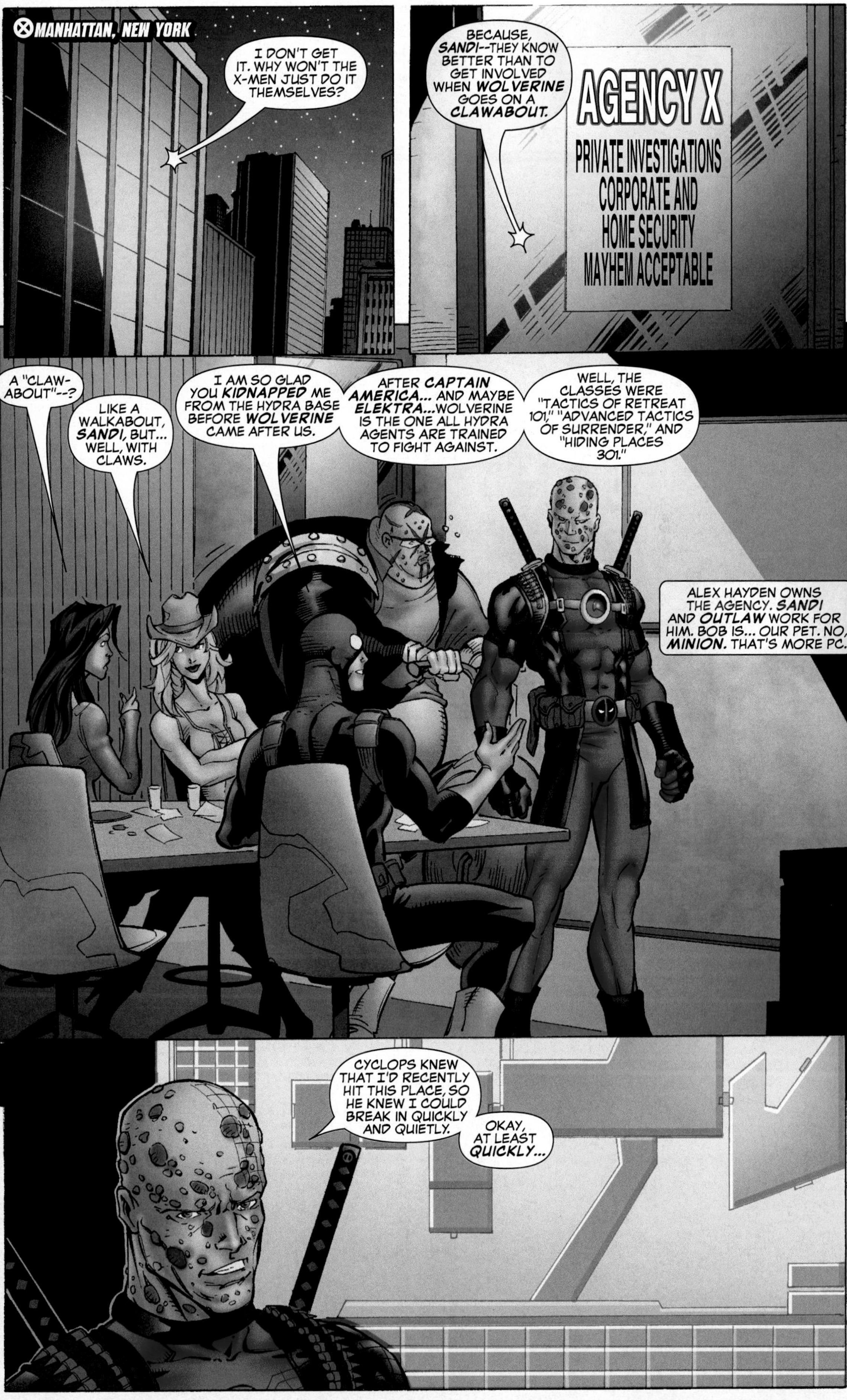
MANHATTAN, NEW YORK
I DON'T GET IT. WHY WON'T THE X-MEN JUST DO IT THEMSELVES?
BECAUSE, SANDI--THEY KNOW BETTER THAN TO GET INVOLVED WHEN WOLVERINE GOES ON A CLAWABOUT.
AGENCY X
PRIVATE INVESTIGATIONS
CORPORATE AND HOME SECURITY
MAYHEM ACCEPTABLE
A "CLAW-ABOUT"--?
LIKE A WALKABOUT, SANDI, BUT... WELL, WITH CLAWS.
I AM SO GLAD YOU KIDNAPPED ME FROM THE HYDRA BASE BEFORE WOLVERINE CAME AFTER US.
AFTER CAPTAIN AMERICA... AND MAYBE ELEKTRA...WOLVERINE IS THE ONE ALL HYDRA AGENTS ARE TRAINED TO FIGHT AGAINST.
WELL, THE CLASSES WERE "TACTICS OF RETREAT 101," "ADVANCED TACTICS OF SURRENDER," AND "HIDING PLACES 301."
ALEX HAYDEN OWNS THE AGENCY. SANDI AND OUTLAW WORK FOR HIM. BOB IS... OUR PET. NO, MINION. THAT'S MORE PC.
CYCLOPS KNEW THAT I'D RECENTLY HIT THIS PLACE, SO HE KNEW I COULD BREAK IN QUICKLY AND QUIETLY.
OKAY, AT LEAST QUICKLY...

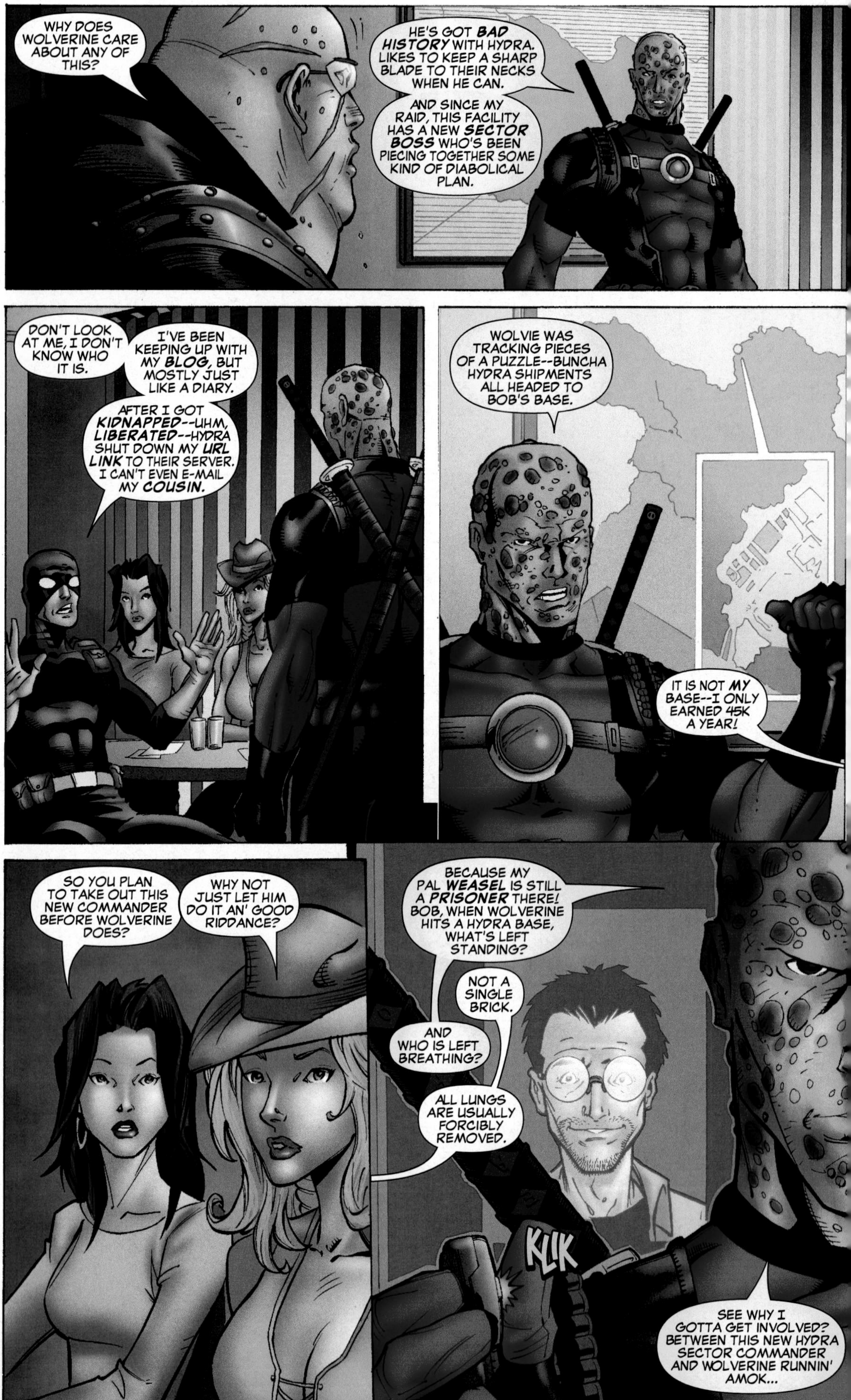
WHY DOES WOLVERINE CARE ABOUT ANY OF THIS?
HE'S GOT BAD HISTORY WITH HYDRA. LIKES TO KEEP A SHARP BLADE TO THEIR NECKS WHEN HE CAN.
AND SINCE MY RAID, THIS FACILITY HAS A NEW SECTOR BOSS WHO'S BEEN PIECING TOGETHER SOME KIND OF DIABOLICAL PLAN.
DON'T LOOK AT ME, I DON'T KNOW WHO IT IS.
I'VE BEEN KEEPING UP WITH MY BLOG, BUT MOSTLY JUST LIKE A DIARY.
AFTER I GOT KIDNAPPED--UHM, LIBERATED--HYDRA SHUT DOWN MY URL LINK TO THEIR SERVER. I CAN'T EVEN E-MAIL MY COUSIN.
WOLVIE WAS TRACKING PIECES OF A PUZZLE--BUNCHA HYDRA SHIPMENTS ALL HEADED TO BOB'S BASE.
IT IS NOT MY BASE--I ONLY EARNED 45K A YEAR!
SO YOU PLAN TO TAKE OUT THIS NEW COMMANDER BEFORE WOLVERINE DOES?
WHY NOT JUST LET HIM DO IT AN' GOOD RIDDANCE?
BECAUSE MY PAL WEASEL IS STILL A PRISONER THERE! BOB, WHEN WOLVERINE HITS A HYDRA BASE, WHAT'S LEFT STANDING?
NOT A SINGLE BRICK.
AND WHO IS LEFT BREATHING?
ALL LUNGS ARE USUALLY FORCIBLY REMOVED.
KLIK
SEE WHY I GOTTA GET INVOLVED? BETWEEN THIS NEW HYDRA SECTOR COMMANDER AND WOLVERINE RUNNIN' AMOK...

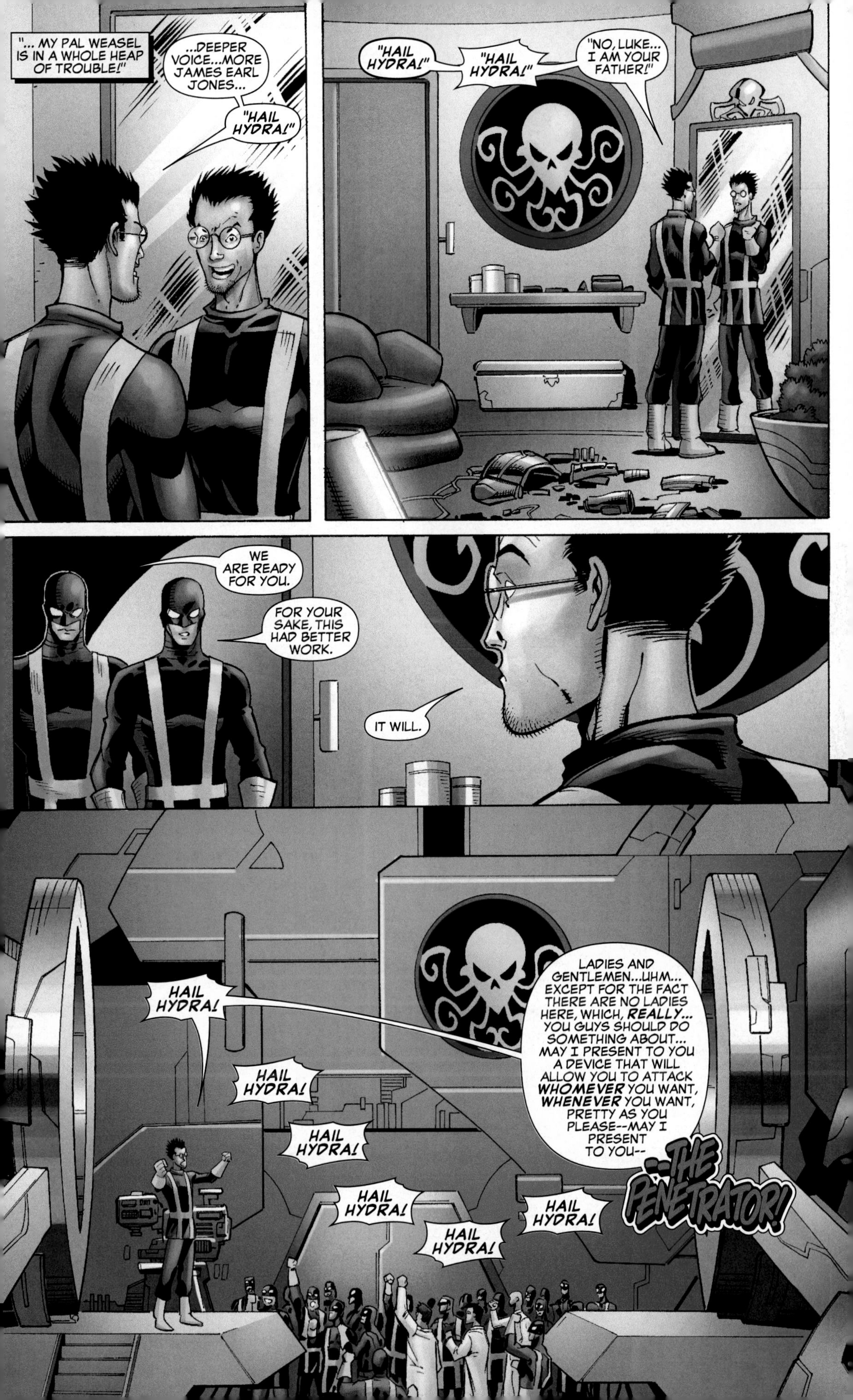
"... MY PAL WEASEL IS IN A WHOLE HEAP OF TROUBLE!"
...DEEPER VOICE...MORE JAMES EARL JONES...
"HAIL HYDRA!"
"HAIL HYDRA!"
"HAIL HYDRA!"
"NO, LUKE... I AM YOUR FATHER!"
WE ARE READY FOR YOU.
FOR YOUR SAKE, THIS HAD BETTER WORK.
IT WILL.
HAIL HYDRA!
HAIL HYDRA!
HAIL HYDRA!
HAIL HYDRA!
HAIL HYDRA!
HAIL HYDRA!
LADIES AND GENTLEMEN...UHM... EXCEPT FOR THE FACT THERE ARE NO LADIES HERE, WHICH, REALLY... YOU GUYS SHOULD DO SOMETHING ABOUT... MAY I PRESENT TO YOU A DEVICE THAT WILL ALLOW YOU TO ATTACK WHOMEVER YOU WANT, WHENEVER YOU WANT, PRETTY AS YOU PLEASE--MAY I PRESENT TO YOU--
--THE PENETRATOR!

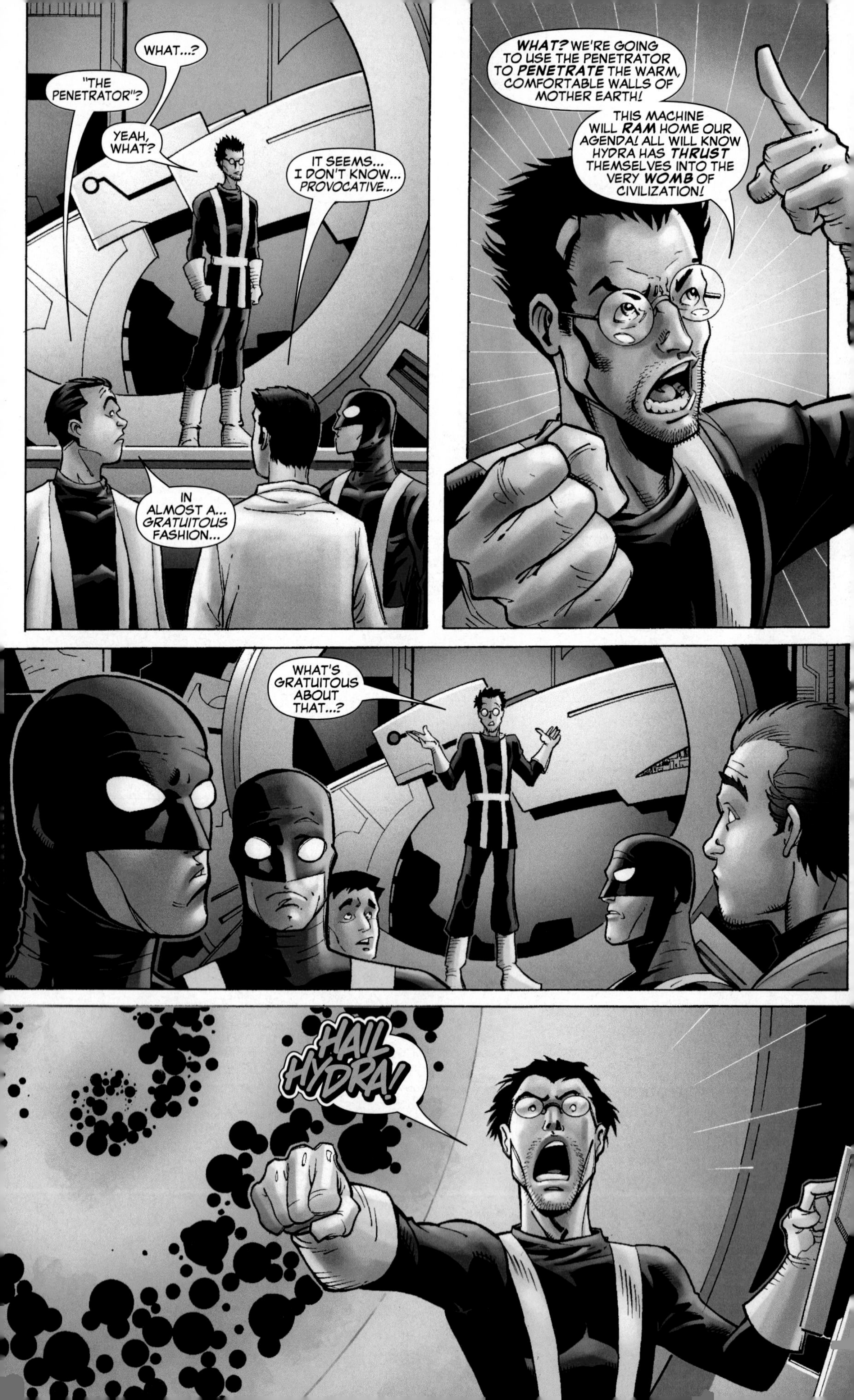
"THE PENETRATOR"?
WHAT...?
YEAH, WHAT?
IT SEEMS... I DON'T KNOW... PROVOCATIVE...
IN ALMOST A... GRATUITOUS FASHION...
WHAT? WE'RE GOING TO USE THE PENETRATOR TO PENETRATE THE WARM, COMFORTABLE WALLS OF MOTHER EARTH!
THIS MACHINE WILL RAM HOME OUR AGENDA! ALL WILL KNOW HYDRA HAS THRUST THEMSELVES INTO THE VERY WOMB OF CIVILIZATION!
WHAT'S GRATUITOUS ABOUT THAT...?
HAIL HYDRA!

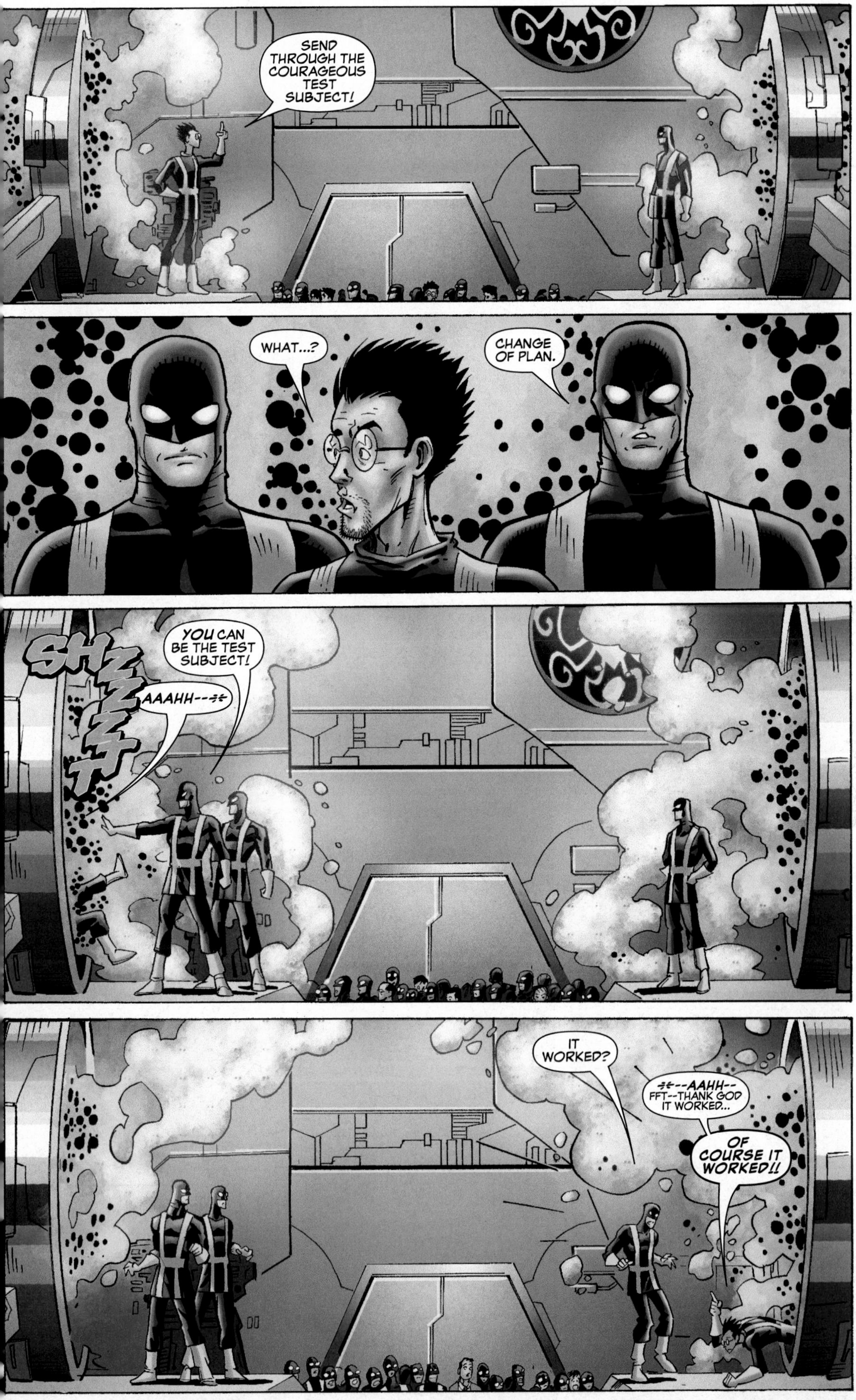
SEND THROUGH THE COURAGEOUS TEST SUBJECT!
WHAT...?
CHANGE OF PLAN.
SHZZZZT
YOU CAN BE THE TEST SUBJECT!
AAAHH--
IT WORKED?
--AAHH-- FFT--THANK GOD IT WORKED...
OF COURSE IT WORKED!!

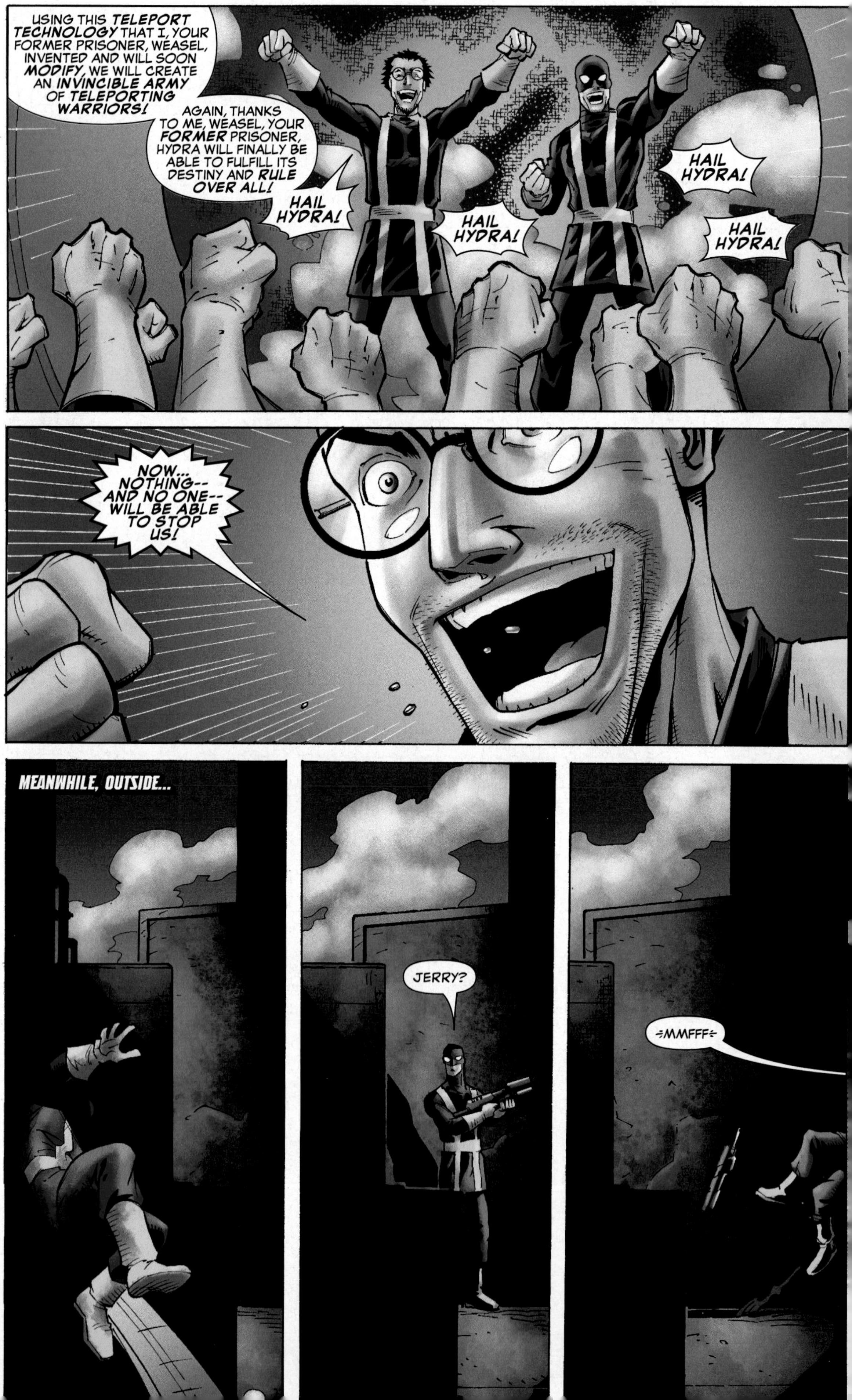
USING THIS TELEPORT TECHNOLOGY THAT I, YOUR FORMER PRISONER, WEASEL, INVENTED AND WILL SOON MODIFY, WE WILL CREATE AN INVINCIBLE ARMY OF TELEPORTING WARRIORS!
AGAIN, THANKS TO ME, WEASEL, YOUR FORMER PRISONER, HYDRA WILL FINALLY BE ABLE TO FULFILL ITS DESTINY AND RULE OVER ALL!
HAIL HYDRA!
HAIL HYDRA!
HAIL HYDRA!
HAIL HYDRA!
NOW... NOTHING-- AND NO ONE-- WILL BE ABLE TO STOP US!
MEANWHILE, OUTSIDE...
JERRY?
=MMFFF=

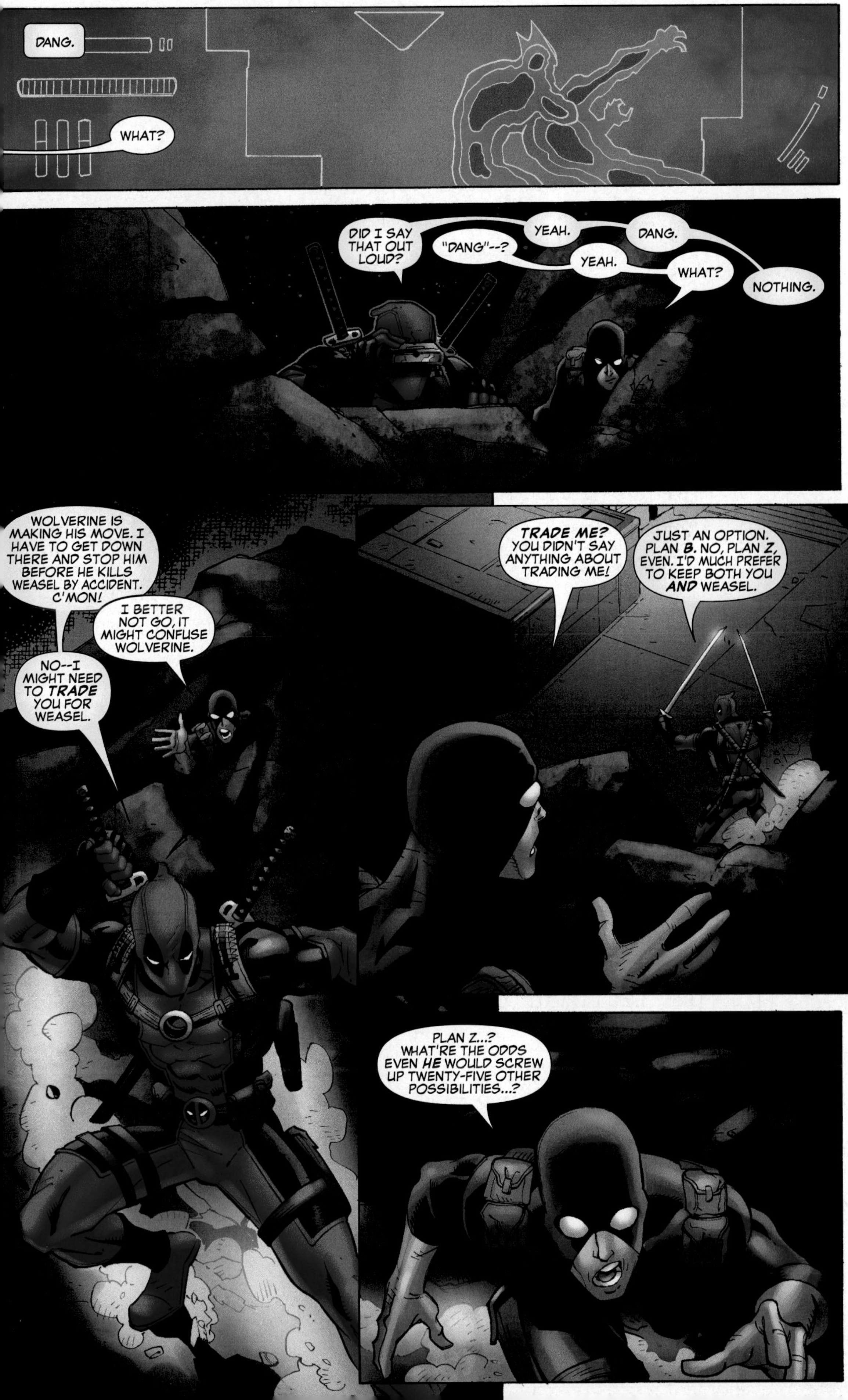
DANG.
WHAT?
DID I SAY THAT OUT LOUD?
YEAH.
DANG.
"DANG"--?
YEAH.
WHAT?
NOTHING.
WOLVERINE IS MAKING HIS MOVE. I HAVE TO GET DOWN THERE AND STOP HIM BEFORE HE KILLS WEASEL BY ACCIDENT. C'MON!
I BETTER NOT GO, IT MIGHT CONFUSE WOLVERINE.
NO--I MIGHT NEED TO TRADE YOU FOR WEASEL.
TRADE ME? YOU DIDN'T SAY ANYTHING ABOUT TRADING ME!
JUST AN OPTION. PLAN B. NO, PLAN Z, EVEN. I'D MUCH PREFER TO KEEP BOTH YOU AND WEASEL.
PLAN Z...? WHAT'RE THE ODDS EVEN HE WOULD SCREW UP TWENTY-FIVE OTHER POSSIBILITIES...?

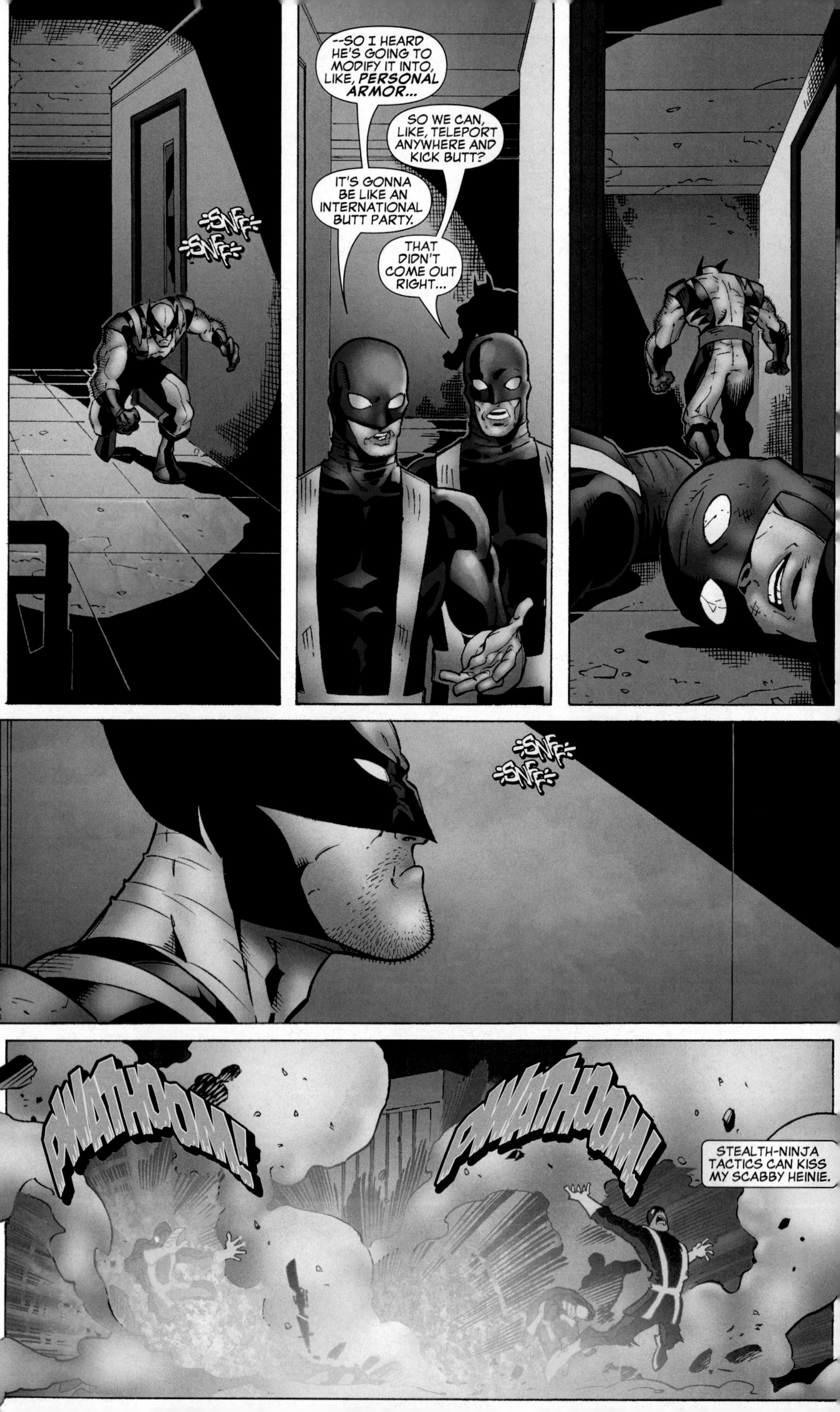
SNFF
SNFF
--SO I HEARD HE'S GOING TO MODIFY IT INTO, LIKE, PERSONAL ARMOR...
SO WE CAN, LIKE, TELEPORT ANYWHERE AND KICK BUTT?
IT'S GONNA BE LIKE AN INTERNATIONAL BUTT PARTY.
THAT DIDN'T COME OUT RIGHT...
SNFF
SNFF
PWATHOOM!
PWATHOOM!
STEALTH-NINJA TACTICS CAN KISS MY SCABBY HEINIE.

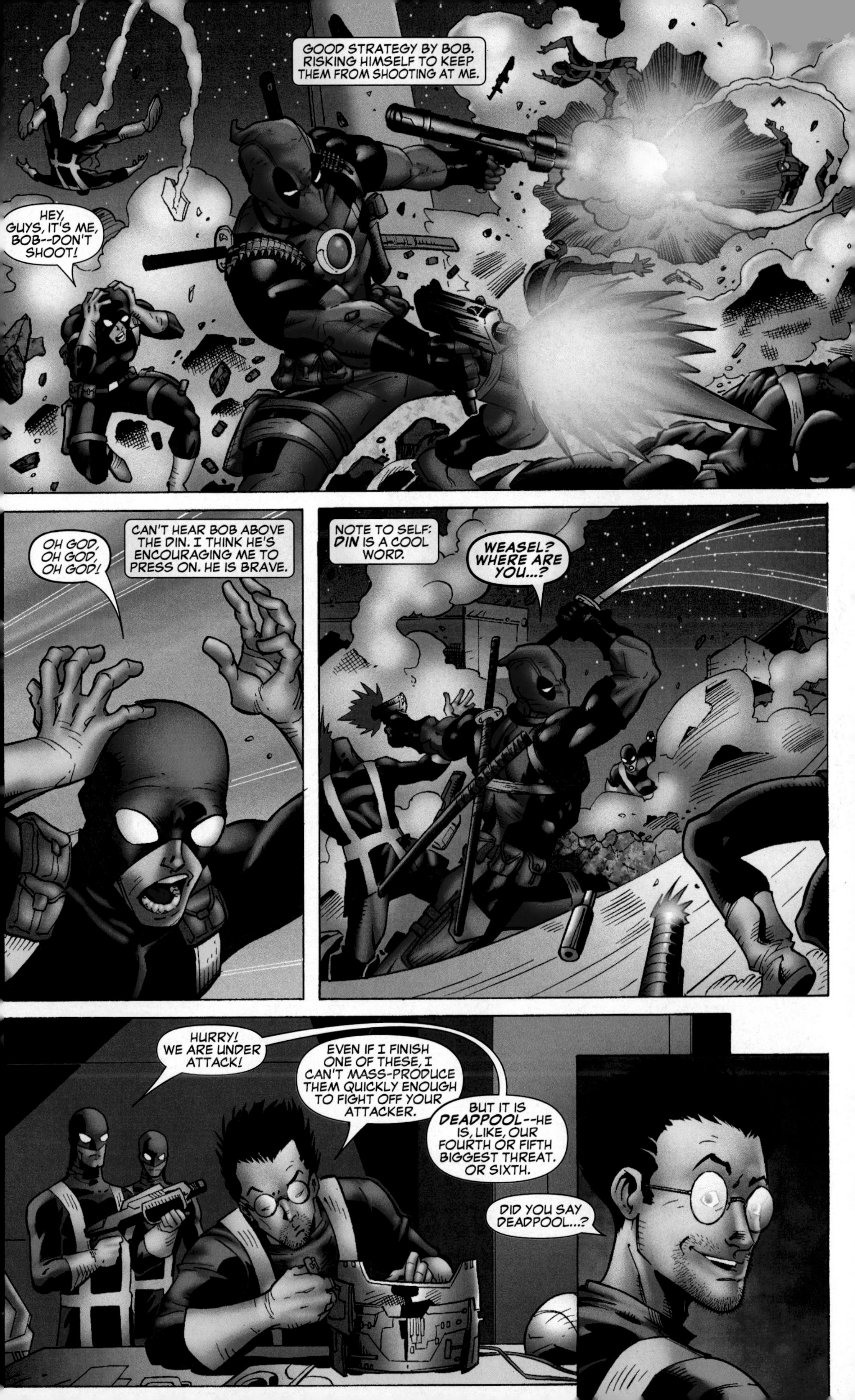

GOOD STRATEGY BY BOB. RISKING HIMSELF TO KEEP THEM FROM SHOOTING AT ME.
HEY, GUYS, IT'S ME, BOB--DON'T SHOOT!
OH GOD, OH GOD, OH GOD!
CAN'T HEAR BOB ABOVE THE DIN. I THINK HE'S ENCOURAGING ME TO PRESS ON. HE IS BRAVE.
NOTE TO SELF: DIN IS A COOL WORD.
WEASEL? WHERE ARE YOU...?
HURRY! WE ARE UNDER ATTACK!
EVEN IF I FINISH ONE OF THESE, I CAN'T MASS-PRODUCE THEM QUICKLY ENOUGH TO FIGHT OFF YOUR ATTACKER.
BUT IT IS DEADPOOL--HE IS, LIKE, OUR FOURTH OR FIFTH BIGGEST THREAT. OR SIXTH.
DID YOU SAY DEADPOOL...?

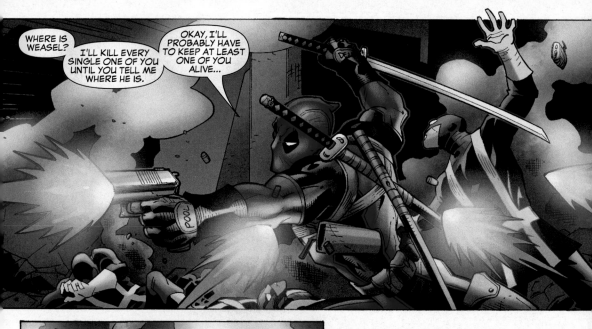

WHERE IS WEASEL?

I'LL KILL EVERY SINGLE ONE OF YOU UNTIL YOU TELL ME WHERE HE IS.

OKAY, I'LL PROBABLY HAVE TO KEEP AT LEAST ONE OF YOU ALIVE...

SORRY. SORRY. SORRY. HARRY--IS THAT YOU?

NO, THAT'S NOT HARRY'S BARELY-CONSCIOUS GROAN... SORRY...

=UUUGHHH=

DEADPOOL!

OH, WHAT NOW...

STOP THIS SENSELESS SLAUGHTER, MERCENARY, OR I WILL BE FORCED TO TELEPORT YOU FAR, FAR AWAY FROM HERE!

THE... PENETRATOR... HE WILL SAVE US ALL...

YES, IT IS I, THE PENETRAITOR!

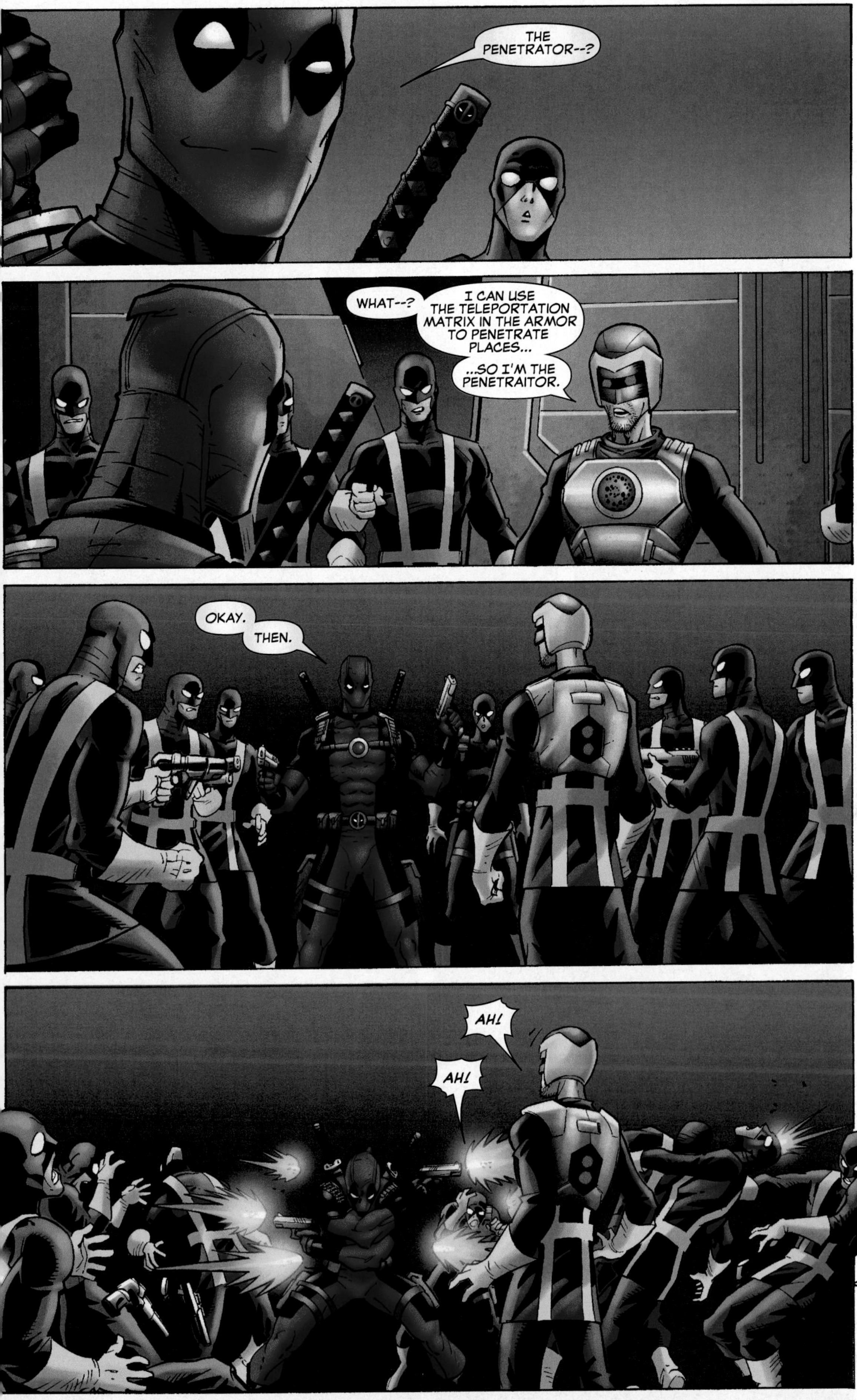
THE PENETRATOR--?
WHAT--?
I CAN USE THE TELEPORTATION MATRIX IN THE ARMOR TO PENETRATE PLACES...
...SO I'M THE PENETRAITOR.
OKAY.
THEN.
AH!
AH!

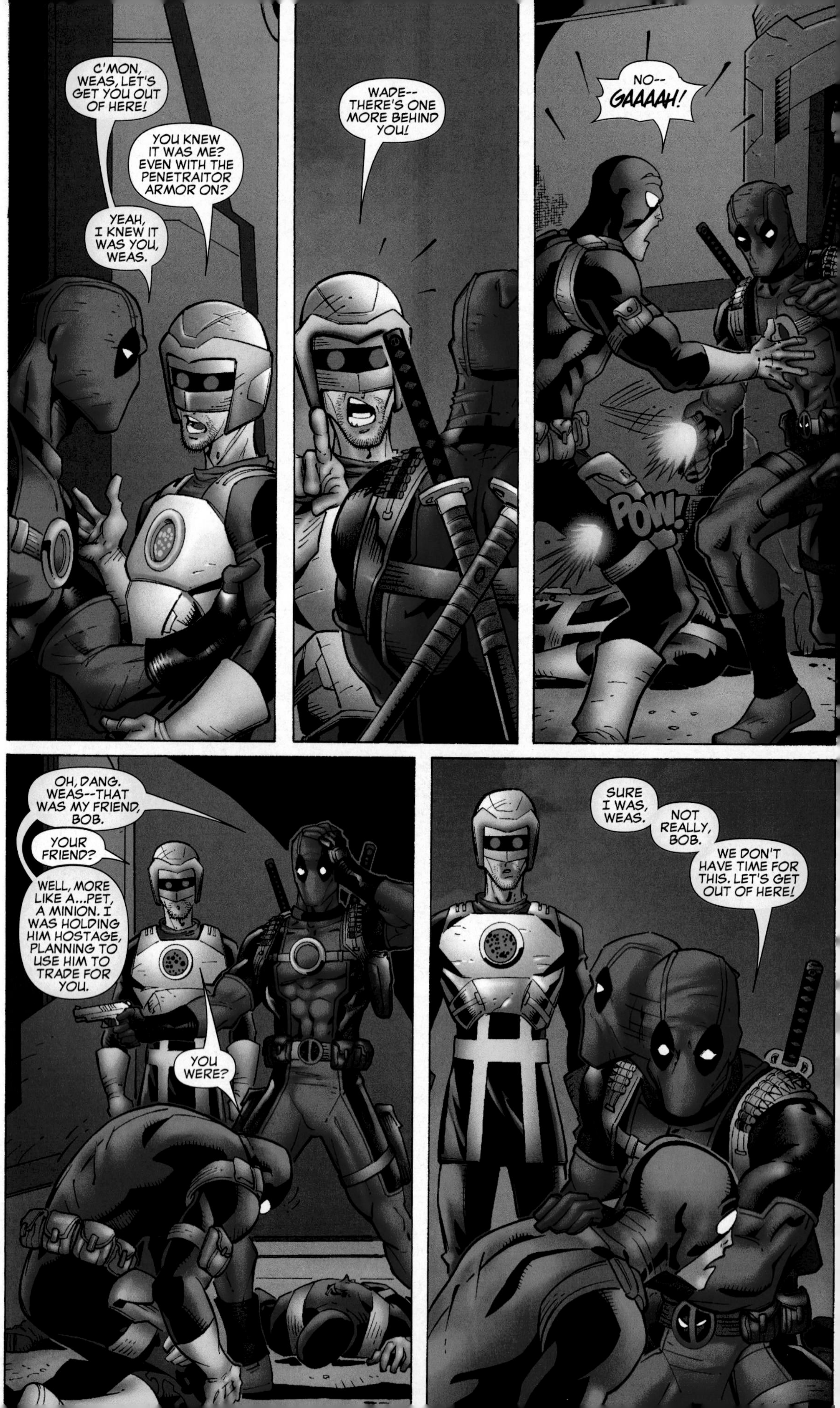
C'MON, WEAS, LET'S GET YOU OUT OF HERE!
YOU KNEW IT WAS ME? EVEN WITH THE PENETRAITOR ARMOR ON?
YEAH, I KNEW IT WAS YOU, WEAS.
WADE-- THERE'S ONE MORE BEHIND YOU!
NO-- GAAAAH!
POW!
OH, DANG. WEAS--THAT WAS MY FRIEND, BOB.
YOUR FRIEND?
WELL, MORE LIKE A...PET, A MINION. I WAS HOLDING HIM HOSTAGE, PLANNING TO USE HIM TO TRADE FOR YOU.
YOU WERE?
SURE I WAS, WEAS.
NOT REALLY, BOB.
WE DON'T HAVE TIME FOR THIS. LET'S GET OUT OF HERE!

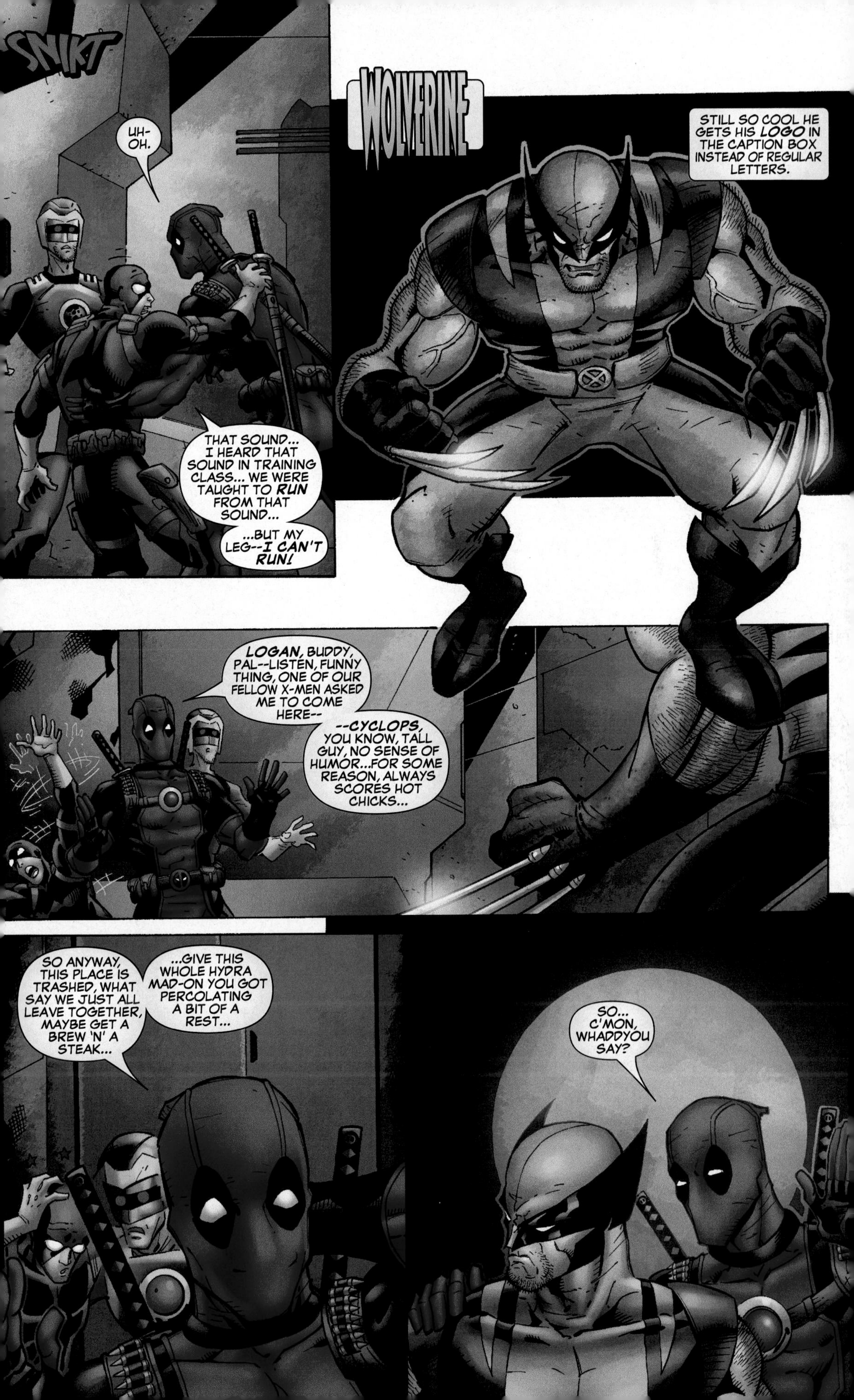
SNIKT
UH-OH.
THAT SOUND... I HEARD THAT SOUND IN TRAINING CLASS... WE WERE TAUGHT TO RUN FROM THAT SOUND...
...BUT MY LEG--I CAN'T RUN!
WOLVERINE
STILL SO COOL HE GETS HIS LOGO IN THE CAPTION BOX INSTEAD OF REGULAR LETTERS.
LOGAN, BUDDY, PAL--LISTEN, FUNNY THING, ONE OF OUR FELLOW X-MEN ASKED ME TO COME HERE--
--CYCLOPS, YOU KNOW, TALL GUY, NO SENSE OF HUMOR...FOR SOME REASON, ALWAYS SCORES HOT CHICKS...
SO ANYWAY, THIS PLACE IS TRASHED, WHAT SAY WE JUST ALL LEAVE TOGETHER, MAYBE GET A BREW 'N' A STEAK...
...GIVE THIS WHOLE HYDRA MAD-ON YOU GOT PERCOLATING A BIT OF A REST...
SO... C'MON, WHADDYOU SAY?

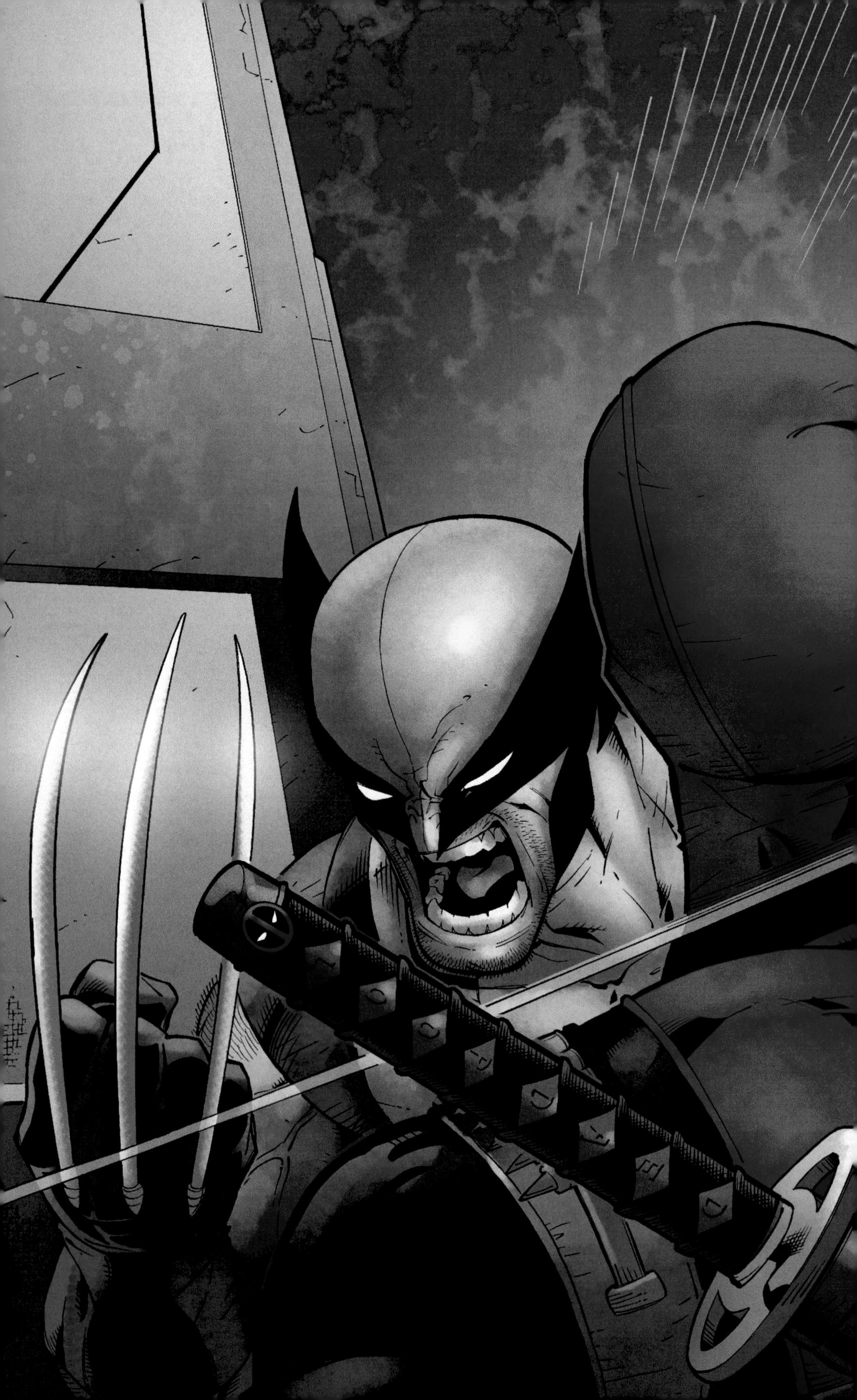

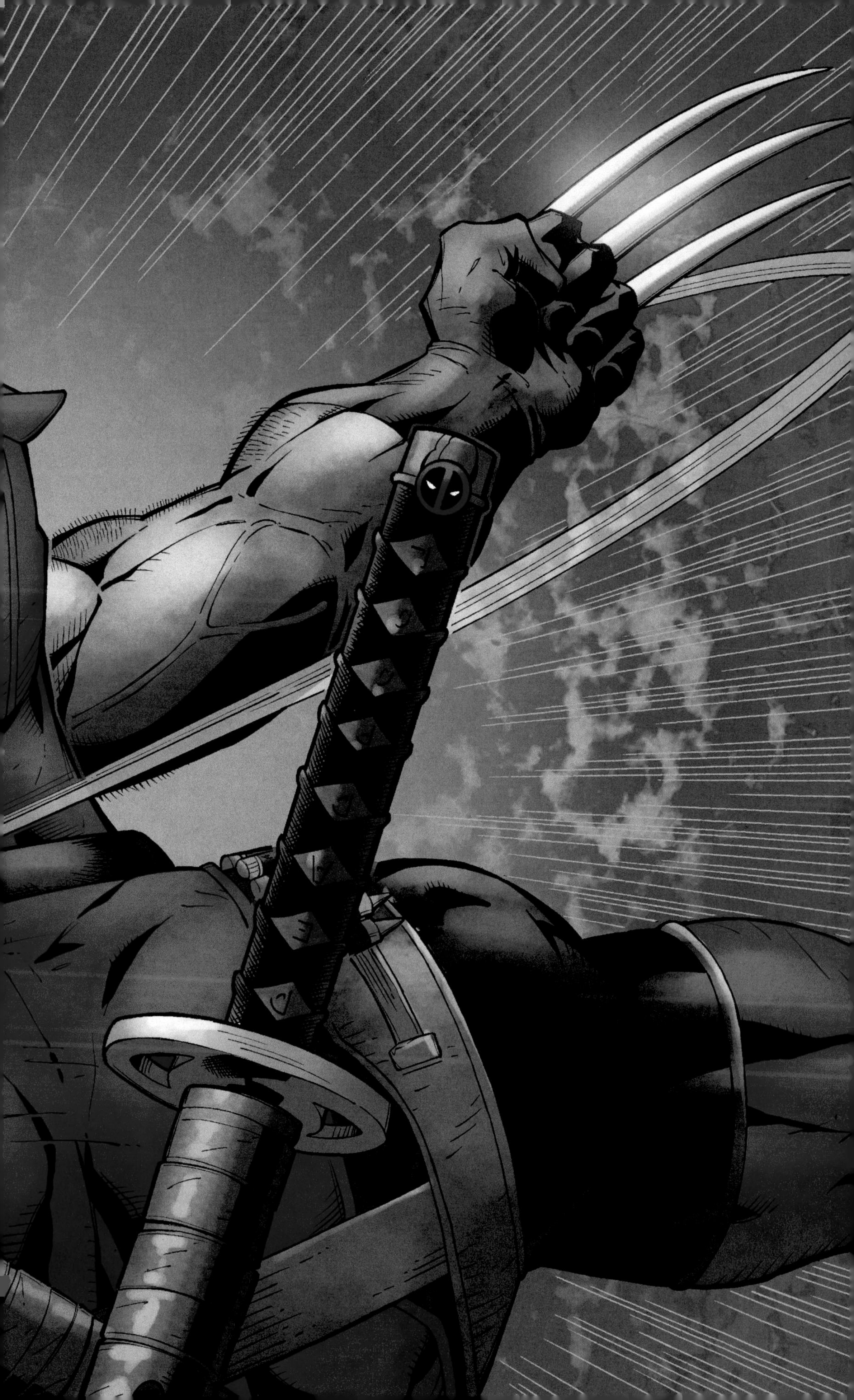

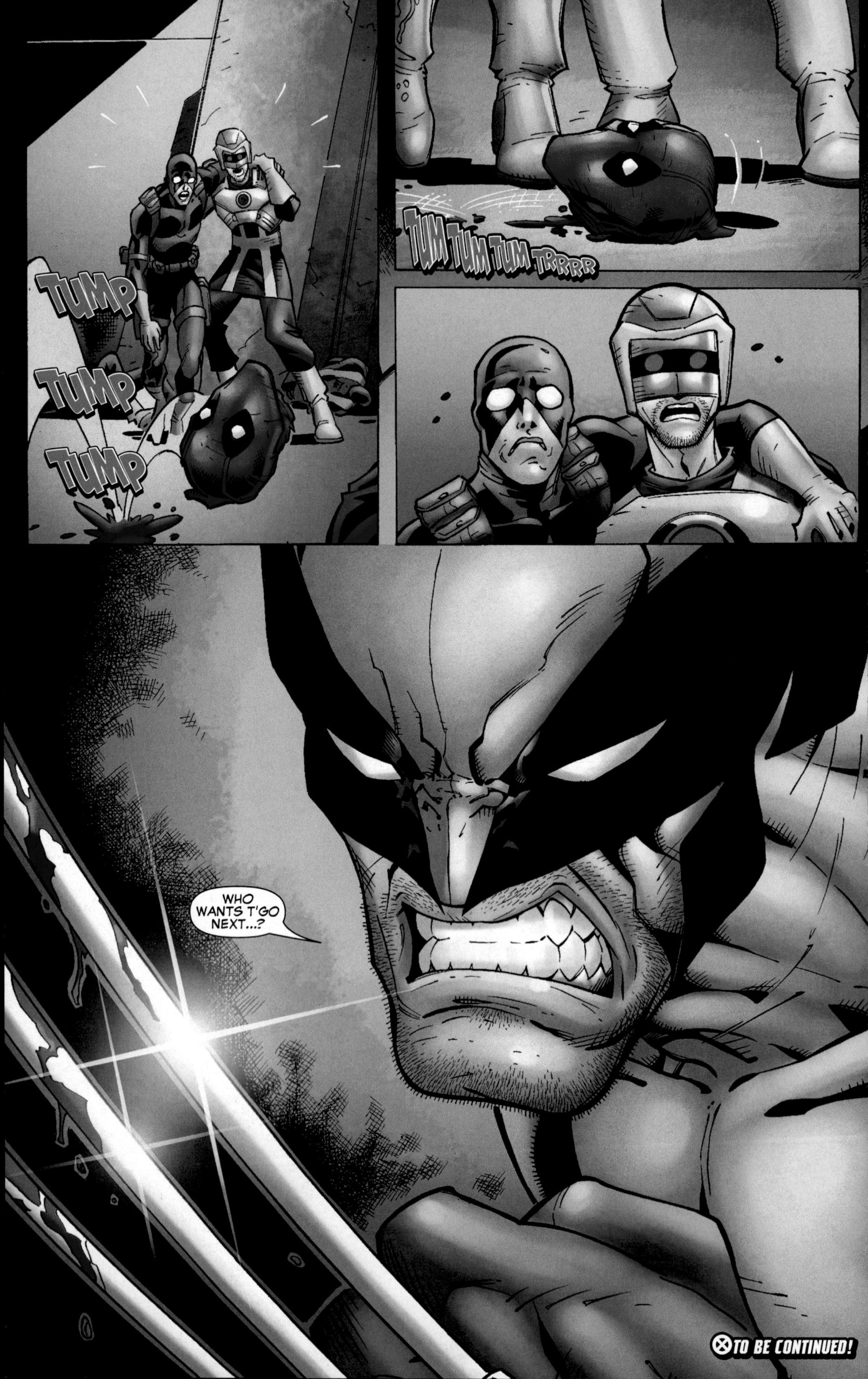
TUMP
TUMP
TUMP
TUM TUM TUM TRRRRR
WHO WANTS T'GO NEXT...?
TO BE CONTINUED!

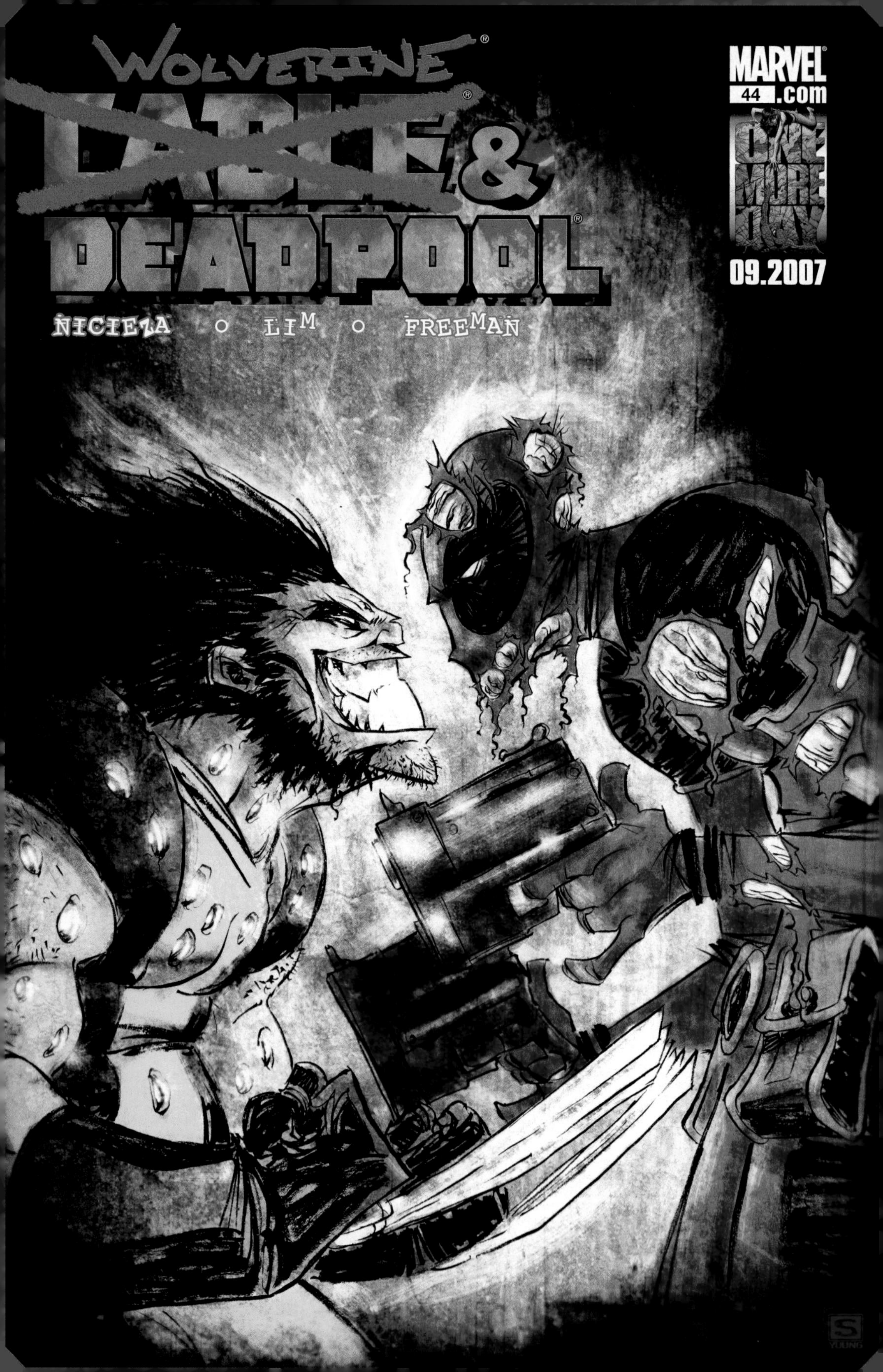
WOLVERINE
CABLE &
DEADPOOL
MARVEL
44 .com
ONE MORE DAY
09.2007
NICIEZA • LIM • FREEMAN

HEAD GAMES

FABIAN NICIEZA-WRITER **RON LIM**-PENCILER
JEREMY FREEMAN AND **JOHN DELL**-INKERS
GOTHAM AND **SOTOCOLOR**-COLORISTS **DAVE SHARPE**-LETTERER **SKOTTIE YOUNG**-COVER
NICOLE BOOSE-EDITOR **JOE QUESADA**-EDITOR IN CHIEF **DAN BUCKLEY**-PUBLISHER

Events Groups Invite Forum Search Mail Browse Home Videos

BOB

HYDRA IS IN YOUR EXTENDED NETWORK

Name: Bob
Age: 33
Eyes: 2
Hair: hanging in there
Ht: 5'10"   Wt: 183 lbs.
Occupation: Agent of HYDRA (Fascist world-dominators)
Marital Status: regrettably, yes
Home: currently kidnapped and living in Manhattan
Favorite TV show: not "24"
Favorite Movie: Austin Powers
Favorite Album: Katherine McPhee--no wait, that's not manly enough, is it...?
Likes: health insurance, world-dominating machinery, jello packs w/fruit inside, playing poker with Outlaw
Dislikes: Captain America, Wolverine, Elektra, Agents of S.H.I.E.L.D.

BOB'S BLOG HAIL HYDRA!

I was stationed in Hydra's secret Pakistani base just south of Hyberadad, when we had our first super hero attack. Well, kind of. It was Wade Wilson, known as Deadpool, the Merc With A Mouth, a fighting machine with a healing factor and a very loud mouth. He forced me to help him escape.

Now, I'm being held hostage in Manhattan, sort of, at a private investigation firm called Agency X. It's run by Alex Hayden, formerly Agent X, now morbidly obese because of some Hydra shenanigans. Wade is Hayden's primo field agent. Sandi is the office manager and Outlaw is the best piece of office furniture I have ever seen.

Deadpool's friend, Weasel, was left behind in Pakistan and now he's in the clutches of Hydra--Hail Hydra! Immortal Hydra! We shall never be destroyed! Cut off a limb and two more shall take its place!--Anyway, now we finally get to rescue him.

Source of all anti-life, Wolverine, the misunderstood mutant misfit berserker from the X-Men, got wind of a Hydra operation to create personal teleportation armors for all its agents (which is really a cool idea. Hail Hydra!). There was a rumor that a new Sector Commander was behind this plot and Wolvie wanted to eviscerate him before he succeeded. Wolverine hates Hydra because of a little mind-control thing we did to him recently (get over it!).

Deadpool and I headed to Pakistan to rescue Weasel before Wolverine mistakenly slaughtered him in one of his patented, claws-barred-yet-licensor-friendly rampages. That's when we encountered the new commander, whose name was The Penetrator. (I'm not making this stuff up.)

Turns out, the Penetrator was actually Weasel! Deadpool was ready to step up to the plate and protect his possibly heinously evil friend when Wolverine decided he'd have none of that silliness, snarled real angry and then...

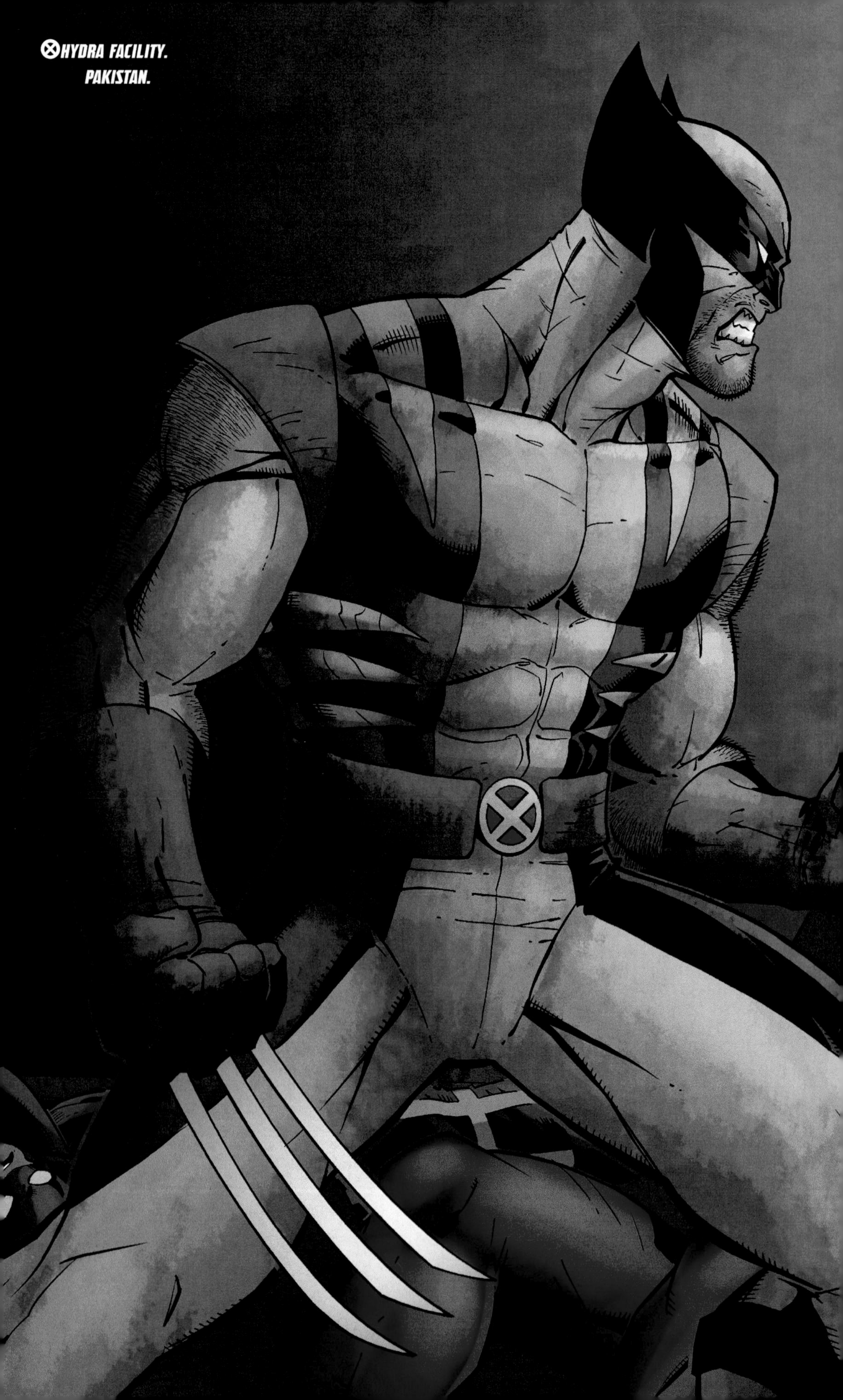
HYDRA FACILITY.
PAKISTAN.

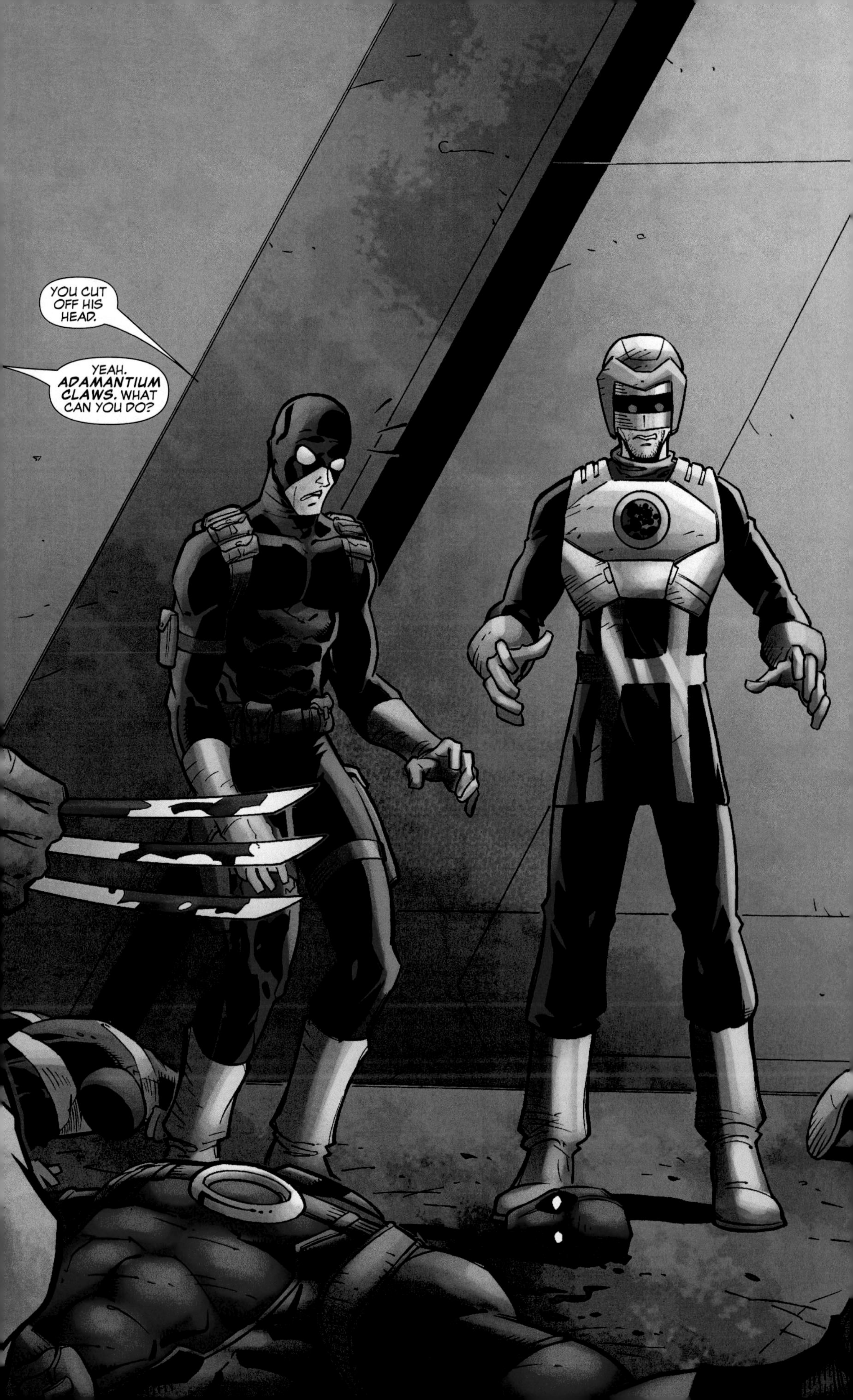
YOU CUT OFF HIS HEAD.
YEAH. ADAMANTIUM CLAWS. WHAT CAN YOU DO?

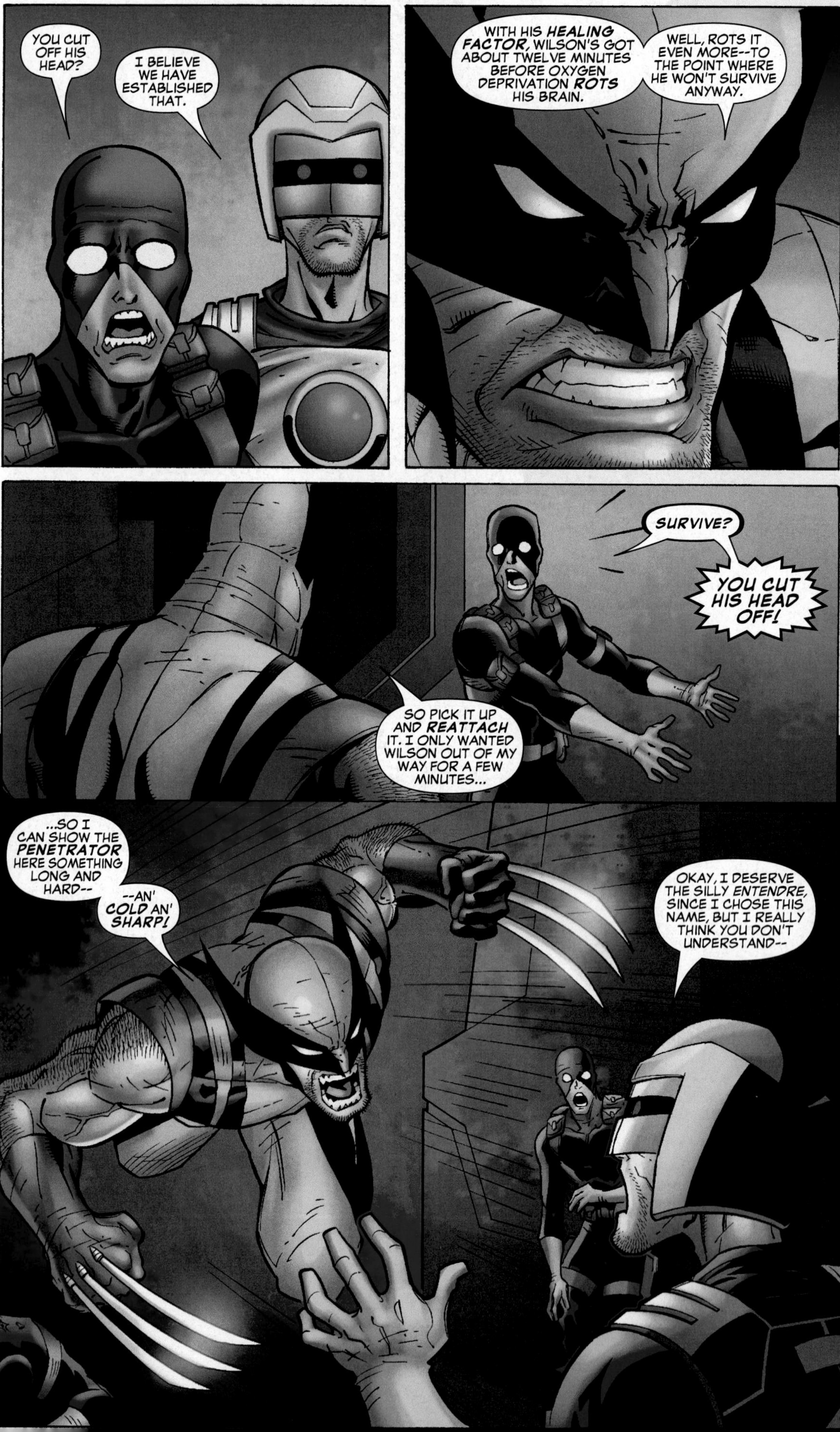

YOU CUT OFF HIS HEAD?
I BELIEVE WE HAVE ESTABLISHED THAT.
WITH HIS HEALING FACTOR, WILSON'S GOT ABOUT TWELVE MINUTES BEFORE OXYGEN DEPRIVATION ROTS HIS BRAIN.
WELL, ROTS IT EVEN MORE--TO THE POINT WHERE HE WON'T SURVIVE ANYWAY.
SURVIVE?
YOU CUT HIS HEAD OFF!
SO PICK IT UP AND REATTACH IT. I ONLY WANTED WILSON OUT OF MY WAY FOR A FEW MINUTES...
...SO I CAN SHOW THE PENETRATOR HERE SOMETHING LONG AND HARD--
--AN' COLD AN' SHARP!
OKAY, I DESERVE THE SILLY ENTENDRE, SINCE I CHOSE THIS NAME, BUT I REALLY THINK YOU DON'T UNDERSTAND--

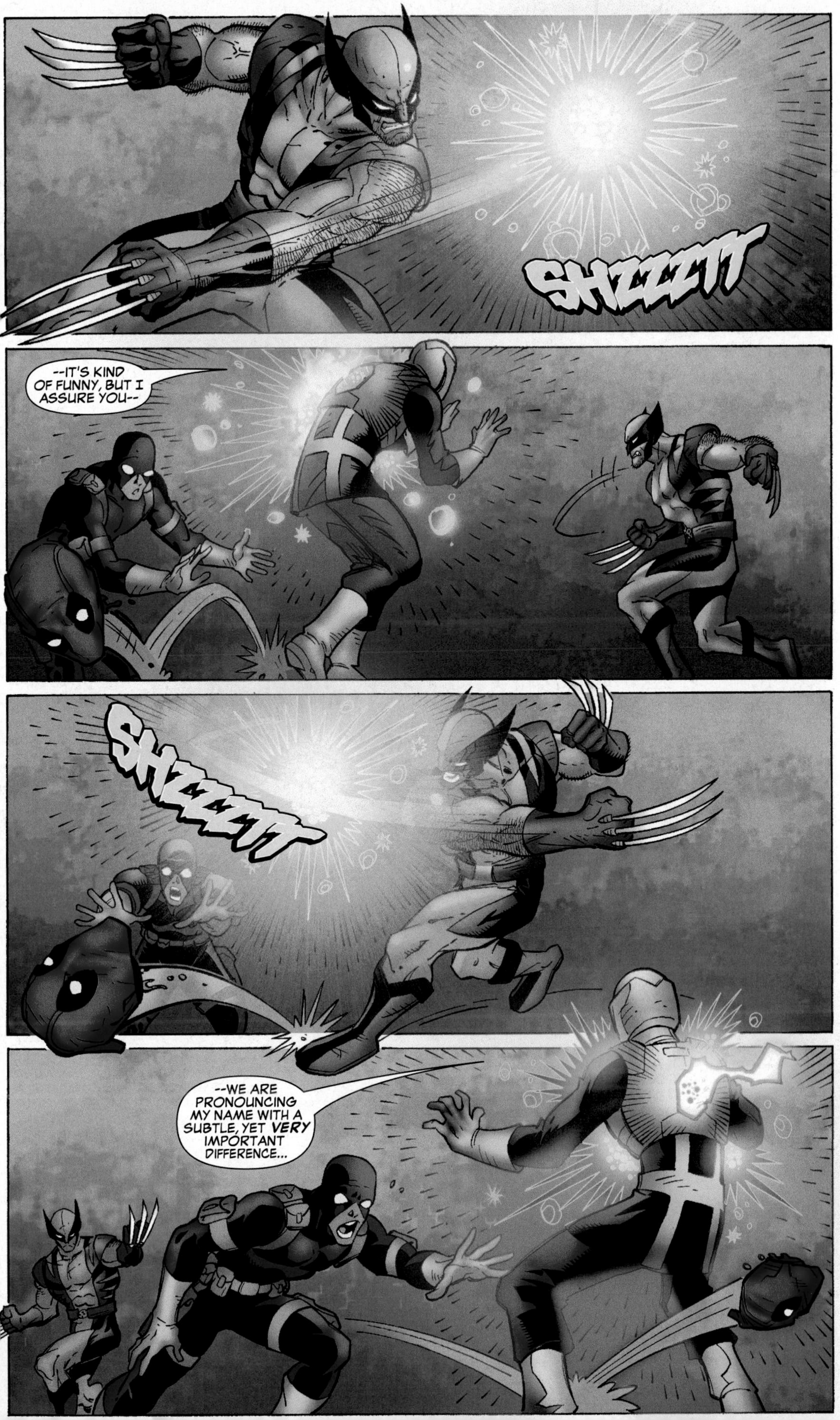
SHZZZTT
--IT'S KIND OF FUNNY, BUT I ASSURE YOU--
SHZZZTT
--WE ARE PRONOUNCING MY NAME WITH A SUBTLE, YET VERY IMPORTANT DIFFERENCE...

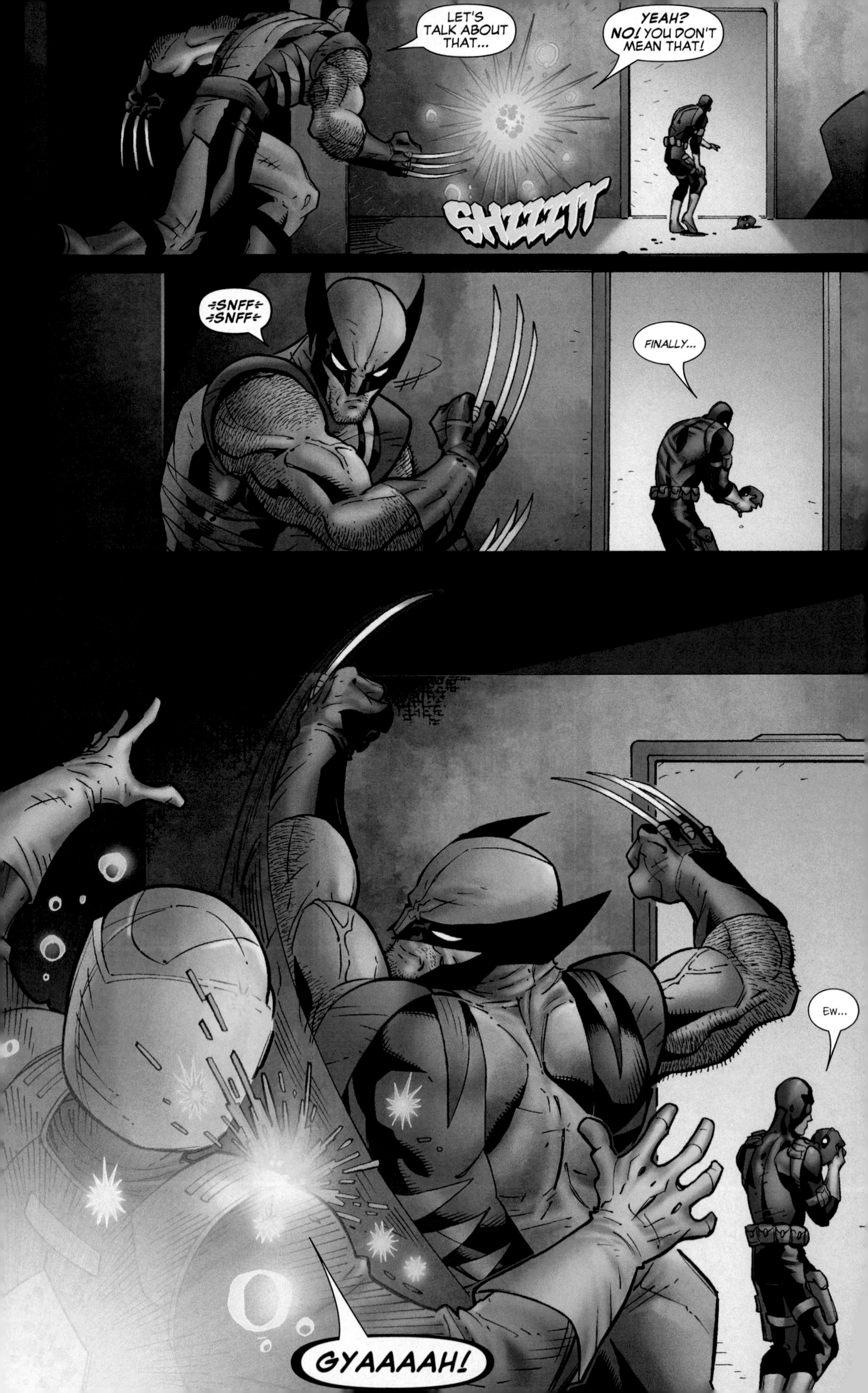
LET'S TALK ABOUT THAT...
YEAH? NO! YOU DON'T MEAN THAT!
SHZZZZTT
SNFF SNFF
FINALLY...
EW...
GYAAAAH!

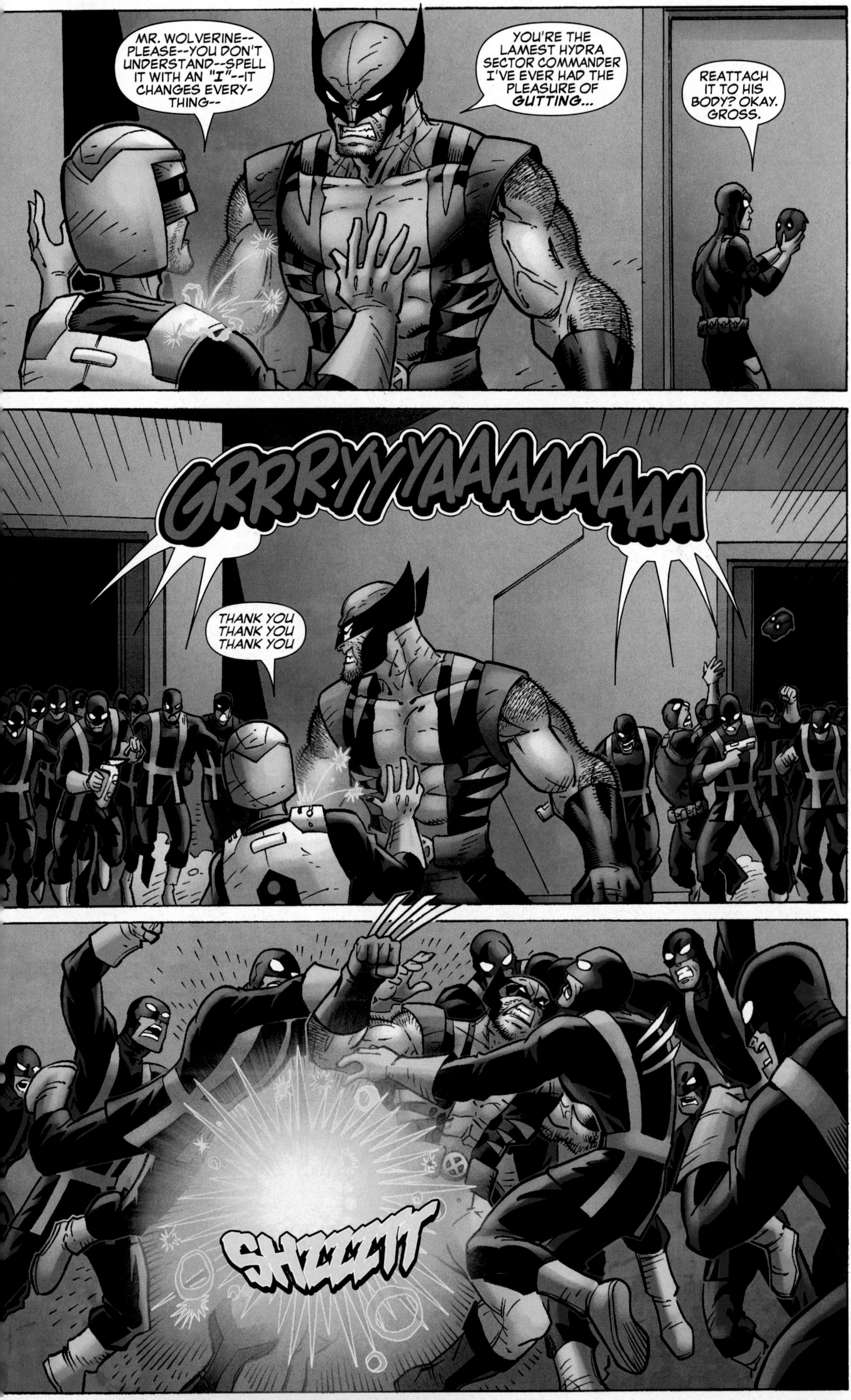
MR. WOLVERINE--PLEASE--YOU DON'T UNDERSTAND--SPELL IT WITH AN "I"--IT CHANGES EVERY-THING--
YOU'RE THE LAMEST HYDRA SECTOR COMMANDER I'VE EVER HAD THE PLEASURE OF GUTTING...
REATTACH IT TO HIS BODY? OKAY. GROSS.
GRRRYYYAAAAAAAAA
THANK YOU THANK YOU THANK YOU
SHZZZTT

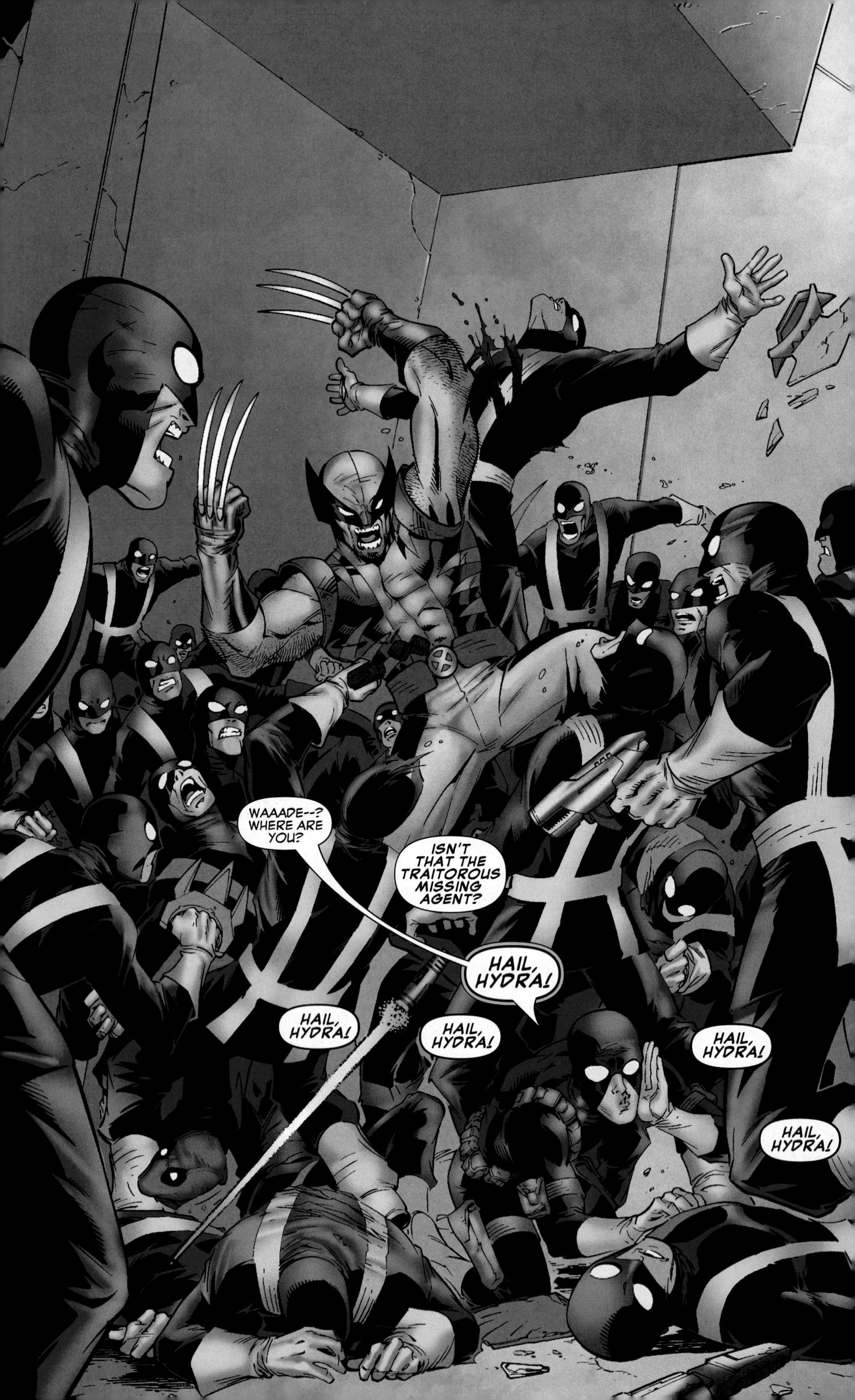

WAAADE--? WHERE ARE YOU?
ISN'T THAT THE TRAITOROUS MISSING AGENT?
HAIL, HYDRA!
HAIL, HYDRA!
HAIL, HYDRA!
HAIL, HYDRA!
HAIL, HYDRA!

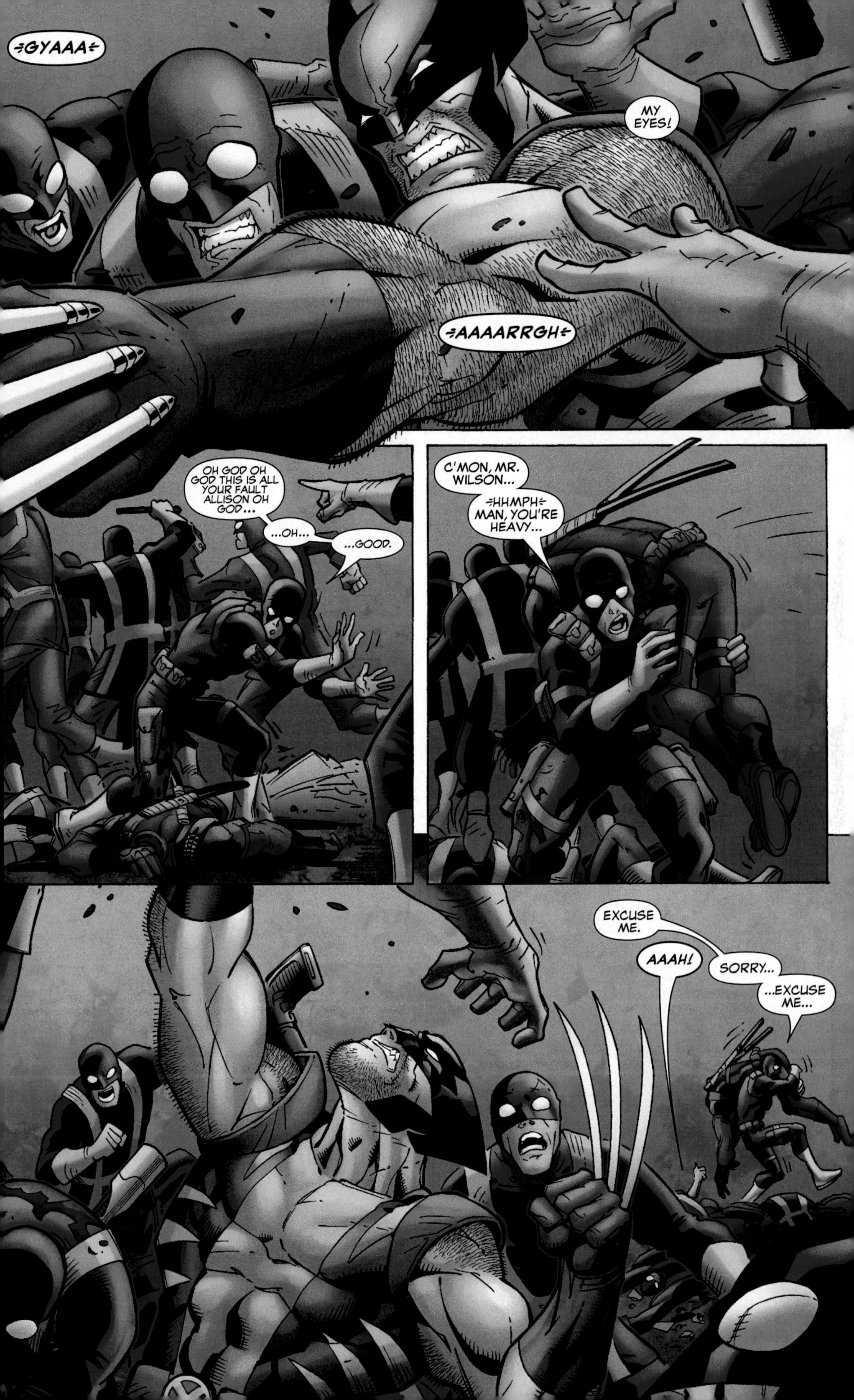
GYAAA
MY EYES!
AAAARRGH
OH GOD OH GOD THIS IS ALL YOUR FAULT ALLISON OH GOD...
...OH...
...GOOD.
C'MON, MR. WILSON...
HHMPH MAN, YOU'RE HEAVY...
EXCUSE ME.
AAAH!
SORRY...
...EXCUSE ME...

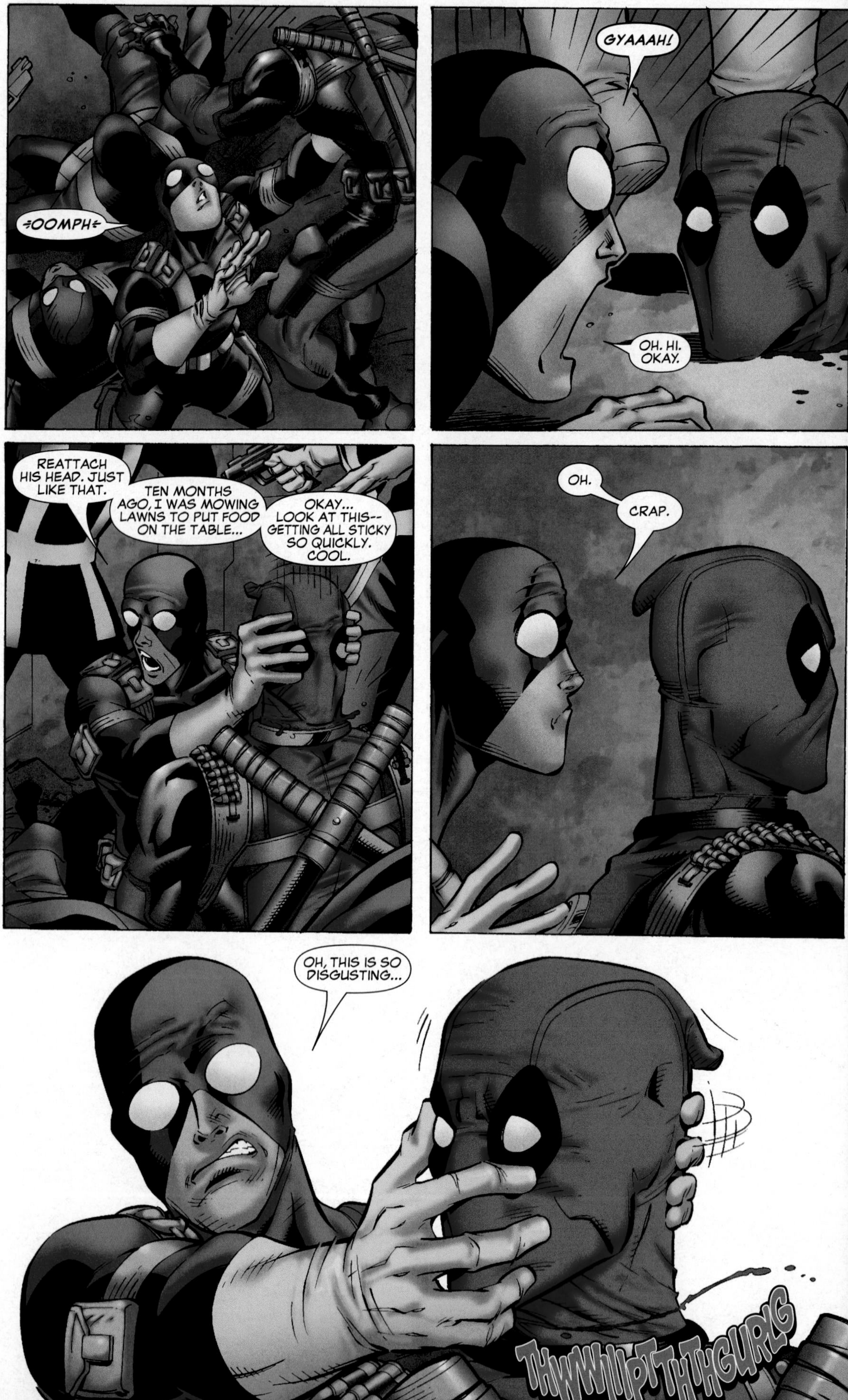

OOMPH
GYAAAH!
OH. HI. OKAY.
REATTACH HIS HEAD. JUST LIKE THAT.
TEN MONTHS AGO, I WAS MOWING LAWNS TO PUT FOOD ON THE TABLE...
OKAY... LOOK AT THIS-- GETTING ALL STICKY SO QUICKLY. COOL.
OH.
CRAP.
OH, THIS IS SO DISGUSTING...
THWWIIIPTTHTHGURLG

POSITIVE THINKING: I AM SWITZERLAND.

I AM SWITZER-LAND.

GYAAAH!

HOW LONG IS THIS GOING TO TAKE...?

SLUCC SLUCC PLIT PLIT THLIPP

MEANWHILE...

NO, THE TACHYON GENERATOR HAS TO ATTACH THERE-- YEAH--

HOW MUCH LONGER?

JUST A FEW MORE MINUTES.

WE DON'T HAVE A FEW MINUTES!

HOW DOES HE KNOW WHERE WE ARE?

HE MUST BE TRACKING YOUR SCENT, PENETRATOR!

HAIL HYDRA! WE NEED A MIRACLE!

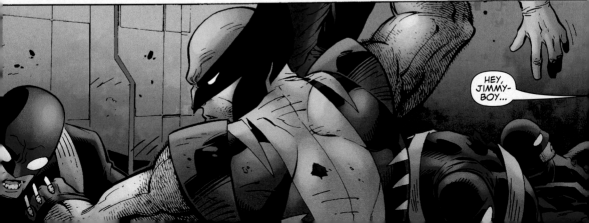

HEY, JIMMY-BOY...

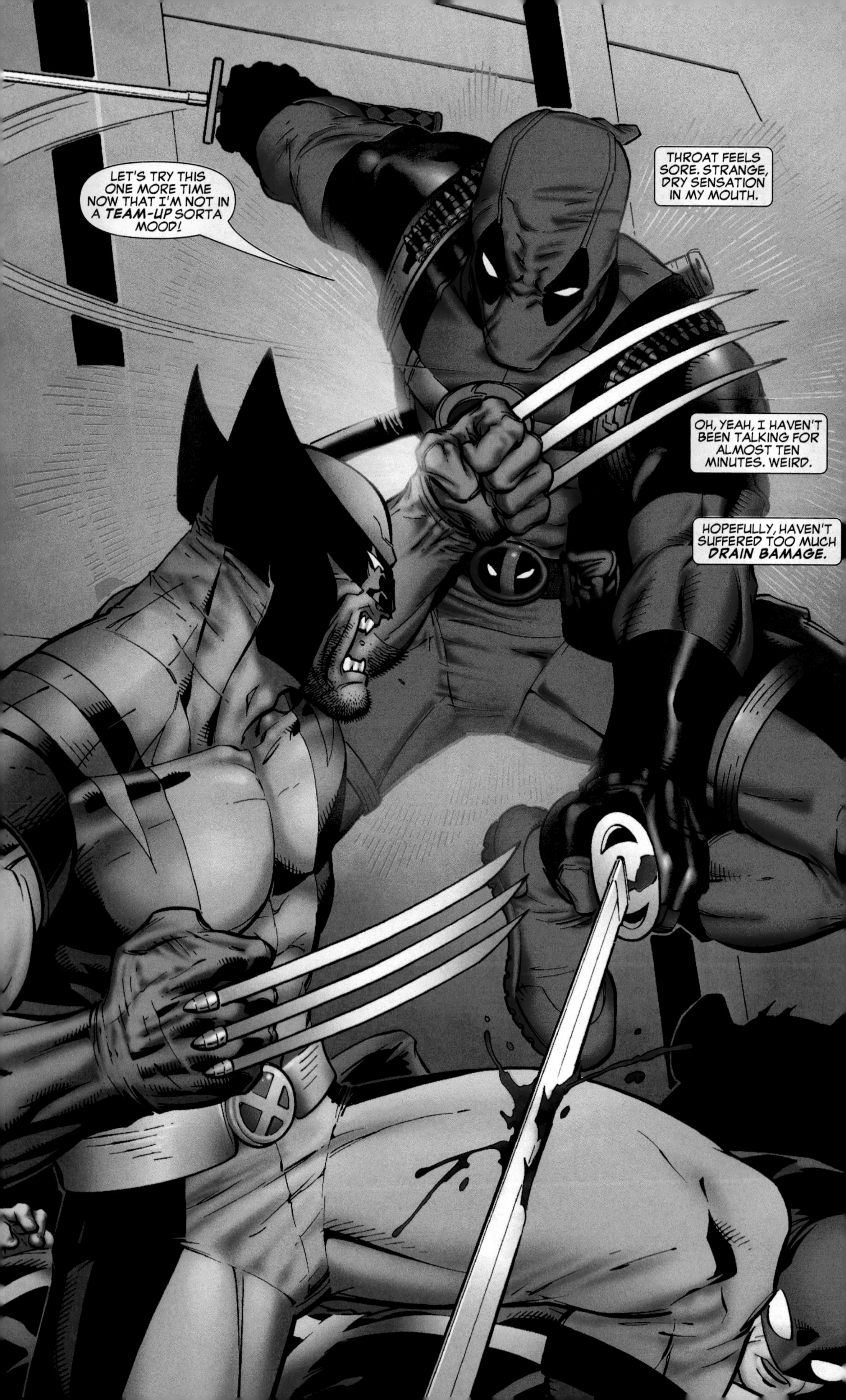
LET'S TRY THIS ONE MORE TIME NOW THAT I'M NOT IN A TEAM-UP SORTA MOOD!
THROAT FEELS SORE. STRANGE, DRY SENSATION IN MY MOUTH.
OH, YEAH, I HAVEN'T BEEN TALKING FOR ALMOST TEN MINUTES. WEIRD.
HOPEFULLY, HAVEN'T SUFFERED TOO MUCH DRAIN BAMAGE.

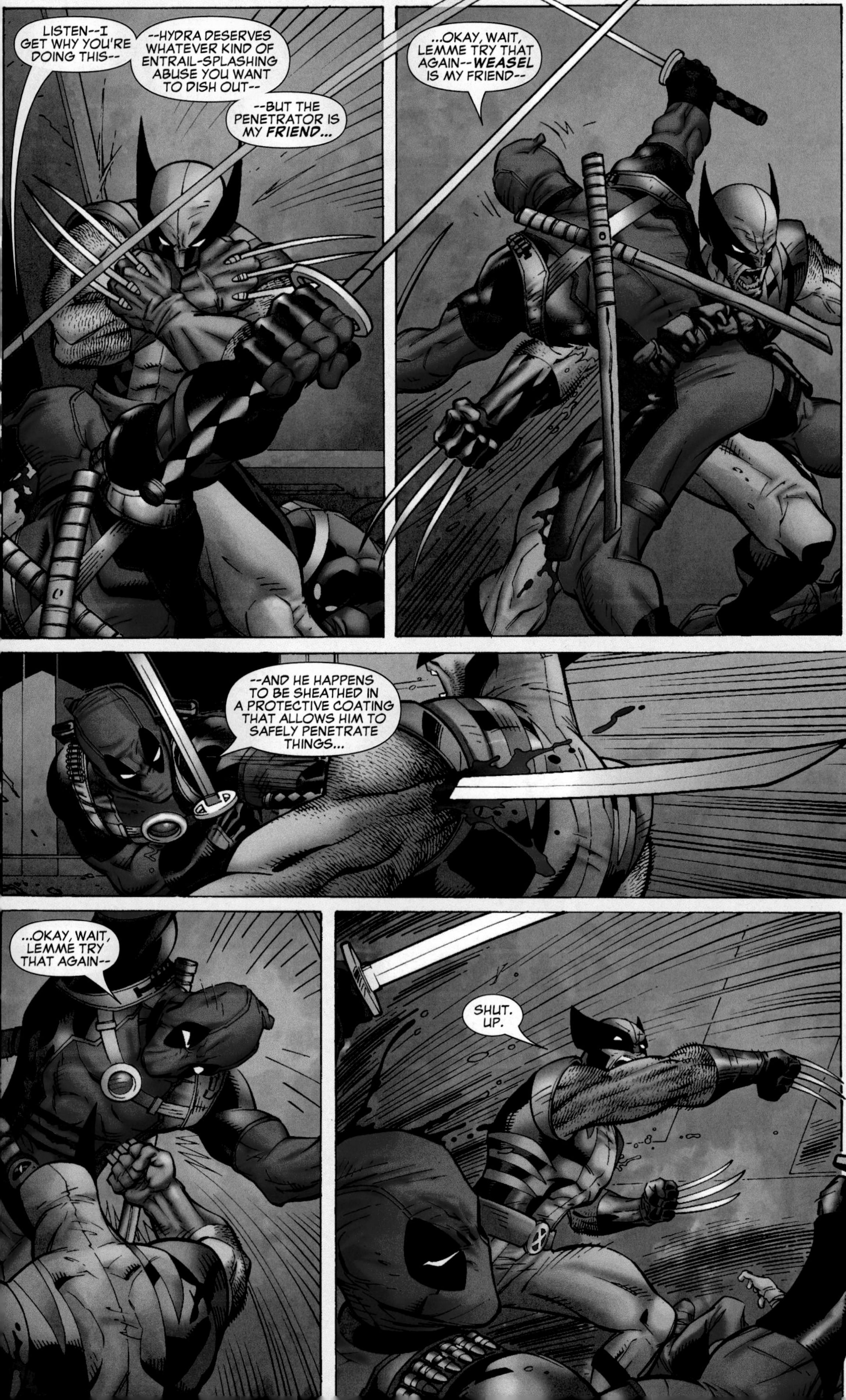
LISTEN--I GET WHY YOU'RE DOING THIS--
--HYDRA DESERVES WHATEVER KIND OF ENTRAIL-SPLASHING ABUSE YOU WANT TO DISH OUT--
--BUT THE PENETRATOR IS MY FRIEND...
...OKAY, WAIT, LEMME TRY THAT AGAIN--WEASEL IS MY FRIEND--
--AND HE HAPPENS TO BE SHEATHED IN A PROTECTIVE COATING THAT ALLOWS HIM TO SAFELY PENETRATE THINGS...
...OKAY, WAIT, LEMME TRY THAT AGAIN--
SHUT. UP.

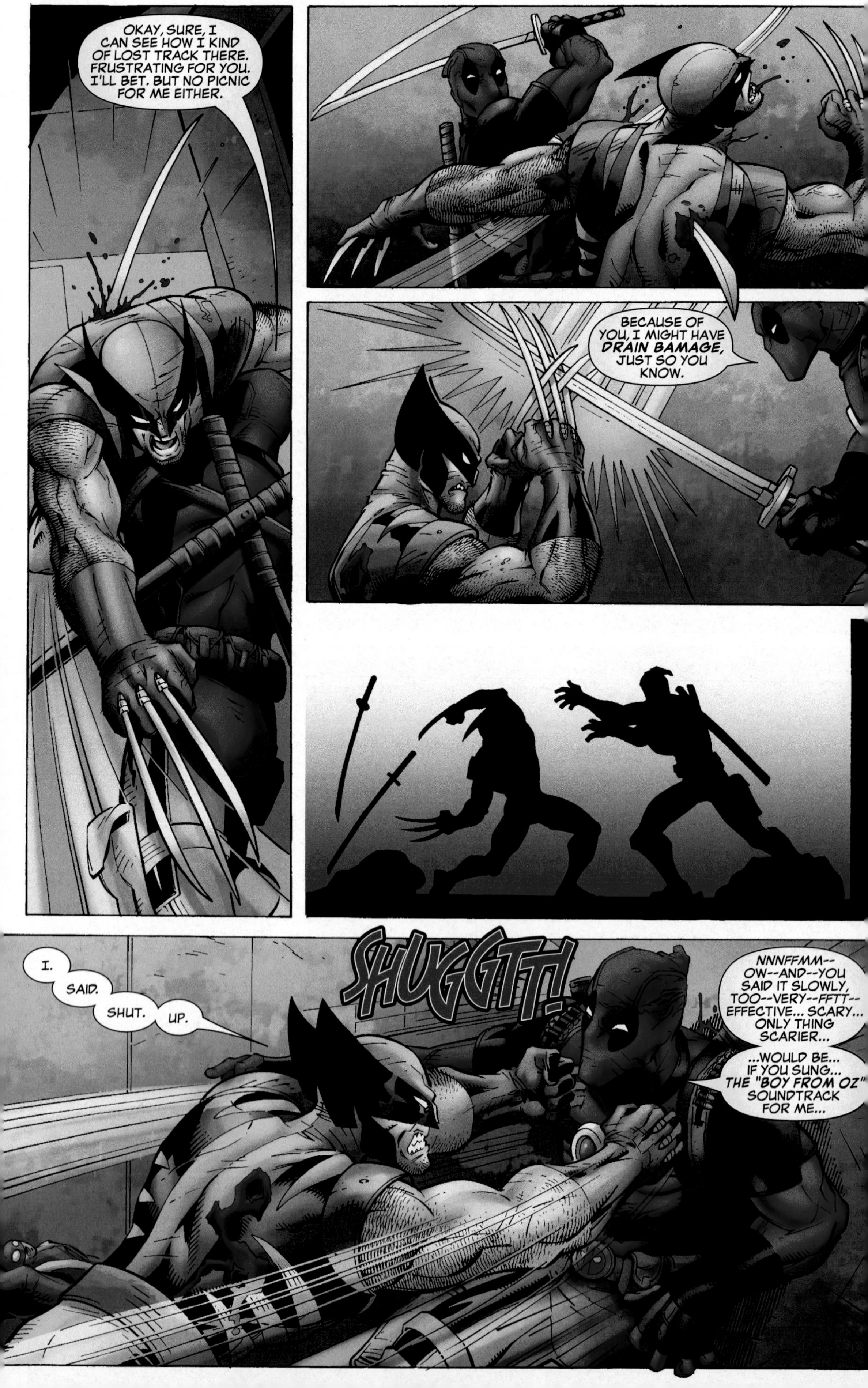
OKAY, SURE, I CAN SEE HOW I KIND OF LOST TRACK THERE. FRUSTRATING FOR YOU. I'LL BET. BUT NO PICNIC FOR ME EITHER.
BECAUSE OF YOU, I MIGHT HAVE DRAIN BAMAGE, JUST SO YOU KNOW.
SHUGGTT!
I.
SAID.
SHUT.
UP.
NNNFFMM--OW--AND--YOU SAID IT SLOWLY, TOO--VERY--FFTT--EFFECTIVE... SCARY... ONLY THING SCARIER...
...WOULD BE... IF YOU SUNG... THE "BOY FROM OZ" SOUNDTRACK FOR ME...

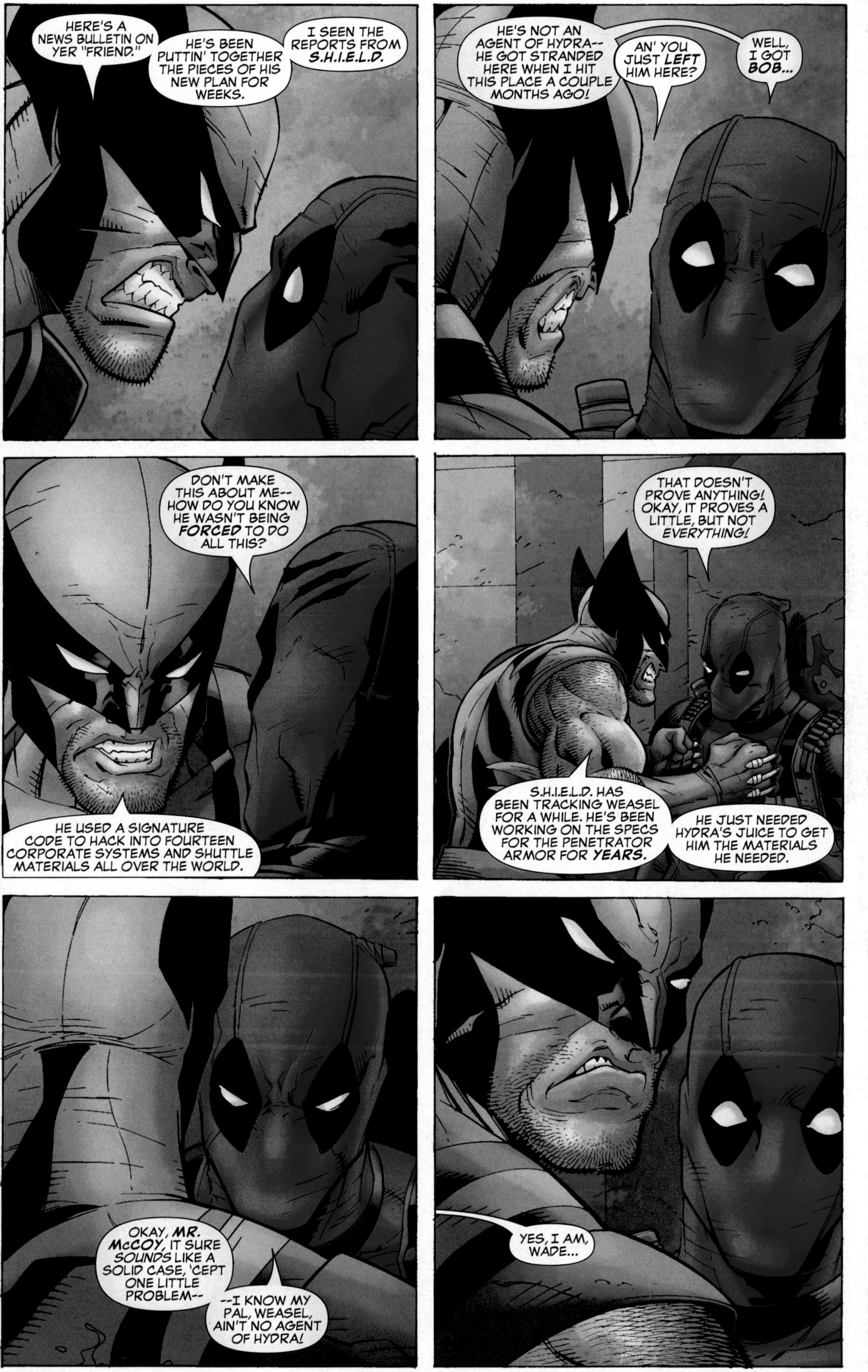
HERE'S A NEWS BULLETIN ON YER "FRIEND."
HE'S BEEN PUTTIN' TOGETHER THE PIECES OF HIS NEW PLAN FOR WEEKS.
I SEEN THE REPORTS FROM S.H.I.E.L.D.
HE'S NOT AN AGENT OF HYDRA-- HE GOT STRANDED HERE WHEN I HIT THIS PLACE A COUPLE MONTHS AGO!
AN' YOU JUST LEFT HIM HERE?
WELL, I GOT BOB...
DON'T MAKE THIS ABOUT ME-- HOW DO YOU KNOW HE WASN'T BEING FORCED TO DO ALL THIS?
HE USED A SIGNATURE CODE TO HACK INTO FOURTEEN CORPORATE SYSTEMS AND SHUTTLE MATERIALS ALL OVER THE WORLD.
THAT DOESN'T PROVE ANYTHING! OKAY, IT PROVES A LITTLE, BUT NOT EVERYTHING!
S.H.I.E.L.D. HAS BEEN TRACKING WEASEL FOR A WHILE. HE'S BEEN WORKING ON THE SPECS FOR THE PENETRATOR ARMOR FOR YEARS.
HE JUST NEEDED HYDRA'S JUICE TO GET HIM THE MATERIALS HE NEEDED.
OKAY, MR. McCOY, IT SURE SOUNDS LIKE A SOLID CASE, 'CEPT ONE LITTLE PROBLEM--
--I KNOW MY PAL, WEASEL, AIN'T NO AGENT OF HYDRA!
YES, I AM, WADE...

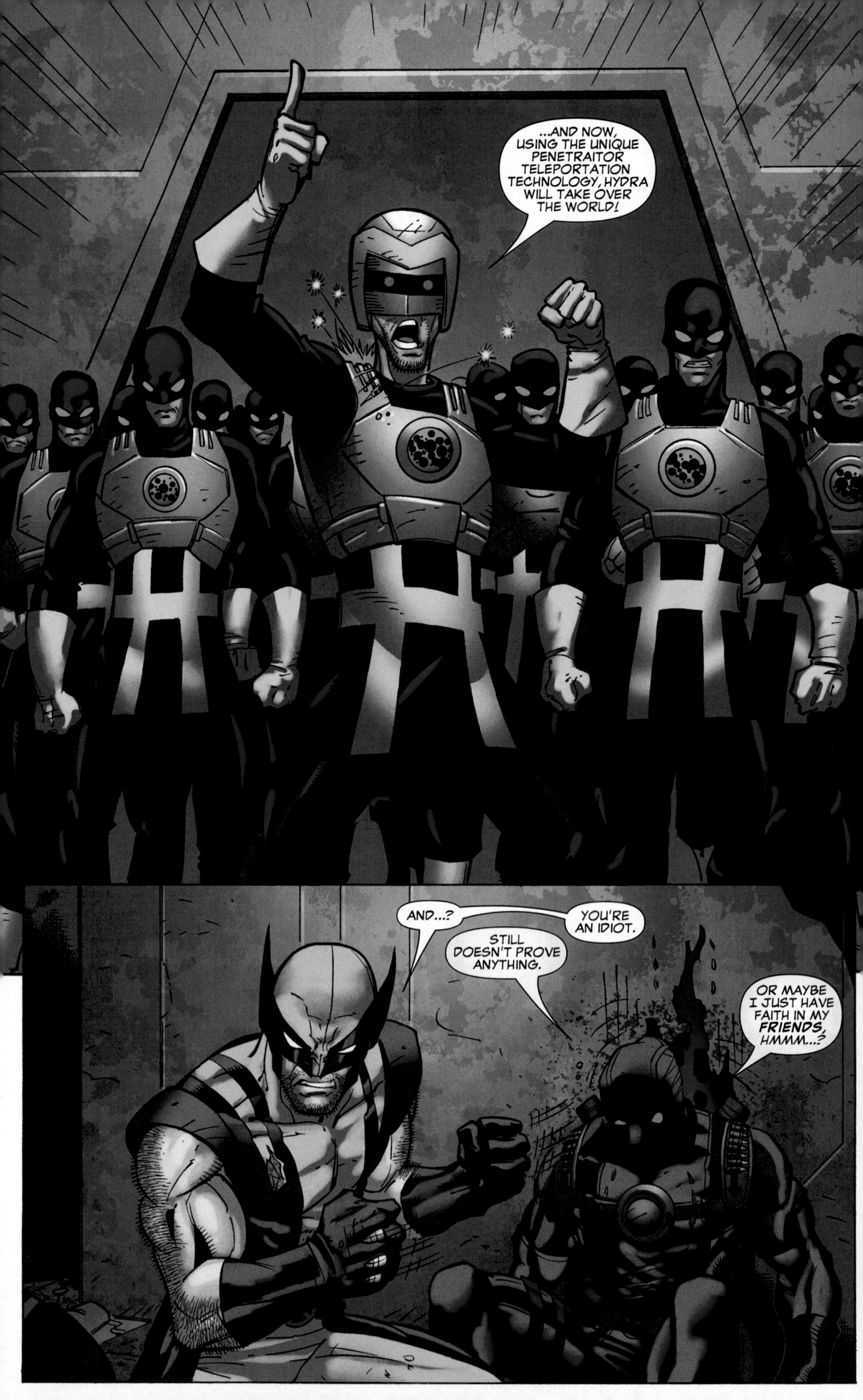
...AND NOW, USING THE UNIQUE PENETRAITOR TELEPORTATION TECHNOLOGY, HYDRA WILL TAKE OVER THE WORLD!
AND...?
YOU'RE AN IDIOT.
STILL DOESN'T PROVE ANYTHING.
OR MAYBE I JUST HAVE FAITH IN MY **FRIENDS**, HMMM...?

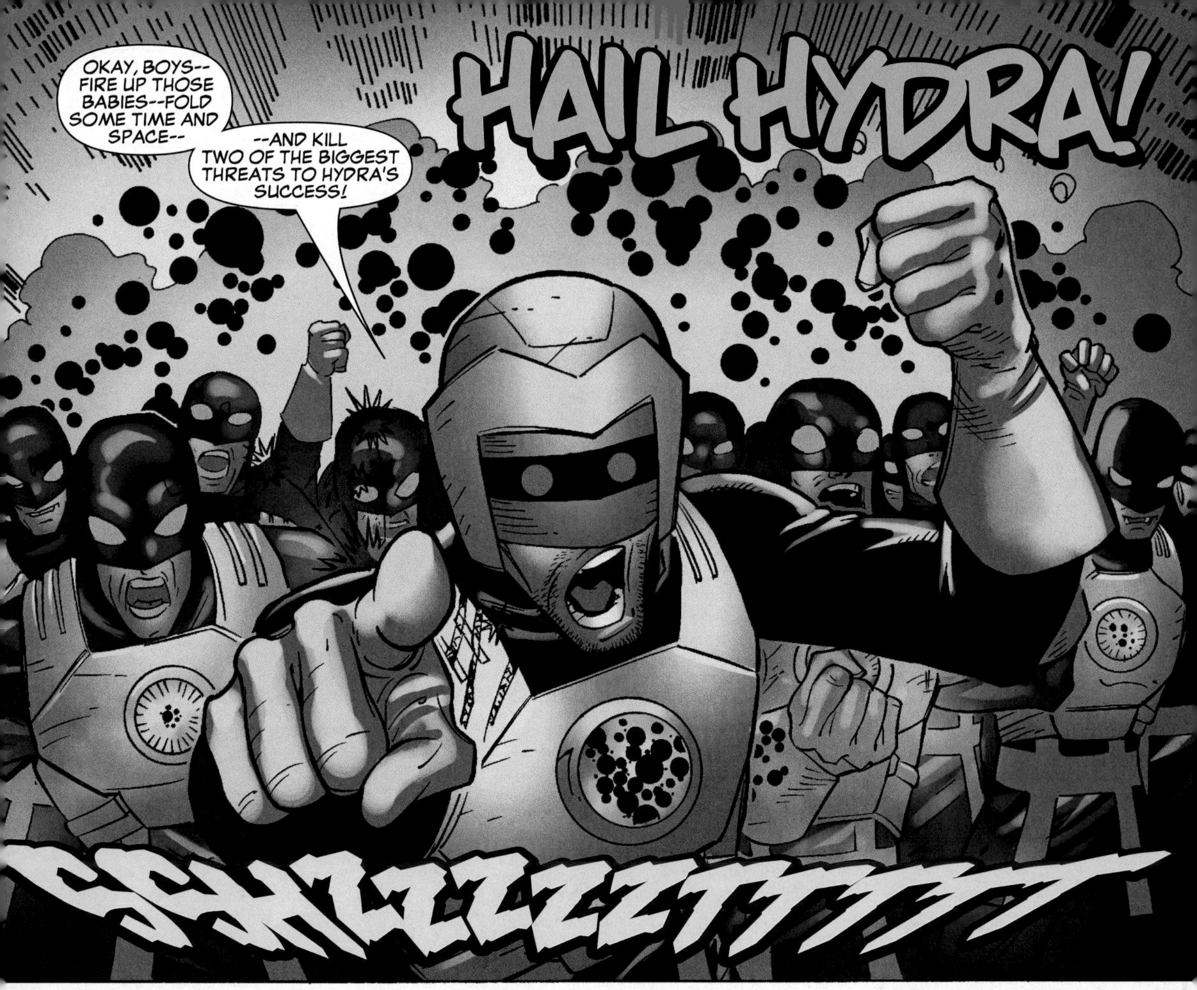
OKAY, BOYS--FIRE UP THOSE BABIES--FOLD SOME TIME AND SPACE--
--AND KILL TWO OF THE BIGGEST THREATS TO HYDRA'S SUCCESS!
HAIL HYDRA!
SSHZZZZZTTTTT

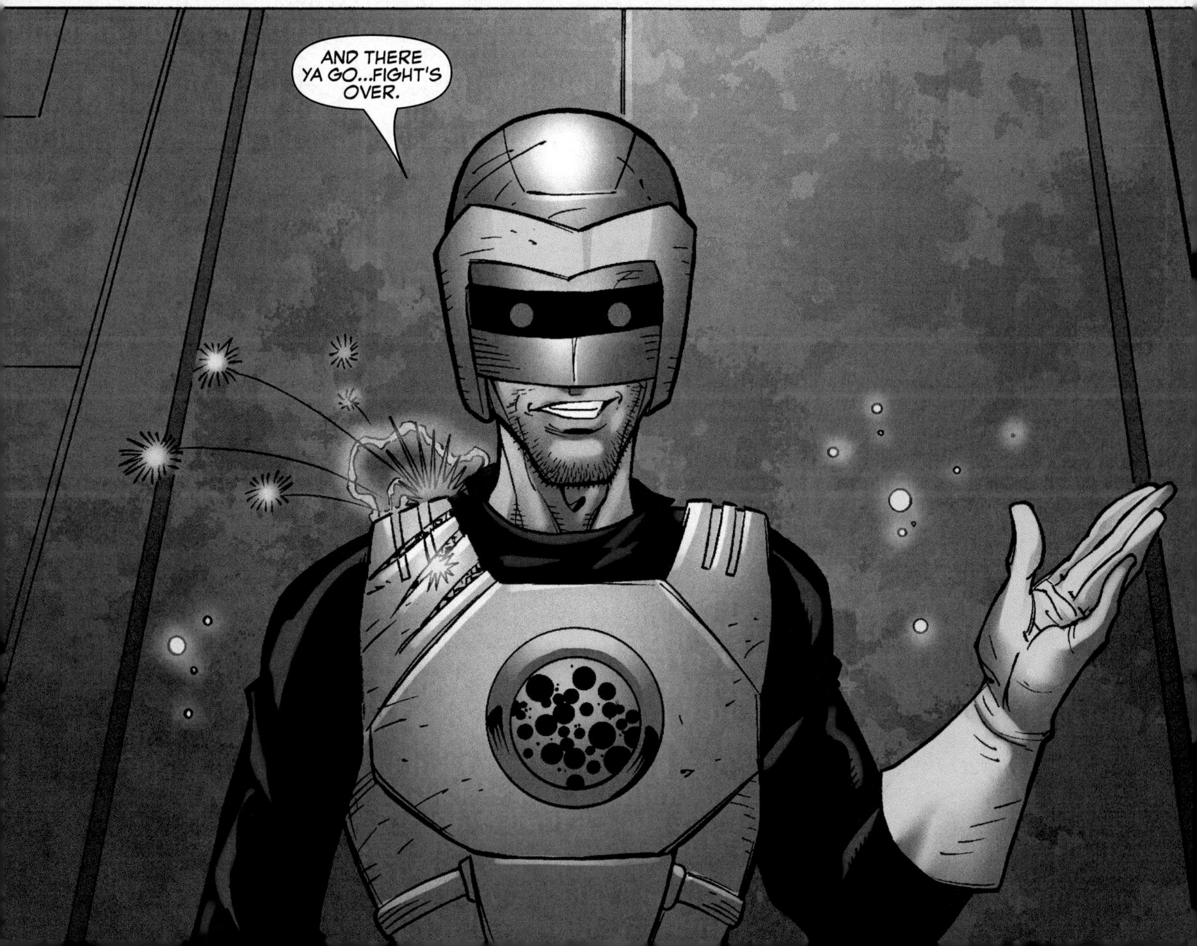
AND THERE YA GO...FIGHT'S OVER.

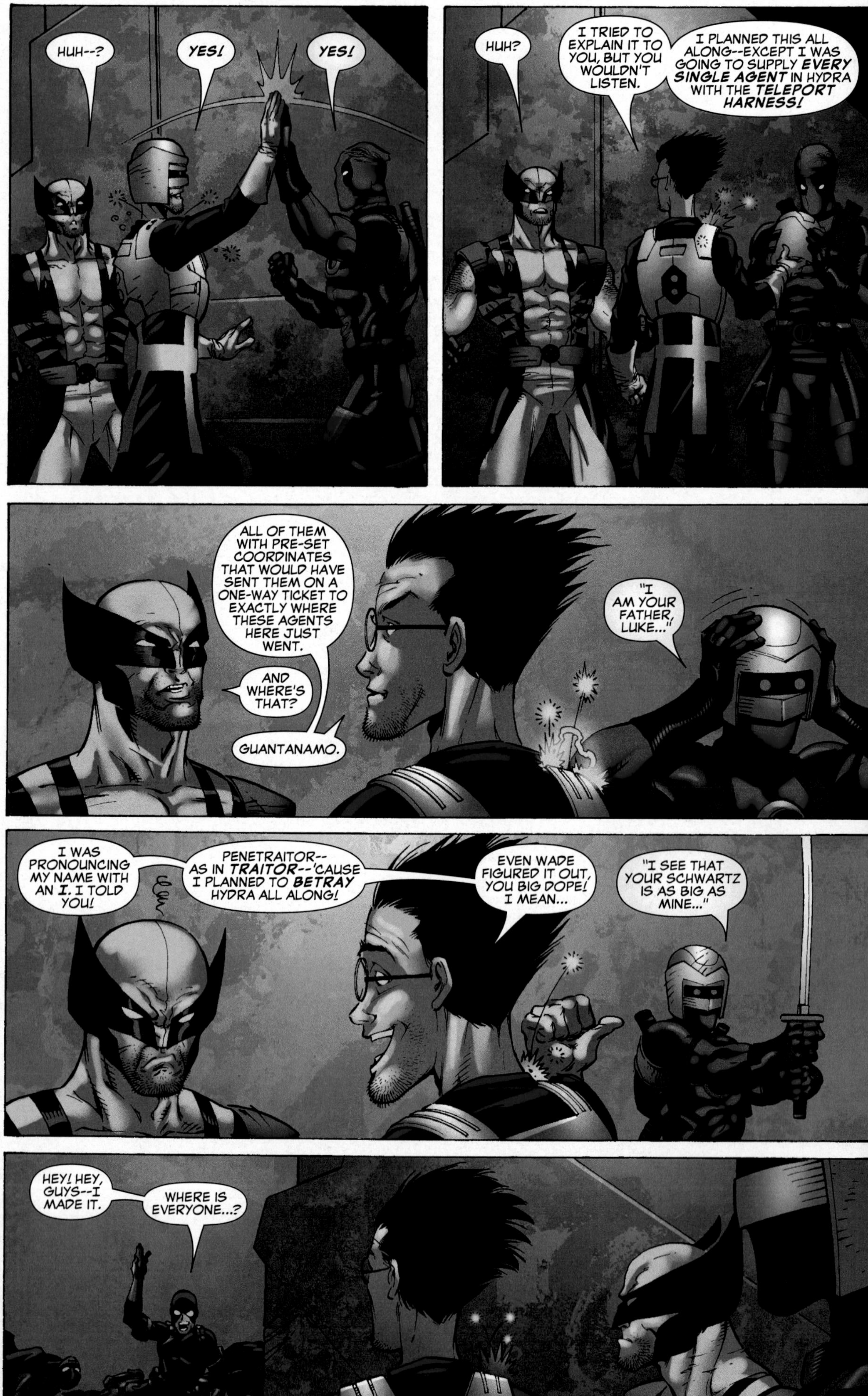
HUH--?
YES!
YES!
HUH?
I TRIED TO EXPLAIN IT TO YOU, BUT YOU WOULDN'T LISTEN.
I PLANNED THIS ALL ALONG--EXCEPT I WAS GOING TO SUPPLY EVERY SINGLE AGENT IN HYDRA WITH THE TELEPORT HARNESS!
ALL OF THEM WITH PRE-SET COORDINATES THAT WOULD HAVE SENT THEM ON A ONE-WAY TICKET TO EXACTLY WHERE THESE AGENTS HERE JUST WENT.
AND WHERE'S THAT?
GUANTANAMO.
"I AM YOUR FATHER, LUKE..."
I WAS PRONOUNCING MY NAME WITH AN I. I TOLD YOU!
PENETRAITOR-- AS IN TRAITOR--'CAUSE I PLANNED TO BETRAY HYDRA ALL ALONG!
EVEN WADE FIGURED IT OUT, YOU BIG DOPE! I MEAN...
"I SEE THAT YOUR SCHWARTZ IS AS BIG AS MINE..."
HEY! HEY, GUYS--I MADE IT.
WHERE IS EVERYONE...?

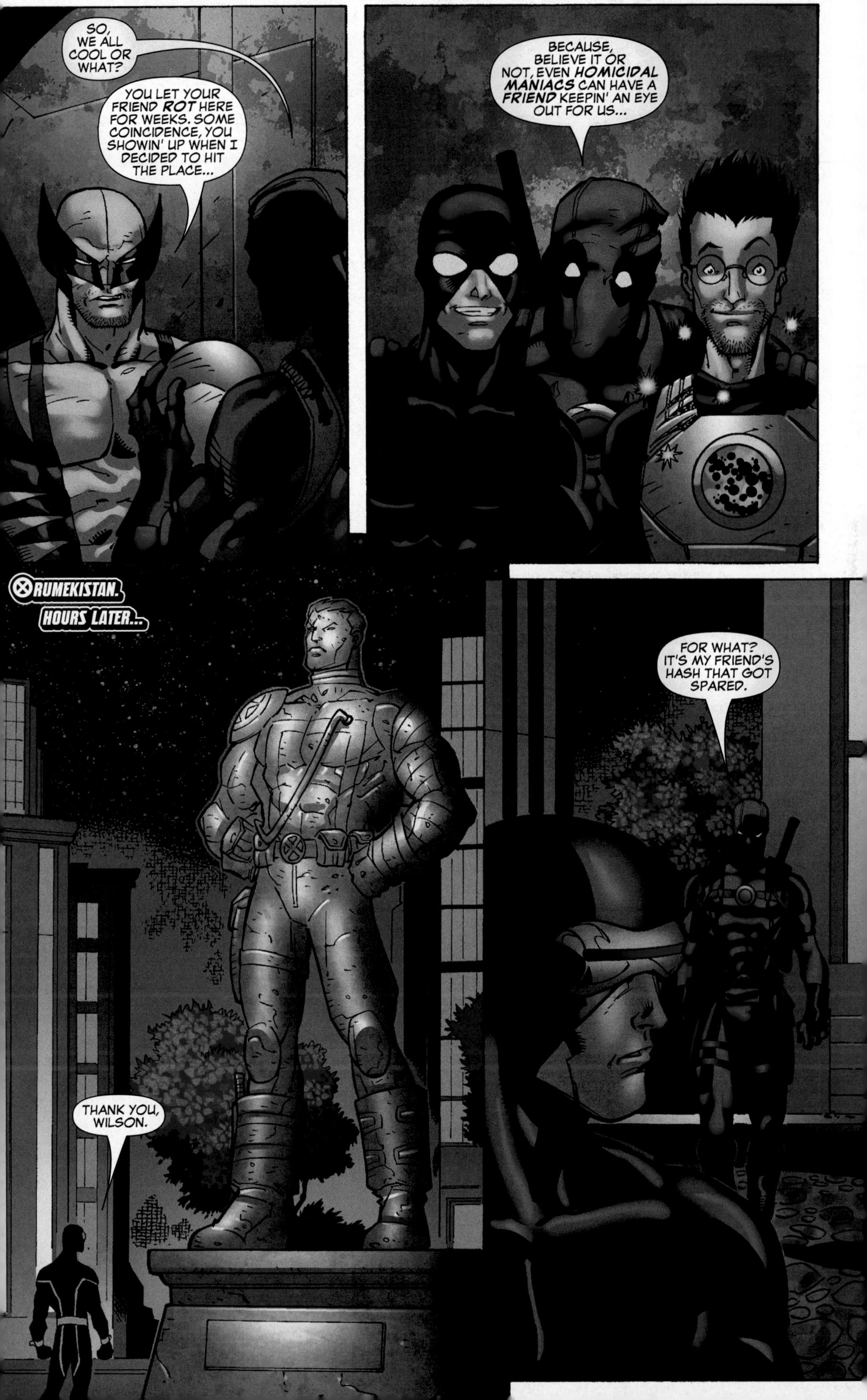
SO, WE ALL COOL OR WHAT?
YOU LET YOUR FRIEND ROT HERE FOR WEEKS. SOME COINCIDENCE, YOU SHOWIN' UP WHEN I DECIDED TO HIT THE PLACE...
BECAUSE, BELIEVE IT OR NOT, EVEN HOMICIDAL MANIACS CAN HAVE A FRIEND KEEPIN' AN EYE OUT FOR US...
RUMEKISTAN.
HOURS LATER...
THANK YOU, WILSON.
FOR WHAT? IT'S MY FRIEND'S HASH THAT GOT SPARED.

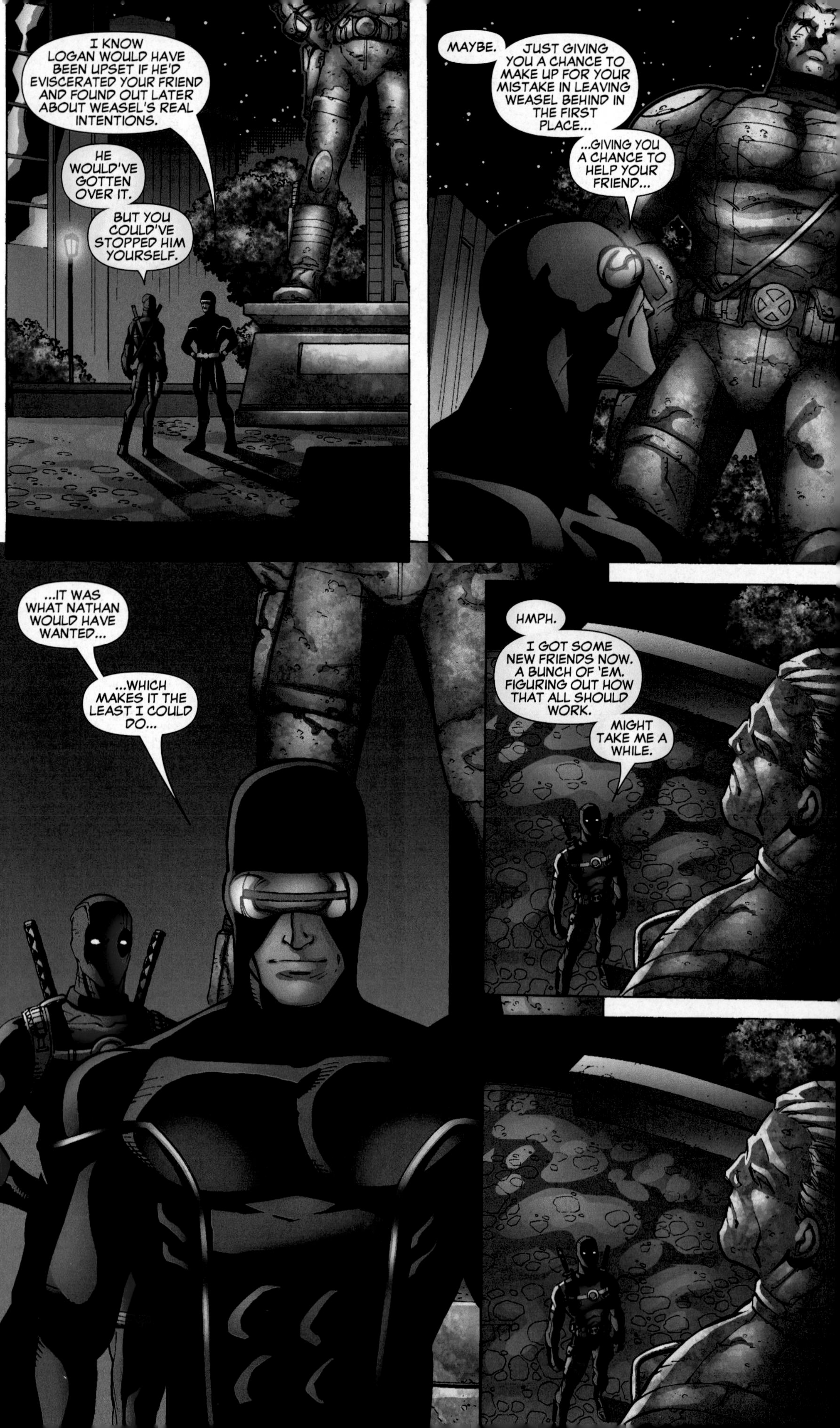
I KNOW LOGAN WOULD HAVE BEEN UPSET IF HE'D EVISCERATED YOUR FRIEND AND FOUND OUT LATER ABOUT WEASEL'S REAL INTENTIONS.
HE WOULD'VE GOTTEN OVER IT.
BUT YOU COULD'VE STOPPED HIM YOURSELF.
MAYBE.
JUST GIVING YOU A CHANCE TO MAKE UP FOR YOUR MISTAKE IN LEAVING WEASEL BEHIND IN THE FIRST PLACE...
...GIVING YOU A CHANCE TO HELP YOUR FRIEND...
...IT WAS WHAT NATHAN WOULD HAVE WANTED...
...WHICH MAKES IT THE LEAST I COULD DO...
HMPH.
I GOT SOME NEW FRIENDS NOW. A BUNCH OF 'EM. FIGURING OUT HOW THAT ALL SHOULD WORK.
MIGHT TAKE ME A WHILE.

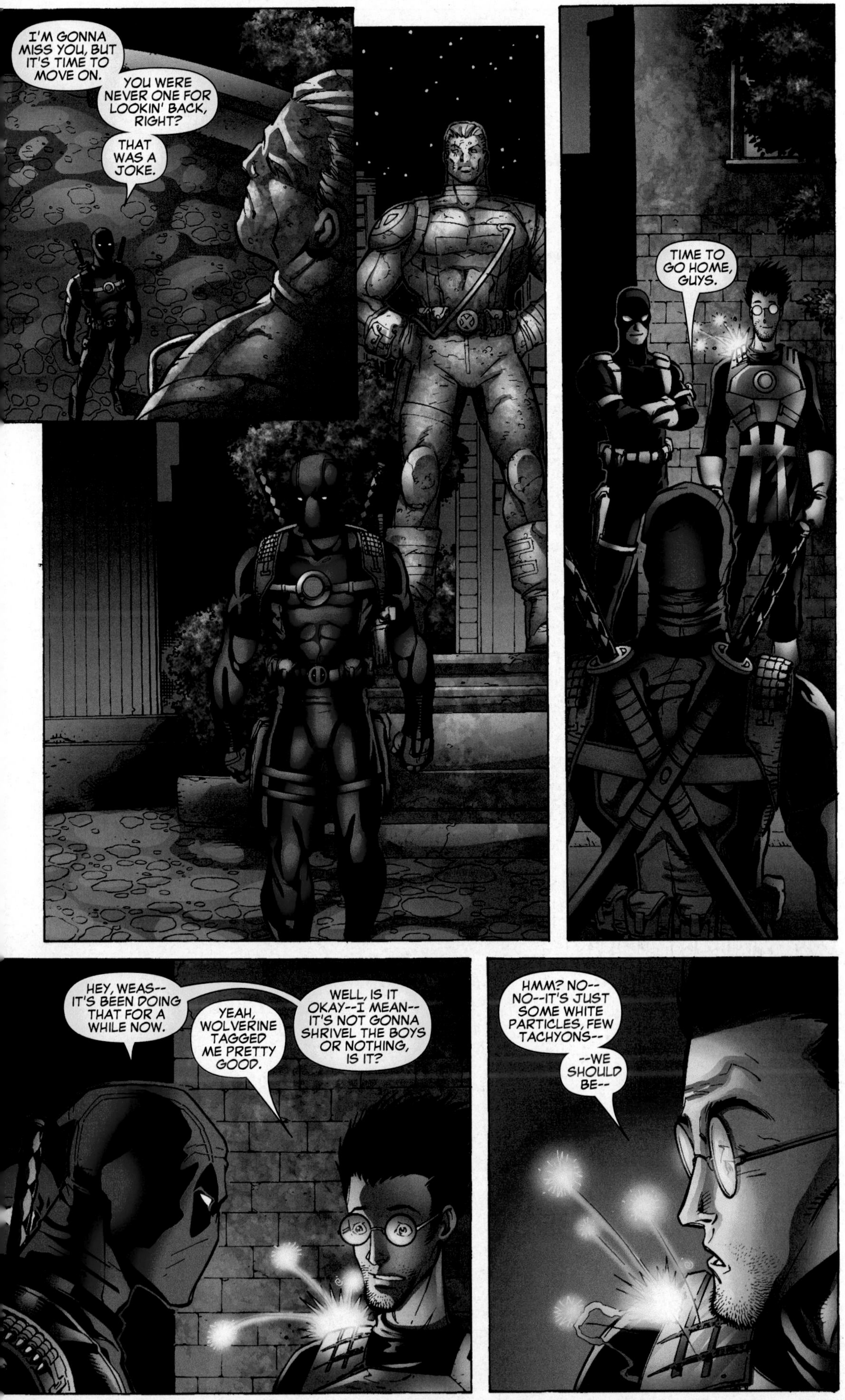
I'M GONNA MISS YOU, BUT IT'S TIME TO MOVE ON.
YOU WERE NEVER ONE FOR LOOKIN' BACK, RIGHT?
THAT WAS A JOKE.
TIME TO GO HOME, GUYS.
HEY, WEAS-- IT'S BEEN DOING THAT FOR A WHILE NOW.
YEAH, WOLVERINE TAGGED ME PRETTY GOOD.
WELL, IS IT OKAY--I MEAN-- IT'S NOT GONNA SHRIVEL THE BOYS OR NOTHING, IS IT?
HMM? NO-- NO--IT'S JUST SOME WHITE PARTICLES, FEW TACHYONS--
--WE SHOULD BE--

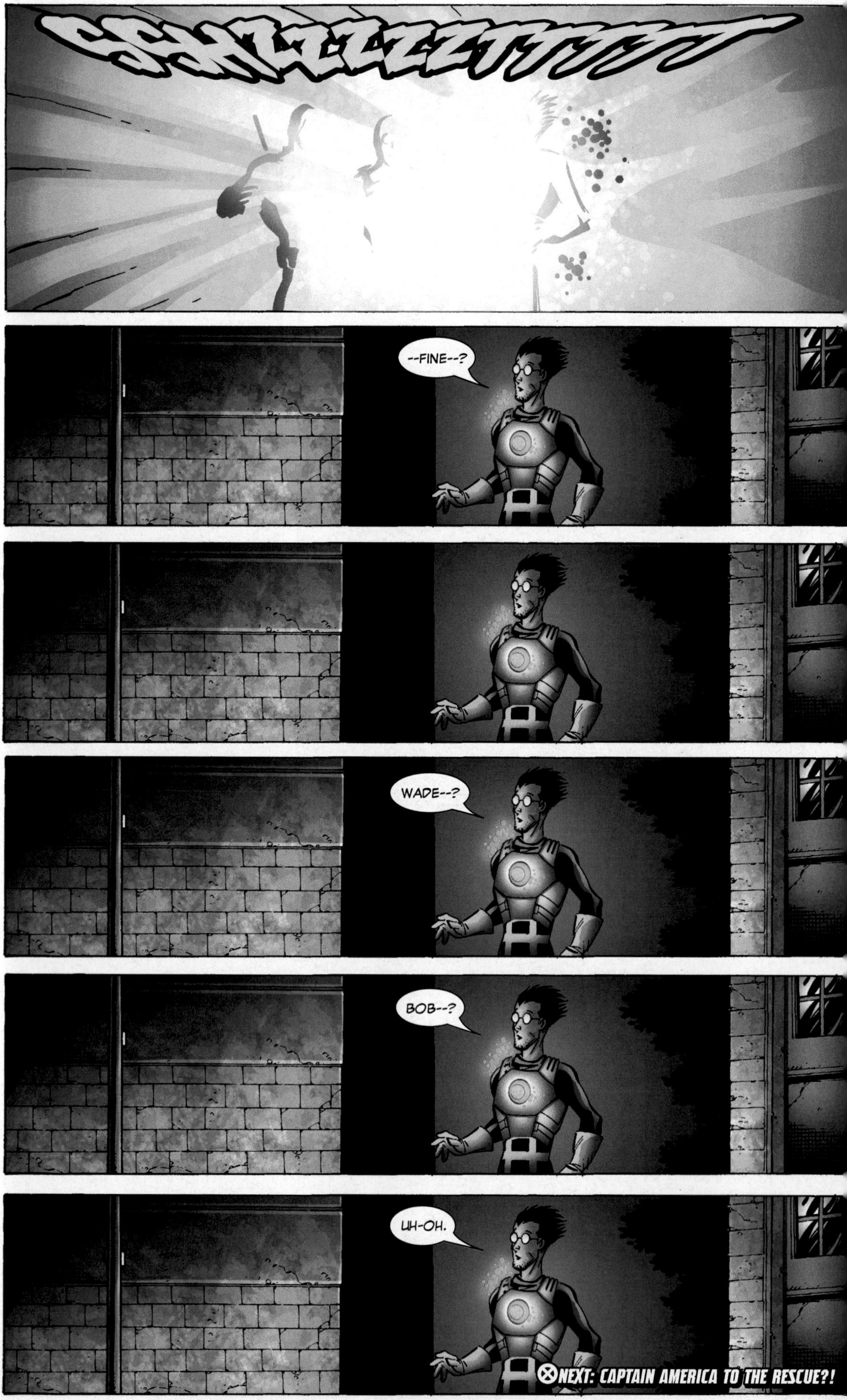
--FINE--?
WADE--?
BOB--?
UH-OH.
NEXT: CAPTAIN AMERICA TO THE RESCUE?!

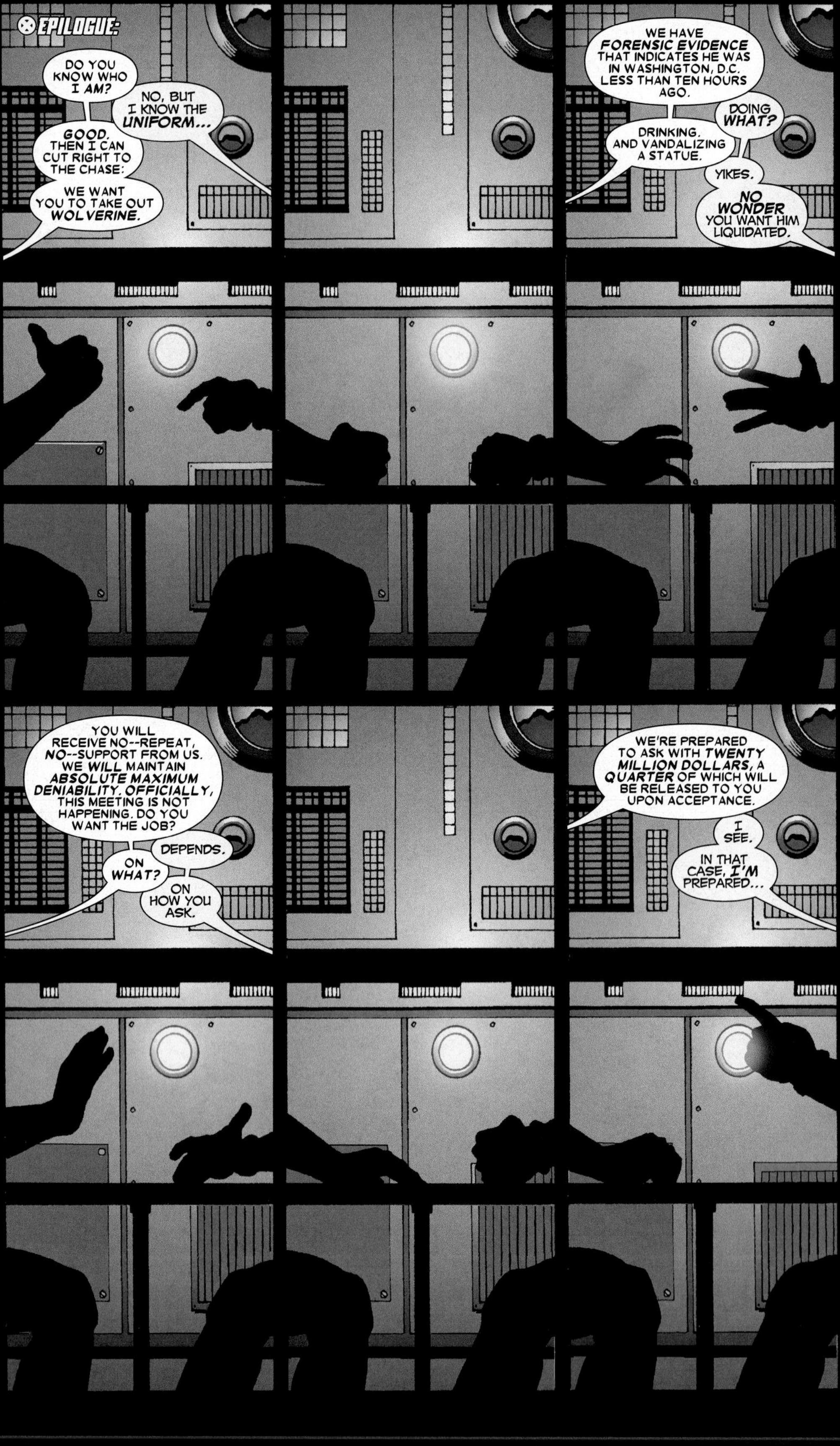
EPILOGUE:
DO YOU KNOW WHO I AM?
NO, BUT I KNOW THE UNIFORM...
GOOD. THEN I CAN CUT RIGHT TO THE CHASE:
WE WANT YOU TO TAKE OUT WOLVERINE.
WE HAVE FORENSIC EVIDENCE THAT INDICATES HE WAS IN WASHINGTON, D.C. LESS THAN TEN HOURS AGO.
DOING WHAT?
DRINKING. AND VANDALIZING A STATUE.
YIKES.
NO WONDER YOU WANT HIM LIQUIDATED.
YOU WILL RECEIVE NO--REPEAT, NO--SUPPORT FROM US. WE WILL MAINTAIN ABSOLUTE MAXIMUM DENIABILITY. OFFICIALLY, THIS MEETING IS NOT HAPPENING. DO YOU WANT THE JOB?
DEPENDS.
ON WHAT?
ON HOW YOU ASK.
WE'RE PREPARED TO ASK WITH TWENTY MILLION DOLLARS, A QUARTER OF WHICH WILL BE RELEASED TO YOU UPON ACCEPTANCE.
I SEE.
IN THAT CASE, I'M PREPARED...

riter: Daniel Way • artist: Steve Dillon • colorist: Avalon's Matt Milla • letterer: VC's Cory Petit • assistant editor: Aubrey Sitterson • editor: Axel Alons

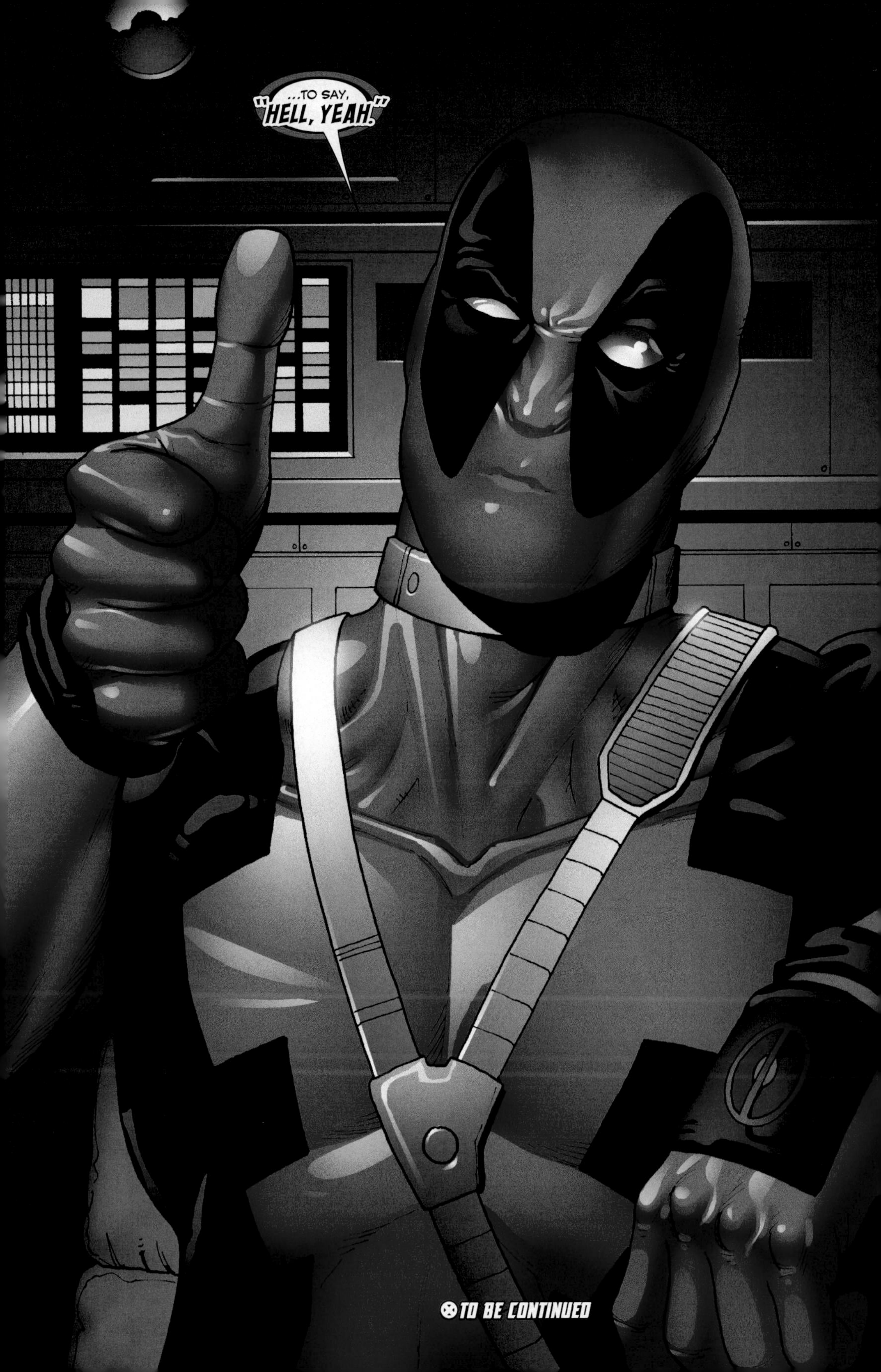
"...TO SAY, "HELL, YEAH.""
TO BE CONTINUED

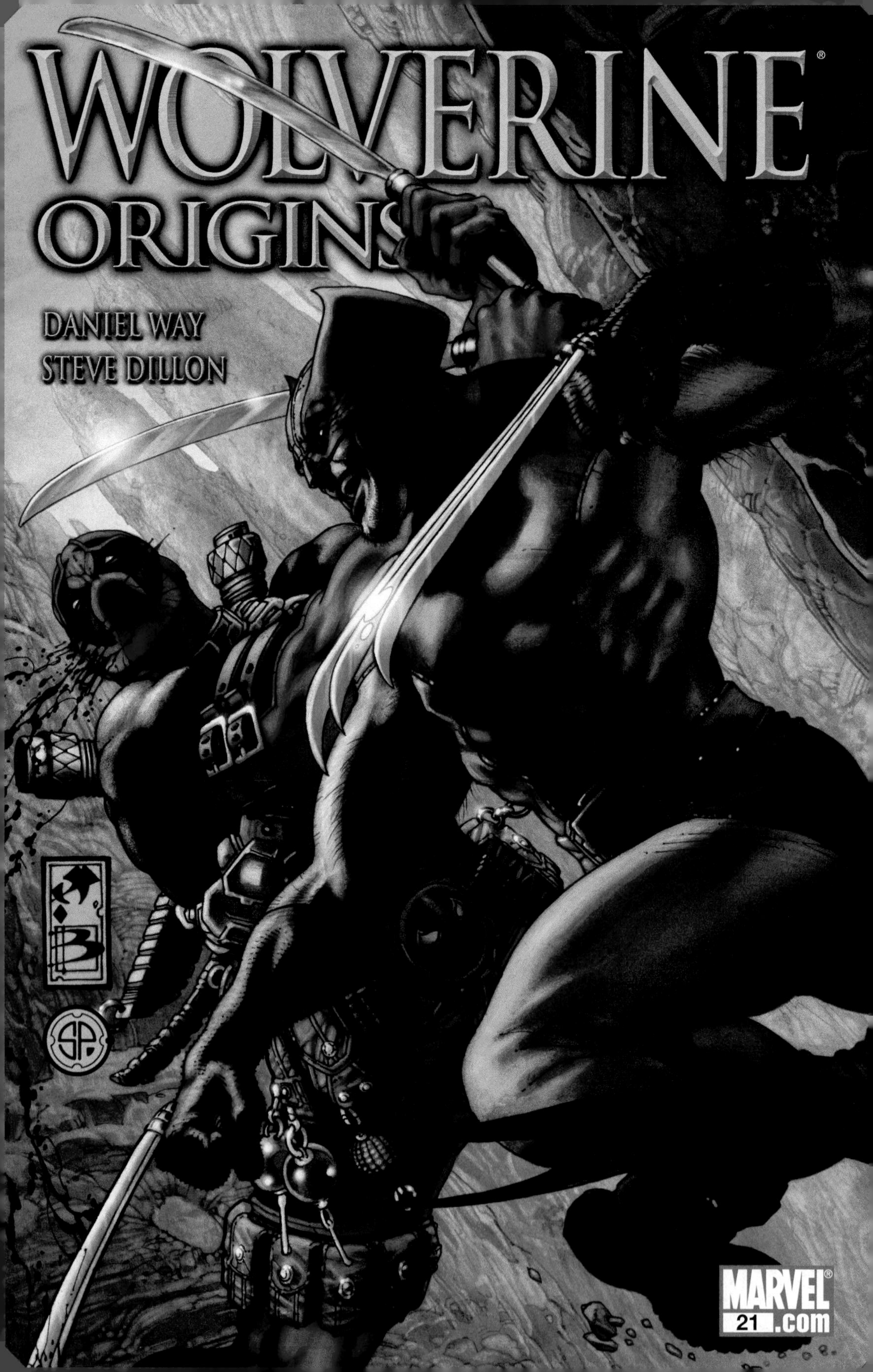
WOLVERINE ORIGINS
DANIEL WAY
STEVE DILLON
MARVEL 21 .com

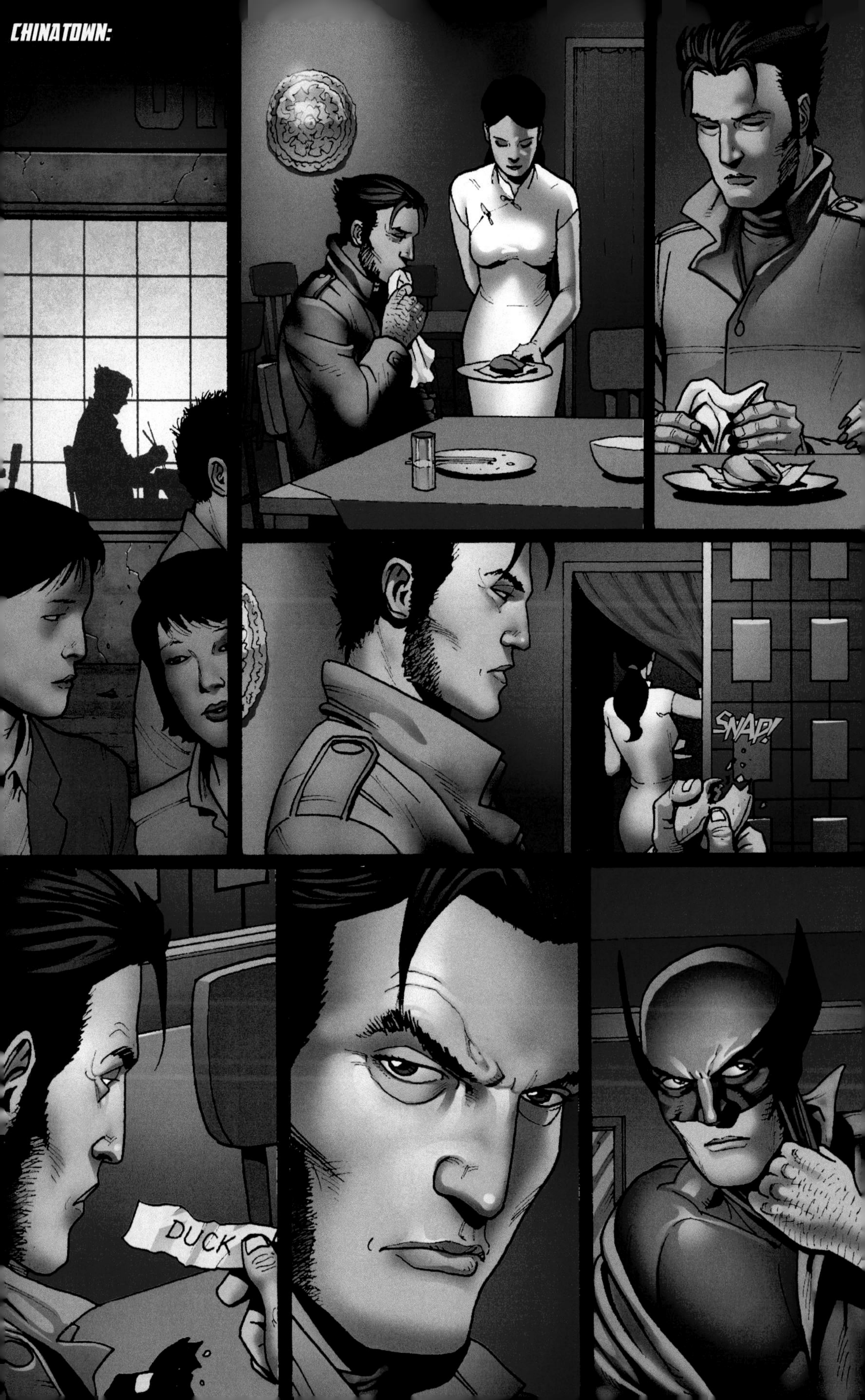

CHINATOWN:
SNAP!
DUCK

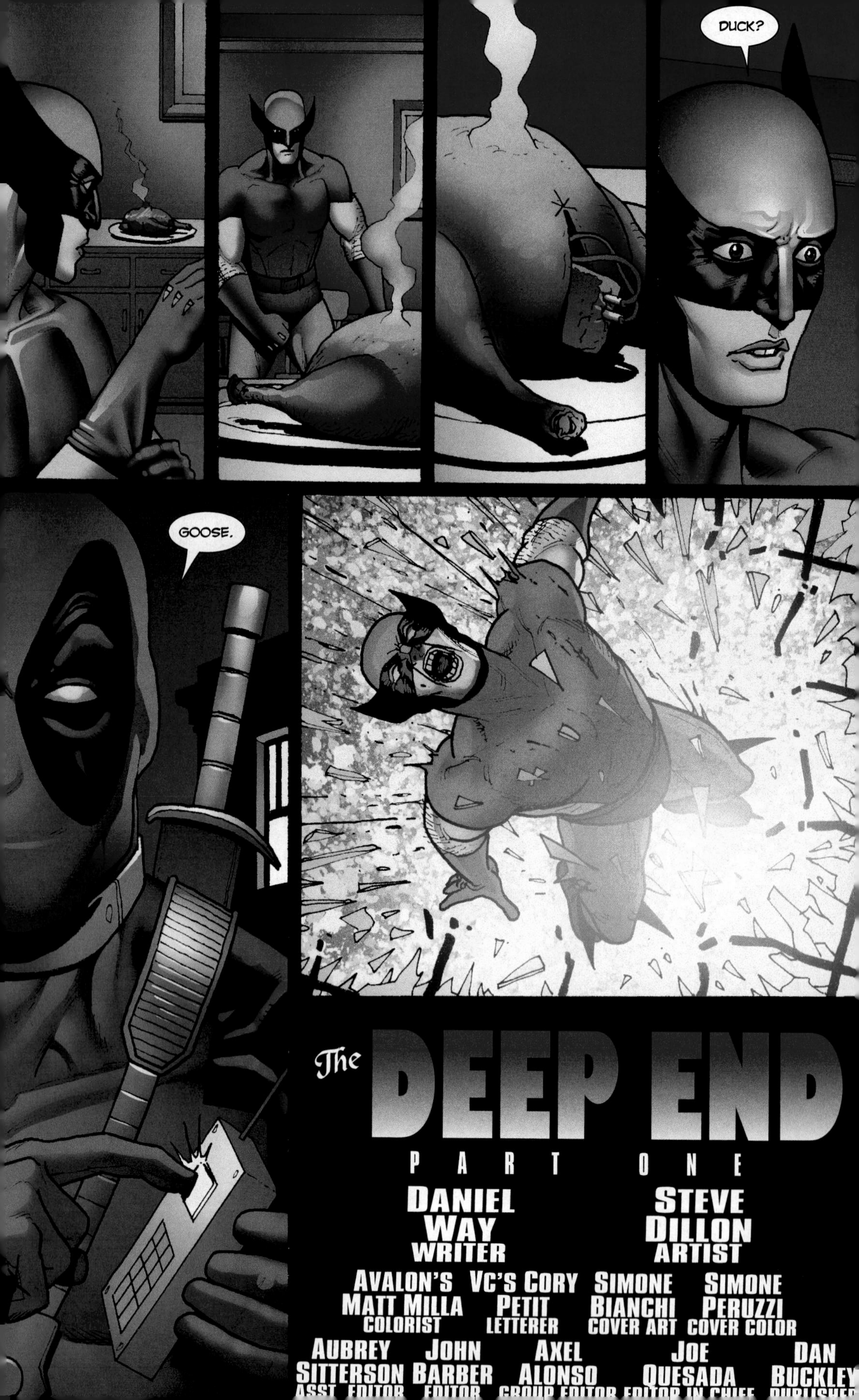
DUCK?
GOOSE.
The DEEP END
PART ONE
DANIEL WAY WRITER
STEVE DILLON ARTIST
AVALON'S MATT MILLA COLORIST
VC'S CORY PETIT LETTERER
SIMONE BIANCHI COVER ART
SIMONE PERUZZI COVER COLOR
AUBREY SITTERSON ASST. EDITOR
JOHN BARBER EDITOR
AXEL ALONSO GROUP EDITOR
JOE QUESADA EDITOR IN CHIEF
DAN BUCKLEY PUBLISHER

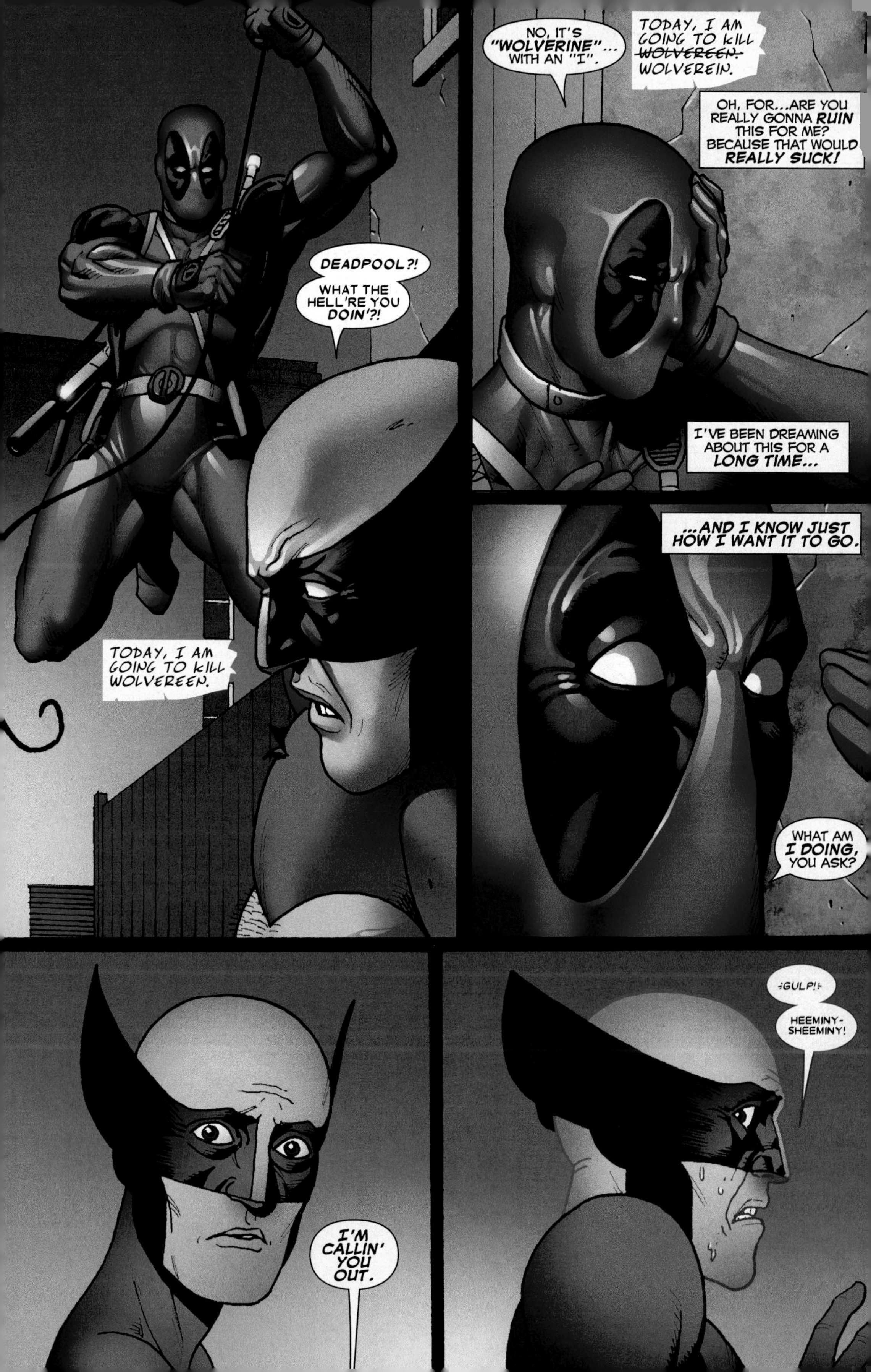
DEADPOOL?!
WHAT THE HELL'RE YOU DOIN'?!
TODAY, I AM GOING TO KILL WOLVEREEN.
NO, IT'S "WOLVERINE"... WITH AN "I".
TODAY, I AM GOING TO KILL WOLVEREEN. WOLVEREIN.
OH, FOR...ARE YOU REALLY GONNA RUIN THIS FOR ME? BECAUSE THAT WOULD REALLY SUCK!
I'VE BEEN DREAMING ABOUT THIS FOR A LONG TIME...
...AND I KNOW JUST HOW I WANT IT TO GO.
WHAT AM I DOING, YOU ASK?
I'M CALLIN' YOU OUT.
-GULP!-
HEEMINY-SHEEMINY!

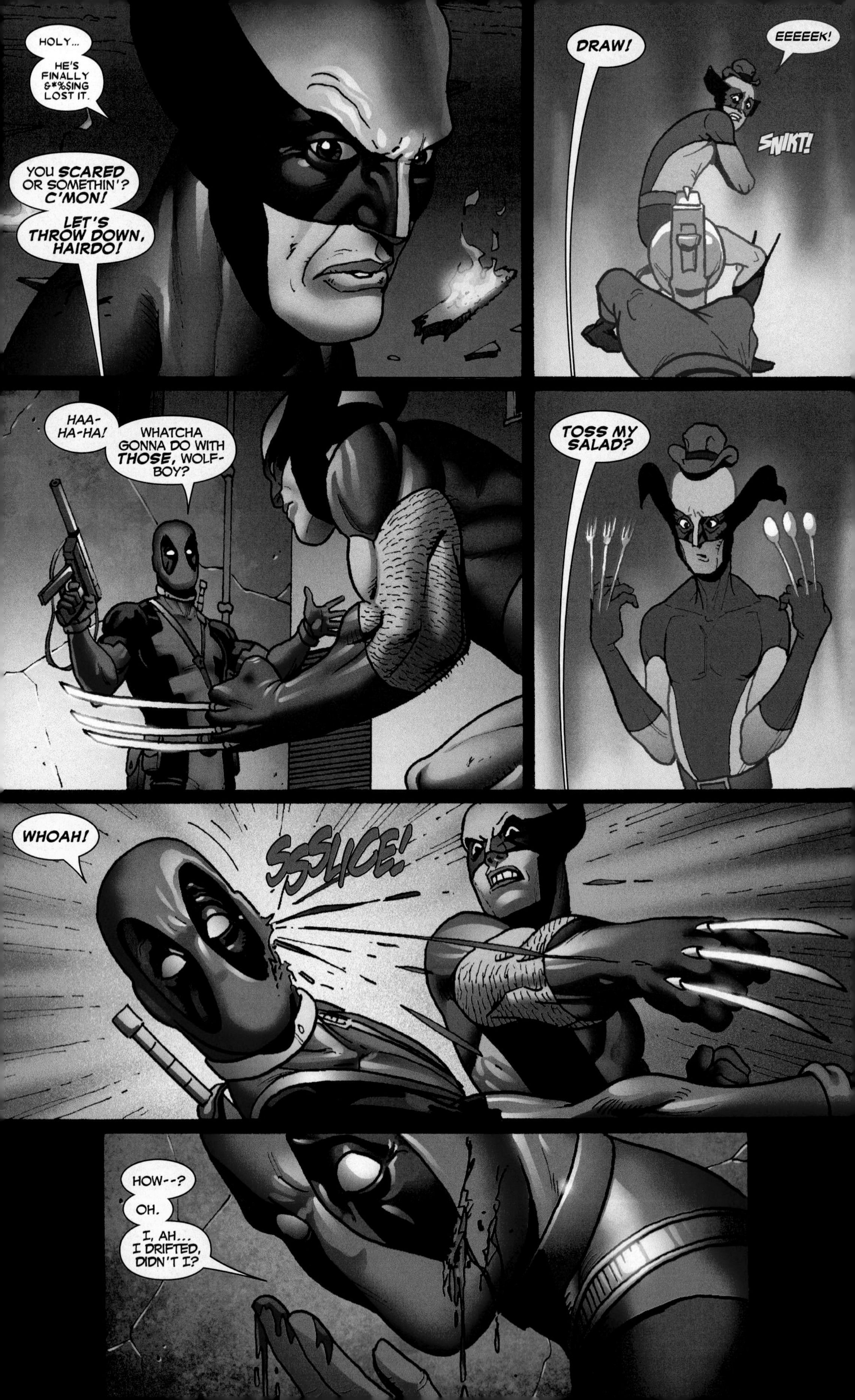
HOLY...
HE'S FINALLY &*%$ING LOST IT.
YOU SCARED OR SOMETHIN'? C'MON!
LET'S THROW DOWN, HAIRDO!
DRAW!
EEEEEK!
SNIKT!
HAA-HA-HA!
WHATCHA GONNA DO WITH THOSE, WOLF-BOY?
TOSS MY SALAD?
WHOAH!
SSSLICE!
HOW--?
OH.
I, AH... I DRIFTED, DIDN'T I?

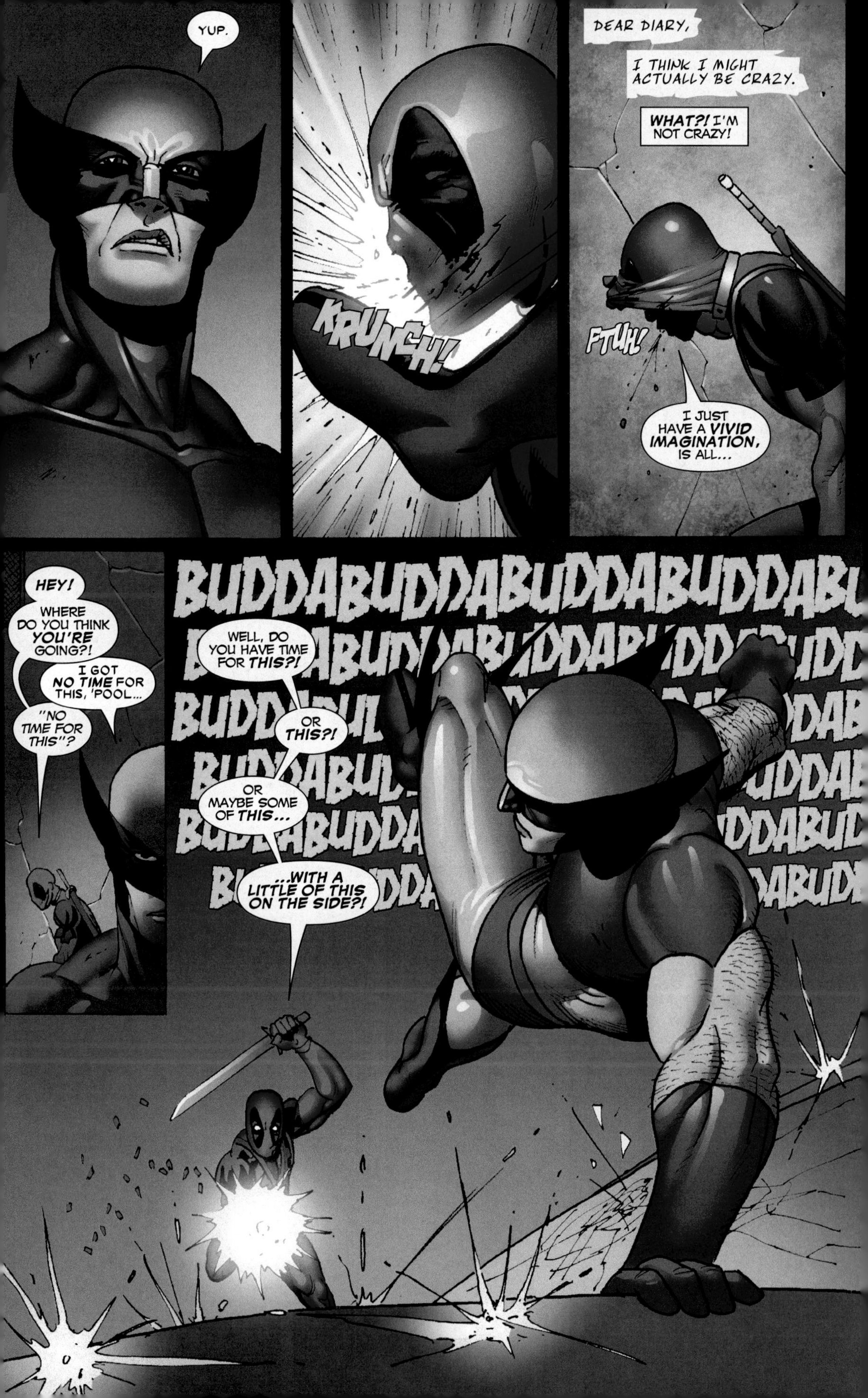
YUP.
KRUNCH!
DEAR DIARY,
I THINK I MIGHT ACTUALLY BE CRAZY.
WHAT?! I'M NOT CRAZY!
FTUH!
I JUST HAVE A VIVID IMAGINATION, IS ALL...
HEY!
WHERE DO YOU THINK YOU'RE GOING?!
I GOT NO TIME FOR THIS, 'POOL...
"NO TIME FOR THIS"?
WELL, DO YOU HAVE TIME FOR THIS?!
OR THIS?!
OR MAYBE SOME OF THIS...
...WITH A LITTLE OF THIS ON THE SIDE?!
BUDDABUDDABUDDABUDDABU

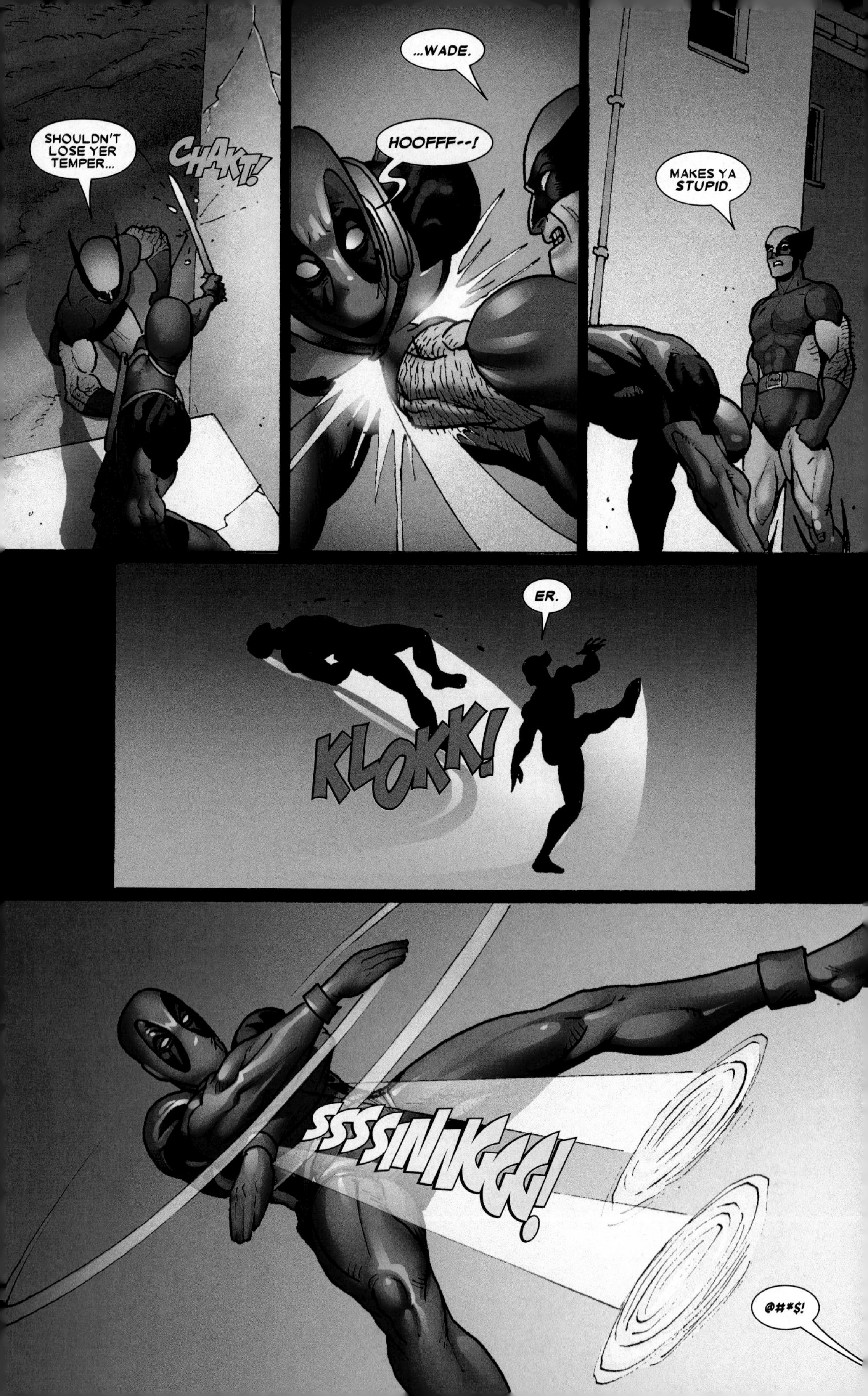
SHOULDN'T LOSE YER TEMPER...
CHAKT!
...WADE.
HOOFFF--!
MAKES YA STUPID.
ER.
KLOKK!
SSSINNGG!
@#*$!

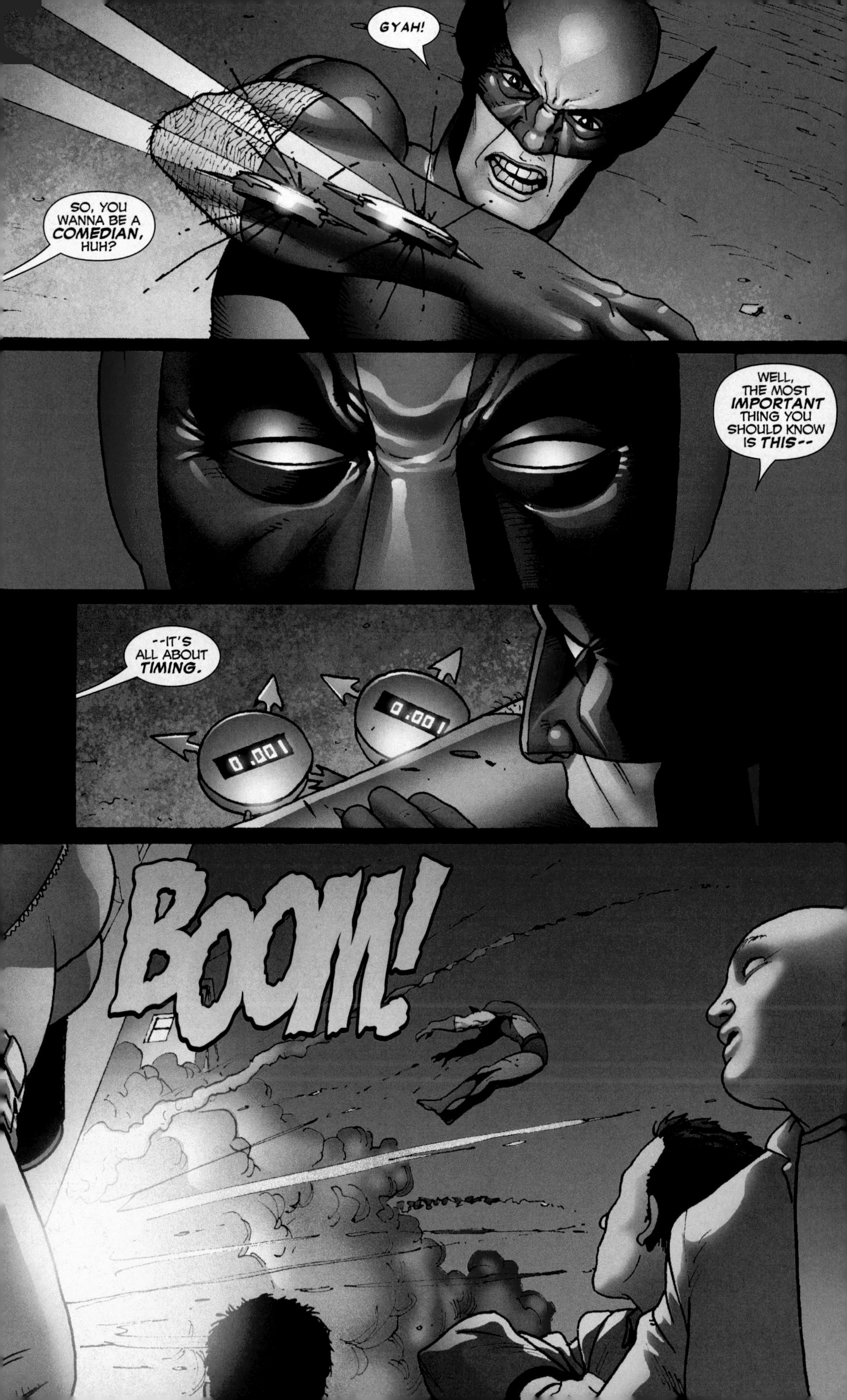
GYAH!
SO, YOU WANNA BE A COMEDIAN, HUH?
WELL, THE MOST IMPORTANT THING YOU SHOULD KNOW IS THIS--
--IT'S ALL ABOUT TIMING.
0.001
0.001
BOOM!

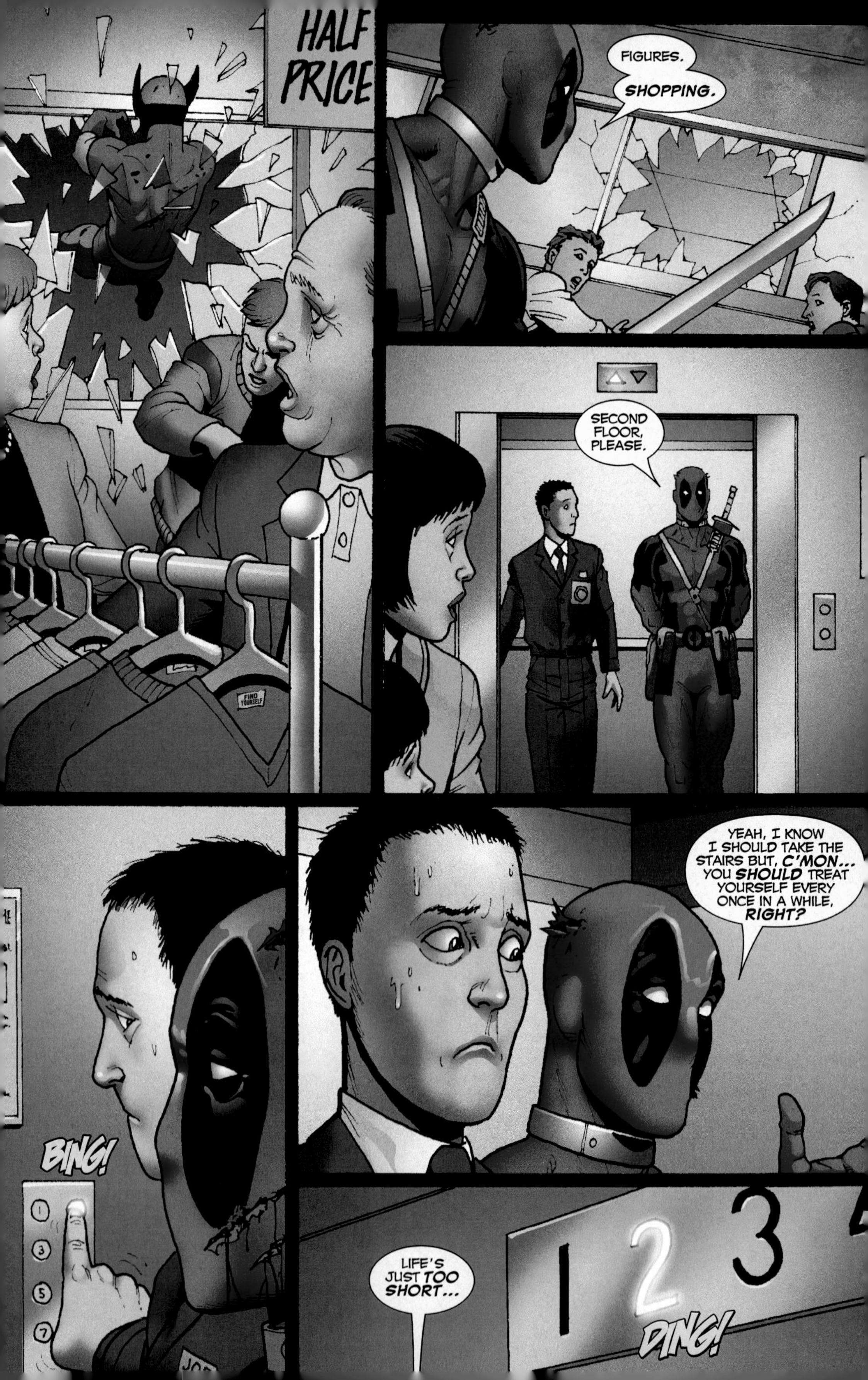
HALF PRICE
FIND YOURSELF
FIGURES.
SHOPPING.
SECOND FLOOR, PLEASE.
YEAH, I KNOW I SHOULD TAKE THE STAIRS BUT, C'MON... YOU SHOULD TREAT YOURSELF EVERY ONCE IN A WHILE, RIGHT?
BING!
LIFE'S JUST TOO SHORT...
1 2 3
DING!

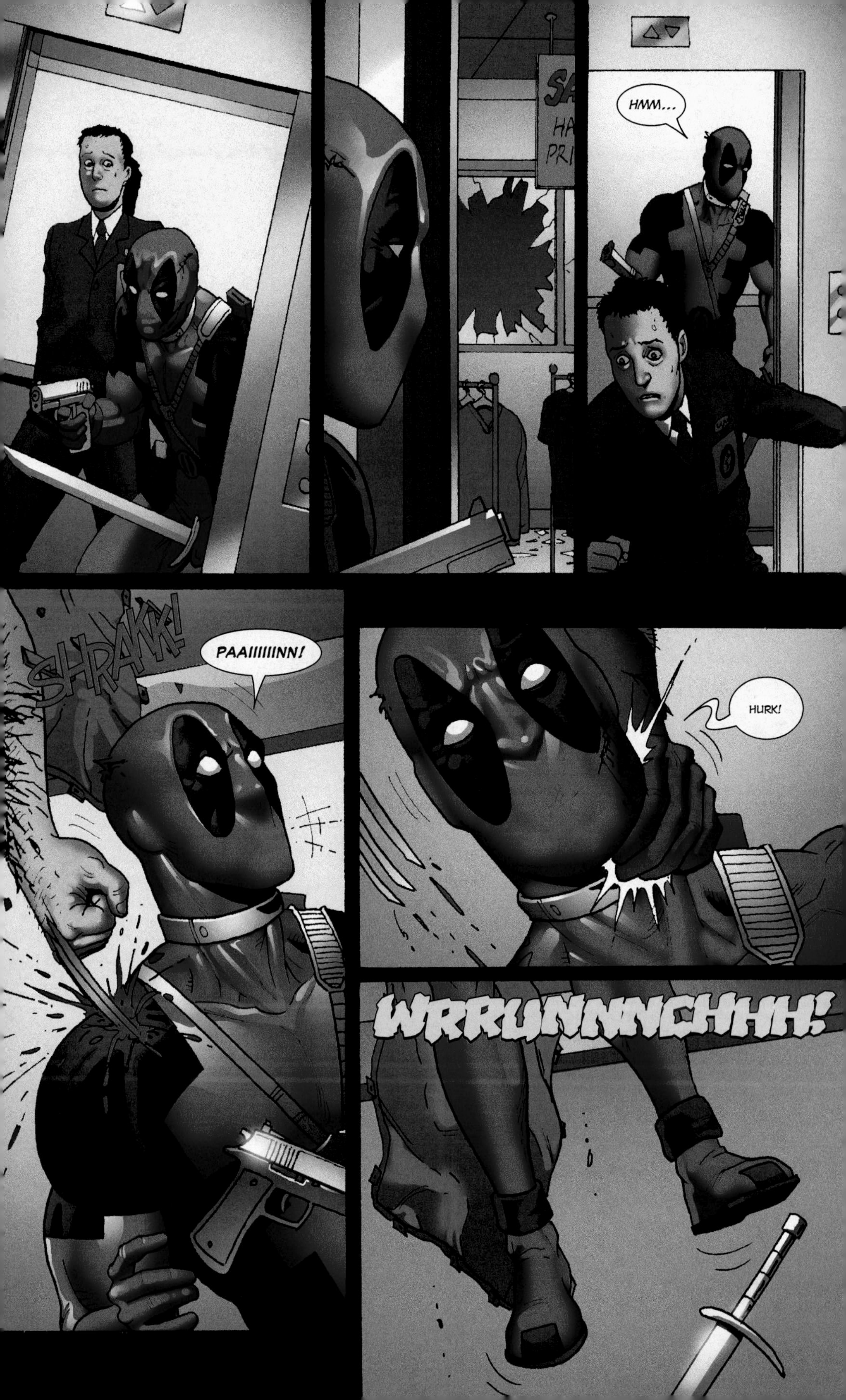
HMM...
SHRAKK!
PAAIIIIIINN!
HURK!
WRRUNNNCHHH!

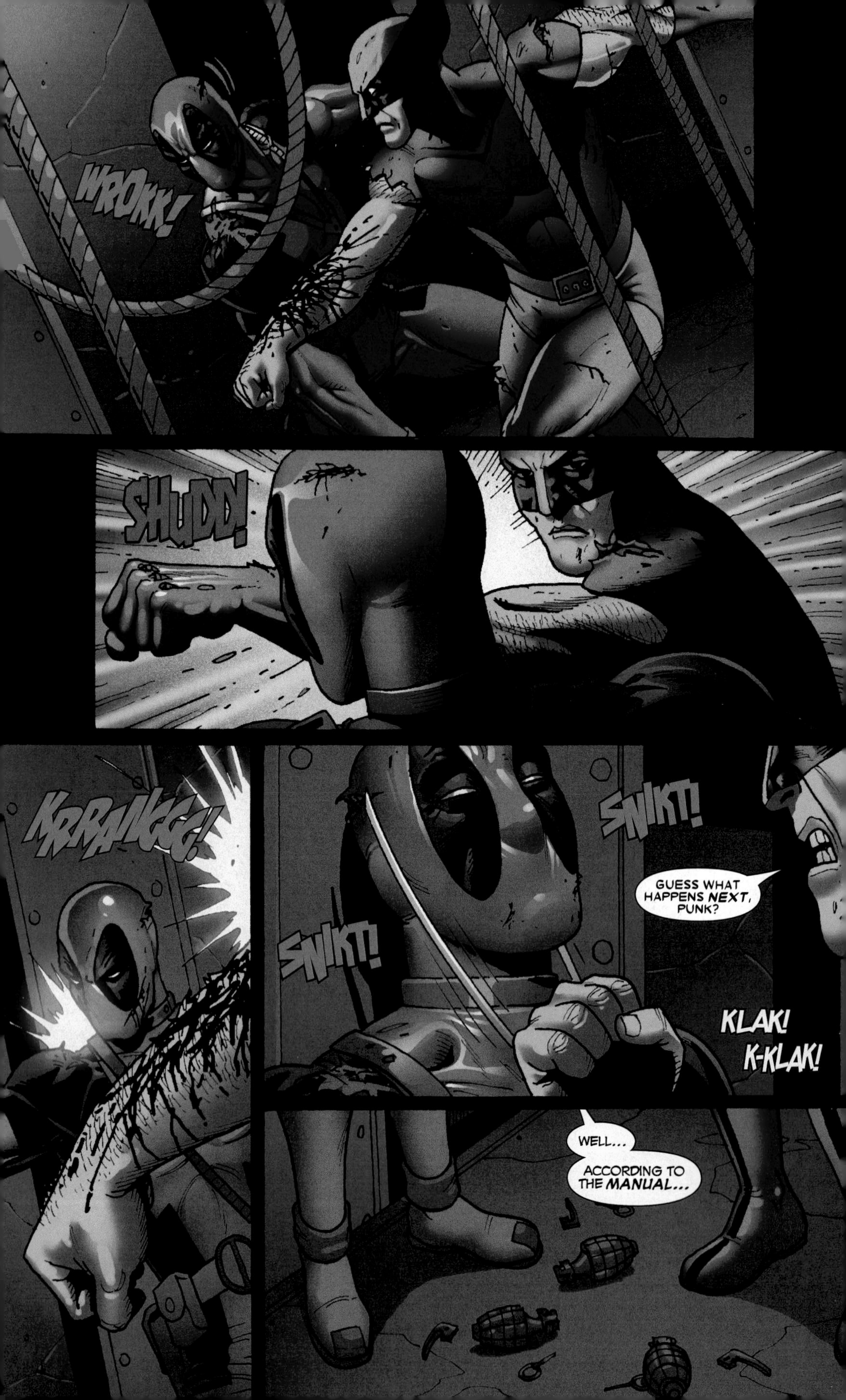
WROKK!
SHUDD!
KRRANGGG!!
SNIKT!
SNIKT!
GUESS WHAT HAPPENS NEXT, PUNK?
KLAK!
K-KLAK!
WELL...
ACCORDING TO THE MANUAL...

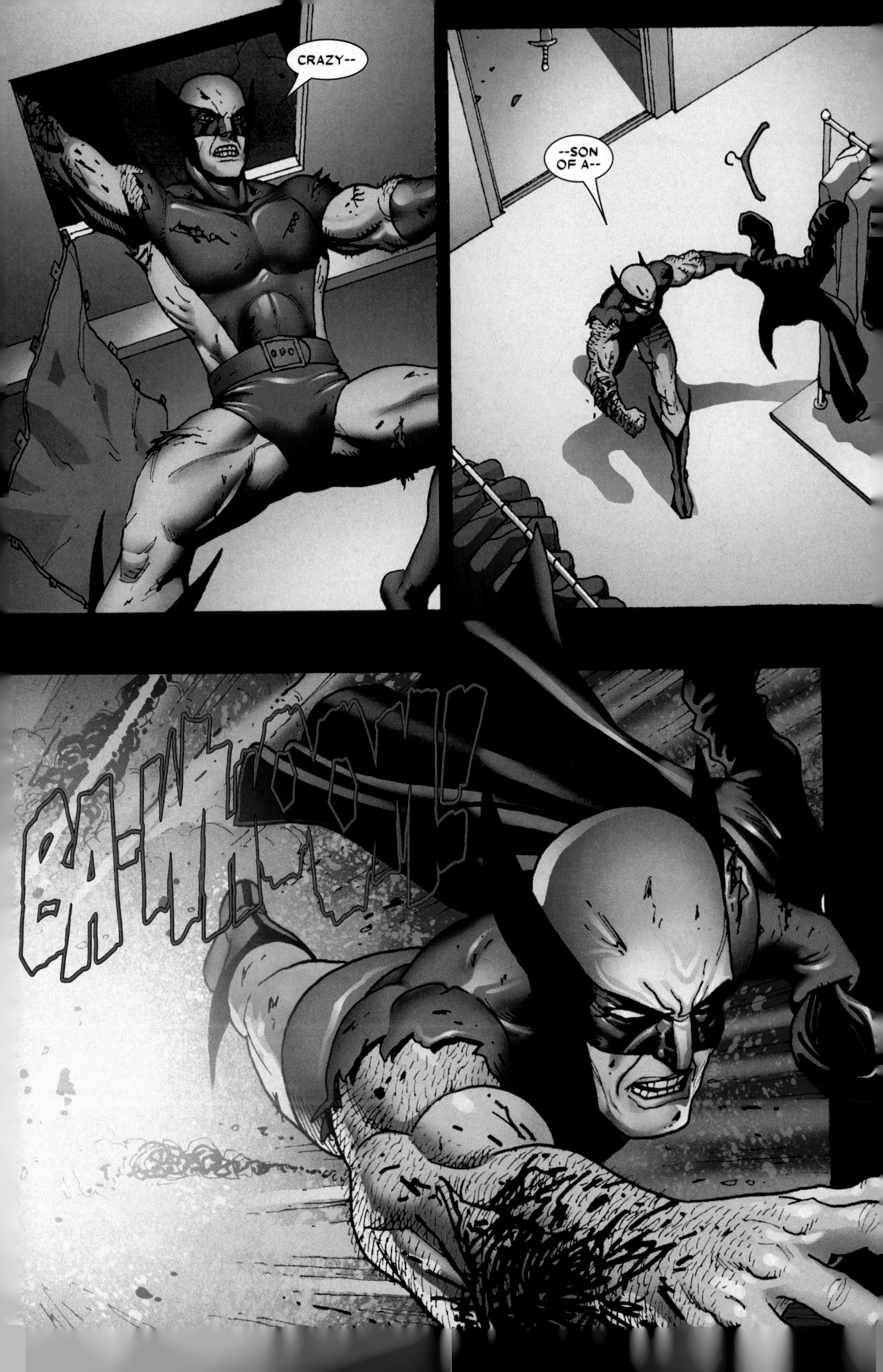
CRAZY--
--SON OF A--

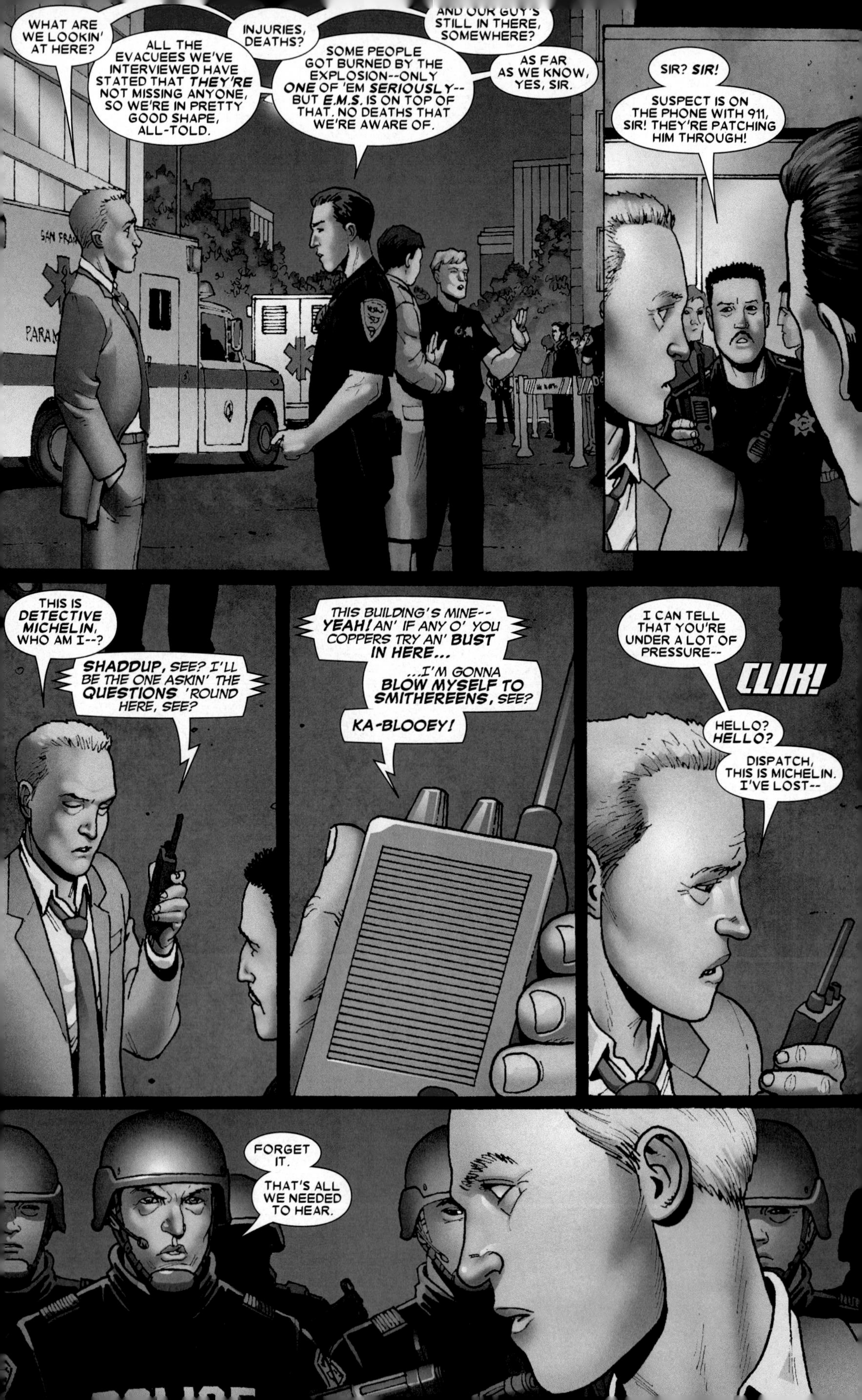
WHAT ARE WE LOOKIN' AT HERE?
ALL THE EVACUEES WE'VE INTERVIEWED HAVE STATED THAT THEY'RE NOT MISSING ANYONE, SO WE'RE IN PRETTY GOOD SHAPE, ALL-TOLD.
INJURIES, DEATHS?
SOME PEOPLE GOT BURNED BY THE EXPLOSION--ONLY ONE OF 'EM SERIOUSLY--BUT E.M.S. IS ON TOP OF THAT. NO DEATHS THAT WE'RE AWARE OF.
AND OUR GUY'S STILL IN THERE, SOMEWHERE?
AS FAR AS WE KNOW, YES, SIR.
SIR? SIR!
SUSPECT IS ON THE PHONE WITH 911, SIR! THEY'RE PATCHING HIM THROUGH!
THIS IS DETECTIVE MICHELIN, WHO AM I--?
SHADDUP, SEE? I'LL BE THE ONE ASKIN' THE QUESTIONS 'ROUND HERE, SEE?
THIS BUILDING'S MINE--YEAH! AN' IF ANY O' YOU COPPERS TRY AN' BUST IN HERE...
...I'M GONNA BLOW MYSELF TO SMITHEREENS, SEE?
KA-BLOOEY!
I CAN TELL THAT YOU'RE UNDER A LOT OF PRESSURE--
CLIK!
HELLO? HELLO?
DISPATCH, THIS IS MICHELIN. I'VE LOST--
FORGET IT.
THAT'S ALL WE NEEDED TO HEAR.

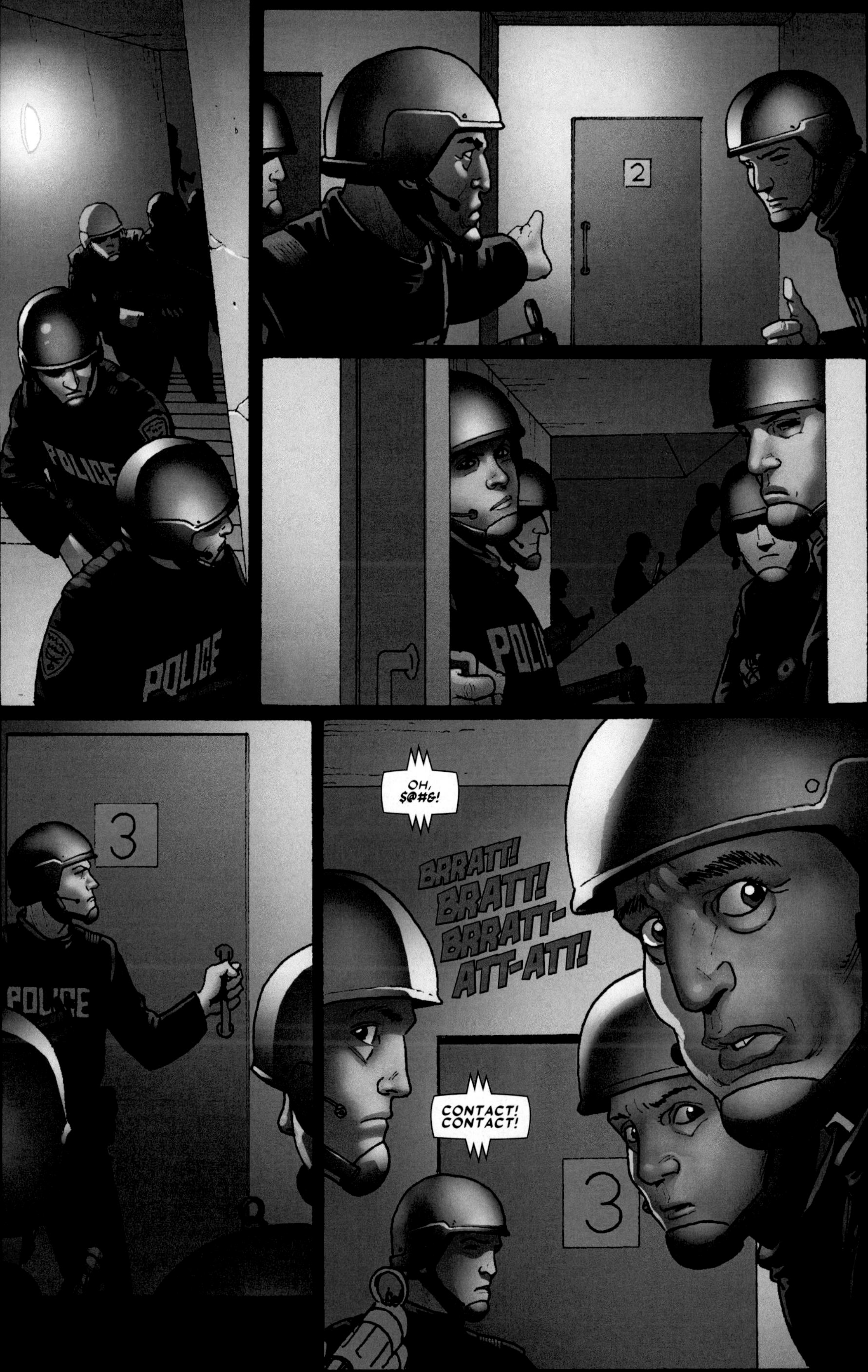
2
POLICE
POLICE
POLICE
3
POLICE
OH, $@#&!
BRRATT! BRATT! BRRATT-ATT-ATT!
CONTACT! CONTACT!
3

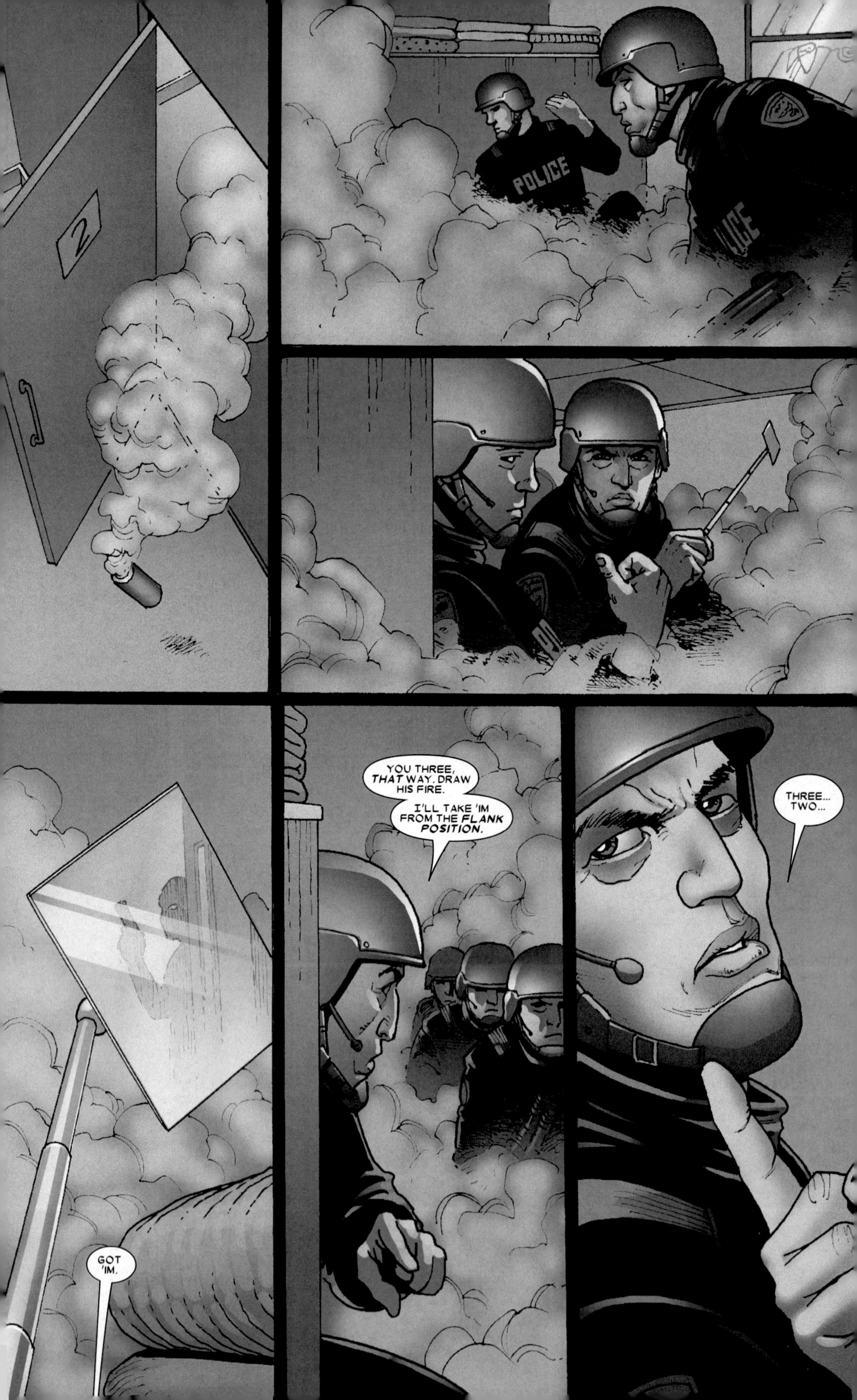
POLICE
POLICE
YOU THREE, THAT WAY. DRAW HIS FIRE.
I'LL TAKE 'IM FROM THE FLANK POSITION.
THREE... TWO...
GOT 'IM.

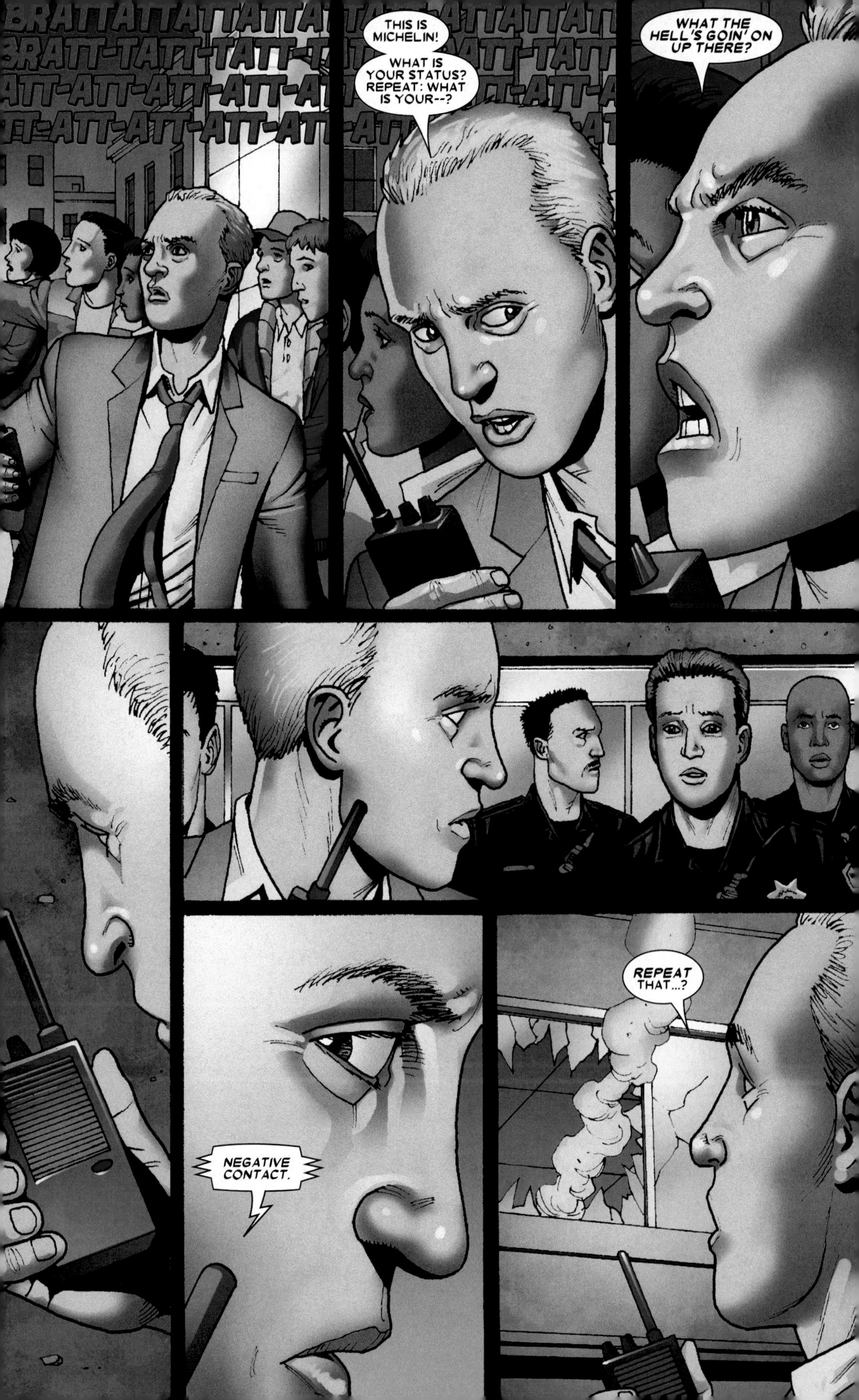
BRATTATTATTATTATTATTATTATT
BRATT-TATT-TATT-TATT-TATT
ATT-ATT-ATT-ATT-ATT
TT-ATT-ATT-ATT-ATT-AT
THIS IS MICHELIN!
WHAT IS YOUR STATUS? REPEAT: WHAT IS YOUR--?
WHAT THE HELL'S GOIN' ON UP THERE?
NEGATIVE CONTACT.
REPEAT THAT...?

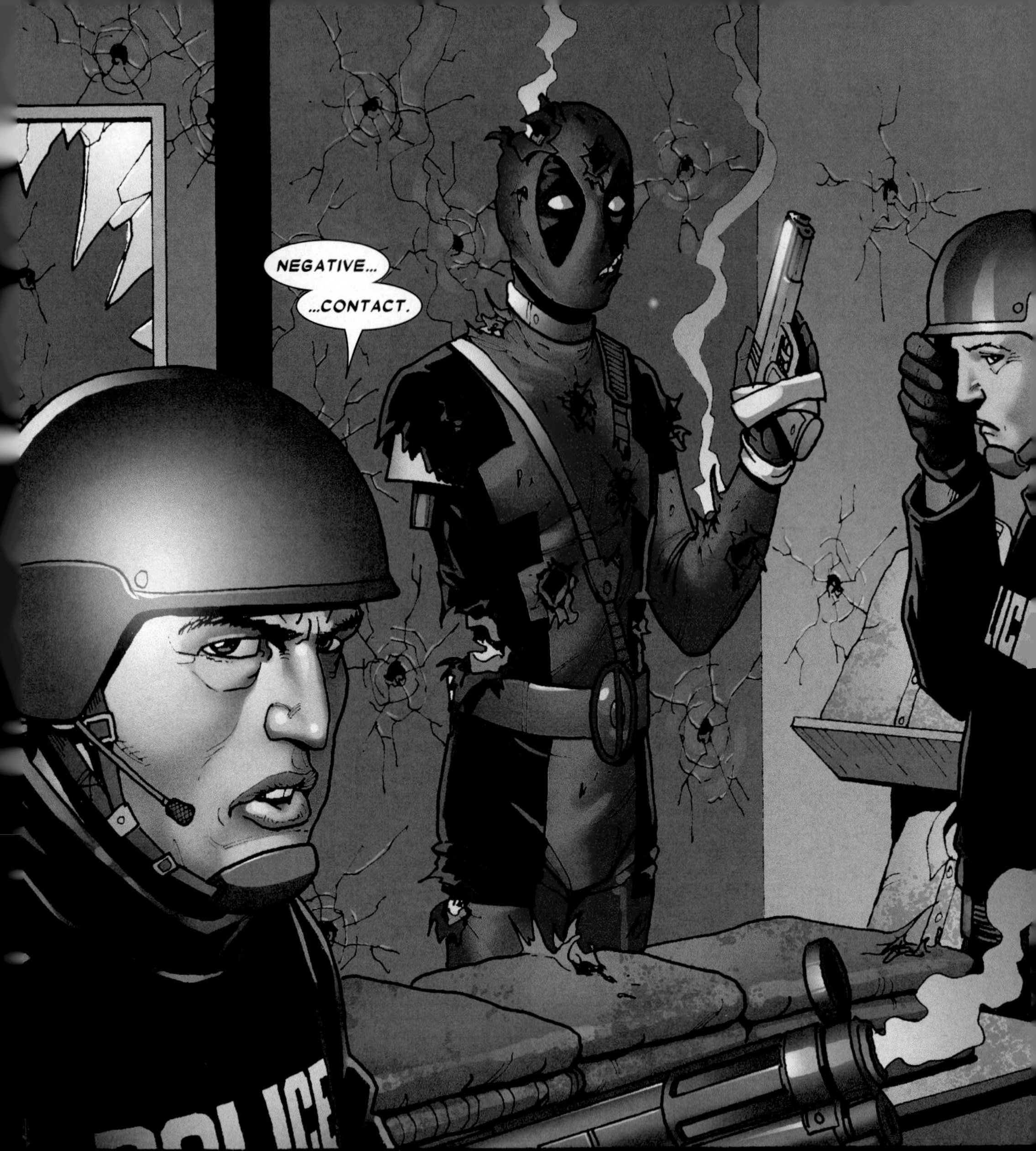
NEGATIVE...
...CONTACT.
POLICE
POLICE
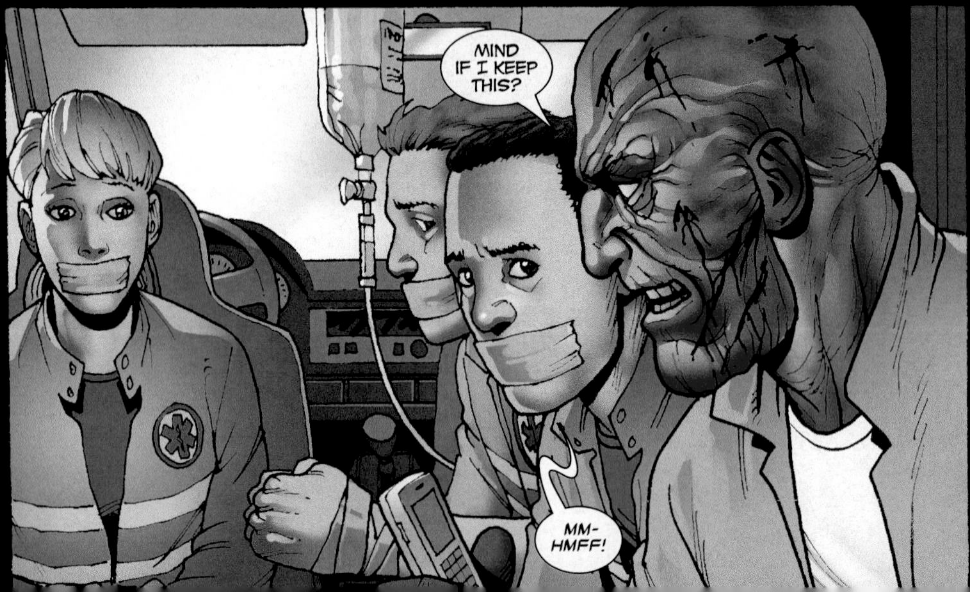
MIND IF I KEEP THIS?
MM-HMFF!

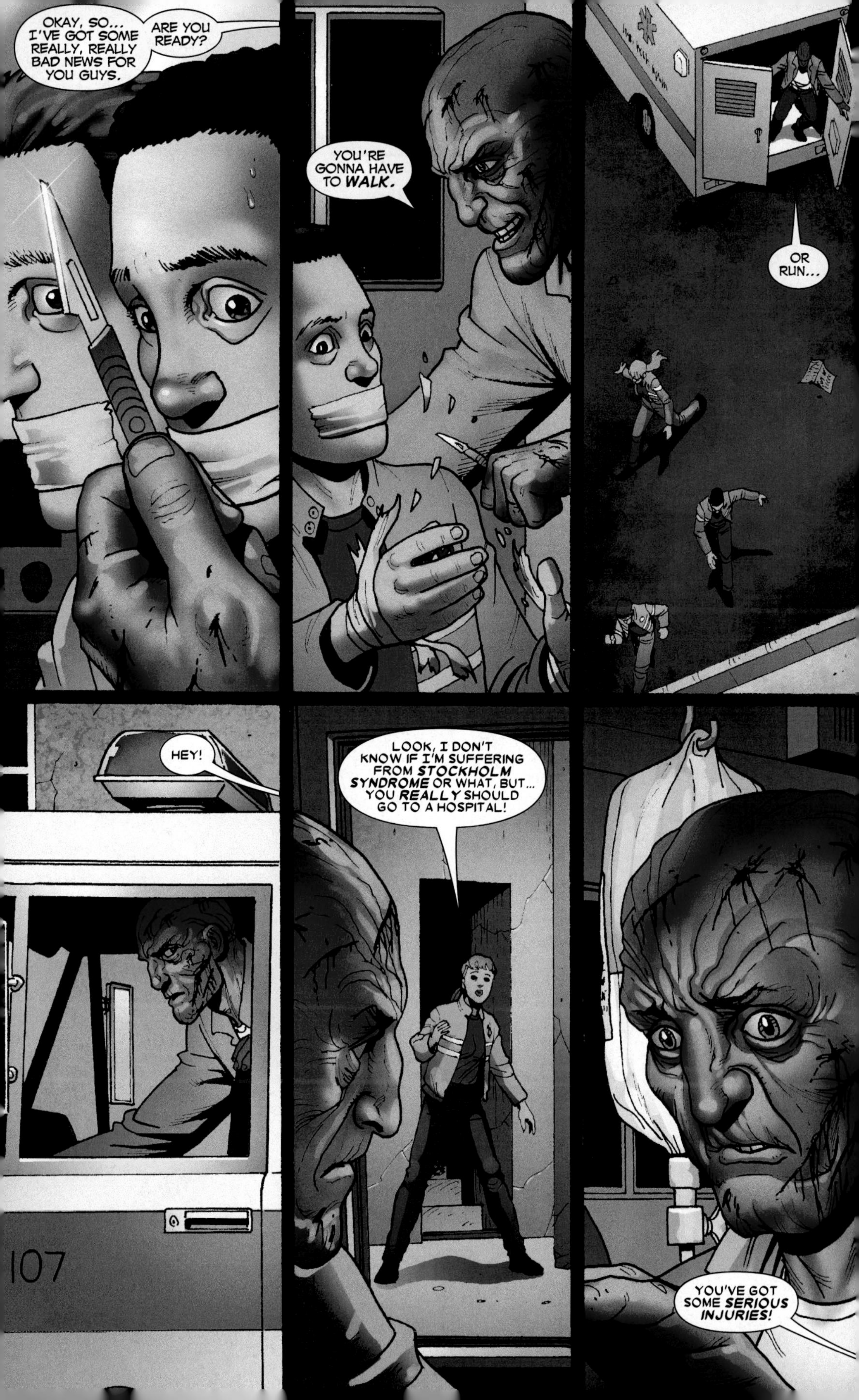
OKAY, SO... I'VE GOT SOME REALLY, REALLY BAD NEWS FOR YOU GUYS.
ARE YOU READY?
YOU'RE GONNA HAVE TO WALK.
OR RUN...
HEY!
LOOK, I DON'T KNOW IF I'M SUFFERING FROM STOCKHOLM SYNDROME OR WHAT, BUT... YOU REALLY SHOULD GO TO A HOSPITAL!
YOU'VE GOT SOME SERIOUS INJURIES!
107

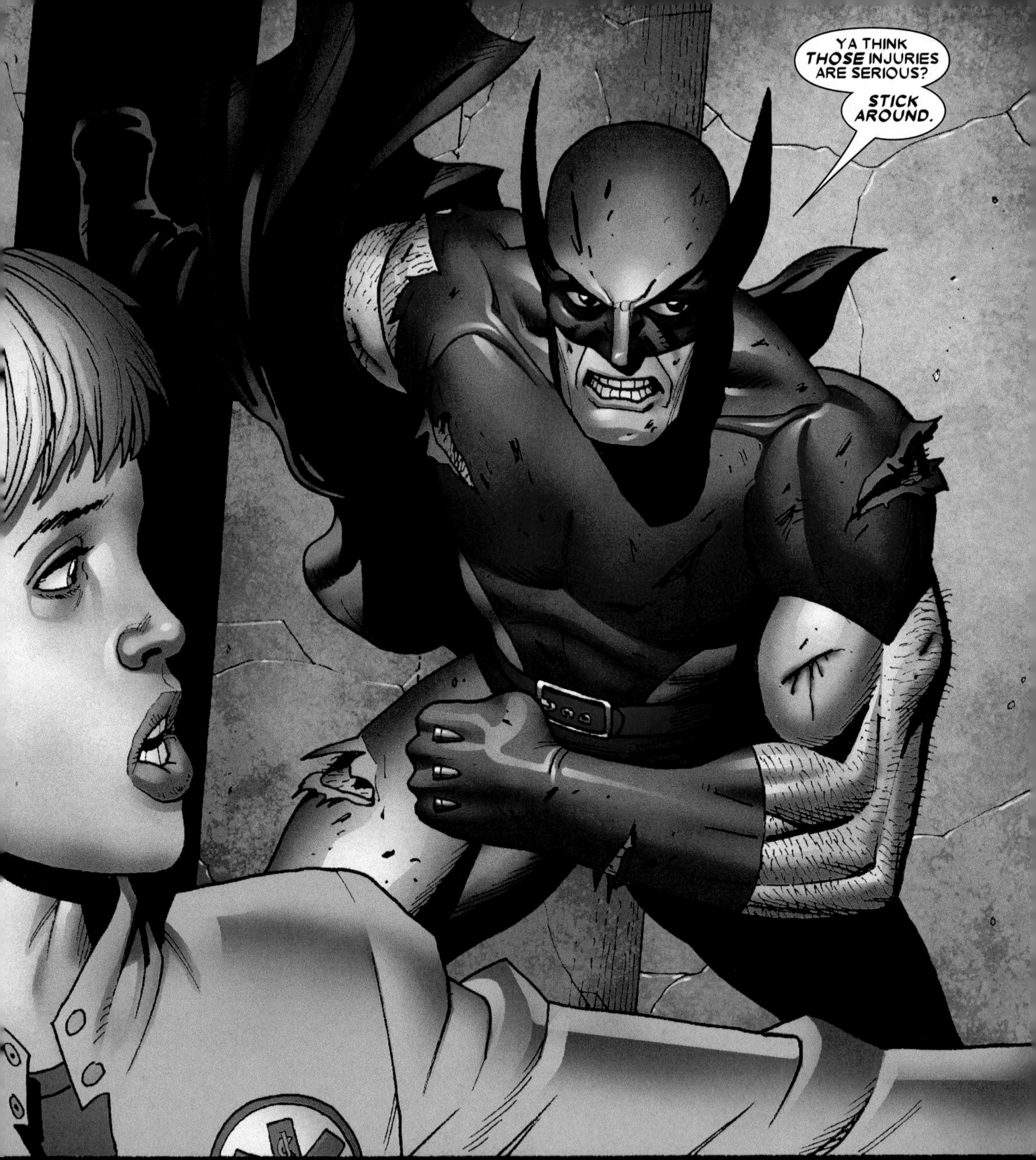
YA THINK THOSE INJURIES ARE SERIOUS?
STICK AROUND.
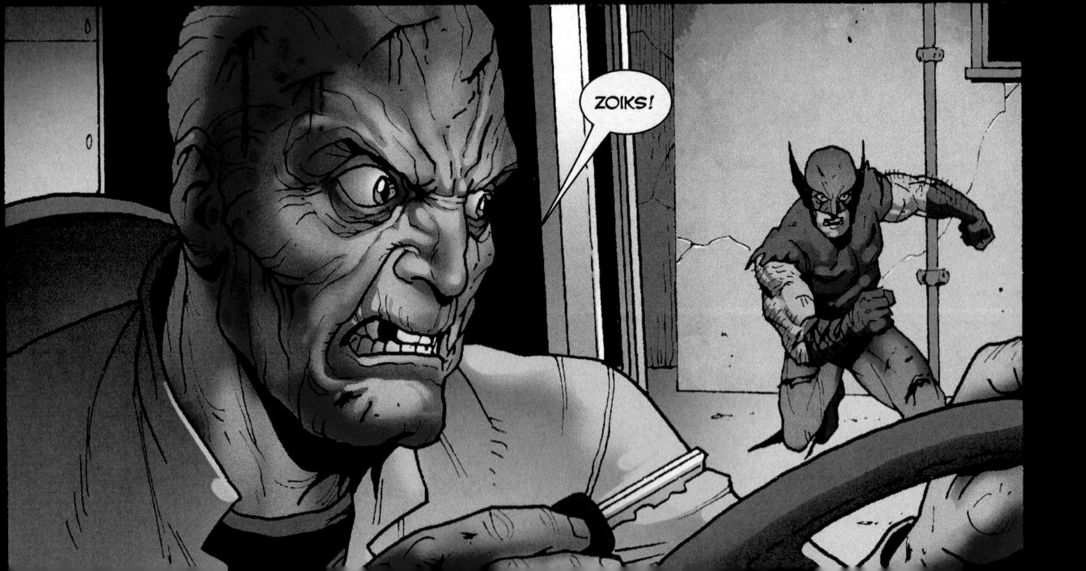
ZOIKS!

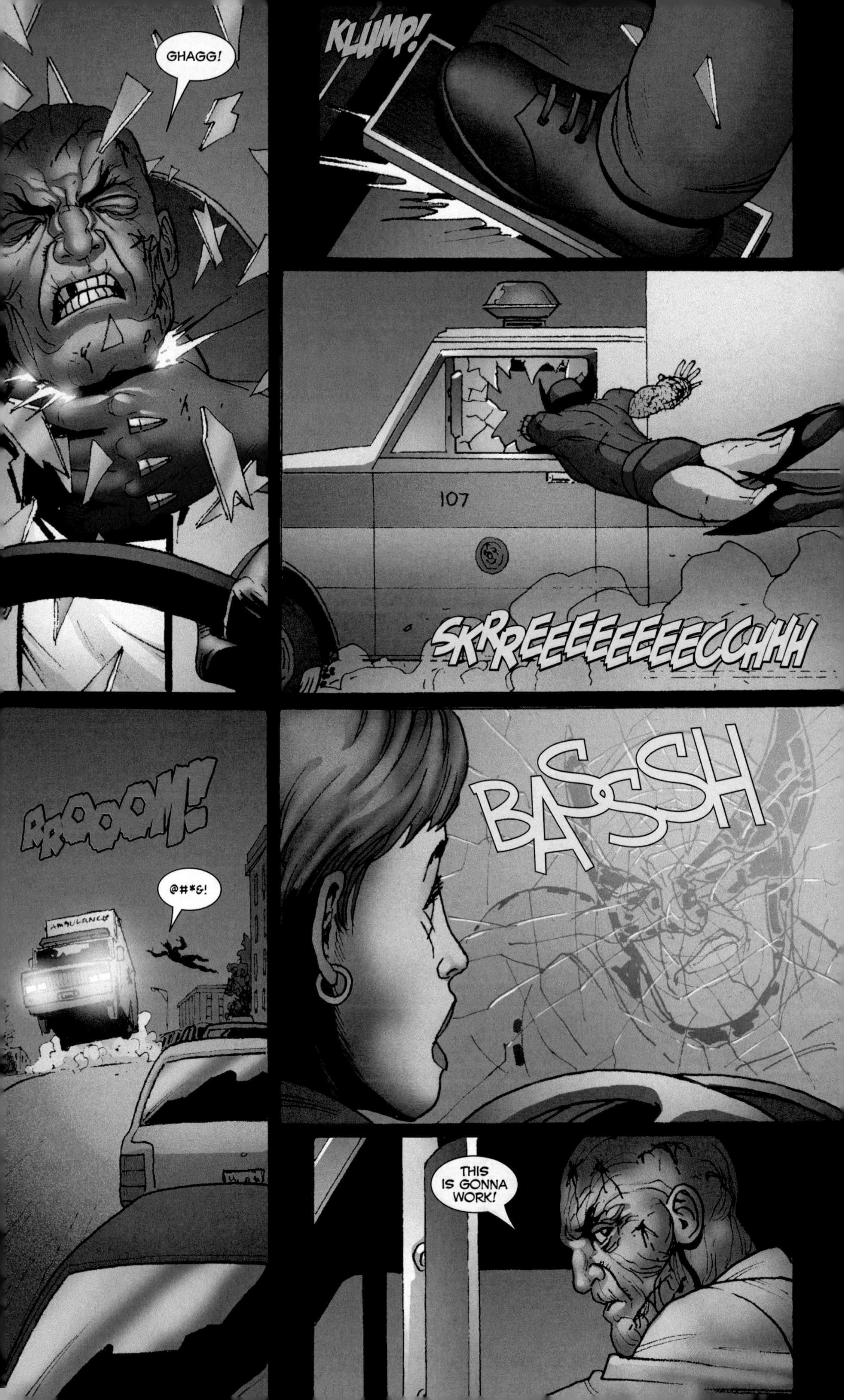
GHAGG!
KLUMP!
SKRREEEEEEEEECCHHH
RRROOOM!
@#*&!
AMBULANCE
BASSSH
THIS IS GONNA WORK!

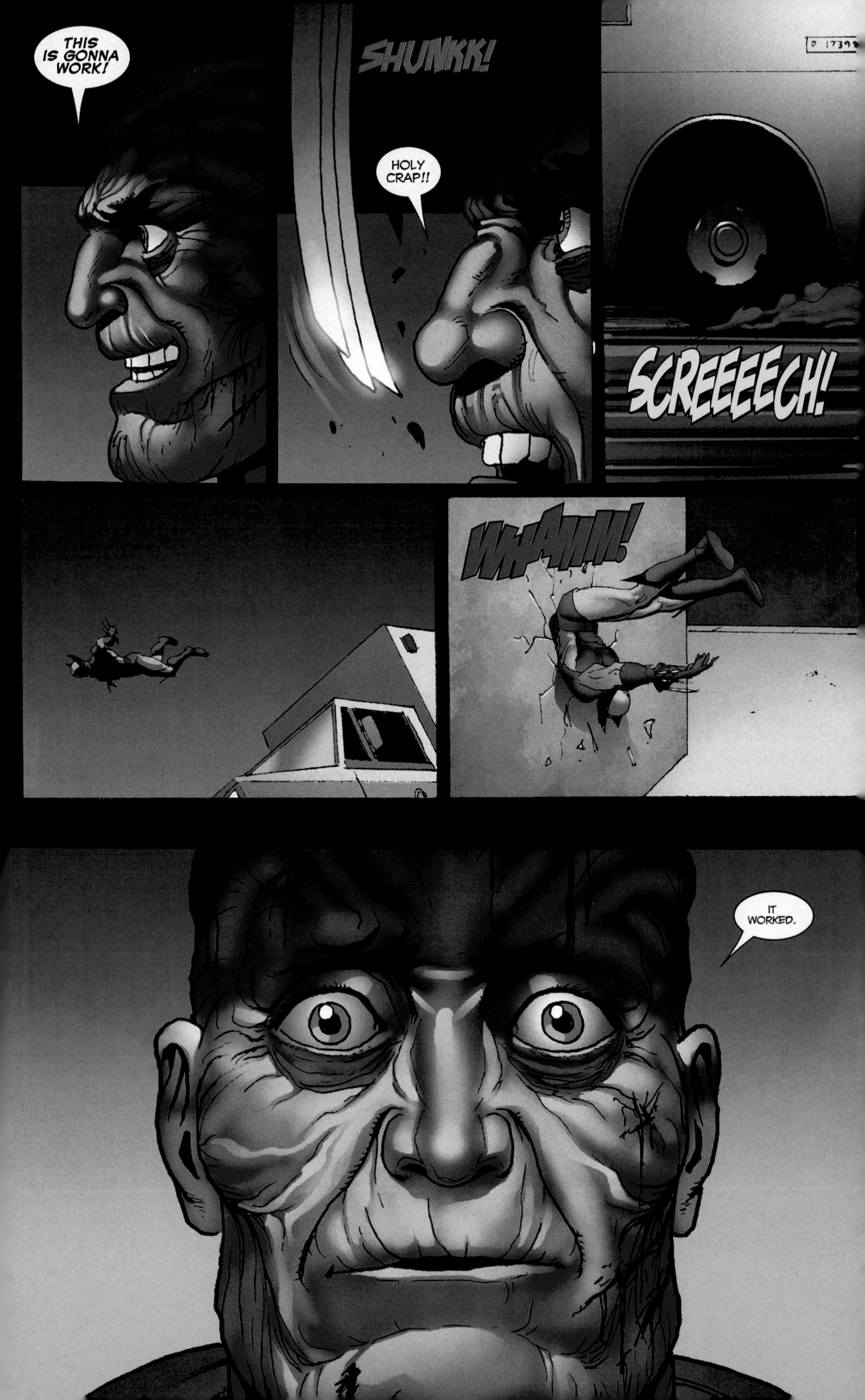
THIS IS GONNA WORK!
SHUNKK!
HOLY CRAP!!
SCREEEECH!
WHAMM!
IT WORKED.

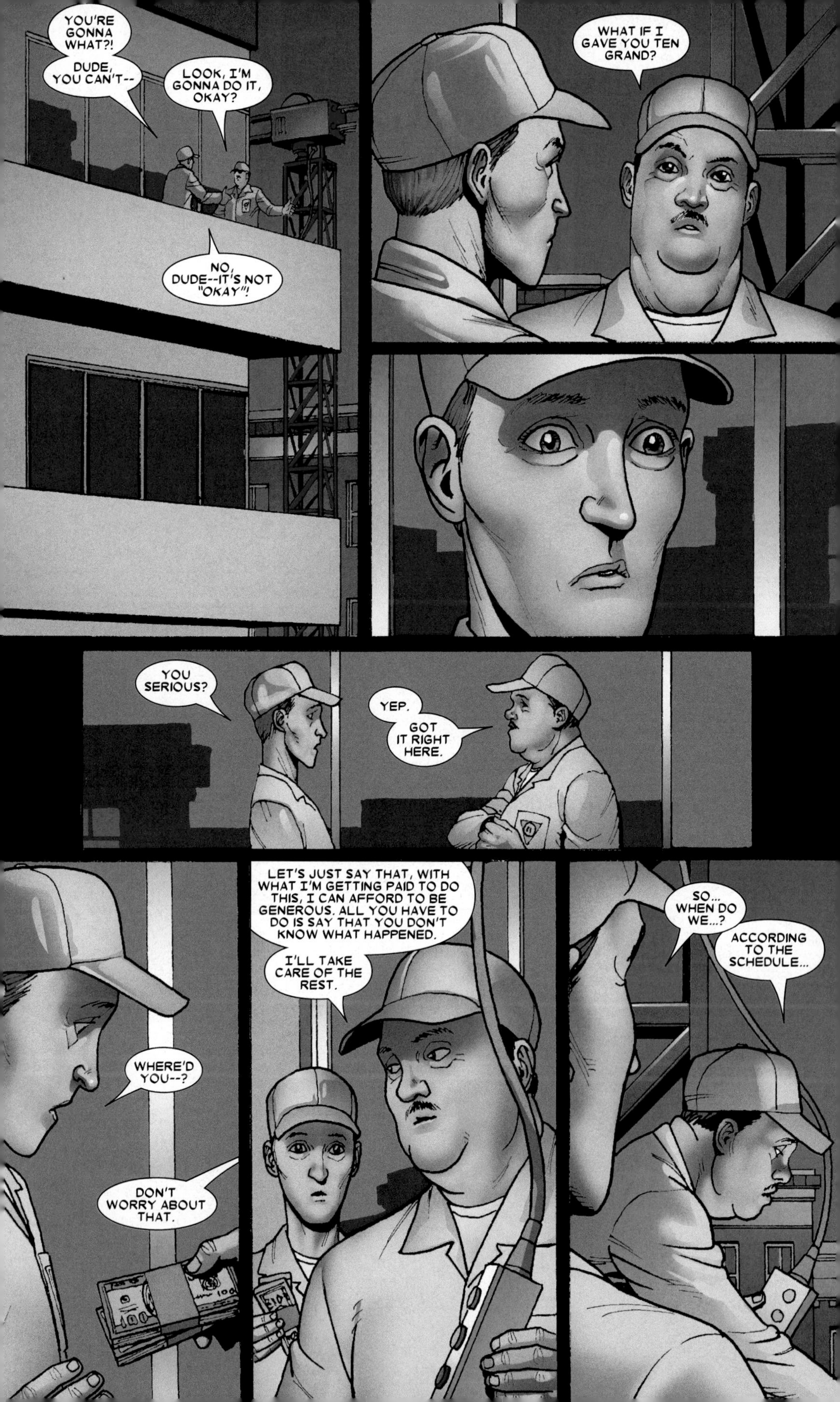

YOU'RE GONNA WHAT?!
DUDE, YOU CAN'T--
LOOK, I'M GONNA DO IT, OKAY?
NO, DUDE--IT'S NOT "OKAY"!
WHAT IF I GAVE YOU TEN GRAND?
YOU SERIOUS?
YEP.
GOT IT RIGHT HERE.
WHERE'D YOU--?
DON'T WORRY ABOUT THAT.
LET'S JUST SAY THAT, WITH WHAT I'M GETTING PAID TO DO THIS, I CAN AFFORD TO BE GENEROUS. ALL YOU HAVE TO DO IS SAY THAT YOU DON'T KNOW WHAT HAPPENED.
I'LL TAKE CARE OF THE REST.
SO... WHEN DO WE...?
ACCORDING TO THE SCHEDULE...

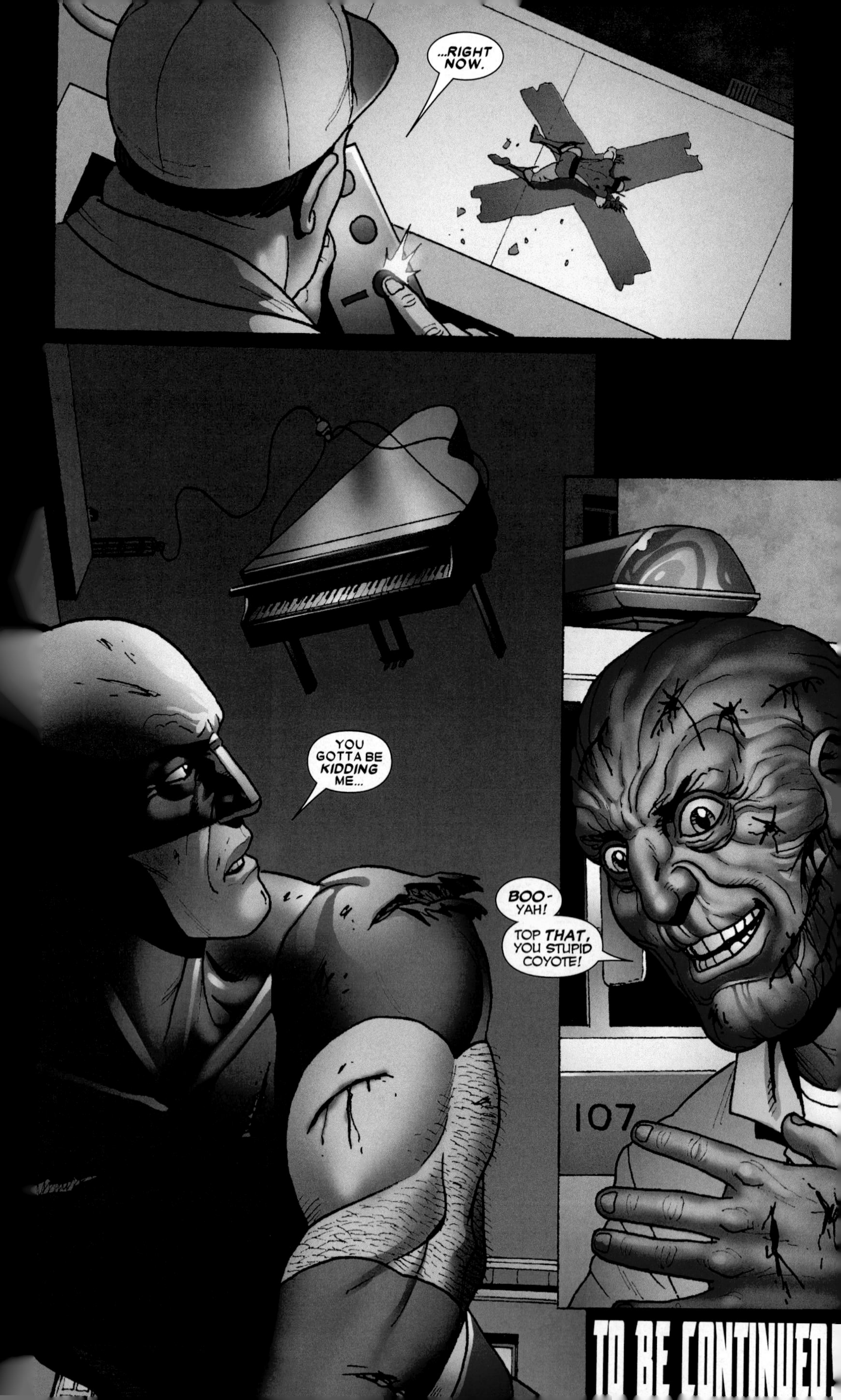
...RIGHT NOW.
YOU GOTTA BE KIDDING ME...
BOO-YAH!
TOP THAT, YOU STUPID COYOTE!
107
TO BE CONTINUED!

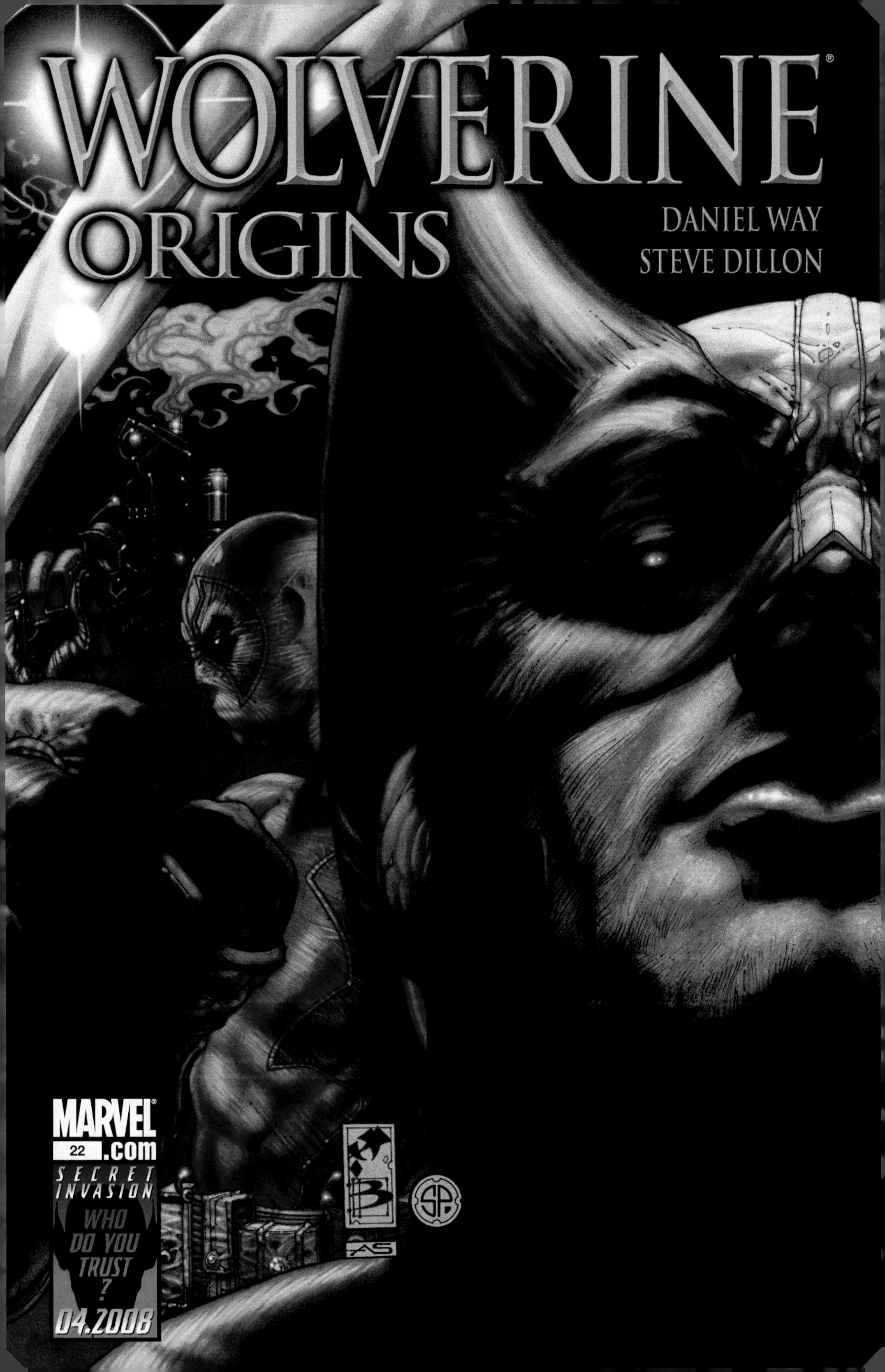
WOLVERINE®
ORIGINS
DANIEL WAY
STEVE DILLON
MARVEL®
22 .com
SECRET INVASION
WHO DO YOU TRUST ?
04.2008

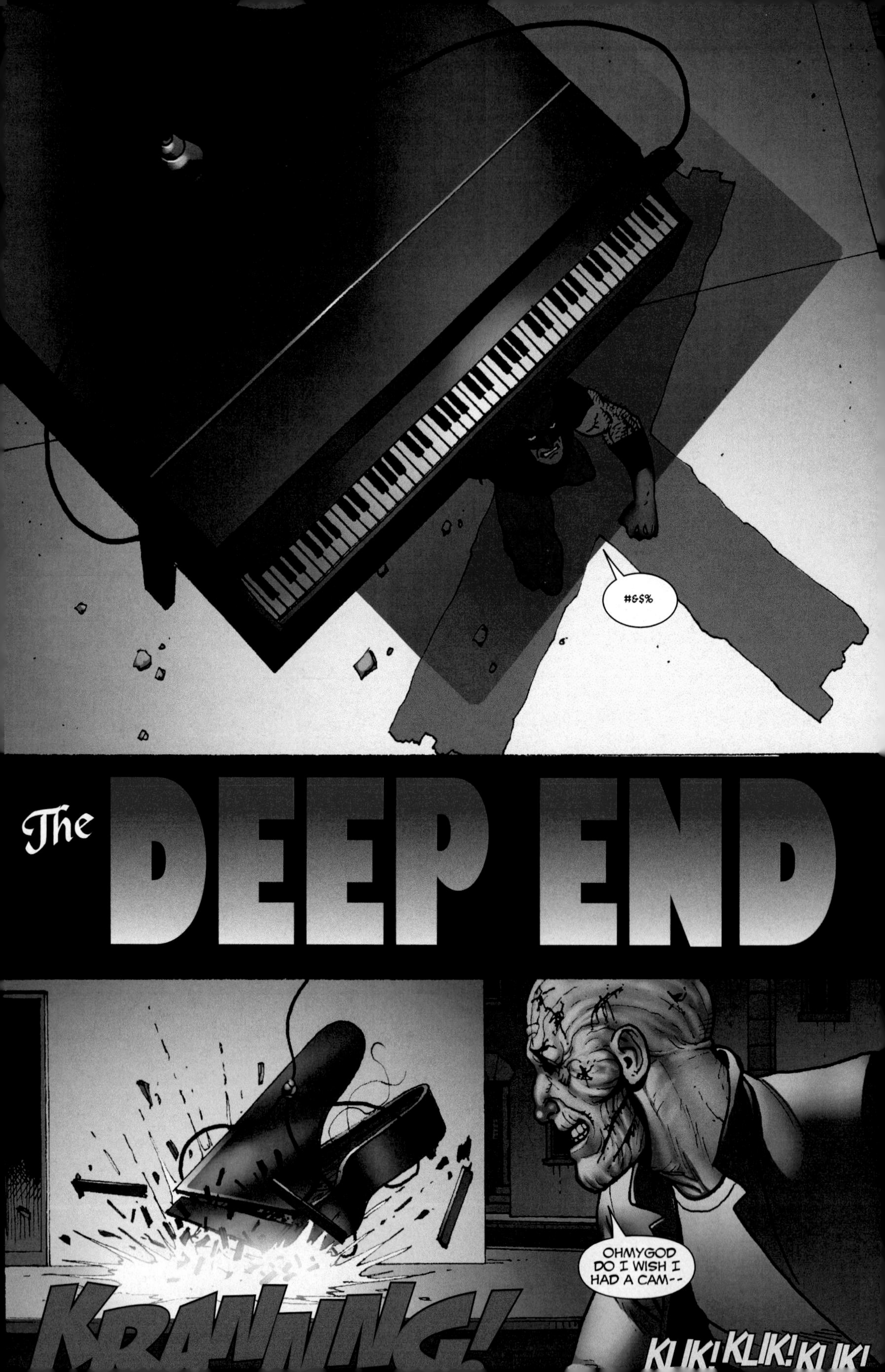
#&$%
The DEEP END
KRANNNG!
OHMYGOD DO I WISH I HAD A CAM--
KLIK! KLIK! KLIK!

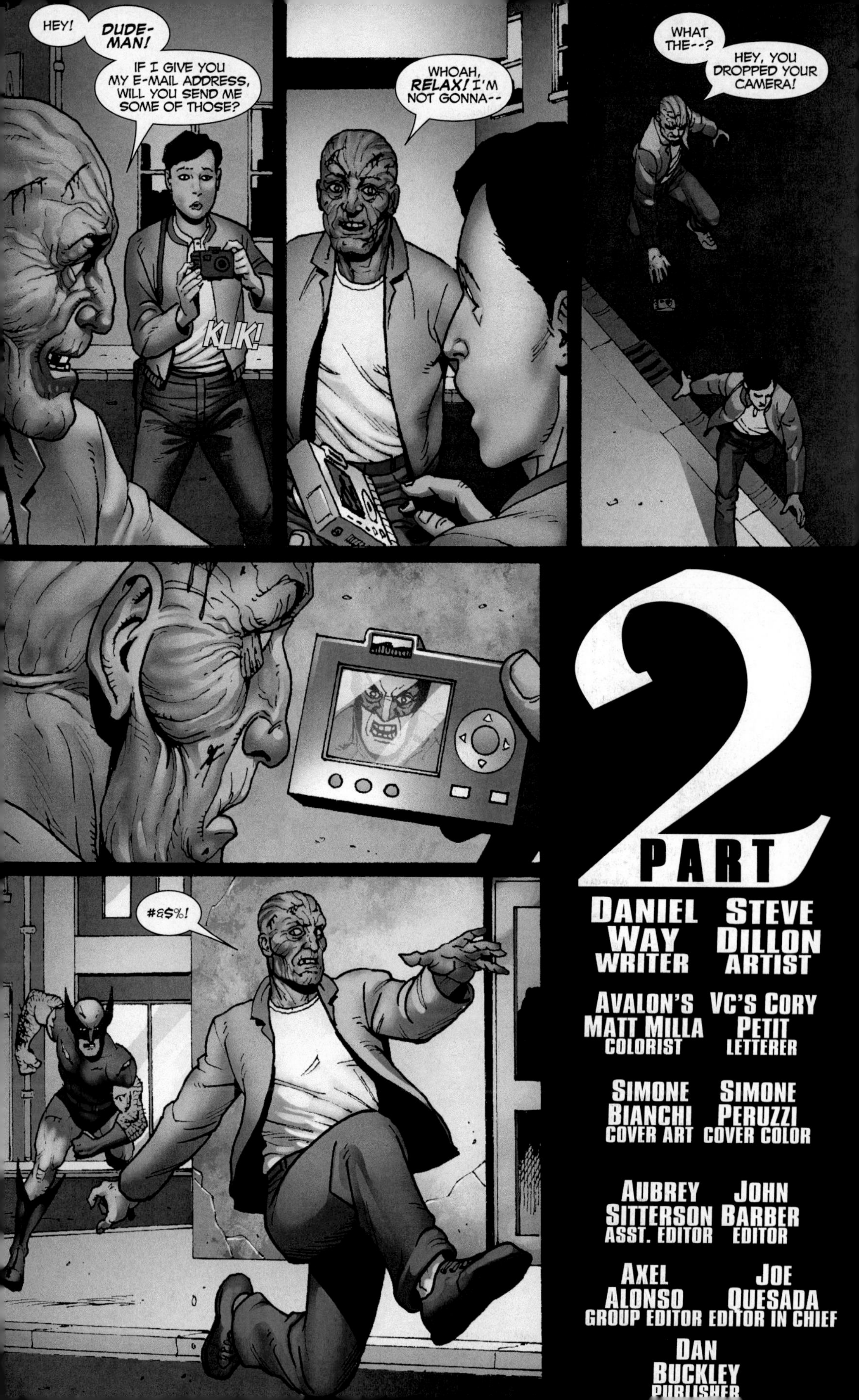
HEY!
DUDE-MAN!
IF I GIVE YOU MY E-MAIL ADDRESS, WILL YOU SEND ME SOME OF THOSE?
KLIK!
WHOAH, RELAX! I'M NOT GONNA--
WHAT THE--?
HEY, YOU DROPPED YOUR CAMERA!
#&$%!
PART 2
DANIEL WAY WRITER
STEVE DILLON ARTIST
AVALON'S MATT MILLA COLORIST
VC'S CORY PETIT LETTERER
SIMONE BIANCHI COVER ART
SIMONE PERUZZI COVER COLOR
AUBREY SITTERSON ASST. EDITOR
JOHN BARBER EDITOR
AXEL ALONSO GROUP EDITOR
JOE QUESADA EDITOR IN CHIEF
DAN BUCKLEY PUBLISHER

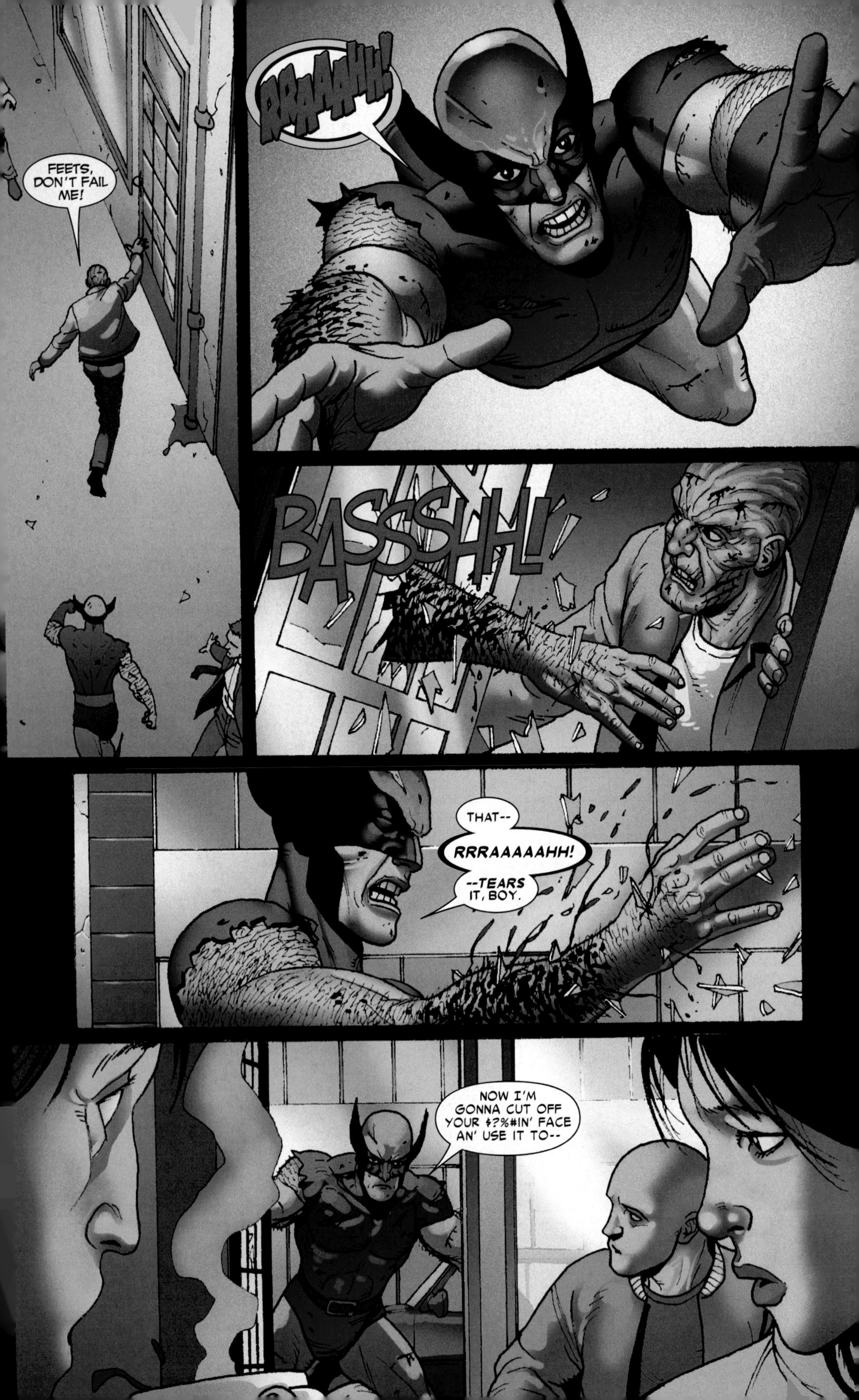
FEETS, DON'T FAIL ME!
RRAAAHH!
BASSSHH!
THAT--
RRRAAAAAAHH!
--TEARS IT, BOY.
NOW I'M GONNA CUT OFF YOUR $?%#IN' FACE AN' USE IT TO--

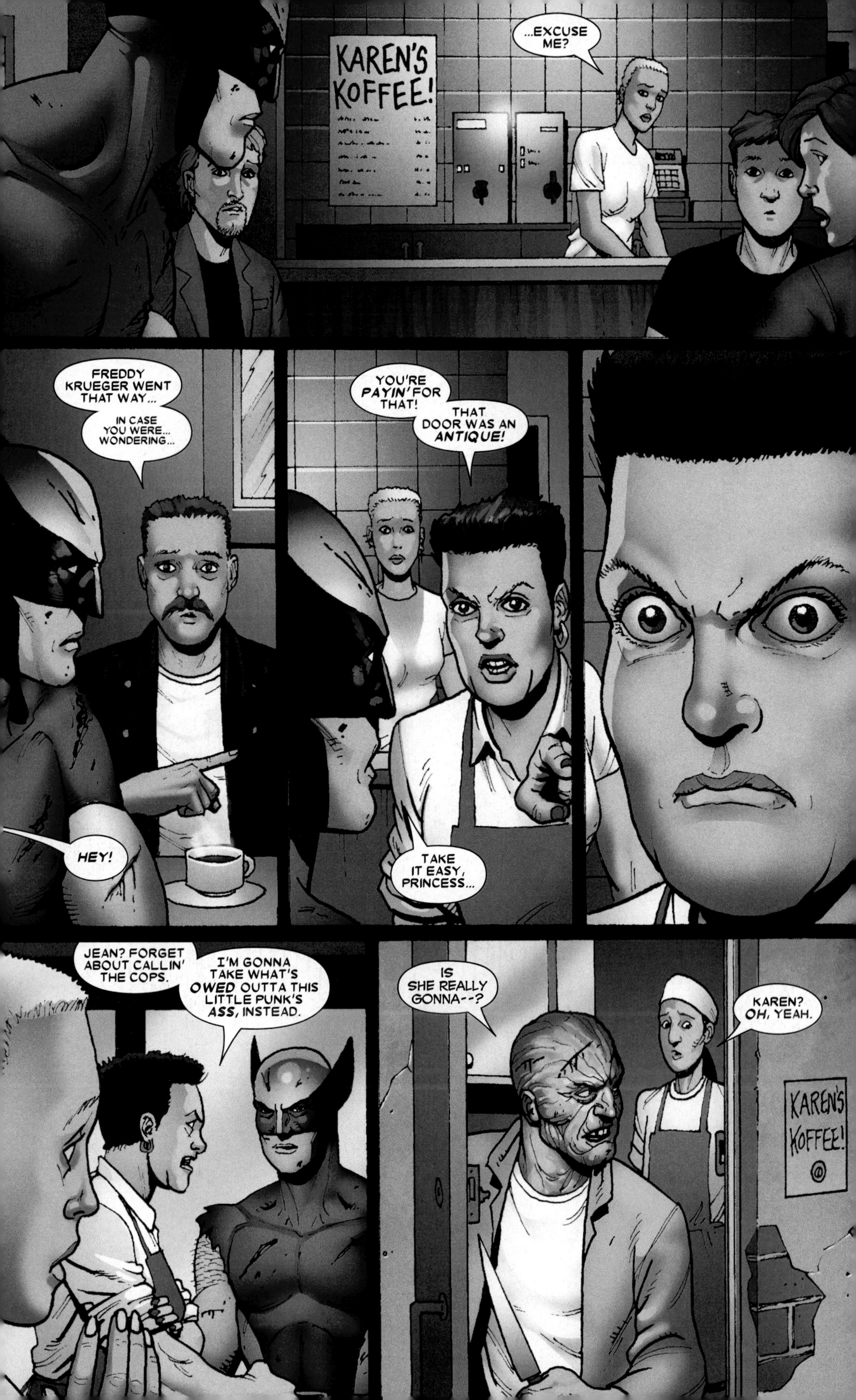
KAREN'S KOFFEE!
...EXCUSE ME?
FREDDY KRUEGER WENT THAT WAY...
IN CASE YOU WERE... WONDERING...
HEY!
YOU'RE PAYIN' FOR THAT!
THAT DOOR WAS AN ANTIQUE!
TAKE IT EASY, PRINCESS...
JEAN? FORGET ABOUT CALLIN' THE COPS.
I'M GONNA TAKE WHAT'S OWED OUTTA THIS LITTLE PUNK'S ASS, INSTEAD.
IS SHE REALLY GONNA--?
KAREN? OH, YEAH.
KAREN'S KOFFEE!

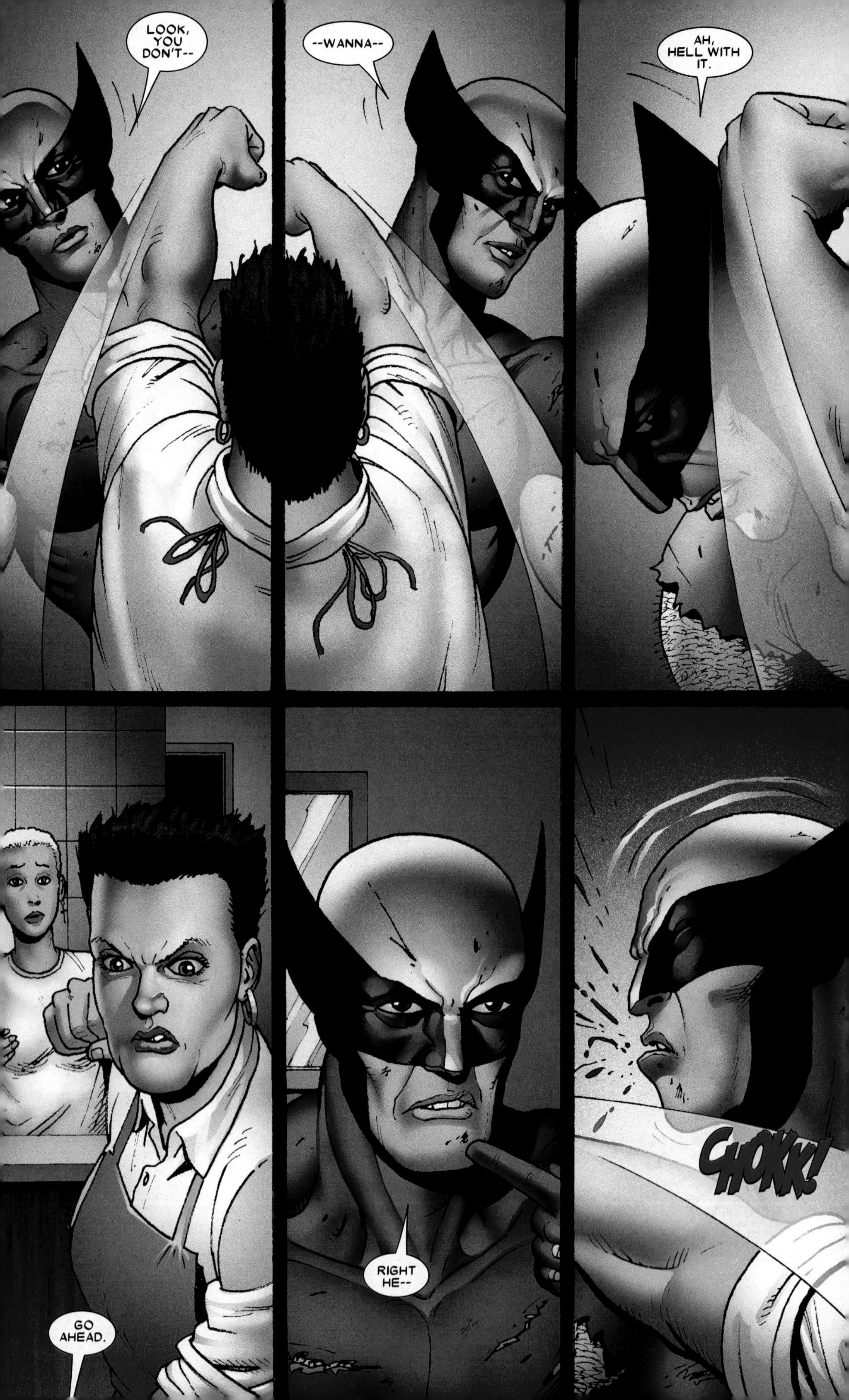
LOOK, YOU DON'T--
--WANNA--
AH, HELL WITH IT.
GO AHEAD.
RIGHT HE--
CHOKK!

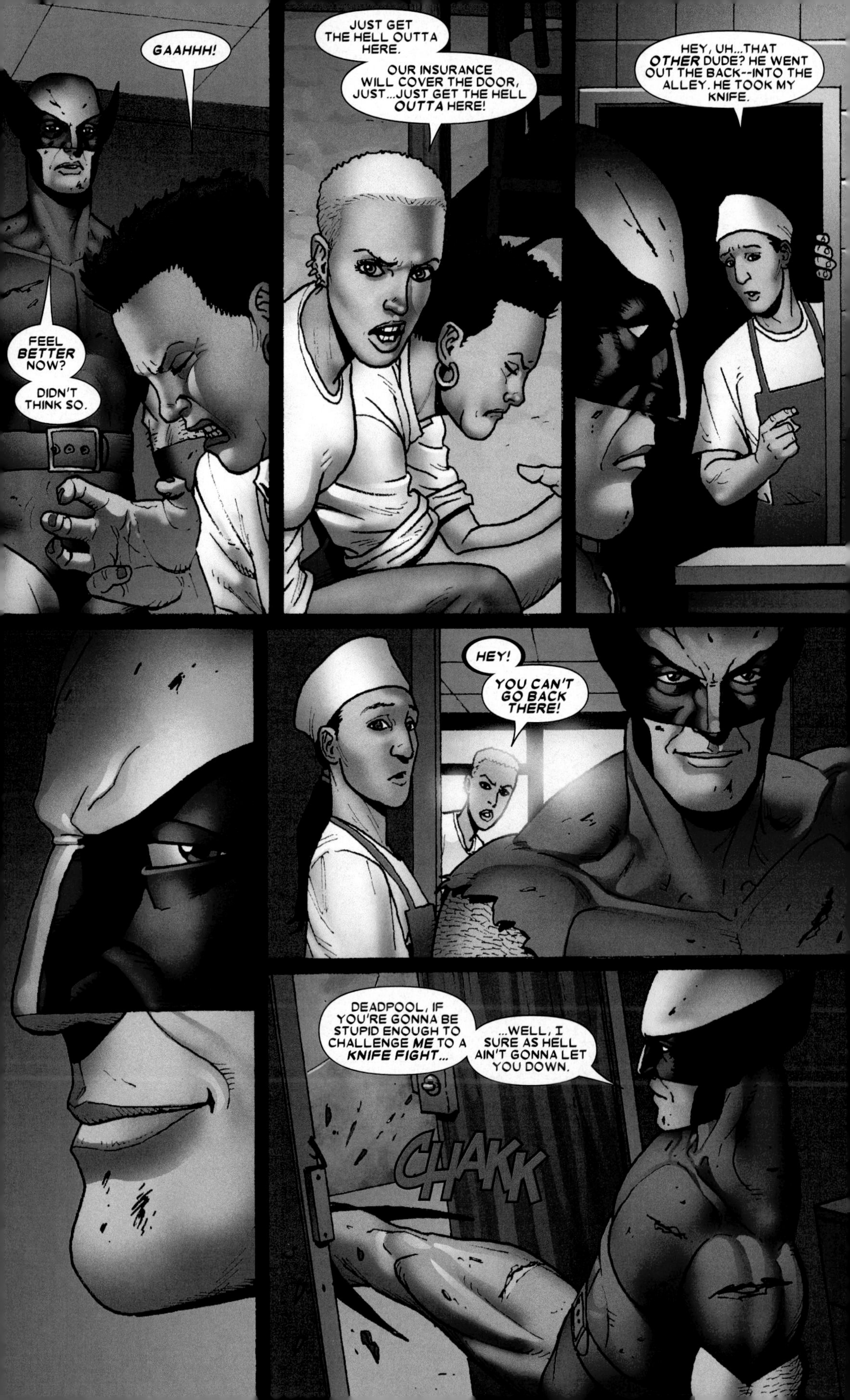
GAAHHH!
FEEL BETTER NOW?
DIDN'T THINK SO.
JUST GET THE HELL OUTTA HERE.
OUR INSURANCE WILL COVER THE DOOR, JUST...JUST GET THE HELL OUTTA HERE!
HEY, UH...THAT OTHER DUDE? HE WENT OUT THE BACK--INTO THE ALLEY. HE TOOK MY KNIFE.
HEY!
YOU CAN'T GO BACK THERE!
DEADPOOL, IF YOU'RE GONNA BE STUPID ENOUGH TO CHALLENGE ME TO A KNIFE FIGHT...
...WELL, I SURE AS HELL AIN'T GONNA LET YOU DOWN.
CHAKK

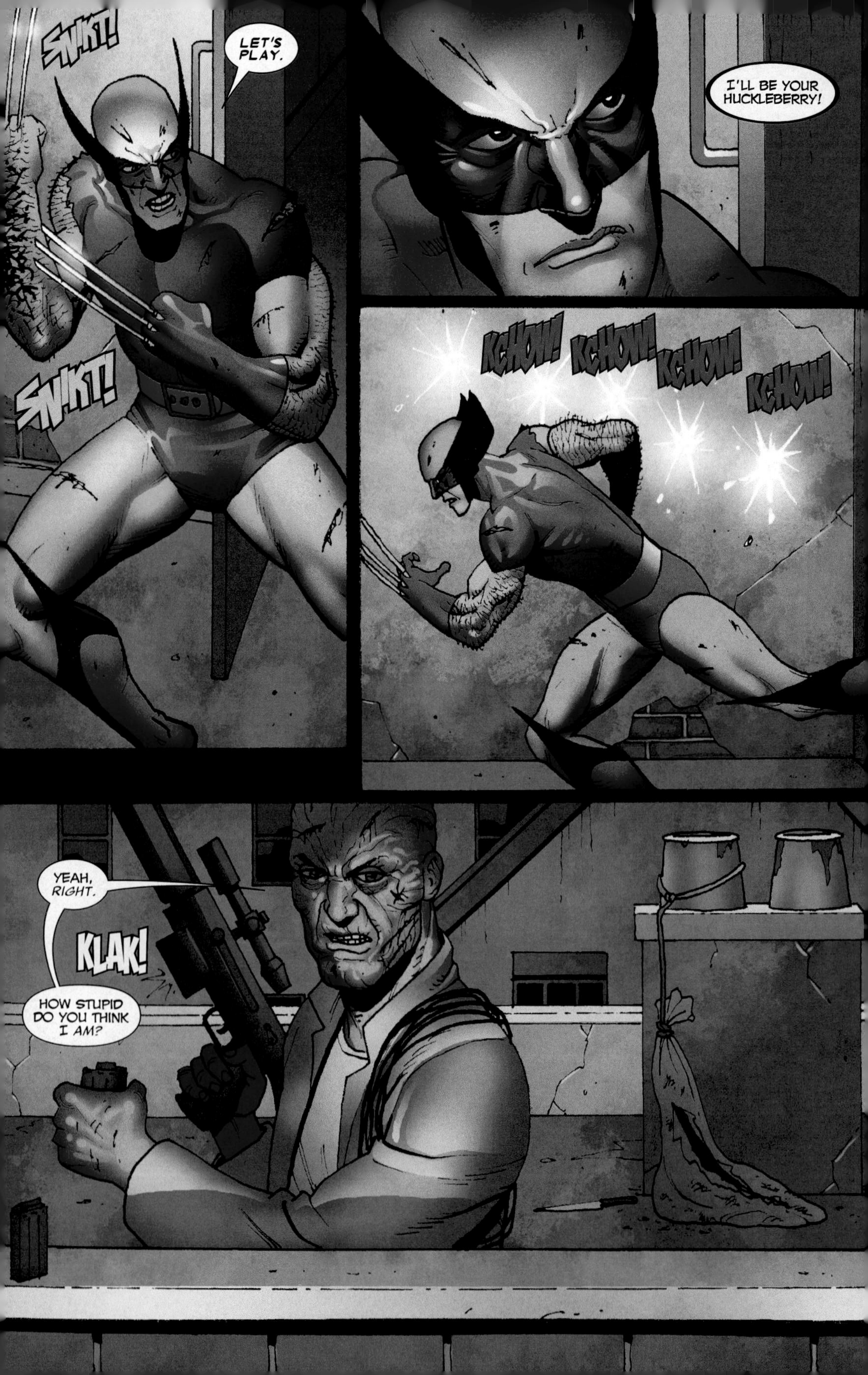
SNIKT!
LET'S PLAY.
SNIKT!
I'LL BE YOUR HUCKLEBERRY!
KCHOW! KCHOW! KCHOW! KCHOW!
YEAH, RIGHT.
KLAK!
HOW STUPID DO YOU THINK I AM?

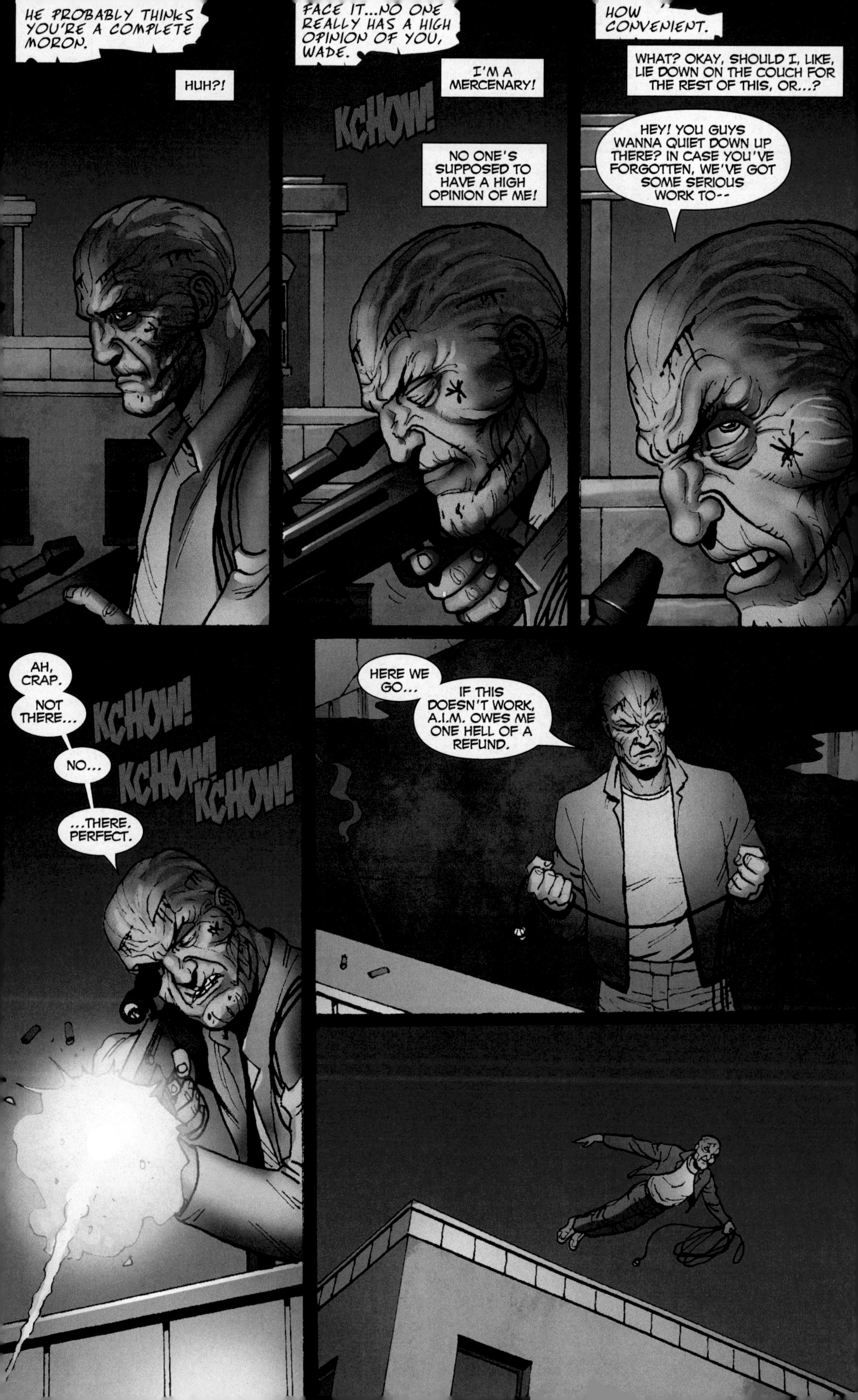
HE PROBABLY THINKS YOU'RE A COMPLETE MORON.
HUH?!
FACE IT...NO ONE REALLY HAS A HIGH OPINION OF YOU, WADE.
I'M A MERCENARY!
KCHOW!
NO ONE'S SUPPOSED TO HAVE A HIGH OPINION OF ME!
HOW CONVENIENT.
WHAT? OKAY, SHOULD I, LIKE, LIE DOWN ON THE COUCH FOR THE REST OF THIS, OR...?
HEY! YOU GUYS WANNA QUIET DOWN UP THERE? IN CASE YOU'VE FORGOTTEN, WE'VE GOT SOME SERIOUS WORK TO--
AH, CRAP.
NOT THERE...
KCHOW!
NO...
KCHOW!
KCHOW!
...THERE. PERFECT.
HERE WE GO...
IF THIS DOESN'T WORK, A.I.M. OWES ME ONE HELL OF A REFUND.

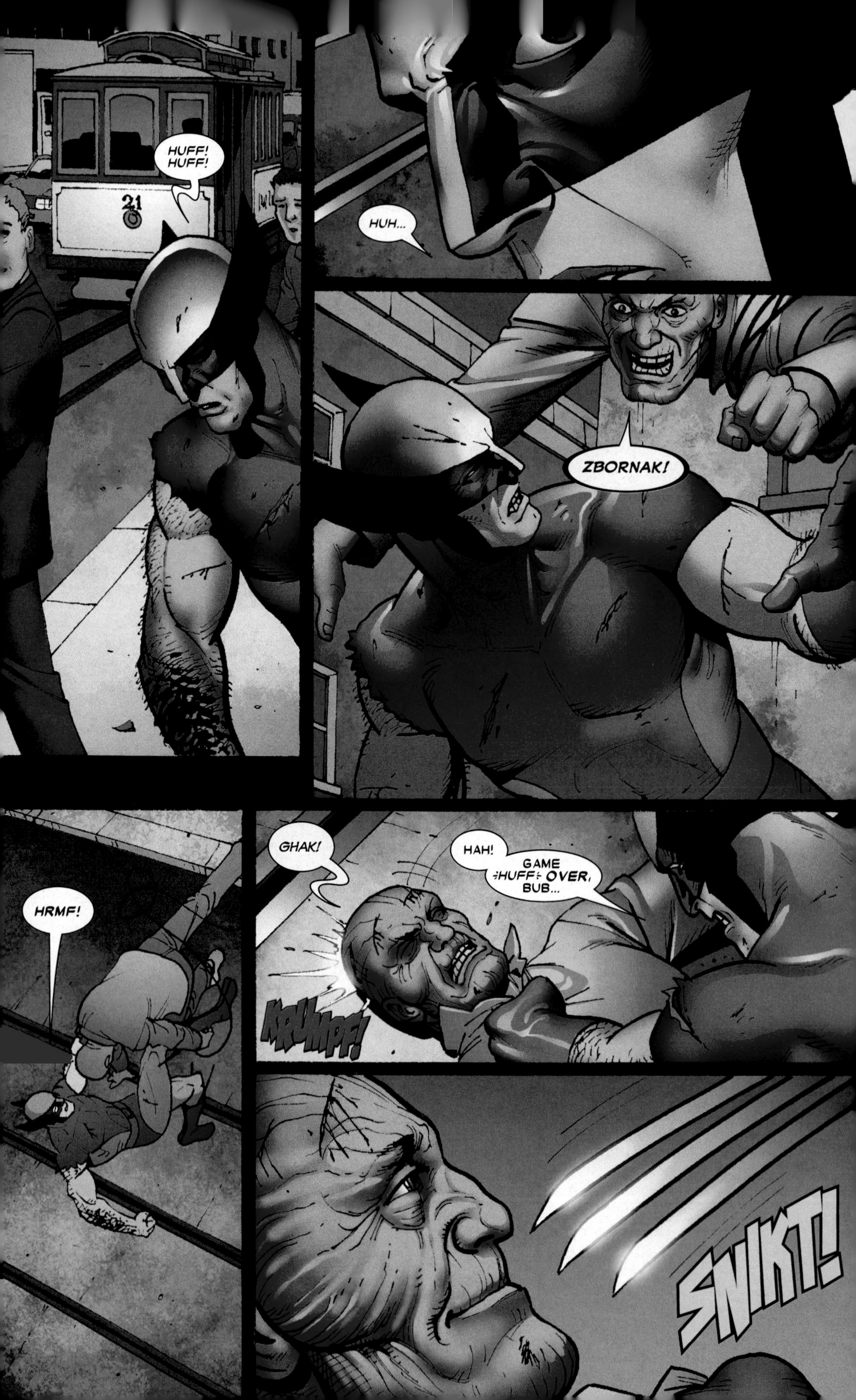

HUFF! HUFF!
HUH...
ZBORNAK!
HRMF!
GHAK!
HAH!
GAME -HUFF- OVER, BUB...
KRUMPF!
SNIKT!

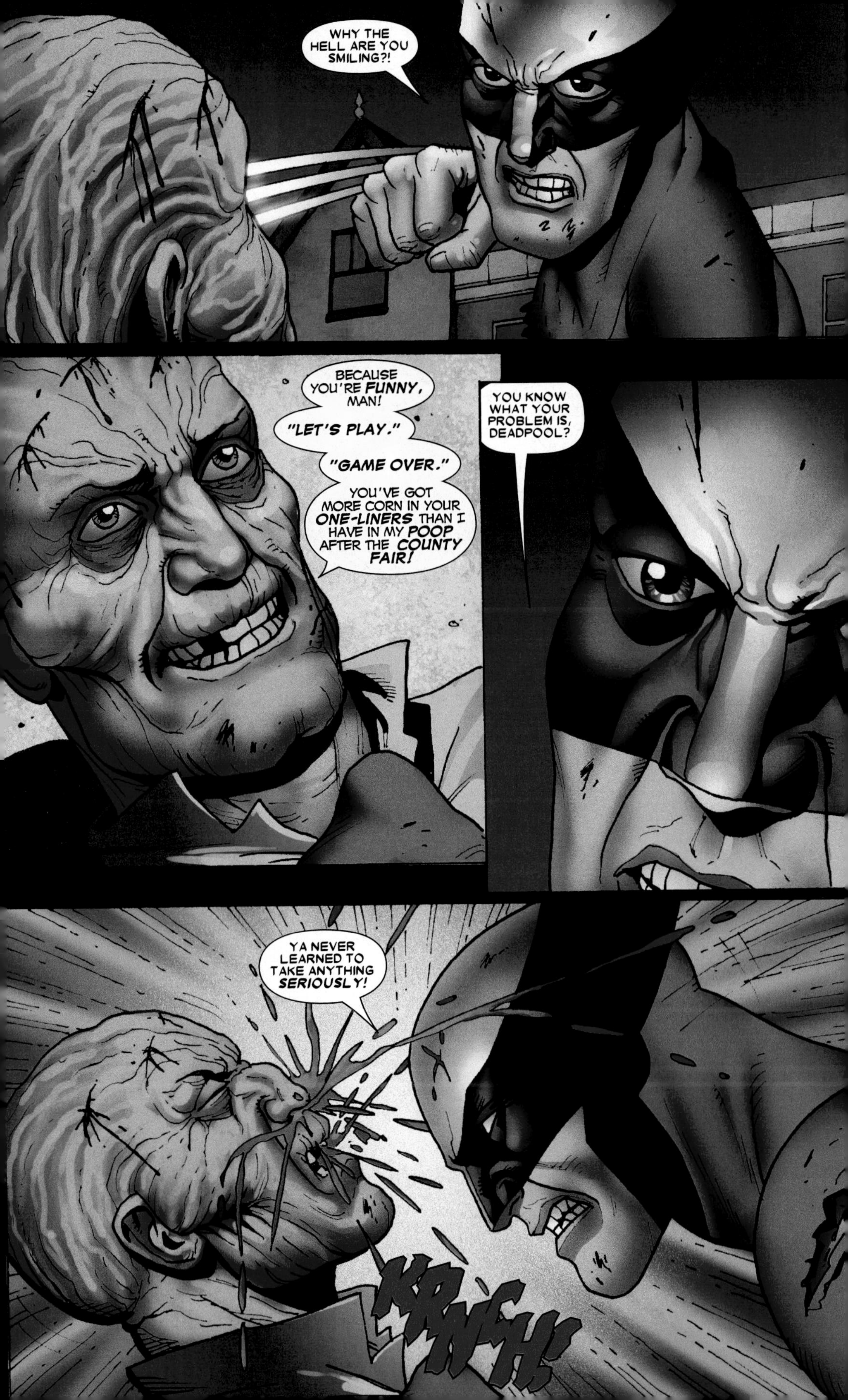
WHY THE HELL ARE YOU SMILING?!
BECAUSE YOU'RE FUNNY, MAN!
"LET'S PLAY."
"GAME OVER."
YOU'VE GOT MORE CORN IN YOUR ONE-LINERS THAN I HAVE IN MY POOP AFTER THE COUNTY FAIR!
YOU KNOW WHAT YOUR PROBLEM IS, DEADPOOL?
YA NEVER LEARNED TO TAKE ANYTHING SERIOUSLY!
KRNCH!

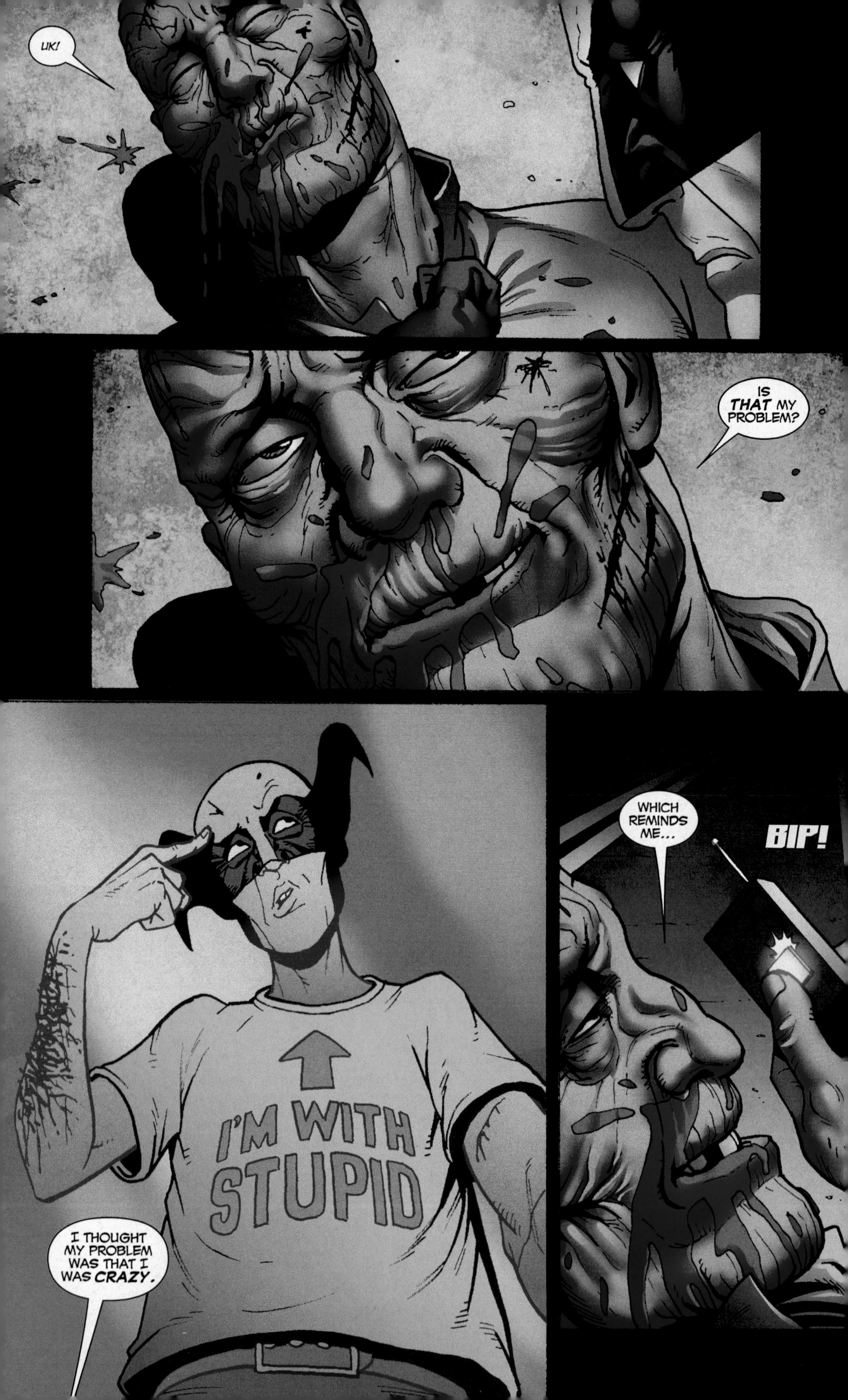
UK!
IS THAT MY PROBLEM?
I THOUGHT MY PROBLEM WAS THAT I WAS CRAZY.
I'M WITH STUPID
WHICH REMINDS ME...
BIP!

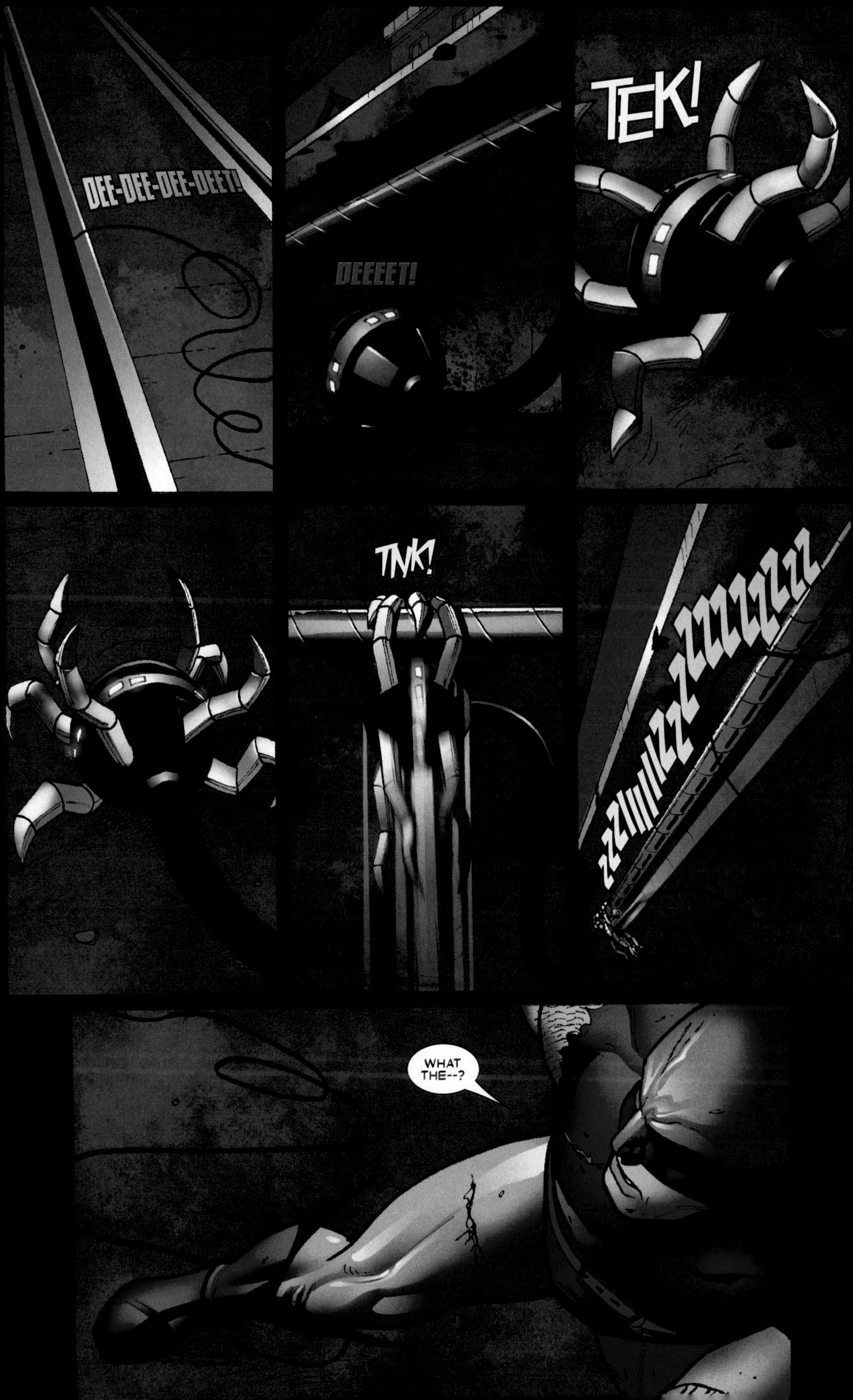
DEE-DEE-DEE-DEET!
DEEEET!
TEK!
TNK!
zzzIIII!!zzzzzzzzzzzzzz
WHAT THE--?

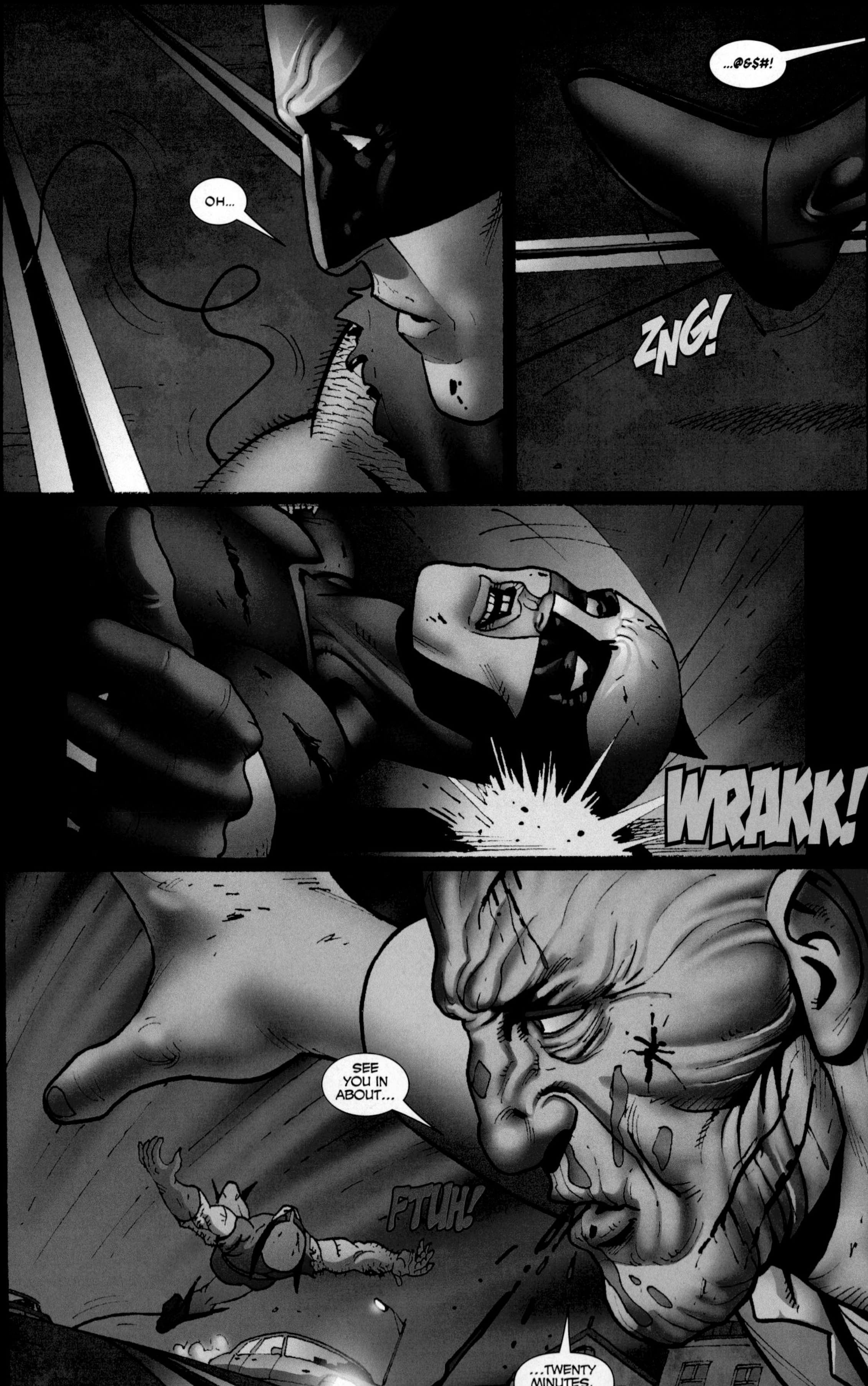

OH...
...@&$#!
ZNG!
WRAKK!
SEE YOU IN ABOUT...
FTUH!
...TWENTY MINUTES, %&*#HEAD.

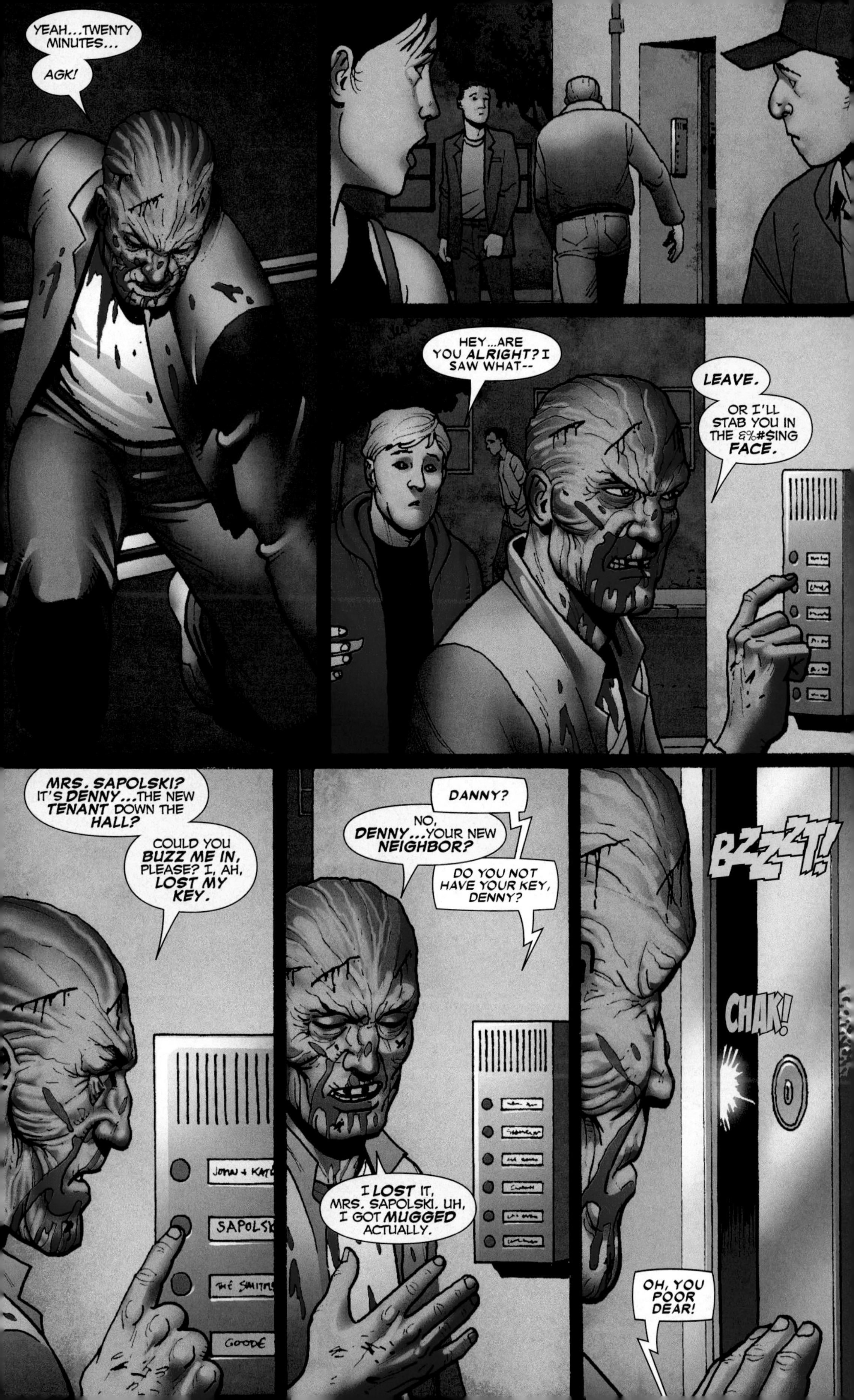
YEAH...TWENTY MINUTES...
AGK!
HEY...ARE YOU ALRIGHT? I SAW WHAT--
LEAVE.
OR I'LL STAB YOU IN THE &%#$ING FACE.
MRS. SAPOLSKI? IT'S DENNY...THE NEW TENANT DOWN THE HALL?
COULD YOU BUZZ ME IN, PLEASE? I, AH, LOST MY KEY.
SAPOLSK
GOODE
DANNY?
NO, DENNY...YOUR NEW NEIGHBOR?
DO YOU NOT HAVE YOUR KEY, DENNY?
I LOST IT, MRS. SAPOLSKI. UH, I GOT MUGGED ACTUALLY.
BZZZT!
CHAK!
OH, YOU POOR DEAR!

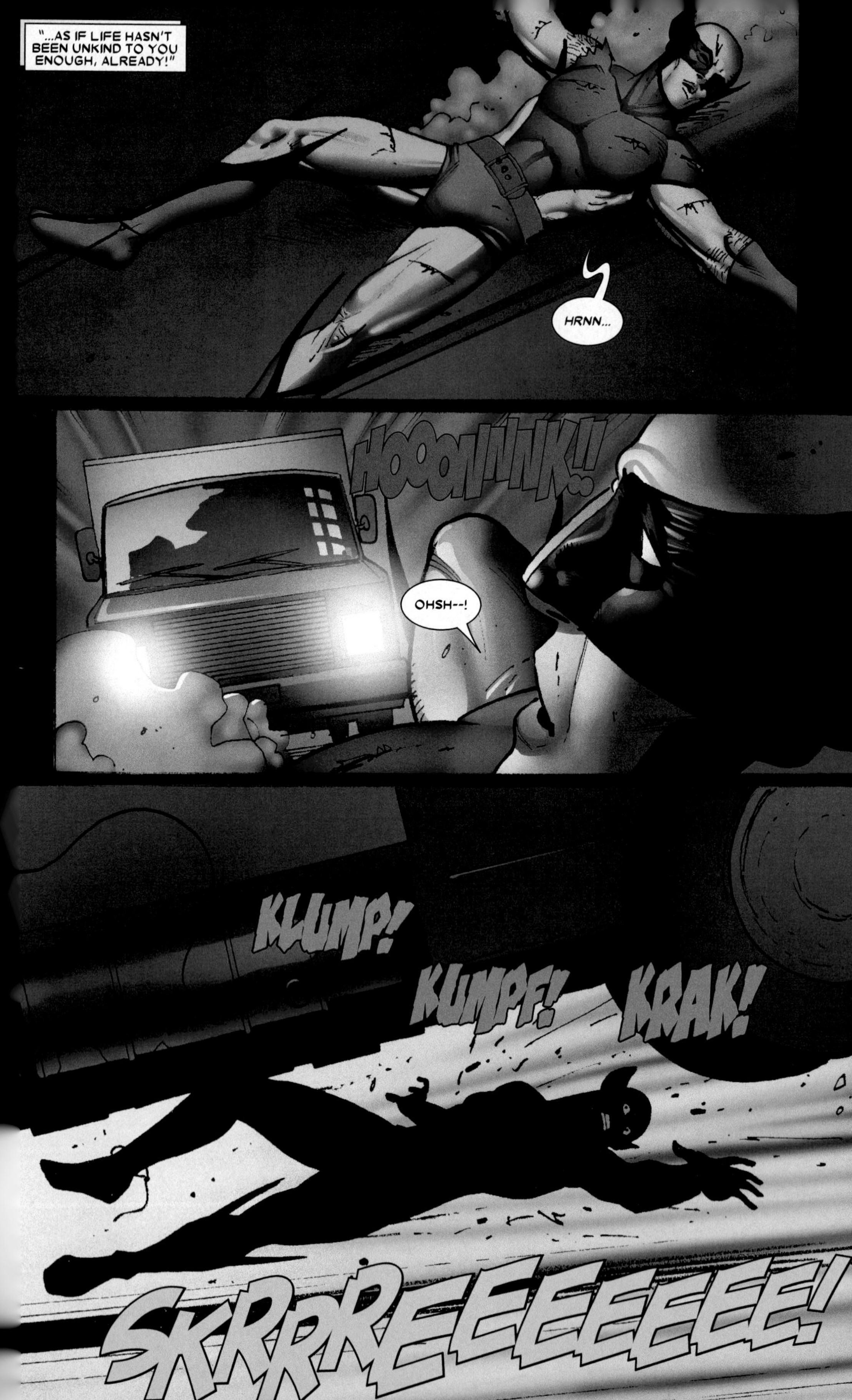
"...AS IF LIFE HASN'T BEEN UNKIND TO YOU ENOUGH, ALREADY!"
HRNN...
HOOONNNK!!
OHSH--!
KLUMP!
KUMPF!
KRAK!
SKRRREEEEEEEE!

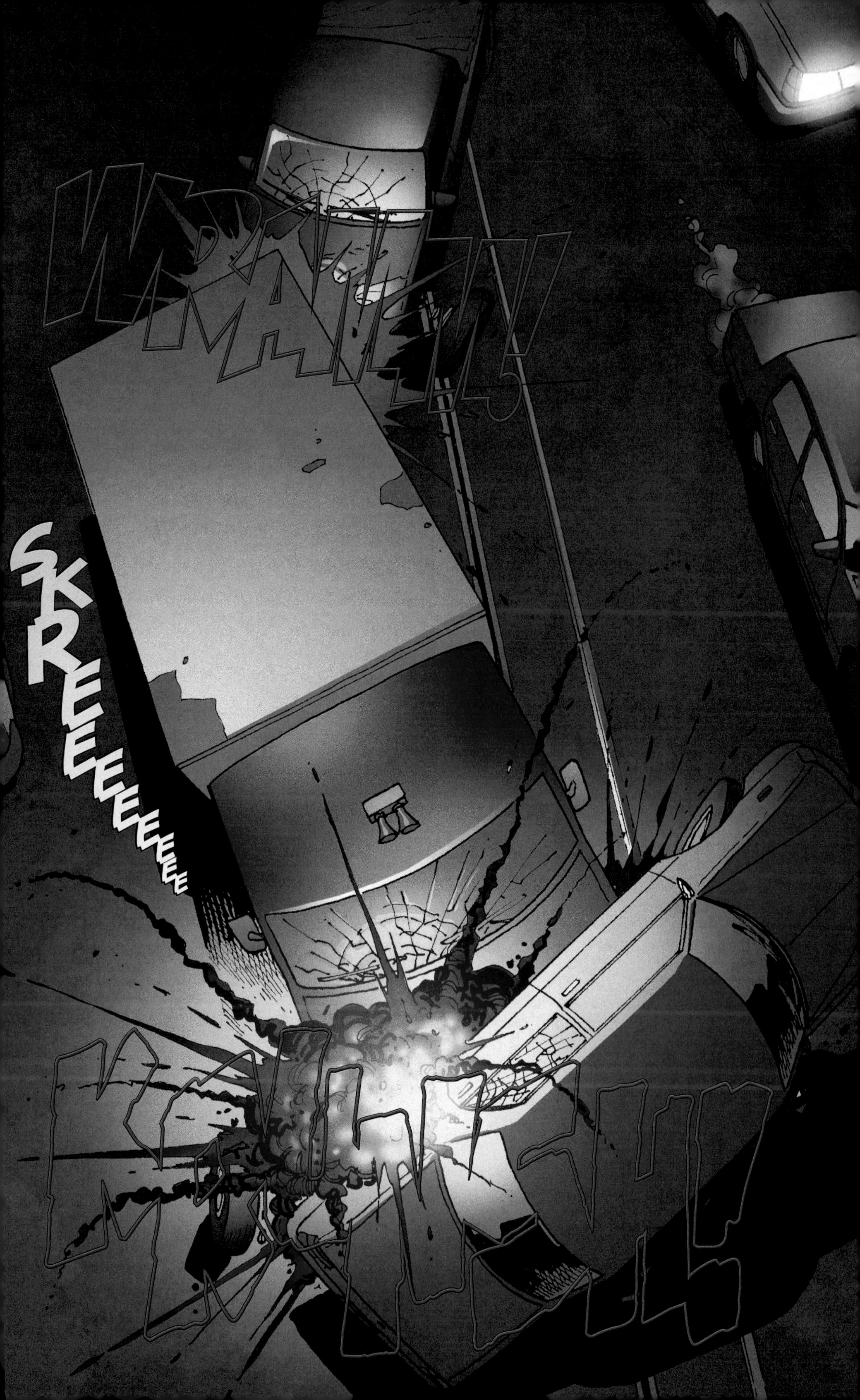
SKREEEEEEEEE

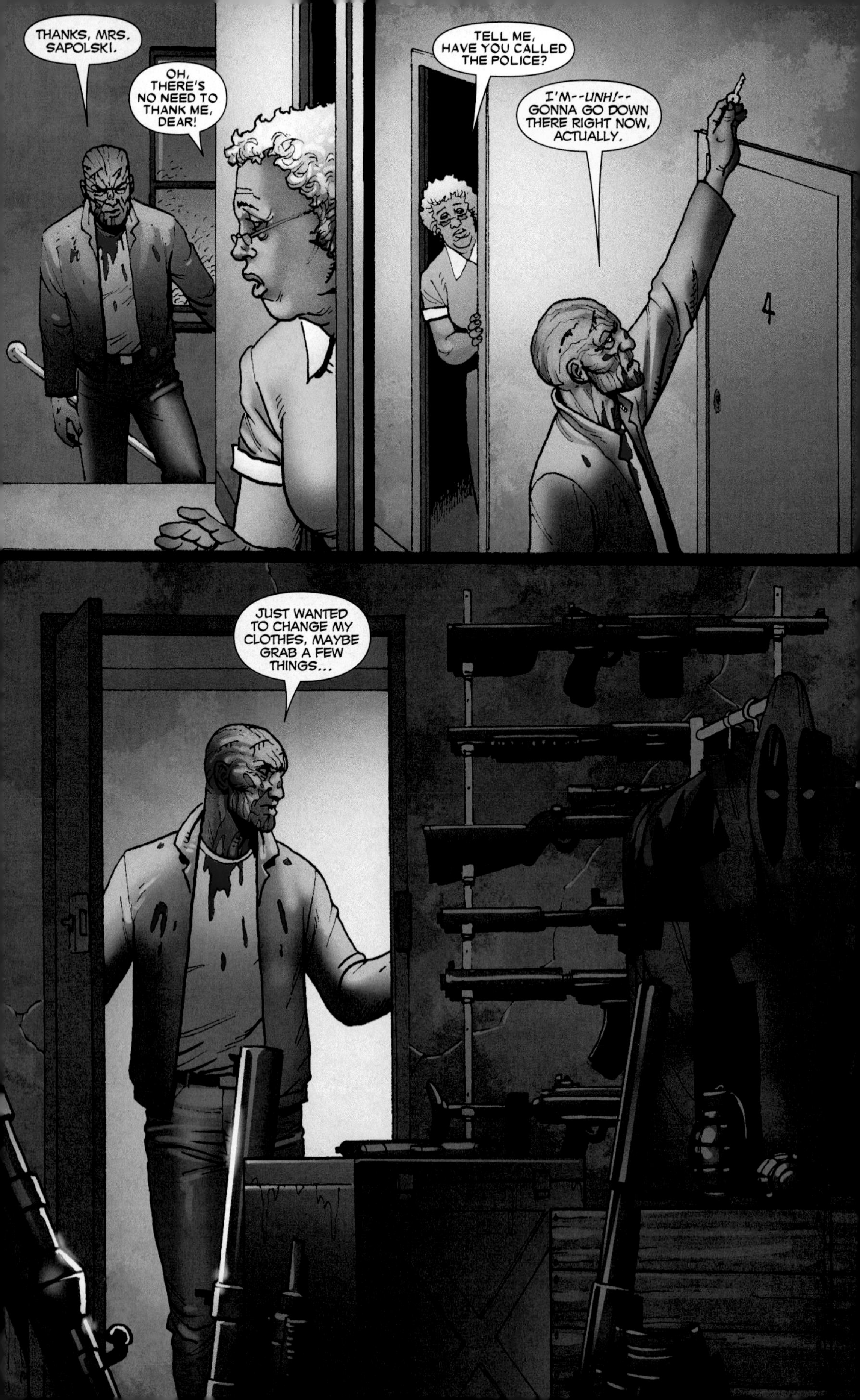
THANKS, MRS. SAPOLSKI.
OH, THERE'S NO NEED TO THANK ME, DEAR!
TELL ME, HAVE YOU CALLED THE POLICE?
I'M--*UNH!*--GONNA GO DOWN THERE RIGHT NOW, ACTUALLY.
4
JUST WANTED TO CHANGE MY CLOTHES, MAYBE GRAB A FEW THINGS...

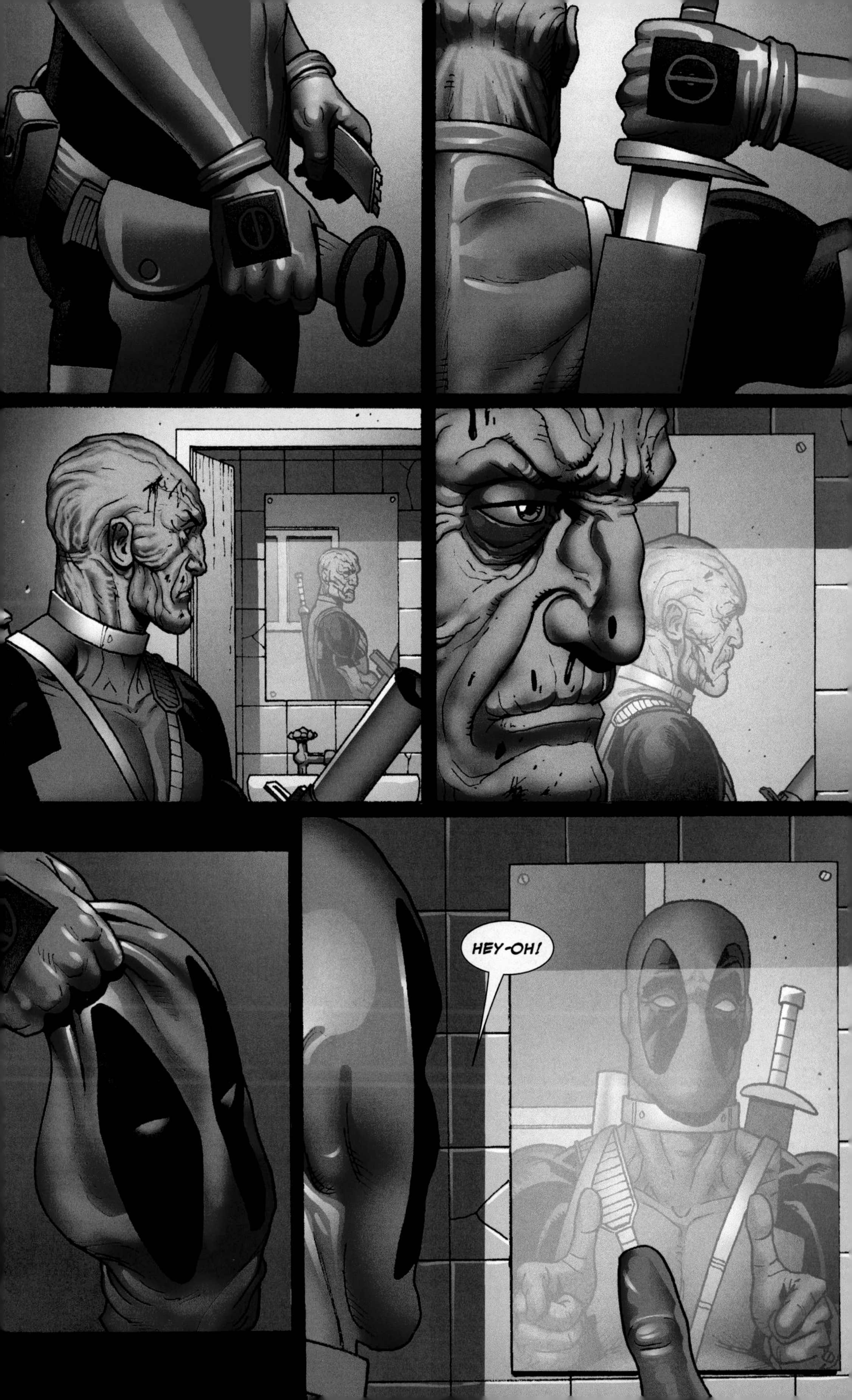
HEY-OH!

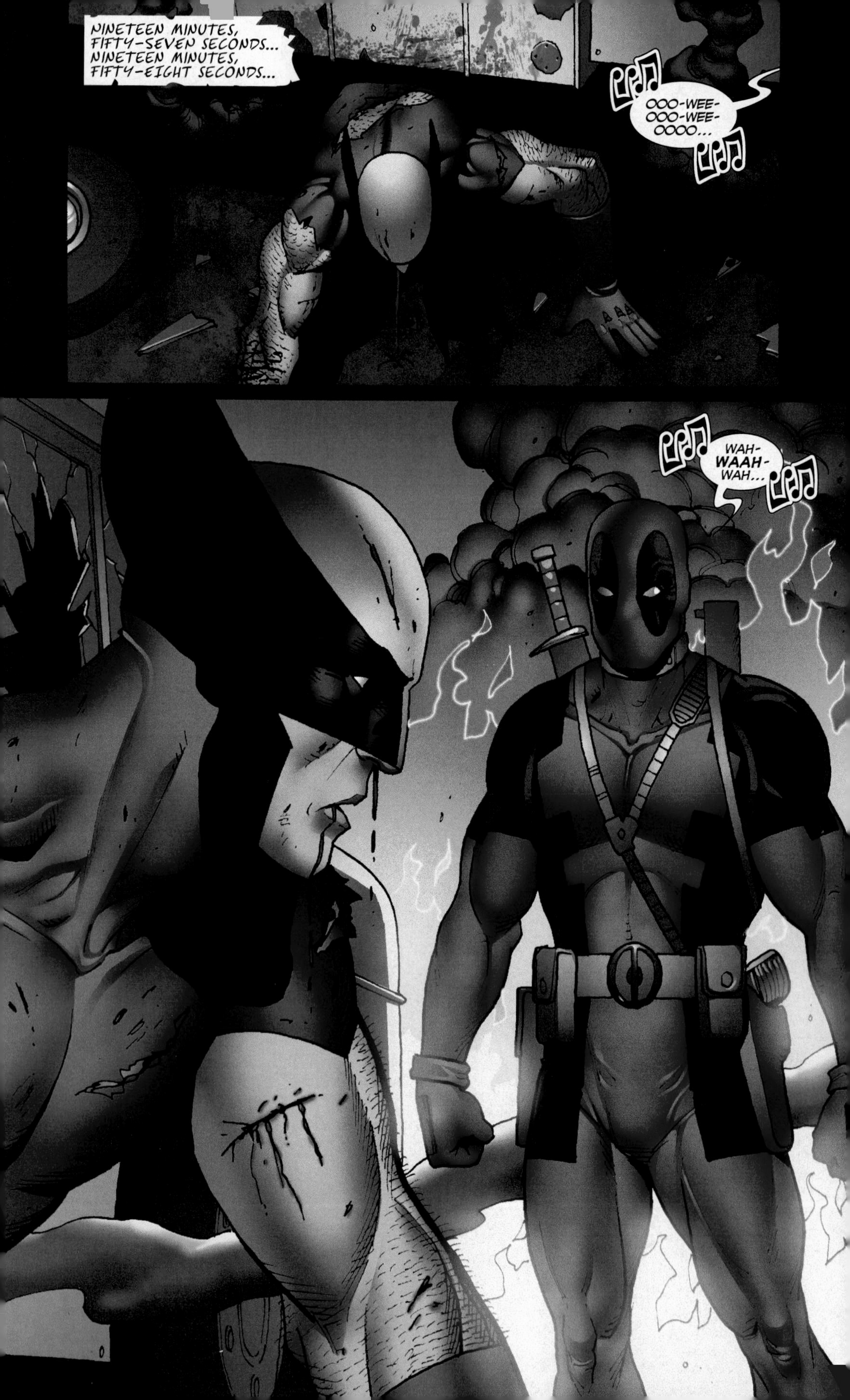
NINETEEN MINUTES, FIFTY-SEVEN SECONDS... NINETEEN MINUTES, FIFTY-EIGHT SECONDS...
OOO-WEE-OOO-WEE-OOOO...
WAH-WAAH-WAH...

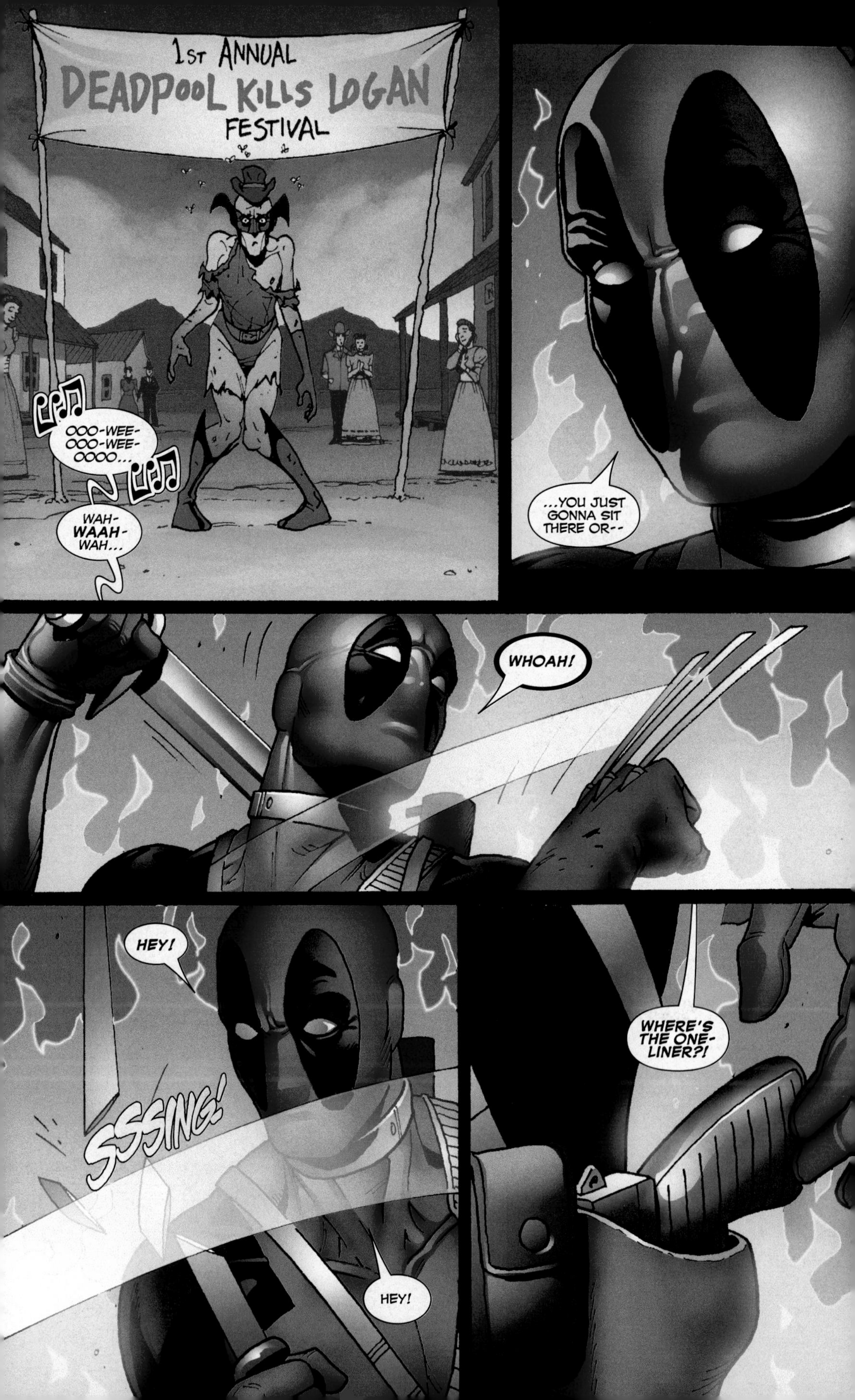
1st ANNUAL
DEADPOOL KILLS LOGAN
FESTIVAL
OOO-WEE-
OOO-WEE-
OOOO...
WAH-
WAAH-
WAH...
...YOU JUST
GONNA SIT
THERE OR--
WHOAH!
HEY!
SSSING!
HEY!
WHERE'S
THE ONE-
LINER?!

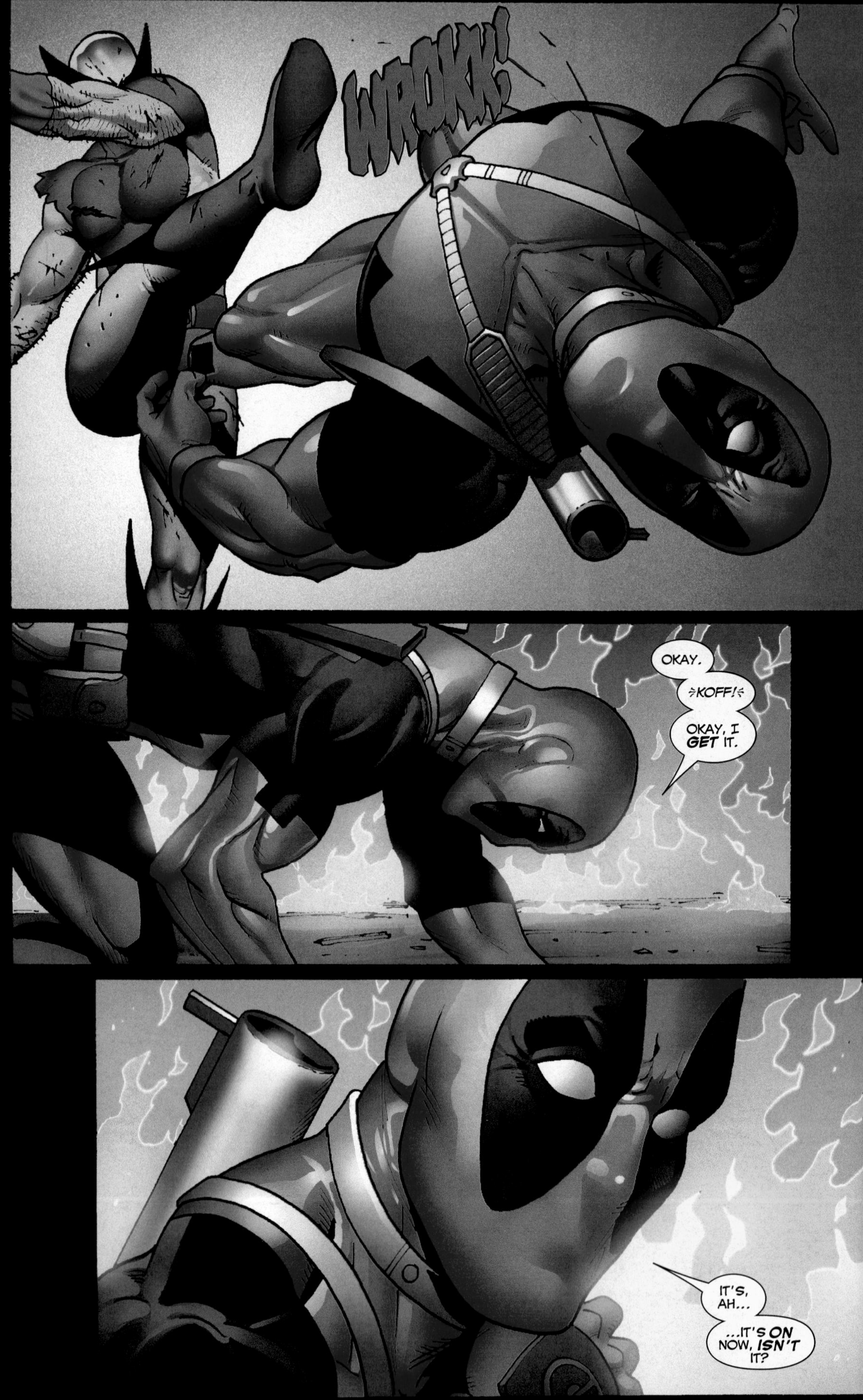
WROKK!
OKAY.
≑KOFF!≑
OKAY, I GET IT.
IT'S, AH...
...IT'S ON NOW, ISN'T IT?

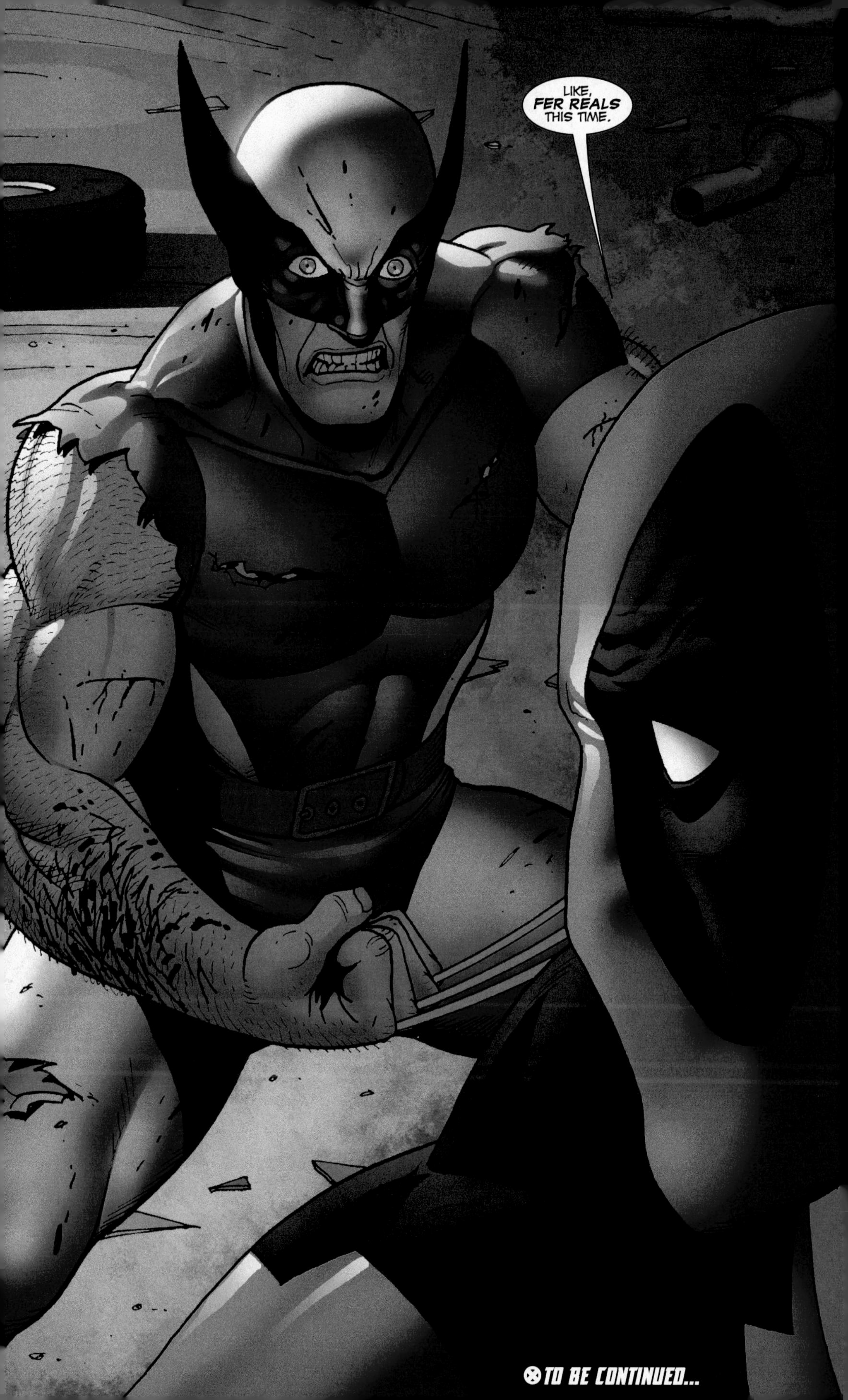
LIKE, FER REALS THIS TIME.
TO BE CONTINUED...

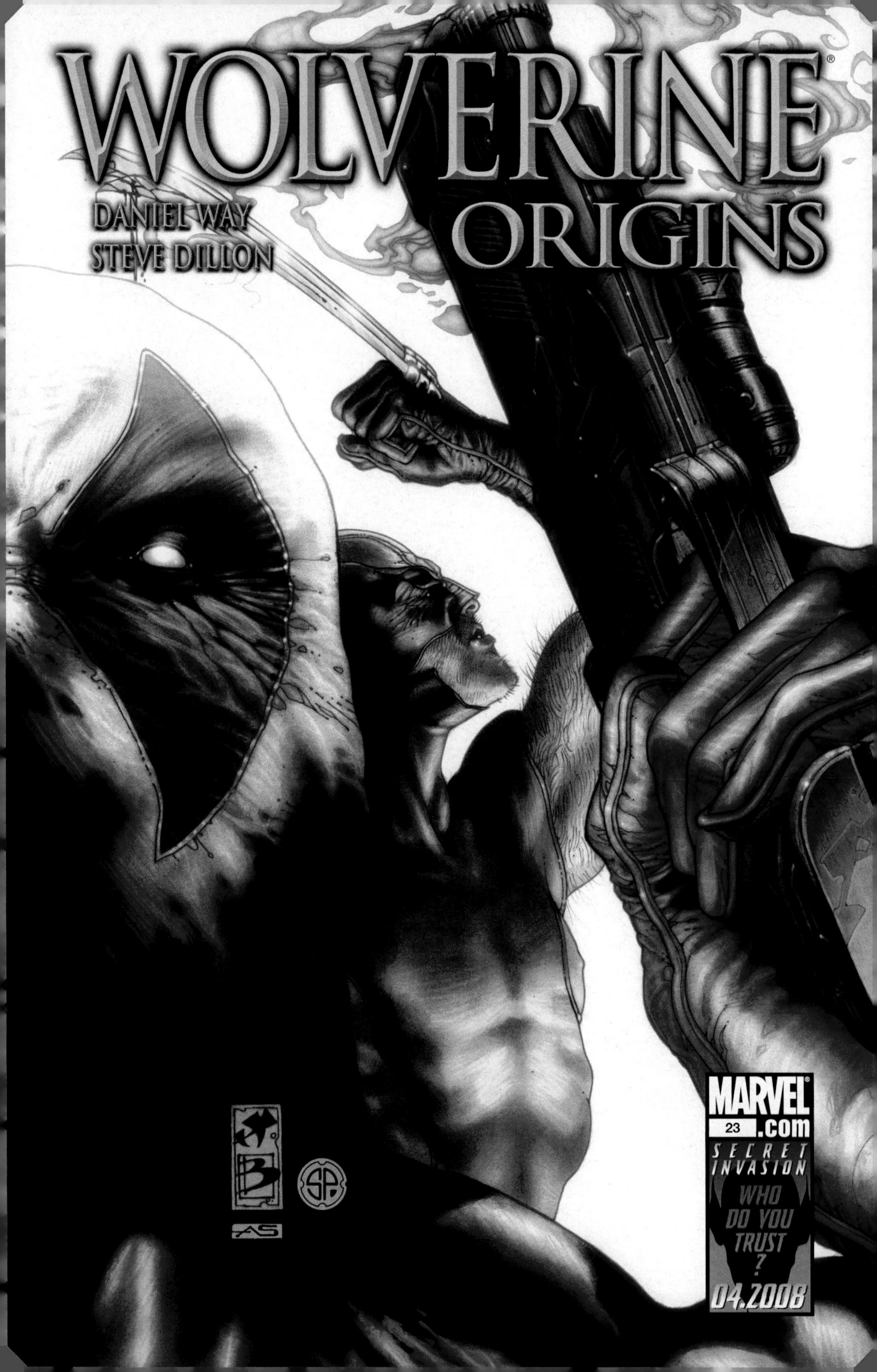
WOLVERINE®
ORIGINS
DANIEL WAY
STEVE DILLON
MARVEL®
23 .com
SECRET INVASION
WHO DO YOU TRUST ?
04.2008

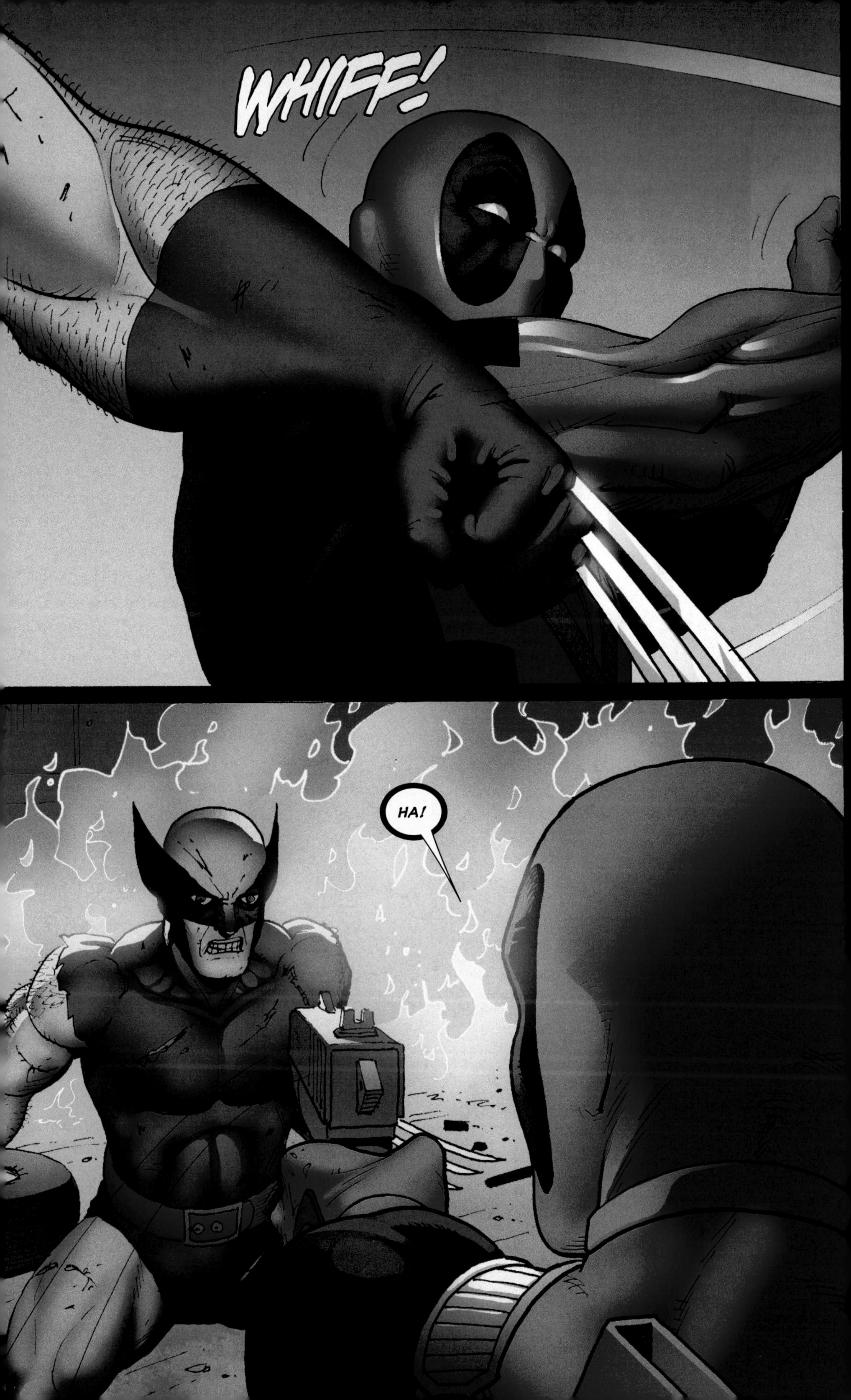
WHIFF!
HA!

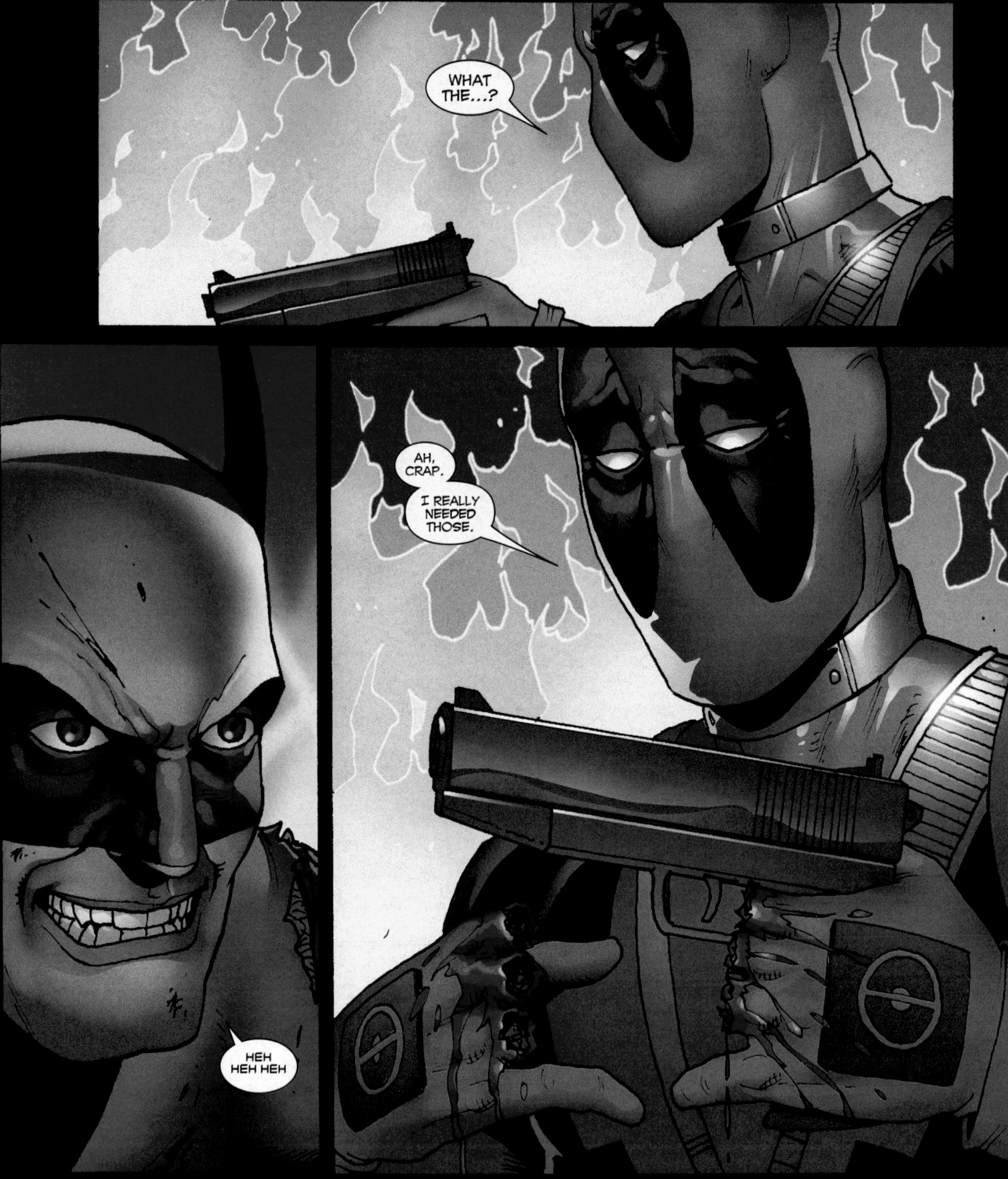

WHAT THE...?
AH, CRAP.
I REALLY NEEDED THOSE.
HEH HEH HEH

The DEEP END PART 3

DANIEL WAY WRITER
STEVE DILLON ARTIST
AVALON'S MATT MILLA COLORIST
VC'S CORY PETIT LETTERER
SIMONE BIANCHI COVER ART
SIMONE PERUZZI COVER COLOR
AUBREY SITTERSON ASST. EDITOR
JOHN BARBER EDITOR
AXEL ALONSO GROUP EDITOR
JOE QUESADA EDITOR IN CHIEF
DAN BUCKLEY PUBLISHER

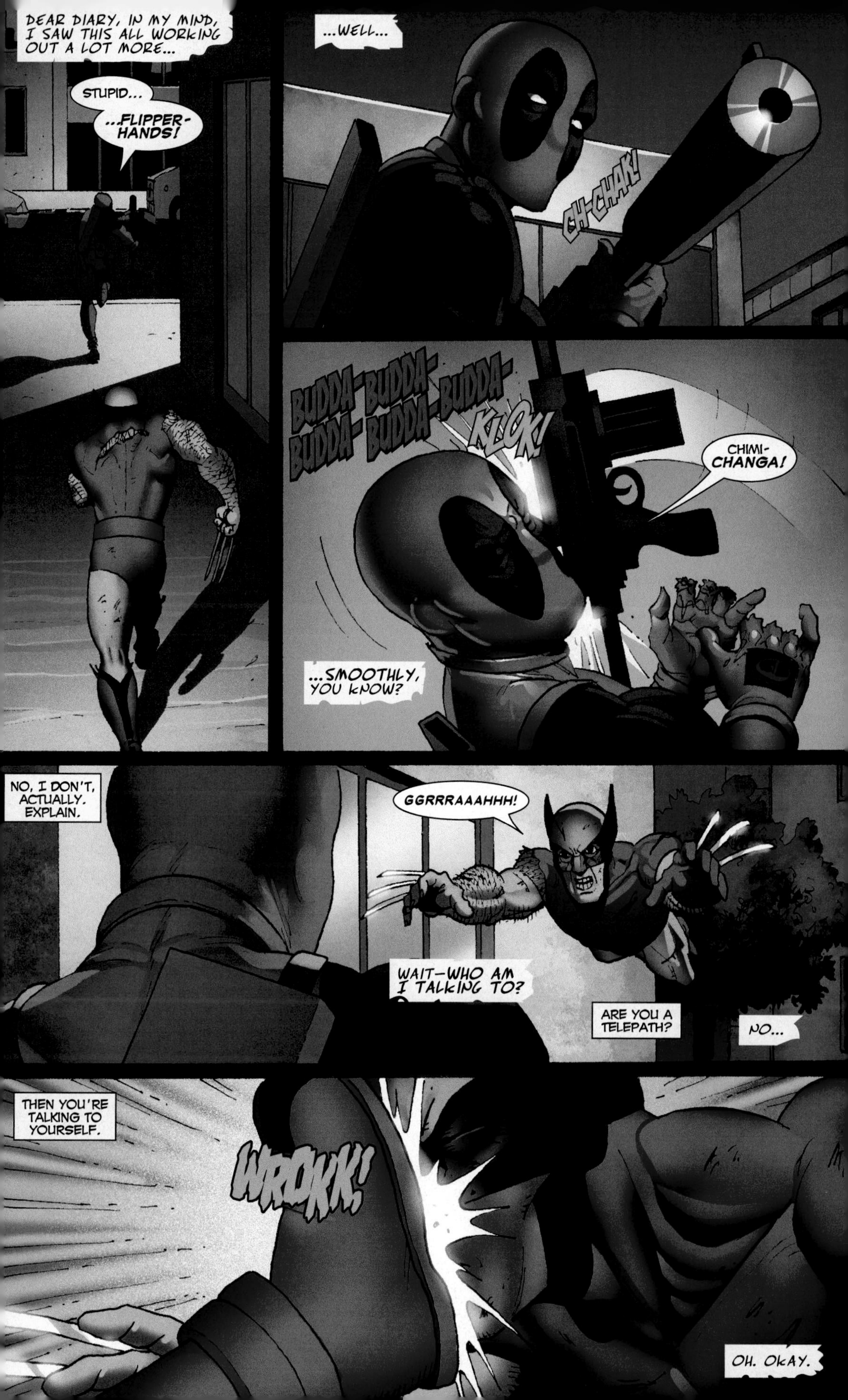
DEAR DIARY, IN MY MIND, I SAW THIS ALL WORKING OUT A LOT MORE...
STUPID...
...FLIPPER-HANDS!
...WELL...
CH-CHAK!
BUDDA-BUDDA-BUDDA-BUDDA-BUDDA-BUDDA-
KLOK!
CHIMI-CHANGA!
...SMOOTHLY, YOU KNOW?
NO, I DON'T, ACTUALLY. EXPLAIN.
GGRRRAAAHHH!
WAIT--WHO AM I TALKING TO?
ARE YOU A TELEPATH?
NO...
THEN YOU'RE TALKING TO YOURSELF.
WROKK!
OH. OKAY.

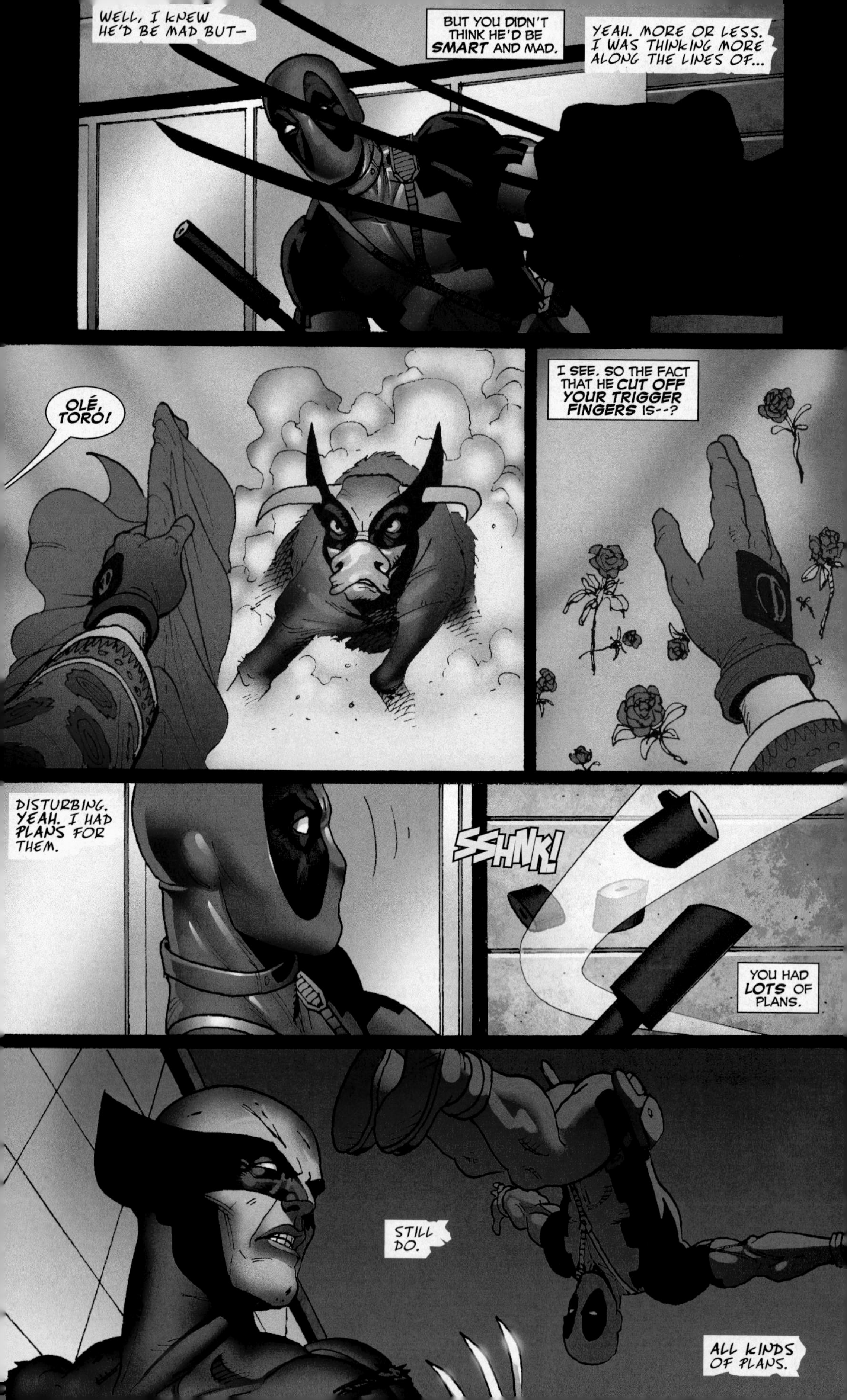
WELL, I KNEW HE'D BE MAD BUT—
BUT YOU DIDN'T THINK HE'D BE SMART AND MAD.
YEAH. MORE OR LESS. I WAS THINKING MORE ALONG THE LINES OF...
OLÉ, TORO!
I SEE. SO THE FACT THAT HE CUT OFF YOUR TRIGGER FINGERS IS--?
DISTURBING. YEAH. I HAD PLANS FOR THEM.
SSHNK!
YOU HAD LOTS OF PLANS.
STILL DO.
ALL KINDS OF PLANS.

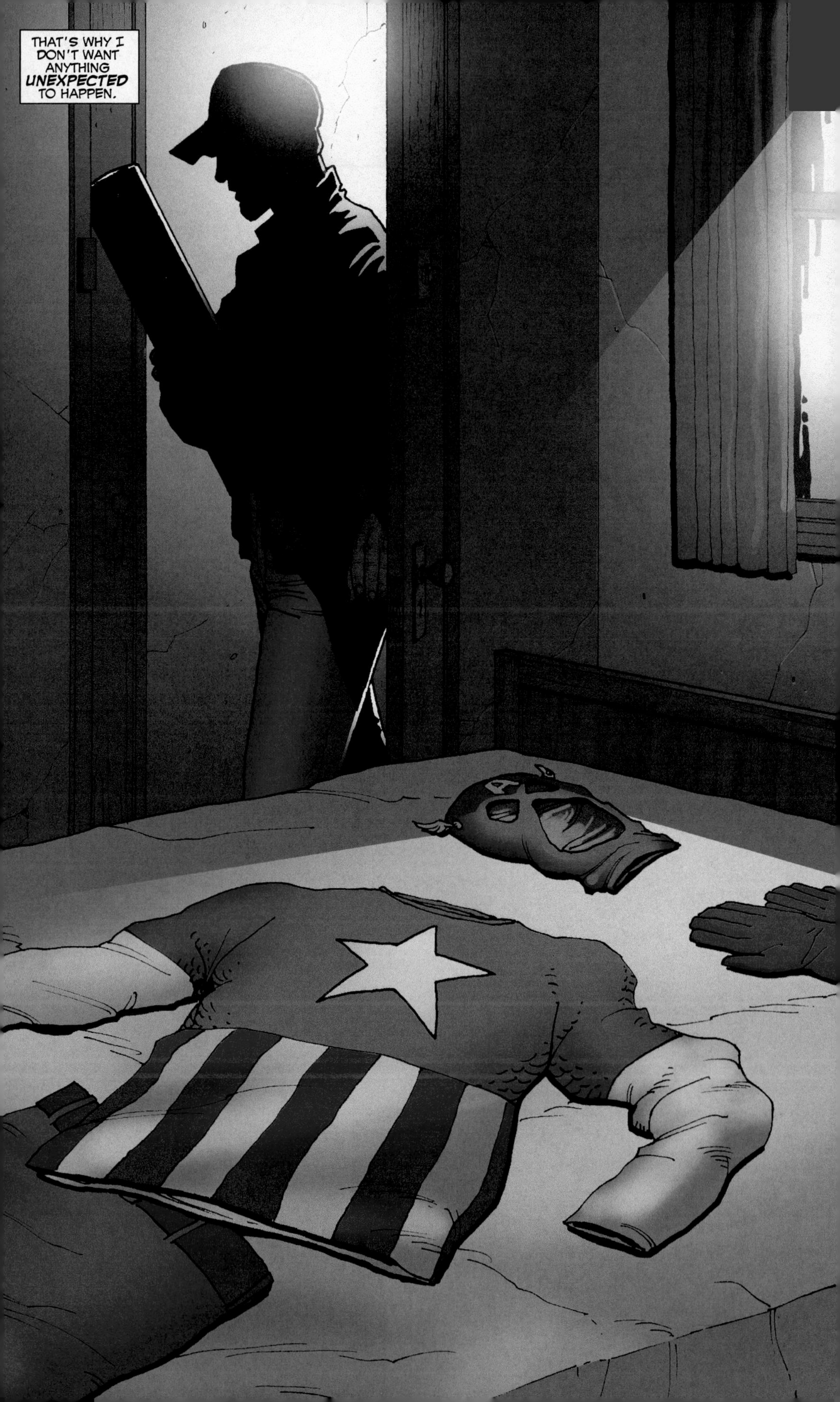
THAT'S WHY I DON'T WANT ANYTHING **UNEXPECTED** TO HAPPEN.

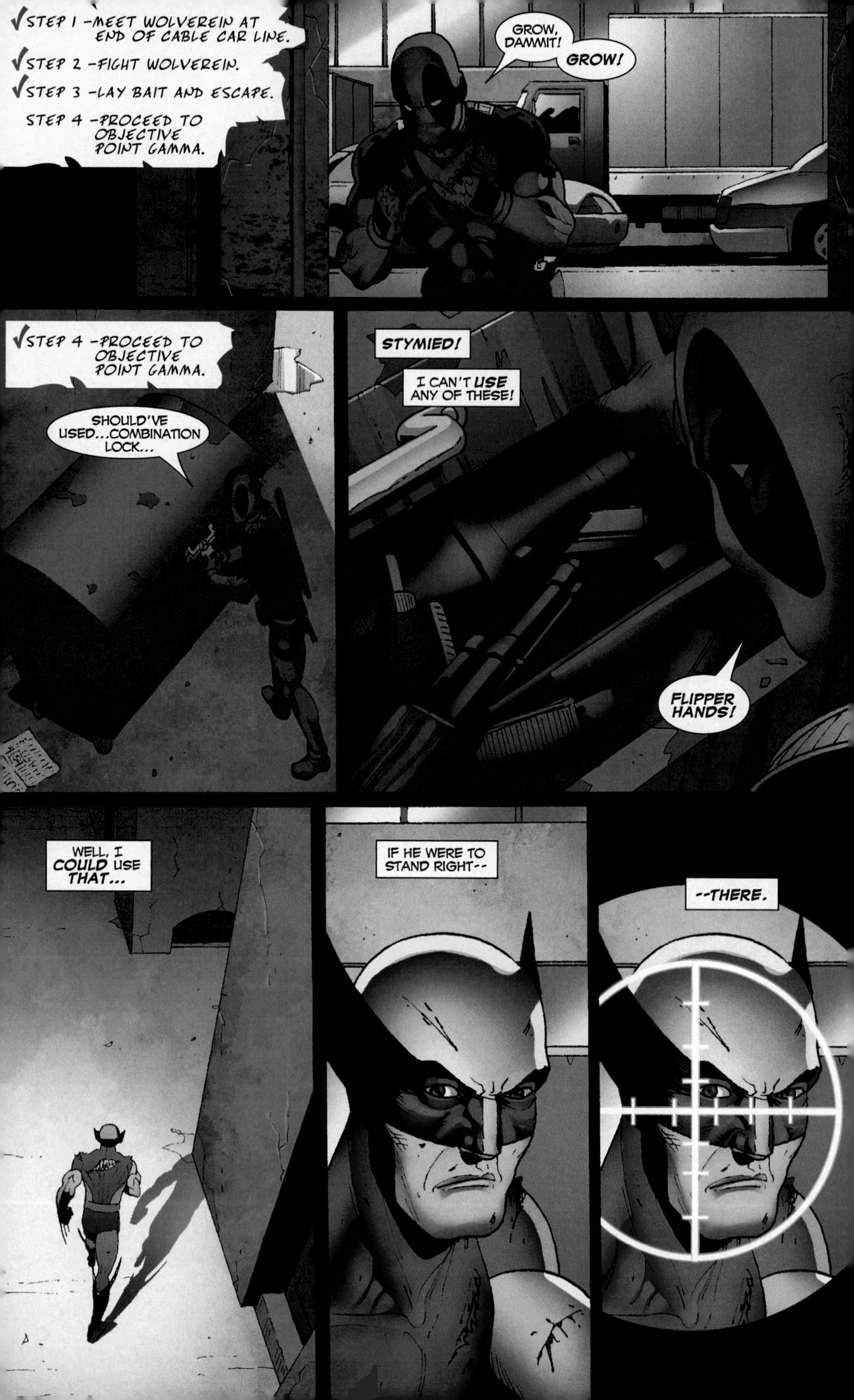
√STEP 1 -MEET WOLVEREIN AT END OF CABLE CAR LINE.
√STEP 2 -FIGHT WOLVEREIN.
√STEP 3 -LAY BAIT AND ESCAPE.
STEP 4 -PROCEED TO OBJECTIVE POINT GAMMA.
GROW, DAMMIT!
GROW!
√STEP 4 -PROCEED TO OBJECTIVE POINT GAMMA.
SHOULD'VE USED...COMBINATION LOCK...
STYMIED!
I CAN'T USE ANY OF THESE!
FLIPPER HANDS!
WELL, I COULD USE THAT...
IF HE WERE TO STAND RIGHT--
--THERE.

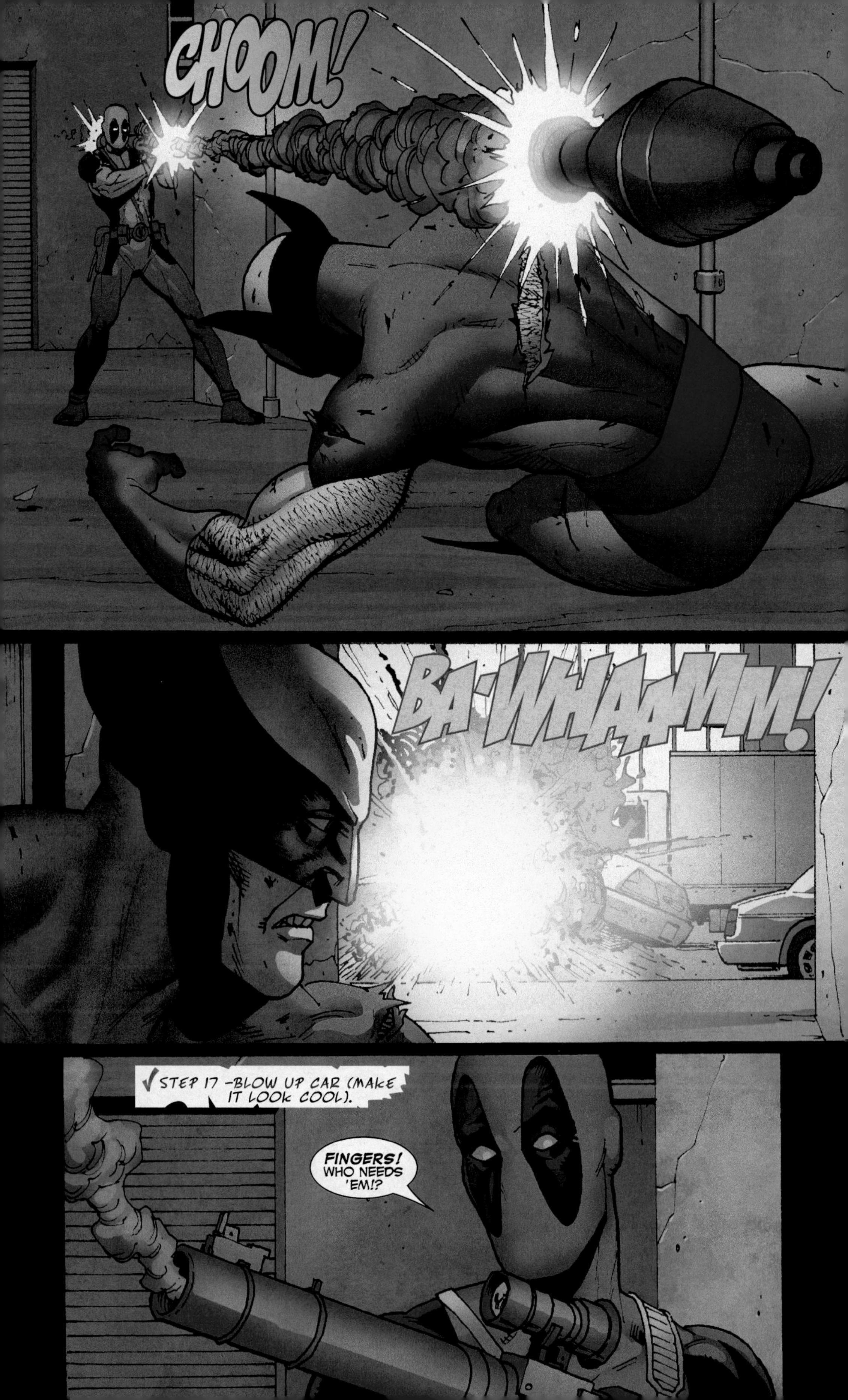
CHOOM!
BA-WHAAMM!
STEP 17 -BLOW UP CAR (MAKE IT LOOK COOL).
FINGERS! WHO NEEDS 'EM!?

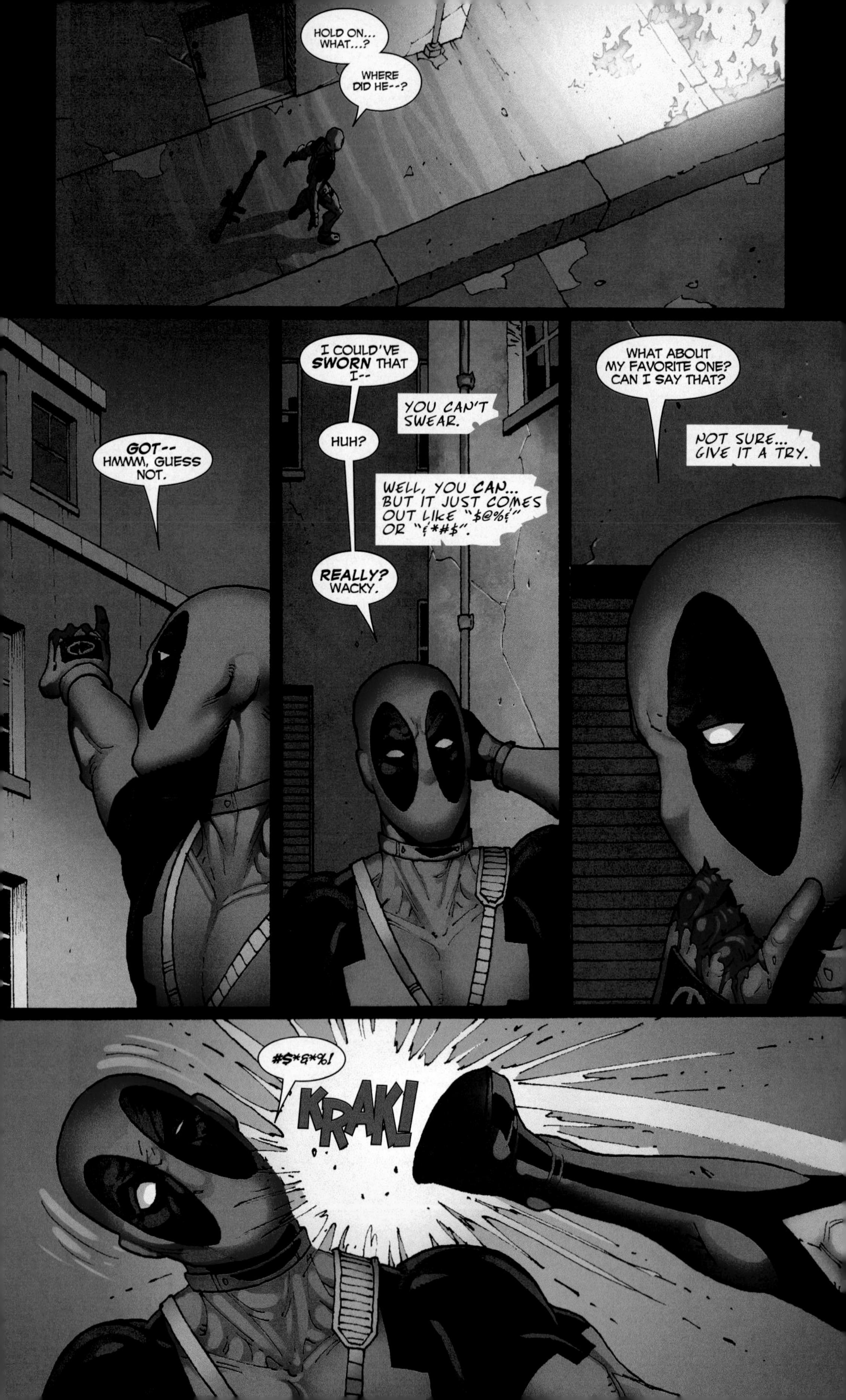
HOLD ON... WHAT...?
WHERE DID HE--?
GOT-- HMMM, GUESS NOT.
I COULD'VE SWORN THAT I--
YOU CAN'T SWEAR.
HUH?
WELL, YOU CAN... BUT IT JUST COMES OUT LIKE "$@%¢" OR "¢*#$".
REALLY? WACKY.
WHAT ABOUT MY FAVORITE ONE? CAN I SAY THAT?
NOT SURE... GIVE IT A TRY.
#$*&*%!
KRAK!

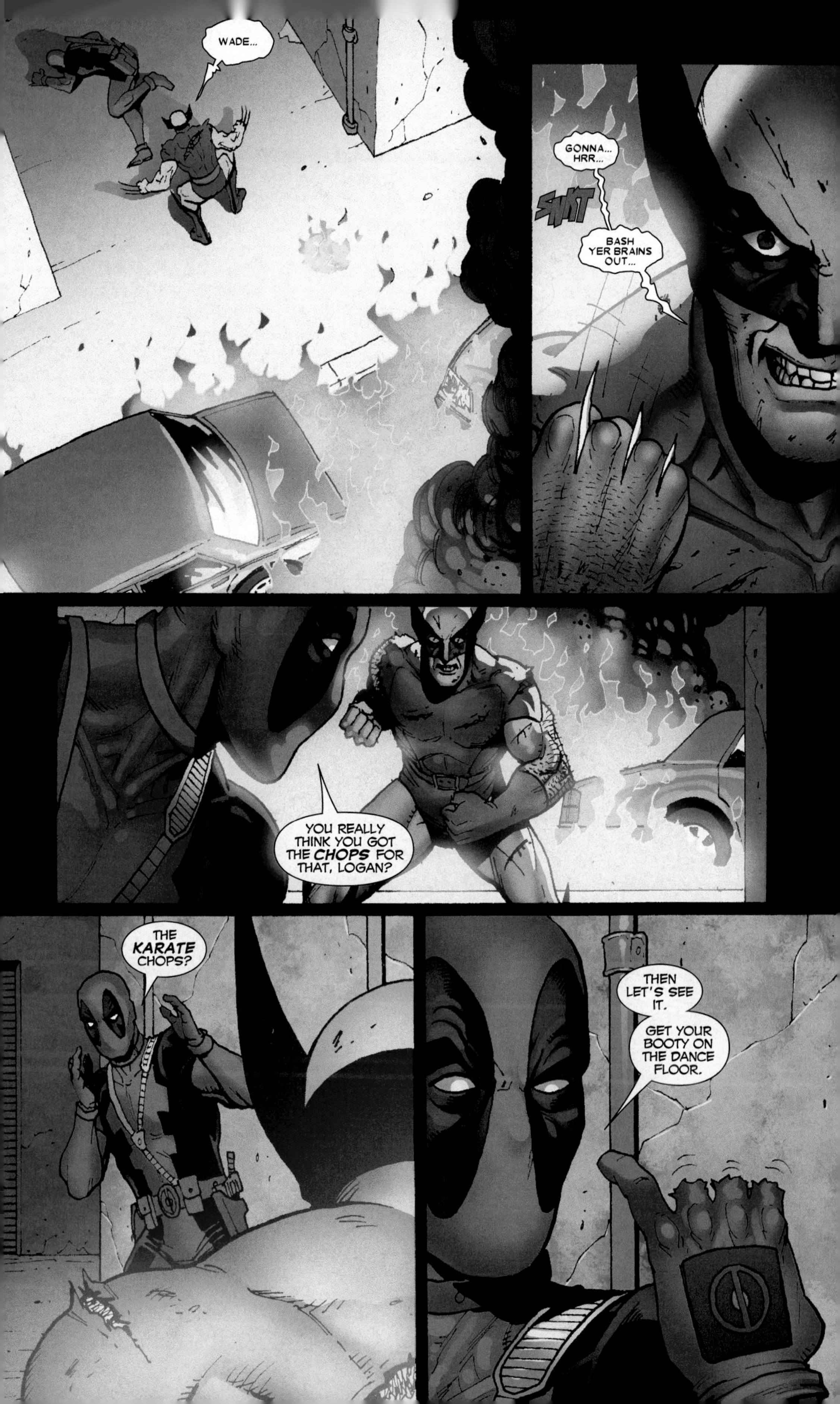

WADE...
GONNA... HRR...
SNKT
BASH YER BRAINS OUT...
YOU REALLY THINK YOU GOT THE CHOPS FOR THAT, LOGAN?
THE KARATE CHOPS?
THEN LET'S SEE IT.
GET YOUR BOOTY ON THE DANCE FLOOR.

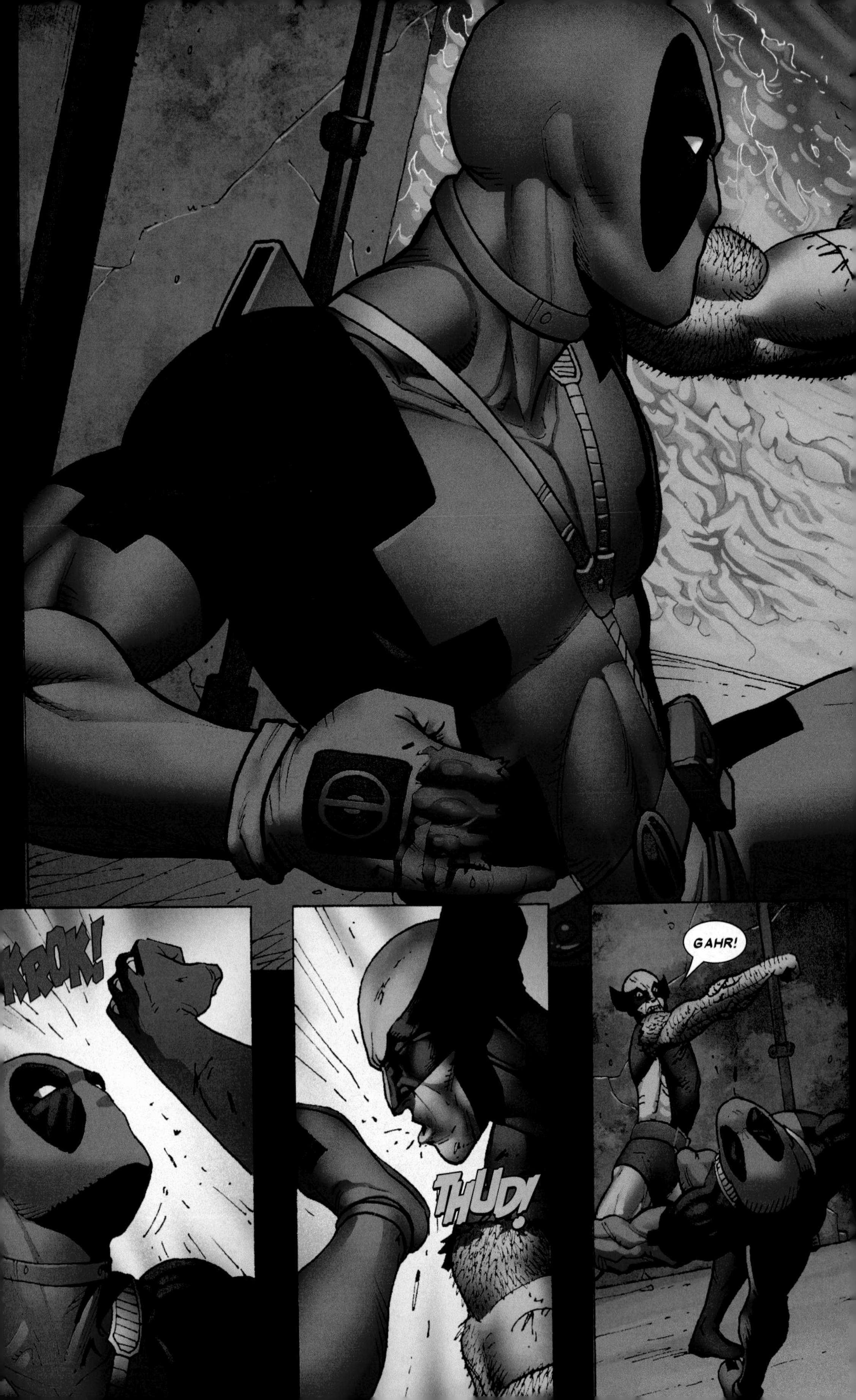
KROK!
THUD!
GAHR!

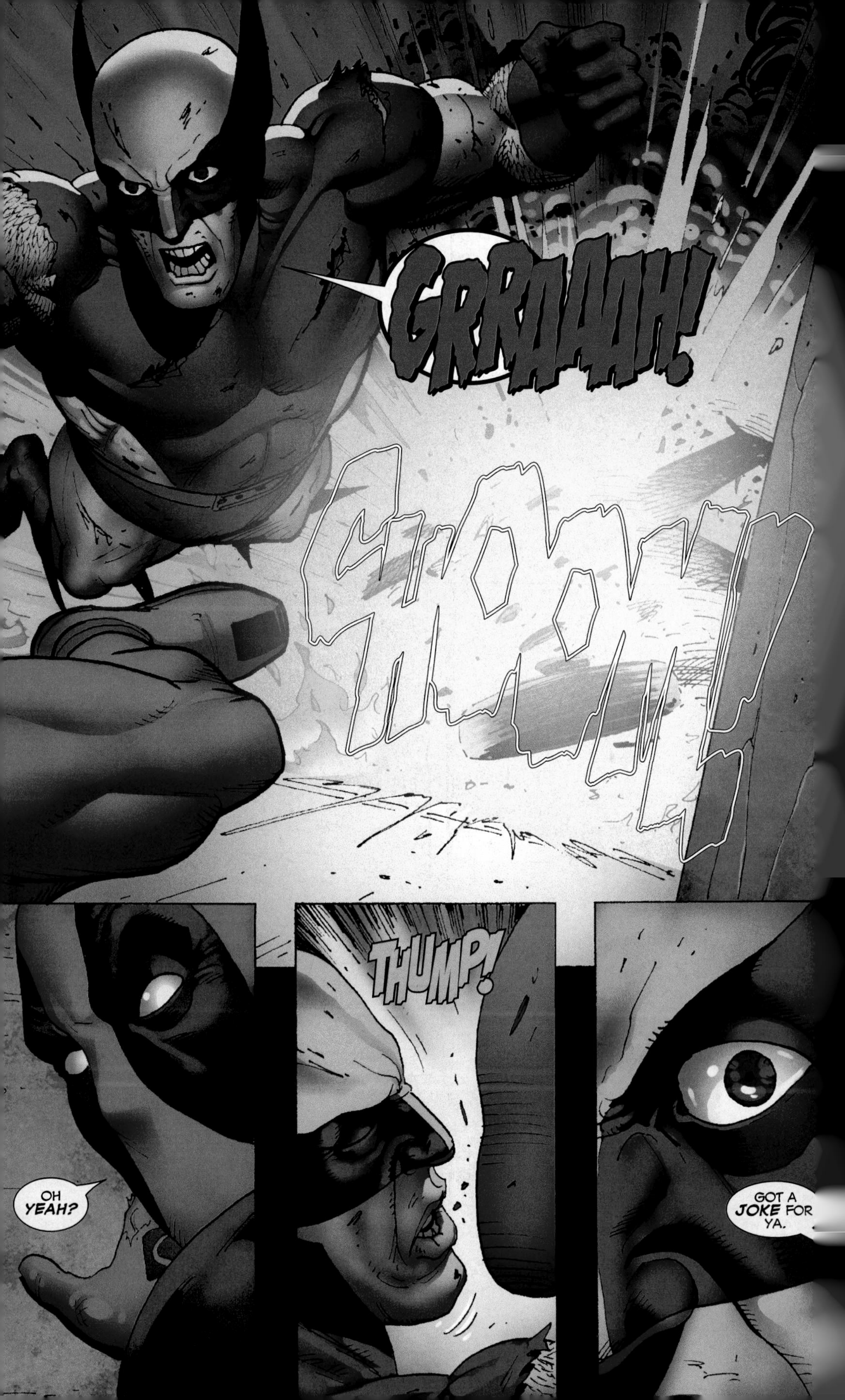
GRRAAAH!
CHOOM
THUMP!
OH YEAH?
GOT A JOKE FOR YA.

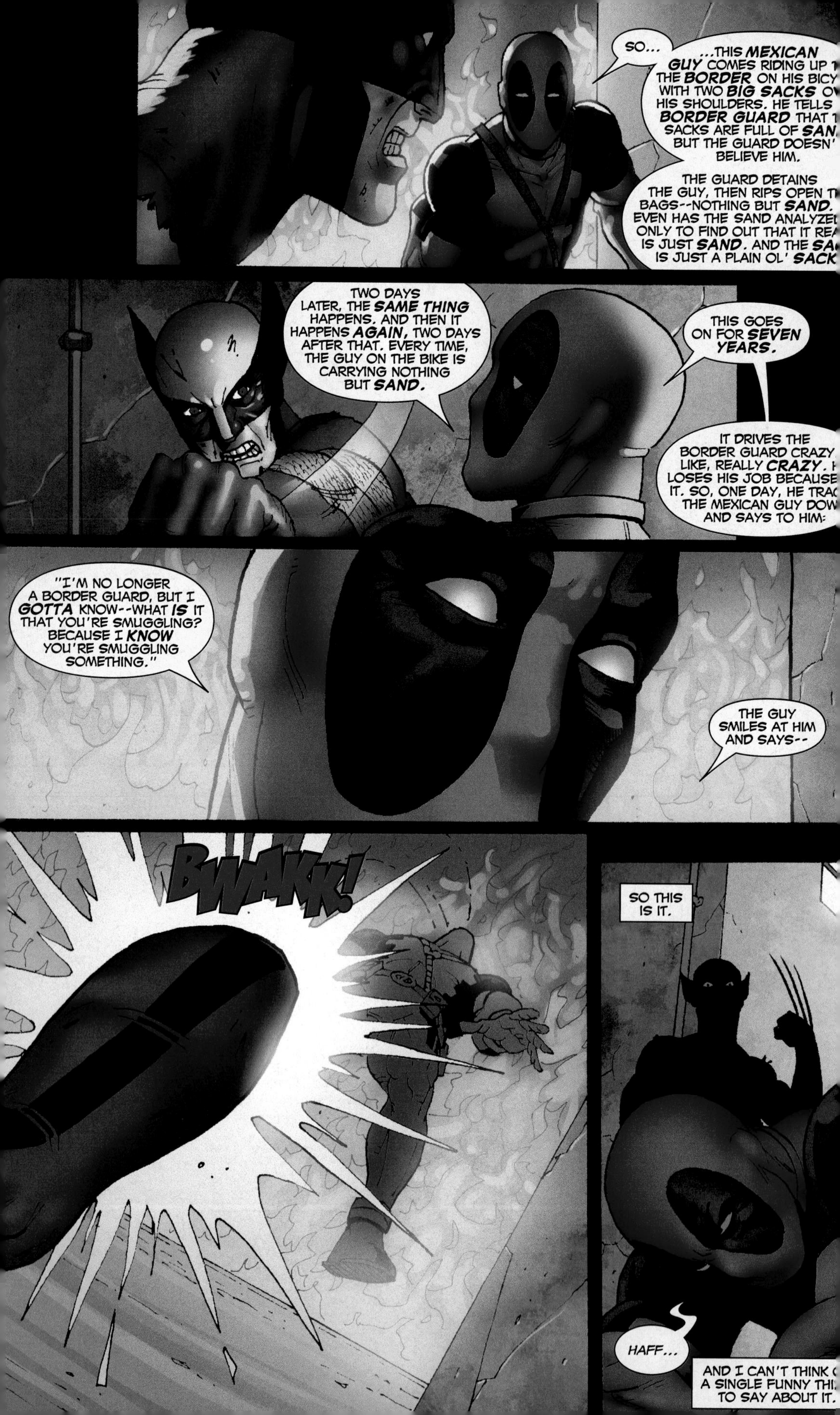
SO...
...THIS MEXICAN GUY COMES RIDING UP T THE BORDER ON HIS BICY WITH TWO BIG SACKS O HIS SHOULDERS. HE TELLS BORDER GUARD THAT SACKS ARE FULL OF SAN BUT THE GUARD DOESN' BELIEVE HIM.
THE GUARD DETAINS THE GUY, THEN RIPS OPEN T BAGS--NOTHING BUT SAND. EVEN HAS THE SAND ANALYZE ONLY TO FIND OUT THAT IT RE IS JUST SAND. AND THE SA IS JUST A PLAIN OL' SACK
TWO DAYS LATER, THE SAME THING HAPPENS. AND THEN IT HAPPENS AGAIN, TWO DAYS AFTER THAT. EVERY TIME, THE GUY ON THE BIKE IS CARRYING NOTHING BUT SAND.
THIS GOES ON FOR SEVEN YEARS.
IT DRIVES THE BORDER GUARD CRAZY. LIKE, REALLY CRAZY. LOSES HIS JOB BECAUSE IT. SO, ONE DAY, HE TRAC THE MEXICAN GUY DOW AND SAYS TO HIM:
"I'M NO LONGER A BORDER GUARD, BUT I GOTTA KNOW--WHAT IS IT THAT YOU'RE SMUGGLING? BECAUSE I KNOW YOU'RE SMUGGLING SOMETHING."
THE GUY SMILES AT HIM AND SAYS--
BWAKK!
SO THIS IS IT.
HAFF...
AND I CAN'T THINK A SINGLE FUNNY THI TO SAY ABOUT IT.

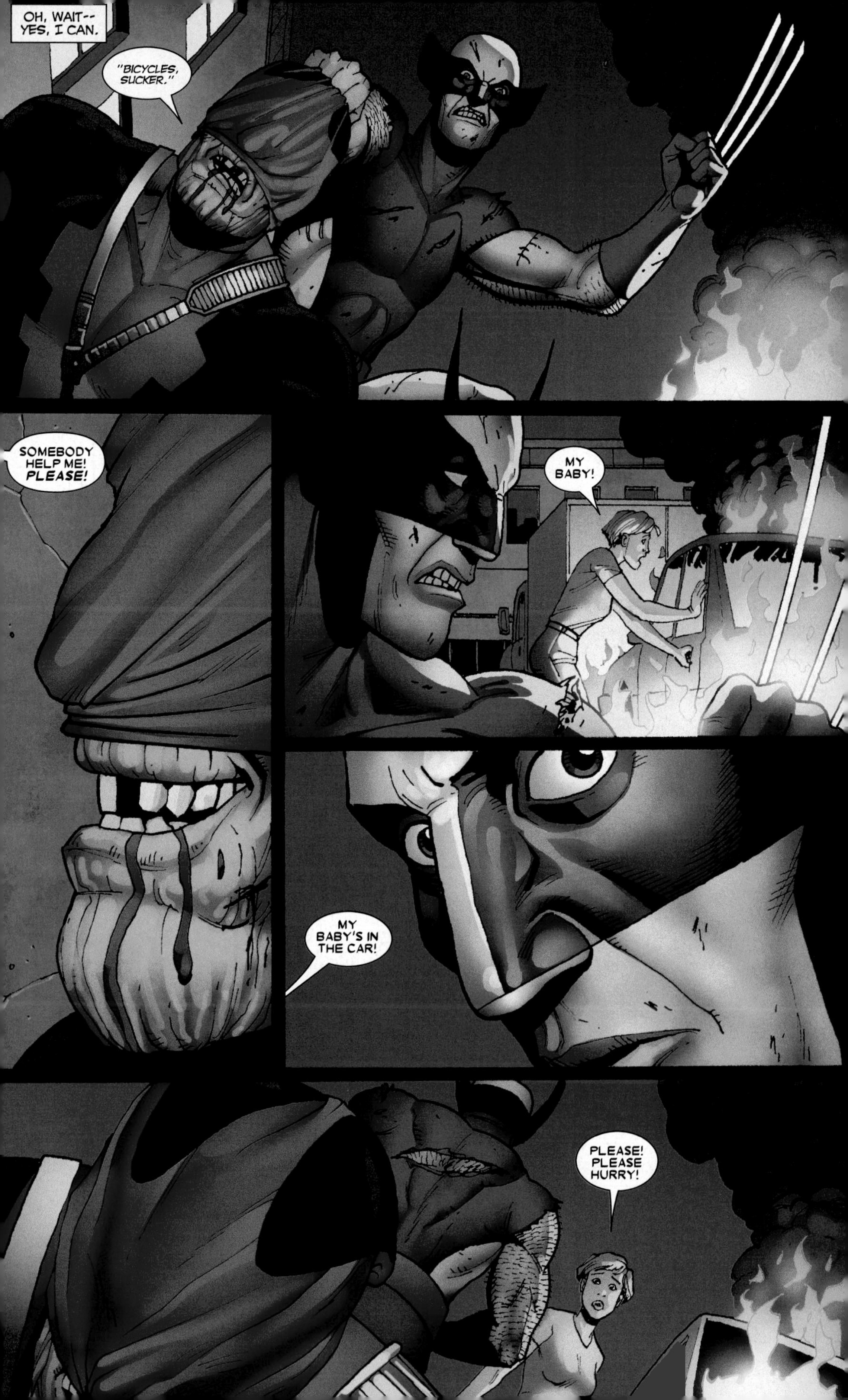
OH, WAIT--
YES, I CAN.
"BICYCLES, SUCKER."
SOMEBODY HELP ME! *PLEASE!*
MY BABY!
MY BABY'S IN THE CAR!
PLEASE! PLEASE HURRY!

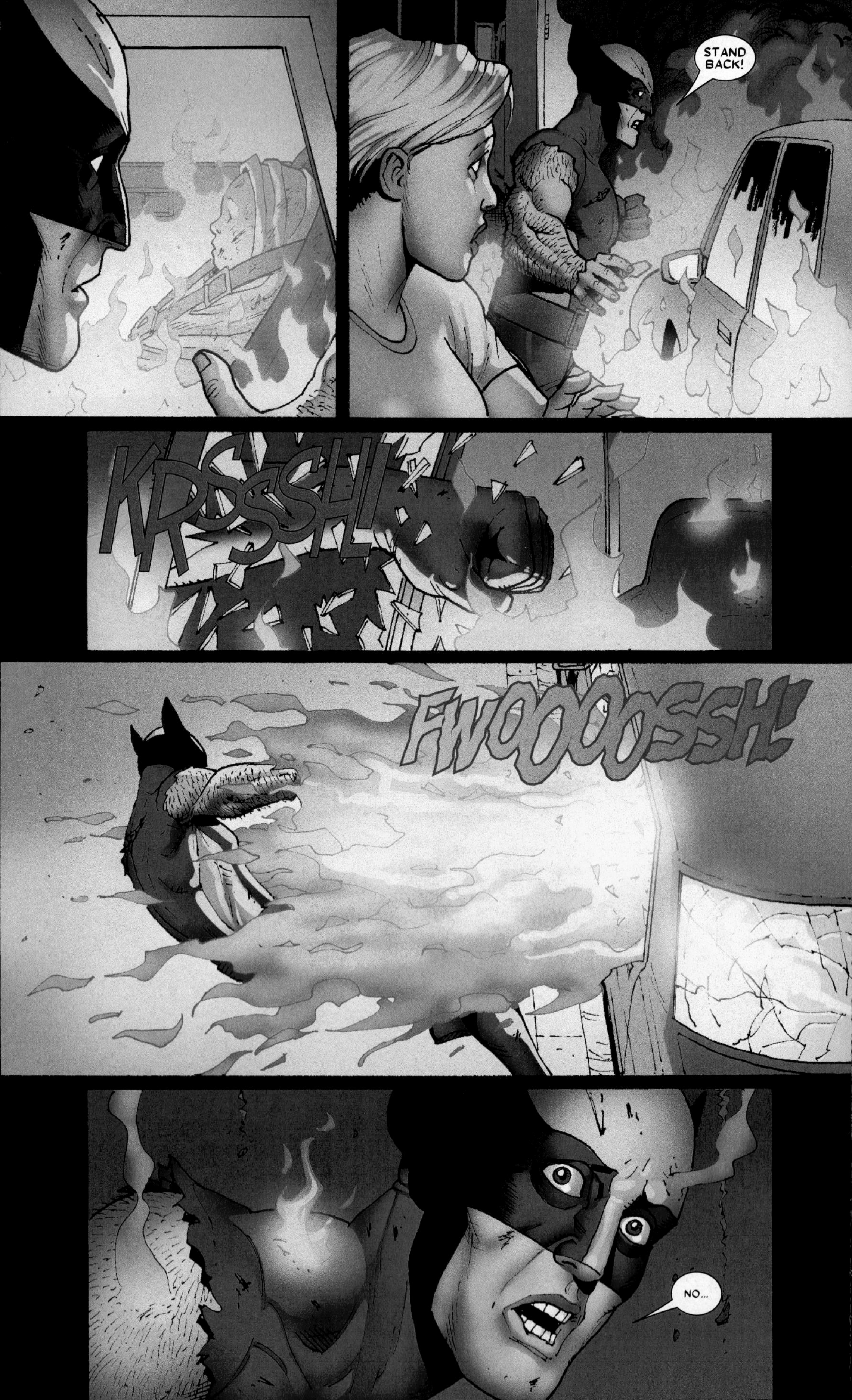
STAND BACK!
KRSSSH!
FWOOOOSSH!
NO...

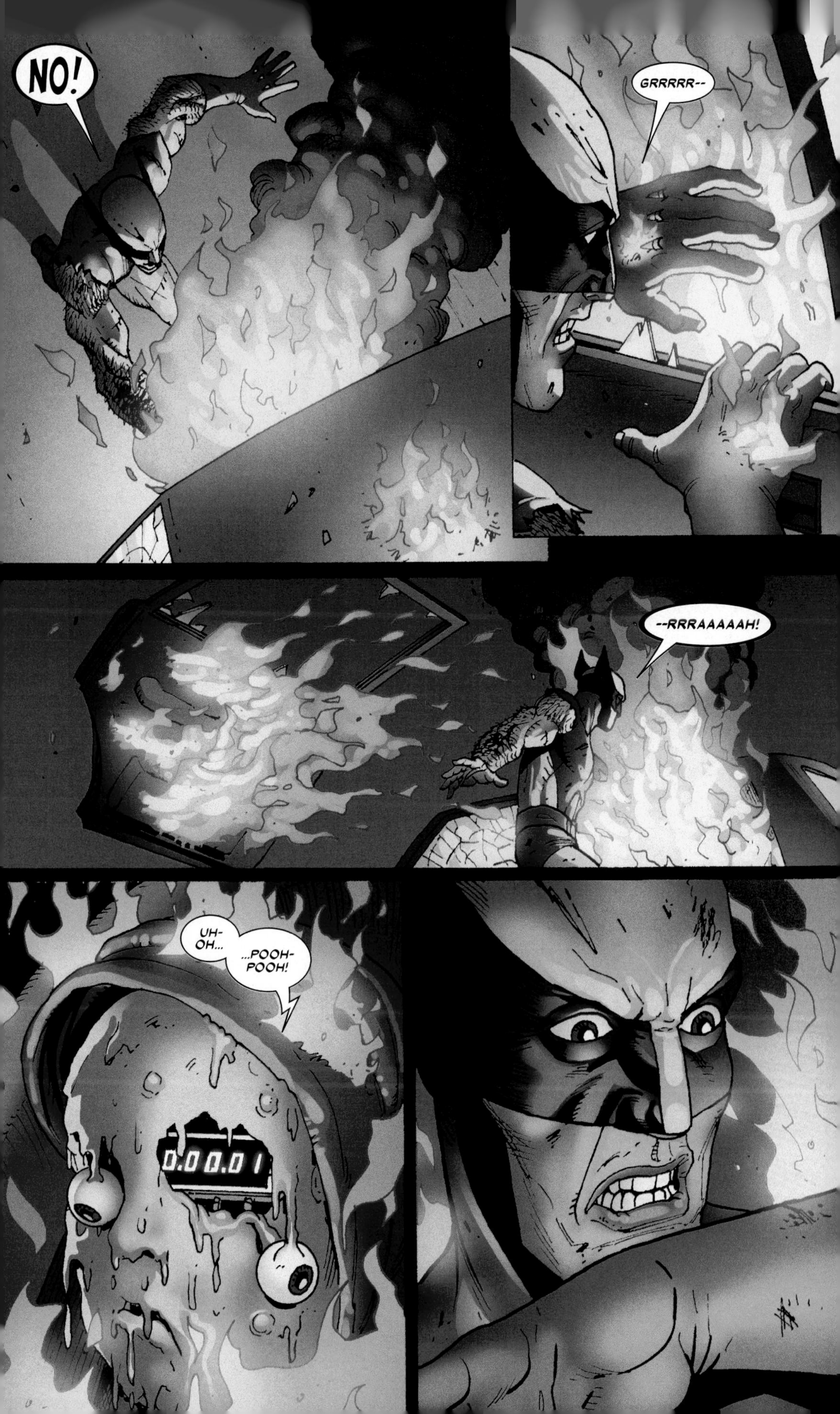
NO!
GRRRRR--
--RRRAAAAAH!
UH-OH...
...POOH-POOH!
0.00.01

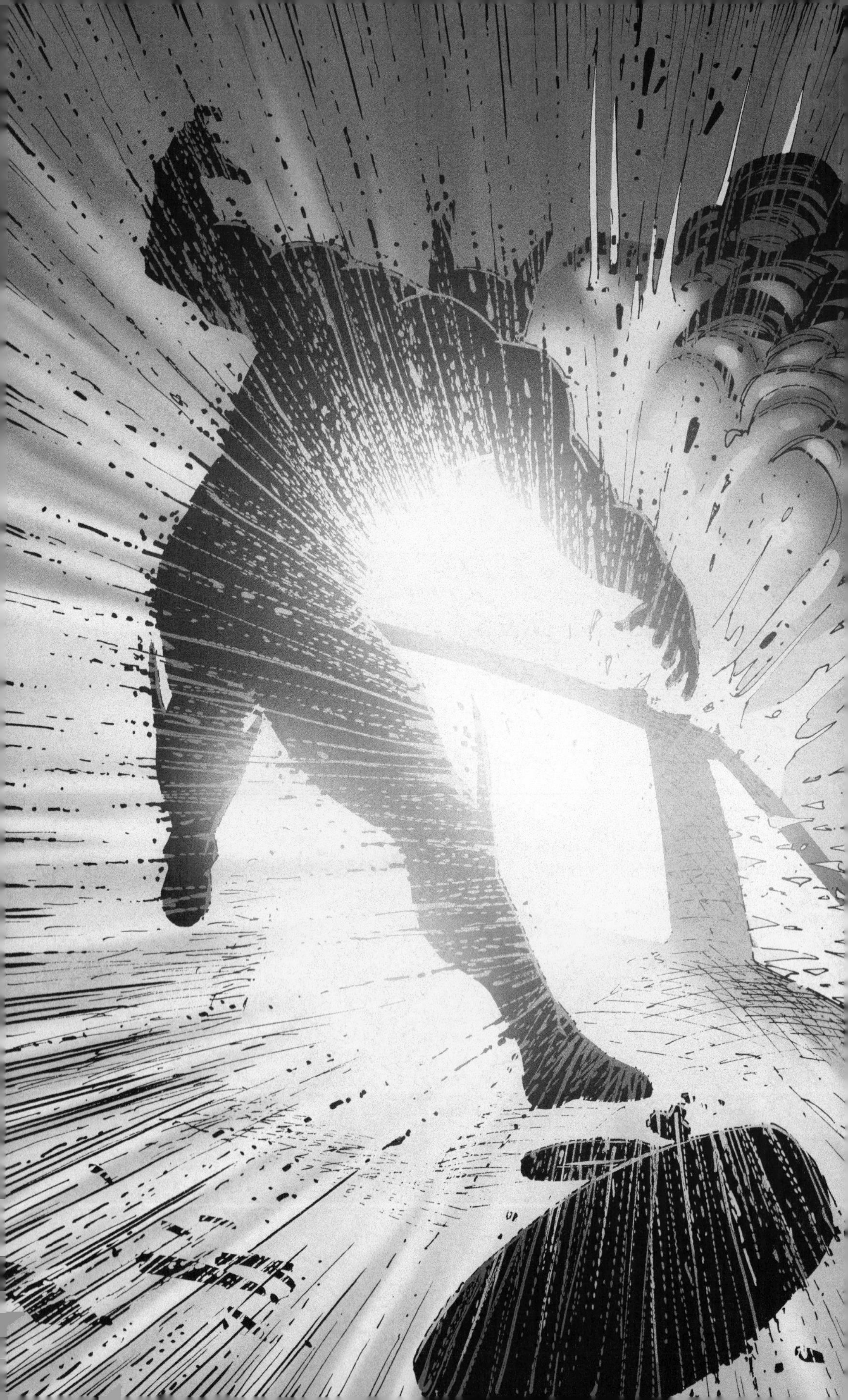

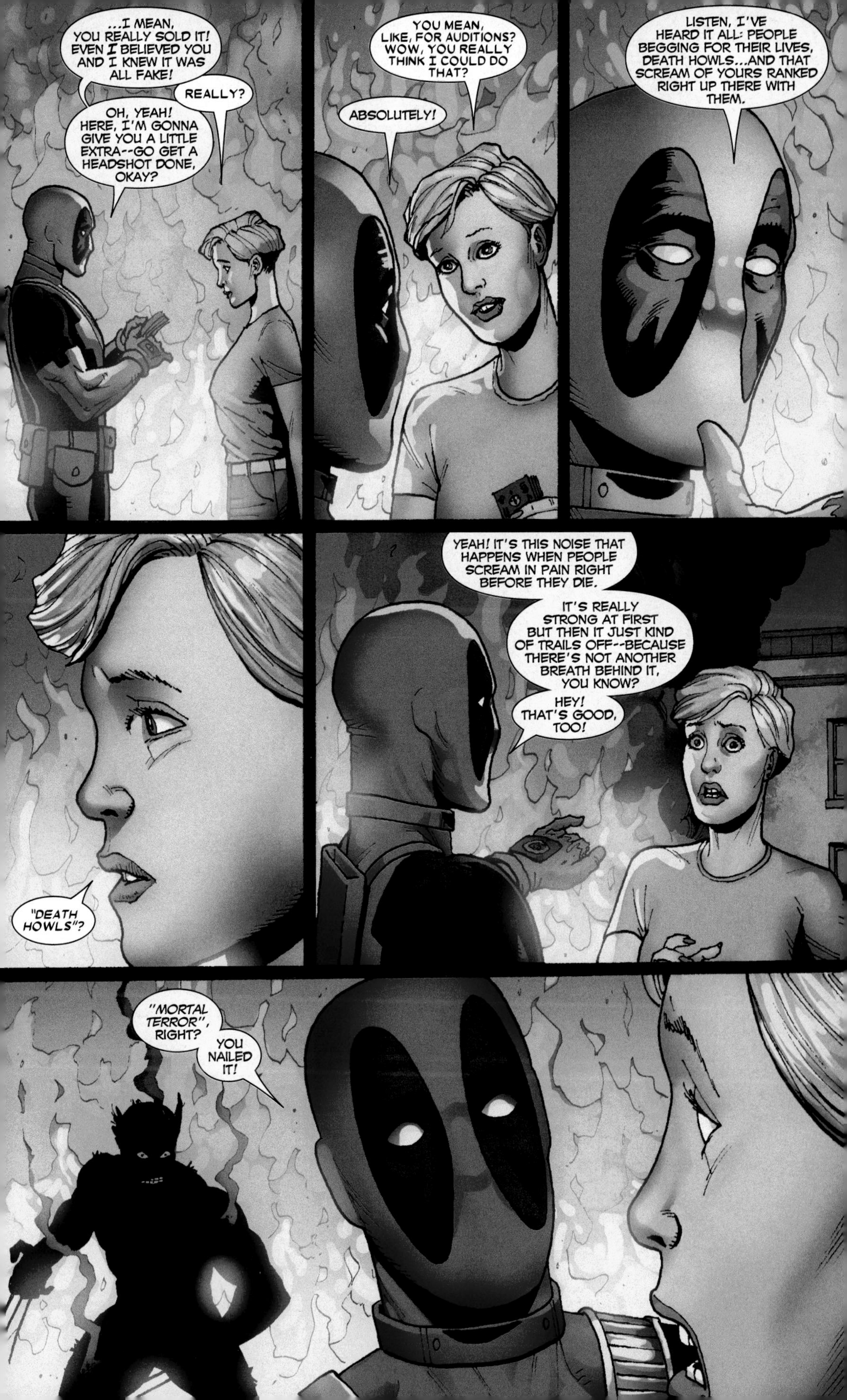
...I MEAN, YOU REALLY SOLD IT! EVEN I BELIEVED YOU AND I KNEW IT WAS ALL FAKE!
REALLY?
OH, YEAH! HERE, I'M GONNA GIVE YOU A LITTLE EXTRA--GO GET A HEADSHOT DONE, OKAY?
YOU MEAN, LIKE, FOR AUDITIONS? WOW, YOU REALLY THINK I COULD DO THAT?
ABSOLUTELY!
LISTEN, I'VE HEARD IT ALL: PEOPLE BEGGING FOR THEIR LIVES, DEATH HOWLS...AND THAT SCREAM OF YOURS RANKED RIGHT UP THERE WITH THEM.
"DEATH HOWLS"?
YEAH! IT'S THIS NOISE THAT HAPPENS WHEN PEOPLE SCREAM IN PAIN RIGHT BEFORE THEY DIE.
IT'S REALLY STRONG AT FIRST BUT THEN IT JUST KIND OF TRAILS OFF--BECAUSE THERE'S NOT ANOTHER BREATH BEHIND IT, YOU KNOW?
HEY! THAT'S GOOD, TOO!
"MORTAL TERROR", RIGHT?
YOU NAILED IT!

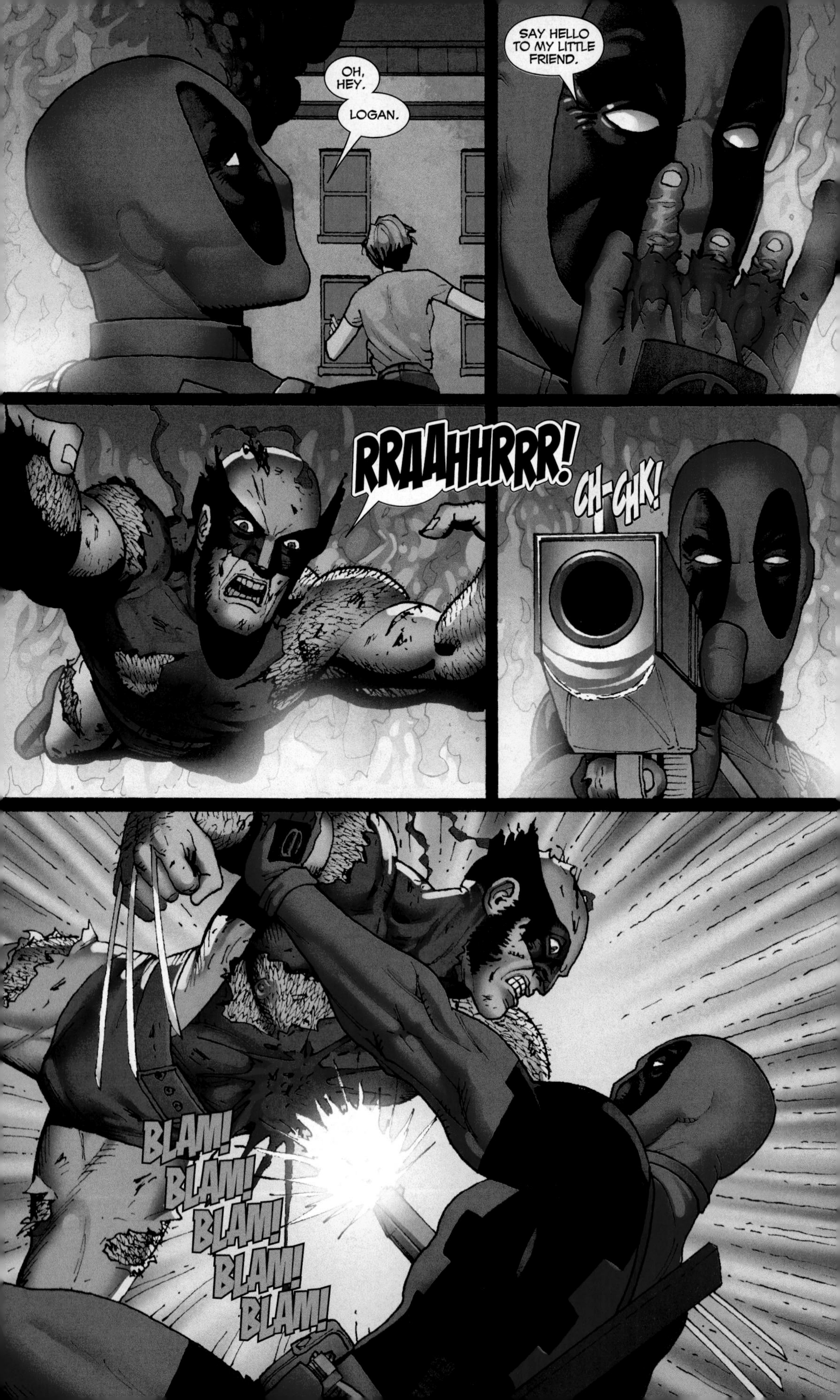
OH, HEY.
LOGAN.
SAY HELLO TO MY LITTLE FRIEND.
RRAAHHRRR!
CH-CHK!
BLAM! BLAM! BLAM! BLAM! BLAM!

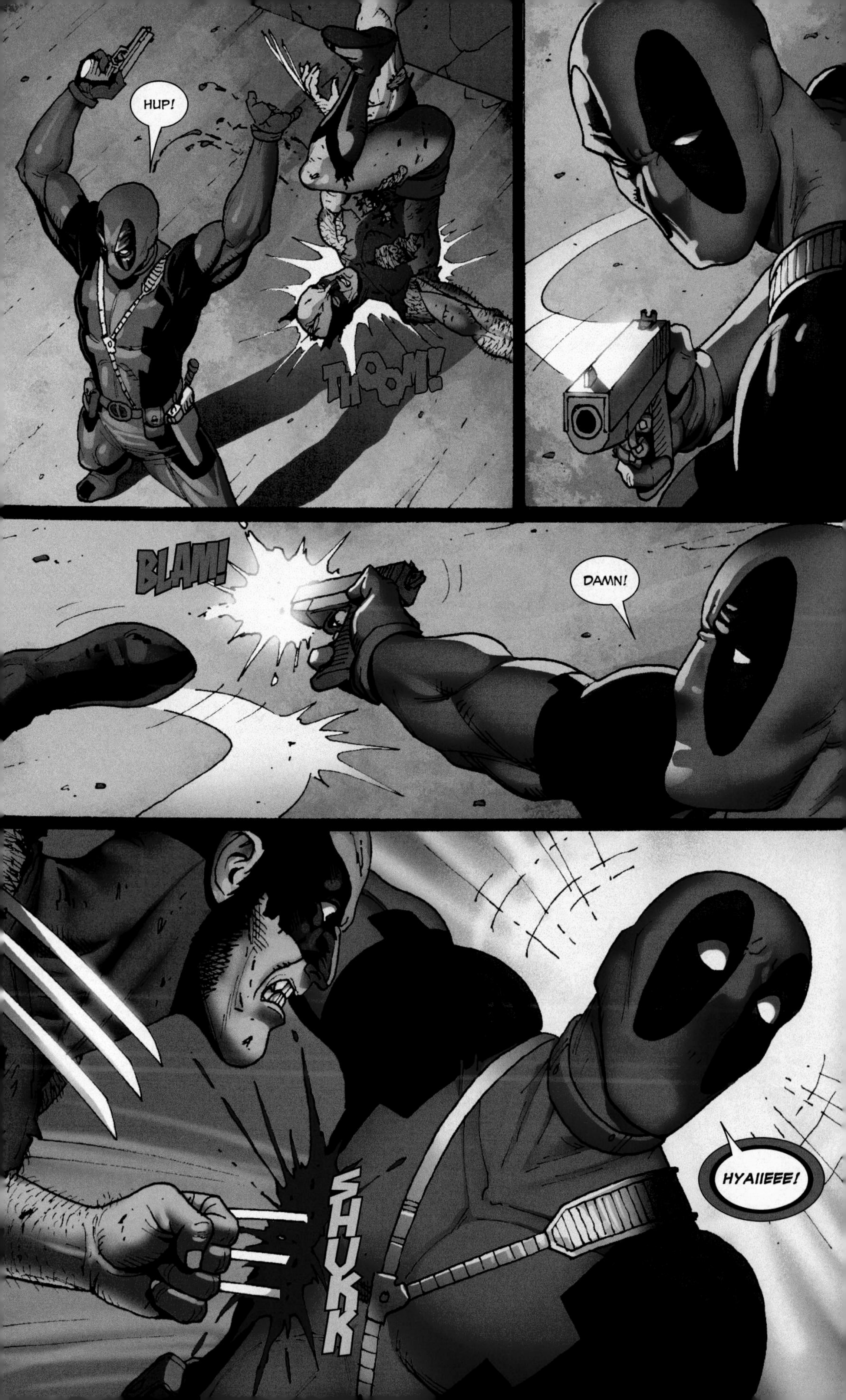
HUP!
THOOM!
BLAM!
DAMN!
HYAIIEEE!
SHUKK

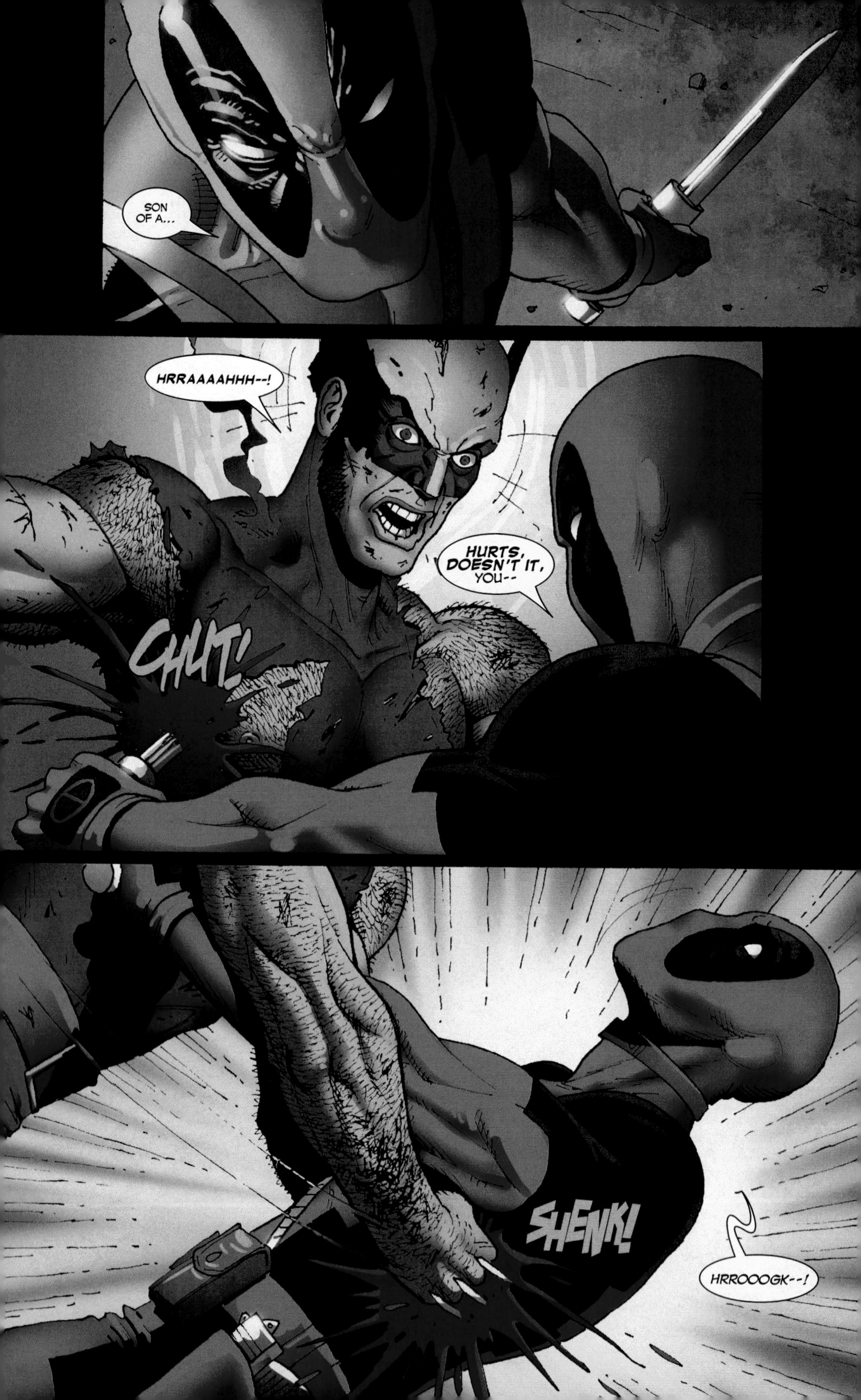
SON OF A...
HRRAAAAHHH--!
HURTS, DOESN'T IT, YOU--
CHUT!
SHENK!
HRROOOGK--!

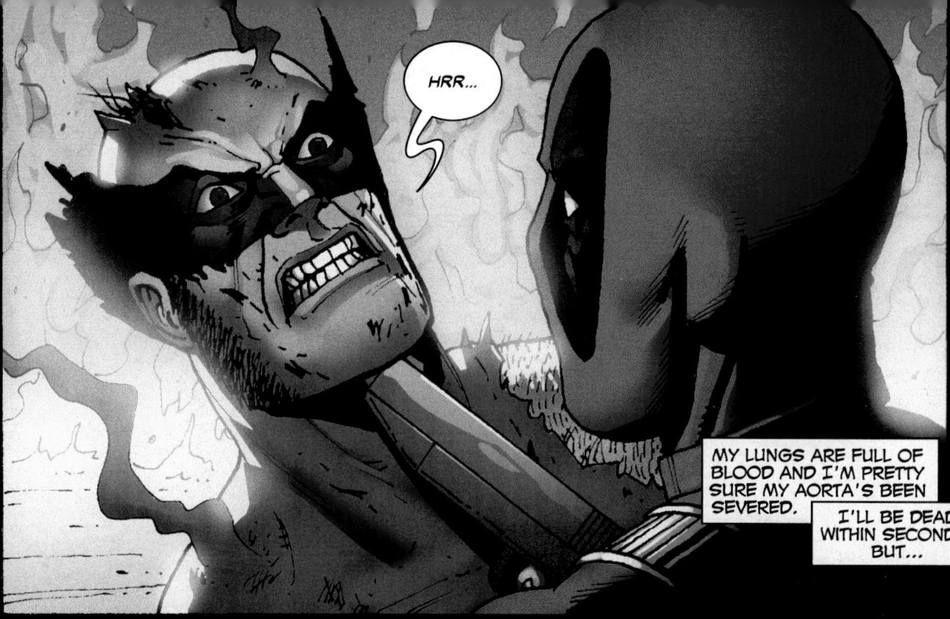
HRR...
MY LUNGS ARE FULL OF BLOOD AND I'M PRETTY SURE MY AORTA'S BEEN SEVERED.
I'LL BE DEAD WITHIN SECONDS. BUT...

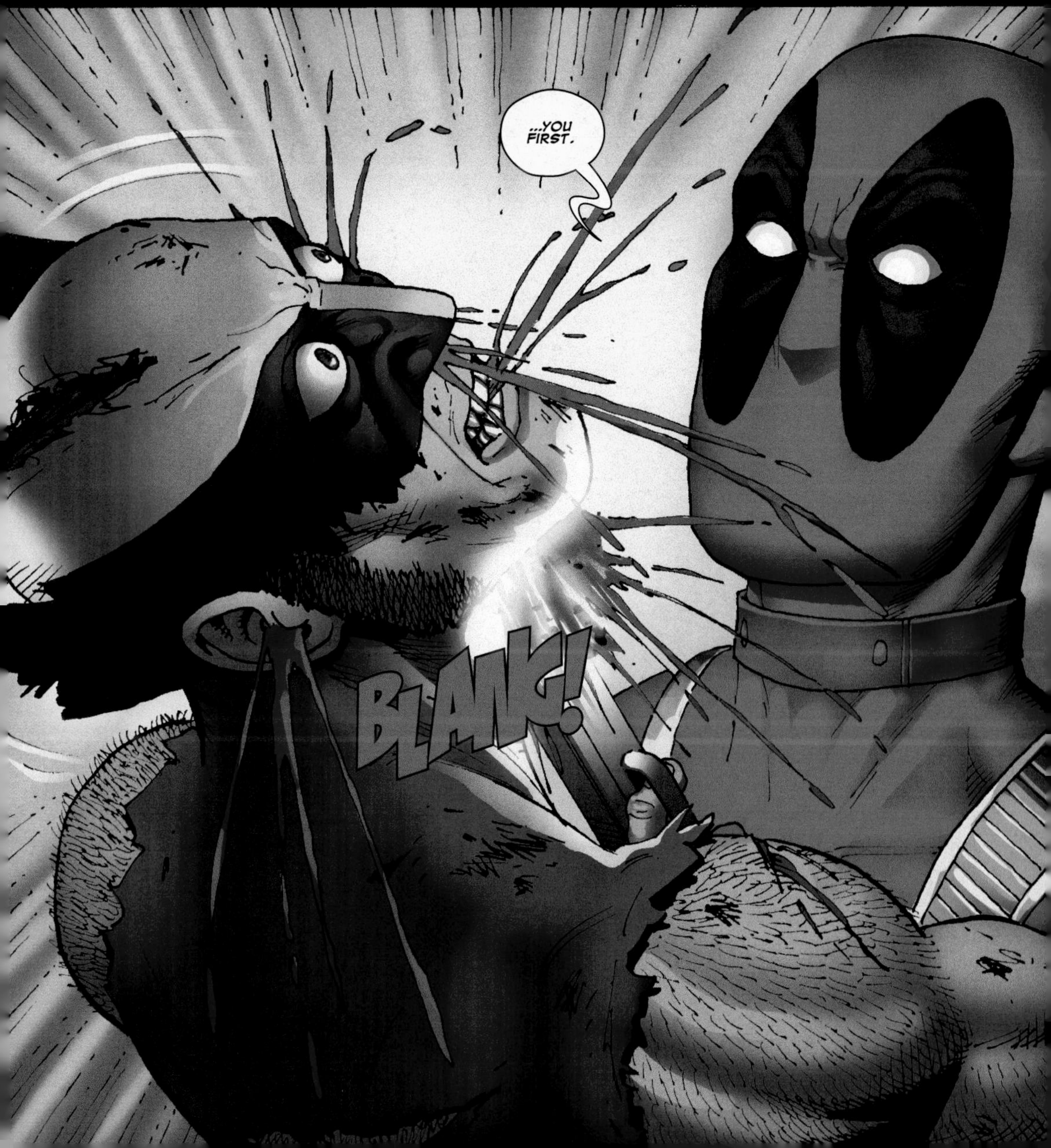
...YOU FIRST.
BLANG!

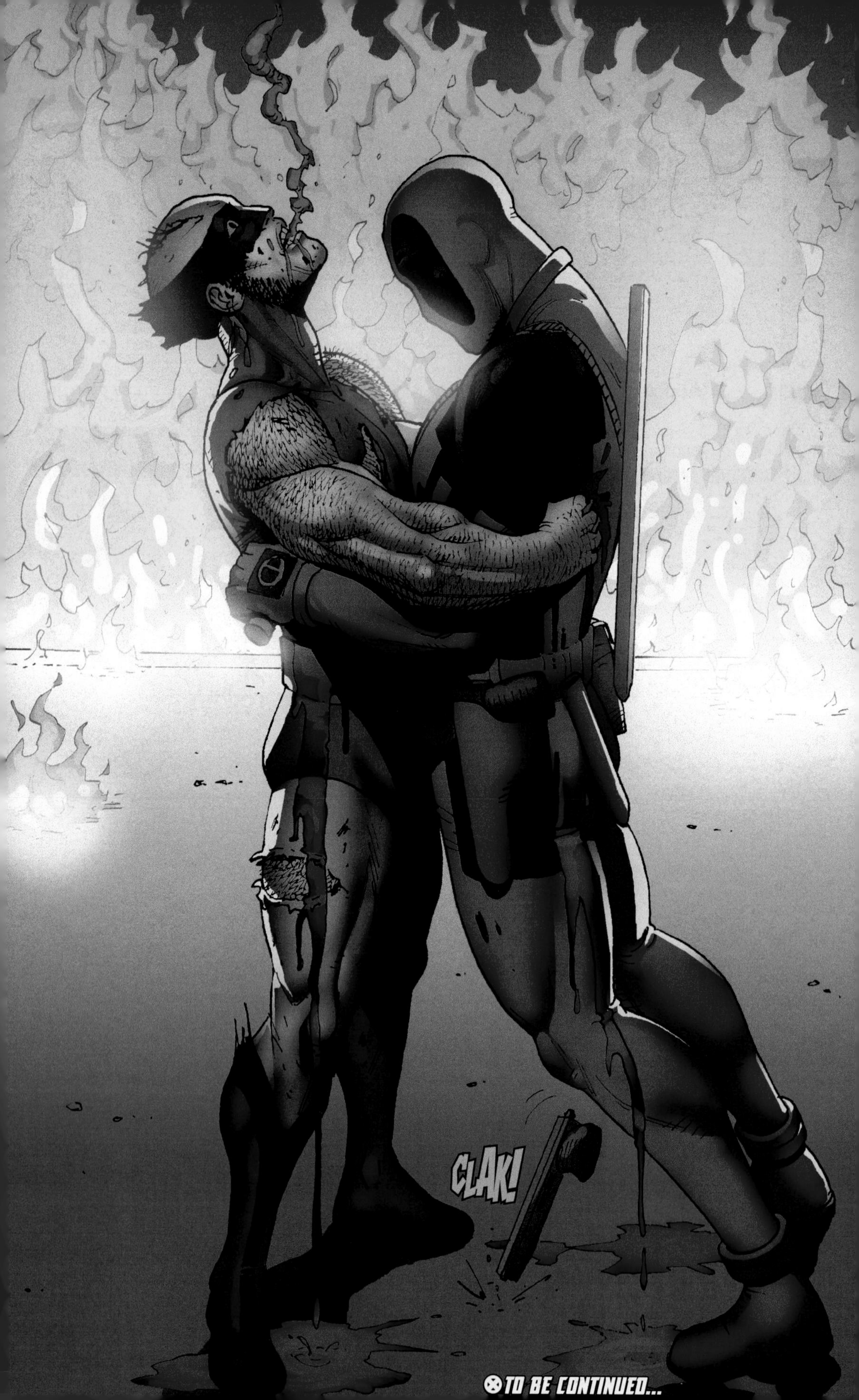
CLAK!
TO BE CONTINUED...

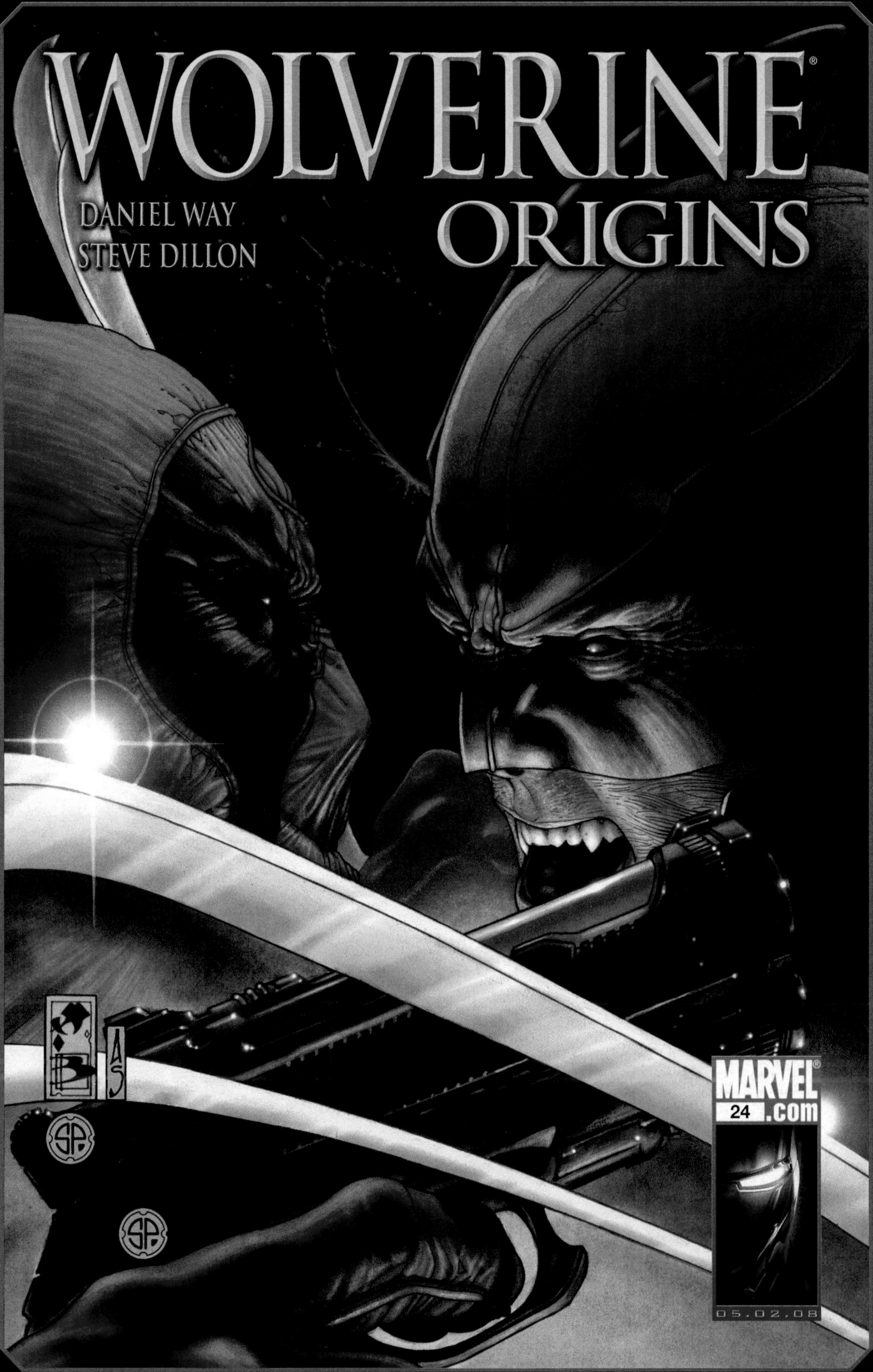
WOLVERINE
ORIGINS
DANIEL WAY
STEVE DILLON
MARVEL
24 .com
05.02.08

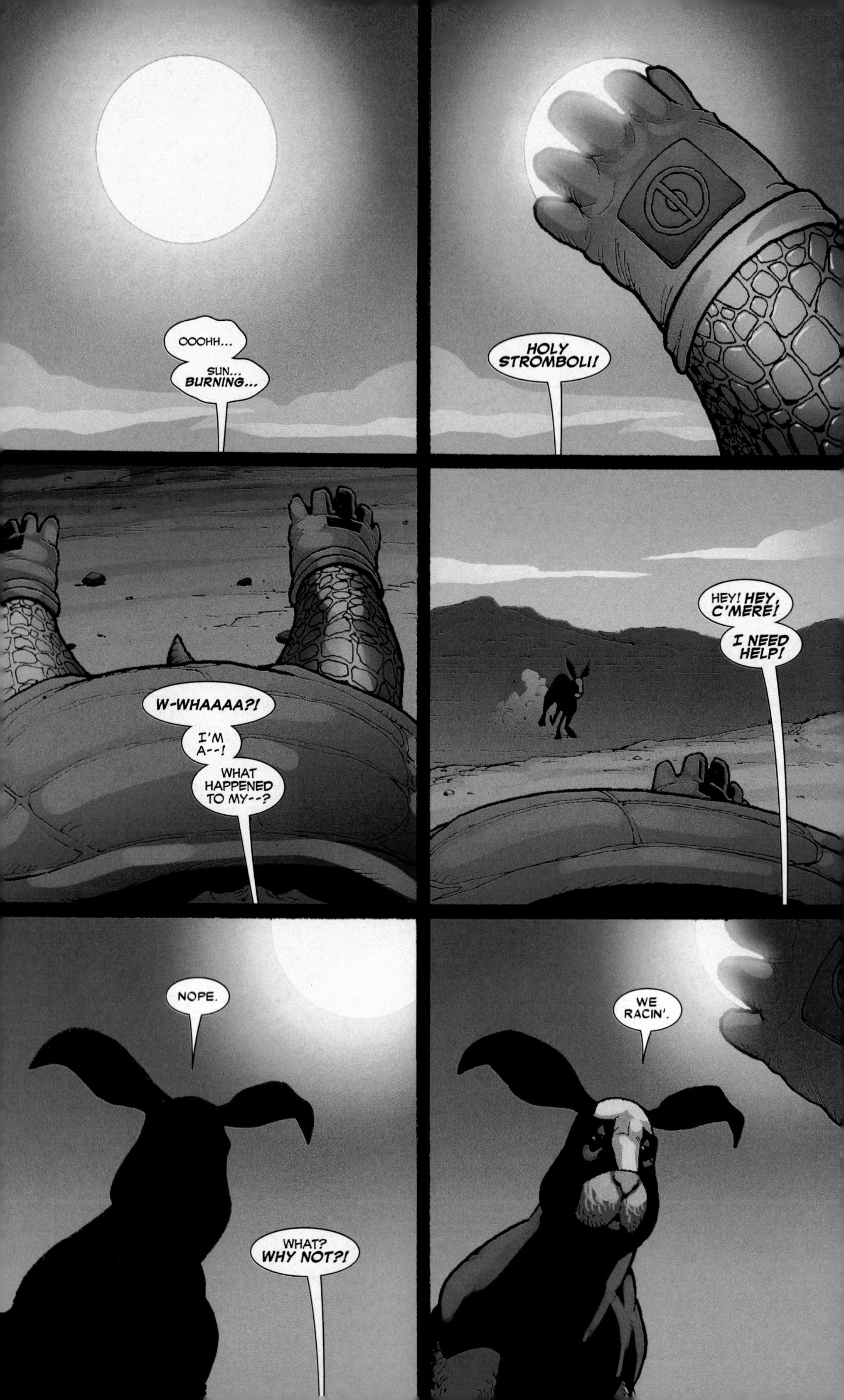
OOOHH...
SUN... BURNING...
HOLY STROMBOLI!
W-WHAAAA?!
I'M A--!
WHAT HAPPENED TO MY--?
HEY! HEY, C'MERE!
I NEED HELP!
NOPE.
WHAT? WHY NOT?!
WE RACIN'.

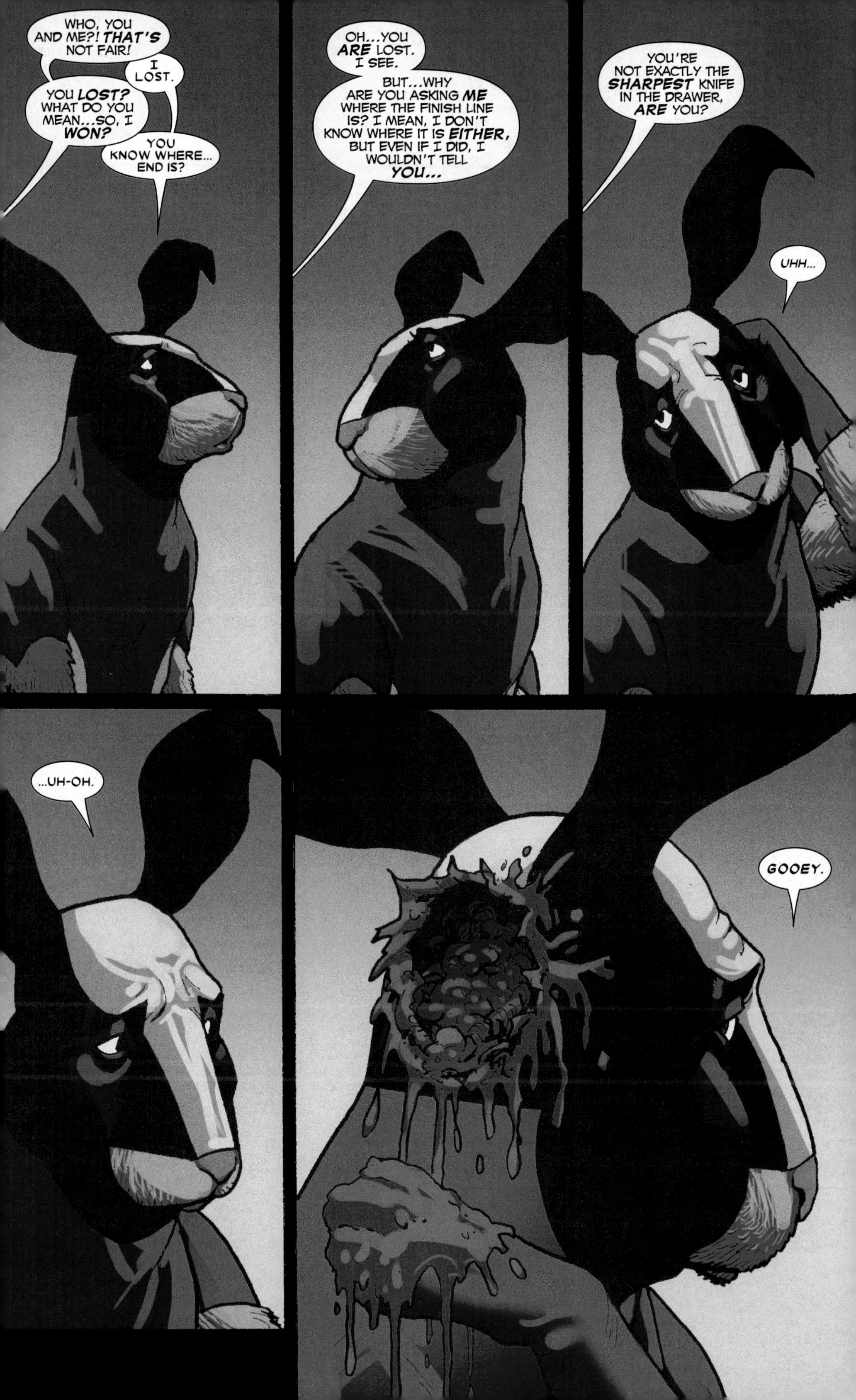
WHO, YOU AND ME?! THAT'S NOT FAIR!
I LOST.
YOU LOST? WHAT DO YOU MEAN...SO, I WON?
YOU KNOW WHERE... END IS?
OH...YOU ARE LOST. I SEE.
BUT...WHY ARE YOU ASKING ME WHERE THE FINISH LINE IS? I MEAN, I DON'T KNOW WHERE IT IS EITHER, BUT EVEN IF I DID, I WOULDN'T TELL YOU...
YOU'RE NOT EXACTLY THE SHARPEST KNIFE IN THE DRAWER, ARE YOU?
UHH...
...UH-OH.
GOOEY.

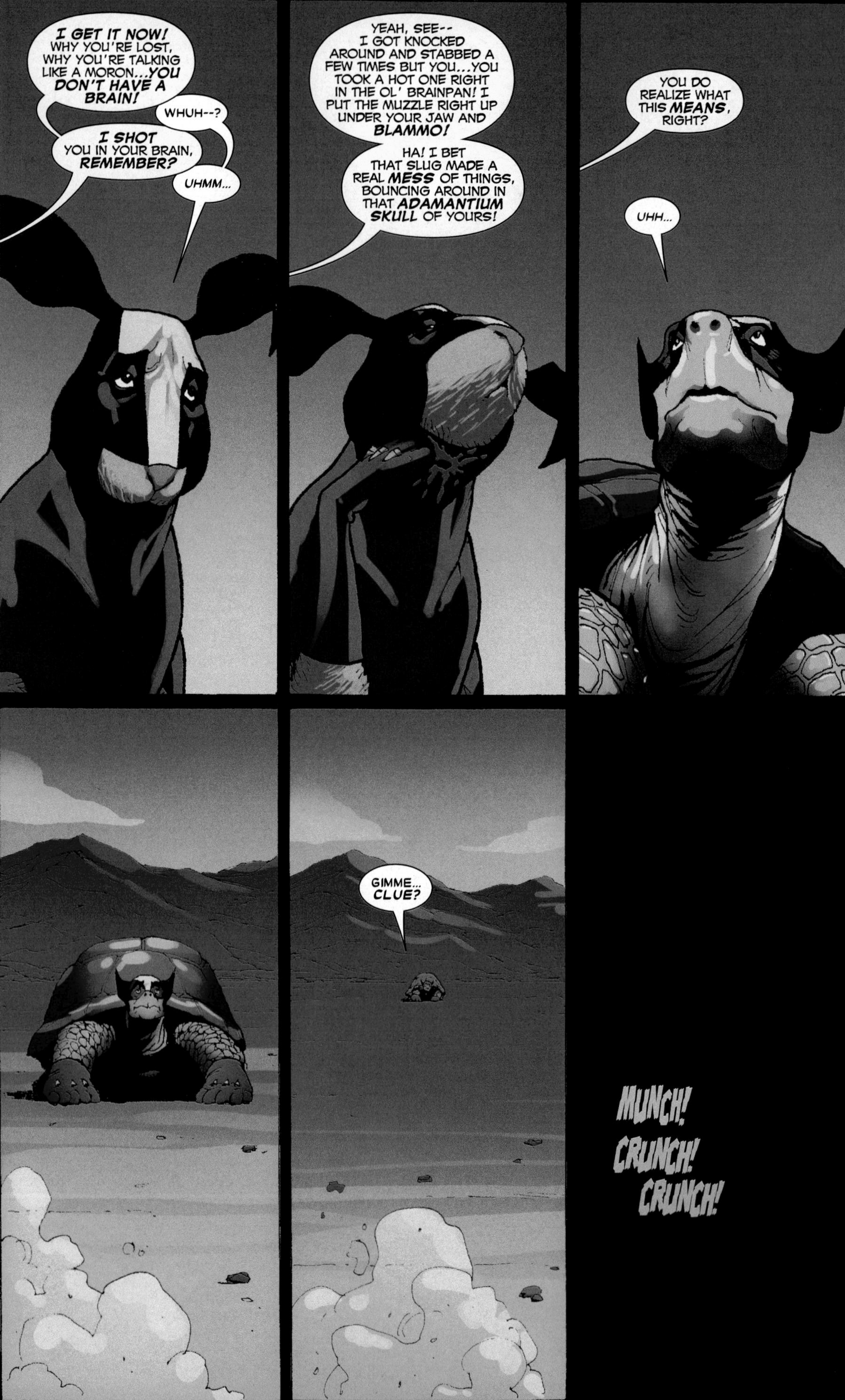
I GET IT NOW! WHY YOU'RE LOST, WHY YOU'RE TALKING LIKE A MORON...YOU DON'T HAVE A BRAIN!
WHUH--?
I SHOT YOU IN YOUR BRAIN, REMEMBER?
UHMM...
YEAH, SEE-- I GOT KNOCKED AROUND AND STABBED A FEW TIMES BUT YOU...YOU TOOK A HOT ONE RIGHT IN THE OL' BRAINPAN! I PUT THE MUZZLE RIGHT UP UNDER YOUR JAW AND BLAMMO!
HA! I BET THAT SLUG MADE A REAL MESS OF THINGS, BOUNCING AROUND IN THAT ADAMANTIUM SKULL OF YOURS!
YOU DO REALIZE WHAT THIS MEANS, RIGHT?
UHH...
GIMME... CLUE?
MUNCH!
CRUNCH!
CRUNCH!

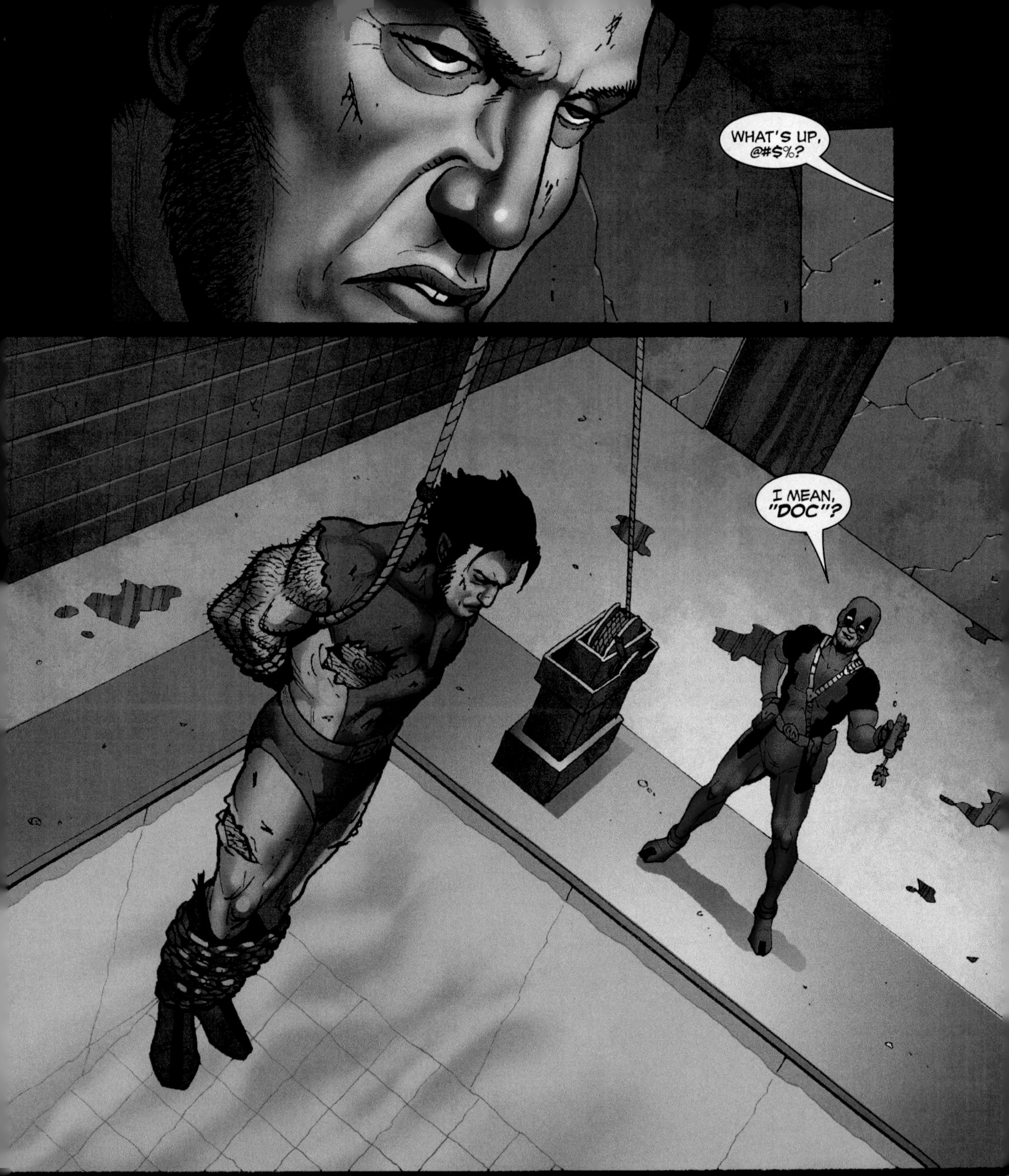
WHAT'S UP, @#$%?
I MEAN, "DOC"?

The DEEP END PART 4

DANIEL WAY WRITER
STEVE DILLON ARTIST
AVALON'S MATT MILLA COLORIST
VC'S CORY PETIT LETTERER
SIMONE BIANCHI COVER ART
SIMONE PERUZZI COVER COLOR
AUBREY SITTERSON ASST EDITOR
JOHN BARBER EDITOR
AXEL ALONSO GROUP EDITOR
JOE QUESADA EDITOR IN CHIEF
DAN BUCKLEY PUBLISHER

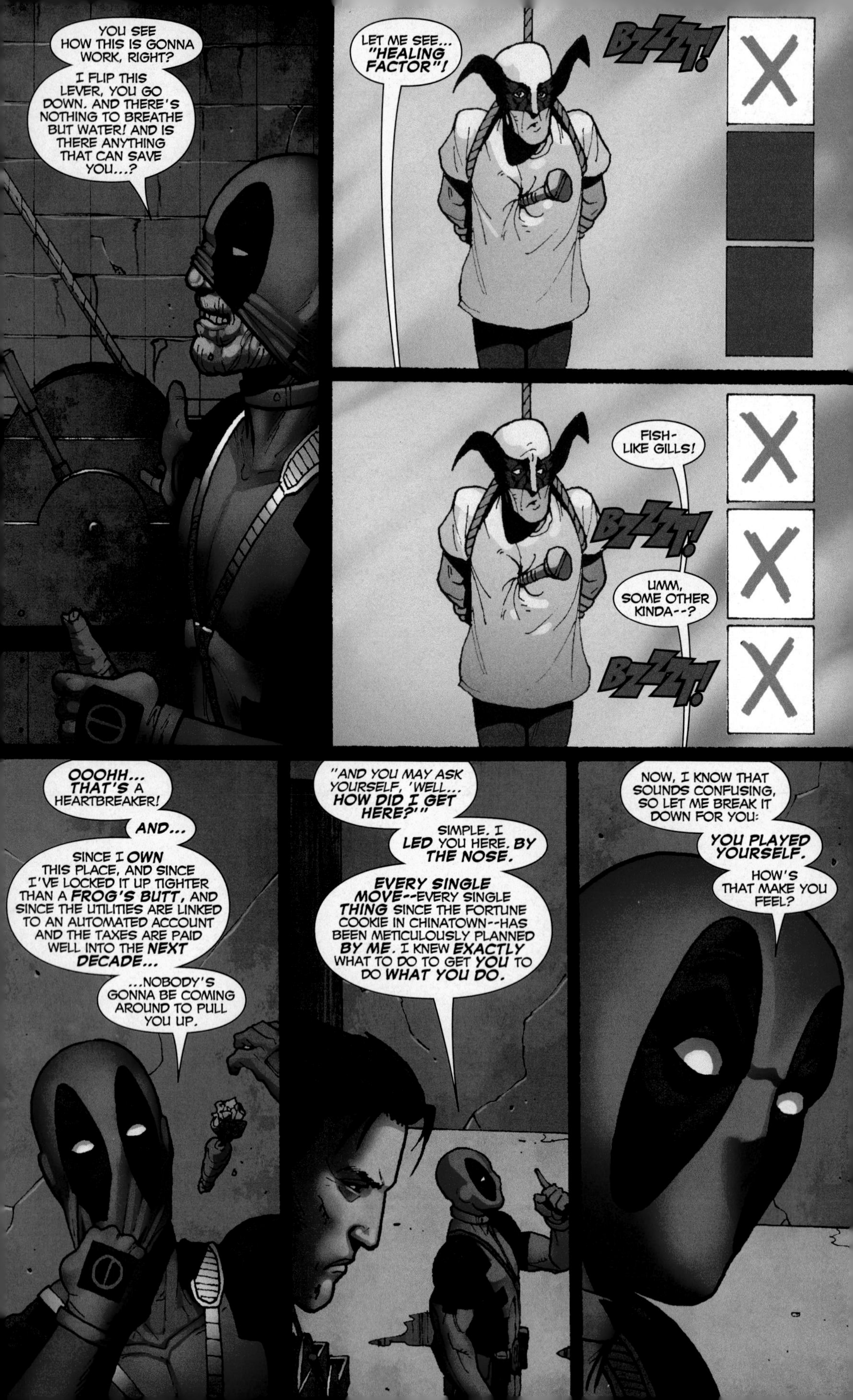
YOU SEE HOW THIS IS GONNA WORK, RIGHT?
I FLIP THIS LEVER, YOU GO DOWN. AND THERE'S NOTHING TO BREATHE BUT WATER! AND IS THERE ANYTHING THAT CAN SAVE YOU...?
LET ME SEE... "HEALING FACTOR"!
BZZZT!
FISH-LIKE GILLS!
BZZZT!
UMM, SOME OTHER KINDA--?
BZZZT!
OOOHH... THAT'S A HEARTBREAKER!
AND...
SINCE I OWN THIS PLACE, AND SINCE I'VE LOCKED IT UP TIGHTER THAN A FROG'S BUTT, AND SINCE THE UTILITIES ARE LINKED TO AN AUTOMATED ACCOUNT AND THE TAXES ARE PAID WELL INTO THE NEXT DECADE...
...NOBODY'S GONNA BE COMING AROUND TO PULL YOU UP.
"AND YOU MAY ASK YOURSELF, 'WELL... HOW DID I GET HERE?'"
SIMPLE. I LED YOU HERE. BY THE NOSE.
EVERY SINGLE MOVE--EVERY SINGLE THING SINCE THE FORTUNE COOKIE IN CHINATOWN--HAS BEEN METICULOUSLY PLANNED BY ME. I KNEW EXACTLY WHAT TO DO TO GET YOU TO DO WHAT YOU DO.
NOW, I KNOW THAT SOUNDS CONFUSING, SO LET ME BREAK IT DOWN FOR YOU:
YOU PLAYED YOURSELF.
HOW'S THAT MAKE YOU FEEL?

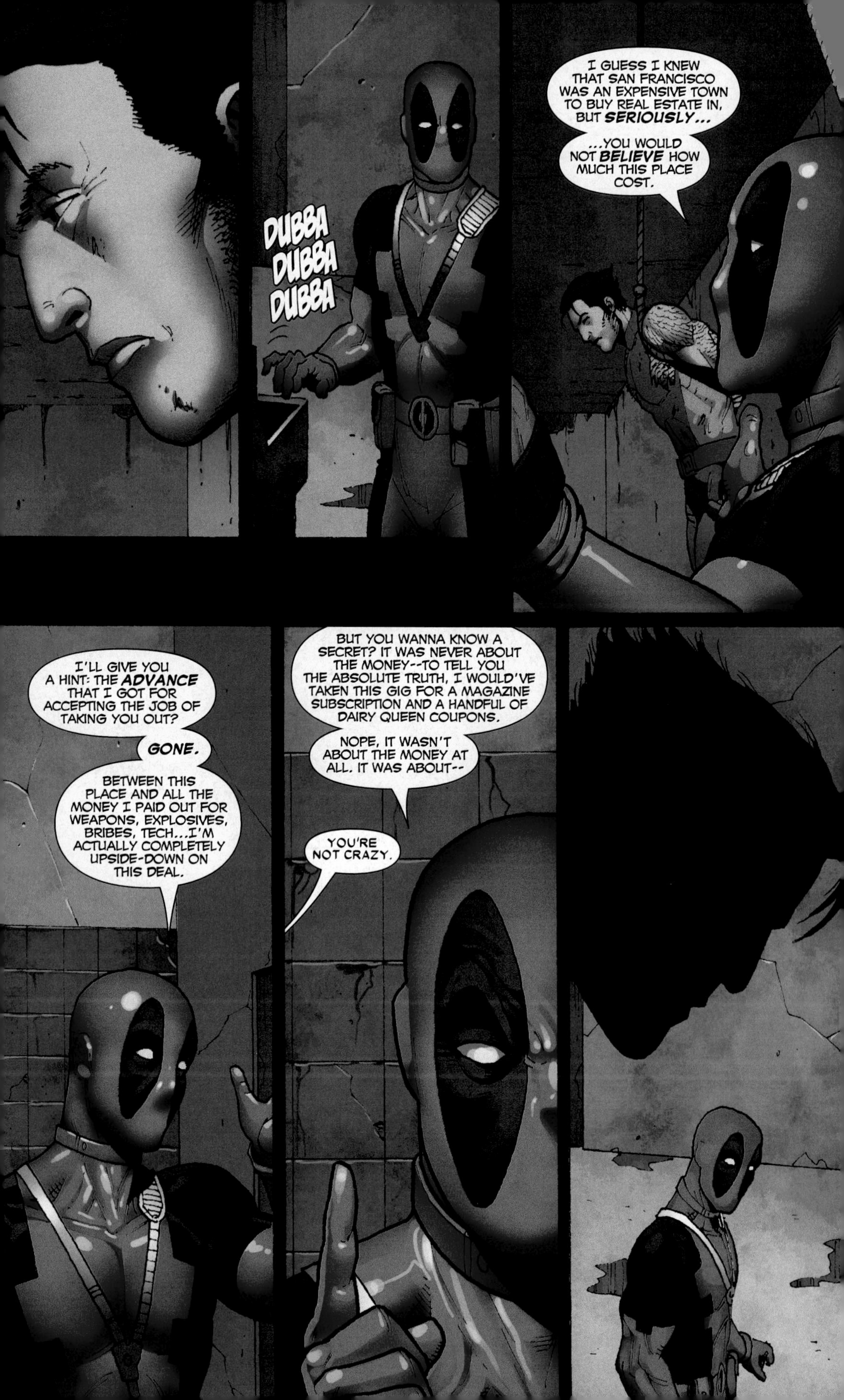
DUBBA DUBBA DUBBA
I GUESS I KNEW THAT SAN FRANCISCO WAS AN EXPENSIVE TOWN TO BUY REAL ESTATE IN, BUT SERIOUSLY...
...YOU WOULD NOT BELIEVE HOW MUCH THIS PLACE COST.
I'LL GIVE YOU A HINT: THE ADVANCE THAT I GOT FOR ACCEPTING THE JOB OF TAKING YOU OUT?
GONE.
BETWEEN THIS PLACE AND ALL THE MONEY I PAID OUT FOR WEAPONS, EXPLOSIVES, BRIBES, TECH...I'M ACTUALLY COMPLETELY UPSIDE-DOWN ON THIS DEAL.
BUT YOU WANNA KNOW A SECRET? IT WAS NEVER ABOUT THE MONEY--TO TELL YOU THE ABSOLUTE TRUTH, I WOULD'VE TAKEN THIS GIG FOR A MAGAZINE SUBSCRIPTION AND A HANDFUL OF DAIRY QUEEN COUPONS.
NOPE, IT WASN'T ABOUT THE MONEY AT ALL. IT WAS ABOUT--
YOU'RE NOT CRAZY.

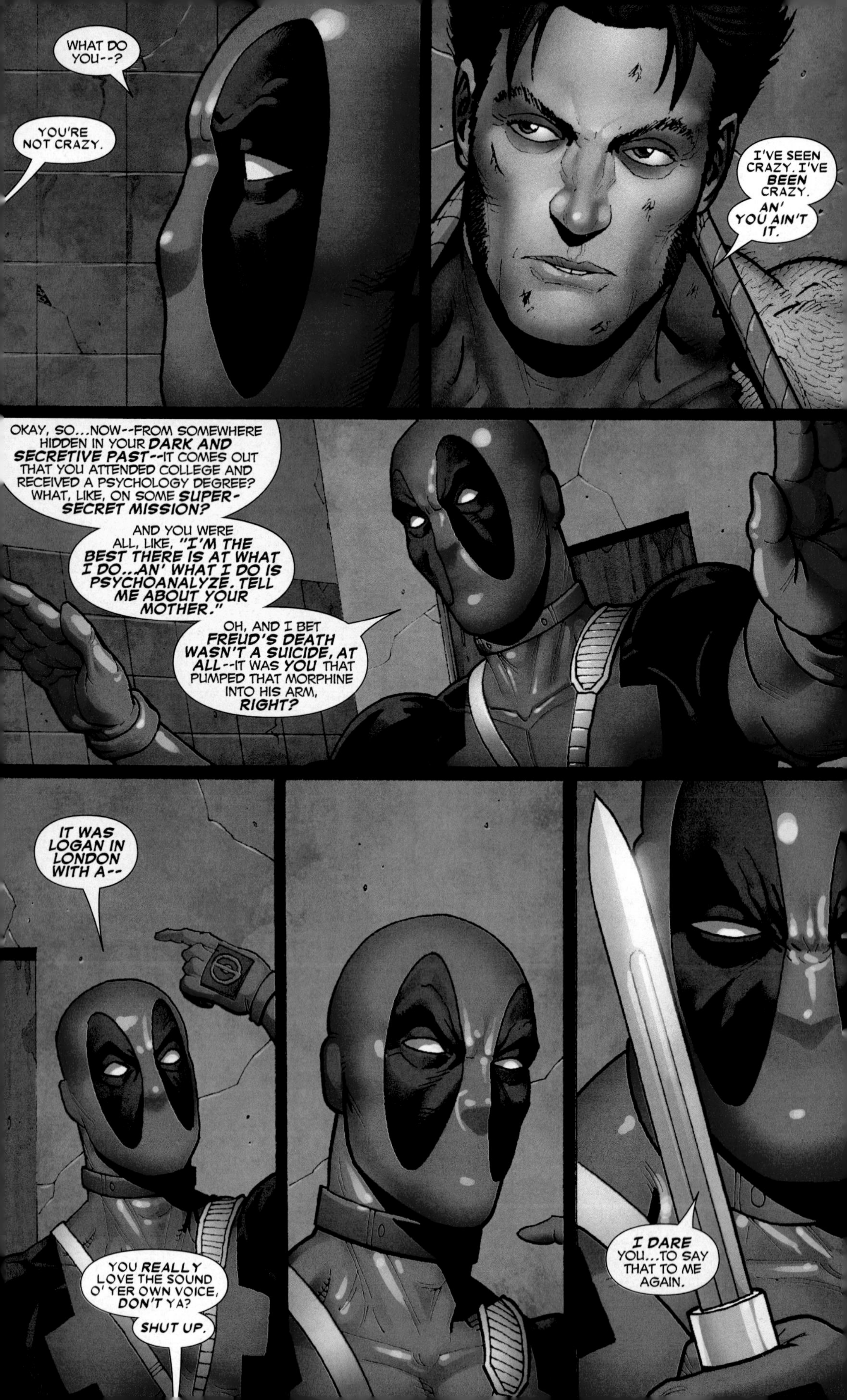
WHAT DO YOU--?
YOU'RE NOT CRAZY.
I'VE SEEN CRAZY. I'VE BEEN CRAZY.
AN' YOU AIN'T IT.
OKAY, SO...NOW--FROM SOMEWHERE HIDDEN IN YOUR DARK AND SECRETIVE PAST--IT COMES OUT THAT YOU ATTENDED COLLEGE AND RECEIVED A PSYCHOLOGY DEGREE? WHAT, LIKE, ON SOME SUPER-SECRET MISSION?
AND YOU WERE ALL, LIKE, "I'M THE BEST THERE IS AT WHAT I DO...AN' WHAT I DO IS PSYCHOANALYZE. TELL ME ABOUT YOUR MOTHER."
OH, AND I BET FREUD'S DEATH WASN'T A SUICIDE, AT ALL--IT WAS YOU THAT PUMPED THAT MORPHINE INTO HIS ARM, RIGHT?
IT WAS LOGAN IN LONDON WITH A--
YOU REALLY LOVE THE SOUND O' YER OWN VOICE, DON'T YA?
SHUT UP.
I DARE YOU...TO SAY THAT TO ME AGAIN.

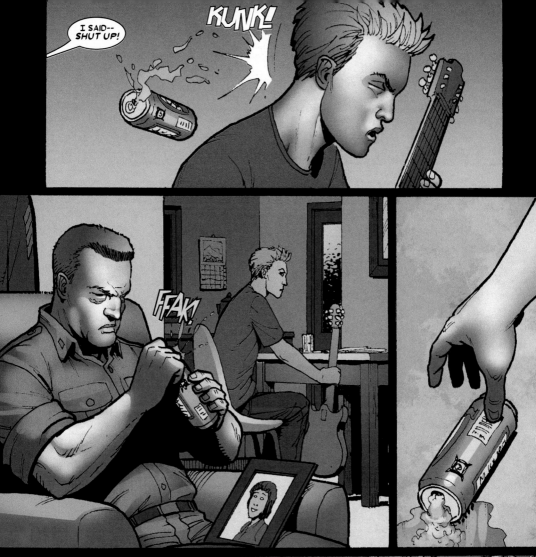

I SAID-- SHUT UP!

KUNK!

FFAK!

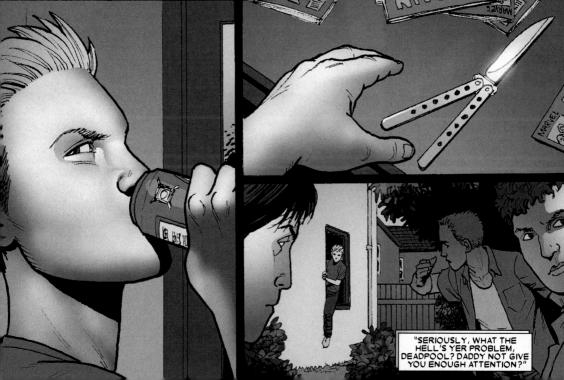

"SERIOUSLY, WHAT THE HELL'S YER PROBLEM, DEADPOOL? DADDY NOT GIVE YOU ENOUGH ATTENTION?"

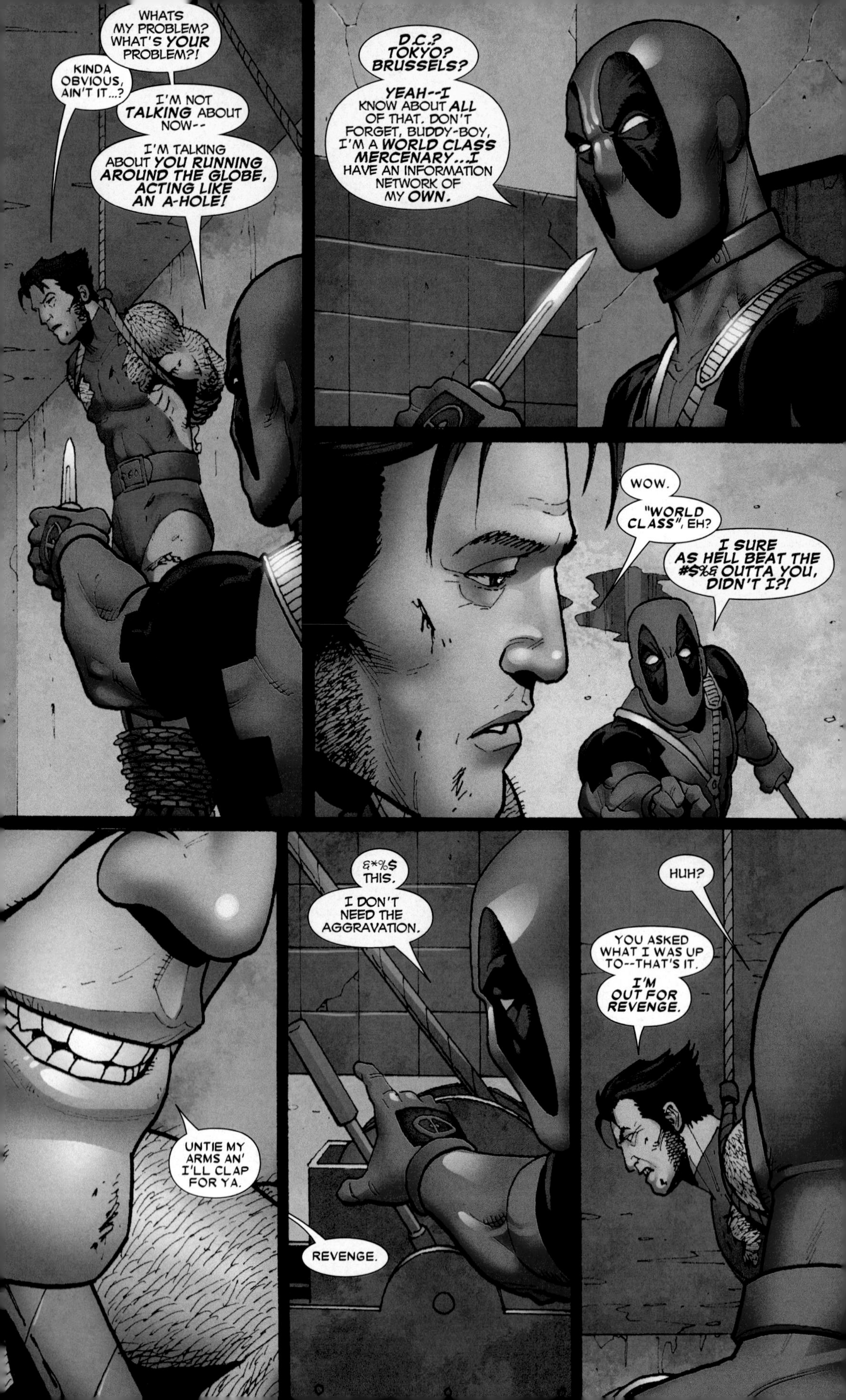

WHATS MY PROBLEM? WHAT'S YOUR PROBLEM?!
KINDA OBVIOUS, AIN'T IT...?
I'M NOT TALKING ABOUT NOW--
I'M TALKING ABOUT YOU RUNNING AROUND THE GLOBE, ACTING LIKE AN A-HOLE!
D.C.? TOKYO? BRUSSELS?
YEAH--I KNOW ABOUT ALL OF THAT. DON'T FORGET, BUDDY-BOY, I'M A WORLD CLASS MERCENARY...I HAVE AN INFORMATION NETWORK OF MY OWN.
WOW.
"WORLD CLASS", EH?
I SURE AS HELL BEAT THE #$%& OUTTA YOU, DIDN'T I?!
UNTIE MY ARMS AN' I'LL CLAP FOR YA.
&*%$ THIS.
I DON'T NEED THE AGGRAVATION.
REVENGE.
HUH?
YOU ASKED WHAT I WAS UP TO--THAT'S IT.
I'M OUT FOR REVENGE.

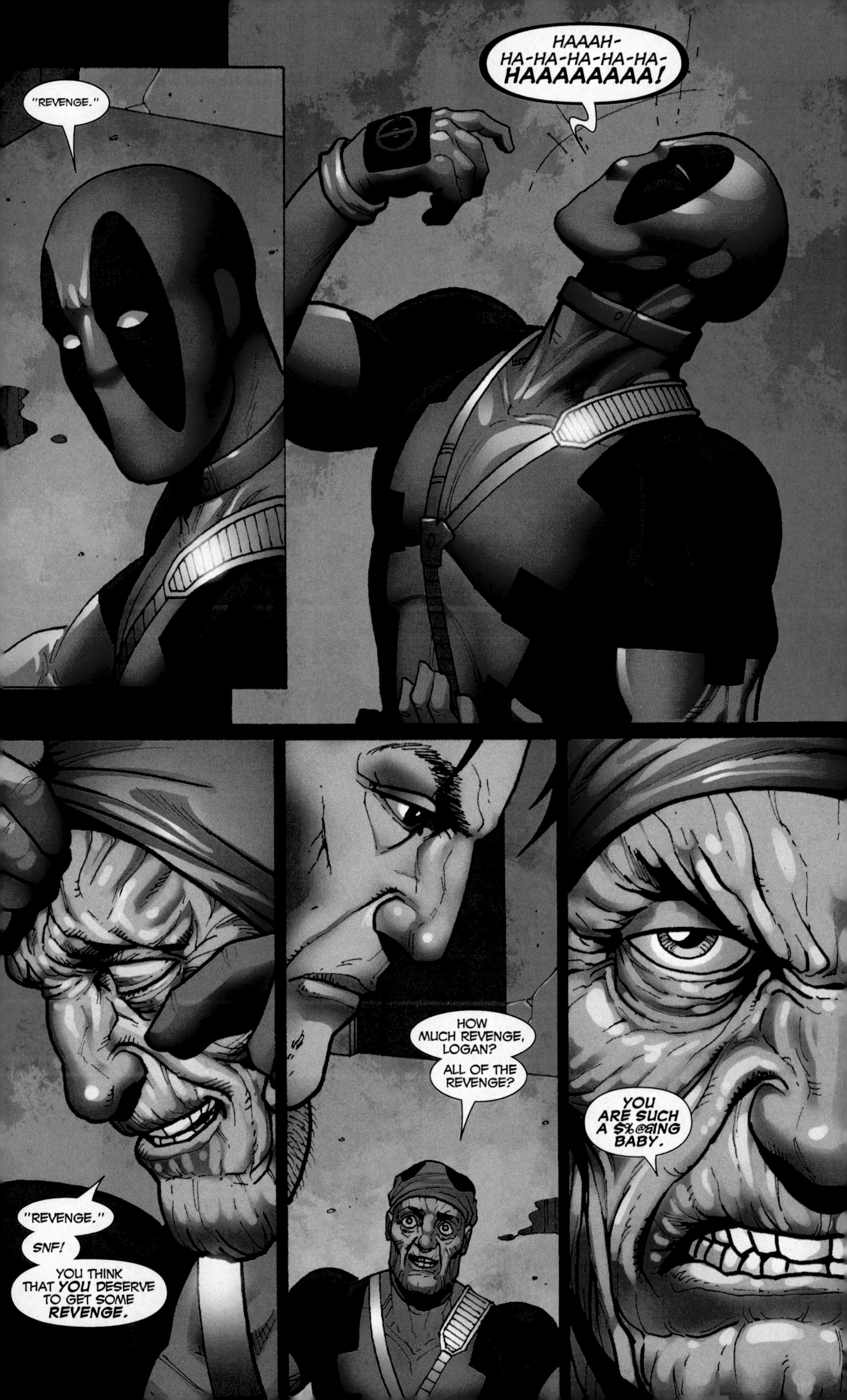
"REVENGE."
HAAAH-
HA-HA-HA-HA-HA-
HAAAAAAAA!
"REVENGE."
SNF!
YOU THINK THAT YOU DESERVE TO GET SOME REVENGE.
HOW MUCH REVENGE, LOGAN?
ALL OF THE REVENGE?
YOU ARE SUCH A $%@&ING BABY.

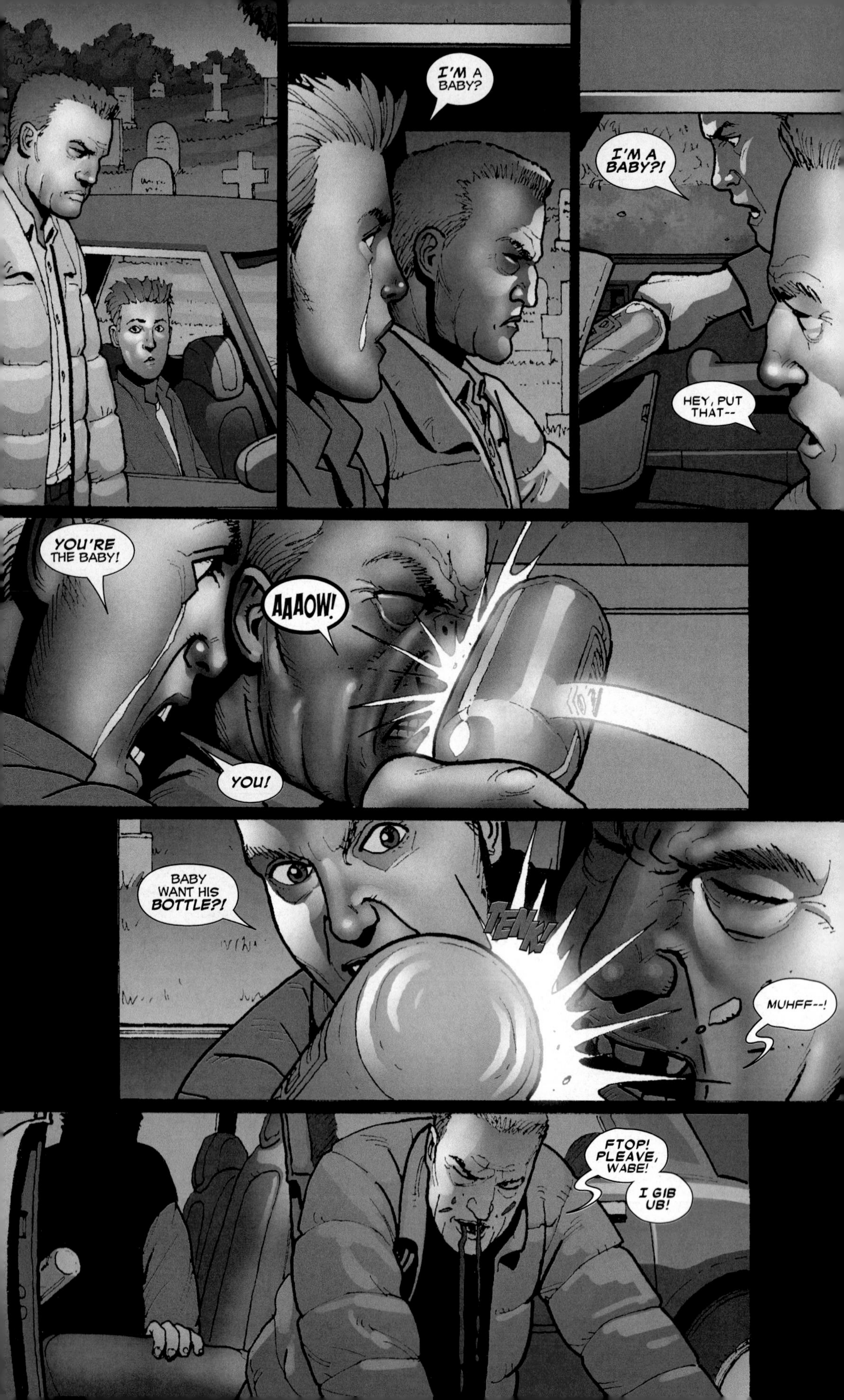
I'M A BABY?
I'M A BABY?!
HEY, PUT THAT--
YOU'RE THE BABY!
AAAOW!
YOU!
BABY WANT HIS BOTTLE?!
TENK!
MUHFF--!
FTOP! PLEAVE, WABE!
I GIB UB!

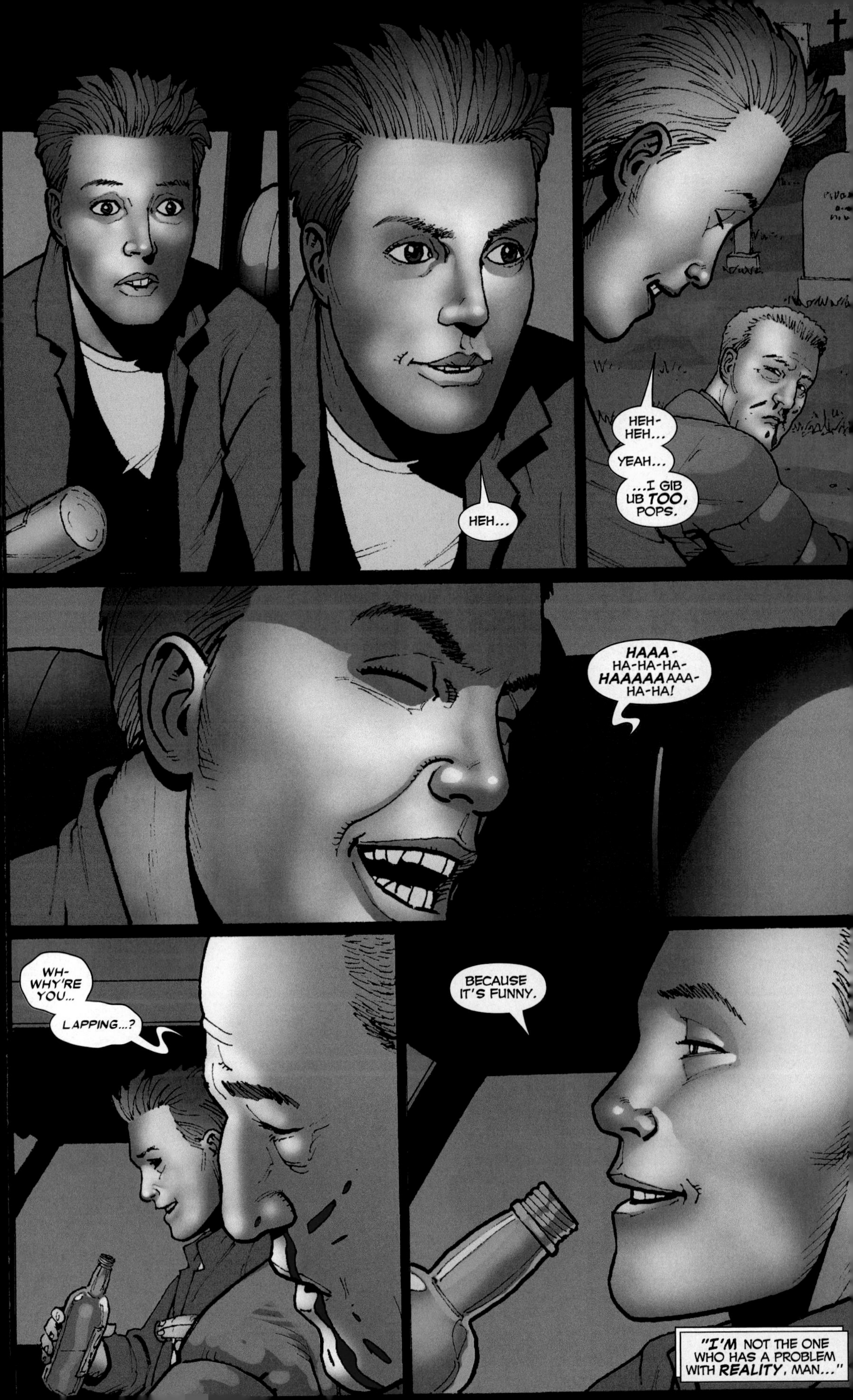
HEH...
HEH-HEH...
YEAH...
...I GIB UB TOO, POPS.
HAAA-HA-HA-HA-HAAAAAAAA-HA-HA!
WH-WHY'RE YOU...
LAPPING...?
BECAUSE IT'S FUNNY.
"I'M NOT THE ONE WHO HAS A PROBLEM WITH REALITY, MAN..."

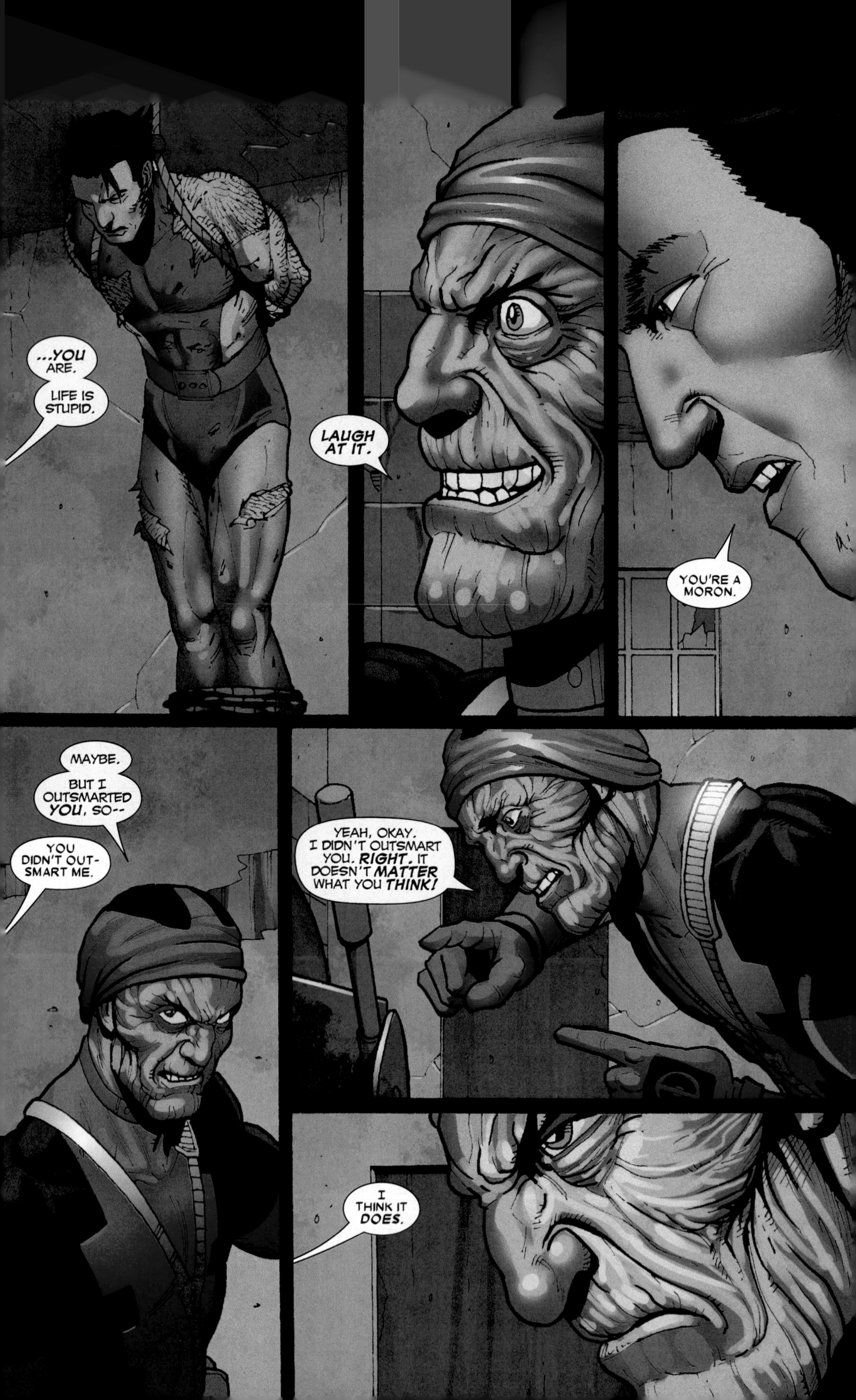
...YOU ARE.
LIFE IS STUPID.
LAUGH AT IT.
YOU'RE A MORON.
MAYBE.
BUT I OUTSMARTED YOU, SO--
YOU DIDN'T OUT-SMART ME.
YEAH, OKAY. I DIDN'T OUTSMART YOU. RIGHT. IT DOESN'T MATTER WHAT YOU THINK!
I THINK IT DOES.

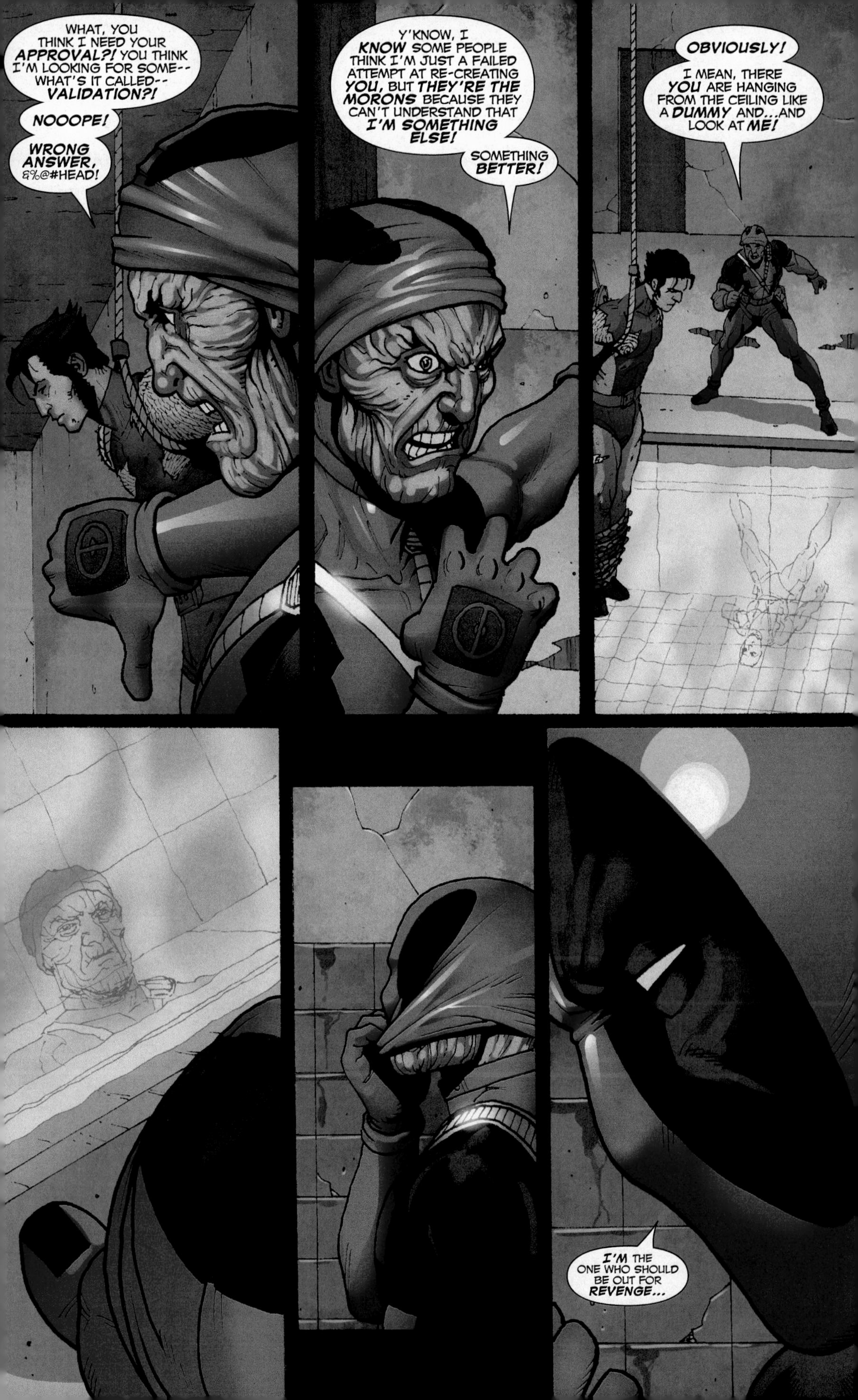
WHAT, YOU THINK I NEED YOUR APPROVAL?! YOU THINK I'M LOOKING FOR SOME-- WHAT'S IT CALLED-- VALIDATION?!
NOOOPE!
WRONG ANSWER, &%@#HEAD!
Y'KNOW, I KNOW SOME PEOPLE THINK I'M JUST A FAILED ATTEMPT AT RE-CREATING YOU, BUT THEY'RE THE MORONS BECAUSE THEY CAN'T UNDERSTAND THAT I'M SOMETHING ELSE!
SOMETHING BETTER!
OBVIOUSLY!
I MEAN, THERE YOU ARE HANGING FROM THE CEILING LIKE A DUMMY AND...AND LOOK AT ME!
I'M THE ONE WHO SHOULD BE OUT FOR REVENGE...

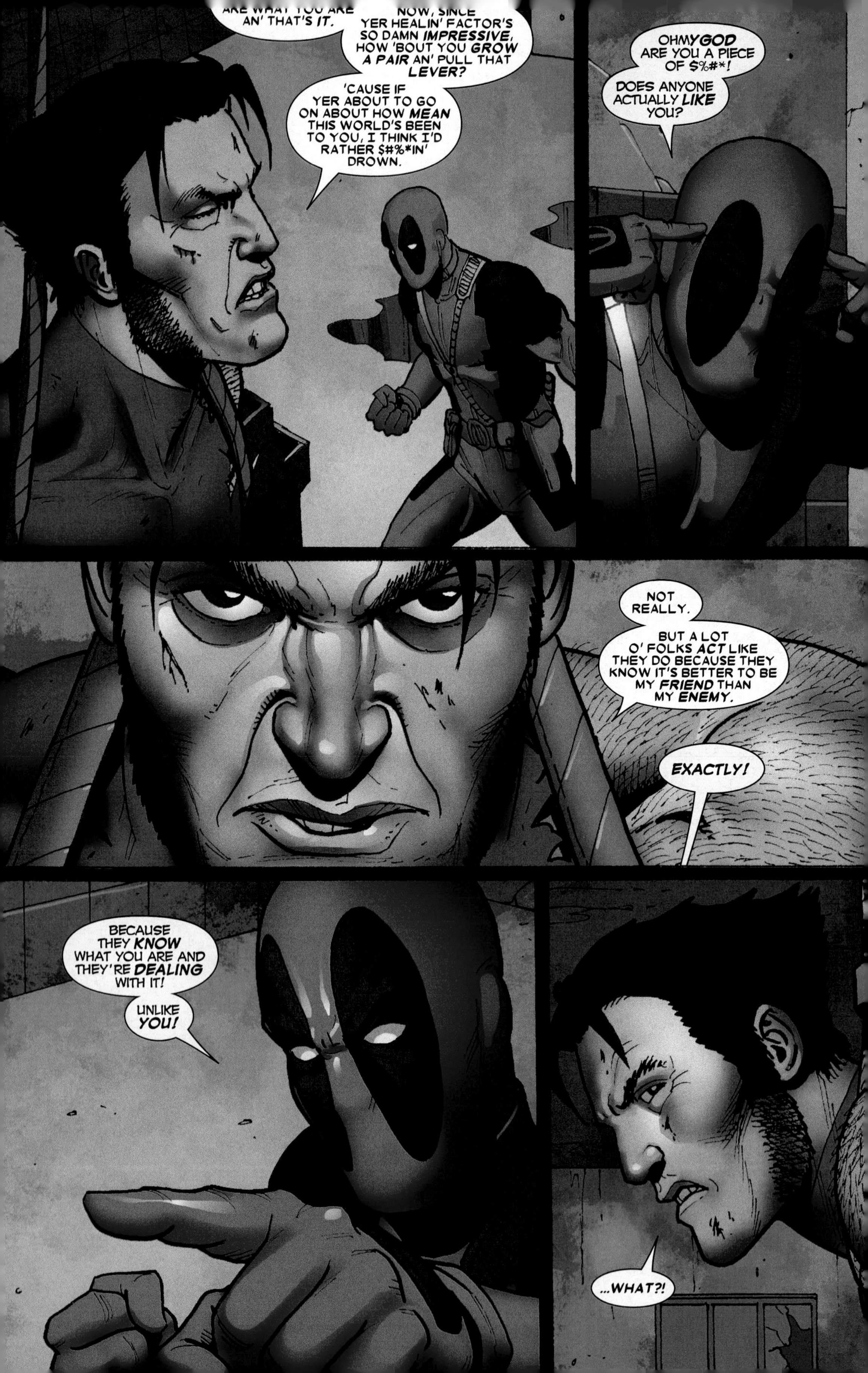

ARE WHAT YOU ARE AN' THAT'S IT.
NOW, SINCE YER HEALIN' FACTOR'S SO DAMN IMPRESSIVE, HOW 'BOUT YOU GROW A PAIR AN' PULL THAT LEVER?
'CAUSE IF YER ABOUT TO GO ON ABOUT HOW MEAN THIS WORLD'S BEEN TO YOU, I THINK I'D RATHER $#%*IN' DROWN.
OHMYGOD ARE YOU A PIECE OF $%#*!
DOES ANYONE ACTUALLY LIKE YOU?
NOT REALLY.
BUT A LOT O' FOLKS ACT LIKE THEY DO BECAUSE THEY KNOW IT'S BETTER TO BE MY FRIEND THAN MY ENEMY.
EXACTLY!
BECAUSE THEY KNOW WHAT YOU ARE AND THEY'RE DEALING WITH IT!
UNLIKE YOU!
...WHAT?!

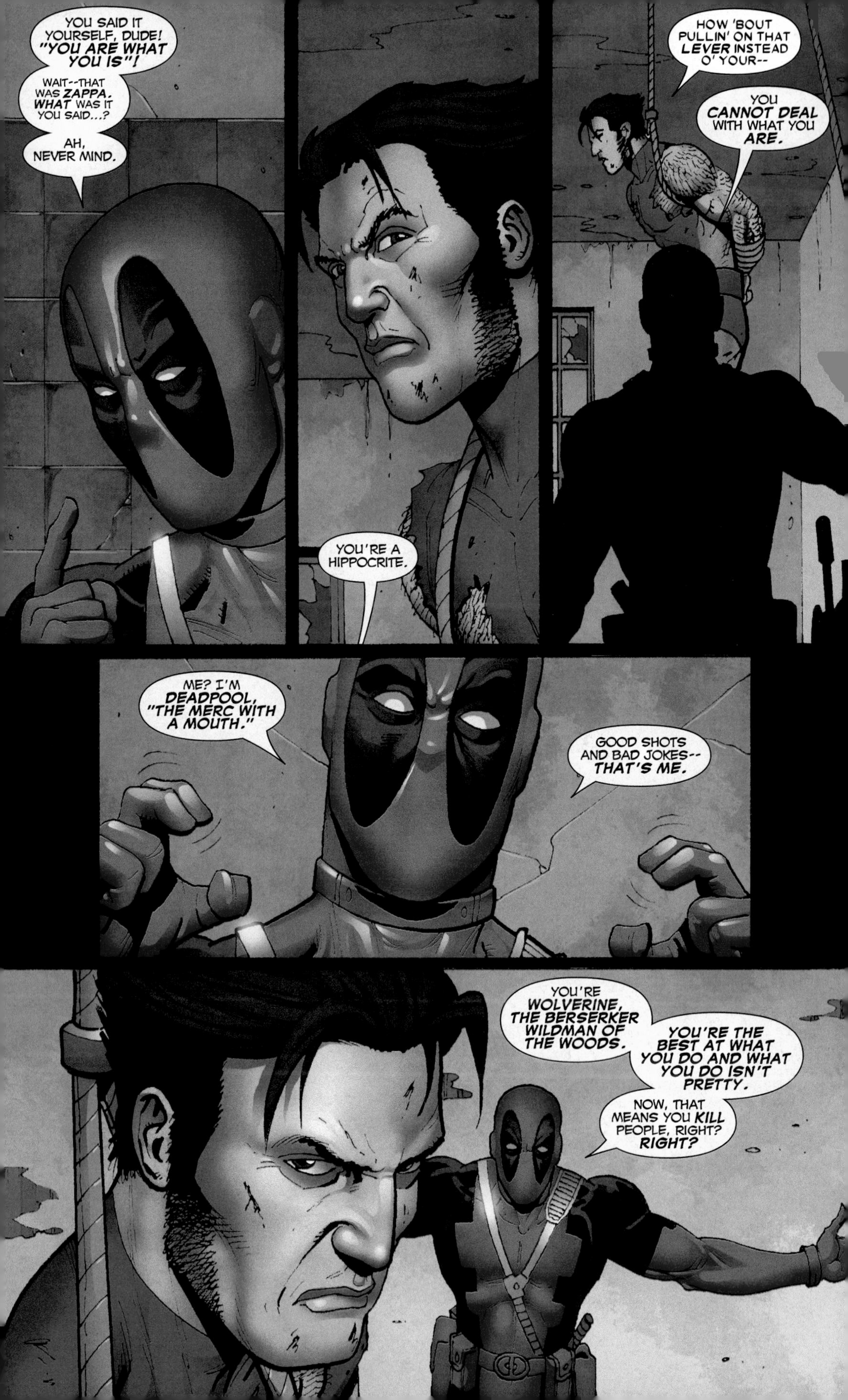
YOU SAID IT YOURSELF, DUDE! "YOU ARE WHAT YOU IS"!
WAIT--THAT WAS ZAPPA. WHAT WAS IT YOU SAID...?
AH, NEVER MIND.
YOU'RE A HIPPOCRITE.
HOW 'BOUT PULLIN' ON THAT LEVER INSTEAD O' YOUR--
YOU CANNOT DEAL WITH WHAT YOU ARE.
ME? I'M DEADPOOL, "THE MERC WITH A MOUTH."
GOOD SHOTS AND BAD JOKES--THAT'S ME.
YOU'RE WOLVERINE, THE BERSERKER WILDMAN OF THE WOODS.
YOU'RE THE BEST AT WHAT YOU DO AND WHAT YOU DO ISN'T PRETTY.
NOW, THAT MEANS YOU KILL PEOPLE, RIGHT? RIGHT?

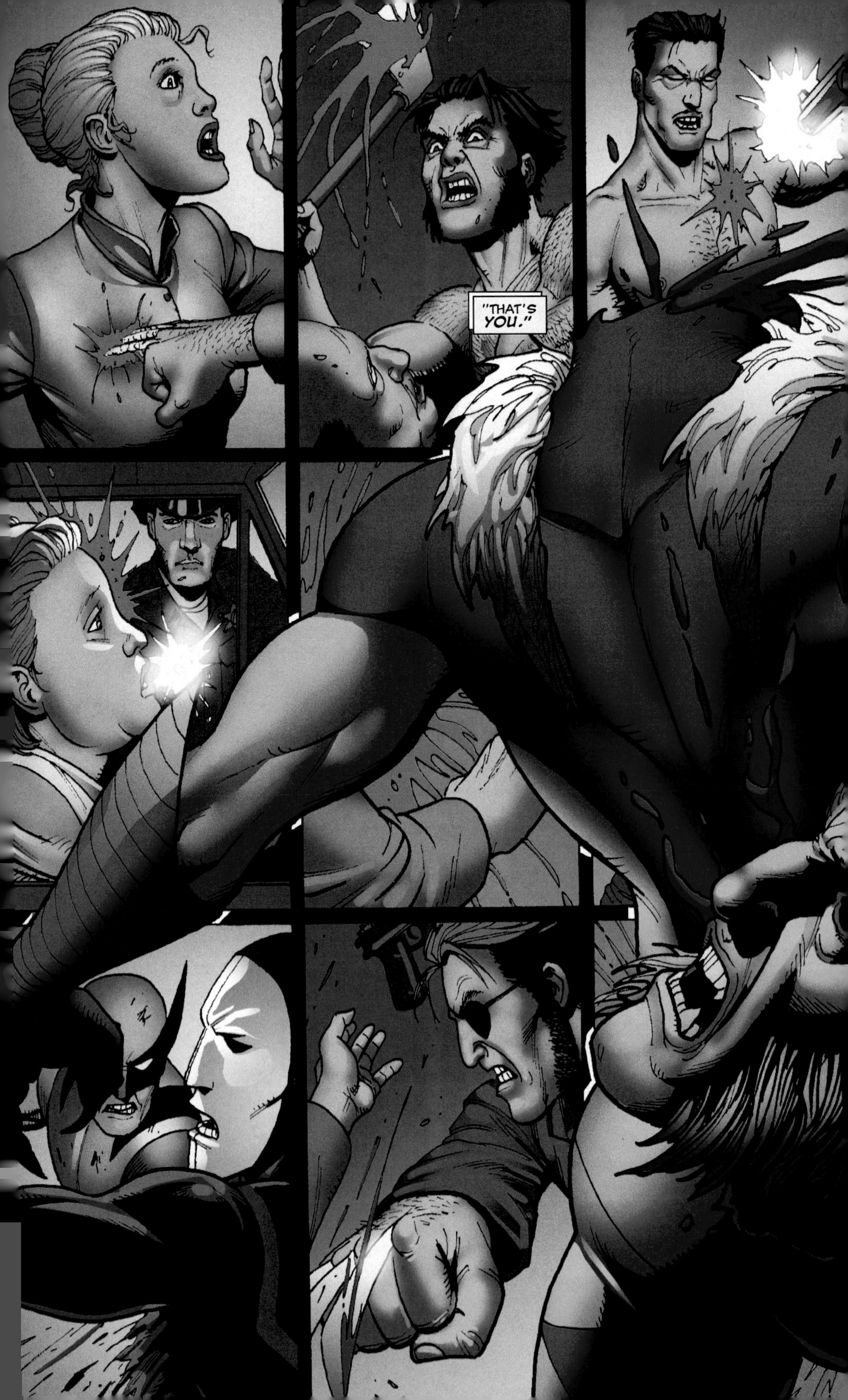
"THAT'S YOU."

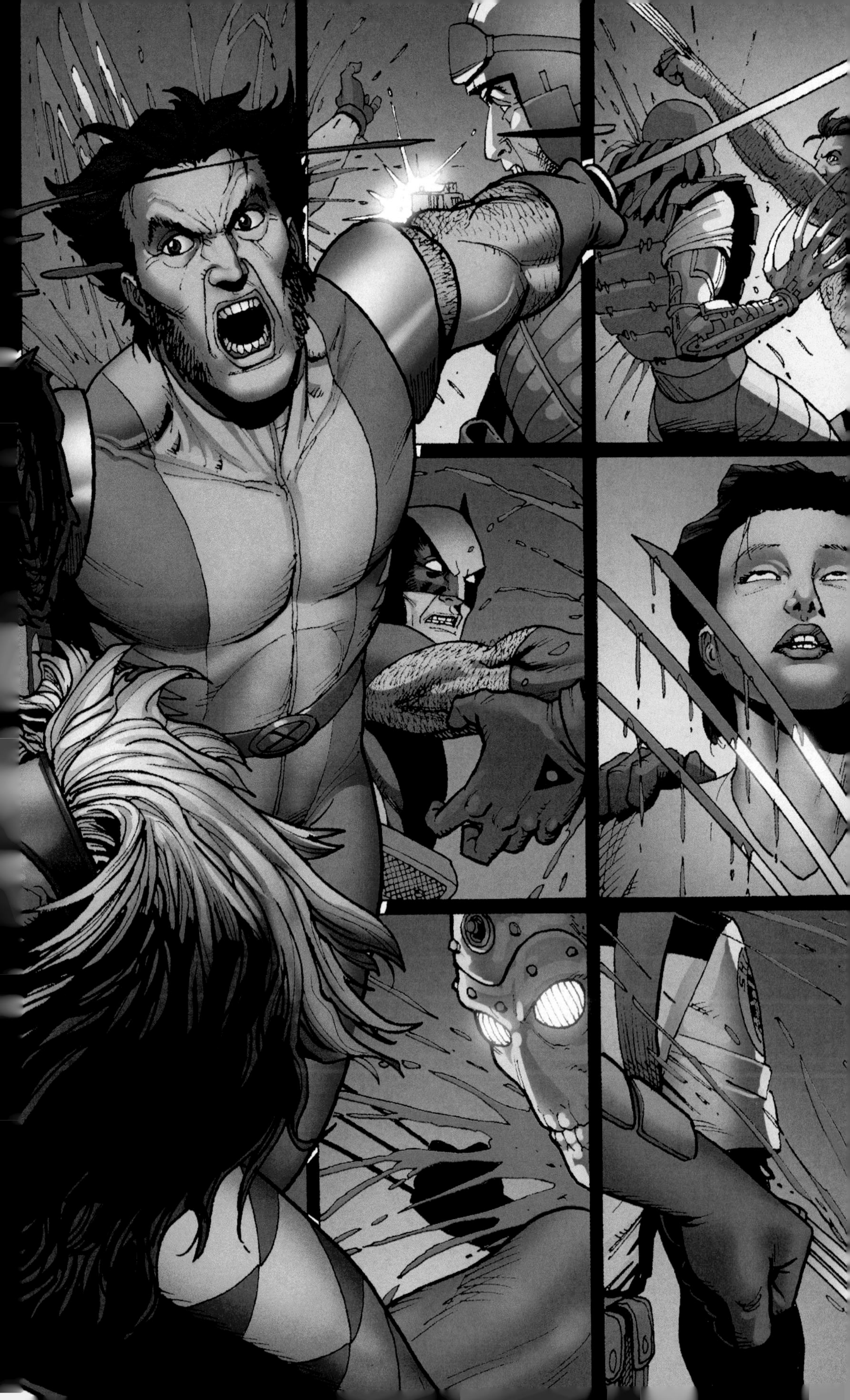

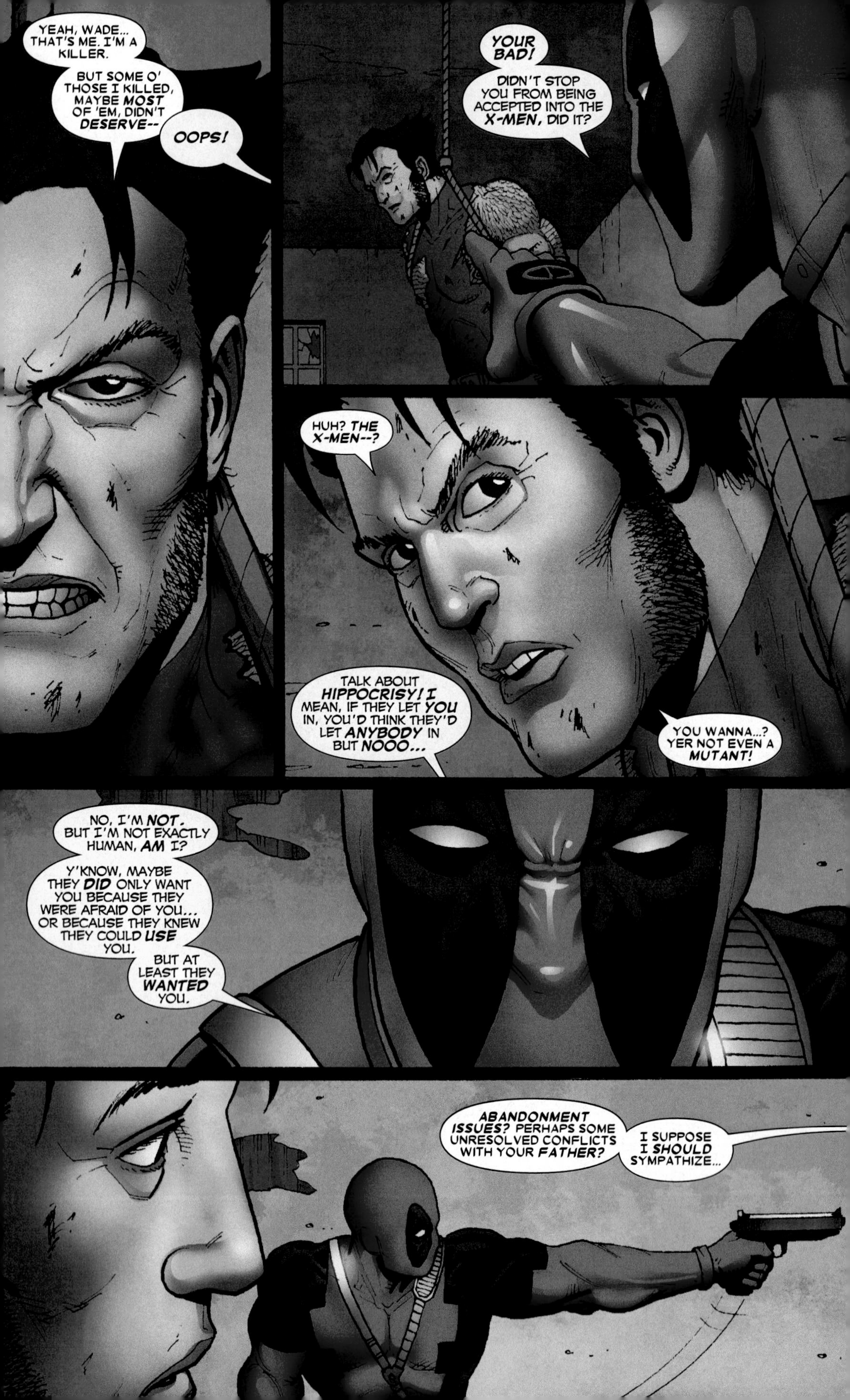
YEAH, WADE... THAT'S ME. I'M A KILLER.
BUT SOME O' THOSE I KILLED, MAYBE MOST OF 'EM, DIDN'T DESERVE--
OOPS!
YOUR BAD!
DIDN'T STOP YOU FROM BEING ACCEPTED INTO THE X-MEN, DID IT?
HUH? THE X-MEN--?
TALK ABOUT HIPPOCRISY! I MEAN, IF THEY LET YOU IN, YOU'D THINK THEY'D LET ANYBODY IN BUT NOOO...
YOU WANNA...? YER NOT EVEN A MUTANT!
NO, I'M NOT. BUT I'M NOT EXACTLY HUMAN, AM I?
Y'KNOW, MAYBE THEY DID ONLY WANT YOU BECAUSE THEY WERE AFRAID OF YOU... OR BECAUSE THEY KNEW THEY COULD USE YOU.
BUT AT LEAST THEY WANTED YOU.
ABANDONMENT ISSUES? PERHAPS SOME UNRESOLVED CONFLICTS WITH YOUR FATHER?
I SUPPOSE I SHOULD SYMPATHIZE...

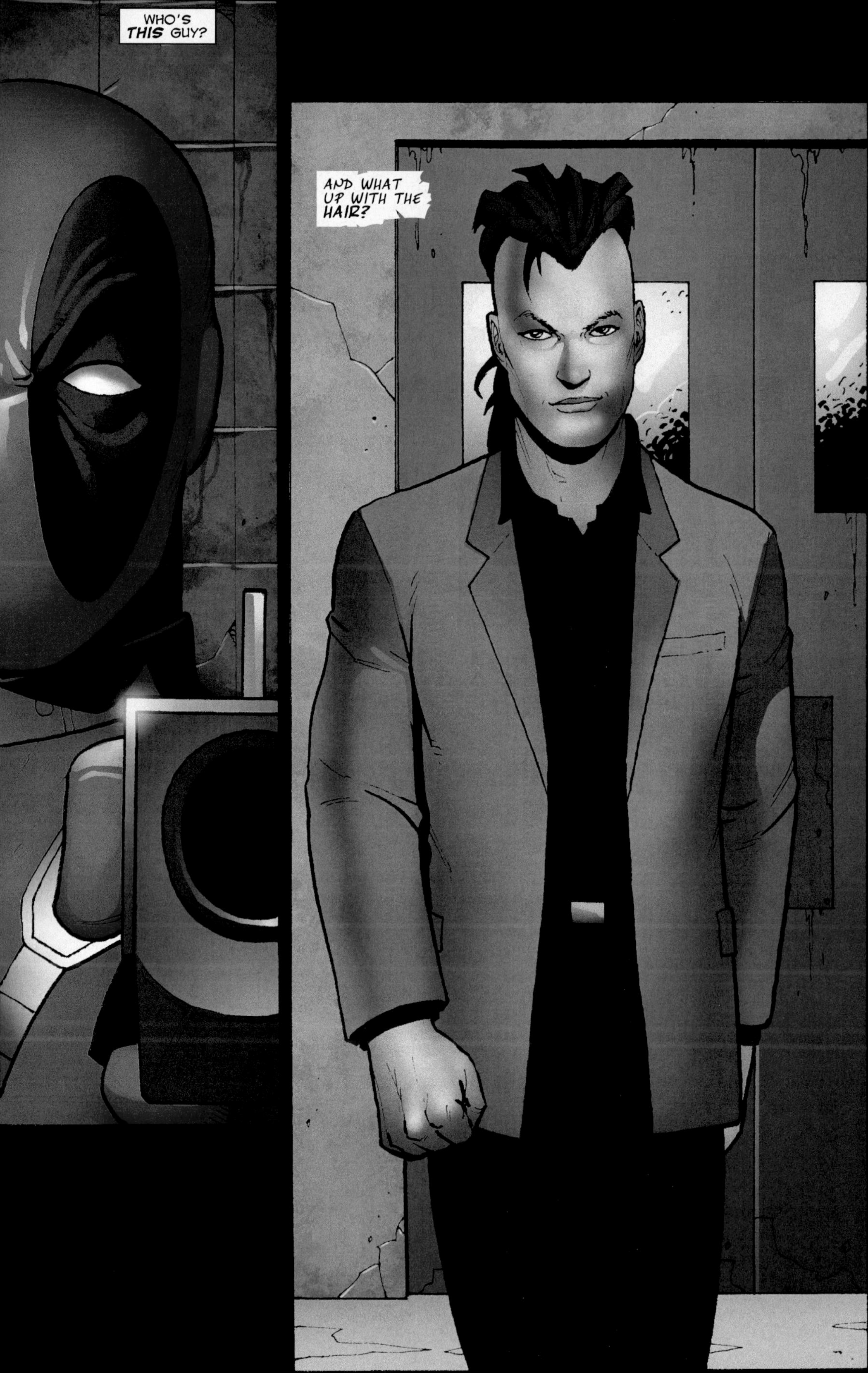
WHO'S THIS GUY?
AND WHAT UP WITH THE HAIR?

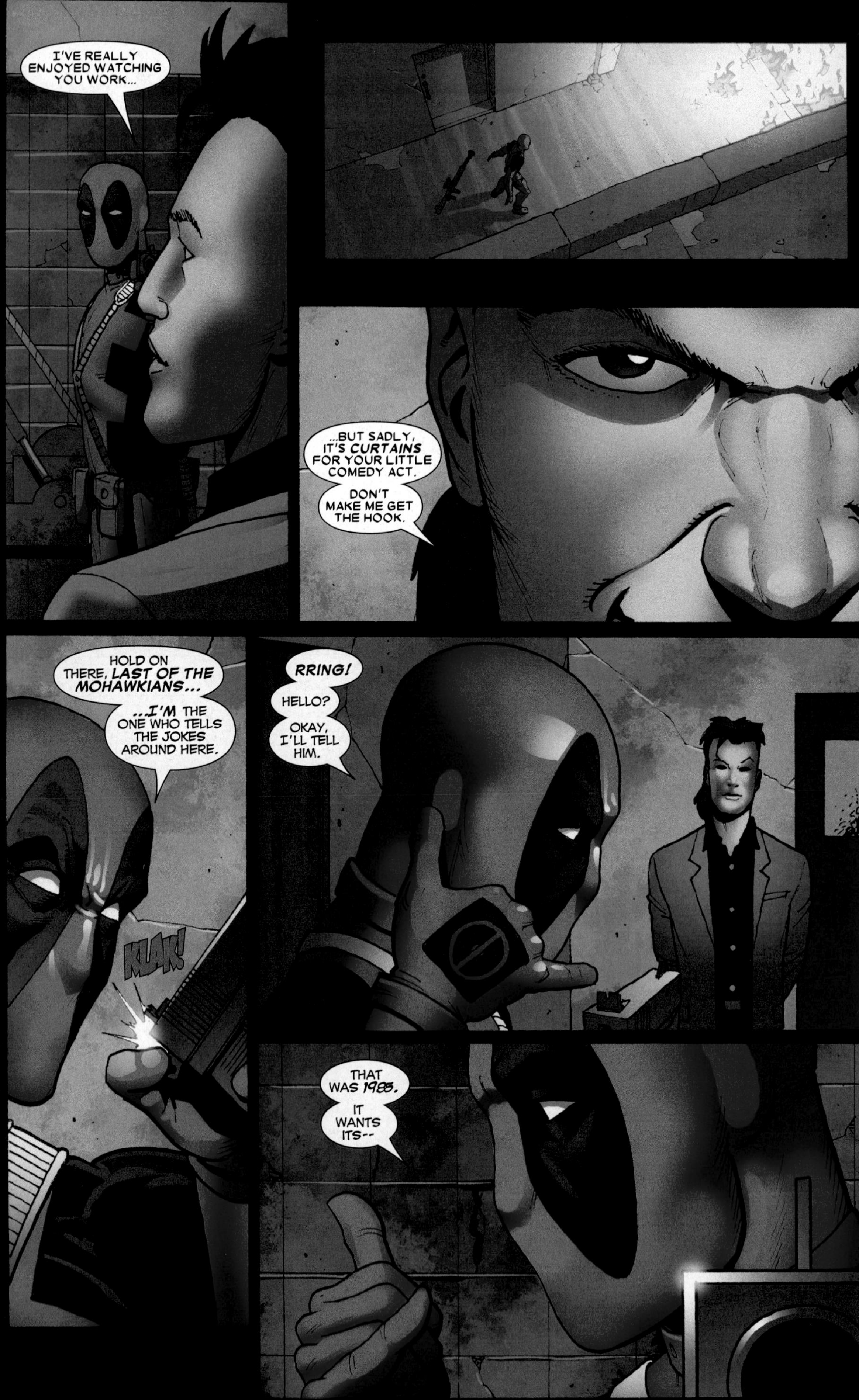
I'VE REALLY ENJOYED WATCHING YOU WORK...
...BUT SADLY, IT'S CURTAINS FOR YOUR LITTLE COMEDY ACT.
DON'T MAKE ME GET THE HOOK.
HOLD ON THERE, LAST OF THE MOHAWKIANS...
...I'M THE ONE WHO TELLS THE JOKES AROUND HERE.
KLAK!
RRING!
HELLO?
OKAY, I'LL TELL HIM.
THAT WAS 1985.
IT WANTS ITS--

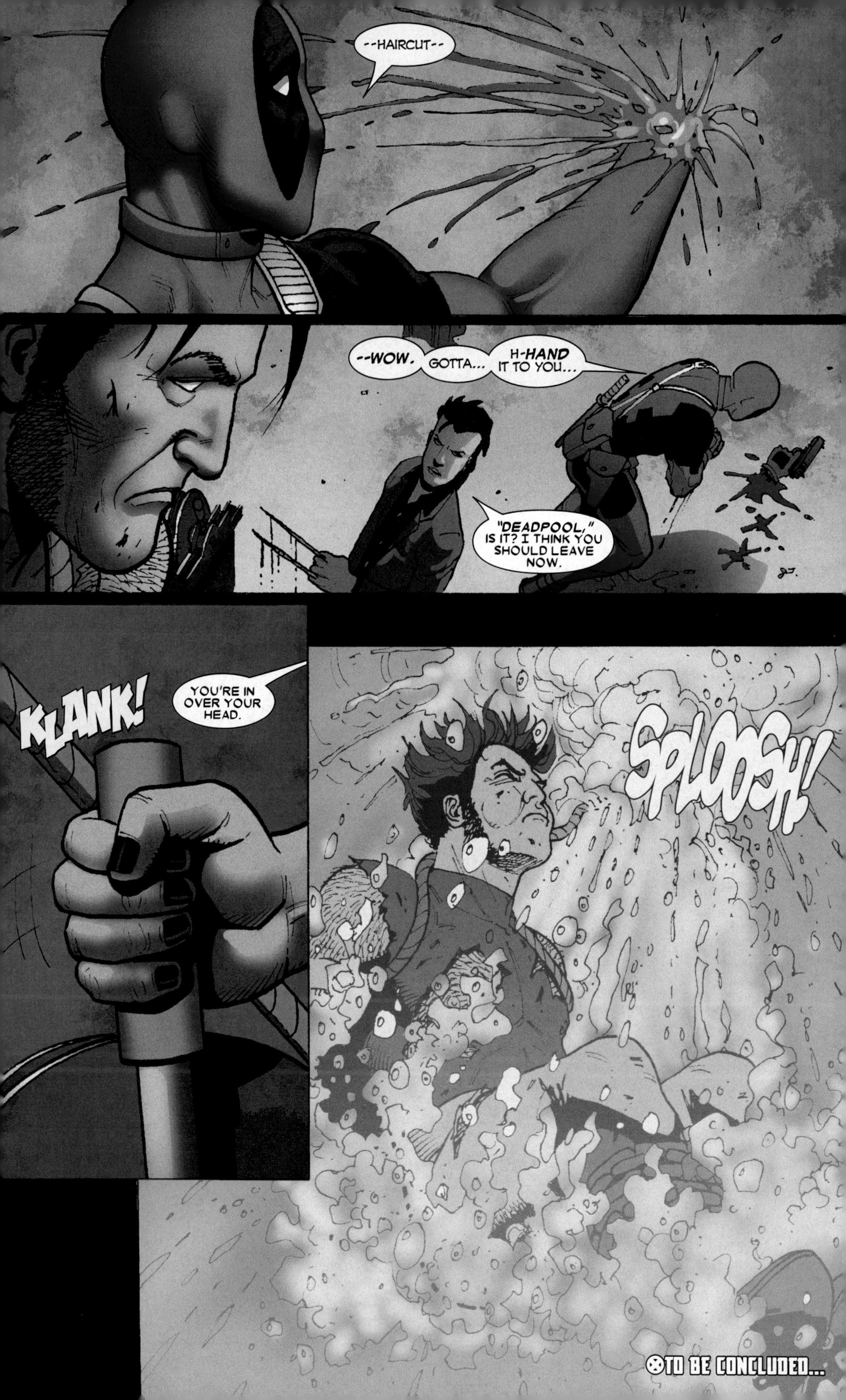
--HAIRCUT--
--WOW.
GOTTA...
H-HAND IT TO YOU...
"DEADPOOL," IS IT? I THINK YOU SHOULD LEAVE NOW.
KLANK!
YOU'RE IN OVER YOUR HEAD.
SPLOOSH!
TO BE CONCLUDED...

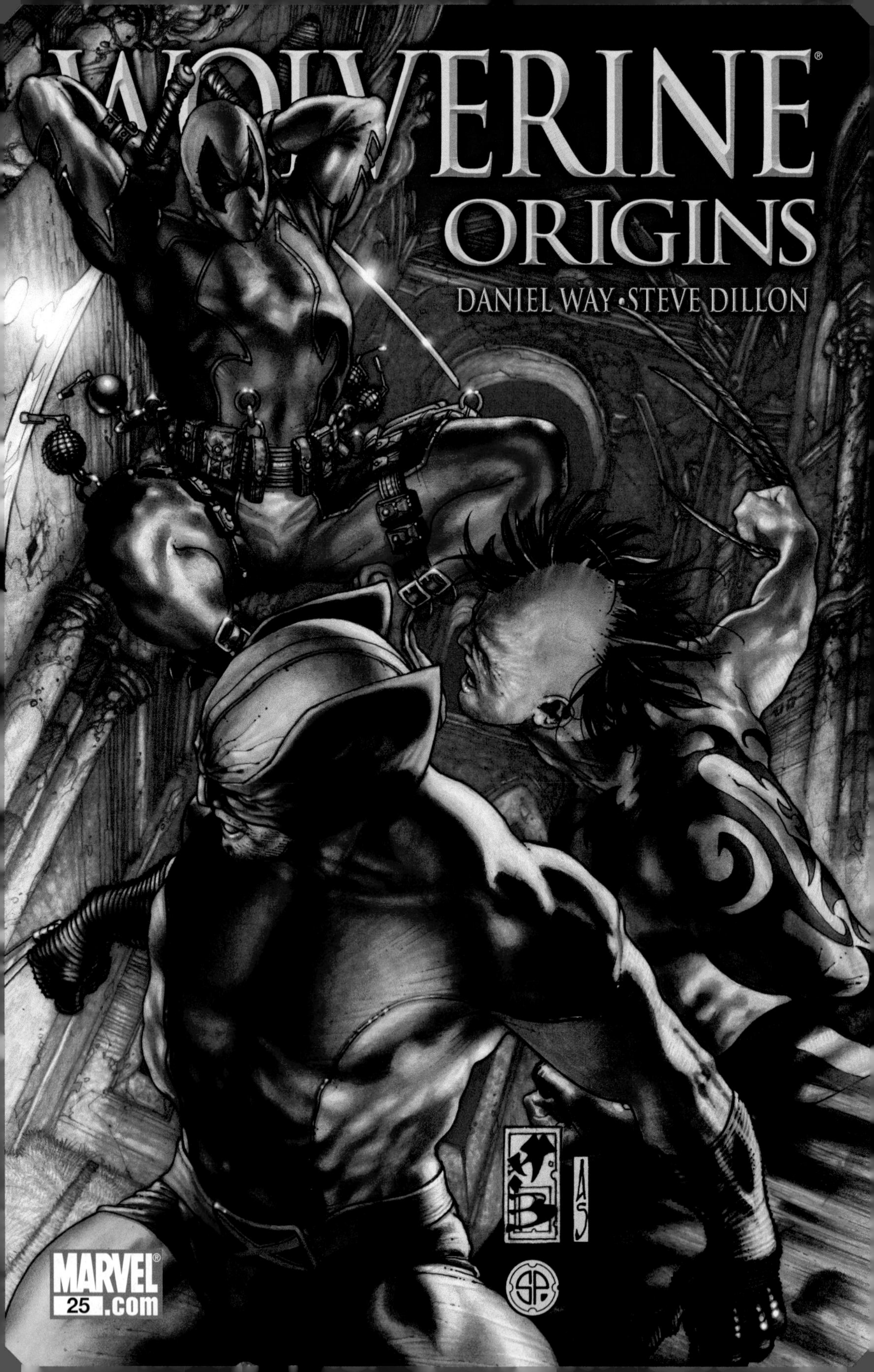
WOLVERINE
ORIGINS
DANIEL WAY·STEVE DILLON
MARVEL
25
.com

THE DEEP END

CONCLUSION

DANIEL WAY
WRITER

STEVE DILLON
ARTIST

AVALON'S MATT MILLA
COLORIST

VC'S CORY PETIT
LETTERER

SIMONE BIANCHI
COVER ART

SIMONE PERUZZI
COVER COLOR

AUBREY SITTERSON
ASST. EDITOR

JOHN BARBER
EDITOR

AXEL ALONSO
GROUP EDITOR

JOE QUESADA
EDITOR IN CHIEF

DAN BUCKLEY
PUBLISHER

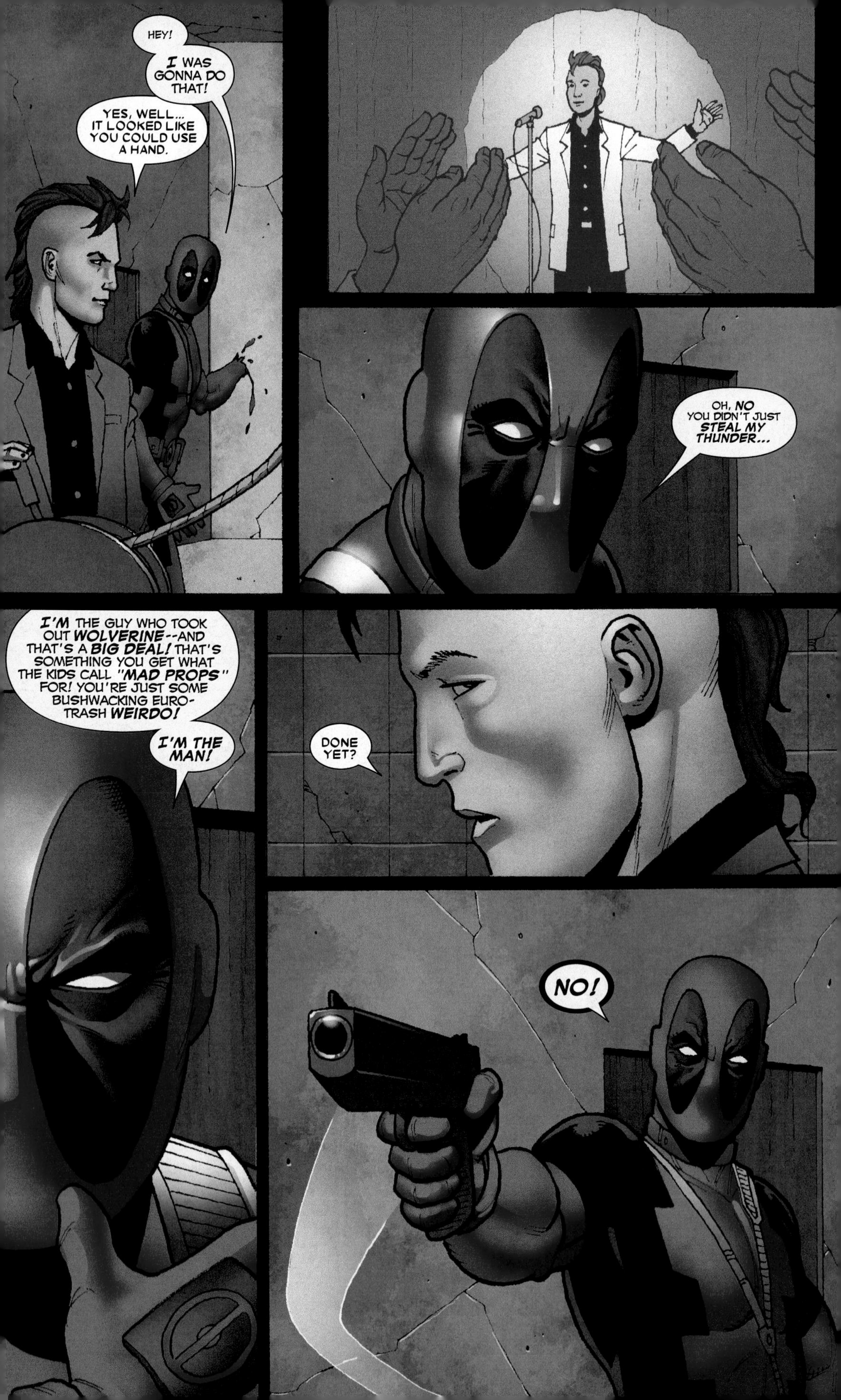
HEY!
I WAS GONNA DO THAT!
YES, WELL... IT LOOKED LIKE YOU COULD USE A HAND.
OH, NO YOU DIDN'T JUST STEAL MY THUNDER...
I'M THE GUY WHO TOOK OUT WOLVERINE--AND THAT'S A BIG DEAL! THAT'S SOMETHING YOU GET WHAT THE KIDS CALL "MAD PROPS" FOR! YOU'RE JUST SOME BUSHWACKING EURO-TRASH WEIRDO!
I'M THE MAN!
DONE YET?
NO!

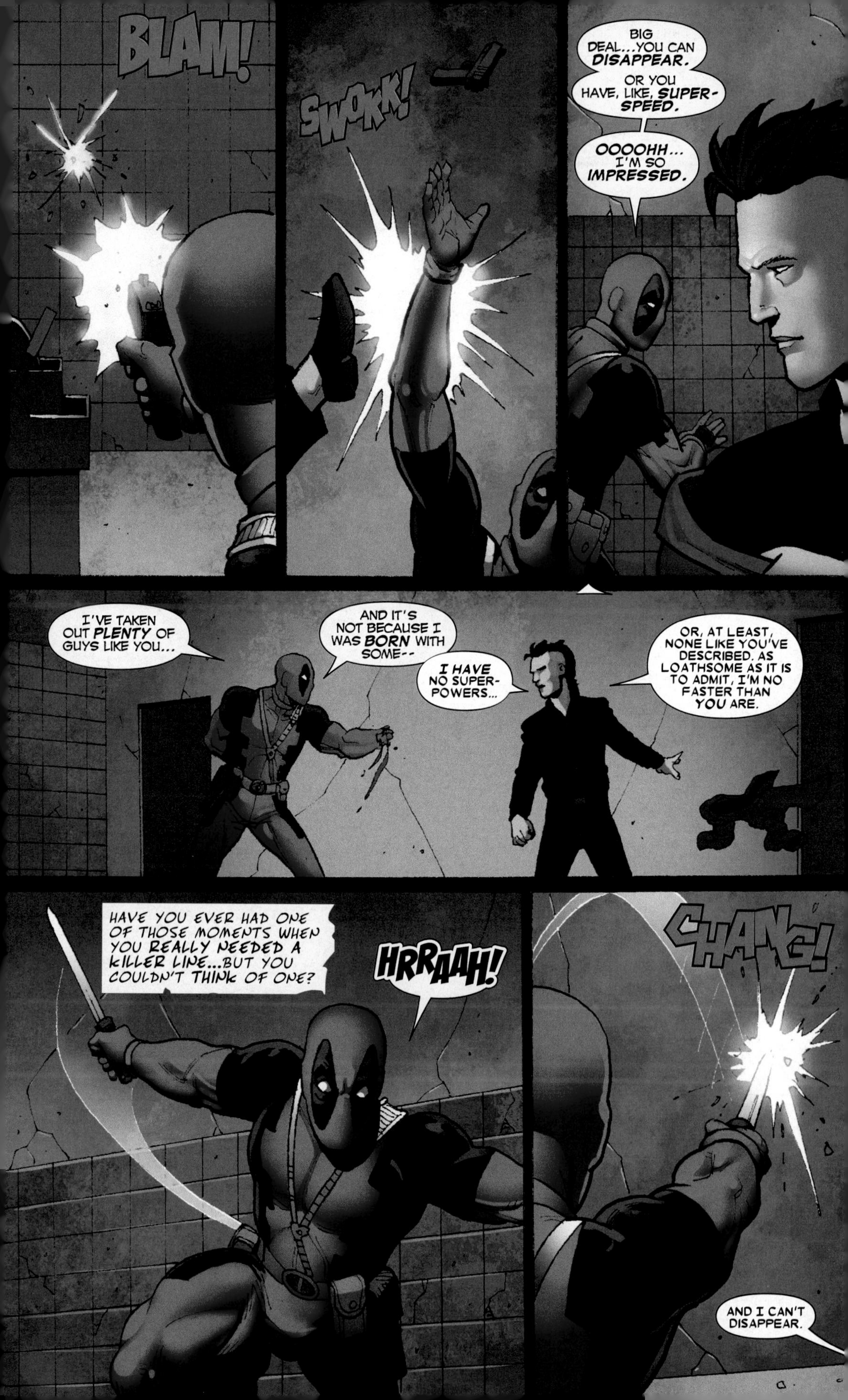
BLAM!
SWOKK!
BIG DEAL...YOU CAN DISAPPEAR.
OR YOU HAVE, LIKE, SUPER-SPEED.
OOOOHH... I'M SO IMPRESSED.
I'VE TAKEN OUT PLENTY OF GUYS LIKE YOU...
AND IT'S NOT BECAUSE I WAS BORN WITH SOME--
I HAVE NO SUPER-POWERS...
OR, AT LEAST, NONE LIKE YOU'VE DESCRIBED. AS LOATHSOME AS IT IS TO ADMIT, I'M NO FASTER THAN YOU ARE.
HAVE YOU EVER HAD ONE OF THOSE MOMENTS WHEN YOU REALLY NEEDED A KILLER LINE...BUT YOU COULDN'T THINK OF ONE?
HRRAAH!
CHANG!
AND I CAN'T DISAPPEAR.

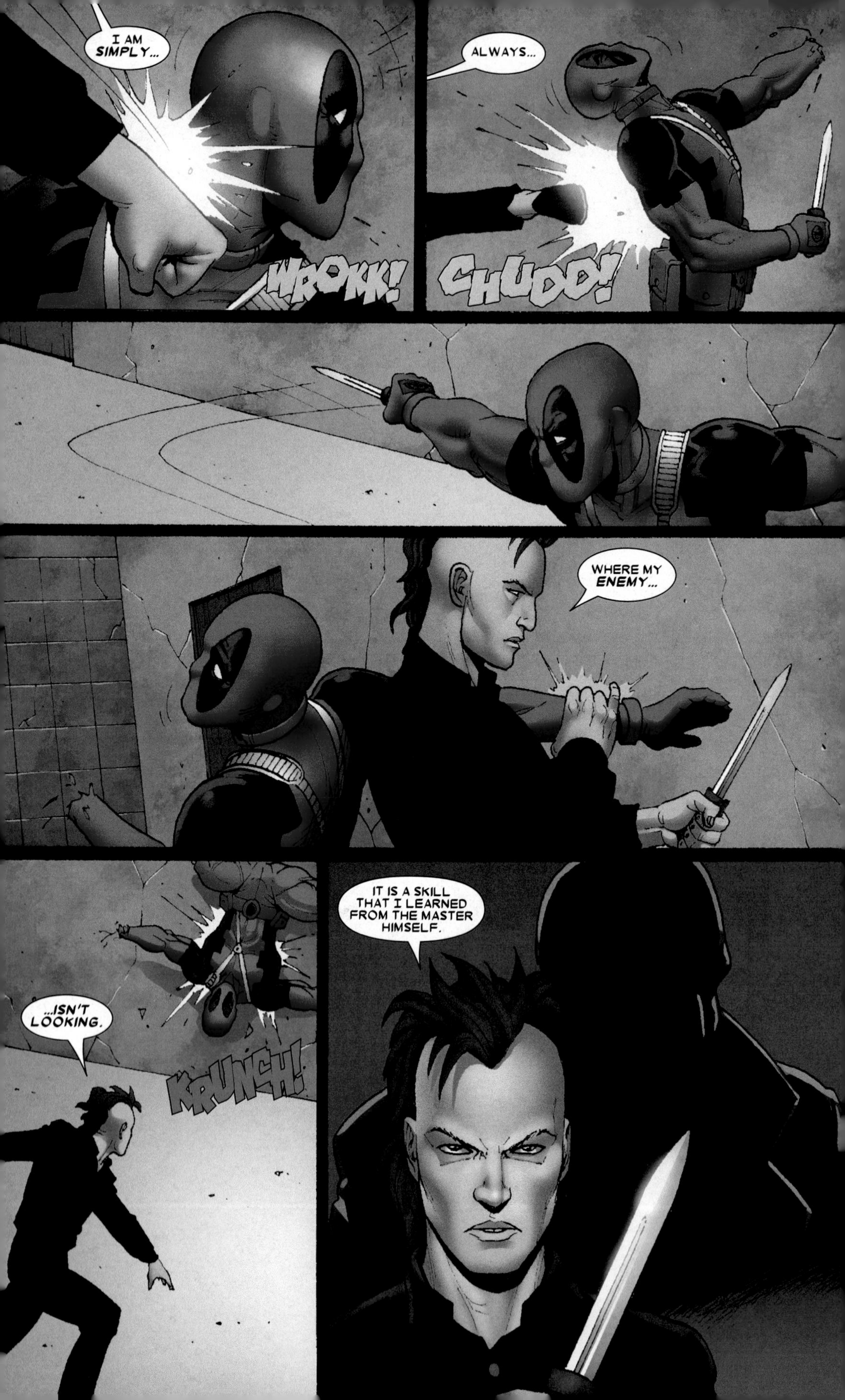
I AM SIMPLY...
WROKK!
ALWAYS...
CHUDD!
WHERE MY ENEMY...
...ISN'T LOOKING.
KRUNCH!
IT IS A SKILL THAT I LEARNED FROM THE MASTER HIMSELF.

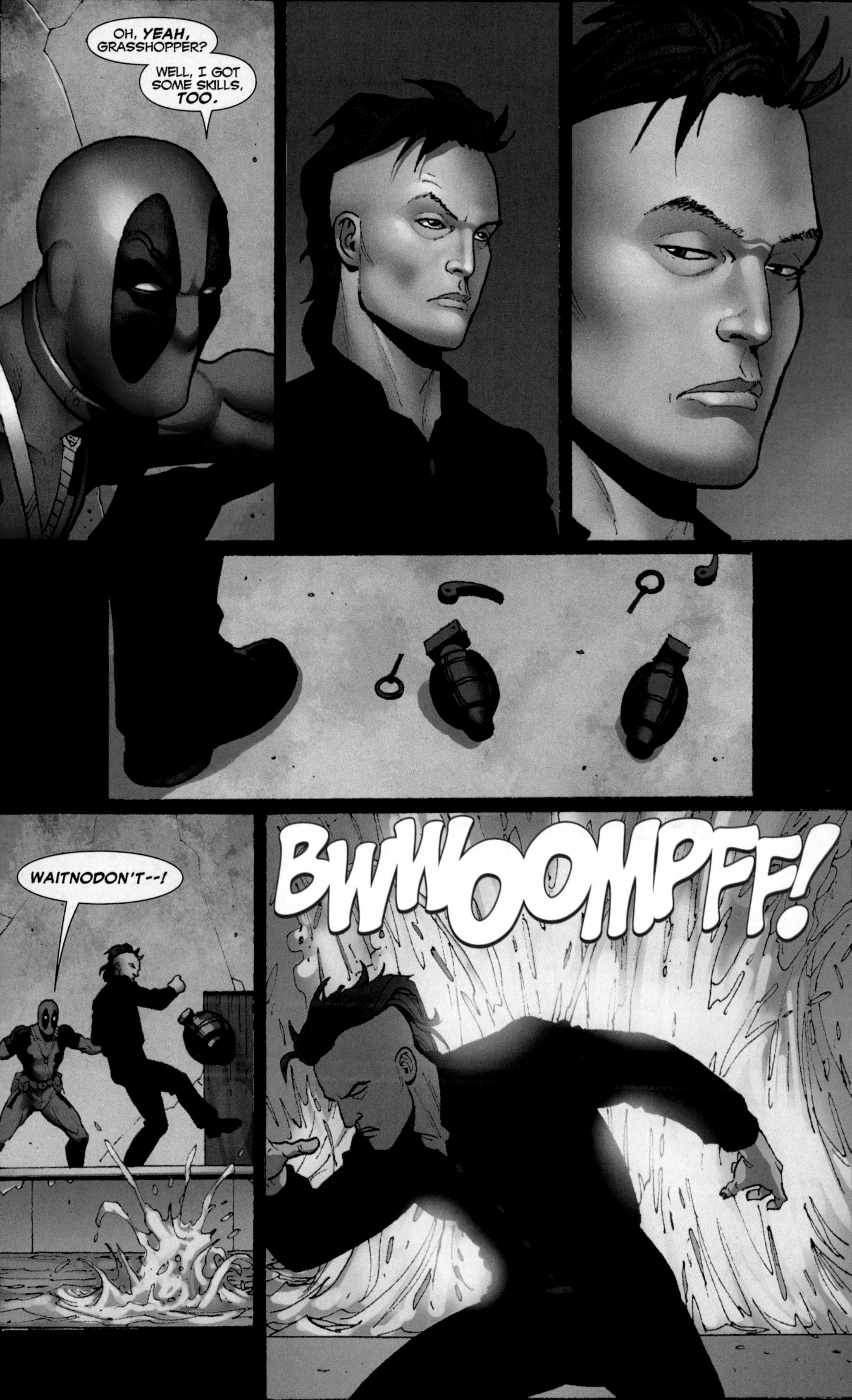
OH, YEAH, GRASSHOPPER?
WELL, I GOT SOME SKILLS, TOO.
WAITNODON'T--!
BWHOOMPFF!

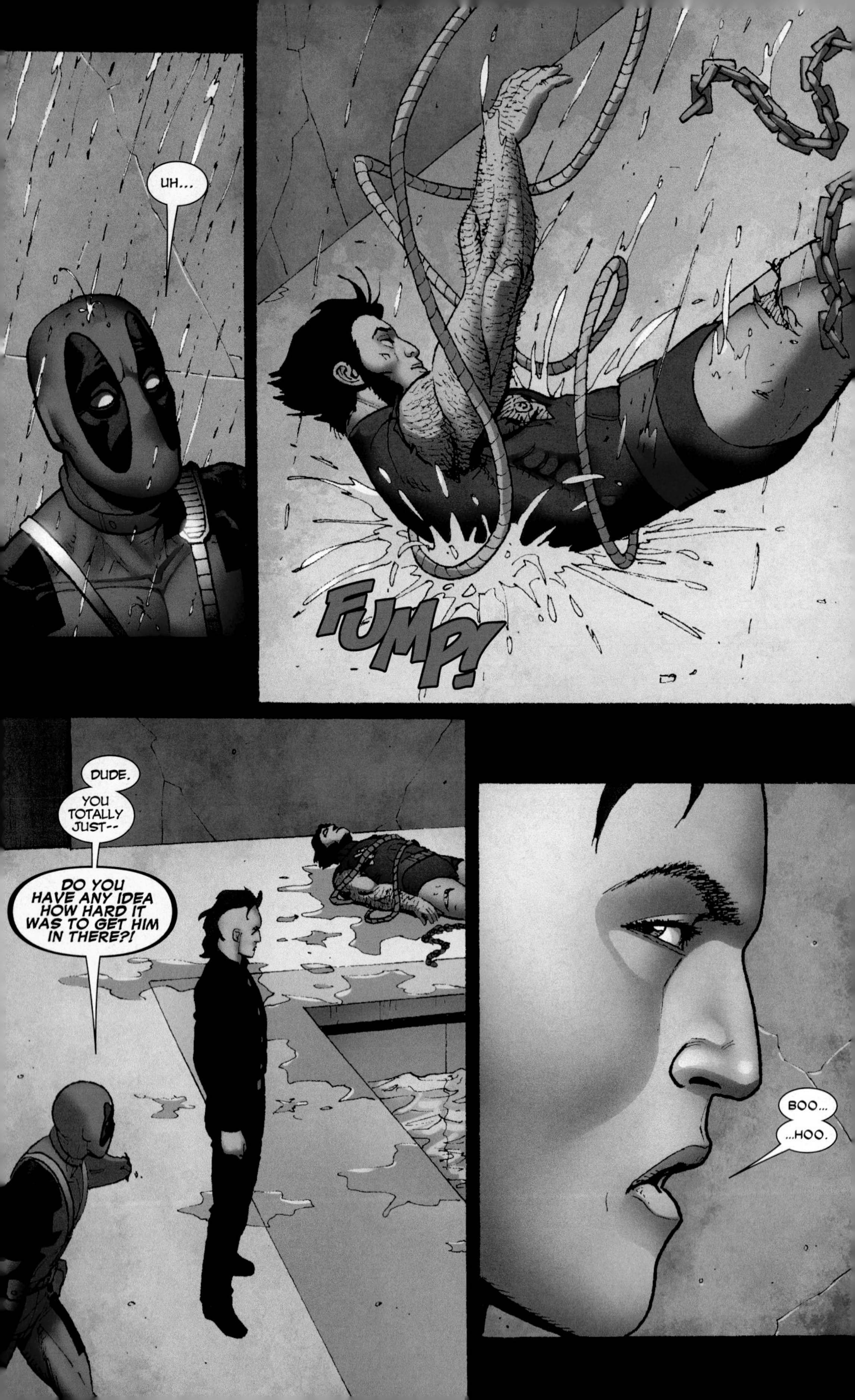
UH...
FUMP!
DUDE.
YOU TOTALLY JUST--
DO YOU HAVE ANY IDEA HOW HARD IT WAS TO GET HIM IN THERE?!
BOO...
...HOO.

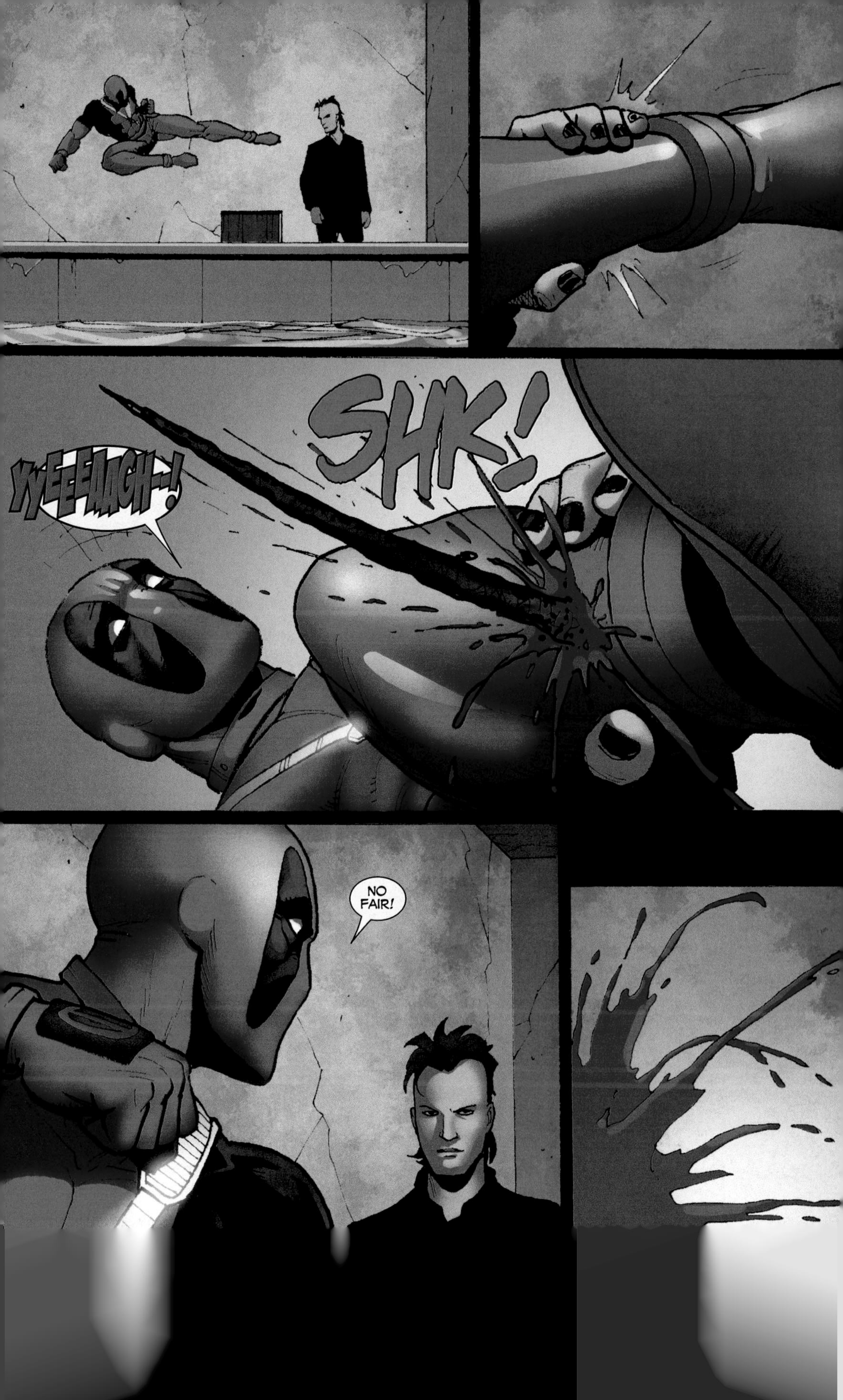
SHK!
YyEEEAAGH--!
NO FAIR!

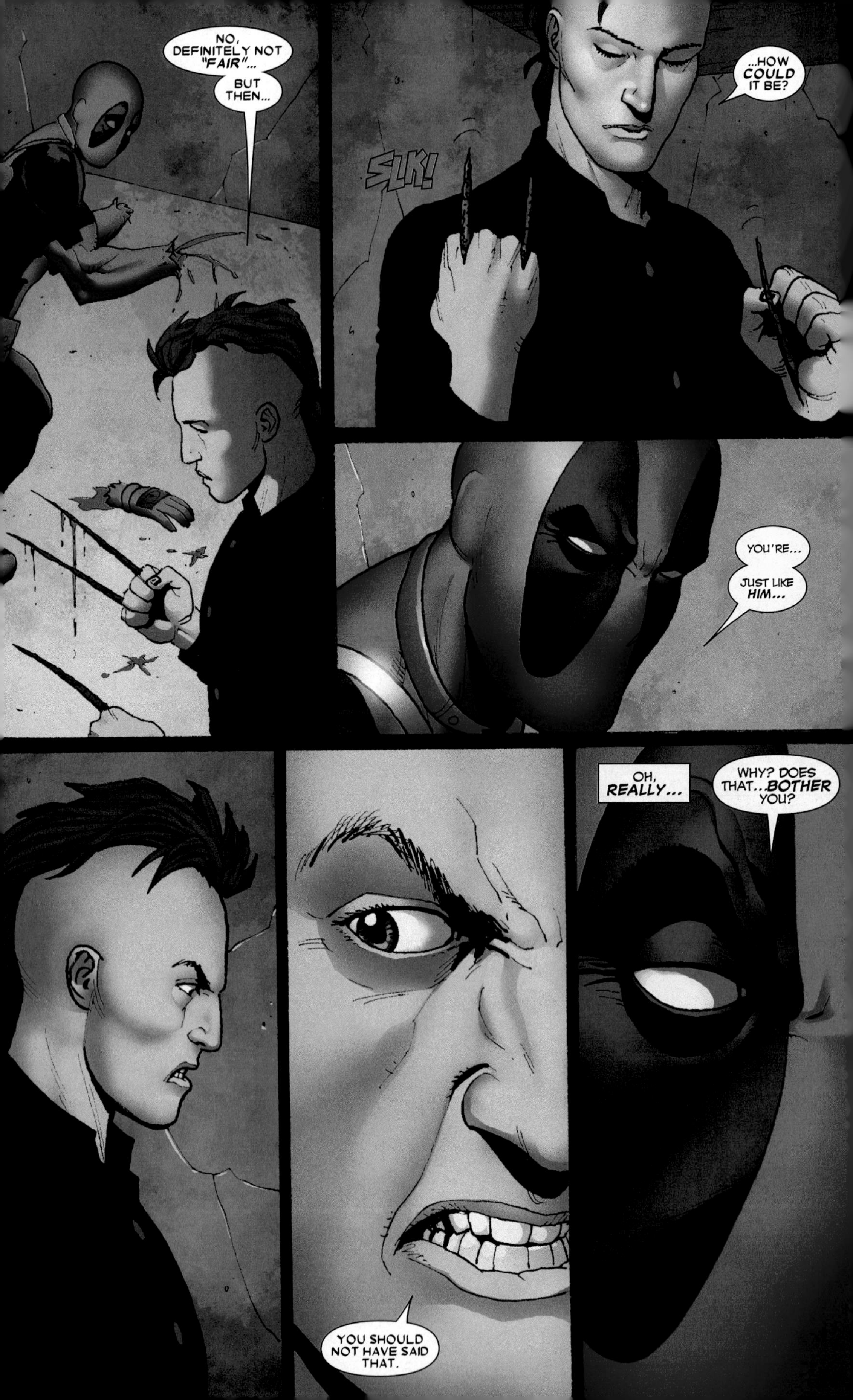
NO, DEFINITELY NOT "FAIR"...
BUT THEN...
...HOW COULD IT BE?
SLIK!
YOU'RE...
JUST LIKE HIM...
YOU SHOULD NOT HAVE SAID THAT.
OH, REALLY...
WHY? DOES THAT...BOTHER YOU?

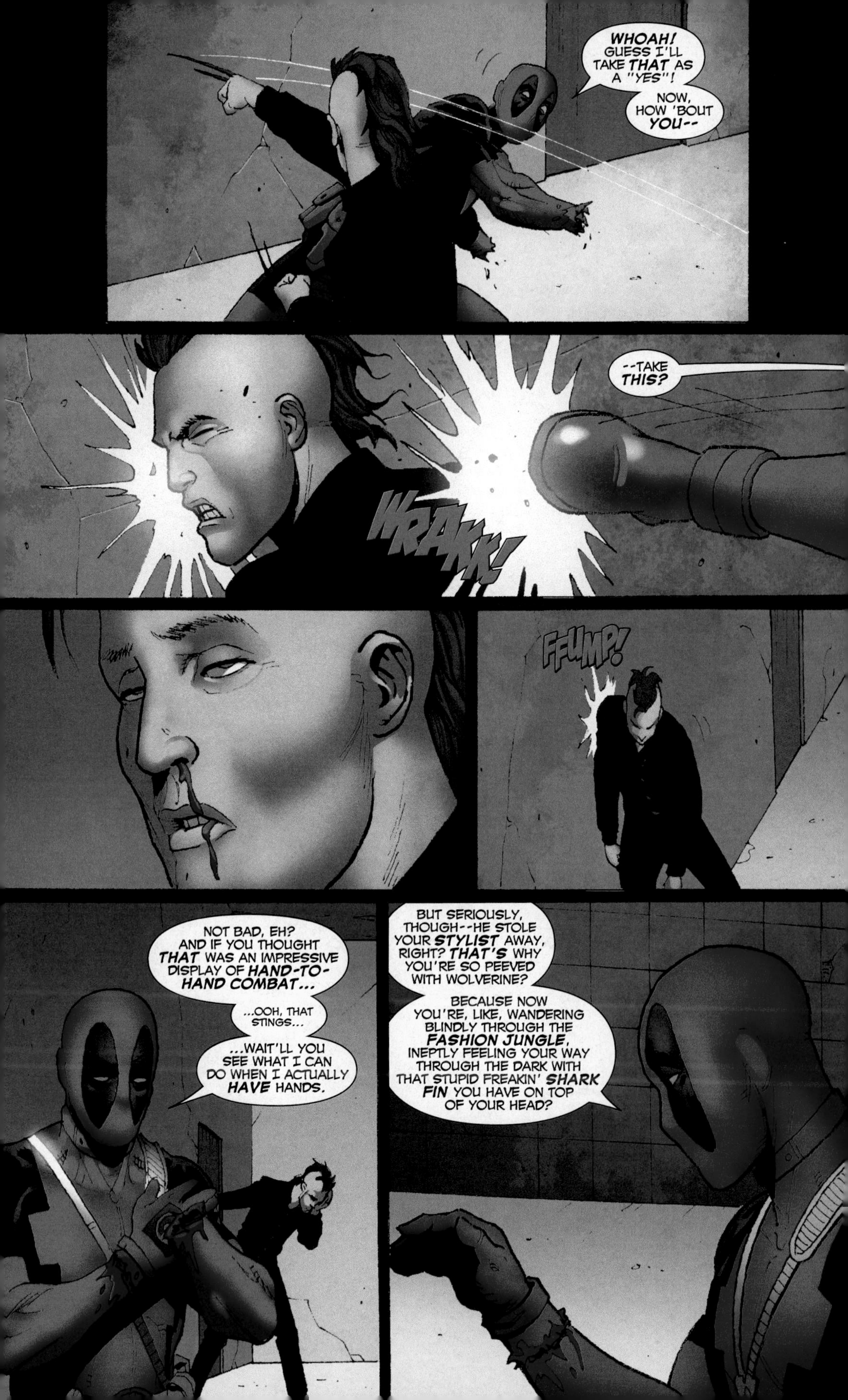

WHOAH! GUESS I'LL TAKE THAT AS A "YES"!
NOW, HOW 'BOUT YOU--
--TAKE THIS?
WRAKK!
FFUMP!
NOT BAD, EH? AND IF YOU THOUGHT THAT WAS AN IMPRESSIVE DISPLAY OF HAND-TO-HAND COMBAT...
...OOH, THAT STINGS...
...WAIT'LL YOU SEE WHAT I CAN DO WHEN I ACTUALLY HAVE HANDS.
BUT SERIOUSLY, THOUGH--HE STOLE YOUR STYLIST AWAY, RIGHT? THAT'S WHY YOU'RE SO PEEVED WITH WOLVERINE?
BECAUSE NOW YOU'RE, LIKE, WANDERING BLINDLY THROUGH THE FASHION JUNGLE, INEPTLY FEELING YOUR WAY THROUGH THE DARK WITH THAT STUPID FREAKIN' SHARK FIN YOU HAVE ON TOP OF YOUR HEAD?

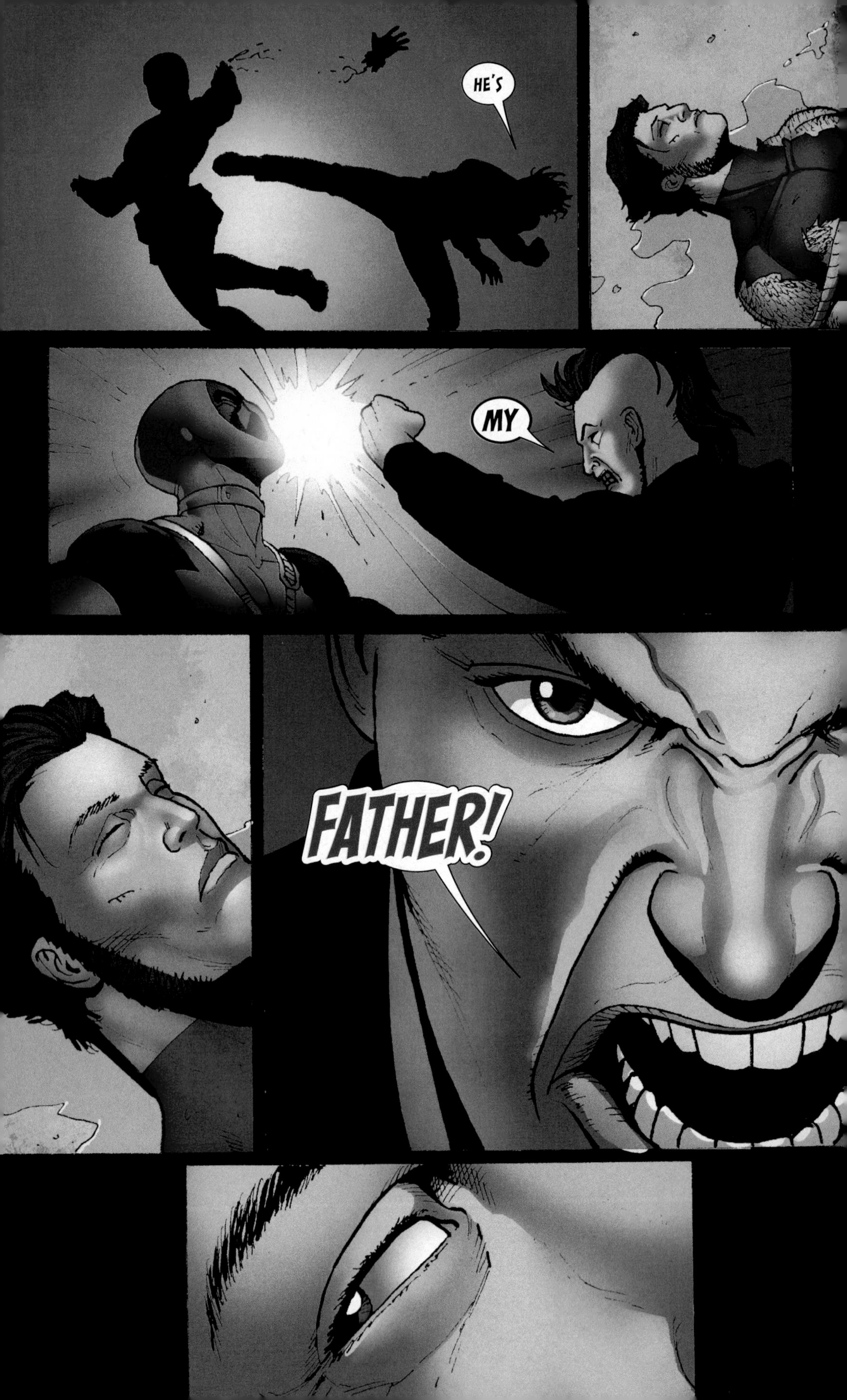
HE'S
MY
FATHER!

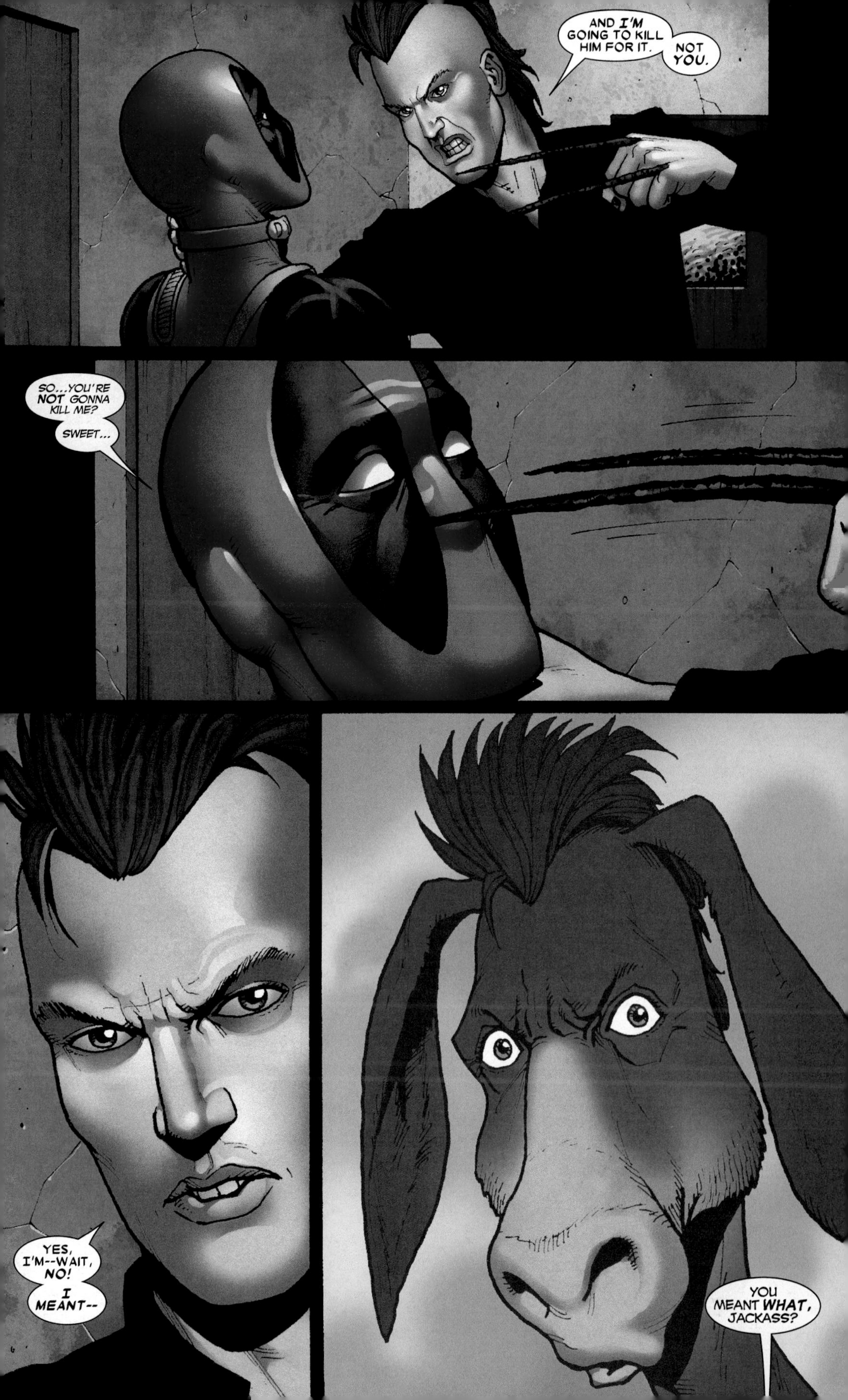
AND I'M GOING TO KILL HIM FOR IT.
NOT YOU.
SO...YOU'RE NOT GONNA KILL ME?
SWEET...
YES, I'M--WAIT, NO! I MEANT--
YOU MEANT WHAT, JACKASS?

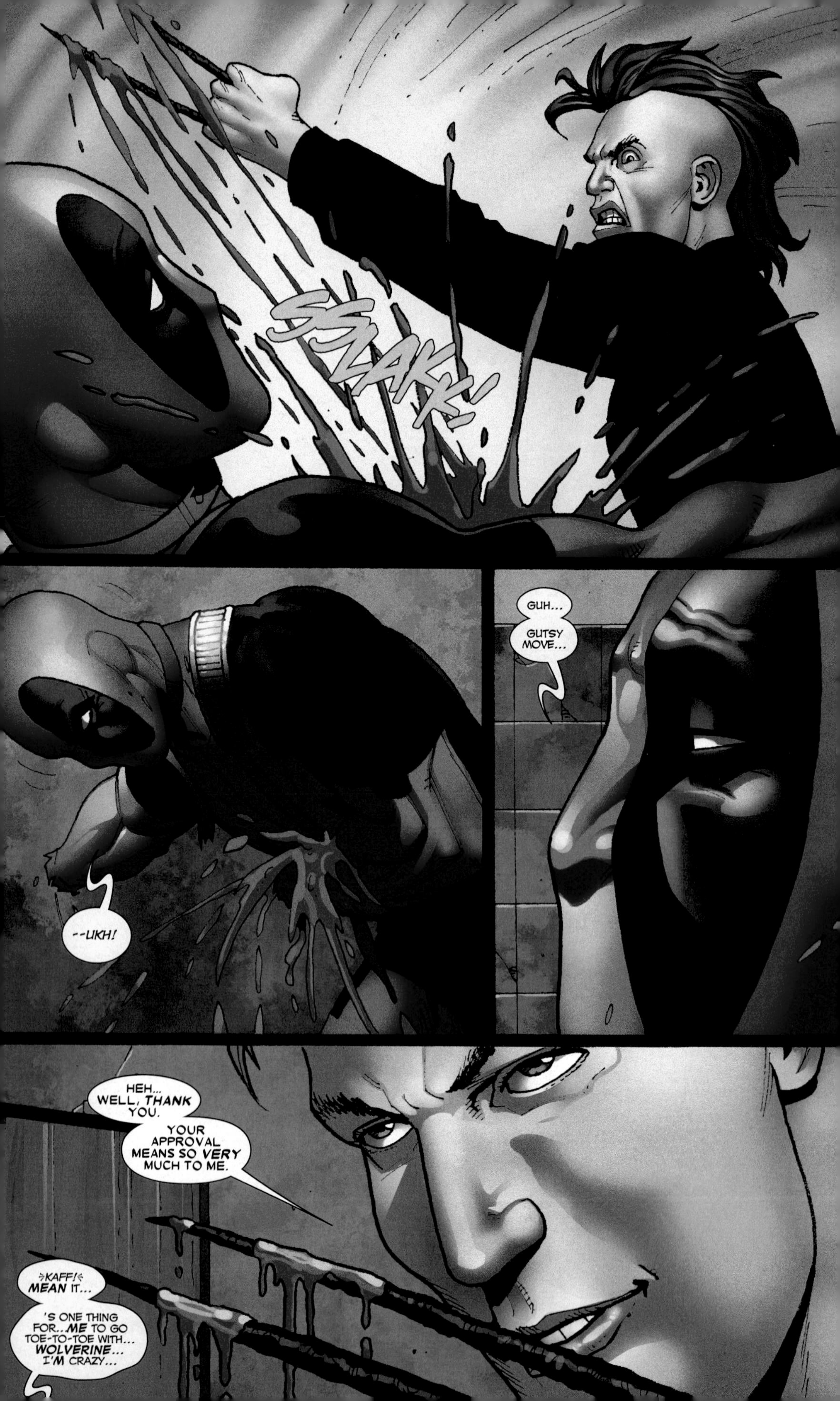
SSNAKK!
--UKH!
GUH...
GUTSY MOVE...
HEH... WELL, THANK YOU.
YOUR APPROVAL MEANS SO VERY MUCH TO ME.
»KAFF!« MEAN IT...
'S ONE THING FOR..ME TO GO TOE-TO-TOE WITH... WOLVERINE... I'M CRAZY...

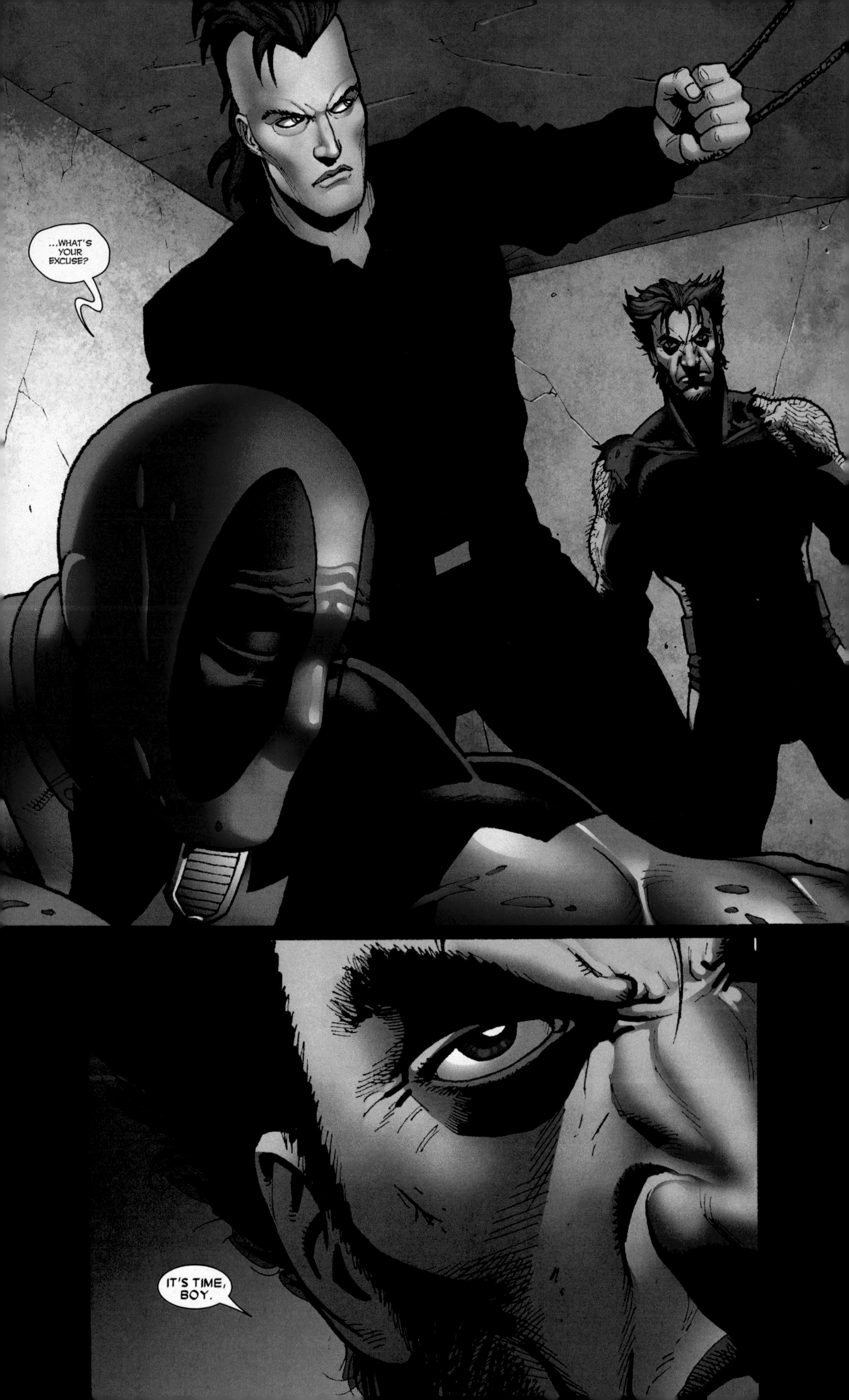
...WHAT'S YOUR EXCUSE?
IT'S TIME, BOY.

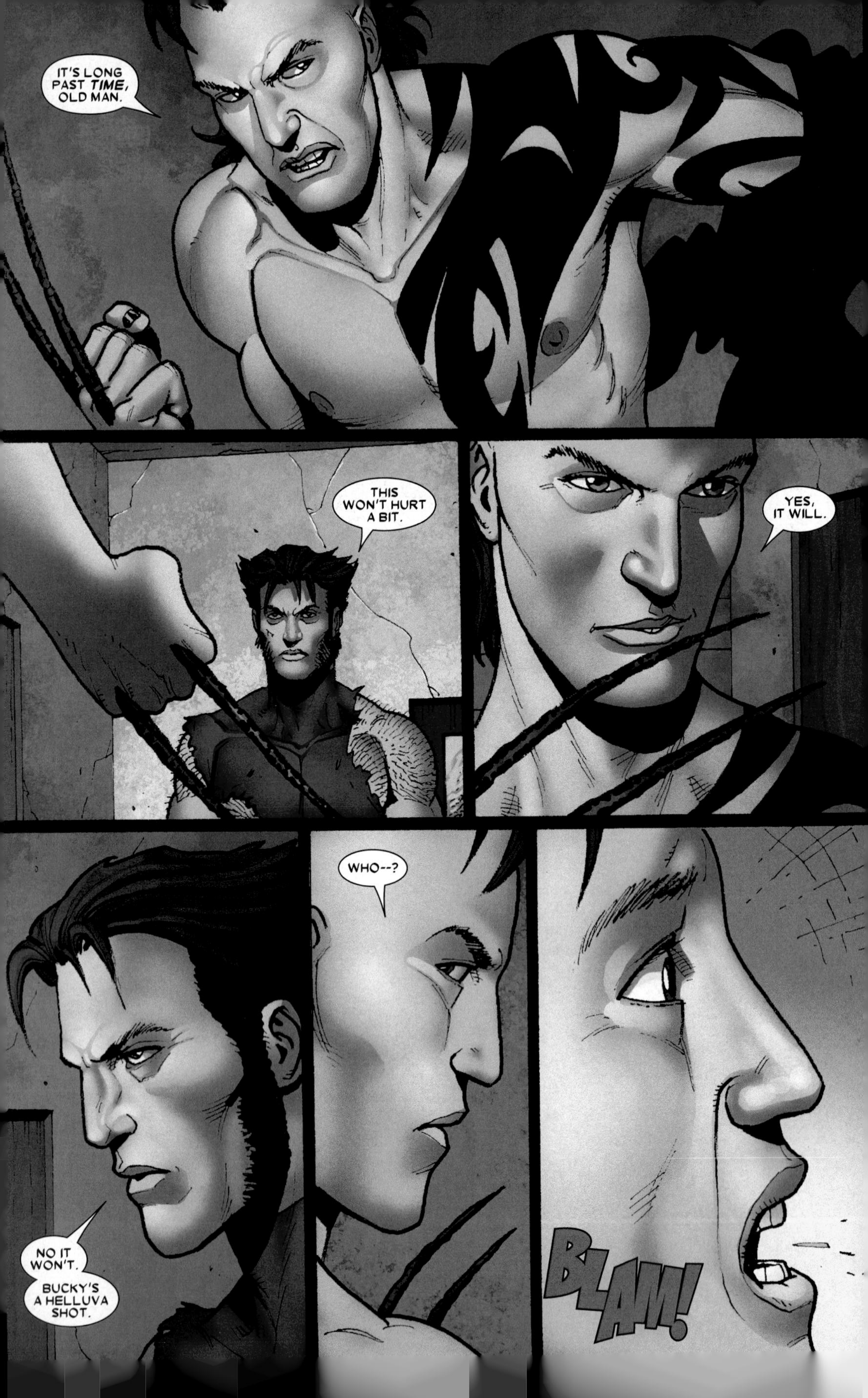
IT'S LONG PAST TIME, OLD MAN.
THIS WON'T HURT A BIT.
YES, IT WILL.
NO IT WON'T.
BUCKY'S A HELLUVA SHOT.
WHO--?
BLAM!

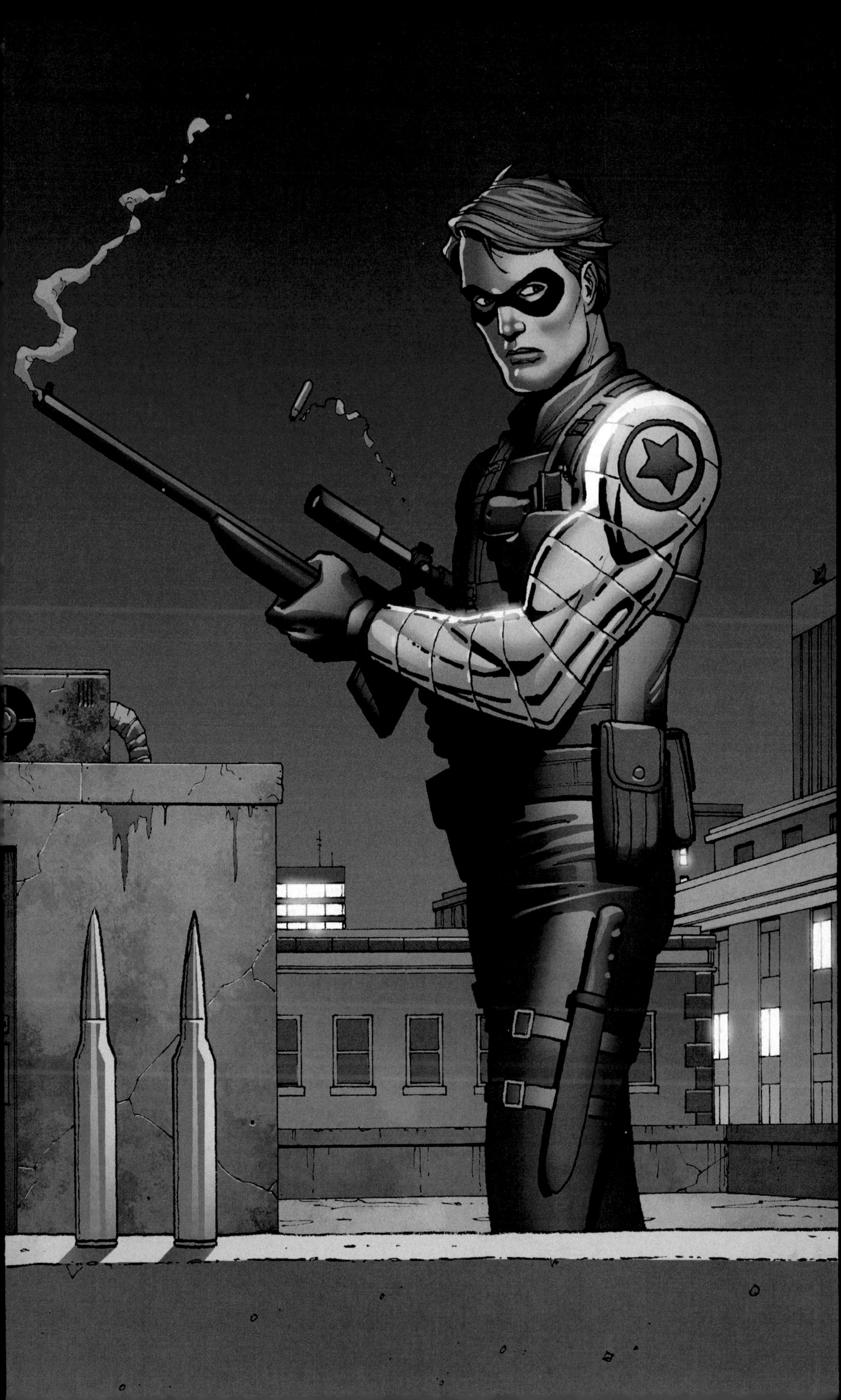

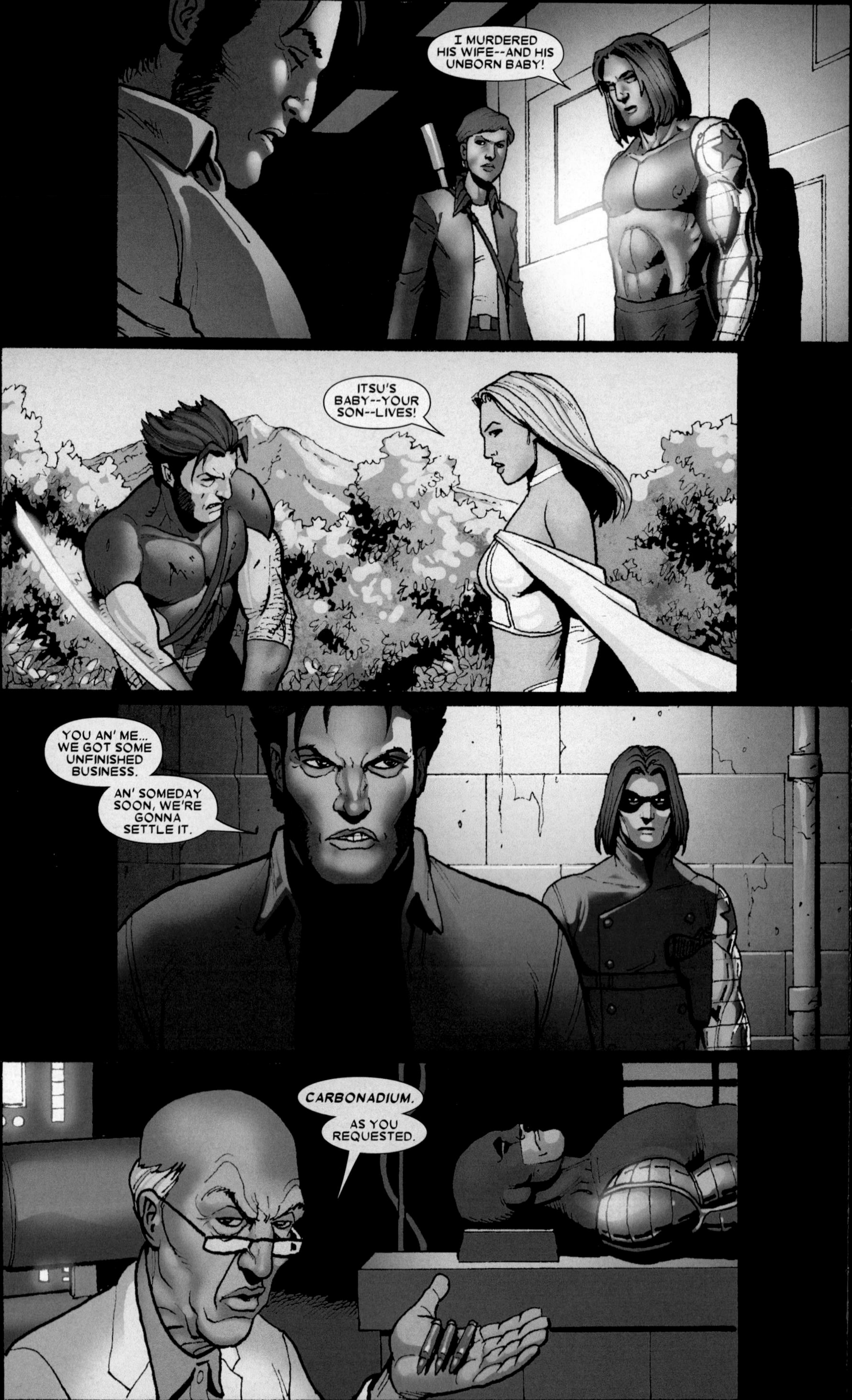
I MURDERED HIS WIFE--AND HIS UNBORN BABY!
ITSU'S BABY--YOUR SON--LIVES!
YOU AN' ME... WE GOT SOME UNFINISHED BUSINESS.
AN' SOMEDAY SOON, WE'RE GONNA SETTLE IT.
CARBONADIUM.
AS YOU REQUESTED.

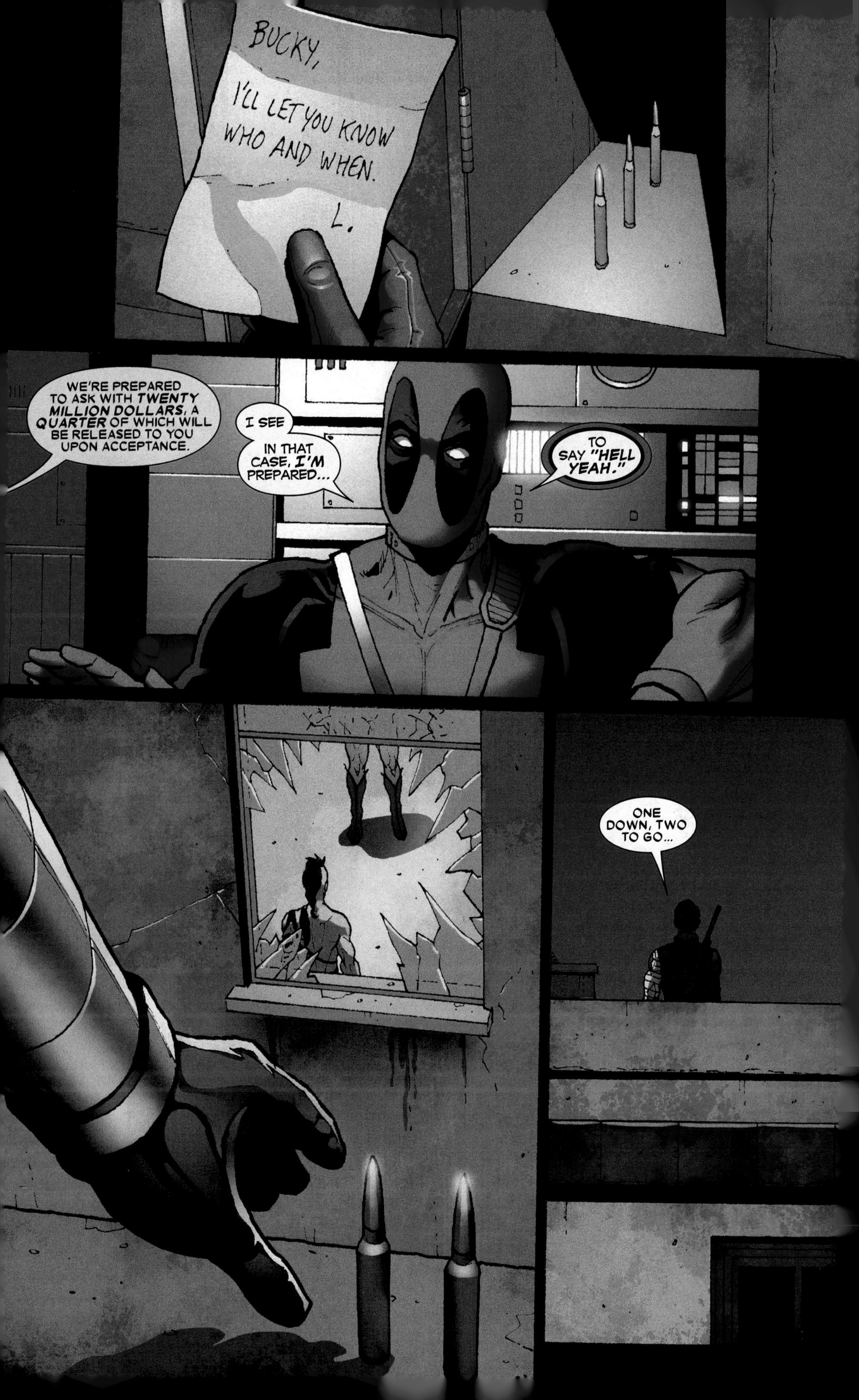
BUCKY,
I'LL LET YOU KNOW WHO AND WHEN.
L.
WE'RE PREPARED TO ASK WITH TWENTY MILLION DOLLARS, A QUARTER OF WHICH WILL BE RELEASED TO YOU UPON ACCEPTANCE.
I SEE
IN THAT CASE, I'M PREPARED...
TO SAY "HELL YEAH."
ONE DOWN, TWO TO GO...

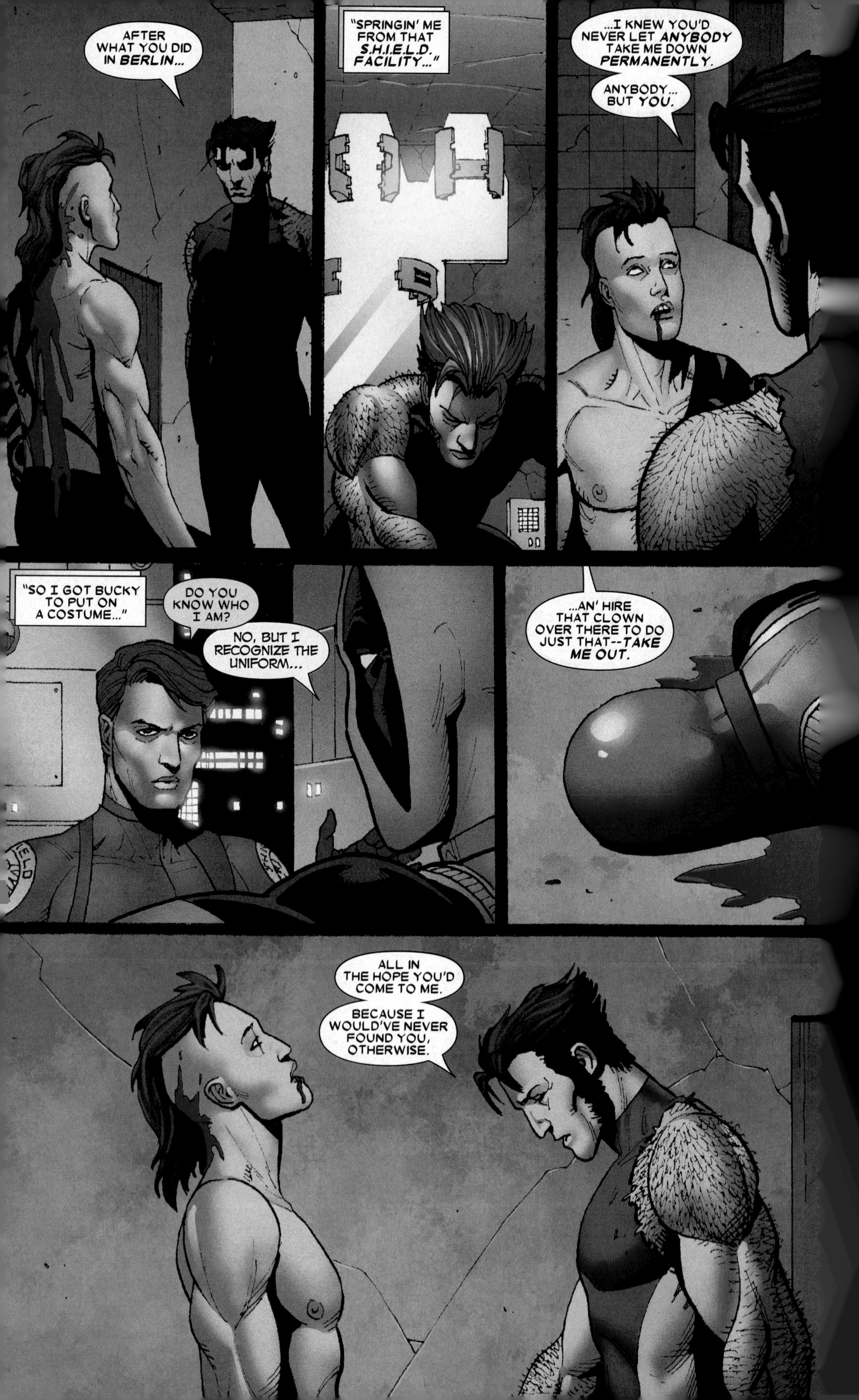
AFTER WHAT YOU DID IN BERLIN...
"SPRINGIN' ME FROM THAT S.H.I.E.L.D. FACILITY..."
...I KNEW YOU'D NEVER LET ANYBODY TAKE ME DOWN PERMANENTLY.
ANYBODY... BUT YOU.
"SO I GOT BUCKY TO PUT ON A COSTUME..."
DO YOU KNOW WHO I AM?
NO, BUT I RECOGNIZE THE UNIFORM...
...AN' HIRE THAT CLOWN OVER THERE TO DO JUST THAT--TAKE ME OUT.
ALL IN THE HOPE YOU'D COME TO ME.
BECAUSE I WOULD'VE NEVER FOUND YOU, OTHERWISE.

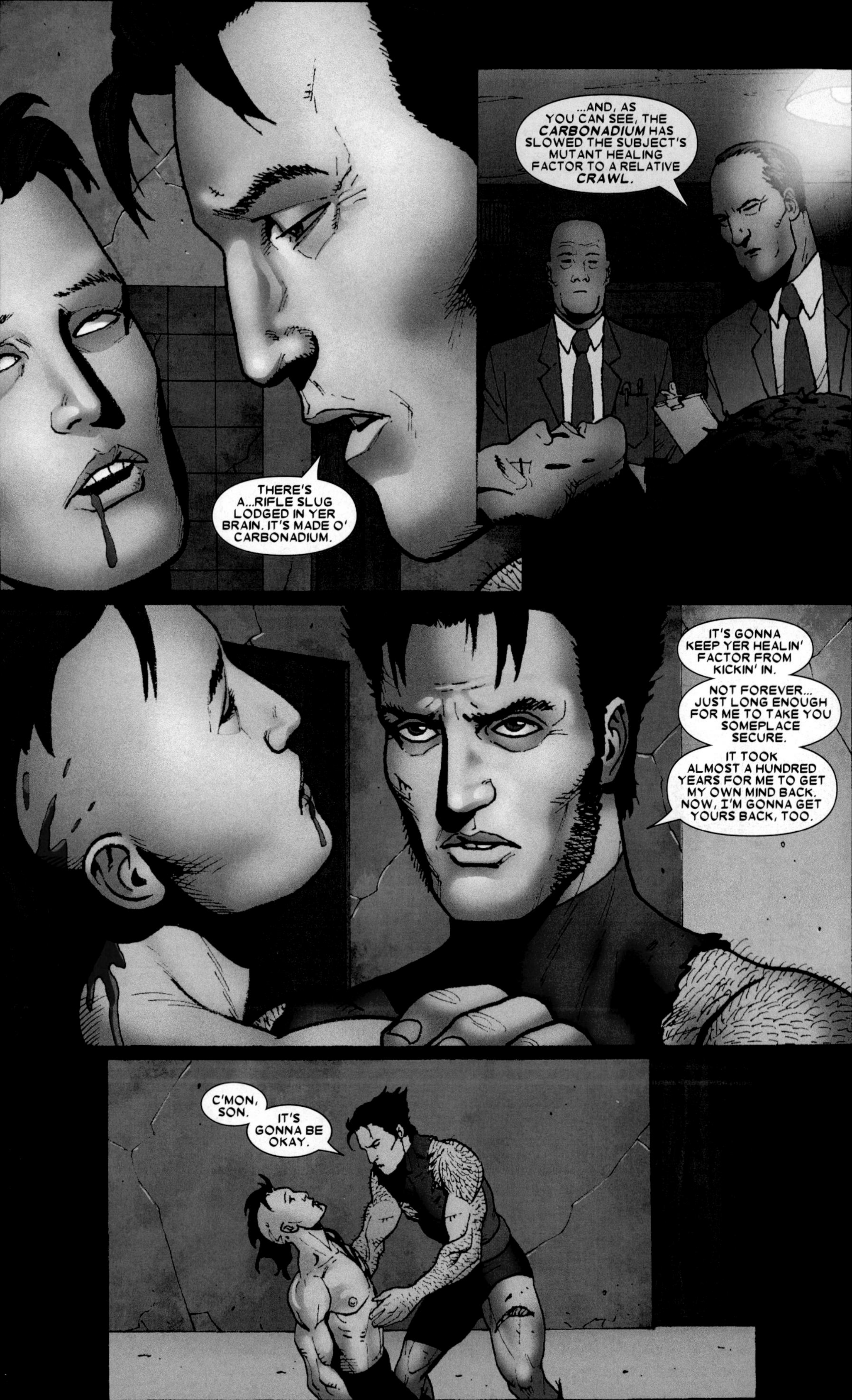
...AND, AS YOU CAN SEE, THE CARBONADIUM HAS SLOWED THE SUBJECT'S MUTANT HEALING FACTOR TO A RELATIVE CRAWL.
THERE'S A...RIFLE SLUG LODGED IN YER BRAIN. IT'S MADE O' CARBONADIUM.
IT'S GONNA KEEP YER HEALIN' FACTOR FROM KICKIN' IN.
NOT FOREVER... JUST LONG ENOUGH FOR ME TO TAKE YOU SOMEPLACE SECURE.
IT TOOK ALMOST A HUNDRED YEARS FOR ME TO GET MY OWN MIND BACK. NOW, I'M GONNA GET YOURS BACK, TOO.
C'MON, SON.
IT'S GONNA BE OKAY.

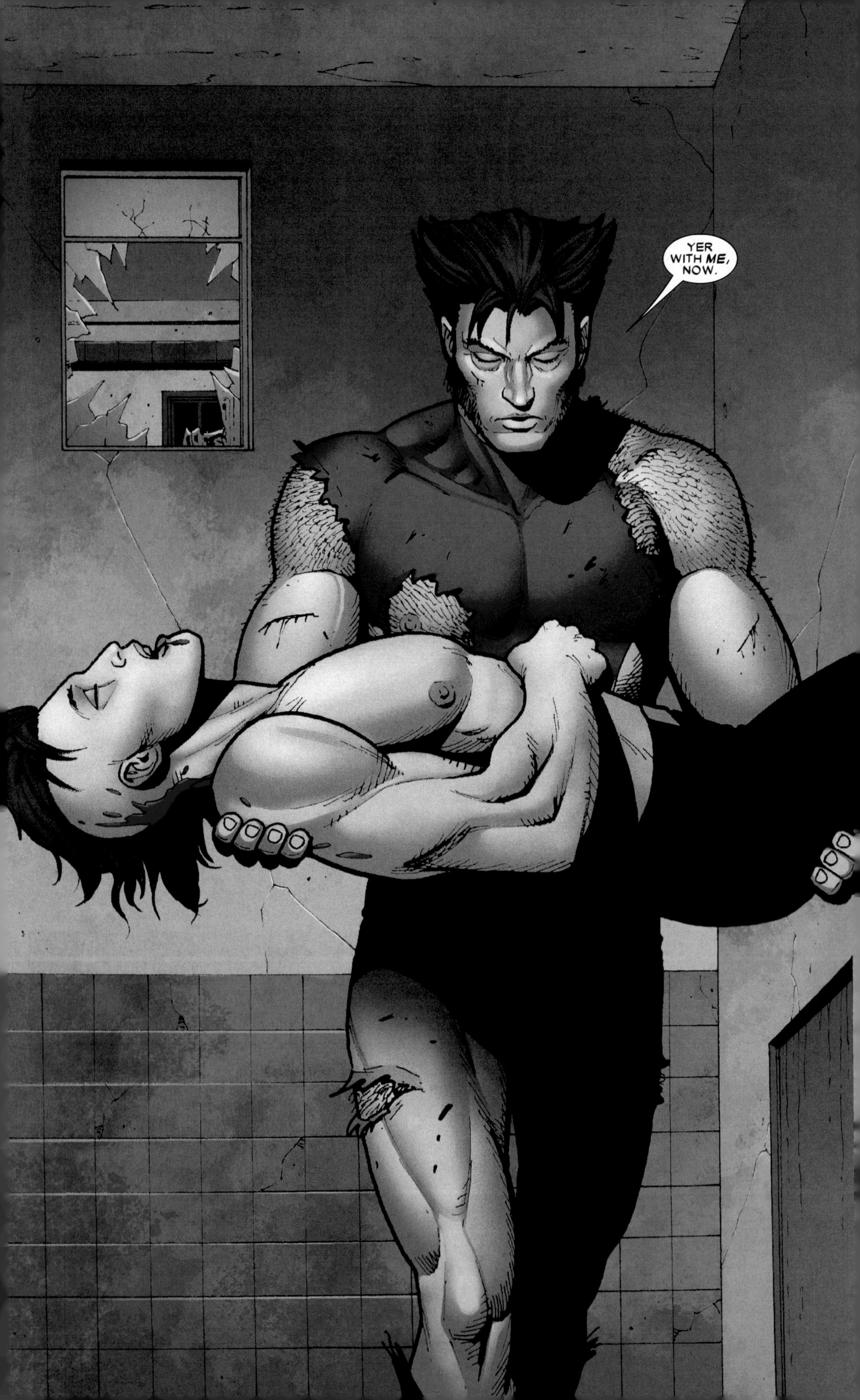
YER WITH ME, NOW.

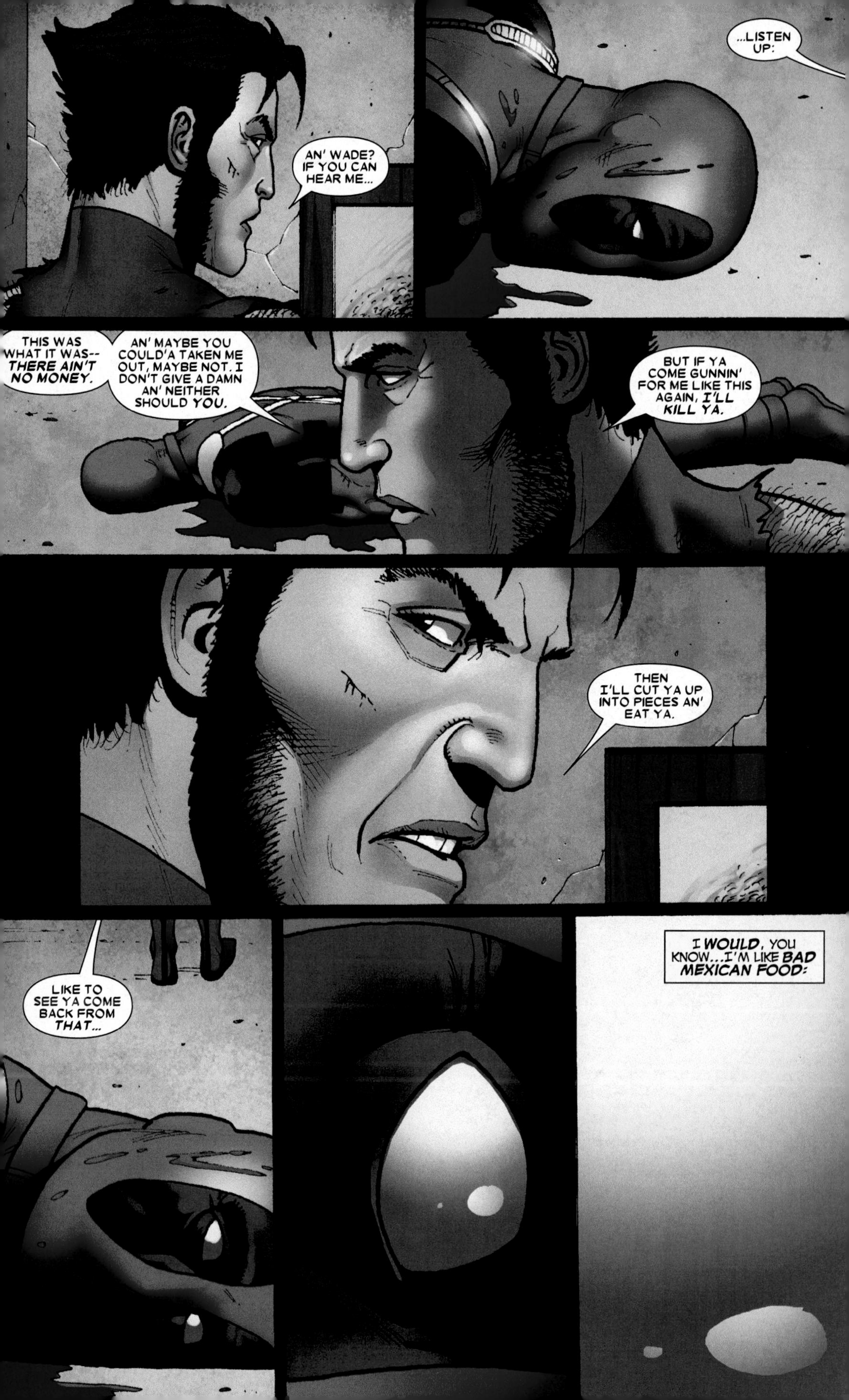
AN' WADE? IF YOU CAN HEAR ME...
...LISTEN UP:
THIS WAS WHAT IT WAS-- *THERE AIN'T NO MONEY.*
AN' MAYBE YOU COULD'A TAKEN ME OUT, MAYBE NOT. I DON'T GIVE A DAMN AN' NEITHER SHOULD *YOU.*
BUT IF YA COME GUNNIN' FOR ME LIKE THIS AGAIN, *I'LL KILL YA.*
THEN I'LL CUT YA UP INTO PIECES AN' EAT YA.
LIKE TO SEE YA COME BACK FROM *THAT...*
I *WOULD*, YOU KNOW...I'M LIKE *BAD MEXICAN FOOD:*

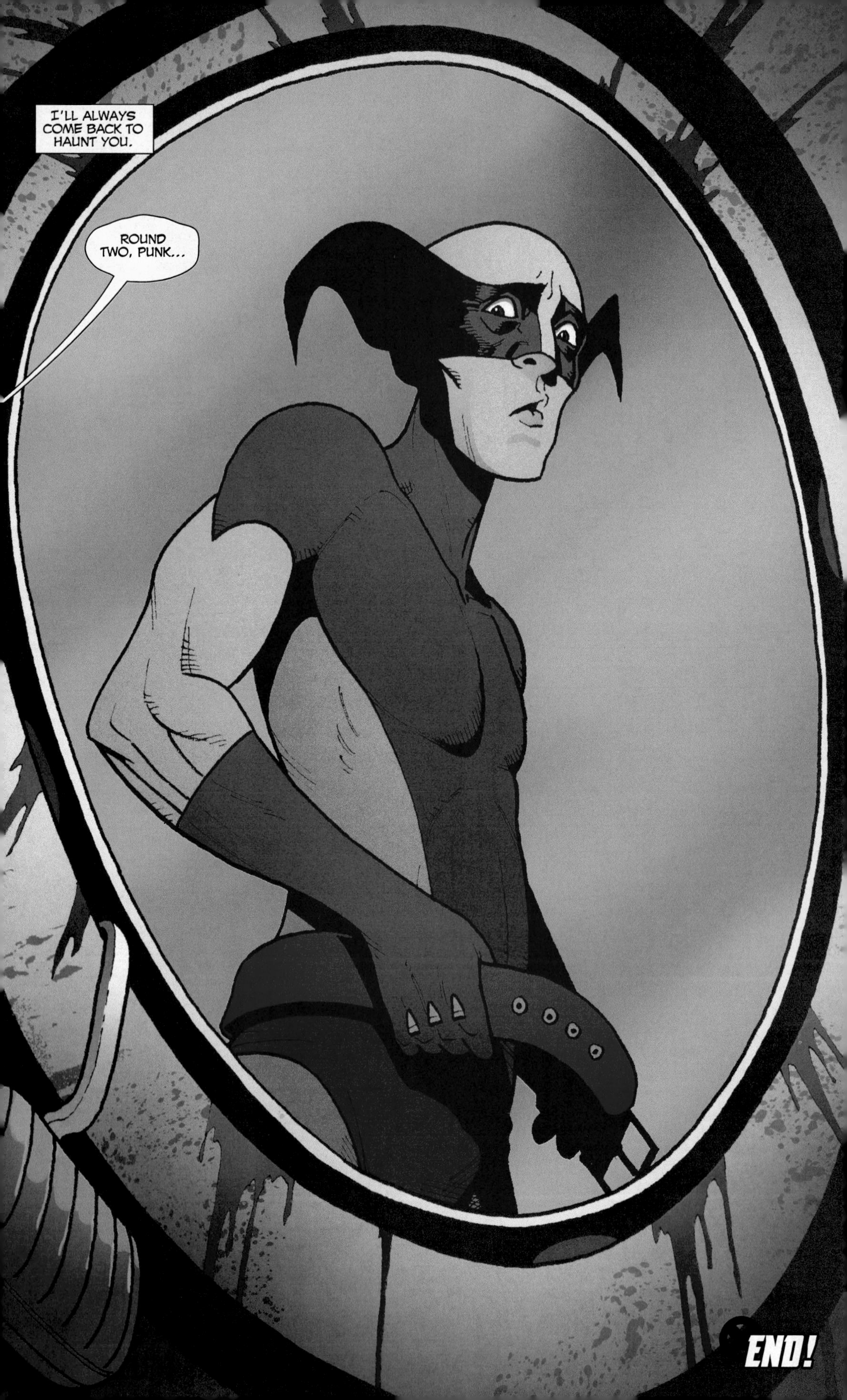
I'LL ALWAYS COME BACK TO HAUNT YOU.
ROUND TWO, PUNK...
END!

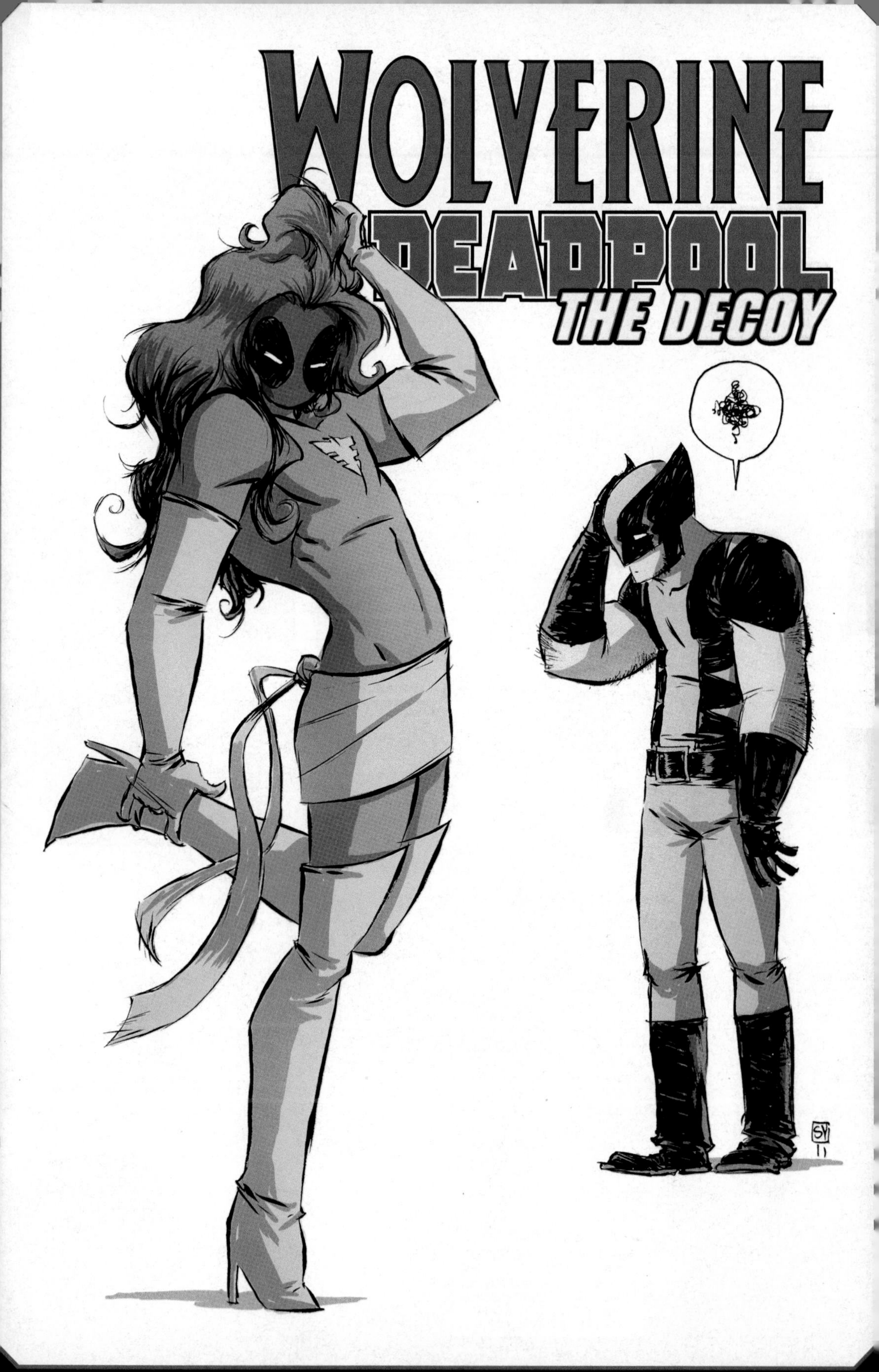
WOLVERINE
DEADPOOL
THE DECOY

writer: **Stuart Moore** • artist: **Shawn Crystal** • colorist: **John Rauch** • letterer: **Jeff Eckleberry** • cover artist: **Skottie Young** • editor: **Sebastian Girner**
vp of digital content & programming: **John Cerilli** • associate producer: **Harry Go** • digital production manager: **Tim Smith 3**

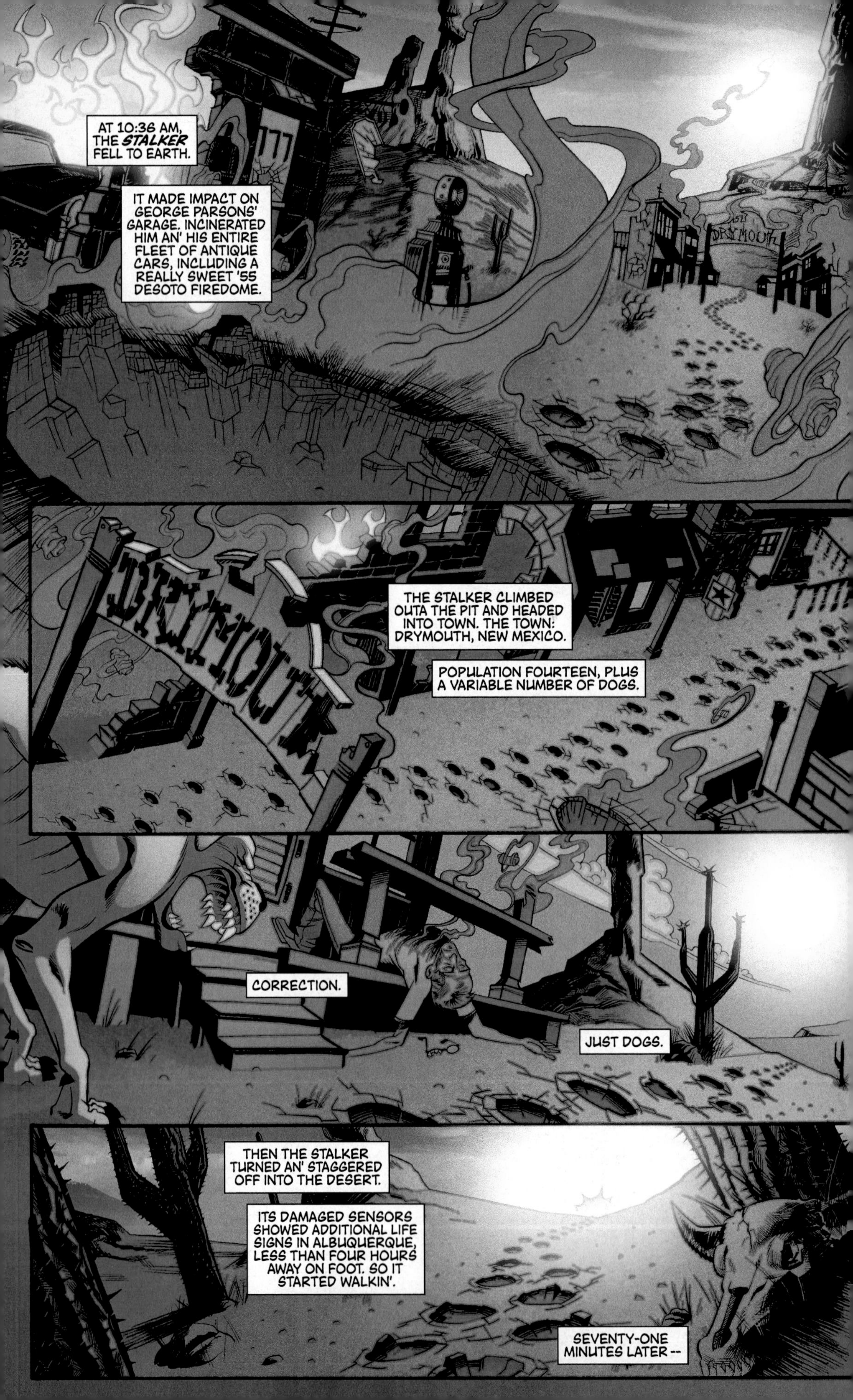

AT 10:36 AM, THE STALKER FELL TO EARTH.
IT MADE IMPACT ON GEORGE PARSONS' GARAGE. INCINERATED HIM AN' HIS ENTIRE FLEET OF ANTIQUE CARS, INCLUDING A REALLY SWEET '55 DESOTO FIREDOME.
DRYMOUTH
THE STALKER CLIMBED OUTA THE PIT AND HEADED INTO TOWN. THE TOWN: DRYMOUTH, NEW MEXICO.
POPULATION FOURTEEN, PLUS A VARIABLE NUMBER OF DOGS.
CORRECTION.
JUST DOGS.
THEN THE STALKER TURNED AN' STAGGERED OFF INTO THE DESERT.
ITS DAMAGED SENSORS SHOWED ADDITIONAL LIFE SIGNS IN ALBUQUERQUE, LESS THAN FOUR HOURS AWAY ON FOOT. SO IT STARTED WALKIN'.
SEVENTY-ONE MINUTES LATER --

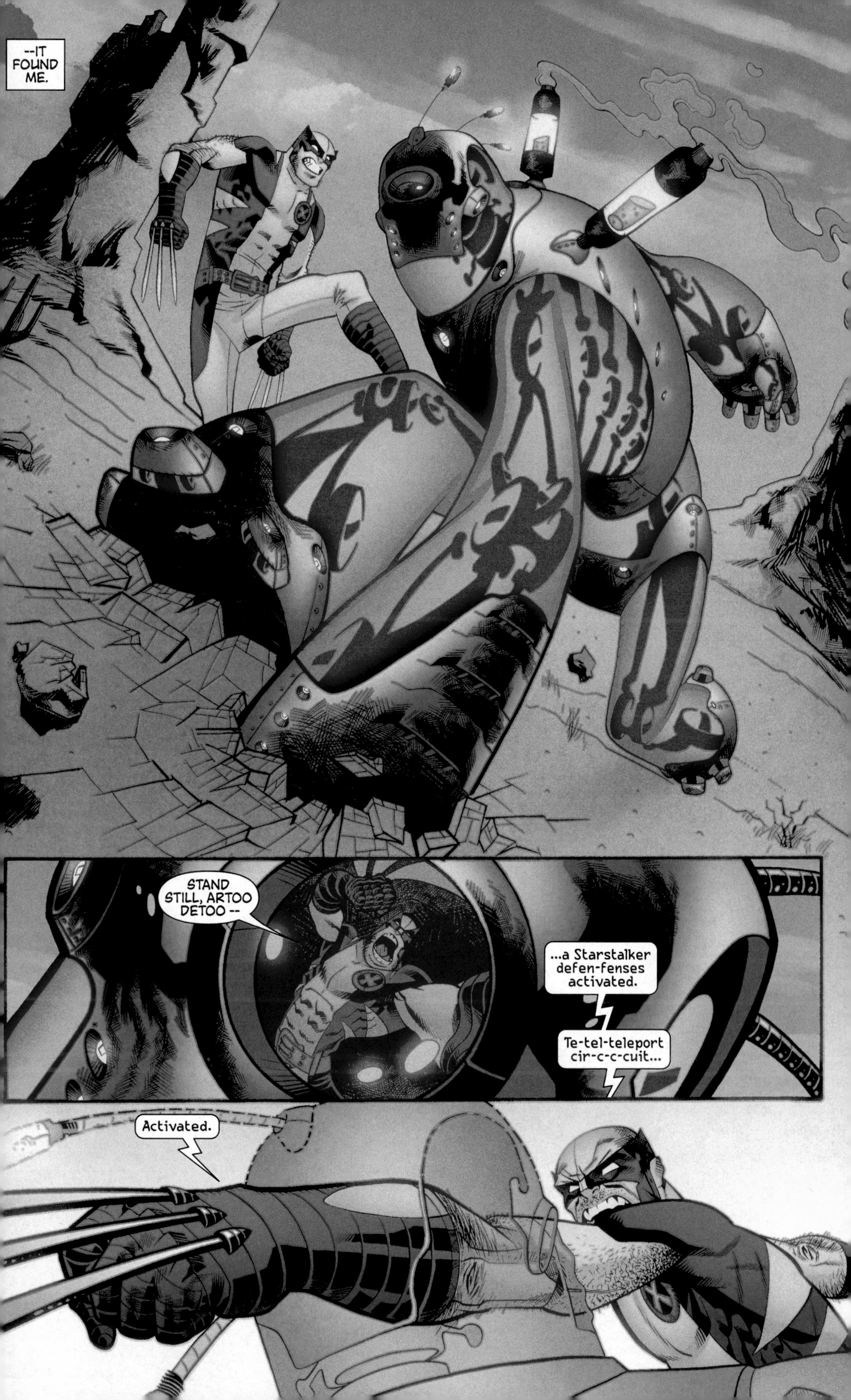
--IT FOUND ME.
STAND STILL, ARTOO DETOO --
...a Starstalker defen-fenses activated.
Te-tel-teleport cir-c-c-cuit...
Activated.

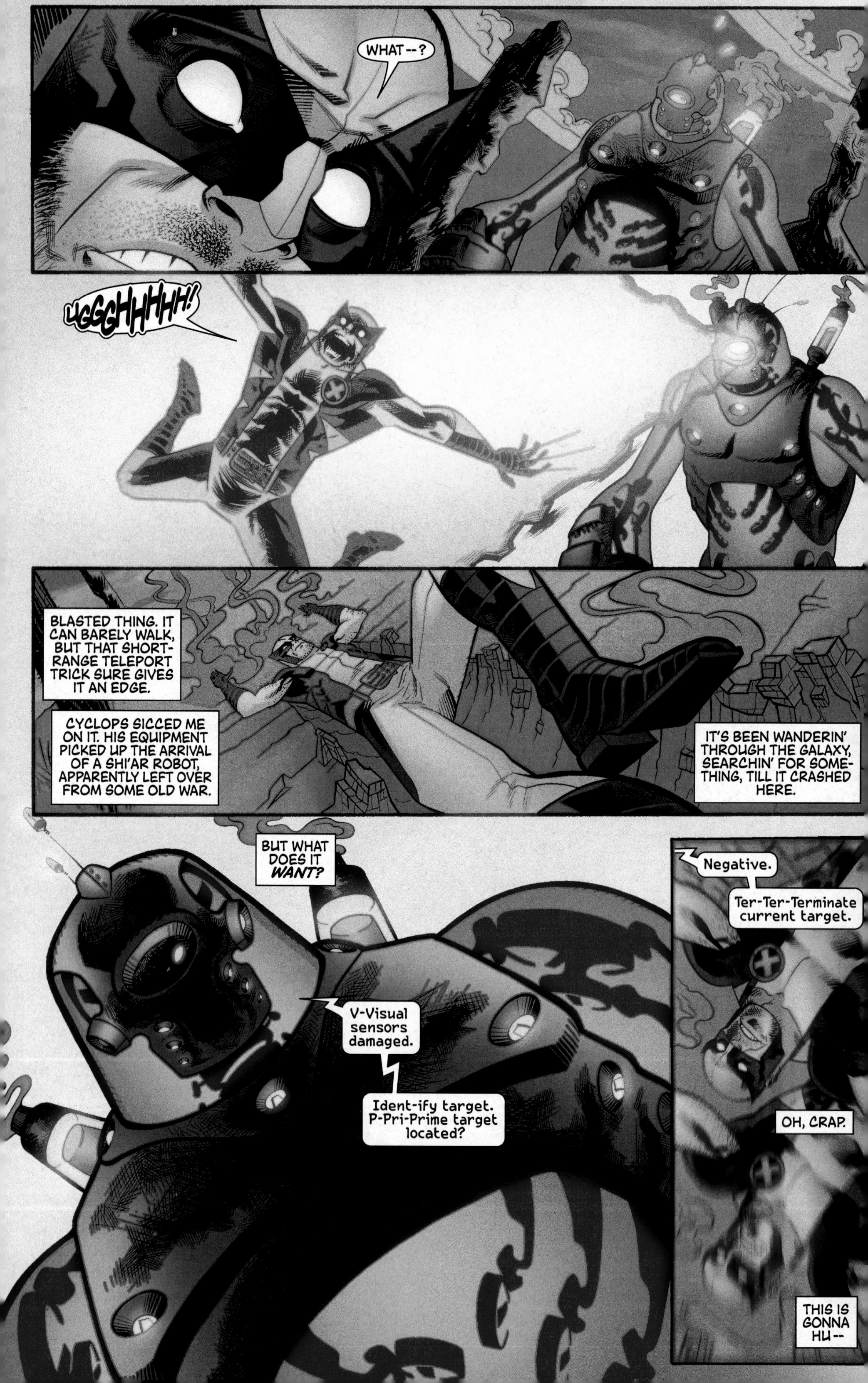
WHAT--?
UGGGHHHHH!
BLASTED THING. IT CAN BARELY WALK, BUT THAT SHORT-RANGE TELEPORT TRICK SURE GIVES IT AN EDGE.
CYCLOPS SICCED ME ON IT. HIS EQUIPMENT PICKED UP THE ARRIVAL OF A SHI'AR ROBOT, APPARENTLY LEFT OVER FROM SOME OLD WAR.
IT'S BEEN WANDERIN' THROUGH THE GALAXY, SEARCHIN' FOR SOME-THING, TILL IT CRASHED HERE.
BUT WHAT DOES IT *WANT?*
V-Visual sensors damaged.
Ident-ify target. P-Pri-Prime target located?
Negative.
Ter-Ter-Terminate current target.
OH, CRAP.
THIS IS GONNA HU--

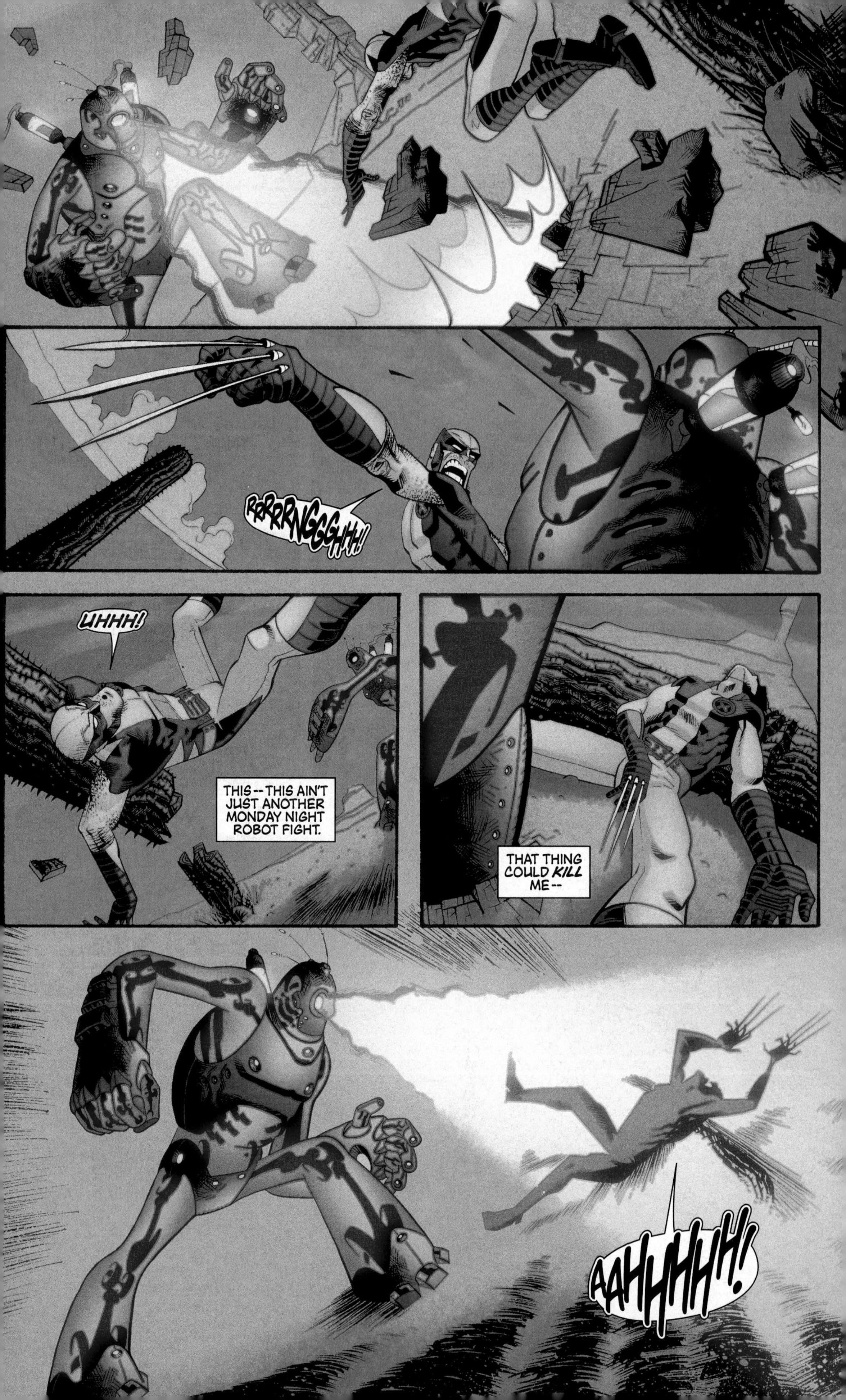
RRRRRNGGGHHH!
UHHH!
THIS -- THIS AIN'T JUST ANOTHER MONDAY NIGHT ROBOT FIGHT.
THAT THING COULD *KILL* ME --
AAHHHHH!

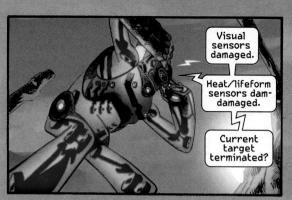

Visual sensors damaged.

Heat/lifeform sensors dam-damaged.

Current target terminated?

Probability 86%

Acceptab-b-b-ble.

Continue search for primary tar-target.

For Jean Grey.

I DON'T BELIEVE IT. *JEAN?*

SHE WAS A FELLOW X-MAN -- AN' I LOVED HER WITH ALL MY HEART. DON'T THINK I EVER GOT OVER HER...

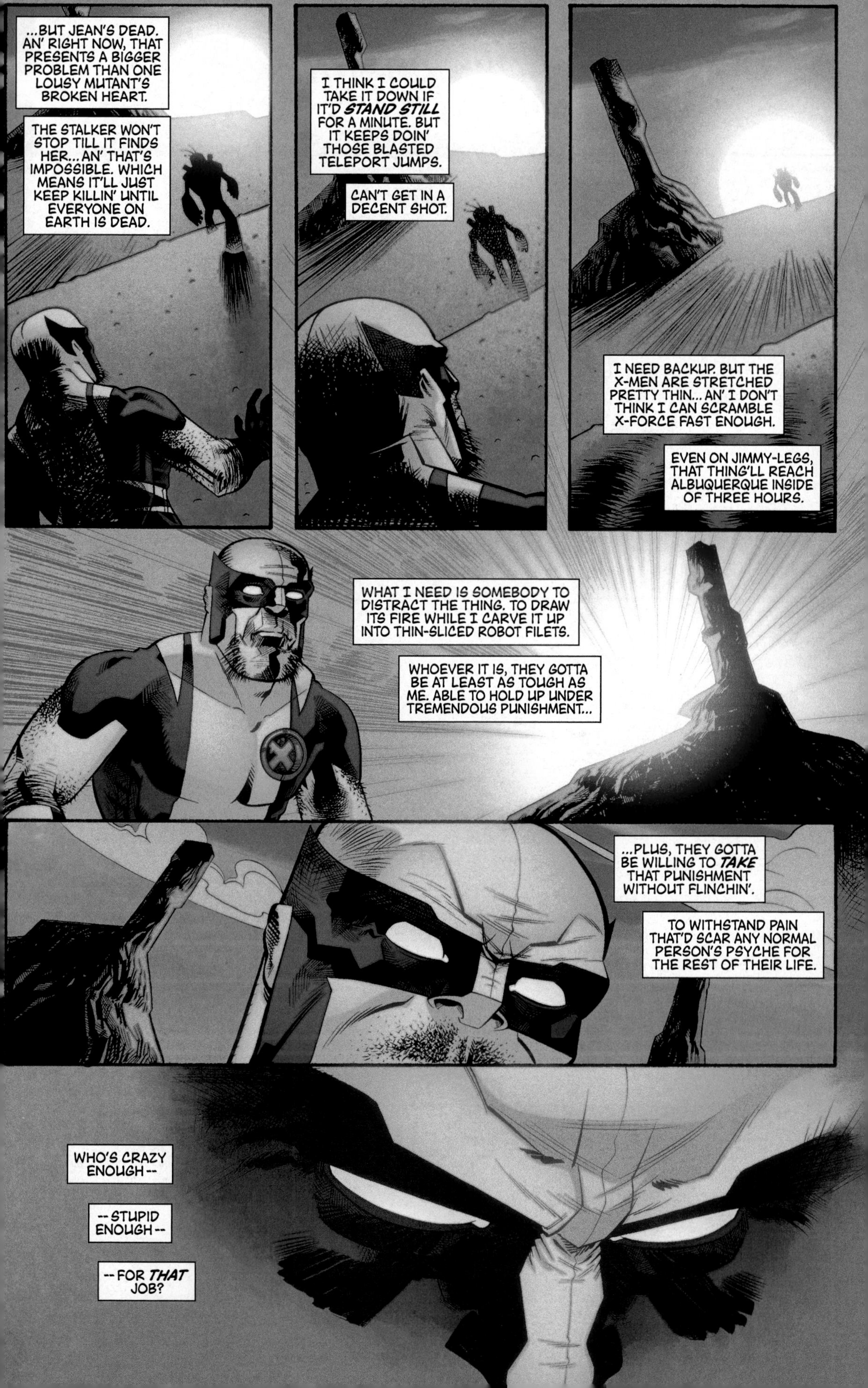
...BUT JEAN'S DEAD. AN' RIGHT NOW, THAT PRESENTS A BIGGER PROBLEM THAN ONE LOUSY MUTANT'S BROKEN HEART.
THE STALKER WON'T STOP TILL IT FINDS HER... AN' THAT'S IMPOSSIBLE. WHICH MEANS IT'LL JUST KEEP KILLIN' UNTIL EVERYONE ON EARTH IS DEAD.
I THINK I COULD TAKE IT DOWN IF IT'D STAND STILL FOR A MINUTE. BUT IT KEEPS DOIN' THOSE BLASTED TELEPORT JUMPS.
CAN'T GET IN A DECENT SHOT.
I NEED BACKUP. BUT THE X-MEN ARE STRETCHED PRETTY THIN... AN' I DON'T THINK I CAN SCRAMBLE X-FORCE FAST ENOUGH.
EVEN ON JIMMY-LEGS, THAT THING'LL REACH ALBUQUERQUE INSIDE OF THREE HOURS.
WHAT I NEED IS SOMEBODY TO DISTRACT THE THING. TO DRAW ITS FIRE WHILE I CARVE IT UP INTO THIN-SLICED ROBOT FILETS.
WHOEVER IT IS, THEY GOTTA BE AT LEAST AS TOUGH AS ME. ABLE TO HOLD UP UNDER TREMENDOUS PUNISHMENT...
...PLUS, THEY GOTTA BE WILLING TO TAKE THAT PUNISHMENT WITHOUT FLINCHIN'.
TO WITHSTAND PAIN THAT'D SCAR ANY NORMAL PERSON'S PSYCHE FOR THE REST OF THEIR LIFE.
WHO'S CRAZY ENOUGH --
-- STUPID ENOUGH --
-- FOR THAT JOB?

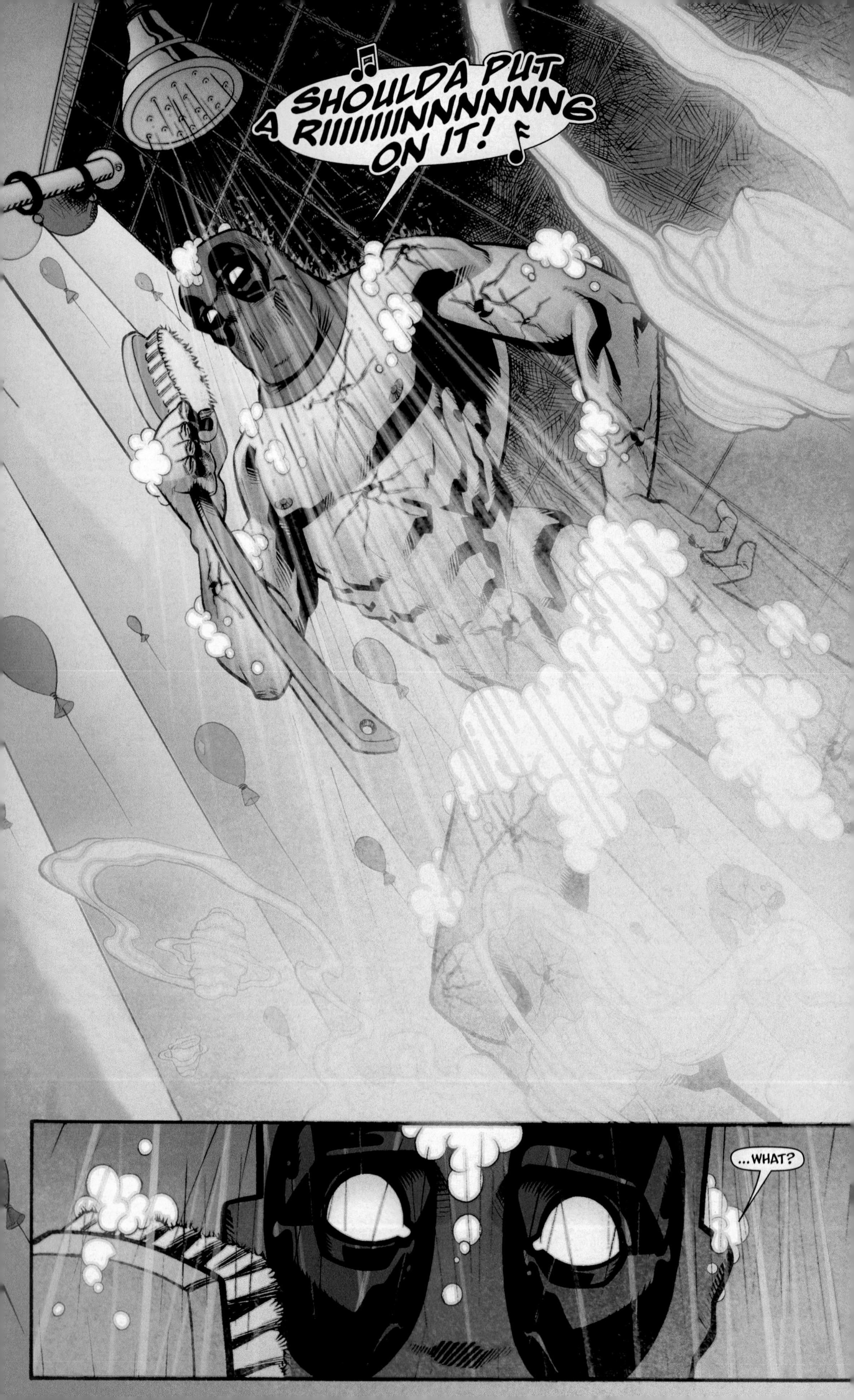
SHOULDA PUT A RIIIIIIIIINNNNNNG ON IT!
...WHAT?

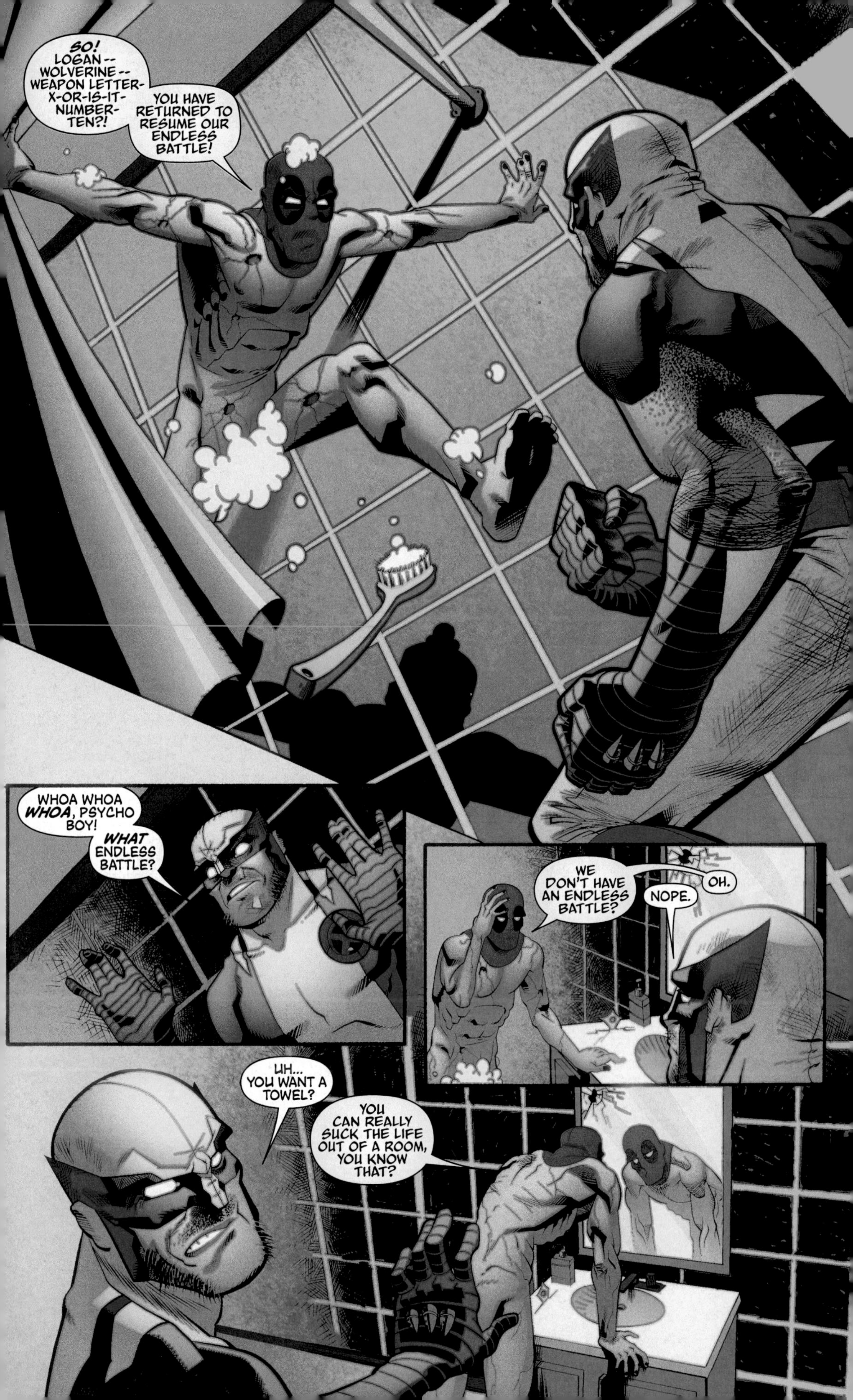
SO! LOGAN -- WOLVERINE -- WEAPON LETTER-X-OR-IS-IT-NUMBER-TEN?!
YOU HAVE RETURNED TO RESUME OUR ENDLESS BATTLE!
WHOA WHOA WHOA, PSYCHO BOY! WHAT ENDLESS BATTLE?
WE DON'T HAVE AN ENDLESS BATTLE?
NOPE.
OH.
UH... YOU WANT A TOWEL?
YOU CAN REALLY SUCK THE LIFE OUT OF A ROOM, YOU KNOW THAT?

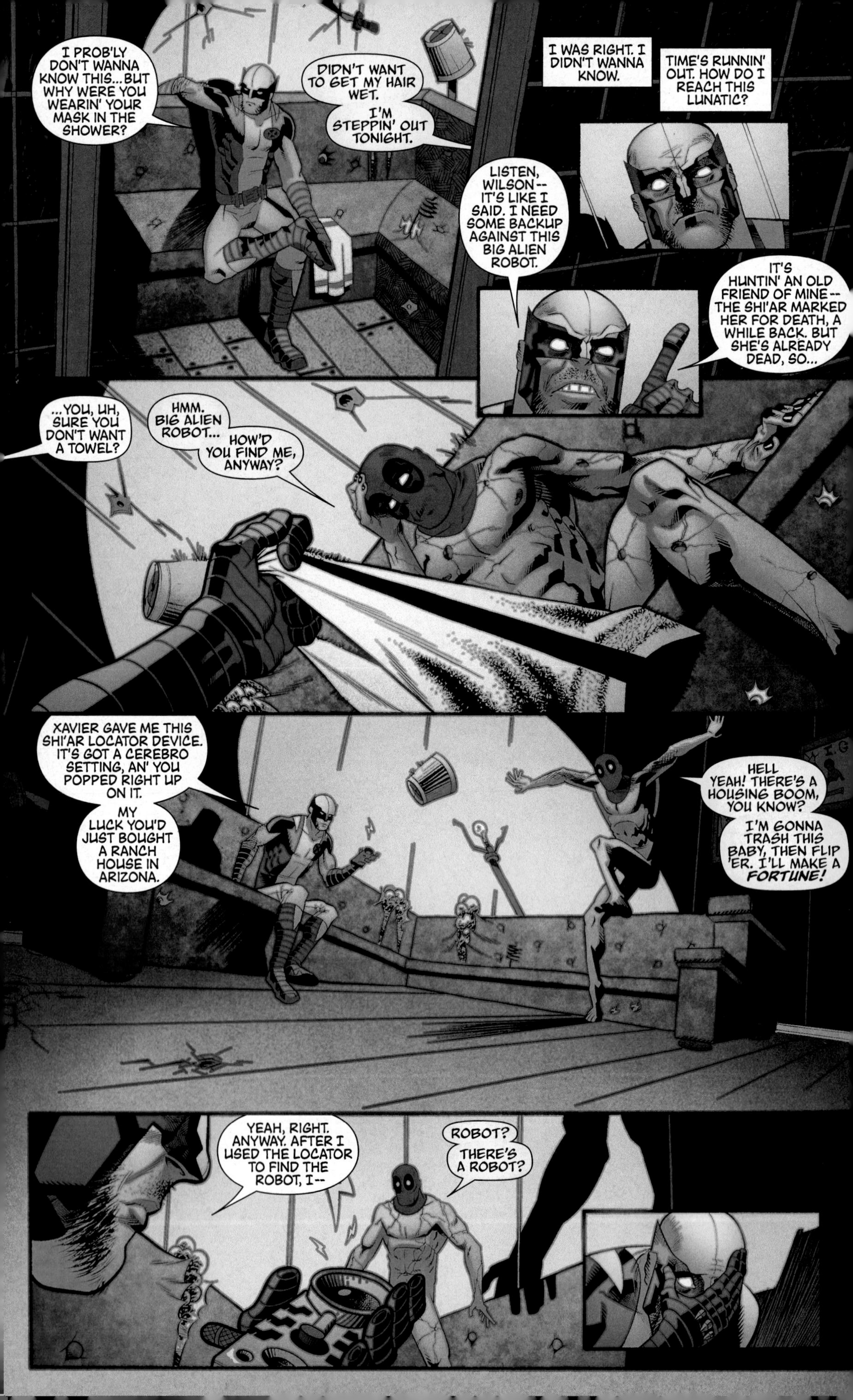
I PROB'LY DON'T WANNA KNOW THIS...BUT WHY WERE YOU WEARIN' YOUR MASK IN THE SHOWER?
DIDN'T WANT TO GET MY HAIR WET.
I'M STEPPIN' OUT TONIGHT.
I WAS RIGHT. I DIDN'T WANNA KNOW.
TIME'S RUNNIN' OUT. HOW DO I REACH THIS LUNATIC?
LISTEN, WILSON-- IT'S LIKE I SAID. I NEED SOME BACKUP AGAINST THIS BIG ALIEN ROBOT.
IT'S HUNTIN' AN OLD FRIEND OF MINE-- THE SHI'AR MARKED HER FOR DEATH, A WHILE BACK. BUT SHE'S ALREADY DEAD, SO...
...YOU, UH, SURE YOU DON'T WANT A TOWEL?
HMM. BIG ALIEN ROBOT...
HOW'D YOU FIND ME, ANYWAY?
XAVIER GAVE ME THIS SHI'AR LOCATOR DEVICE. IT'S GOT A CEREBRO SETTING, AN' YOU POPPED RIGHT UP ON IT.
MY LUCK YOU'D JUST BOUGHT A RANCH HOUSE IN ARIZONA.
HELL YEAH! THERE'S A HOUSING BOOM, YOU KNOW?
I'M GONNA TRASH THIS BABY, THEN FLIP 'ER. I'LL MAKE A FORTUNE!
YEAH, RIGHT. ANYWAY. AFTER I USED THE LOCATOR TO FIND THE ROBOT, I--
ROBOT?
THERE'S A ROBOT?

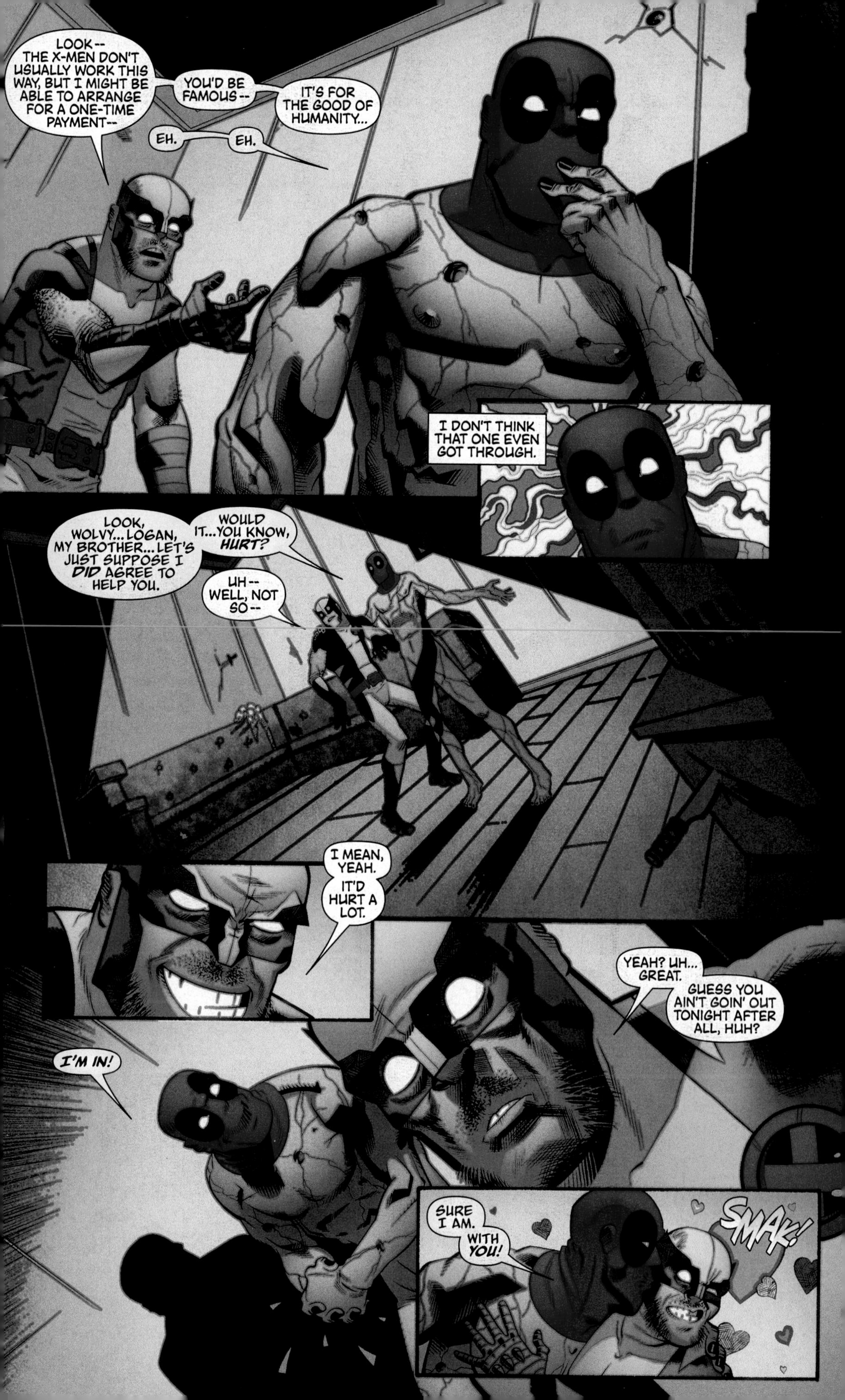
LOOK-- THE X-MEN DON'T USUALLY WORK THIS WAY, BUT I MIGHT BE ABLE TO ARRANGE FOR A ONE-TIME PAYMENT--
YOU'D BE FAMOUS--
IT'S FOR THE GOOD OF HUMANITY...
EH.
EH.
I DON'T THINK THAT ONE EVEN GOT THROUGH.
LOOK, WOLVY... LOGAN, MY BROTHER... LET'S JUST SUPPOSE I DID AGREE TO HELP YOU.
WOULD IT... YOU KNOW, HURT?
UH-- WELL, NOT SO--
I MEAN, YEAH.
IT'D HURT A LOT.
YEAH? UH... GREAT.
GUESS YOU AIN'T GOIN' OUT TONIGHT AFTER ALL, HUH?
I'M IN!
SURE I AM.
WITH YOU!
SMAK!

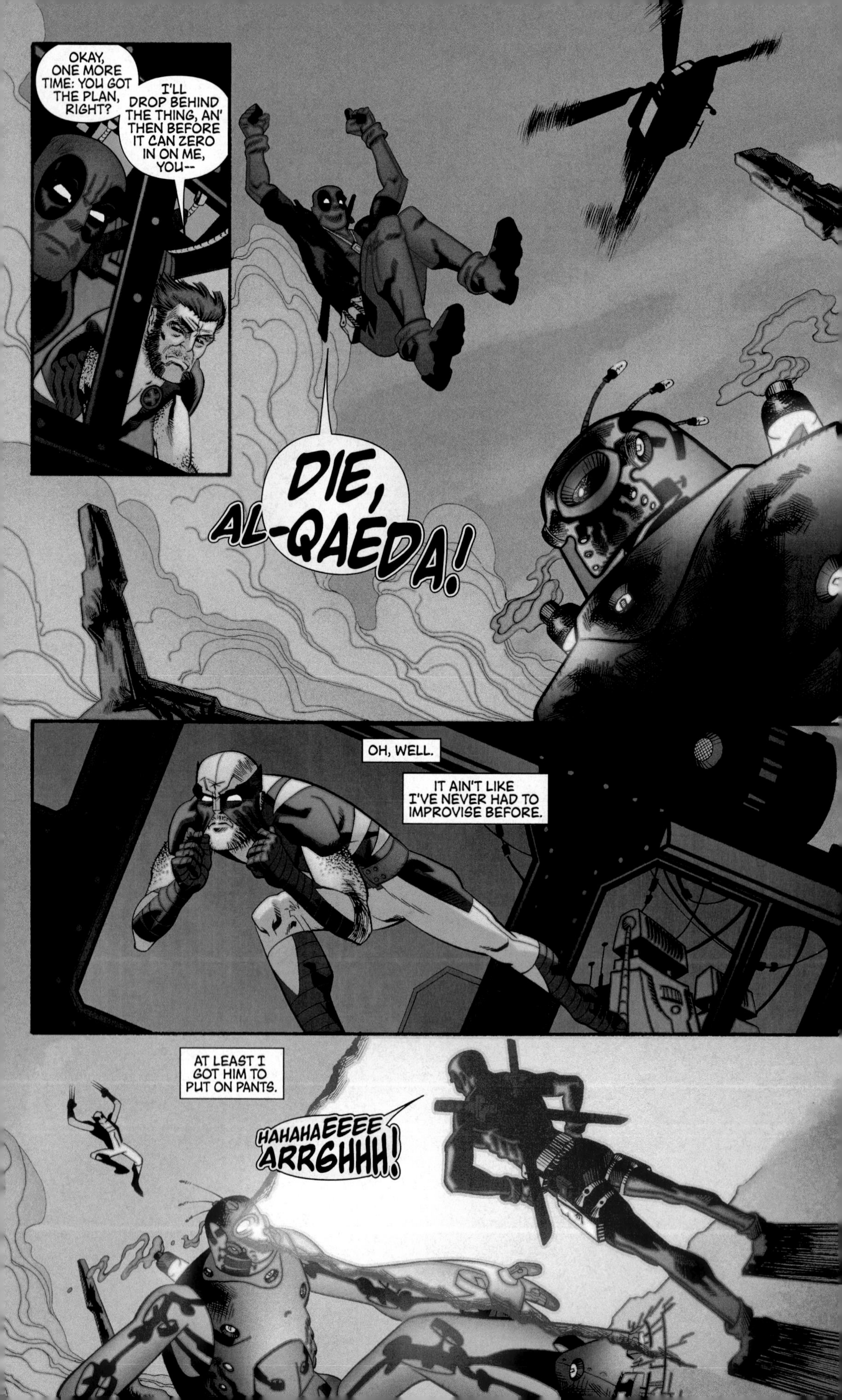
OKAY, ONE MORE TIME: YOU GOT THE PLAN, RIGHT?
I'LL DROP BEHIND THE THING, AN' THEN BEFORE IT CAN ZERO IN ON ME, YOU--
DIE, AL-QAEDA!
OH, WELL.
IT AIN'T LIKE I'VE NEVER HAD TO IMPROVISE BEFORE.
AT LEAST I GOT HIM TO PUT ON PANTS.
HAHAHAEEEE ARRGHHH!

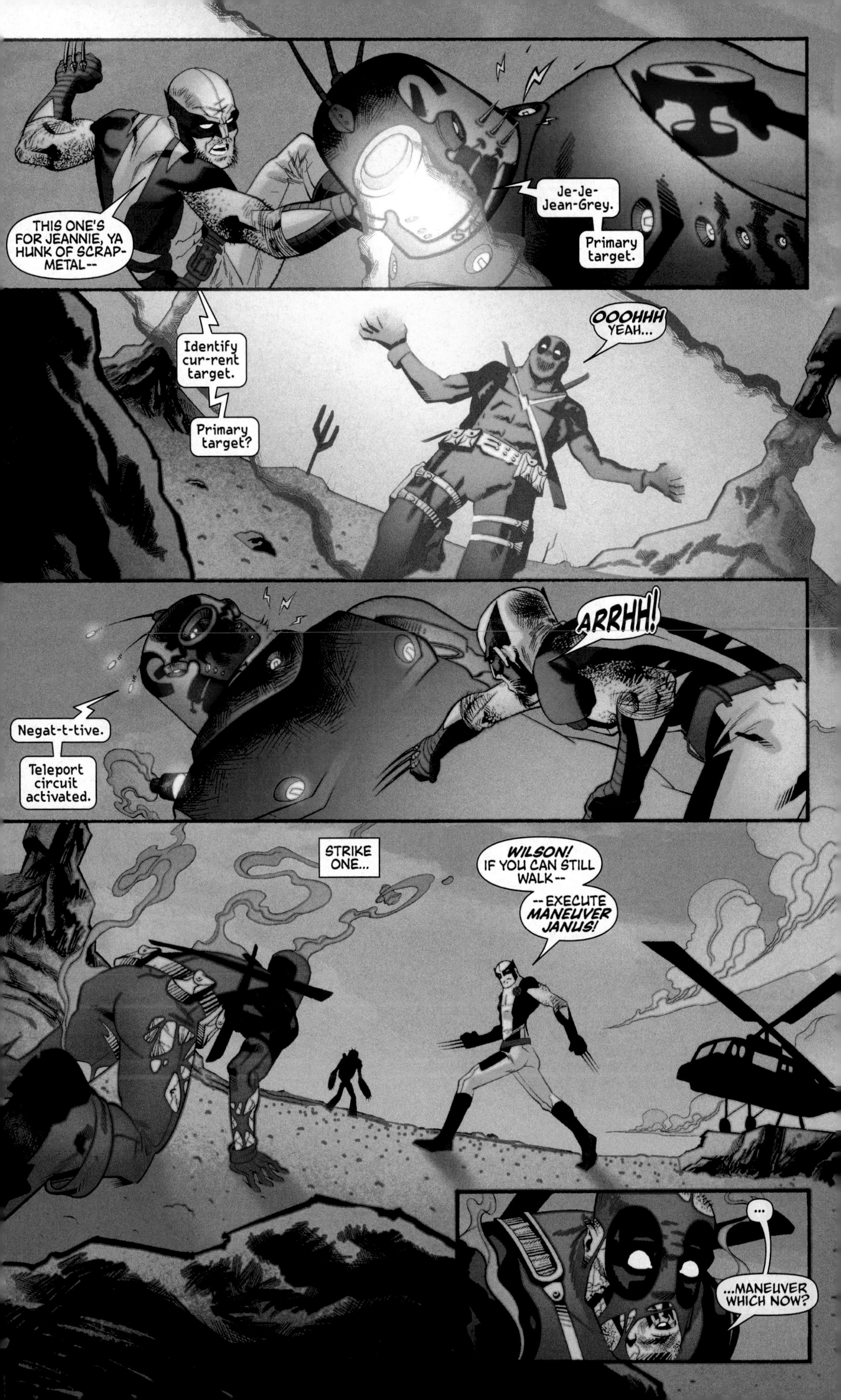
THIS ONE'S FOR JEANNIE, YA HUNK OF SCRAP-METAL--
Je-Je-Jean-Grey.
Primary target.
Identify cur-rent target.
Primary target?
OOOHHH YEAH...
ARRHH!
Negat-t-tive.
Teleport circuit activated.
STRIKE ONE...
WILSON! IF YOU CAN STILL WALK--
--EXECUTE MANEUVER JANUS!
...
...MANEUVER WHICH NOW?

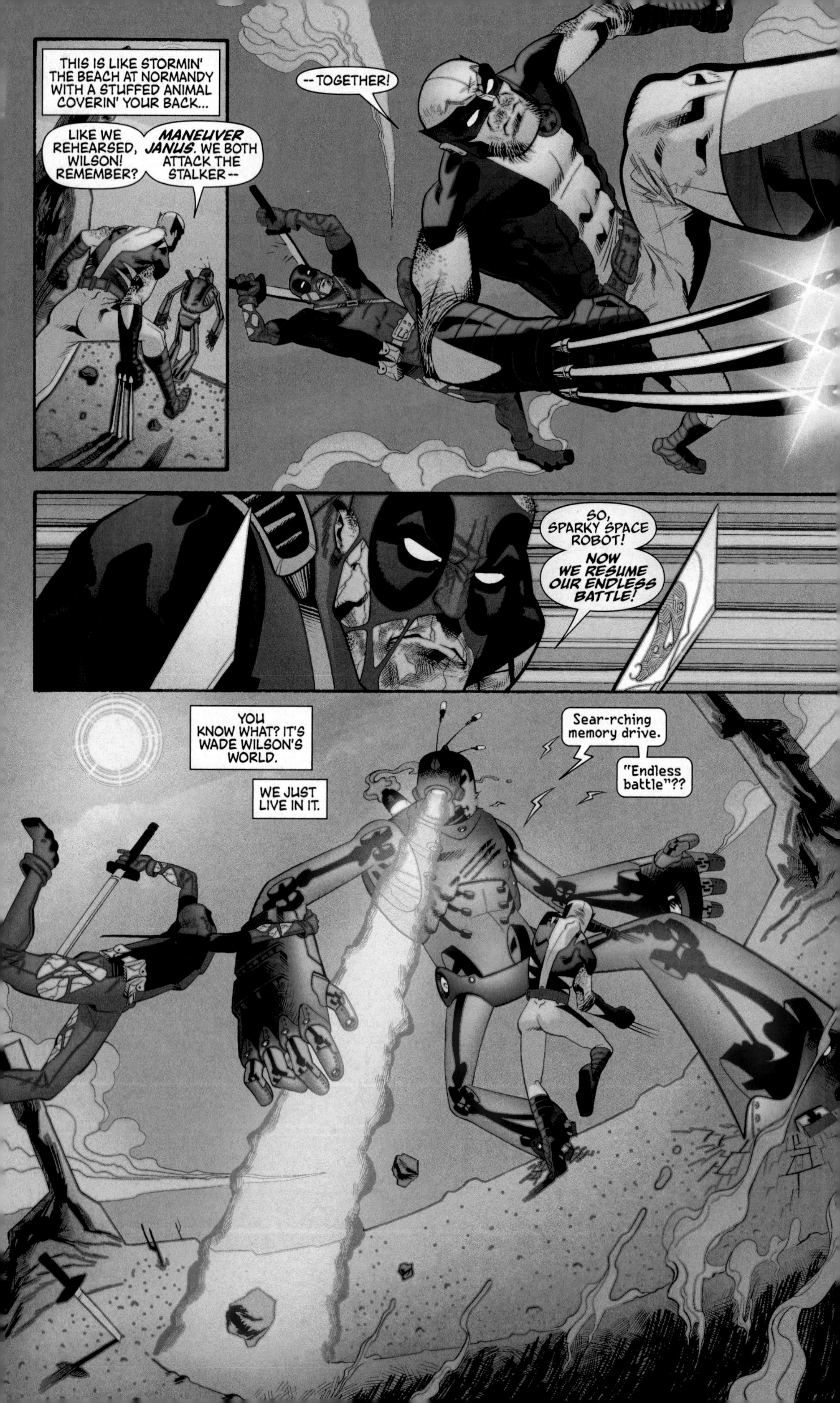
THIS IS LIKE STORMIN' THE BEACH AT NORMANDY WITH A STUFFED ANIMAL COVERIN' YOUR BACK...
LIKE WE REHEARSED, WILSON! REMEMBER?
MANEUVER JANUS. WE BOTH ATTACK THE STALKER --
-- TOGETHER!
SO, SPARKY SPACE ROBOT! NOW WE RESUME OUR ENDLESS BATTLE!
YOU KNOW WHAT? IT'S WADE WILSON'S WORLD.
WE JUST LIVE IN IT.
Sear-rching memory drive.
"Endless battle"??

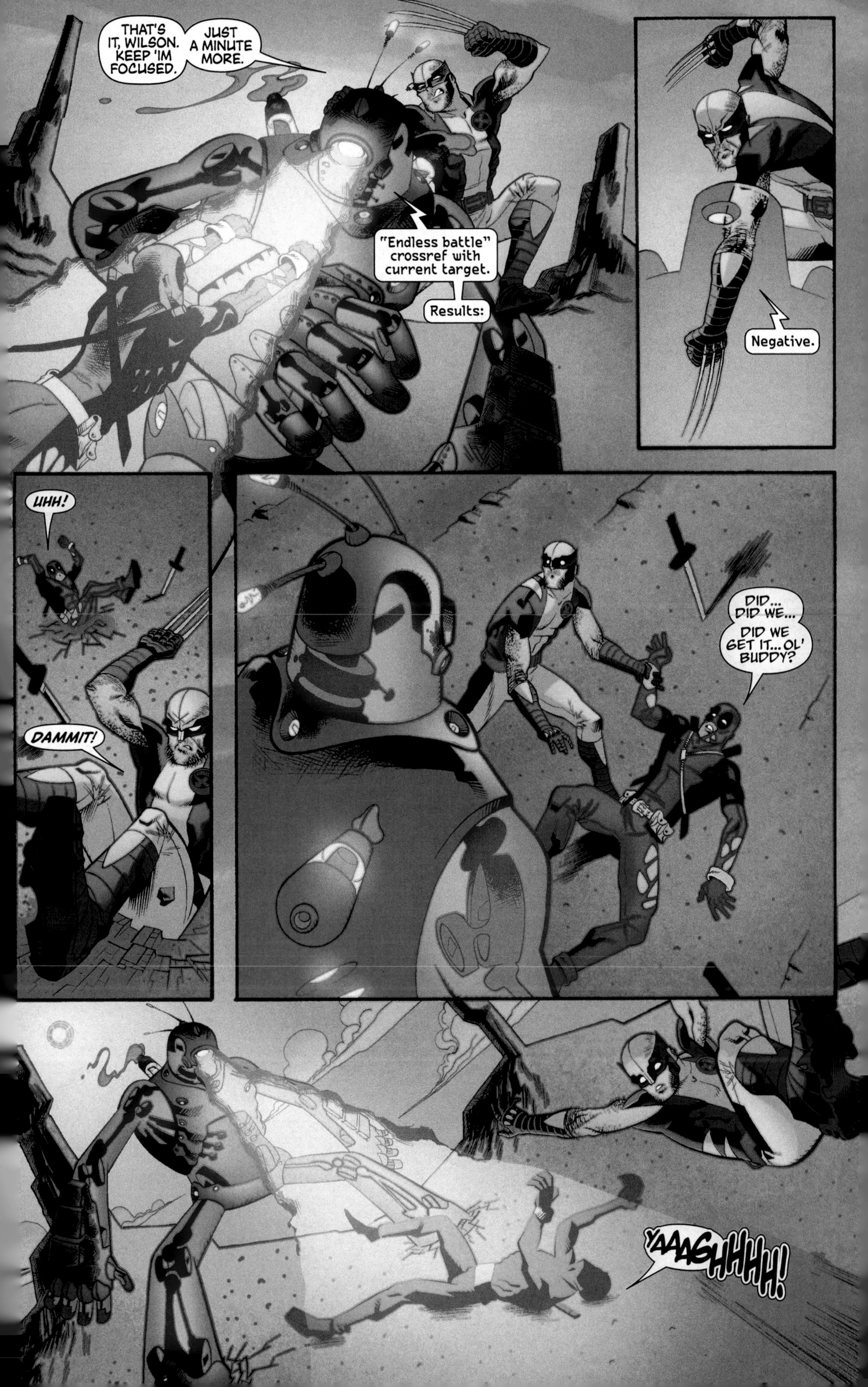
THAT'S IT, WILSON. KEEP 'IM FOCUSED.
JUST A MINUTE MORE.
"Endless battle" crossref with current target.
Results:
Negative.
UHH!
DAMMIT!
DID... DID WE... DID WE GET IT...OL' BUDDY?
YAAAGHHHH!

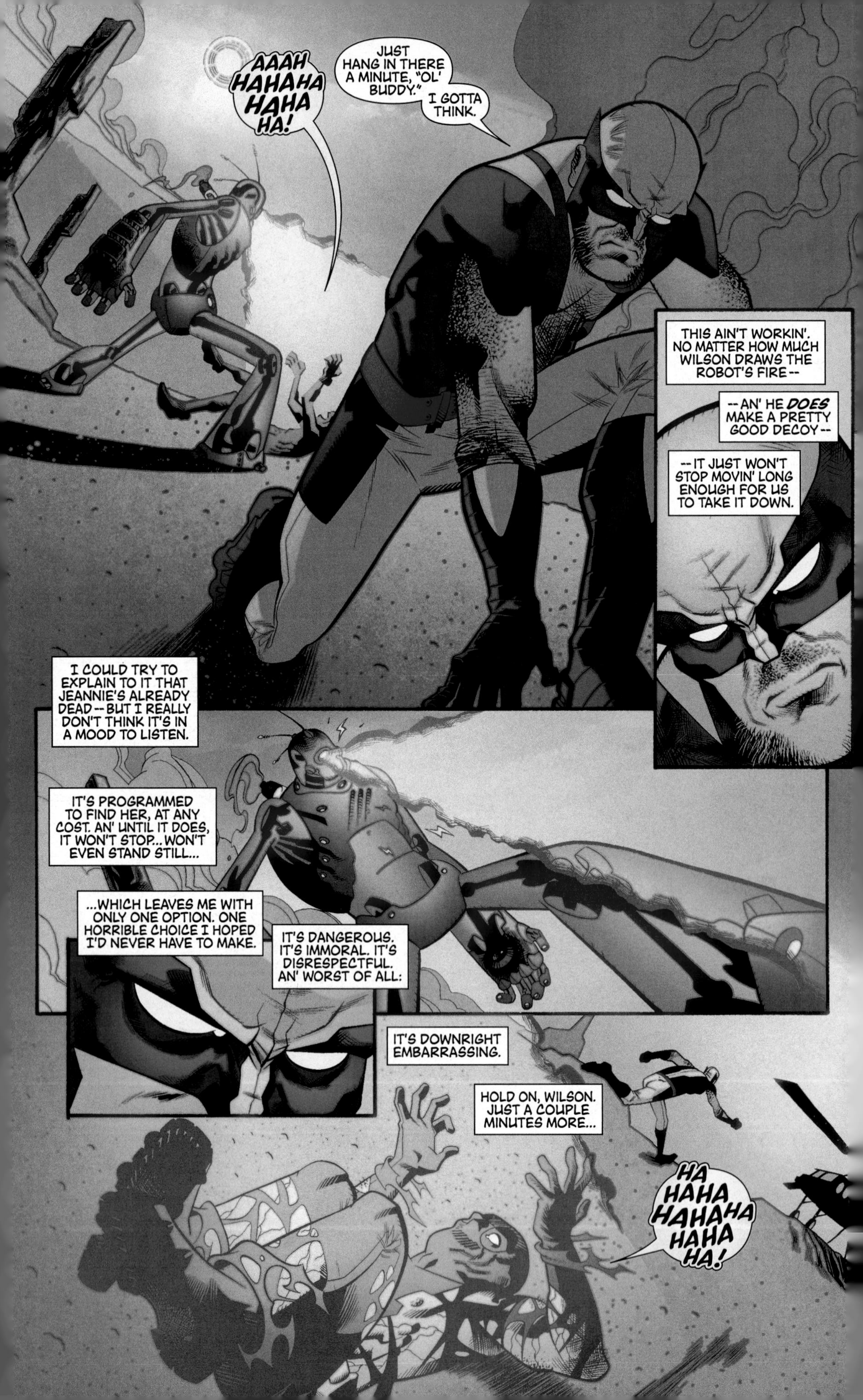
AAAH HAHAHA HAHA HA!
JUST HANG IN THERE A MINUTE, "OL' BUDDY."
I GOTTA THINK.
THIS AIN'T WORKIN'. NO MATTER HOW MUCH WILSON DRAWS THE ROBOT'S FIRE --
--AN' HE DOES MAKE A PRETTY GOOD DECOY --
--IT JUST WON'T STOP MOVIN' LONG ENOUGH FOR US TO TAKE IT DOWN.
I COULD TRY TO EXPLAIN TO IT THAT JEANNIE'S ALREADY DEAD -- BUT I REALLY DON'T THINK IT'S IN A MOOD TO LISTEN.
IT'S PROGRAMMED TO FIND HER, AT ANY COST. AN' UNTIL IT DOES, IT WON'T STOP... WON'T EVEN STAND STILL...
...WHICH LEAVES ME WITH ONLY ONE OPTION. ONE HORRIBLE CHOICE I HOPED I'D NEVER HAVE TO MAKE.
IT'S DANGEROUS. IT'S IMMORAL. IT'S DISRESPECTFUL. AN' WORST OF ALL:
IT'S DOWNRIGHT EMBARRASSING.
HOLD ON, WILSON. JUST A COUPLE MINUTES MORE...
HA HAHA HAHAHA HAHA HA!

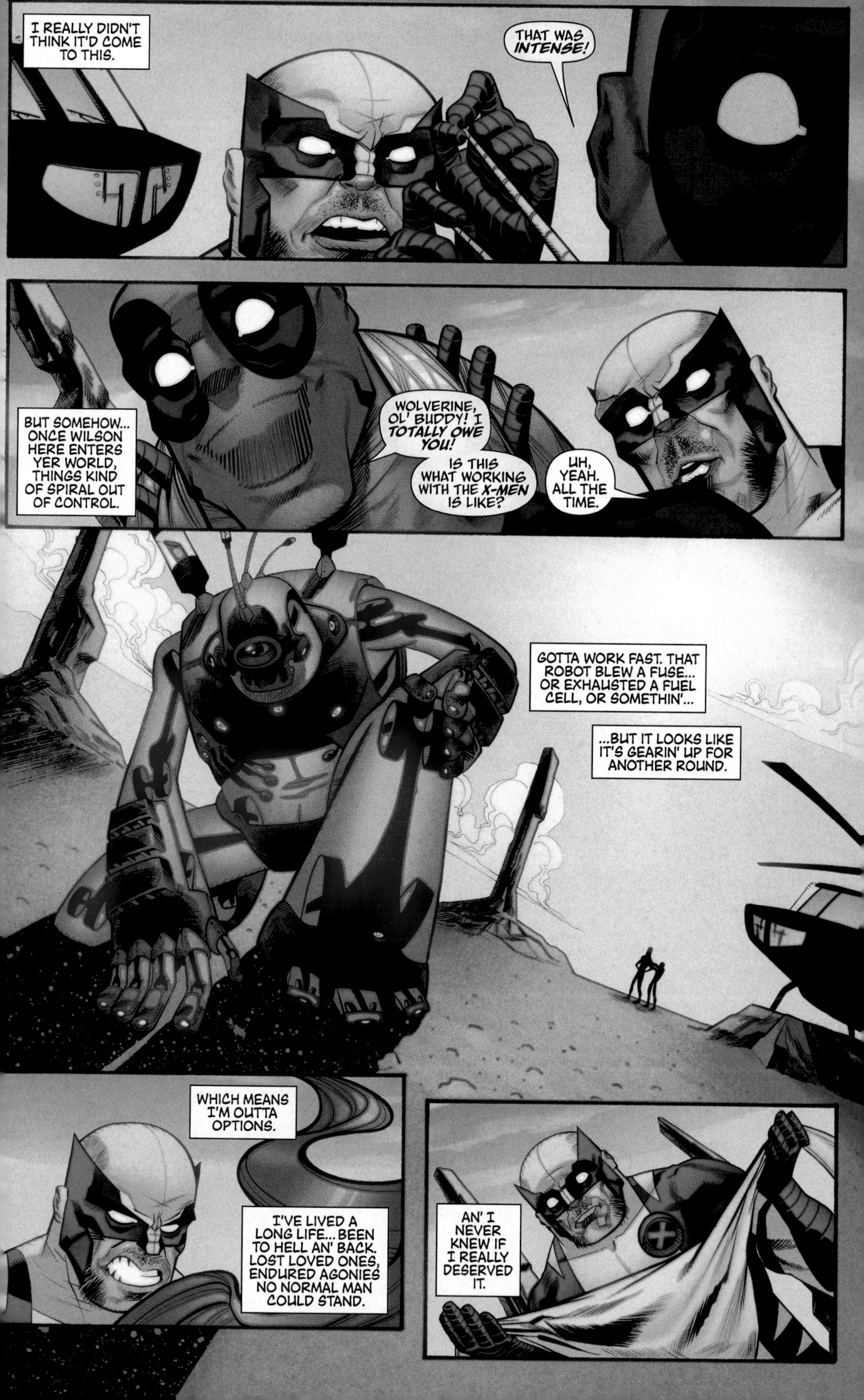

I REALLY DIDN'T THINK IT'D COME TO THIS.
THAT WAS INTENSE!
BUT SOMEHOW... ONCE WILSON HERE ENTERS YER WORLD, THINGS KIND OF SPIRAL OUT OF CONTROL.
WOLVERINE, OL' BUDDY! I TOTALLY OWE YOU!
IS THIS WHAT WORKING WITH THE X-MEN IS LIKE?
UH, YEAH. ALL THE TIME.
GOTTA WORK FAST. THAT ROBOT BLEW A FUSE... OR EXHAUSTED A FUEL CELL, OR SOMETHIN'...
...BUT IT LOOKS LIKE IT'S GEARIN' UP FOR ANOTHER ROUND.
WHICH MEANS I'M OUTTA OPTIONS.
I'VE LIVED A LONG LIFE... BEEN TO HELL AN' BACK. LOST LOVED ONES, ENDURED AGONIES NO NORMAL MAN COULD STAND.
AN' I NEVER KNEW IF I REALLY DESERVED IT.

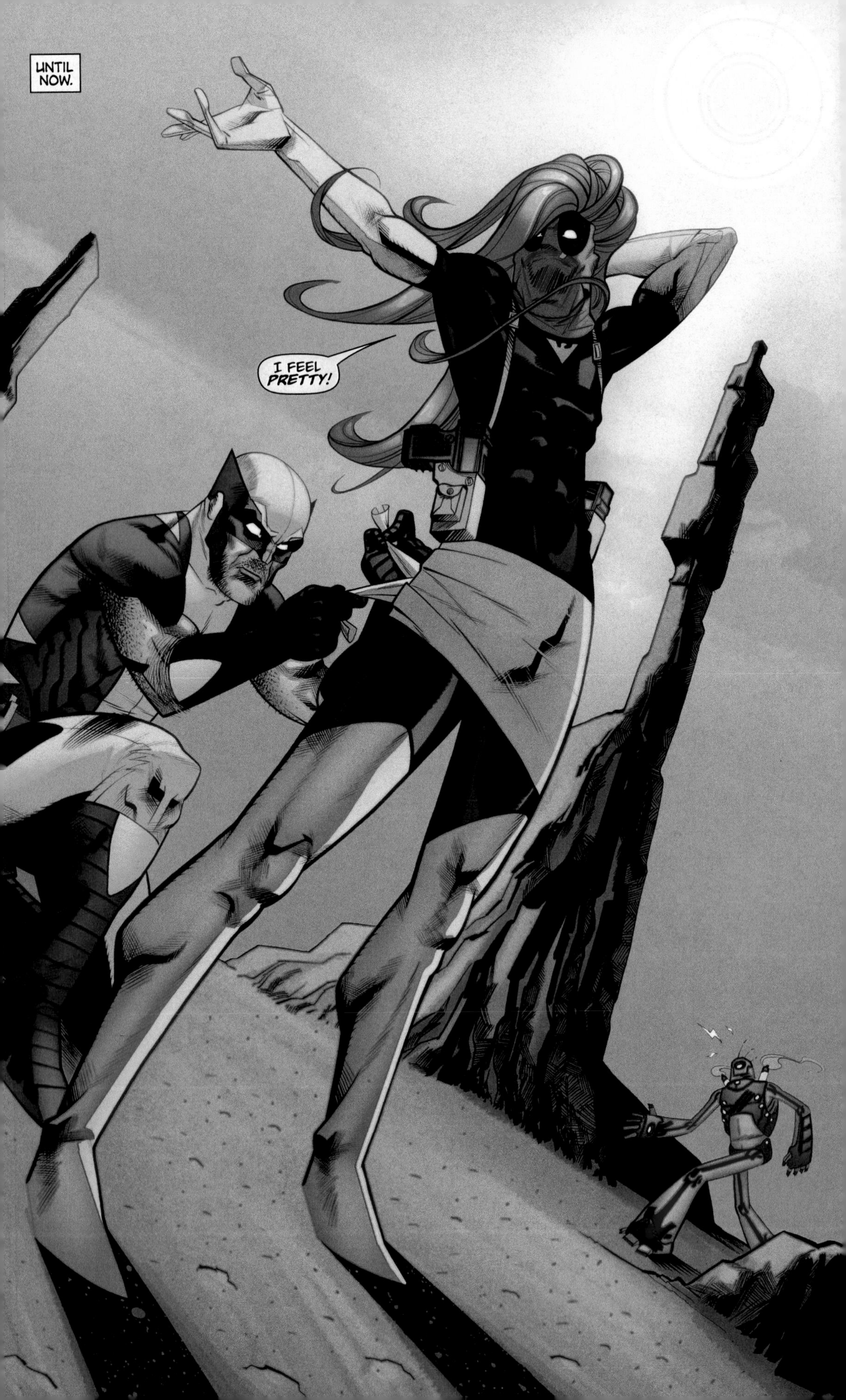
UNTIL NOW.
I FEEL PRETTY!

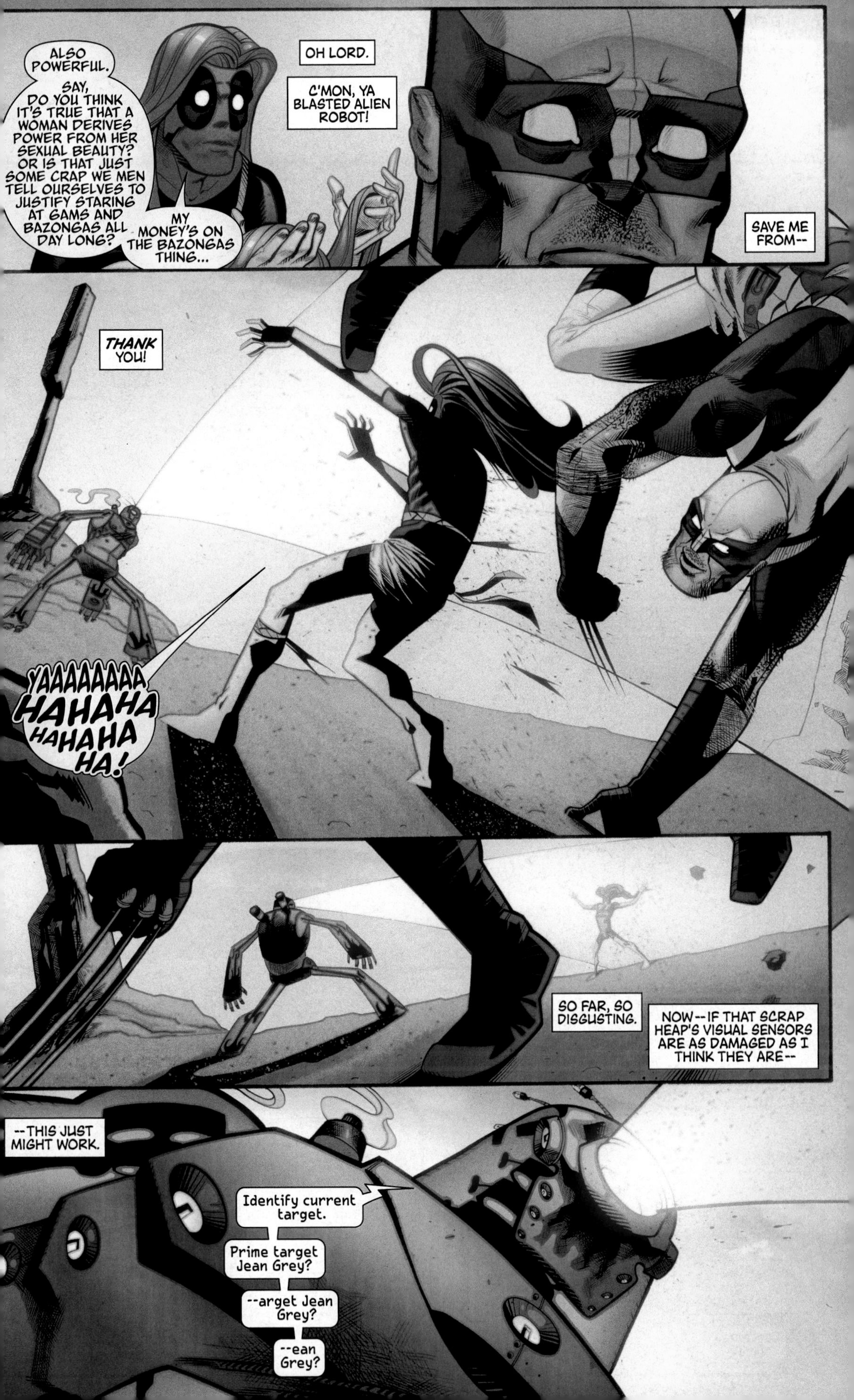

ALSO POWERFUL.
SAY, DO YOU THINK IT'S TRUE THAT A WOMAN DERIVES POWER FROM HER SEXUAL BEAUTY? OR IS THAT JUST SOME CRAP WE MEN TELL OURSELVES TO JUSTIFY STARING AT GAMS AND BAZONGAS ALL DAY LONG?
MY MONEY'S ON THE BAZONGAS THING...
OH LORD.
C'MON, YA BLASTED ALIEN ROBOT!
SAVE ME FROM--
THANK YOU!
YAAAAAAAA HAHAHA HAHAHA HA!
SO FAR, SO DISGUSTING.
NOW--IF THAT SCRAP HEAP'S VISUAL SENSORS ARE AS DAMAGED AS I THINK THEY ARE--
--THIS JUST MIGHT WORK.
Identify current target.
Prime target Jean Grey?
--arget Jean Grey?
--ean Grey?

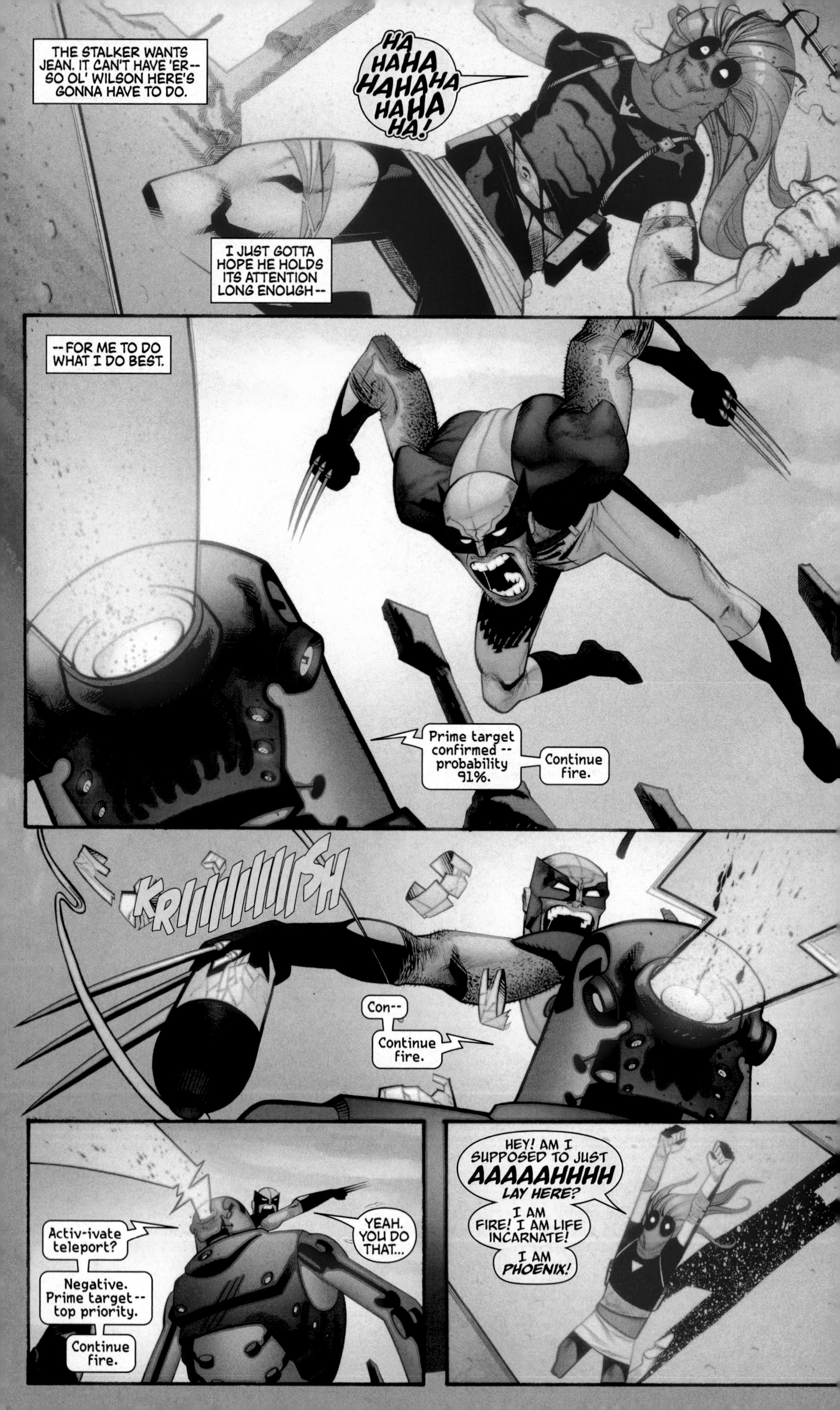

THE STALKER WANTS JEAN. IT CAN'T HAVE 'ER-- SO OL' WILSON HERE'S GONNA HAVE TO DO.
HA HAHAHA HAHAHA HAHAHA HA!
I JUST GOTTA HOPE HE HOLDS ITS ATTENTION LONG ENOUGH--
--FOR ME TO DO WHAT I DO BEST.
Prime target confirmed -- probability 91%.
Continue fire.
KRIIIIIIIISH
Con--
Continue fire.
Activ-ivate teleport?
Negative. Prime target -- top priority.
Continue fire.
YEAH. YOU DO THAT...
HEY! AM I SUPPOSED TO JUST AAAAAHHHH LAY HERE?
I AM FIRE! I AM LIFE INCARNATE!
I AM PHOENIX!

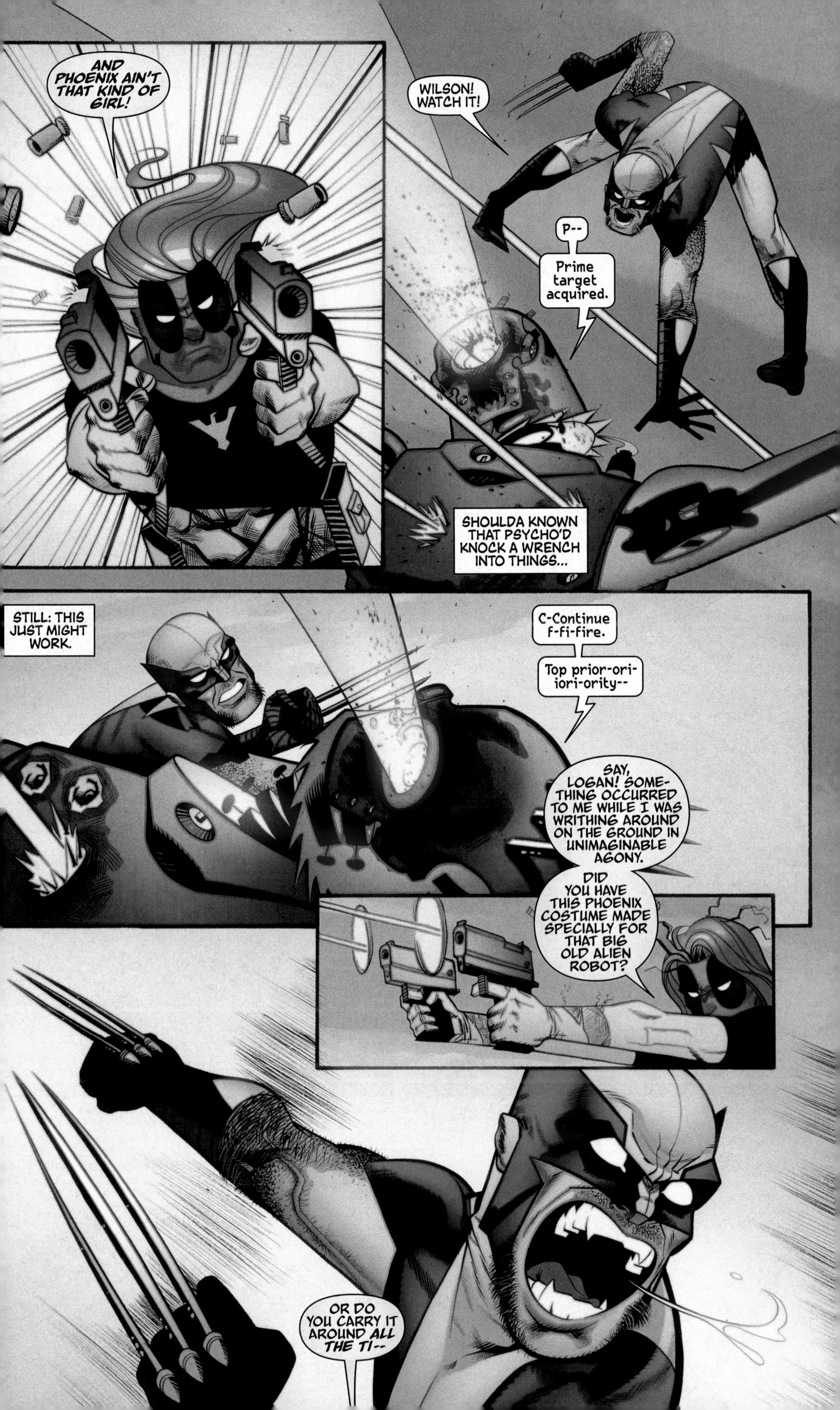
AND PHOENIX AIN'T THAT KIND OF GIRL!
WILSON! WATCH IT!
P--
Prime target acquired.
SHOULDA KNOWN THAT PSYCHO'D KNOCK A WRENCH INTO THINGS...
STILL: THIS JUST MIGHT WORK.
C-Continue f-fi-fire.
Top prior-ori-iori-ority--
SAY, LOGAN! SOMETHING OCCURRED TO ME WHILE I WAS WRITHING AROUND ON THE GROUND IN UNIMAGINABLE AGONY.
DID YOU HAVE THIS PHOENIX COSTUME MADE SPECIALLY FOR THAT BIG OLD ALIEN ROBOT?
OR DO YOU CARRY IT AROUND ALL THE TI--

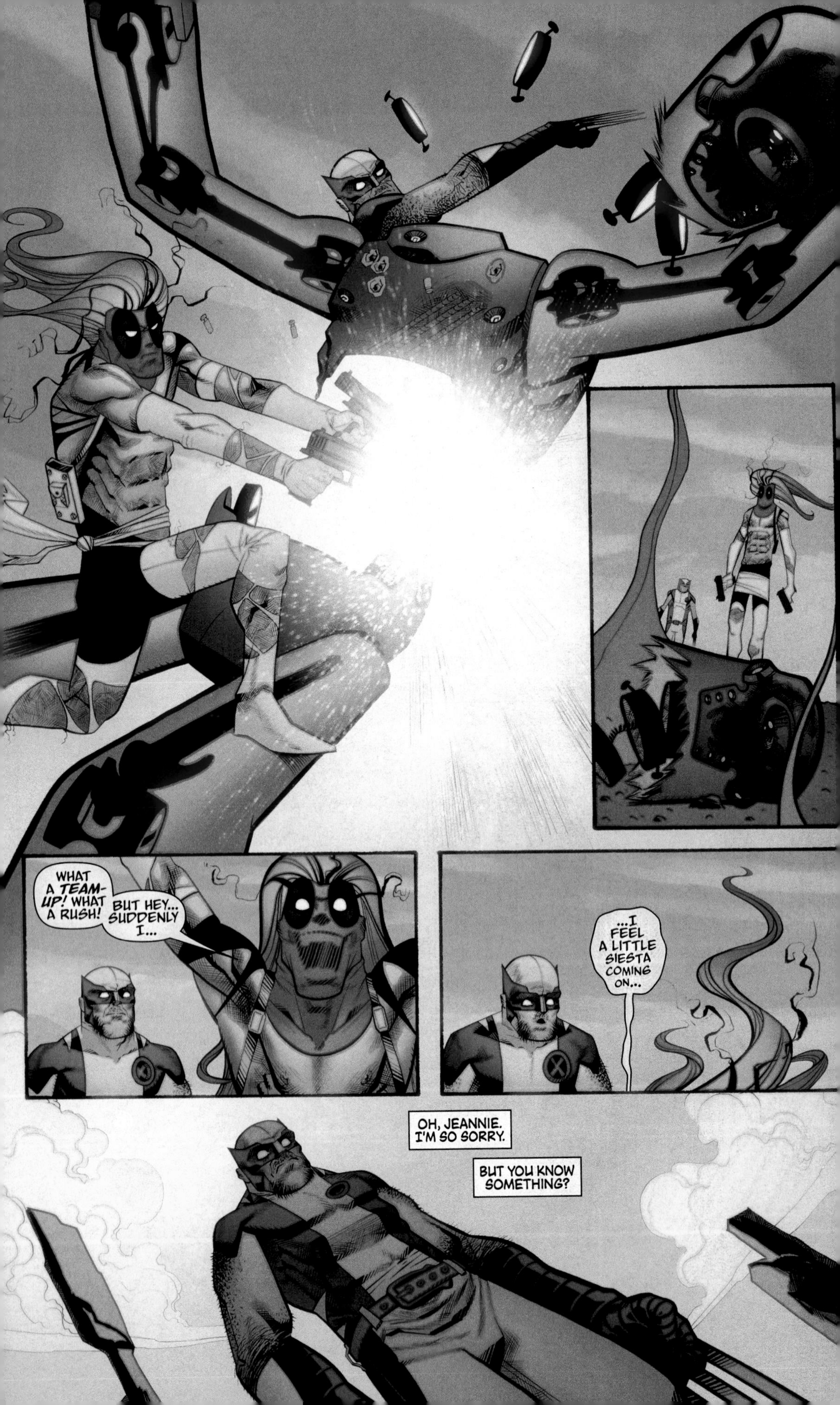
WHAT A TEAM-UP! WHAT A RUSH!
BUT HEY... SUDDENLY I...
...I FEEL A LITTLE SIESTA COMING ON...
OH, JEANNIE. I'M SO SORRY.
BUT YOU KNOW SOMETHING?

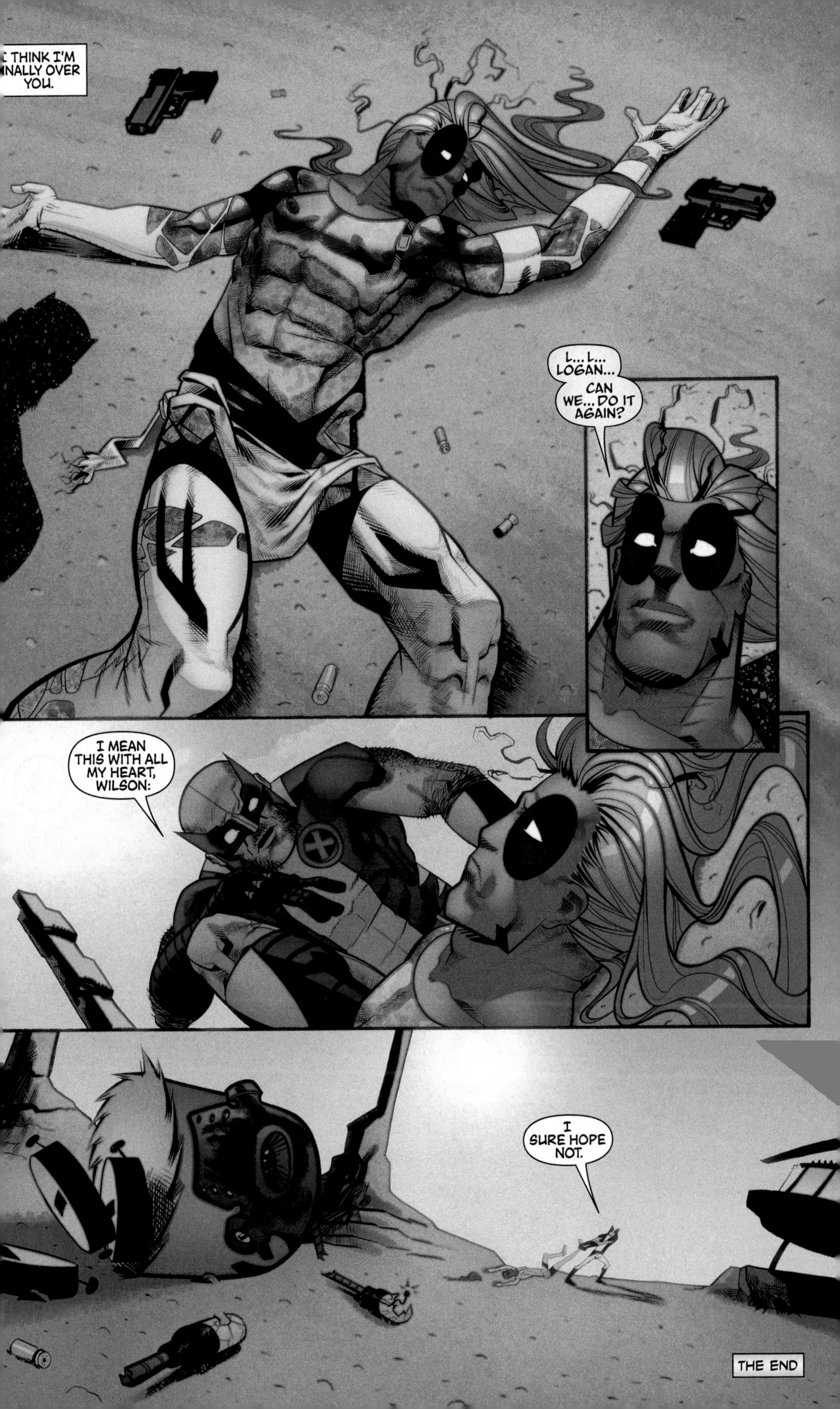
I THINK I'M
NALLY OVER
YOU.
L... L...
LOGAN...
CAN
WE... DO IT
AGAIN?
I MEAN
THIS WITH ALL
MY HEART,
WILSON:
I
SURE HOPE
NOT.
THE END

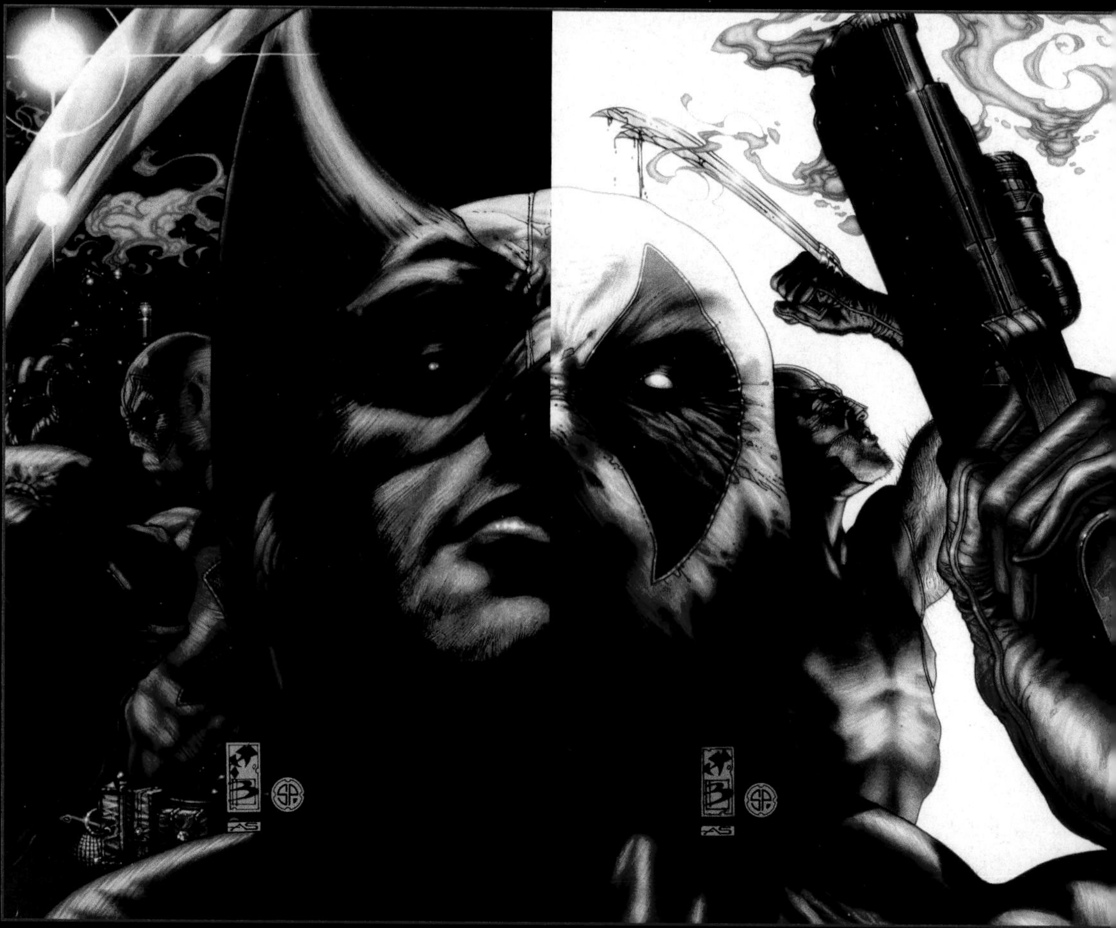

Wolverine: Origins #22-23 combined cover art by **Simone Bianchi, Andrea Silvestri** & **Simone Peruzzi**

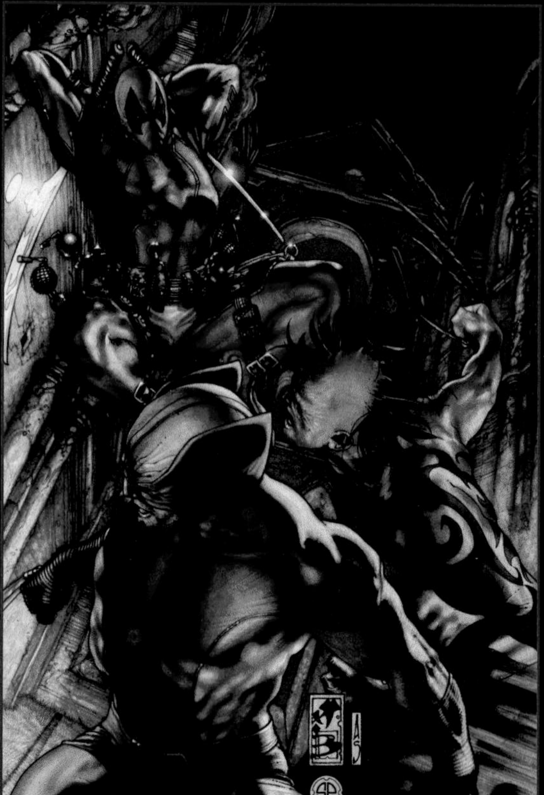

Wolverine: Origins #25 Skrull variant by **Simone Bianchi, Andrea Silvestri** & **Simone Peruzzi**